HAROLD T. CHRISTENSEN, Ph.D., University of Wisconsin, is Professor of Sociology at Purdue University. He has also taught at Brigham Young University and the University of Hawaii. He has served as editor of *Marriage and Family Living* (now *Journal of Marriage and the Family*) and is a frequent contributor to the scholarly journals. He is the editor of *Handbook of Marriage and the Family*. In 1967 he received the Burgess Award for outstanding research on the family.

KATHRYN P. JOHNSEN, Ph.D., Purdue University, is Associate Professor of Sociology at that institution. She is the author of numerous research studies and professional journal articles.

MARRIAGE AND THE FAMILY

HAROLD T. CHRISTENSEN

KATHRYN P. JOHNSEN

BOTH OF PURDUE UNIVERSITY

THIRD EDITION

THE RONALD PRESS COMPANY · NEW YORK

Library of Congress Catalog Card Number: 71–155205
PRINTED IN THE UNITED STATES OF AMERICA

To our Families

Our parents, our spouses, our children
their spouses and future spouses
and to the generations of tomorrow

Preface

This is a functional textbook designed for use in undergraduate courses on marriage and the family. It is functional in the sense that it will give students a practical understanding of the social and psychological factors that influence their interpersonal relationships and the kind of marriage and family life they may be able to establish. It is firmly grounded in both theory and empirical research findings. It is so written, however, that the theoretical and empirical underpinnings can be directly translated into personal experience.

This text is a revision of *Marriage Analysis,* by Harold T. Christensen. In recent years there have been far-reaching changes in the American society, and the book has been rewritten to reflect these changes and to come to grips with growing student concern with the relationship between the society in which they live and their control over their own lives.

Social changes have accelerated at an increasing rate. These changes contribute to value conflicts within the culture, which in turn specifically relate to ideas about "right" or "good" male–female relationships, husband–wife relationships, and parent–child relationships. It becomes highly important, then, for individuals to understand the process by which values develop, are reinforced or changed, and their consequences for marriage and family interaction. This *Principle of Value Relevance* is used throughout this text as a tool for understanding the different consequences stemming from similar behavior.

Parts I and II of this book focus on the influence of society upon the framework within which family interaction takes place and the processes by which selected values are transmitted to individuals growing up in a particular family. They emphasize the variety of social and social psychological factors influencing the male–female relationship well before the individual develops an interest in the opposite sex.

Parts III, IV, and V follow logically through the life cycle of the family from its inception in dating and mate selection to its termination in death, separation, or divorce. The treatment of each stage, though relying heavily on research, stresses the importance of individual values, the fit between the systems of men and women in paired relationships, and the consequences of this fit for both the individual and the relationship. No particular system is supported; readers are presented the evidence and allowed to arrive at their own positions. The emphasis is on variation in systems present at each stage. Through a discussion of the variations and their consequences, the students' attention is drawn to the importance of values for themselves, their family, and their society. They are provided the perspective from which they may draw their own conclusions, understand the influences that bear upon them, and evaluate the effects on their behavior, marriage, and life in general.

The text concludes with a look into the future as it attempts to extend the trends of today to the family of tomorrow. It is intended to emphasize the importance, for the future direction of the family, of the interactions of each individual family as it responds to societal pressure and change.

Throughout the book, students' views are interspersed for illustrative purposes. Unless otherwise cited, they are taken from the author's files of student papers or from classroom discussions. Some of the statements have been slightly edited for clarity, but never to change the meaning.

In the preparation of this text there has been consistent close communication between the authors. Certain excerpts from the earlier work have been retained intact. But the rewriting has been thorough, so much so as to make this, in effect, another book. Major responsibility for the reorganization and new writing has been assumed by Kathryn Johnsen.

HAROLD T. CHRISTENSEN
KATHRYN P. JOHNSEN

Lafayette, Indiana
August, 1971

Contents

PART I   SOCIAL CONTEXT

1	Introduction	3
2	The Family as a Changing Institution	20
3	The Family as a Reflection of Social Class	45
4	The Problem of Values	68

PART II   THE INDIVIDUAL

5	The Development of a Sense of Self	91
6	Habits of Interaction	106
7	Masculinity and Femininity	121

PART III   PREMARITAL INTERACTION

8	Dating Patterns	149
9	Premarital Sex	177
10	Mate Selection	211
11	Engagement	238

PART IV   MARITAL INTERACTION

12	Husband–Wife Roles	261
13	Communication and Conflict Resolution	286
14	The Sexual Relationship	317
15	The Economic Relationship	338
16	The In-Law Relationship	356
17	Special Problems in Mixed Marriages	370
18	Childbearing	389

CONTENTS

PART V   FAMILY INTERACTION

19   Childrearing   421
20   Postparenthood and the Aged   446
21   Separation, Divorce, and Widowhood   462

PART VI   CONCLUSION

22   The Challenge of the Future   493

     Appendix: Family Changes Reflected in Statistical Trends   511
     Bibliography   523
     Name Index   537
     Subject Index   541

I

SOCIAL CONTEXT

1

Introduction

People learn to value a particular type of family life and consider it the only normal way of doing things. Today, the majority of people in our society value a family life which gives them _personal satisfaction._ They expect to build this family from a *happy* marriage relationship. For some, this expectation is amply fulfilled; for some, it is partially fulfilled; for others, marriage provides little more than misery and frustration. This book is directed toward an analysis of the factors which contribute to these different marital experiences.

A functional textbook on marriage and the family is expected generally to provide guidelines for heightening the probability of success and decreasing the probability of failure in marriage. This is a realistic expectation provided there is first agreement on what a successful marriage is and what guidelines will be most useful. This chapter is devoted to discussions of: (1) the criteria useful in defining success in marriage; (2) the analytical framework used in subsequent chapters; and (3) the perspective the authors attempt to maintain throughout the book.

THE CRITERIA FOR EVALUATING SUCCESS

Marriages are highly personal relationships, but they do not take place in a vacuum. They take place in a society which has developed ideas about how husbands and wives are supposed to act toward each other. They take place in a society which has developed certain ways of meeting the everyday needs of food, shelter, and clothing and has established certain levels of living as legitimate expectations.

These established ways of doing things help form the individual's expectations for marriage and the criteria by which he judges its success

3

or failure. These criteria for evaluating marital success not only differ from society to society, but they also change over a period of time in the same society. We do not ask the same things of marriage today that we did a hundred years ago. Our society has changed and so have our expectations for marriage and family life. These expectations change partially in response to changes in the economic system, adapting to a changing technology, labor needs, and living conditions.

The direction the adaptation takes is guided, however, by strong value systems limiting the choice among alternatives. The speed and scope of the adaptation is held in check by the past history of the marriage and family forms of that society (Vincent, 1966a, p. 18). Every marriage is affected by the social pressures surrounding it and by the history of family forms preceding it. It is impossible, then, to understand the individual marriage without understanding something about the society in which it takes place.

Society Changes

In a complex, industrialized society, change becomes a normal state. As the technological base expands, the rate of technological development increases, continually calling for changes in other related activities. For example, the expanding base of technological knowledge which made possible the mass production of numerous items created a need for an increase in people living near and working in factories. As the number of people living within a relatively small area grew, they created a market for more mass-produced goods which they could not produce for themselves. As additional industries developed to meet these challenges, the availability of pre-processed foodstuffs and clothing had an impact on the activities demanded of the housewife and the expectations for her contributions to family life. The ability to bake bread, knit, sew, and perform tasks once considered essential criteria for judging the "good" wife have now begun to be considered hobbies or artistic skills if they remain at all. The "good" wife has begun to be evaluated on characteristics beyond the essentials of cooking, sewing, and housekeeping. Standards of home making have risen, calling for a higher quality of goods and more labor-saving devices, each demanding new developments in industry. Thus, changes in one area induce changes in related activities in an ever widening network.

The Unevenness of Change

Although the over-all face of society may look like the proverbial bag of worms—in constant motion and change—there is both regularity and variation in the rate of change in different parts of the society.

Not everyone has enjoyed the benefits or felt the demands of the expanding economic system. Obviously the housewife whose husband is employed in a low-paying, unskilled job considers skill in preparing low cost meals and in sewing a more necessary and essential part of her job than the wife of a highly paid executive. Many of the same criteria used for evaluating a good wife which applied to the wife in the pre-"ready-to-serve" food era apply to the working man's wife. For her, the evaluation of a successful marriage and family centers around meeting the necessities of food, shelter, and clothing. For the executive's wife, these things are taken for granted and a successful marriage and family centers around an enhancement of the environment and is evaluated in terms of personal satisfactions and occupational status.

Individual families are subjected to varying exposures to change depending upon their life conditions. The young man who enters the same local industry as his father at about the same level, marries a local girl with a high school education, and lives out his life in the same community, will be subjected to significantly fewer pressures to change from his parents' expectations for successful family relationships than the young man from a similar family background who goes to college, enters an industry in a managerial capacity, marries a college girl, and is subjected to a series of residential changes as he rises in the managerial hierarchy. Thus, we find differences in marital expectations according to social class position.

There are differences in affiliations with ideological groups supporting past family forms reflected in the range of religious and ethnic groups. Even when contact with the economic system presents comparable pressures for change, individual families differ in the amount of resistance they offer to adaptation. The devout Catholic, for example, is perhaps not as willing to limit family size as an adaptation to economic demands for a more flexible and mobile family unit as the Protestant or non-religious person with more liberal birth control views.

These variations in the amount of resistance to change encountered in the various segments of society result in an uneven rate of change in ideas about what a marriage *should* be. Thus, different criteria for assessing the successful marriage are in existence at the same time. It becomes, then, impossible to construct a specific list of guidelines for achieving a successful marriage applicable to all families in the society.

Perhaps one could assess the individual histories of a particular husband and wife, the development of their relationship, the present economic, social, and religious placement of the marriage and then prepare a blueprint for marriage which might satisfy these individuals. There would be no guarantee that they could behave toward each other in the prescribed way, however, or that some change in the external situation would not upset the blueprint the next day. As far as general applicability is concerned, any *specific* suggestions for behavior expected to contribute to marital success would not be practical. They may well reflect only the social class positions and life histories of the writers with a rather limited range of relevancy.

Definitions of Success

Although the individual approach may be unworkable, there *are* observable consistencies to be found. There are certain processes which are generally applicable to human relationships. There are recognizable pressures which confront some groups and not others. There are certain shared expectations for marital success which appear to vary with class positions. There are associations which have been found between age at marriage, religious affiliation, religious mixtures, education, and divorce —one indicator of marital failure.

We can use these generalizations to describe the different pressures to which marriages are subjected, to point out the potential conflicts inherent in certain marital combinations, and to aid in developing a definition of marital success which allows for individual variation in goals and personal desires. When we begin to define a successful marriage, we must first ask, *from whose perspective?*

Perspective of the Law. Legally in our society marriage is a contract between a man and woman, which determines their minimal obligations to each other, legitimizes the bearing of children, and designates their legal rights as husbands and wives. A successful marriage from this point of view is one which honors the obligations of the contract and remains intact, regardless of the evaluation of the relationship made by the individuals within it. It is this legal criterion of success—lack of separation or divorce—which is used in many sociological investigations of the factors associated with marital failure. This is legitimate, and obviously alerts us to certain high risk factors in marriage.

From the point of view of this book, however, a marriage in which one or both partners are continually miserable in the relationship would not be considered successful even though they stayed together to observe a fiftieth wedding anniversary. We must look at broader points of view than the legal one for a general definition of success.

Perspective of Society. The successful marriage must produce certain consequences which are functional for society. Functional, as used here, means a contribution to the integration, organization, and continuity of the society. Such a marriage must be sufficiently adapted to the legitimate norms of society that it does not impede the accomplishment of major societal goals. We would not count as functionally successful those marriages which continually pursued criminal goals, no matter how successfully they achieved them or how devoted the two people were to each other. They might be a perfectly matched couple but they would not have a successful marriage from the societal point of view.

Perspective of the Individual. The successful marriage must produce certain consequences for the individual which are functional for him. This means it must contribute to *his* sense of continuity and integration. It must be sufficiently adapted to his needs to allow him to function within his social context.

The successful marriage, of course, cannot be defined solely in terms of its satisfaction of individual desires or in terms of its conformity to social norms. A marriage which emphasized either of these factors to the exclusion of the other would not be a successful marriage from the point of view of this book.

The Link Between Society and the Individual. One of the main integrating factors of the individual is his concept of self; that is, his concept of who he is, his self-worth, his strengths and weaknesses. An adequate and integrated self-concept allows one to retain a feeling of continuity and meaning while interacting with a variety of persons in widely differing situations and activities. In the course of a relatively short period of time, one may be called upon to outmaneuver a competitor in landing a contract, deliver a lecture on the value of fair play, settle a dispute between two battling youngsters, discipline a recalcitrant child or employee, comfort a distressed spouse, and explain the loss of a sale to the boss. An integrated self-concept furnishes the consistency which cushions the feelings of elation, defeat, or inadequacy connected with individual events.

The self-concept can be seen as the link between societal needs and individual needs. Societies cannot continue unless individuals are motivated to participate in essential activities. The individual's self-concept and his attempts to enhance it are major factors in motivating him to activity. When the standards (norms) he uses to evaluate himself are in agreement with the norms used by others to evaluate him, continual interaction serves to confirm (validate) his concept of self. Since the self-concept promotes behavior that is in accord with it, an acceptable concept of self both enhances a person's participation in societal activities and promotes his own feelings of self-worth, integration, and continuity.

From this perspective, then, *a successful marriage is one in which the interaction between the spouses continually confirms for them positive self-concepts which are functional for the social context within which the marriage takes place.* In other words, the individual feels better about himself, better able to carry out his daily activities because of the continual support gained from the marital relationship. To broaden the definition to include the children coming from the marriage one need only substitute the word *family* for marriage, and the word *family members* for spouses.

The concept of social context must be kept in mind or the definition becomes very limiting. Social context includes not only the values and goals of the larger society but the individual's values and goals as well. The successful marriage, then, aids in his own sense of integrity and continuity as he resists certain societal pressures and adapts to others. Since individual values vary, as do social pressures, all people do not ask the same things of the marriage relationship. Consequently, success is defined in terms of how well the relationship meets the needs and expectations of the individuals and how appropriate these expectations are for integrating the members into the society. A particular type of marital relationship may bring satisfaction to a couple in one segment of society during a certain part of their life cycle. The same type of marital relationship may bring stress, conflict, and dissatisfaction in a different segment of society or at another point in the life cycle.

For the individual, then, the probability of success is enhanced by an understanding of the impact of the social context on definitions of marital success; an awareness of the sources of his own expectations for the marriage relationship; knowledge of the processes by which self-concepts are developed, changed, and confirmed; and a recognition of the possible sources of conflict in expectations stemming from large changes in society over time as well as from changes in the life cycle of the individual family. In general, this describes the focus of the book. It becomes functional for the individual as he learns to apply the general knowledge to his own particular situation. He gains the tools to allow him to perceive more objectively and thereby obtain a measure of control over his own experiences.

ANALYTICAL FRAMEWORK OF THE BOOK

Marriage analysis suggests the intent of taking apart the marriage relationship and viewing its elements separately in order to understand how they interrelate with each other. The analytical framework of this text spells out the way in which the dissection will be made. From the sociological and social–psychological perspectives (which this book represents) attention is focused on certain elements rather than others. Marriage is seen as a special kind of interaction taking place in a social context. We will be focusing on the components of the social context and the factors influencing the interactions. Attention will not be drawn to budgeting, nutrition, child care, or to other specific activities except to the extent that changed or conflicting expectations and evaluations concerning them have an impact on marital interaction. This in no way suggests the greater importance of one perspective of one over another. It merely reflects the perspective of the theoretical orientation we have chosen.

Social Context

The phrase *social context* connotes a space marked off in the larger society where the probability is increased that a particular combination of norms and values will prevail. The normative content of this space is influenced by a number of factors, each serving to limit the range of norms and values to which the individual is exposed. The influential factors of special interest to us include: (1) the central value system of the society, (2) occupation, (3) religion, (4) education, (5) government, and (6) family culture.

Central Value System. The central value system of a society furnishes the broadest range of norms and values. The term *value* refers to worth, the goodness or badness ascribed to an object, an activity, or a class of objects or actions. For example, in our society a central value ascribes goodness to a monogamous marriage. One husband for one wife is considered the only "right" marital relationship. There is nothing inherently right or good in that particular marriage form, it is made "right" by the cultural value ascribing goodness to it.

Norm is used to mean a shared guideline for behavior. Norms tell us what we should or should not do in certain kinds of situations. Generally, they spell out a range of acceptable means by which a valued goal is achieved. There are norms, for instance, which provide us with guidelines concerning how to keep our valued monogamous marriage sexually exclusive. We *should* marry someone we love. A woman *should* keep herself attractive after marriage. A husband *should not* develop an intimate relationship with his secretary. Norms describe what should or should not happen—they do not necessarily describe actual or average behavior. The fact that the norms are violated in actual behavior does not generally reflect a change in the *standards* of acceptable behavior. The fact that many people engage in shoplifting does not mean that there has been a general decline in the belief that it is wrong to steal.

As far as the family is concerned, the central values of a society determine in general the marriage form which is considered "normal"; outline broad guidelines for mate selection; provide the range of expectations for the permanence of the union, the general obligations, and privileges assigned to family members; and roughly indicate the importance of the family in relation to other institutions. Institution is defined in terms of norms also. Roughly an *institution* is a collection of norms organized around an important and recurring social activity. Thus, collections of norms develop around the control of sexual behavior; mate selection; childbearing and rearing; and the relationships between husband, wife, and children. This collection of norms, taken together, comprises the *institution of the family.* In the same way, there are institutions developed around work, religion, education, and any other activity which recurs over and over. The term institution refers to the way in which activities should be carried out, not to an organization of individuals directed toward some goal, as it is occasionally used.

The Economic Institution.   One important and recurring activity in any society is the production and distribution of food, shelter, clothing, and other necessities to societal members. A group of norms develops in every society prescribing the preferred organization of activities to meet these needs. The result is the economic institution. The current, active, economic system in a society broadly provides the external environment to which the family must adapt in order to meet the basic needs of its members. The economic institution roughly indicates whether individual families will be relatively self-sufficient or interdependent. It determines whether families will be geographically mobile or rooted to the same plot of ground. It largely dictates whether families will live closely grouped or widely scattered.

Any large change in the economic institution over time will have an impact on the general expectations for family relationships. At any one point in time, however, the individual's point of contact with the economic system will influence his perception of "good" family relationships. Families integrated into the economic system at financially insecure levels or families which are involved in the production of foodstuffs in rural areas may see good family relationships as implying a high degree of cooperative activity in meeting food, shelter, and clothing needs—"Everyone contributes something for the good of the family." Those integrated at a higher, more secure financial level may see good family relationships as meaning the sharing of leisure time activities, or non-interference with personal goals—"The main thing is that everybody's happy." As will be discussed in more detail later, family organization, authority pattern, the evaluation of children, expectations for family relationships—all depend at least partially upon the means by which the family meets its basic biological needs.

The Religious Institution.   Since the family is wholly dependent upon the economic system for its basic biological needs, it is vulnerable to pressures to adapt to the needs of that system. It is tempting to view the economic institution as all important in forcing adaptive changes in the family. These pressures, however, are partially countered by the religious institution. The religious institution, when it supports an absolutistic value system, is one means for preserving past family forms by placing value on the form itself whether or not it is functional for the economic system. By providing a framework of values it makes a particular family relationship appear intrinsically "good." Thus, it contributes to continuity and stability of relationships, and limits the range of possible means of adaptation. Though childless marriages or nonpermanent unions may be temporarily functional for particular parts of the economic system, the religious values making a permanent union and childbearing "good" in and of themselves offer resistance to widespread adaptation in this way.

Our society shares broad central religious values. It also supports different beliefs reflected in a range of denominations. There is general consensus concerning basic Judeo–Christian beliefs. At the same time there is wide variation in beliefs concerning, for example, the "goodness" of childbearing, per se. At one extreme, children are gifts from God and should be ever welcome. At the other end, children are luxuries and should be "bought" only when they can be amply provided for.

The religious institution also changes over time, however. New meanings develop for old symbols. The importance of religion in guiding behavior varies as does its place in the hierarchy of other social institutions. Individual denominations differ in their resistance to social change. Thus, at any point in time the range of family norms and values to which a given family is exposed varies depending upon the religious affiliation as well as the strength of the commitment to it.

The Educational Institution. The educational institution is closely interrelated with the needs of the economic institution. As demands for certain knowledge and skills change, norms concerning the nature and function of education change. As the need for training beyond that which can be given by the family grows, the educational system expands, aiding the family in training its members for societal participation. At the same time, it lessens the influence the family has over the value system of its members. Depending upon its relationship with the religious institution it either hastens or slows down changes in family values held in check by religious values. In our society, the strong value separating the religious and educational institutions tends to nullify partially the braking effect exerted by religious values. The amount of time an individual family exposes itself to the educational system partly determines its point of contact with the economic system: the greater the education the better the job. The amount of time spent in contact with the educational system, then, influences the expectations for family relationships—through values as well as through the potential level of living.

The Political Institution. Every society must be concerned with the maintenance of order and the distribution of power. The norms which develop to guide this behavior form the political institution. The central value system of a society is reflected in the way the power positions are distributed—through descent, force, popular elections, and so forth. In our own society, the policies reflected in major legislative programs have a direct influence on the family. There is little family policy, per se (Schorr, 1962). Rather, it creeps in as unanticipated consequences of other interests such as public welfare, poverty programs, social security, Medicare, veterans programs, and related concerns. As only one example of legislative influence exerting itself on the family institution, consider the impact of social security, Medicare, and old-age assistance programs on the expectations for care of aged parents. This was at one time considered the sole responsibility of the family. Many aging parents occupied a position in the family of a son or daughter. Whether or not they made their home with a child, however, the norms of the period placed responsibility for their welfare on the shoulders of their grown children. Regardless of the other effects of the social security and Medicare legislations, one consequence has been the removal of this responsibility from the family. The norm is now debatable. Again, however, variation is noted in the resistance to change. A study conducted among high school students in Texas (Moore and Holtzman, 1965) revealed a significant difference in attitudes toward the care of aged parents between religious denominations. Catholic students were much more likely to see this as their own responsibility than were the more liberal Protestant groups. The question of care of the aged was not isolated from other expectations for family relationships. Those seeing care of the aged as the children's responsibility were also more likely to think the parents should give up everything for their children and less likely to insist on privacy for themselves within the family. Thus, government policy influences expectations for family relationships through attempting to perform services seen as legitimate functions in keeping with central values of the society.

The Family Itself. Through daily interaction within its own social context combined with the individual past histories of husband and wife, a given family develops its own culture. In some ways the family's culture will be very similar to all other families in the society, in some ways it will be similar to certain other families, in others it will be quite unique. Children born into this family will see the world initially through the screen provided by this family's culture. The range of available expectations for family relationships contained in the central value systems, and in the economic, religious, political, and educational institutions, is restricted by the particular family's experiences in these systems and the selective incorporation of norms into its own behavior.

An individual marriage takes place in a social context defined broadly by central values and the political institution and more selectively by the particular segments of the economic, religious, and educational systems with which it has had contact. The changing needs of these institutions place demands for adaptation on the family that result in a framework of norms and values which furnish guidelines for the structuring of family goals, authority patterns, emotional relationships, and definitions of marital success. Part I of this book is devoted to a discussion of the changes in these institutions and the resultant consequences for the family.

The Individual

The social context describes the normative world in which the family exists. The interactional aspect in marriage directs attention to the individuals, and the personalities they bring with them. *Personality* is used here as an umbrella concept—the totality of all the attitudes, habits, ideas, and traits (both inborn and acquired) that makes a person what he is.

Each individual personality considered as a totality is unique from every other individual. However, if the concern is with those aspects of the personality particularly relevant to marital interaction, there are again consistencies in development and in the consequences for marital interaction. The aspects of personality singled out for analysis are those values and attitudes concerning masculinity, femininity, family relationships, and activities directly related to the family; those habitual ways of perceiving, interpreting, and reacting to behaviors in others; and most important of all the perception and continual evaluation of one's self—the self-concept.

The Self-Concept. Through interaction with "significant others," the individual develops a self-concept. For most persons, the first significant others are parents and family members. The family members represent a particular social context from which they interpret and evaluate the child. In so doing, they transmit to him expectations for personality characteristics and behaviors appropriate to that social context. He develops concepts of the characteristics associated with masculinity and femininity at different age levels as well as concepts of appropriate behavior associated with different status positions such as father, mother, husband, son, daughter, student, employee, and so on. From recurring interactions that transmit expectations and evaluations of self and others he develops a hierarchy of values which guide his expectations of self and others in future relationships.

Habits of Perception, Interpretation, and Reaction.   Every individual is exposed to masses of data coming into him in the form of expectations, evaluations, descriptive information, and feelings. In order to make sense out of the overwhelming amount of information, he learns to screen out what appears to be irrelevant, anxiety-provoking, or disturbing. He learns to attach meaning to those gestures or verbalizations he allows himself to perceive, to hierarchically evaluate them, and to react to them. He cannot react to another person's action without first interpreting its meaning. Interaction takes place in terms of its interpretation rather than in terms of the action itself. The reaction, for example, that a husband gets to his bringing home a box of candy to his wife will depend on whether she interprets it as an admission of guilt, something he ought to do occasionally as a husband, or a spontaneous, thoughtful expression of love. His satisfaction with her reaction will depend on whether or not he interpreted the act in the same way. These interpretations are learned initially through interaction with persons who have already developed interpretations of behavior within a social context. Interaction with others within the same context, where meanings may be similar, reinforces the original interpretations. Thus, an individual develops habits of perception, interpretation, and reaction. The development of these aspects of the personality and their consequences in marriage and family relationships will be taken up in Part II of the book.

Marital Interaction

Marital interaction is only one type of interpersonal relationship. It has many things in common with other relationships, such as friendships, partnerships, lovers, father–daughter, and mother–son. It differs from other relationships in the combination of areas of activity it covers, and the goals it attempts to achieve. Interaction implies at least two individuals. Each individual has been developed in a different social context. The resulting interaction—the marital relationship—is viewed as the consequence of the peculiar combination of value hierarchies, habitual perceptions, interpretations, and reactions carried by the participants subjected to external pressures connected with the meeting of everyday needs.

Certain external pressures, such as the demands of a military career, force recurring activities—numerous geographical moves, perhaps. This would be expected to accentuate one pattern of interaction and de-emphasize others, which may make this relationship something different in this social context from what it may have been in some other context.

The development of any continuing relationship involves the establishment of interactive patterns which tend to become stabilized. These patterns highlight certain aspects of the personalities and rarely call others into play. The recurring focus on particular aspects of the personality and the evaluation of them leads to changes in the self-concept. The marriage relationship is, then, something different than the sum of the two individual personalities. It is a consequence of the interplay between personalities which themselves have the potential for being changed, evaluated, and confirmed in the relationship itself.

Viewed in this way, the personalities contribute to and become part of the interaction. A woman, for instance, with a great need for order may interject a strong emphasis on keeping things neat, clean, and in their place. If her husband shares this personality trait, the maintenance of an orderly household may become a satisfying, overriding characteristic of the relationship. If, on the other hand, he views this as of secondary importance and as evidence of rigidity or superficiality on her part, much conflict can be introduced into the interaction. As the relationship develops, however, the interaction becomes part of the personality—the repetitive evaluation occurring in the interaction may make her progressively more nagging and critical, or freer and more relaxed, enjoying with her husband what may then be seen as "comfortable disarray." In a real sense, it can be said that a person is never the same after a marriage relationship, whether this be viewed positively, negatively, or humorously. Parts III and IV of this book will be devoted to a discussion of the interaction between personality, relationship, and social context variables as they apply to mate selection and marital interaction.

The Principle of Value Relevance

This book attempts to maintain a consistent perspective. It does not take a moralistic stance, which would imply that the authors subscribe to a value system from which they judge beliefs or behaviors to be right or wrong. Nor do the authors attempt to influence behavior in order to bring it in line with a set of beliefs. Privately they may hold such beliefs, but the perspective of the book is not from these positions.

This is a scientific perspective in that it recognizes that judgment of "good" or "bad" made on any behavior rests on assumptions concerning the nature of man, the potential for his development, and the ultimate goals of his activities. These assumptions, in turn, are supplied and confirmed by widely shared belief systems which have ramifications in their effect on individual attitudes, behavior, and evaluations of self. From the perspective of this book, these belief systems are recognized and become part of the data, subject to analysis. They must be explained and used as variables in explaining other behavior. The interest here is only in describing and attempting to explain relationships between numerous factors which have an impact on marriage and family relationships.

The perspective can be summed up as *the principle of value relevance*. In essence, this principle states that an act or thing is neither good nor bad in and of itself—it is made good or bad by the attitudes of the persons actively involved and of the social groups within which they interact. In reality, these attitudes have the effect of endowing the object with inherent good or bad qualities for those persons who subscribe to them. For these persons, the attitude appears to be a universal assessment and provides for them needed guidelines and a feeling of security in their behavior. From the scientific perspective, however, the belief which makes the behavior appear universal and to possess ultimate "good" must be examined—not from the standpoint of assessing its "rightness" or "wrongness," but of examining the effect of the belief on family continuity, harmony, conflict, integration or disintegration. In other societies where only one set of values is seen as "right," or where extreme pressure is exerted to enforce conformity, the effect of conflicting values may not be so important in the marriage relationship. But in our society, where the right to one's own beliefs is a central value, the effect of these beliefs and potential conflict between them is of crucial importance in understanding family life.

Application to Family Analysis.   The value relevance position forces us to look at the family from two conceptual frameworks. One, the *structural-functional framework*, considers the norms guiding family behavior and their relationship to other societal structures supporting various value systems. For example, we are interested in the effect of the economic structure on family norms. In our expanding society the economic structure supports a value system under which change is equated with progress —and is evaluated as good. We are also interested in the impact of the religious structure, part of which supports a value system under which change may be equated with loss of moral standards—and is evaluated as bad. Consider, then, the present dilemma concerning changes toward more freedom in premarital sexual behavior. From one value system comes the predisposition to emphasize the "rightness" of this behavior as the change is seen to increase individual freedom, to herald the increasing equality of the sexes, and to emphasize the break with tradition (seen as restricting and impeding progress). From the other value system comes a predisposition to emphasize the "wrongness" of this behavior as a deviation from chastity norms (with such behavior seen as immoral and threatening to the whole structure of monogamous and permanent marriage relationships based on sexual exclusiveness).

The second conceptual framework is that of the *symbolic interaction approach*. This framework focuses on the attempts of individual families to integrate the values stemming from contact with various institutions, and to transmit them to children through socialization. The structural–functional approach focuses attention on the social context and changes therein, while the symbolic interaction approach focuses attention on individual development, subsequent marriage and family relationships, and the place of values in interaction.

Sources of Value Conflict. The focus of values and their relationship to marital success leads to a consideration of the different points at which value conflict may occur and place strain on an individual relationship.

The culture itself provides one source of conflict. The family is dependent upon the culture for a definition of its values. What is right in one culture may be wrong in another, or at a different time in the same culture. To give one illustration, our forefathers tended to regard marriage as successful if it were permanent and provided many children, regardless of other satisfactions, whereas modern couples are more willing to sacrifice both of these factors when necessary for the sake of personal happiness.

As stated earlier, when cultural change is taking place it does not occur uniformly across a society; sub-cultural differences appear, resulting in conflicting values supported by different groups. Differences in value hierarchies appear between age groups. Teen-agers, for example, are not likely to hold the same hierarchy of values as their parents. In family interaction, then, the interpretation of identical behavior is likely to vary, decreasing communication and understanding between family members.

Within the marital pair value conflict is most likely. Because modern society is highly heterogeneous, the probability that husband and wife were developed in social contexts supporting different value systems is increased. When conflict over values occurs, there exists no universal measure for deciding which is correct. The probability is increased that different images appear in the couple's minds when the term good wife or good husband is used, depending upon the goals seen to be important in the good marriage or family. Rather than there being any universal criteria for determining the best characteristics of a wife or husband, the evaluation depends on the demands of the particular external situation, the values of the social groups within which the marriage is acted out, and the individual values of the participants. To the extent that value systems are not shared, it can be assumed that communication and understanding between the participants is decreased and conflict increased.

Within the individual himself there exists the possibility of value conflict. There are at least three types of value conflict which can occur within the individual. The first is a conflict between personal and cultural norms. In our society there is an expectation that an individual will experience change in at least some of the factors comprising his social context. He is likely to change his social class position from that of his parents, change his religion, part of the country, and numerous affiliations with informal social groups. Values acquired in one social context may be subjected to conflict and pressures for change as he moves into new contexts.

The second type of value conflict occurs from the actual internalization of cultural conflict. As long as value conflicts exist in the larger society, the possibility is always present that the individual may incorporate these conflicts within himself. It is quite likely today, for example, for the college-educated woman to hold to some degree two conflicting values: (1) that it is "good" for a woman to remain at home, devoting her life to husband and children; and (2) that complete devotion to family affairs is restricting, a waste of her capabilities, and for the "good" of her family she should maintain contact with the outside world in some kind of work. Whichever value she acts out in her own life, there is a strong possibility that she will experience some doubt or guilt over her decision. She is likely to have the feelings that she is neglecting her family if she works, since she thinks she *should* be devoting full time to them. If she stays at home, she is likely to feel she is wasting her capabilities—not doing enough with her education.

The third type of conflict involves a situation in which a person may be forced, by external circumstances, to act out values with which he does not agree and for which he is not suited. Consider the husband who, because of career demands, must involve his wife in a great amount of social activity. He may not enjoy this kind of life, feel that he is using his family for his own gain, yet think he must do this in order to provide financial security.

Value conflicts, from whatever source, find their way into marriage and family relationships. The way they are perceived and worked out in the relationship is related to the individuals' assessment of the marriage itself. Hence rather than proceeding from the orientation of any one value system, the perspective of the remainder of the book will be on *values as data*. Values are seen as useful in analyzing and suggesting the sources of marital harmony or disharmony.

SUMMARY

Marriages are highly personal relationships, but they take place in a social context. The social context provides a limited range of norms and values which form expectations for the marriage relationship and the criteria used for evaluating the successful marriage.

The social context is a space marked off in the larger society defined by the individual's particular contact with the economic, educational, religious, political, and family institutions. Within this context the individual develops a self-concept which influences his behavior, his expectations for marriage, and his sense of integrity and continuity. Since the activities a person engages in have an impact on his concept of self and feelings of self-esteem, marital success is defined in self-concept terms. Since not everyone wants or needs the same thing from marriage, the successful marriage is seen as one in which the interaction between the spouses continually confirms for them positive self-concepts which are functional for the social context in which the marriage takes place. This focuses attention on the variety of marital types which may be successful or unsuccessful depending upon the needs of the individuals and the social contexts within which they interact.

The analytical framework of this book utilizes the structural–functional and symbolic interaction approaches. These perspectives focus on the effect of social change on norms and values guiding family behavior, as well as the processes by which these values are instilled in the individual as he grows up in a particular family culture.

The perspective of this book is in accord with the principle of value relevance and it treats values as data rather than as support for any one value position. It recognizes that values and value conflict are crucial in understanding family interaction. The way they are perceived and worked out in the relationship is related to the individuals' assessment of their marriage and family. A major task of the remainder of this book is to assess the importance of values in understanding the sources of marital harmony or disharmony.

QUESTIONS AND PROJECTS

1. Arrange a panel discussion on the topic of what makes a successful marriage. Is there much variation in ideas among the group? Is there any uniformity to the discrepancies—between males and females, between married and unmarried persons, etc.?

2. What is meant by the term social context? How does this concept relate to the question of *relevance* in family life education?

3. Describe the relationships between institutions. What are their contributions to change in family norms and values?

4. What is the principle of value relevance? Give illustrations.

5. Why are values such an important consideration in a study of marriage and family interaction?

2

The Family as a Changing Institution

It is commonplace to speak of *marriage* and *family* in the same breath, as if they were synonymous. Actually these terms refer to separate, though closely related, social institutions. Marriage is society's way of sanctioning and controlling adult sexual behavior. It differs from *mating* in that the latter is simply a biological act, largely instinctive and temporary. Marriage is the institutionalization of that act, together with the many psychological and sociological overtones that surround it. Marriage fixes responsibility for sex and makes order out of what otherwise would be chaos. Marriage plus children make a family.

Nearly everyone belongs to at least two families during his lifetime; his *family of orientation* and his *family of procreation*. The first he is born into and the second he establishes through marriage. He is a child in the one and a parent in the other. Thus there is continuity from generation to generation.

UNIFORMITY AND DIVERSITY IN FAMILY FORMS

No society has ever been without marriage and the family. They are what is known as "universal social institutions." Both have antiquity and universality. Societies vary regarding details of custom; but always, in all ages and all cultures, some sort of family life has been the norm. Love and procreation outside of marriage have been exceptions in the history of mankind, never the rule.

There must be a reason. Is it that man is born with the urge to marry, that family life is instinctive? Anthropologists, sociologists, and psy-

20

chologists say not; for while the drive to mate is a part of one's original nature, the institutions for realizing and controlling this urge are a part of man's culture, and are learned. Why, then, are marriage and family life so ubiquitous? The answer to this question lies in the similarity of needs among men and the apparent tendency of man everywhere to organize similar institutions to meet these common needs. Institutions are promoted and perpetuated for the sake of specific functions they can perform in the light of recognized human needs.

Universal Functions

The long dependency period of the human infant requires some arrangement for his protection and feeding until he is able to care for himself. In every society this recurring need has resulted in the development of a set of norms prescribing how and by whom the infant will be cared for. This set of norms partially forms the family institution of a society. Each activity, however, is closely linked to and has consequences for other activities, resulting in a complex web of interdependent institutions. The consequences which an institution has for the integration between other institutions and the continuity of society are called the *functions* of that institution. Certain family functions appear in every society in some form, no matter how varied the family form. The functions which are recognizable in all known societies are called the *universal functions of the family*.

Some of these are no doubt essential to the perpetuation of a society. Whether they could result equally well from some other type of human grouping rather than one based on kinship is a moot question. Every society *has* grouped people together in terms of the adult sex relationship and blood kin. This arrangement has had universal consequences for other aspects of every society. In order to see clearly the interconnection between various institutions, the universal functions will be examined one by one.[1]

Responsible Reproduction. For a society to continue over one generation there must be some orderly way of replacing aging and dying members. The major portion of this replacement normally comes from reproduction. Reproduction can occur without benefit of a social institution such as marriage. The need, however, is not just for reproduction—the need is for young adults trained to take over as the elders become incapacitated or die. The existence of a family group bound together by

---

[1] This discussion of universal functions follows the scheme presented by Goode (1959, pp. 178–96).

blood ties serves to place responsibility for the new infant on an organized group. As the family exercises control over who comes into it through marriage and subsequent reproduction, it has the effect of structuring the choice of marriage mates, ordering the satisfaction of sexual and emotional needs, and legalizing parenthood.

The way this is done gives rise to the family organization considered "right" and "normal" to the individuals reared in that society. The smallest unit or "least common denominator" in family organization, the _nuclear family_, consists of husband, wife, and immediate children. It exists everywhere throughout the world and is the typical pattern in the United States. In many societies, however, nuclear families are clustered together, like atoms in a molecule, to form larger aggregations. Two principles govern the manner in which nuclear families combine. (1) They may be joined at the focus of the marriage relationship, making for plural marriages where one of the spouses is a member of every nuclear family. This is known as _polygamy_, which means that one spouse has two or more mates. If it is a husband with several wives, the technical term is _polygyny;_ whereas if it is a wife with several husbands, the technical term is _polyandry_. Though this latter practice is the rarer of the two, there are at least a half-dozen societies in which it has been known to exist. (2) If the blood bond becomes the point at which nuclear families are joined, there develops what is known as an _extended or consanguine family._ This is an organization that cuts across several generations. An example is the traditional Chinese family, consisting of the oldest living male, his wife or wives, his unmarried children, his married sons, together with their wives and unmarried children, his married grandsons, together with their wives and unmarried children, and also great-grandsons if there are any. Daughters, on marrying, leave their own families and join those of their husbands. This is an example of an extended family traced by patrilineal descent. Kinship can also be traced by matrilineal descent, in which the family consists of the oldest living female, her husband, unmarried children, married daughters, and so forth. There are variations on these lines of descent but in general extended families represent an expansion of the parent–child relationship; polygamous families represent an expansion of the husband–wife relationship. Both are fairly common in various parts of the world. Most common, however, is the nuclear family founded upon _monogamy_ (the marriage of one man to one woman).

Although there is great variation in the structuring of the marriage relationship regarding the number of spouses and place of residence, all family forms result in ordering the satisfaction of sexual and emotional needs, and in placing the offspring from the sexual unions in the midst of a small group which has the responsibility for it. The designation of which individuals are family members also structures the kinds of relationships the child will have as it starts its long journey toward eventual adult participation in the society.

Biological Maintenance.   A necessary requirement for the continuance of a society is the meeting of the essential biological needs of its members. They must be fed, clothed, and protected from bodily harm.   The gathering together of individuals in family groups results in spreading the responsibility for meeting these individual needs.   The family organization determines who is entitled to share in the family's goods, how long he can expect to share, and what he must contribute to the maintenance of other family members.

In some societies the family becomes self-sufficient, meeting all the biological needs of its members.   Our own pioneer families approximated this extreme.   The great distances between families and the difficulty of transportation made them largely dependent upon their own efforts.

On the other hand, the family may be completely dependent on a societal network of coordinated activities to produce and distribute commodities which must be bought.   In this case, typical of present-day America, the survival of the family does not depend on the cooperative efforts of all the members but on the continuation of the economic system which produces the necessities as well as offers the opportunity to earn the money needed to purchase them.

However the raw materials are obtained, some preparation and distribution of goods among family members is necessary.   The amount and kind of preparation varies tremendously, but everywhere the meeting of individual biological needs results in some kind of division of labor within the family.   Every society has made labor divisions along age and sex lines.   Different tasks become differentiated according to whether they are seen to be "man's work," "woman's work," "boy's work," or "girl's work."   In the family, these develop into the social roles applying to the positions of husband, wife, son, and daughter.

No matter how extended these roles become, they start from such questions as who takes care of the baby; who provides the food and clothing, whether this means growing raw material or providing money to purchase them; who does the cooking; who feeds the chickens; who mends the clothes; and so on.   When these divisions are made, however, they have ramifications which extend to numerous other relationships.   Seldom do these sex-based divisions of labor exist without the development of concepts of masculinity and femininity to support them.

Societies, for example, vary within and among themselves from the extreme of making woman the "work-horse" of the family to enshrining her on a throne of fragility.   Each of these positions carries with it supporting beliefs about the biological nature of woman and ideals of femininity. In early America, at the same time the pioneer woman was working alongside her husband in the fields, her urban counterpart was swooning in her drawing room at the slightest excitement or exertion.

The degree to which the biological needs of the family are met solely by the cooperative efforts of all members has implications for the internal authority structure of the family. If there are crucial tasks which must be performed for the family to survive, then someone must be responsible for assigning them and seeing that they are carried out. If the failure of one of the members is immediately felt by all the family, that authority structure is reinforced. If the cooperative efforts of all members are not required to meet these crucial needs, there is less necessity for a strong centralized authority structure. Imagine for a moment a strong father in a family dependent upon firewood for cooking and warmth. He assigns to one of his sons the task of filling the firebox by a certain time every day without fail. The boy's failure to do this would probably result not only in a painful response from his father, but he would be as cold and hungry as the rest of the family. Now imagine a strong father in a family living in a modern, centrally heated home. He assigns to his son the task of coming straight home from school every day without fail to bring in wood for the fireplace in the recreation room. This boy's failure to do so may result in the same painful response from his father, but no crucial loss occurs to him or any other family member because of his failure. The action becomes more arbitrary and provides little justification for the need of a strong authority structure.

Some authority structure is present in every family institution. The nature and strength of it will vary, partially, in response to the way the family meets its biological needs. Where the responsibility resides in the father—or eldest male in the extended family—we have the *patriarchal* authority structure so well-known in our past. If the authority is vested in the mother—or eldest female—it is called a *matriarchal* authority structure. Where it is shared between father and mother, it is spoken of as an *equalitarian* authority pattern.

Status Placement. The cooperation necessary for societal survival would not be possible without the ability to predict the behavior of the members in various situations. Part of this predictability comes from an organization of norms guiding the way individuals act toward others in different status positions. Every society has developed some arrangement for ranking individuals in terms of the positions they occupy, characteristics they possess, or tasks they perform. The hierarchical evaluation of individuals is supported by a system of role relationships which emphasizes the legitimacy of the system. The subject bows to the king; the young employee speaks respectfully to his older employer; the tribesman pays homage to the old chief; the "untouchable" crosses the road when a caste Hindu approaches; the Japanese mother bows her infant's head to a person of higher rank. The acting out of the expected behavior may not connote agreement with it, but it does convey a recognition of its legitimacy.

Societies vary drastically in the rigidity of the ranking order—or stratification system—and in the elaborateness of the supporting interactions. Every society, however, supports some differential treatment of individuals, depending upon their positions within it. The prestige awarded the individual occupying the position generally extends to the family members —the prince is treated differently than the pauper. Thus, the infant, by being born into a family, is born into a ready-made place in the society according to his family's position within it. The way he is treated by numerous others outside the family group will be partly ordered because of the existing stratification system. The ordering of these relationships produces the necessary predictability of others' behavior so that the growing child can form a concept of who he is, where he belongs, and where he may hope to go in his society.

Depending upon one's value system, certain stratification systems may be evaluated as fair or unfair; but regardless of the judgment made, they all have the consequence of providing some order in human relationships. This order contributes to the integration of the individual's concept of self, whether the resulting self-concept is evaluated as good or bad.

In some societies, the status placement function of the family extends through adulthood, with the family's class or caste largely determining the occupations the children can aspire to and the field of eligibles from which a mate may be selected. Others, not quite so restrictive, still exert control over the adult status of their children by arranging their marriages. Many of these are economic arrangements uniting families similar in rank, thereby reinforcing the existing stratification system. Some societies, like our own, have freer systems. The individual's adult status is not wholly determined by the family of orientation and marriages are not arranged. Even here, however, potential relationships are ordered through place of residence, school attendance, and social group restrictions. This limiting of the people one may hope to meet shows the continuing effect of the status position of the family on adult occupation and mate selection. A person is much more likely to date and select a marriage partner from his own general social class position than one much higher or much lower. The great attention attracted by the rare Cinderella marriage illustrates the lack of cultural prohibition against them (our value system favoring equality) and the force exerted by the status placement function of the family which almost precludes its occurrence. The status placement function, then, contributes to the continuity over time of predictable individual behavior necessary for societal order, and aids in maintaining the status quo both through the restriction of social groups with which the children have contact and by transmittal to them of the values and expectations expressed in that part of the society to which the family belongs. Although there is great variation among societies, the family in all of them tends to hold its members in well-established class positions, as well as make it seem right and natural to them.

Socialization. As stated earlier, any society must have orderly replacement of its members to exist. This means the young members must be trained in the skills utilized by the society. They must learn how to communicate their thoughts and feelings, how to act. In other words, the biological organism must become a human being, able to participate in the activities of his society. It is this process of transforming the biological organism into a social being that is called socialization. It is the process of acquiring the characteristics, values, attitudes, and behaviors which are associated with being a responsible member of society. This only happens through group interaction within a cultural framework. The family, as it cares for its own offspring, provides the continued interaction for this to take place. As the young child is slowly introduced to the family activities, he learns the expectations held of him in accord with his sex, his age, and his status in the community. Since his family is part of an ongoing society, the things he learns within it provide the training for participation in the larger community as well.

Societies differ widely in the amount of socialization which occurs within the family. On the whole, the more simple the society the greater the proportion of socialization which takes place informally within the family group. In extremely complex societies, such as our own, the family is not able to socialize the child for full participation. It is aided by other institutions such as the educational and religious institutions. Socialization includes not only the formal acquisition of skills associated with education, but the "taking on" of morals—the internalization of them so that they become a functioning part of the member's personality. This is done informally by the family as it transmits the meanings of activities, the beliefs concerning its own place in the scheme of things, and morally "right" and "wrong" behavior; and formally through organized religious groupings.

Whether the socialization process is carried out solely by the family or aided by other agencies, the family appears to be the primary influence in developing the personality of the child, which itself is the outcome of the impact of socialization on the unique combination of inherited characteristics in the biological organism. There probably could develop other means of caring for and socializing children, but some continuity of contact with the same individuals over time seems necessary for the acquisition of a stable, integrated personality. A stable family grouping has a consequence of heightening the probability that the necessary contact will occur, thus providing a steady supply of young adults prepared to participate in societal activities and to perpetuate the society by wanting to reproduce the family form in which they were reared.

Emotional Maintenance. Some kind of human interaction appears necessary not only for socialization of the young, but also for the maintenance of stability among adults. Some feeling of belonging somewhere, of being important to someone appears to be a universal human need. The placing of individuals together in terms of kinship at least offers the opportunity for this need to be met. Man's long period of dependency before he is able to care for himself results in the development of some kind of continuing need for dependable, predictable relationships. When this need is met, the individual feels a measure of security. The type of relationship he seeks and interprets as being emotionally secure is probably related to the family structure and kind of nurturing care he received in his family of orientation.

Social Control. All of the foregoing family functions result in a measure of control exerted over individual behavior, thereby contributing to societal order. Not only does the family exert overt control over its members by demanding certain behaviors and restricting others, it lessens the need for overt control by developing internal controls within the individual personality through the socialization process. The amount of social control provided by the family varies with the degree to which the family is the sole agency providing for biological and emotional maintenance, for socialization, and for status placement.

In the days of Rome, long before the beginning of the Empire, there was in existence the archetype of the extended patriarchal family. The ruling patriarch of this family held the power of life and death over the males in the family for life, and over the females until they were transferred to some other family through marriage. The individual family powers were so inclusive that no central government could emerge. Not until they were threatened by invaders was their need for cooperation great enough to force the family patriarchs to relinquish enough power to allow the formation of a loose central government.

At the other extreme, the Israeli kibbutz represents a family form which has been reduced almost entirely to the reproductive function. Biological maintenance, as well as the major portion of emotional maintenance, socialization, and status placement is supplied by the total community. Although the parents and children maintain a certain amount of contact during leisure hours, the basic needs of all are supplied through the cooperative efforts of all members. Here, the social control of the family is at a minimum, being transferred to nurses, teachers, and the informal control of the peer group.

An Adaptive, Conservative Institution

When the universal functions of the family—including responsible reproduction, biological maintenance, status placement, socialization, emotional maintenance, and social control—are viewed together, we see that they result in continuous, ordered interaction which develops individuals capable of participating in the society, places them within it, and maintains them as actively contributing adults. Tied as it is to other institutions, the family is continually mediating between the demands of these other institutions and the demands of its own individual members. The norms forming the institution are constantly subjected to change as many individual families adapt to changing conditions, thereby presenting to their growing children new models of the correct way to do things.

The Adaptive Aspect. Around the turn of the century, the urban middle class family in our society was embedded in a relatively stable external world. Transportation and communication systems were, by our standards today, poorly developed. Of necessity activities tended to be carried out close to home. We have mental images of the punctuality and relative formality of family mealtimes. Children were expected to be gathered around when father returned home from work. Few conflicting interests were present to pull mother and the children away from the schedule geared to father's demands.

Consider the changes which have taken place in this one activity of family meals as millions of individual families have had to adjust to lengthening distances between work and home, demands of the public schools for children's time, church group meetings, civic activities, little league practices, choir rehearsals, and the numerous demands from other groups which require the participation of many individuals in order to exist. Family mealtimes have become informal; time schedules have become flexible. For many, the whole family is gathered together around the table only a few times a week. A father, coming from a family where mealtime schedules were ritualistically observed and valued, may find himself fighting a losing battle as he tries to maintain the customs of his youth. If he insists that his teen-age children be present at dinner regardless of scheduled football practices, play rehearsals, or an extra help session called by the algebra teacher, he is likely to find himself under attack not only by family members but by the school system as well.

It is the formal organization of other groups which puts added pressure on the individual families to adapt. Clark Vincent (1966a) sees this adaptive function as one of the important characteristics of our modern families.

Since individual families have no formal organization, they are at a disadvantage when pressured by organized groups to give up their members at times when the organized group can attract the greatest number of participants—not when it is convenient for the individual families. Thus, the church choir picks a practice time when the director is available, the rehearsal room is not in use by other church groups, and when competing groups do not have scheduled meetings—not in accord with the schedules of individual families. Thus, if families motivate their members to participate, they must adapt to the demands of the organized groups. As many families adapt to similar external situations new norms begin to develop, and the institution is in the process of adaptation.

The Conservative Aspect. Although the family institution is an adaptive one, it is also conservative. That is, it tends to hold to and promote the status quo. As we grow up in a family we see and interpret the world through that family and that portion of society in which it is embedded. As we obtain emotional support and a feeling of security within it, we have a tendency to want to reproduce it as adults (Kirkpatrick, 1963, pp. 195–99). We gain a measure of security by reproducing the situation in which we felt secure as children. To the extent, then, that the universal family functions are adequately produced by the family institution, the probability is heightened that the individuals will see that way of doing things as "right," "good," and "proper," and will try to reproduce it in the next generation. The father in the previous illustration may be forced to give in somewhat to the demands for flexible mealtime schedules, but he may feel that the family is falling apart and insist on family meals being taken together on certain days—when nothing outside can interfere. The family then becomes a mediating institution: mediating the demands from a changing society through older values and mediating the demands of the society to protect the individual.

Evaluation of the Family

Present day concern about our society's ability to survive is oriented around the functions of the family. The continual concern with strengthening the family can be seen to be organized around securing these family functions. Many social problems are traced to either the failure or extreme success of the family functions. The growing problem of illegitimacy suggests the weakening of the function of *responsible* reproduction. The hurry with which some young people rush into marriage and begin their childbearing period—or the over-emphasis on this function—is viewed by others as alarming. The rise of delinquent and criminal behavior brings concern about the failure of the *socialization* and *social control* functions. The increasing number of youths demonstrating for racial equality, peace, and so forth brings concern from some about the failure of the family to transmit values supporting the ongoing system. The same behavior brings praise from other quarters for the successful transmission of the central values of democracy and individual freedom. The problem does not appear to be that families do not transmit values, but that they transmit too well the "wrong" ones. Which ones are seen as wrong varies with the point of view of the observer.

The proportion of hospital beds occupied by the mentally ill questions the adequacy of the family in providing emotional maintenance. The present attempts to combat poverty attack the failure of some families to provide *biological maintenance* while being too successful in their *status placement* and *reproduction* functions. In other words, the successful transmission of the values and skills which provide support for the continuation of the stratification system may be seen as "bad" if there is a desire to upset the system. Recognition of this can be seen in the attempts to counter the early influence of the family by an extension of the educational system through the Head Start program.

The family functions appear to play a crucial part in the survival of a society in its present form. Where the family system is extremely strong, then it becomes a powerful force to combat if wide-scale societal change is attempted, since all of its functions contribute to stability and the continuance of the status quo. Once a change is made, however, the family again begins to function and can as readily transmit the new values. If the family system is extremely weak, then the adaptation to demands for change may be very rapid with little commitment to the preservation of the system. The family appears crucial to societal survival. Whether this is the result of our own socialization within a family system which limits the awareness of other arrangements; or whether it is a *necessary* institution we cannot know at present. No society which has left a history has developed an alternate form with which to compare. The kibbutz comes closest to developing an alternate form, but its history is not yet long enough to give conclusive evidence of its survival over time in its present form.

CHANGES IN THE AMERICAN FAMILY

It makes a difference in talking about long-term changes in the family, whether we are speaking of norms—what one ought to do—or what families actually do or did in the past. If we are talking about what families actually did, we are on shifting sands. We do not know much about what families actually did. We are much safer talking about norms and values.

Then we may draw upon articles, novels, memories, stories told from generation to generation and be fairly comfortable in the expectation that deviations from actual descriptions are in the direction of the norms. It is well to keep in mind that behavior is not always in conformity to the norms. We well know that husbands and wives are supposed to love each other, to cooperate with each other, and present a united front to their children and the community. We know just as well, that few families manage this all the time and that some seem to manage it seldom or not at all. The norms are still there, however, furnishing a standard for measuring our own and others' behavior. The young husband who tells his wife: "I don't mind helping you with the dishes, but for heaven's sakes don't tell anybody I do it," is reaffirming the norms concerning the division of labor at the same time he is deviating from them.

It is relatively easy to see the variation of behavior during our own time, but as we look back over distances in time the various shades and hues run together and the emerging picture appears of a single color, with life amazingly uncomplicated and in simple conformity to the norms. As we talk about the family in earlier times, then, it will be well to remember that probably behavior has never been in complete accord with the norms. But as the family institution has adjusted to changing social and physical environments, it has maintained some central threads through the long course of history.

Historical Roots of Family Values

It is not surprising that the modern American family has deep roots in the Judeo–Christian tradition. The Hebrew family form as well as the Christian adaptations of it are well documented in the Old and New Testaments of the Bible. These writings continue to provide support for forms developed long ago.

The Christian Influence.   One of the greatest influences on the American family has been Christianity. The family form supported by the edicts of the Church fathers associated with early Christianity has been described by Kirkpatrick as a reaction by a repressed minority group to the decadence associated with the latter period of the Roman Empire (Kirkpatrick, 1963, pp. 104–6). The ancient Roman family appeared as an archetype of the patriarchal system. The extreme powers of the patriarch were reinforced by property laws and a family-centered religion in which the father served as priest arranging for the worship of household gods as well as family ancestors. This system was broken by the long period of the Punic Wars, in which the absence of the men cleared the way for women to take over responsible positions, obtain rights to hold property, and also weakened the male-dominated family religion.

With the supports for the Roman family gone, the growing wealth of Rome and the importation of slaves contributed to a period in which the family was greatly weakened. Marriage rates declined; divorce rates increased; abortion, child exposure, and infanticide were common means for decreasing the responsibility accompanying childrearing. Prostitution and increased sexual freedom were characteristic. This was the situation which confronted the early Christians as they began to emerge as a force in the pagan Roman Empire. Kirkpatrick sees the Christian tradition emerging as they reacted against the disorganized Roman family in four important ways.

1. They reacted against the sexual freedom and licentiousness with hostility toward sex and partially to marriage itself. Celibacy was seen as the highest state of man. Marriage was seen as the next best state if one could not manage complete abstinence. This negative attitude toward sex was finally entrenched through the establishment of celibacy as a requirement for the clergy.

2. As another consequence of the aversion toward sex, the status of women suffered a devastating blow. Possibly, since their high status in Rome was accompanied by a decay of social responsibility, their rise in status was seen as a causative factor. The biblical account of the Garden of Eden favored woman's decline. It cast her in the role of temptress as she urged Adam to eat of the forbidden fruit, which probably symbolized sexual temptation to the early Christians. Given their aversion to sex and their image of the woman as a constant evil forever tempting man to fall from his high state of celibacy, it is not surprising that she was again subjugated to the man "for whom she was created."

The one status left open to her was marriage, where the husband was urged to "give honor to the wife as unto a weaker vessel." There she provided, at least, a moral sexual outlet for the man not able to abstain and could breed celibates and virgins. Even marital sex was not to be seen as pleasure but was for the purpose of reproduction—an idea which has only recently been tempered. The historical hostility toward sex apparent in our society has its roots in this extreme reaction to a period of history far removed from the modern world.

3. The practices of infanticide and abortion brought strong reactions from the early Christians. The concern for children found in the teachings of Jesus coupled with the designation of marriage as the one acceptable sexual outlet influenced these reactions to take the form of encouraging childbearing and kindness to children.

4. The fourth reaction to Rome was the Christians' opposition to divorce. There is some doubt concerning the complete abolishment of divorce in this early period, but certainly the free and loose divorce laws of Rome were countered by strong opposition, which included the male

as well as the female. As marriage came more and more under the control of the church, divorce and remarriage were prohibited. Separation from bed and board was allowed under certain circumstances, such as adultery, heresy of one of the parties, or cruelty. Under certain other circumstances the marriage could be nullified, but for all practical purposes marriage was a sacrament, instituted by Christ, and to be presided over by the church. Its dissolution was not to be an individual choice.

The Romantic Tradition.   Although many modern ideas concerning the nature of marriage and its permanence can be traced to Judeo–Christian beliefs and practices, the notion that marriages should be preceded by a love bond must be traced elsewhere. Certainly the human capacity to love is not restricted to Western civilization. Nor is love between man and wife an innovation of the modern family system. What does seem to be unique is the extent to which love as a romantic sexual attraction has been made a prerequisite to marriage in the American society.

Love, as an idealized glorification of the loved object, was a product of the nobility during the Middle Ages. Supposedly, it spread as a consequence of the Crusades. The men were gone long periods of time, leaving their wives alone to manage the affairs of the castle. The love songs of the wandering troubadours were probably a welcome break in the othewise monotonous life of these noble ladies. Marriages were contracted by the families, with little regard for individual preference. So the fantasies of love, of "champions," and chivalrous knights tended to be focused outside of marriage. In fact, the great love stories stemming from that period picture all-consuming love as divorced not only from marriage but also from the sexual union which could result in reproduction. In its initial form, it was characterized by the glorification of the noble gentlewoman. She was placed in her turret window where she epitomized purity, beauty, and sexual inaccessibility. Thus, the glorified feeling of love was based on the idealization of frustrated and unfulfilled desires which became more beautiful the more hopeless the situation.

During the late Middle Ages, however, the romantic love ideal and the continuance of marriages arranged on the basis of economic or political liaisons, contributed to taking the lady out of the turret window and firmly uniting the ideas of sex and love—but still outside of marriage. The love trysts (meetings stolen and secretive) sustained the distance and longing associated with the feeling of love. Marriage was an economic arrangement—a legal prerequisite to reproduction—the constant, monotonous, practical nature of which spelled death to love, if it had ever been present (see Biegel, 1951; Ehrmann, 1964).

The concept of love based on glorification of the woman and nurtured in a relationship which kept the love-partners from seeing anything but

the courtly aspects of their personalities had certain important consequences. Although the woman's status was legally and politically low,
the elevation of her "nature" to one of purity, mysticism and beauty placed
her on a pedestal of adoration. According to Biegel (1951, p. 328):
". . . it introduced voluntary fidelity, restraint, and the magnanimous
gentleness of the male consciously into the relation between the sexes,
qualities that were not considered essential or even possible in a marriage
based on the semi-patriarchal concept of the Middle Ages."

This idea of love spread outside of the court society; the religious beliefs, the tradition of thrift, and the economic struggles of the bourgeois
class would not support the illicit relationships of the aristocracy. Slowly,
the language of romantic love began to be addressed to the unmarried
maiden who was being sought as a wife.

Certainly the ideal of love as the basis for marriage and the lasting
bond between husband and wife is part of our concept of marriage today.
Confusion over the meaning of love, whether it is the unfulfilled longing
and idealization of the loved one or the mutual understanding and affectionate acceptance associated with a long, close, satisfying relationship,
allows it to be both blamed for our high divorce rate and extolled for
saving the monogamous system from complete disorganization. The ideas
forming the basis for the union between love and marriage had their beginnings in the Middle Ages, but today they are solidly welded together,
with love expected to come first and to furnish the basis for the family as
reflected in the childish chant heard on schoolyard playgrounds:

> Jimmy and Mary sitting in a tree
> K-i-s-s-i-n-g.
> First comes love, then comes marriage.
> Then comes Jimmy with a baby carriage.

For a concept, such as love, to become a permanent part of a culture,
it must have support from other aspects of the culture. Van den Haag
suggests that romantic love varies from society to society depending on
the emphasis placed on the individual and sexual restrictions. He says:

Love flowers best in a monogamous environment morally opposed to un-
restrained sex, and interested in cultivating individual experience. In such an
environment, longing may be valued for itself. Thus, love as we know it is a
Christian legacy, though Christianity in the main repudiates romantic love
where the object is worldly, and accepts passion only when transcendant, when
God is the object—or when muted into affection: marital love (Van den Haag,
1962).

Changes Occurring in the New World

Alterations in the family system that developed in Western Europe and
England occurred as settlers migrated to the New World. These settlers

were not representative of the nobility, but were, in the main, working class people. They represented a Protestant minority who had been oppressed for their protest against the interpretation of Christianity forced upon them by the Catholic Church. Many of the changes in the family form can be seen as consequences of this hostility and the hardships imposed by the rigorous tasks of shaping a new life from a large expanse of hostile but promising land.

Marriage as a Civil Contract.   Just as the early Christians had rebelled against the freedom and disorganization of marriage in Rome and gradually brought marriage under the control of the Church the Protestants in the New World rebelled against the oppressive regulation of the Catholic Church and brought it under civil control. The nature of marriage changed from a sacrament ordained by God to a civil contract between a man and woman. Ministers were actually prohibited from performing marriages in some areas until 1700. Regulations were imposed, however, but by the state.

The view of marriage as a man-made contract instead of a religious sacrament opened the way for complete divorce. This served a necessary purpose for the sparsely settled new land. Men needed women to help them in building homes, to contribute to the population through childbearing, and to meet everyday essential needs. A number of the settlers were married men who had left their wives behind. Some were unable to send for their wives as intended, and some of the wives refused to join their husbands. Divorce allowed these men to remarry in the new land and contribute to its growth. Divorce was not prevalent, however, and tended to be granted only for adultery, desertion, cruelty, and refusal of conjugal duty. Marital sex, thus, became viewed as a rightful part of marriage.

The Encouragement of Marriage.   The importance of children, both as extra hands and for increasing the small population, had an impact on the early Christian view which placed celibacy above marriage. The Protestants were in strong disagreement with the Catholic's celibacy requirement for priesthood. The need for reproduction and the extreme hardships faced by a single person in the harsh environment of the struggling settlers led to the encouragement of early marriages and the ridicule of bachelors and single women. Bachelors were subjected to additional taxation and controls intended to hurry them into the married state. Women began to be labeled "old maids" at about the age of twenty-three if they were as yet unmarried.

The hard life, recurrent pregnancies, lack of sanitation, and the rather primitive medical practices took a high toll among women. The pressing need to replace the departed wife by someone to care for the children and perform other household tasks led to an encouragement of early re-marriage. Immediate remarriage a few days or weeks after the death of a wife was not uncommon. Widows were considered highly desirable as marriage partners. They had experience with household tasks and occasionally brought with them their deceased husband's economic assets to which they were entitled. The whole physical environment including the harsh existence, necessity for hard work for survival, and the avail-ability of free land for those with the will to endure the hardships and loneliness, encouraged early marriage, remarriage, and prolific reproduc-tion.

The Higher Status of Women.   These same aspects of the physical en-vironment, especially among the pioneers, brought a change to the status of women. Their contributions were essential and they were scarce. The importance of children emphasized their maternal and wifely image rather than their image as evil temptresses. Although still subjected to harsher treatment than the male for sexual promiscuity or adultery they won more freedom than the essentially patriarchal structure of the family appeared to give them. The loneliness of the pioneer environment and need for cooperative effort forced husband and wife to rely on each other for com-panionship. The availability of free land made it possible for a young couple to be free of family intervention in a way hardly possible when available land was held in the family name under the control of the father. The attributes of the individual became more important than the family name. In individual families, the patriarchal authority structure was still strongly supported, but the long dependence of the children on the family was shortened and the large extended family pattern of the past did not reappear.

Of course, conditions differed in different areas as the colonies devel-oped and united into a single country. In the South, the presence of slaves and large plantations furnished the conditions for a more leisurely life for the master's wife and daughters. Here, the romantic love concept, courtly love, and chivalry were kept alive among the upper class families. The large plantations, almost completely self-sufficient, allowed the de-velopment of extended families and supported family control to a much greater extent than in the West. In both places, however, the status of women was elevated—in one through the romantic theme emphasizing her gentleness, purity, and dependency, and in the other through her im-portant contribution to the family's survival through her essential work and companionship relationship with her husband.

We find vestiges from both these male–female relationships today in discussions concerning the position of women. Perhaps one of the reasons we have difficulty in deciding whether woman's place is "in the home" (as wife, mother, or ornament) or working shoulder to shoulder with men as a contributor to the economy can be found in the firm foundation for both points of view in our early history.

The Tempering of the Patriarchal System. Legally, of course, the early American family was patriarchal. The strong religious beliefs especially prevalent among the Puritans in the New England colonies supported the dominance of the male. They also supported the idea that love should exist between husband and wife. These beliefs legitimized the authority structure through "divine will" and at the same time tempered it as far as husband and wife were concerned. A loving wife was obedient to her husband—a loving husband was kind to his wife. Although love was expected to be a part of marriage, it was discouraged as a factor in mate selection. A man decided it was time to marry, selected a marriage mate on the practical base of availability as well as economic and domestic considerations. But then a short waiting period was recommended to allow the "longing" to result in conjugal love. There is ample evidence in letters and writings of the period that this rational approach to mate selection, followed by a conscious development of love, resulted in deep feelings of devotion (Morgan, 1964). The elements of our modern system were all present—only the time schedule has been reversed.

As our society continued to expand, changes in the economic, religious, and political systems brought changes to the family. But many of the basic values concerning family life and some of the most bitter arguments concerning what it *should* be, have their roots in the unique form which developed as the Christian beliefs, forged in Western Europe, underwent changes as our forefathers coped with the physical and social environment of the New World.

Recent Changes in Family Functions

With this rather brief overview of the historical development of some of our basic ideas concerning marriage and the family in mind—the monogamous system, attitudes toward sex, attitudes toward love, preferred authority structure, divorce and remarriage—let us consider the major changes in family functions as the family has continued its development since the pioneer days.[2]

More Dependency on Institutions. The shift from an agricultural to an industrial economy has resulted in numerous changes in the family. Partly the changes are related to urbanization which developed concur-

[2] A statistical treatment of family changes is included in an Appendix for those students who are interested and for those instructors who wish to employ it.

rently with the industrial expansion; partly to the growth of public education which could develop only in an urbanized setting; partly to the
tremendous technological advances; and partly to the general rise in level
of living. It is impossible to separate these. Rather we see a chain of
events which, taken together, have produced a profound change in our
family system in a relatively short period of time.

The family, now, is interlocked with other societal systems to a much
greater extent than in its agricultural context. Probably the most drastic
change has been the family's altered place in the distribution chain which
provides food, shelter, and clothing needs. The congregation of millions
of families in the urban setting has made the family dependent upon a
network of industries and a vast transportation system for providing these
necessities rather than on the cooperative work of its own members. In
the agricultural setting the family produced most of its raw materials,
transforming them into consumable goods for immediate or future use. It
was truly a "production unit" requiring cooperation, planning, and consistent work to provide a continuous supply of these necessities. In the
modern urban setting, the family is still a link in the distribution chain
but at a much later point. It buys goods ready for consumption with the
monetary rewards for the work of one member—usually the adult male.
These goods are then distributed among family members without regard
for their contributions to the family economy. It becomes a "unit of
consumption," totally dependent on a successful economy and an efficient
transportation system.

The family still provides these essentials, but not as a cooperative unit,
and not without help from the industrial network. Think for a moment
of the near disaster which occurs when the power supplying one of our
large cities is interrupted, or when a city becomes isolated through a snow
storm or other occurrence which cuts off transportation.

Greater Equality among Family Members.   The change to a consumption unit has lessened the need for a strong central authority within the
family. The educational and economic opportunities available for both
sexes have lessened the dependence of the female on the male. There has
been a tremendous increase in the number of women gainfully employed.
Although more than one-third of all workers are women (about 38 per
cent in 1969), the proportion of all women 16 years of age and over who
are in the work force amounts to better than two-fifths (about 42 per
cent in 1969). This is not restricted to single or childless women; as a
matter of fact, there are approximately three times as many married as
single women working, and employment for them has been increasing
at a more rapid rate. In 1890, less than one wife in twenty was in the
work force; in 1950, it was one in five; in 1960, it was one in three; by

1969 it was two in five. While only about two-fifths of the wives were working, nearly half (49 per cent) of the wives who had children between the ages 6 and 18 were in labor force in 1969 (Bureau of the Census, 1970; Population Reference, 1963). These changes have disturbed the traditional roles of men and women, replacing them with new ones of a more democratic nature. Woman is becoming emancipated from the lowly status that has been hers, with few exceptions, throughout the ages. Man's ego and assumed superiority are being challenged, forcing him to move over. The sexes are becoming more nearly equal in opportunity and more nearly alike in functioning. There now is less differentiation of role according to sex; more women are doing things formerly reserved for men, and more men are doing things formerly reserved for women. Furthermore, differentiated or not, there is less of a cultural prescription concerning what men and women should do. Today people are more nearly on their own because patriarchal sanctions are being removed before democratic patterns and procedures have been adequately established within the family to take their place. All of this means a greater amount of confusion and disorganization, temporarily at least, until new patterns can be established within the culture. In the meantime, brides and grooms will continue to be forced to work out arrangements and role differentiations following the wedding which were formerly dictated by the culture.

Along with greater equality between the sexes has came a change in the family control over children. Not only has the need for strong control over children's behavior to secure their cooperation in essential family activities declined, but the family now shares with and sometimes competes with other authority structures for the control over its children's behavior. As the educational system has grown and become compulsory, the family has had to share part of its control over the children after they reach school age. Before school age the parents probably have more exclusive control over their children than ever before because of the rise of the nuclear family system. But as the child is brought under the influence of early reading texts, a succession of teachers, and friendship groups, he is subjected to competing authority structures, a variety of values, and demands for conformity behavior, which may or may not resemble those of his family. Awareness of different family relationships and authority structures tends to decrease the legitimacy of any of them. In this confusion, new psychological insights into the nature of the child and his emotional needs have led the way toward developing more equalitarian norms between parent and child. Concern over making the child "mind" is giving way to understanding him and helping him develop generally. Control over him is seen to be more effective if he *wants* to conform to his parents' wishes than if he is *forced* to obey. He is seen to have certain "rights" to be accepted and respected as an individual in his own right. Family solidarity is seen to come more from interpersonal cohesion and less from external restriction and pressures. The family remains responsible for its children but shares its authority over them with other societal systems.

Greater Sexual Freedom. One consequence of lessened familial control, the general emphasis on individual freedom, and the decline in the negative evaluation of sex, has been an increase in sexual freedom. Males and females are thrown together at an early age and encouraged to enjoy each other's companionship. The growing equality between the sexes has allowed greater communication and closer relationships prior to marriage. Young people can escape more easily the watchful parental eye now than in their grandparents' day. Affectional interchange has become expected before marriage. In fact, the affectional relationship is expected to be established before thoughts of marriage to this particular person occur. Given these expectations, the privacy associated with the dating relationship, and the lessened familial control, it is not surprising that a greater percentage of young persons extend the affectional interchange to include varying degrees of petting and sexual intercourse prior to marriage.

Traditionally, men have claimed sexual freedom for themselves. But the same freedom was denied women. A *double standard of morality* operated to condemn women's indiscretions more severely than men's. A woman who engaged in premarital intercourse was not considered marriageable material by the same male who might claim freedom for himself. Recent trends have been toward a single standard, with each sex judged equally. Even though the single standard is being approached, it has not yet been reached. The growth of a single standard, however, has allowed greater sexual freedom between persons who are committed to a relationship and expect to be married. By far the greatest increase in premarital intercourse, especially for females, has been among engaged couples.

More Emphasis on the Nuclear Unit. Not only has the internal organization of the family changed, but the number of people it is responsible for has dwindled, and the length of time it is responsible for them has decreased. As our society became stabilized after the "taming" of the West, the agricultural base of the economy contributed to the growth of the quasi-extended family. Never characterized by the gathering together of many related families under one roof, there was a tendency for married children to settle near the parent, taking over the land as the parents aged and died. The parents, who met the children's needs until they were old enough to do so themselves, could look forward to care in their old age by their grown-up children. More and more, however, the family responsibility extends only to the nuclear unit, with the expectation that after the children are grown the parents should be responsible for themselves.

The political system shares with the family the responsibility for the aged with the growth of social security insurance, welfare programs and Medicare. The first of these programs was born during the late depression years of the 1930's. At that point, a failure in the economic system threatened the security of families dependent upon it for essential needs. The political system responded with programs to aid families unable to meet their own needs. Once established, however, these programs became factors themselves—shaping expectations and reassigning responsibility for the maintenance of the family and supporting the idea that the nuclear family *should not* be disturbed by the presence of aging members. The trend continues as the economic system responds to this emphasis on the exclusiveness of the nuclear family with the rapid development of retirement towns and homes for the aged.

This rather temporal arrangement of family responsibilities hints that the most important functions of the changed family are early socialization and emotional support. As the society becomes more and more complex, demanding greater impersonal and technical participation by its individuals, the family becomes mainly a psychological haven. This is reflected in the growing expectations for "happiness" in marriage, when the family is seen as a means of emotional satisfaction rather than primarily as a means of meeting material needs.

Effects of Crisis Situations. The changes discussed up to this point have been somewhat gradual, and their effects cumulative. In addition, occasionally there are sudden disturbances of great magnitude whose effects upon social institutions are also far-reaching. They frequently come without warning and require immediate adjustments, for which family members are not always prepared. Some of these crisis situations are natural calamities such as floods, droughts, epidemics, and earthquakes. Others, such as war and economic depression, are more of man's own making. Despite all efforts to eliminate them, periodic recurrences of both war and depression are still to be expected. Furthermore, when they do occur, they tend to be more severe than in earlier periods; the advancement and complexity of the general culture seem to make for a greater intensity of the social upheavals within it.

Someone has described modern war as a social earthquake. Its impact can be felt by nearly everyone and every institution within society, including the family. In wartime, marriage rates, birth rates, and divorce rates all increase. Reasons for these trends are many, chief of which are emotional hysteria, more money, relaxed morals, hurried courtships, and long separations.

Depression has the opposite effect upon marriage, birth, and divorce rates; it sends them all downward. The main reason is lack of money. Without economic security more people come to feel that they cannot afford to get married or to have children or to seek a divorce. However, as the depression lifts, all of these rates return to normal and above, showing that the effects have been temporary only. Actually, economic depression has many negative effects upon the family, due to such things as loss of status, worry over income, and frustration over long-range goals.

Both war and depression work to unsettle the sex norms of society, which in turn tends to unstabilize the family itself. It is usual for illegitimacy rates to increase during both of these crises. During depression, delayed marriage results in increased sexual activity before the wedding, which leads to larger numbers of illegitimate births. During war, there are more separations between mates and a greater stimulation to sexual activity, with increased illegitimacy as one of the results.

The American Family Today

Over the last half century, then, the family functions have changed drastically. The family has joined forces with the economic and political systems to provide the meeting of biological needs. It has joined forces with the educational system and religious system in socializing the children so that the child becomes subject to competing authorities thus reducing the social control exerted by the family alone. The authority structure within the family has undergone change as the importance of emotional satisfaction has influenced a change toward more equality among family members. Status placement becomes related more to the success of the socialization process than to having a particular family name. The child's future placement will depend on the transmission of values that encourage his taking advantage of the educational opportunities needed to train him for participation and to maximize his adaptation to demands from a changing economy.

The family emerges as a small temporal unit, specializing in emotional support and the meeting of psychological needs—strong enough to produce some social control but not strong enough to interfere with the children forming small independent units of their own (see Seeley, *et al.*, 1963, Chapter 7). We cannot say it is less important than in the past; it is still a vital link between the individual and the society, but the hierarchical importance of its several functions has changed, giving it a new relationship to other social institutions.

It is against the backdrop of norms, values, limitations, and opportunities provided by the social context that the individual seeks satisfaction in his family relationship.

SUMMARY

Marriage and the family, important to both social stability and personal happiness, are universal social institutions. No known society has been without them (though details of practice have shown great diversity in both time and space). These institutions result in six basic functions everywhere: responsible reproduction, socialization, biological maintenance, status placement, social control, and emotional maintenance. Family forms differ in the emphasis on certain functions, the rigidity of family control, and the interdependence with other institutions. Family form is both affected by and affects the direction and rapidity of change in other aspects of the society.

At any given time the family form reflects the economic and social development of the society, the central value systems of that society, and its own social and ideological history. Our own family system has its roots in the Judeo–Christian tradition, colored and extended by the romantic love complex born in the Middle Ages and developed in Western Europe during the seventeenth and eighteenth centuries. Further adaptation occurred in the New World as the hardships of building a new country made unique demands on the inhabitants. As the industrial revolution called for new patterns of mobility and widened the skills needed for an expanding economy, the family underwent changes as it continued to provide individuals able to participate in the changed society.

These adaptations have resulted in a family form which emphasizes the nuclear unit of parents and offspring. The authority structure has shifted from a patriarchal system to a more equalitarian one. More equalitarian relationships are seen not only between husband and wife, but also between parent and child. The family shares control over family members with other institutions. Greater sexual freedom has occurred with lessened family control, encouragement of heterosexual interaction, and greater equality between the male and female. The family has emerged as a small unit, specializing in socialization and emotional maintenance.

QUESTIONS AND PROJECTS

1. Explain the meaning of the phrase universal functions of the family. What does this imply about the effect of an extremely strong family system on social change?

2. Explain how the family is both a conservative institution and an adaptive institution.

3. Which family functions appear to be most emphasized in the middle class family today? What evidence do you have for choosing these?

4. Do you think the changes taking place in family functions over the last century have weakened the family? Why? Do you think this is good or bad? Explain your position.

5. How has the family's increased dependency on other institutions affected the socialization function of the family? Do you think this is good or bad? Why?

6. Give as many reasons as you can for the trend toward greater equality between family roles.

7. How strong is romantic love today as a prerequisite to marriage? What evidence do you have for your position?

8. Try to imagine other kinds of adaptations the family could have made to the changes occurring in other institutions. For example, what other roles for women could have developed rather than her incorporation into the economic system? If you can imagine alternatives, why do you think they did not develop?

9. Consider each of the family functions listed in this chapter and decide whether or not you think they could be performed as well under some other system, without marriage. Give reasons for your answers.

10. Has the automobile strengthened or weakened family relationships? What about television? Contraception? Explain your answer.

11. Make a list of social trends which you think will be of long-range benefit to the family, and another list of trends which are likely to prove detrimental. Why do you think the trends on your lists would be either detrimental or beneficial?

12. Discuss the question, "Is marriage as a legal contract necessary today if there are no children contemplated?" Is there a sex difference in the advantages and disadvantages? Is there an age difference? Would you come to the same conclusions if children were contemplated?

3

The Family as a
Reflection of
Social Class

The major trends discussed in previous chapters have not occurred uniformly across the United States. There are ethnic and religious pockets in which family patterns have changed little over the last several generations. Other cultural pockets vary in the amount of change which has taken place. Change, as has been pointed out, appears to be associated with education, geographical mobility, exposure to the mass media, and pressures from the economic system.

These factors tend to result in social class differences concerning the norms and values guiding marriage and family behavior. Since the individual absorbs his expectations for marital interaction from his parental family, value differences between the classes heighten the probability that individuals with different class backgrounds will hold somewhat different expectations for marriage. When they get together in the same marriage they may find themselves evaluating the success of their marriage from different points of view.

For this reason we will look at the most prominent social class differences, realizing that the distinctions between classes are not sharp and that representatives of each family type can be found at all class levels. Certain types are just more prevalent where the educational and economic factors are similar and either inhibit or encourage contact with the sources of change.

The emphasis will be mainly on differences within and between the middle and working classes. Although there is an upper class category observable in the American society, it is very small—including less than 1 per cent of the total population. In terms of wealth, power, prestige, and influence, however, it is a very important part of the society. Upper class membership is defined generally in terms of wealth and family name. Wealth that is enough to maintain the upper class way of life must have been in the family for at least two generations. Usually wealth has been associated with the family name for three, four, or more generations.

THE UPPER CLASS

Little is known, empirically, about the family behavior of these people. Many of the names are well known, such as the Rockefeller's, the Roosevelt's, the Ford's, the Kennedy's, and so forth. Socialization of the child in an upper class family is significantly different from other class positions in that financial problems are not part of the experience. Social striving is lacking since the family is already at the top. This preferred place in society accrues to the child as a member of the family, and his association with it is to be respected and protected. The kinship group then becomes more important here than at any other class level. When marriage occurs, it is likely to be a means for joining together two upper class families. Obligations to the extended family take precedence over individual preferences. Since the name descends through the male, a semi-patriarchal system is supported, with the wife's main obligations being the supervision of child care and of the household, and participation in social activities.

Children are important to carry on the family name and position of influence. They are carefully supervised and trained to upper class values through the use of private educational institutions and control of friendship groups. If James Upper fails to carry on the family tradition, the family name suffers, the position of wealth and power may be shaken, or he may lose his place in the family. If Jim Lower fails to live up to his family tradition, he will quite possibly move up—and he may move faster alone, unfettered by his origins—or he may pull his family up slightly with him. Family control is much greater, then, in the upper class. It has more resources with which to exert control, and more to lose if uncontrolled behavior brings shame to the family name or dissipates its wealth.

In general, the upper class family is extended in form, patriarchal in authority structure, and stresses the functions of responsible reproduction, socialization, and status placement. Its form is less influenced by demands from the economic system because of its secure financial basis and power in the society; its values are not as threatened by competing authorities since it can use private educational systems over which it can maintain some control and can restrict interaction of its members to other upper class families which support similar values. The family control and emphasis on extended family goals rather than individual satisfaction support a stable family system, reflected by the low divorce rate—lower than any other class position.

This brief resumé of the upper class is intended only to provide a comparison with other positions. The lack of close contact with other classes, the carefully guarded privacy of familial interaction, and the extreme difference in economic situation make it highly unlikely that this family form represents a model toward which the American family is moving. If the upper class is able to maintain control of the socialization process, it may remain a unique island in our society. If it cannot maintain this control, we can expect the family form to gravitate toward the upper-middle class, which will be discussed later in this chapter.

THE WORKING CLASS

Studies of working class families present both consistencies and discrepancies, partly due to the variety of persons included under this rubric. Sometimes the term is applied to the "multiple problem" family which includes the intermittently employed or unemployed male, families broken by death, divorce, or desertion, or the never-married female and her fatherless children. Sometimes the term is applied to the skilled workman with a high degree of job security. His level of income many times surpasses the salary of the middle class white-collar worker, who in turn may possess more education.

Economic Structure

Certainly the life experiences of these two groups differ considerably, and from our orientation we would expect value differences to occur. There are however, certain similarities in the economic structure which tend to characterize the life condition of those members of our society who are in relatively skilled or unskilled manual jobs. To the extent that the working class person's experience approaches this model we would expect closer conformity to the family values associated with it. Five major characteristics are associated with this position in the economic structure.

1. The occupations classified as working class generally require no academic education beyond high school. Here is also where the majority

of persons with less than high school education find employment. For the most part, then, the exposure to the educational system and its pressures for value change is at a minimum.

2. The males are not likely to experience geographical mobility in the placement of their first job. Many times first job placement comes about from the aid of a relative who helps the young man to be "taken on" in the same factory or introduces him to a similar trade. Although this trend appears to be changing, there is still a high probability that they will stay near family members and experience a work world very similar to the one they anticipated from association with their fathers (Handel and Rainwater, 1964). The lack of geographical mobility further reduces the probability of exposure to new family norms by keeping the young couple in almost daily contact with parents, cousins, and siblings who are likely to reinforce the "rightness" of the family norms they grew up with.

3. They are more likely than middle class youths to live at home until they marry (Komarovsky, 1964, p. 25). They are quite likely to feel the pull of being considered a child at home and under the family's domination while holding down a man's job. Marriage is many times entered into in order to gain independence from the parents and solidify an "adult" status. They are more likely than the middle class youths to drift into marriage or to marry as a result of premarital pregnancy which very quickly moves them into the parent roles, as well as husband and wife roles.

4. Obviously there is a wide range of economic security and level of income represented in the working class category. In general, however, persons at this level share a dependence on other people's decisions (company's and/or union's) and on what may be seen as quirks of fate (job loss, strikes, temporary lay-offs) for their job security. The job becomes a dominating factor not because of the feeling of satisfaction the man gets from it but because of the immediate dependency of the family on the weekly paycheck. Even if they have not personally experienced the loss of car or furniture from the inability to keep up payments, they are likely to know families who have. Thus, the ever-present possibility that sudden illness, accident, or temporary layoff may upset their economic security is a continuing source of anxiety.

5. Their jobs are likely to be ones which require them to follow routine or specific orders of a "boss" or foreman. The work is likely to be monotonous and demand few decisions or creative endeavor on the worker's part. The ability to know what is wanted and follow instructions is likely to be an outstanding requirement of successful performance of the job. Characteristic of the perceptions of their jobs is a statement by a hand truckman reported by Komarovsky in her intensive study of a small group of working class families:

I'm glad enough to get away from there. When I get away from the plant, I'd rather just let that rest 'til the next day. After all, it's no great fun; it's just something I got to make a living by. That's all.

And from a steeple jack: "I just mix paint all day and put it on. It is monotonous" (Komarovsky, 1964, pp. 151–152).

Family Values

To the degree that the life situation of an individual couple fits these general circumstances of the working class condition, we may expect them to express the following values in their relationship:

1. Although they are interested in improving their standard of living, the precariousness of their economic situation leads them to emphasize stability and security rather than striving for status and prestige—"getting by" rather than "getting ahead."

2. Part of the stability and security is achieved through kinship interaction and mutual aid. These kinship interactions occupy a major portion of leisure time activity.

3. They value a traditional division of labor between the sexes, with strong support for male dominance, and automatic obedience on the part of children.

4. There is some distrust of higher education, mainly because of lack of knowledge about what could be done with it, and fear of disrupting the security of family, peer-group, and community relationships. They are likely to be somewhat distrustful of new ideas and "too much talk" (Miller and Riessman, 1964, pp. 29–30).

5. Success or failure is more likely to be associated with luck than with any personal skills or exertion. Thus, they are saved the negative self-evaluations which accompany failure in the middle class but also miss the positive evaluations accompanying success. They are not likely to see how they may improve their occupational position by learning new skills since "it's all luck anyway."

Husband–Wife Roles

The extreme separation of the worlds of the two sexes is attested to by Komarovsky's intensive interviews. Both the restricted exposure to the norms promoting equality of the sexes and the continued association with parents and extended family members support the ideals of male dominance. The tendency toward early childbearing reinforces the dependency of the female on the male. The male's lack of real satisfaction from the work world and some feeling of inadequacy in providing security for his family leads him to lean heavily on traditional male prerogatives to support his feeling of masculinity. This appears to be more pronounced

among those with less than high school education and those with the
lowest income. The norms are reinforced by the female, who well expects to spend her life taking care of the house and children with few
outside interests. She expects little help from her husband in the household chores and child care. Most of the men do help occasionally if it
is considered really necessary, but it is expected by neither sex (Komarovsky, 1964, p. 53).

Communication Between Husband and Wife

The segregation of marital roles carries over into communication. The
middle class expectation of friendship and deep communication between
husband and wife does not extend to the working class. The separation
of work roles, and the necessary focus on getting these jobs done, create
separate worlds of interest for males and females. This, in turn, supports
stereotypical thinking about the sexes which is likely to impede close
communication. A number of comments were reported by Komarovsky
which illustrate the lack of communication or even the expectations of it.
A woman with eight years of schooling states:

Well, men and women are different. They each go their separate ways.
A man does his work and a woman does her work and how can they know
what it's all about (Komarovsky, 1964, p. 114).

A husband with grammar school education puts it this way:

What is there about women that they want to talk about things when there
is really nothing to talk about? . . . They talk about screwy things. Keep
quacking, like beating a dead horse (Komarovsky, 1964, p. 149).

When asked if they ever talked about things they'd seen on television,
two typical responses were: "We both see it, why talk about it"; and
"What's there to talk about other than say it's good or bad?" (Komarovsky,
1964, p. 155).

Even talk about the man's job is restricted. Sometimes the husband
deliberately avoids talking about his job, to keep from hearing about his
wife's day:

If you don't want to know what happens with the washing and with the
neighbor's kids, you shouldn't ought to tell her about what goes on at the
plant, either.

or

She don't want to know what I did in the warehouse and I don't want to
know if the baby is sick, so long as it ain't really sick (Komarovsky, 1964, p.
154).

Again, the amount of communication is related to education, with the
high school graduates showing a greater tendency to share experiences,

feelings, and thoughts. There is somewhat less differentiation of roles among the high school graduates. The high school fathers are more active in child care; there is more discussion of the job; there is more of a tendency for husband and wife to share some leisure time activity; the high school wives are more likely to have some outside interests such as a church group or the P.T.A. which gives them something to talk about beside home activities.

Leisure Time Activities

Associated with the communication barrier between husband and wife is the strong tendency to utilize same-sex groups for leisure time activities and communication. The women maintain strong relationships with their mothers, sisters, and same-sex in-laws, who sometimes operate as go-betweens in the husband–wife communication. The difficulty in understanding husbands is relieved by talking the matter over with older females who commonly give the reassuring comment: "That's the way men are; women have to take it." This reinforcement for stereotypical thinking actually aids in keeping down discontent. If a wife firmly believes that no man cares about things that are important to women, then she would not be expected to hold it against a particular man that he doesn't want to listen to her.

The men, on the other hand, tend to seek out groups of male friends, which may include brothers but rarely other family members. But their tendency to associate talking about themselves or their marriages with "griping" restricts their use of friends as confidants. The fear that complaints about his wife would be interpreted as a lack of an ability to control her restricts the male to exchanges of confidences which support the stereotypical concepts of masculinity and femininity. Thus, the talk includes such things as sports, cars, and jobs in which women have no interest; general complaints about unmet sexual needs; the extravagance of wives; male secrets from which wives are excluded; and the giving of support to resist what is seen to be the excessive demands of women. As males grow older, even this kind of companionship declines (Komarovsky, 1964, pp. 205–19). It does not seem to be replaced by greater communication with their wives, however. Several studies disclose that, regardless of social class, communication between husband and wife declines with the passing years (Pineo, 1961; Blood and Wolfe, 1960, pp. 156–58).

Effect of Geographical Mobility

Rainwater and Handel report that job opportunities and higher pay have encouraged geographical mobility on the part of the upper portion of the working class in recent years. This has had the effect of breaking up the extended family and friendship ties and giving them relief from pressing money problems. When these changes are present there is a tendency to rely more on nuclear family members for companionship than on relatives or friends. As this occurs, a breakdown in the highly segregated sex roles seems to follow, as well as a more active interest in the children on the part of the father. These changes tend to increase the male's involvement with the family and create greater overlap in the activities of the husband and wife, opening the way for more communication. Although these husbands may not define themselves as being as powerful as the more traditional working class man, they have more real influence over what goes on at home because they are there more, and are more involved in making and carrying out everyday decisions. Their wives are likely to consult them more and are less likely to say that they must make all the decisions around the house than are the wives of the more traditional husbands (Rainwater and Handel, 1964, pp. 70–74).

Sexual Relationships

Just as communication appears related to exposure to newer equalitarian norms and a breakdown of stereotypical thinking about sex differences, so do the sexual relations. To the extent that the general characteristics associated above with the working class situation are present, the traditional ideas that sex is for the male's pleasure only appear to prevail. As far as the female is concerned, it is the wife's duty to submit to her husband's demands with little expectation for enjoyment herself. Rainwater and Handel (1964) find mutuality in sexual relations associated with the breakdown of the highly segregated sex roles in marriage. Where the husband is more involved in family affairs and there is greater cooperation in carrying out the role activities in marriage, the working class couples become indistinguishable from middle class couples in patterns of sexual relations. The less segregated sex roles are associated, in this sample, with more secure and higher paying jobs. It may be that a feeling of adequacy on the part of the male makes him more able to consider the feelings of his wife.

This suggestion is supported by Komarovsky's study. She quotes one wife, married to an extremely traditional male, who seemed to equate sexual consideration with money: "I guess when a man's got other pleasures, he ain't so selfish about this one."

There are other supports for the traditional male prerogatives in the working class culture, however. This woman seemed to think many other women she knew felt the same way she did:

They pity the men. That's the only thing they got. Most of the people is Catholics, and they say it goes against God if you don't give in to a man and give him his one pleasure.

And again:

> . . . my ma said I had to give in to him (Komarovsky, 1964, pp. 89–91).

Marital Satisfaction

It should not be assumed that the marriages are perceived as unsatisfactory because the interaction level is low between husband and wife. Since economic pressures are great, and continued job security is likely to be seen as the result of luck, most unhappiness is attributed to lack of money and bad luck rather than to shortcomings in the mate or marital relationship. Applying the principle of value relevance, it is not the type of relationship itself which is the deciding factor in marital satisfaction but the degree to which it meets the expectations the participants have of marriage, and the similarity to other marriages of which they are aware.

The reasons for marital instability are not very likely to be value conflicts between husband and wife about the marital roles. Marital instability is more related to the life conditions which make it difficult to carry out the expected roles. It is one thing to agree that the husband should provide the necessities of life for his family and quite another for him to do this when education and skills are low. Part of the uninvolvement of the husband in family life may be related to his awareness that at any time he may fail in providing for his family's needs.[1] Thus, he is freer to desert, separate, or divorce when the pressure becomes too great than the more involved upper-working class or middle class male. However, this very lack of involvement, and the culturally supported separation of the sexes, prevent husband and wife from turning to each other for companionship and emotional support in the face of the external difficulties.

THE LOWER-MIDDLE CLASS

Work orientations and amount of education again provide differences in exposure to the factors influencing changes even within the broad middle class category. Different points of contact with the economic system roughly distinguish between the lower-middle and upper-middle class families, exposing them to varying views of the world and their place in it.

As in our treatment of the working class society, we can sketch out the major characteristics of the economic situation of the lower- and upper-middle classes. The more the individual family's experience approximates one of these models, the greater should be its agreement with the values

---

[1] For a discussion of the lower class family patterns as a "solution" to other, more pressing problems, see Hyman Rodman (1964).

and family relationships associated with the class position. Kahl (1957, p. 202) suggests that the basic split in our stratification order is between the "big people" and the "little people." This split becomes most obvious between the lower- and upper-middle classes.

Kahl sees the little people as those who carry out the instructions of the big people, who make most of the decisions. The little people include both the working class and lower-middle class, but there are important differences between them.

Economic Structure

Although many lower-middle class persons may make less money than some upper-working class persons, the structure of their economic world is quite different. They work at the various clerk and sales jobs; they may be small businessmen; some of them are semi-professionals or semi-managers. "They are at the bottom of the various ladders that lead upward; the working classes are not on the ladders at all" (Kahl, 1957, p. 202). But by being at least on the bottom rungs of the ladders, they still have a view of the people on the top rungs. They carry out the instructions of these people and perceive themselves as more like those above them than like the working class. The major factors characterizing this lower-middle class position are as follows:

1. They have greater job security although not necessarily more money than the upper-working class. They are likely to be salaried and less dependent on daily attendance at the job for a dependable paycheck.

2. Since they tend to have desk jobs rather than jobs requiring physical exertion, there is less anxiety concerning temporary loss of pay from minor physical disabilities, or bad weather which may prevent outside manual work but not inside paper work.

3. Most have high school education, and many have exposure to some college or additional special training.

4. The tremendous changes in the economic structure over the last fifty years have opened up numerous jobs of this kind which were unknown or performed in a vastly different way a generation or two ago. Their work situation is likely, then, to differ from the work experience of their fathers, who may be of little help to them in securing jobs.

5. Although their jobs are more secure than in the working class situation, their advancement is limited. Working with big people, they aspire to "getting ahead" but most will not get very far and "after they have outlived the romantic dreams of youth, they know it" (Kahl, 1957, p. 203).

6. They are conscious of being "in-between." They know they are not and never will be big people, but feel they are further along and have

more respectable jobs than the working class.[2] They are more secure in their ability to provide a "respectable" life, yet are aware of the limitations for advancement.

Family Values

To the extent that an individual family experiences the characteristics of this model in their economic situation, we would expect a tendency for them to express the following family values in their relationships:

1. The "in-betweenness" evidenced in the economic position leads them to emphasize the major difference they see between themselves and the working class—respectability. They are probably the most regular church-goers in the society, although they may not count themselves as formal members.

2. They value education highly for their children. Though they may not get too much higher than the lower rungs of the ladders leading upward, they can hope that their children will go where they cannot. They value moral and well-behaved children and are more interested in their children being "good" than in freely expressing themselves.

3. The lessened anxiety in providing the essentials for their family, the limited horizon, and the lack of success satisfaction from the job, allow the male to become involved in the family and encourage him to turn to it as the major focus of his life.

4. Home ownership is valued as a symbol of respectability and stability; home becomes the center of their lives, with most of their leisure being spent there.

Husband–Wife Roles

Husband–wife roles in the lower-middle class begin to show the effect of newer family norms. The heightened exposure to education tends to break down the highly segregated sex roles and encourages more equalitarian relationships. There is a greater break with the kinship group and with the older norms they reinforce. There are not however, the pressures from the economic system to move far away from the extended families in search of career advancement. Thus, they have not moved as far toward the newer norms as the upper-middle class, where geographical distance and extreme education come together to create the greatest departure from traditional family norms.

[2] This difference in status is recognized by many in the working class also. Komarovsky cites the dilemma of some in her sample who wrestle with the problem of whether to take a lower paying white-collar job because of the higher status and greater possibilities of advancement or stick with the higher paying but lower status, working class jobs (Komarovsky, 1964, pp. 282–84).

Rainwater (1965, pp. 30–31) furnishes a comparison of the upper-middle, lower-middle, upper-lower, and lower-lower classes in terms of the type of husband–wife role relations. He categorizes the relationship as *a joint conjugal role relationship* if husband and wife undertake many activities with a *minimum* of task differentiation and separation of interests. Couples with a joint relationship plan the affairs of the family together, exchange many household tasks, and spend much of their leisure time together. Even if there is a division of labor in task assignments they expect to be interested in and sympathetic to each others separate duties. The *intermediate conjugal role relationship* characterizes those who are neither sharply joint nor highly segregated in their activities. The *roles* of husband–wife and father–mother are much more central to their relationships than the more person-centered relationship of the joint couples. They may spend as much or more time "together" as those in joint relationships but they spend it differently. They are more likely to watch TV together, read magazines, or pursue some personal interest in the same room, but with little "talk" about what they see or what they do. The more traditional division of labor in the family is maintained, with the husband's contributions being mainly the male-oriented ones of home maintenance and repairs. *Segregated conjugal role relationships* refer to relationships in which most activities are separate and different but are fitted together to form a functioning unit. They are quite likely to have separate friendship groups and separate leisure time activities.

Rainwater found a strong association between social class and type of husband–wife relationship. The lower-middle class group showed a strong preference for the intermediate role relationship which we would expect from the intermediate exposure to the general societal pressures associated with change in the family relationships. Table 3–1 gives the social class differences in prevalence of particular role relationships for Rainwater's sample.

As far as decision-making is concerned, lower-middle class marriages

Table 3–1

Social Class and Conjugal Role Relationship

Social Class (whites only)	Role Relationship		
	Joint	Intermediate	Segregated
Upper-middle	88%	12%	—
Lower-middle	42	58	—
Upper-lower	19	58	23%
Lower-lower	4	24	72

Source: Lee Rainwater, *Family Design: Marital Sexuality, Family Size, and Contraception* (Chicago: Aldine Publishing Co., 1965), p. 32.

are likely to be more equalitarian than marriages in either the working class or the upper-middle class. Blood and Wolfe (1960, p. 33) show that the husband's power is at its lowest point in the intermediate social status positions. This does not mean that the wives are dominant, it merely means that husbands and wives are likely to make an equal number of decisions alone (segregated) or make the majority of decisions together (joint).

Sexual Relationships

Sexual relationships in the lower-middle class seem to reflect the move toward more equalitarian norms in other areas. There is little of the traditional feeling that sexual gratification is mainly for the male while it remains a duty for the wife. According to Rainwater, those in the lower-middle class were more likely than those in any other class to specifically mention that the husband tried to ensure his wife's gratification (Table 3-2). He sees this as representing a mid-way point in acceptance of the

Table 3-2

Spontaneous Mention that Husband Endeavors To Ensure His Wife's Gratifications

	Husband	Wife
Upper-middle class	12%	7%
Lower-middle class	42	48
Upper-lower class	23	19
Lower-lower class	6	14

SOURCE: Lee Rainwater, *Family Design: Marital Sexuality, Family Size, and Contraception* (Chicago: Aldine Publishing Co., 1965), p. 107.

newer norms of sexual equality. The lower class male sees the female's sexual desires as much weaker than his own and there is little he can do about the "nature of women," so he does not concern himself with her desires. The upper-middle class male, while interested in his wife's gratification, is more likely to accept the idea of sexual equality and not expect her to require attention from her husband to arouse her desires. Located in-between these two concepts of female sexuality is the lower-middle class male who believes that the woman is less free sexually than the man, and is dependent on her husband for stimulation and consideration.

The social class differences in sexual attitudes appear greatly affected by the marital role types prevalent in certain strata. Within the lower classes, for example, 68 per cent of the wives in highly segregated marital roles, and 32 per cent in intermediate roles had either slightly negative or rejecting attitudes toward sex. There were only 14 per cent so rated in the middle classes where intermediate and joint roles predominate (Rainwater, 1965, p. 65).

THE UPPER-MIDDLE CLASS

The distinguishing feature of the upper-middle class is the orientation toward a career. As Kahl (1957, pp. 193–201) describes them, they do not have jobs—they occupy positions; they do not work—they pursue careers. These are the professionals, the managers, the bureaucratic officials, and the big businessmen. The term career implies that the man has been trained, probably in college, for a particular specialty. As his career is launched, he sees himself in his present position as preparing for future advancement. While the working class and lower-middle class man may change jobs many times, the jobs may not be connected with each other; they are lateral movements which are not likely to mean either more money or more prestige (Wilensky, 1960, pp. 554–55). The job change in a career, however, supposedly implies an advancement in the same line of work or a lateral move to maximize the opportunity for advancement.

Economic Structure

The major characteristics of the upper-middle class economic condition follow.

1. There is a great amount of job stability with much of the anxiety about actual job loss removed, but more anxiety about success in the career. Success in the career requires personal initiative and involves greater autonomy in decision-making than in the lower status jobs.

2. The upper-middle class members are active participants in the economic system and have a greater sense of control over their own future, as well as a greater sense of personal failure if they do not succeed.

3. The career orientation means a way of life, in which the family and community activities become factors in the successful pursuit of the career.

4. The career is likely to be seen as important and challenging, providing the potential for a high amount of personal satisfaction associated with the work.

5. A high degree of geographical mobility is likely to be associated with the development of the career. Many talents are interchangeable between companies. An executive in one company may "sell" his executive talents to another company for more money, prestige, or future security. Within large companies, young professionals being groomed for advance-

ment may be moved around for greater knowledge of the whole enterprise.

6. The growth of occupations of this kind has brought many sons of lower-middle and working class families into the upper-middle class through university training. Their parents are of little help in promoting their new careers, and they are likely to be removed from them geographically as well as socially.

Family Values

The predominant values associated with this orientation include:

1. A strong belief in the existence of free competition and the rightness of individualistic effort. The energy and devotion necessary for success is not the result of luck but of one's own ability and efforts.

2. The husband's career is the central focus for the whole family. An understanding and cooperative wife is an asset. He wants to succeed "for her," so that she and other family members can have enough goods and prestige to keep them "respectable." Respectability has a different meaning here than in the lower-middle class. Here it is likely to mean the display of one's success through housing, clothes, and entertainment appropriate for the particular locale and social group (Kahl, 1957, pp. 193–98).

3. Education is important, but so are leadership characteristics developed in community activities. The well-rounded personality is as important, if not more so, as high excellence in a specialized field.

4. The development of individual personalities is seen to be an important function of the family. These are believed to be developed best in a "democratic" family, where persuasion rather than force is the main form of control.

5. Individual happiness is an important goal of family life. Harmony and affection between family members is idealized as the mark of a successful family (Seeley, Sim, and Loosley, 1963, pp. 164–65).

Husband—Wife Roles

This class has the highest exposure to the newer norms of family life through extensive education. At the same time, geographical and social distance from the extended family reduces the support for older family norms. Kahl suggests this is an unstable group. Many have climbed from lower status backgrounds. Even sons of the upper-middle class are likely to have shifted from the occupation of their fathers. Sons of businessmen become engineers, sons of engineers become lawyers, sons of university professors become businessmen. People within the group are constantly shifting from position to position and town to town. They are, consequently, not likely to be able to behave appropriately in their present position by repeating behavior learned in their parent's home (Kahl, 1957, p. 199). They learn by imitating those around them, consulting the "experts"—from the interior decorator to the child psychologist—either through personal contact or the numerous magazines devoted to keeping them posted on the latest fashions and fads.

This becomes mainly the wife's job. Her responsibility for home and children remains strong; in fact she is likely to take on more responsibility around the home than the lower-middle class woman since her husband must devote so much time to furthering his career. The upper-middle class suburb described in *Crestwood Heights* epitomizes the career orientation and its consequences for family life. The changed nature of the traditional domestic role of the wife is vividly portrayed. She must not devote herself *wholly* to husband and children, but they must remain her first and most important responsibility—she must become the emotional hub of the family. She is expected to provide an atmosphere of warmth, security, and unconditional love for her children. She is to provide food, sex, and interesting activity to attract and please her husband and she must enjoy these equally with him. "She does not simply provide food, or sex, or parties; she must enter into them with equal ardor and gratification or the husband will not be satisfied" (Seeley *et al.*, 1963, Chapter 7).

For the home to be a proper exhibition of status and an aid to the male career, it must always give an unlived-in appearance. The house cannot be decorated once and for all time. The current styles in home furnishings and arrangements must be studied either to be able to defend the present arrangement or know when to "sweep these aside in favor of new ones."

Family Norms

In summing up the norms for this family, the authors suggest that they represent the ideal of family life which is "in the Crestwood air," whether or not all families live up to them. Such norms emphasize respect for each individual member almost to the point of denying the actual age gap between parents and children. They encourage responsibility which means community service for the adults and service to the family group for the children. They stress the importance of family harmony, judged by verbal and physical acts of affection—the giving of presents being a highly regarded token of love. Equally strong is the insistence on separate activities for each of the members with a high degree of efficiency in operating the household.

The husband's role is primarily one of attention to the development of his career. He is away from home so much that much of the responsibility within the house is delegated to his wife. However, he remains the head of the household and is held accountable for the "success" of his family. Since the family's activities are visible, his wife's and children's behavior reflect on the abilities of the husband–father to successfully run this "business," with either beneficial or disastrous effects on his career (Seeley *et al.*, 1963, pp. 174–77).

There is, however, pressure upon him to become involved in family activities, to provide companionship for his wife, and to participate in the childrearing activities. In the upper-middle class are found the greatest pressures for equalitarian relationships stemming from these norms as well as from the high degree of coordination of activities necessary for their way of life. Yet the husband's power appears *greater* in this class than in any other stratum. This seems partly related to his standing in the community, where he is likely to be in authoritative positions. He not only gains prestige in the eyes of his fellow citizens but also in the eyes of his wife and children.[3] The necessary decision-making in his career carries over into familial relationships. Many familial decisions reflect on his "career," which takes first place in importance for the whole family.

Obviously, not all upper-middle class people share the "career" orientation associated with the family norms and values just discussed. Many professionals either do not desire the high success we have described above, or have discovered they will not make it and have settled for a lower rung on the ladder. To the extent that their job orientation resembles that of the lower-middle class we would expect departures from the family values described above. We are merely describing the pressures which are exerted by certain types of occupational settings and the consequences of these pressures on family values.

THE NEGRO-AMERICAN VARIATIONS

All of the factors influencing marriage and family relationships in the various social classes apply to Negro and Caucasian marriages alike. There are however, additional factors associated with the Negro-American subculture which produce some differences between Negro and Caucasian families within the same social class. The same lack of exposure to education, anxiety associated with job instability, and lack of geographical mobility which reinforce the older family norms among lower-working class whites impinge upon the lower-working class black—except to a greater extreme. He is not only likely to have less exposure to education but is excluded to a greater degree from contact with the white middle class culture. When economic slumps or changes in the economic structure re-

---

[3] For a comparison of the awareness of the prestige associated with the father's job among blue-collar families, see William G. Dyer (1964).

sult in job lay-offs, he is the one likely to be laid off first. In the competition for dwindling unskilled jobs he is likely to have more trouble being
hired.

Black—White Differences

There are two major differences between the black and white lower-
working classes. First, the lack of exposure to new norms reinforces the
continuation of older family norms for the Negro as well as the Caucasian,
but there are differences in the norms being reinforced. The slavery history of the Negro aided in reducing the commitment of the male to the
family. The position of responsibility and authority over family members
resided with the slave-owner not with the Negro male. Marriages were
neither encouraged nor honored universally since the economic assets from
selling slaves outweighed the assets from stable family units. The most
stable unit was the mother—child unit. This structure continued to develop
after slavery, with the family often being comprised of the grandmother
and one or two daughters and their children. The male commitment continued to be tangential since his placement in the economic structure was
more tenuous than that of the female to whom domestic service was open.
These family norms still continue where social isolation from the larger
community, lack of economic stability, and discrimination prevent the
male from feeling secure in his breadwinning role and weaken his position
in the family. Thus, while the Caucasian working class tends toward
a male-dominant power structure (even though the wife may be forced to
make many day to day decisions because of husbandly default) the Negro
working class has developed a female-dominant family structure, especially
at the lower levels. The Negro wife tends to be the dominant person
whether or not her husband is present (Rainwater, 1965, p. 53; Blood and
Wolfe, 1960, pp. 34–36).

Second, the close, supportive kinship groups which operate as stabilizing influences among working class Caucasians is not as strong among
Negroes. Where it does exist, it tends to be a female group. The lack
of strong kin-groups, as well as the weak involvement of the male, leads
to higher illegitimacy rates, a higher desertion rate, and a higher rate of
common-law relationships among Negroes than among their Caucasian
counterparts.

As there is greater education, more job stability, and more exposure
to the Caucasian middle class culture as evidenced by upper-lower and
middle class position, the Negro-American family structure begins to resemble that of the white family in similar positions. However, there is
some evidence that the Negro male's power does not equal that of the
Caucasian male in any social status, although it does go up as his educa-

tion, income, and occupational prestige increases (Blood and Wolfe, 1960, pp. 34–36). It may be that the lesser rewards he receives from comparable skills and education prevent him from acquiring the esteem in the eyes of his family (and in his own) that his Caucasian counterpart acquires.

The stability of the Negro marriage does not approach that of the Causasian, however, even in the higher class positions. Perhaps until full exposure to the social factors supporting stability is achieved through complete social participation, the vestiges of the loose family structure, born in slavery days, will continue to produce a higher percentage of unstable marriages among the Negro-American population.

Stability of Marriage

Bernard (1966b) has analyzed the stability of marriages as it relates to race, income, education, and occupation using 1960 census data. She defined a stable marriage as one in which a male (aged 45–54) had been married only once, and was still living with his wife. This excluded the very new marriages which may become unstable in the future. In about 90 per cent of the cases this was the first marriage for the wife also. Tables 3–3 and 3–4 show the effect of education and income respectively. Although the influence is obvious among both the whites and non-whites,

Table 3–3

Proportion of Ever-Married Men Aged 45–54 in Stable Marriages (by years of schooling)

Years of Schooling	Proportion in Stable Marriages	
	Non-white *	White
0–4	53.5	73.0
5–7	57.3	76.4
8	57.5	78.4
9–11	55.9	77.3
12	59.1	79.6
13–15	54.8	78.2
16	65.2	83.5
17+	71.3	85.7

SOURCE: Jessie Bernard, "Marital Stability and Patterns of Status Variables," *Journal of Marriage and the Family,* 28 (November, 1966b), p. 423.

* Non-white includes other races besides Negro, although Negroes comprise 90 per cent of the non-white population except in the West. The Japanese showed the highest per cent of stable marriages (81.7), and Filipino's the lowest (49.3). Negroes showed 52.2 per cent in stable marriages.

Table 3–4

**Proportion of Ever-Married Men Aged 45–54
in Stable Marriages
(by income)**

Income in 1959	Proportion in Stable Marriages	
	Non-white	White
No income	38.5	57.9
$1 to $999	49.9	64.8
$1,000 to $2,999	55.6	73.7
$3,000 to $4,999	58.2	78.0
$5,000 to $6,999	62.8	80.5
$7,000 to $9,999	68.0	82.0
$10,000 and over	69.0	84.7
Median income	$3,079	$5,613

SOURCE: Jessie Bernard, "Marital Stability and Patterns of Status Variables," *Journal of Marriage and the Family,* 28 (November, 1966b), p. 423.

the non-whites must climb to the highest educational levels to reach the stability associated with the lowest levels among the whites. To at least some extent, a perception of the society and one's place in it as stable and predictable seems a prerequisite for a high percentage of stable marriages.

Comparable studies using data more recent than 1960 are not available at this writhing. Whether or not the gap between whites and non-whites has been closing is not known. If separation due to marital discord can be used as an indicator of relative stability, there appears to be little change. Estimates from 1965 for the United States indicate that 1.7 per cent of white married men are separated compared with 9.5 per cent of non-white married men. Comparable percentages among married women were 2.4 for white and 15.3 for non-white (Department of Health, Education, and Welfare, 1969). Incomes, obviously, have risen over the last decade. The disparity between white and non-white median incomes was still quite apparent in 1968.[4] There is, however, no reason to suspect that the relationship between income and marital stability has changed, especially within the age group with which Bernard's study was concerned.

At the present writing it is hazardous to predict the future of the Negro-American family. Certainly it is impossible now and will continue to be impossible to suggest that a single family type describes *the* Negro-American family (see Billingsley, 1969). Variation will occur according

[4] The median family income for 1968 was $8,937; for non-white families it was $5,590 (Bureau of the Census, 1970).

to the integration into the economic system, education, mobility, and religion just as it does with any other ethnic group. Already sharp differences are appearing between the family structures supported by the Black Muslims and the Negro Christians—both within the working class segment of society. The Black Muslims appear to be reestablishing patriarchal norms and traditional husband–wife roles which contrast sharply with the more female-dominant families among the Christians. Here religious beliefs and teachings are influencing the family structure within similar economic contexts (Edwards, 1968, pp. 604–11).

The conscious efforts to establish racial pride noticeable in the rising use of the word *black* rather than *Negro* with its connotation of subjugation to white supremacy, may be of extreme importance in changing the family structure. Pride in racial identification will in all likelihood be translated into a more positive self-concept for the black male, which will enable him to establish a more prominent place for himself in the family. As the economic system and increasing educational attainments open the way for him to meet his breadwinner obligations in a respectable, predictable way, his power and prestige in the family should increase. As with the white male, recognition and prestige in the community should be accompanied by heightened authority and respect in the family.

The current situation is in flux. It is therefore impossible to forecast the direction the major trends will take. We can be sure, however, that the family structure will be dependent partly upon the kind of integration into the economic system the black family achieves, the amount of exposure it has to the educational system, and the amount and kind of contact it has with the white culture. The black family does not develop in a vacuum any more than the white family does.

SUMMARY

During a period of rapid social change, members of society differ from each other in the exposure they have to new norms and values. The amount of exposure is related to level of education, type of occupational setting, geographical mobility, and the value systems of the social groups with which they associate. These factors tend to cluster together in rough socioeconomic groupings, producing social class differences in values concerning family relationships. The social class groupings reflect different levels of economic stability and different sources of anxiety contained in the economic structure. These differences affect the ability to carry out the expectations for family life with consequences for family stability.

We find an emphasis on extended family relationships and a patriarchal structure more likely to exist at the extreme top and extreme bottom of the social class ladder. In both instances there is insulation from the demands for adaptation stemming from the economic system—in the upper class because of the power and wealth which decreases dependency, and in the lower class because of insufficient integration and rewards from the economic system. Traditional norms in both cases are reinforced by extended family interaction.

It is the large middle class which is exposed to the newer norms through higher education and is subjected to the greatest pressures from the economic system for adaptations. Their higher degree of geographical and social mobility tends to cut them off from the extended family and forces them to look to the nuclear family for emotional support and satisfaction of ego-needs. In these classes, especially at the upper levels, is found the greatest emphasis on individual happiness and achievement.

The black family is subject to the same pressures as the white family. At present blacks are over-represented in the working class because of lower education and restricted opportunity in the economic system. The older family norms which still exist are more likely to result in female-dominant families than in the male-dominant ones found in the white working class. Since social changes involving the black American are so extensive, speculations about their effect on the black family are extremely hazardous at the present writing. To the extent that the black population becomes integrated into the economic system on an equal footing with the whites, we would expect that the family structure will resemble that of the white family at the same class level, as is already apparently true at the middle and upper-middle class levels.

The economic and normative structure used to describe the ideal typical class position does not describe the life situation of all persons categorized as belonging to a particular class in terms of their education and occupation. A wide range of within class differences can be observed. However, the general economic and social environment provides the framework within which the individual family members work out their patterns of interaction with each other and with the larger society.

In the next chapter we will attempt to assess the strengths and weaknesses as well as the pressures and supports that families experience at different class levels. We will look at the types of conflicts which are most likely to be experienced, and their consequences for marital stability.

QUESTIONS AND PROJECTS

1. What are the major elements in the economic structure which tend to characterize the life conditions of working class families?

2. What are the main points of difference between the economic structure of working class families and upper-middle class families?

3. Which functions of the family seem to be emphasized in each of the social class positions? Can these differences be explained by the life conditions associated with class position?

4. Distinguish between the husband–wife roles associated with each of the social class positions. Can you state any reasons for these differences?

5. How can you account for the differences between lower-class black and lower-class white family structure?

6. What kind of marital difficulties would you expect to find in interclass marriages? Under what conditions might you expect an interclass marriage to be more compatible than an intraclass marriage?

7. If you were to marry someone whose father had an almost identical occupation to your father's, could you be assured that you would share the same marital expectations? Why or why not?

4

The Problem of Values

With rapid changes occurring in the social institutions and in their relationships to each other, it is not surprising that a number of value conflicts are present within the society. Neither is it surprising that different value systems are transmitted by individual families as they differ in exposure to these changes through social class position and type of occupation. With the increased ease of transportation and communication it is highly probable that persons will marry who have absorbed different ideas about husband–wife roles, parent–child relationships, and the overall goals of marriage. It is also likely, given a changing society, that as children grow and experience a world somewhat different from the world their parents grew up in there should exist value conflicts between parent and child.

TYPES OF CONFLICT

Value conflicts fall into four different categories: (1) conflicts among norms within the general society; (2) conflict between family and societal norms; (3) conflicts between expectations and realizations; and (4) conflicts among values held by different family members.

Conflict Among Societal Norms

Some basic conflicts in our central value system are reflected in conflicting norms concerning selection of marriage mates, marriage, and child-rearing. A few of the conflicts become apparent by reviewing pairs of statements, both of which have widespread support in the society.

1. Premarital sex is morally wrong.
   versus
   Sex is an individual "right" and should be an individual decision.
2. Love is the only true basis for marriage.
   versus
   Matching of interests, values, and personalities is more important than love in mate selection.
3. The man should definitely "wear the pants" in the family.
   versus
   Authority should be equally shared between husband and wife.
4. Working mothers are the root of juvenile delinquency.
   versus
   Women should have equal rights to work.
5. Parents should stay together even though they are unhappy, for the sake of their children.
   versus
   Children are hurt more by parental bickering than divorce.
6. Children need guidance, love, and understanding rather than strict discipline.
   versus
   Strict discipline is necessary to develop character in children.

Such a list is only suggestive, but it is enough to indicate that doubt and anxiety are likely to be present in individuals exposed to conflicting values. The conflicts may be internalized during the socialization process, introducing tension and conflict into the personality itself and affecting behavior. The more value conflicts present in the general culture the more likely are internal conflicts, tension, and insecurity.

Conflict Between Family and Societal Norms

Tension can also arise when the values developed in the family are out of line with the norms of the society in which the family operates. This can come about through inadequate socialization, through movement into a social group subscribing to different norms than those one has grown up with, or through rapid changes occurring in the society itself. As changes occur quickly, they can force family members to change themselves too rapidly or affect the members differently, changing some more rapidly than others. Consider the young mother who is exposed to psychologically oriented childrearing methods through the local nursery school. As she attempts to introduce these at home, where the father is firmly rooted in the "spare the rod, spoil the child" philosophy, stress in the childrearing activities is likely to increase—thereby raising doubts and fears in the parents and confusion in the child.

Conflict Between Expectations and Realizations

No one, of course, has his every wish fulfilled. But if wish frustration becomes great, it may mean that basic goals are left unrealized. The experience is frequently disorganizing. We build up vague, general expectations for marriage as well as quite specific ones. General satisfaction seems much more related to the *gap* between the expectations and reality than to the *actual* behavior or circumstances. For example, more important to satisfaction than the actual level or kind of marital affection is the degree to which affectional interaction meets the expectations. More important than amount of money or degree of occupational success is the gap between expected standard of living and present level of income. The complaint, "My husband never gives me any money for clothes," may mean just that or it may mean that he doesn't provide enough for the amount or kind of clothing his wife desires. The resulting dissatisfaction is just as real in both cases.

Value Conflicts Between Husband and Wife

Closely related to discrepancies between expectations and reality is value conflict between husband and wife. Values are expressed in behavior. Where conflict exists, the resulting interaction inevitably leaves one or both partners with unfulfilled expectations. When the society contains conflicting values and the people in that society are highly mobile, the probability of people marrying with divergent values is increased. Supposedly, the mate selection process operates to weed out those with greatly differing values. But many values, highly important in the daily interaction of marriage, are not brought to light or have a different meaning in the interaction before marriage. A student of one of the authors commented:

> Of course, I knew before we married that his family was a tight knit one. I thought it would be nice to be part of a close family group, since mine wasn't like that. But I didn't expect that he'd want to go over there every weekend—every holiday; or that we couldn't buy a piece of furniture without asking what they thought of it first. He talks to them about everything—we don't have any privacy! If I complain about it, he says I don't like his family—that I'm ungrateful, they're just interested in us. I like them alright—I didn't marry them, though!

PARADIGM OF INTERNAL-EXTERNAL VALUE CONFLICT

It is impossible to say what is good or bad for marriage without taking values into account. It is how a thing relates to one's individual values, to the spouse's values, or to those of the prevailing culture that really counts—more perhaps than the thing itself. This is what is meant by the *principle of value relevance*. How people see things or define the situation often determines their action or the consequences of this action. This perception of the situation is affected by values. Value conflicts which affect the family can come externally from the general society or from differences between family and societal norms. They can come internally from the discrepancy between expectations and realization or from disagreements among family members.

We can visualize the interaction between these internal and external sources of value conflict or value consensus in paradigm form, as shown in Figure 4–1. Although the categories are actually continua rather than

Intramarital Interaction Between Husband and Wife	Interaction Between Married Pair and External Groups	
	Value Consensus	Value Conflict
Value Consensus	A Maximum harmony	B Pair agreement strained by external conflict
Value Conflict	C Pair disagreement mollified by external support	D Maximum dissonance

Fig. 4–1. Paradigm of internal–external value conflict. (Adapted from Christensen, 1969, p. 994.)

dichotomies, as shown, they are presented in this form to help explain the relationship between values and marital harmony. The consensus–conflict categories pictured on the left-hand side of the figure refer to internal, husband–wife interaction; while across the top the same categories refer to the agreement of the values of the couple with those of the external groups with whom the marital pair interacts (Christensen, 1964, pp. 988–98).

Of course it is not expected that any marriage is characterized by either total consensus or total conflict. Realistically, most couples will have some values in agreement and some upon which they disagree. Some value conflicts may never enter the interaction, causing little if any discomfort; for instance, the childless couple who disagree on parochial or public school education. Some values become relevant only at certain periods of the family life cycle. For example, a couple may agree that a woman should not work while there are pre-school children at home, and only face the conflict concerning whether she should work at all when the children are in school. In the same vein, the social group values are probably never either in complete agreement or total conflict with the couples' values. Actually, we are talking about the weight of social group support, so that value conflict in cell B of Figure 4–1, for example, means either that the social group values are in conflict with the couple's values, or that there is conflict in the social groups themselves with approximately equal support for different values.

Let us use the example of the working wife to illustrate the four types of interaction pictured in the paradigm.

Type A: Both husband and wife believe that the wife should not work. They live in a neighborhood where few women work, and have friends and families who agree with them that wives should not work. There is no pressure here for any behavior save that which is in accord with their values. The spousal values, in agreement, have continual support from external groups reinforcing the "rightness" of the values. Maximum harmony should exist as far as these values are concerned.

Type B: Again we have consensus between husband and wife that wives should not work. But this time we place them in an apartment unit where many wives work. They have friends who believe that it's a wife's duty to help out financially, especially if there are no children. The agreement between husband and wife serves as reinforcement against the outside pressures, but some strain is likely since reinforcement for the rightness of the values is lacking from their social groups. Especially if circumstances make one of them feel that more money is needed, the outside support is available to suggest this alternative as an acceptable way of getting it, thus opening the way for internal value conflict to develop. Conditions in this situation are potentially disruptive to marital harmony, but husband and wife *can* maintain their consensus and resist the external pressures.

Type C: In this situation, the potential dissonance is more apparent. One spouse believes the wife should work, the other thinks she should not. If, however, the supporting social groups have consensus supporting either one of the positions, one of the spouses has support while the other does not. Depending upon a number of factors, the combined weight of spousal opposition and social group consensus may bring the deviant party into line, so to speak, moving them to

Type A. Or, the pair conflict may continue but with the weight of outside consensus keeping it from being expressed in behavior. The wife, for example, who wants to work is probably much less likely to do so if she has no support from either her husband, family, or social groups than if she has some ally among them.

Type D: Conditions suggesting the maximum disruption or dissonance are found in this combination. Here, there is disagreement between husband and wife *and* conflict in the social supports. Both are likely to get partial support for their positions, aiding in keeping the argument alive. It also heightens the probability that disagreement will come into the open, furnishing a recurrent source of irritation and resulting guilt feelings.

Probably few marriages fit neatly into any of these types. The paradigm merely serves to highlight the interplay between a given marriage and its network of extended family and friendship groups.

The value-conflict paradigm can also serve as a framework within which we compare the stresses and strains impinging upon people in different social contexts. We have already seen in the previous chapter that marital instability differs according to education, income, and occupation —the measures of social class position. We can now look at the various pressures stemming from the economic system which have an impact on the type of value conflict most likely to be experienced at different class levels.

Pressures on the Working Class Family

The conditions impinging on the working class family are exceedingly complex and do not lend themselves to any easy analysis of the reasons for the greater marital disruption associated with lower levels of education and low paying jobs. Any analysis must account for the stable families as well as the unstable ones.

From our value conflict paradigm, we would be led to conclude that the high value consensus present, both within the working class family and in their external social groups, would produce harmonious relationships. However, this appears too simple and is not borne out by the higher disruption rate. The external situation must allow the values to be acted out, and the values must be suitable to the given life conditions. We must, then, imbed our paradigm in a more complex setting, so that the effect of realistic economic pressures can be seen.[1]

---

[1] Miller (1964a) suggests typologies of lower class families in terms of the interplay between economic and familial stability. We have elaborated the scheme, taking into consideration the effect of value consensus on famility stability.

In Figure 4–2, let us assume that the values are those associated with the lower-working class, so that consensus means there is agreement on the values of high segregation of sex roles, low communication, and so forth. Conflict, then, assumes the intrusion of middle class values of companionship, equalization of authority, and so on as presented in

Intramarital Interaction Between Husband and Wife	Economic Condition	Interaction Between Married Pair and Social Group	
		Consensus (+)	Conflict (–)
Value Consensus (+)	Secure (+)	A (+++) Stable	B (++ –) Strained
	Insecure (–)	C (+ – +) Resigned	D (+ – –) Externally unstable
Value Conflict (–)	Secure (+)	E (– ++) Contained	F (– + –) Internally unstable
	Insecure (–)	G (– – +) Trapped	H (– – –) unstable

Note: Parenthesized symbols in each cell indicate, in order, the husband–wife interaction, economic condition, and interaction between marital pair and social group. For example: Read Cell C (+ − +) as a type in which there is husband–wife consensus, economic insecurity, and social group values in agreement with husband–wife values.

Fig. 4–2. Paradigm of internal–external value consensus with economic stability intervening.

Chapter 3. Type A represents the situation in which the marital roles are highly segregated and the husband is adequately meeting his bread-winner responsibilities. The family has ample support for the way they are enacting their adult roles from their friends and extended family members. Even though the marriage falls short of the middle class expectations for communication and emotional support, these people should be satisfied and highly stable.

If through job loss, accident, or some other circumstance they move to Type C, we would expect little blame of the spouse for the economic difficulties, but a resignation to the "bad luck." Short-term financial aid may be expected from the supporting social groups with little loss of face, but marital disruption is also a possibility if the economic pressures become insurmountable. The values of "luck" and non-recognition of the opportunities for improving skills may operate here to hold the family together but prevent them from improving their economic position.

If, however, the Type A's elect to move to a "better" neighborhood as a result of the economic security then we may expect pressure of a different kind (Type B). Here, the greater probability of exposure to different (middle class) values may introduce new expectations for the marriage and family relationships (Hurvitz, 1964). The same behavior once considered satisfactory may now begin to be seen as falling short of the new middle class values. Since it is the wife who is more likely to be exposed to them from her new neighbors,[2] it is likely to be the husband who receives the complaints; however, he may be nonplussed by the change in his wife.

These pressures, introduced from exposure to new values, may have a number of consequences. A new consensus between husband and wife, in line with the new values, may develop, with a change in their relationship. If the conflict remains, however, the family's stability becomes highly vulnerable to possible job loss and financial insecurity (Type H). Now, financial insecurity is likely to be evaluated by the wife from middle class values that place blame on the husband for not improving his skills rather than protect him through blaming "circumstances" or "luck." The family is now vulnerable to both internal and external strain with rapid loss of stability associated with Type H.

The potential for different kinds of pressures and conflicts can be present in a marriage from the beginning, with the actual eruption of difficulty being influenced by the shifting economic situations and/or social group support. Komarovsky points to the problems occurring in working class marriages where the wife either has more education than her husband or comes from a higher social class.[3] In either case she is more likely than her husband to have been exposed to the more equalitarian and individualistic norms associated with education and the higher socioeconomic groups. When these marriages are imbedded in a strong social group supporting the working class norms and there is economic security (Type E) the internal conflict is likely to be contained. If, however, the financial position is threatened, the wife is likely to feel trapped by the values which keep her husband from improving his position and excuse his economic failure by blaming his "bad luck" (Type G). If she gains support for her values from outside groups—say her family—the husband's

_____

[2] The tendency for wives to have more exposure to newer equalitarian family norms seems supported in other social classes as well. (See Seeley et al., 1963, pp. 193–203.)

[3] The highest level of education represented by her sample was high school graduate. Thus, where the wife has more education, the husband must have not completed high school (Komarovsky, 1964, pp. 261–67).

self-esteem, protected by patriarchal, working class norms, is likely to suffer, with heightened instability associated with a movement to Type H.

Complexities in Analysis

The above discussion of the variety of combinations of stresses and strains present in the working class family makes it apparent that a simple analysis of this family type is impossible. On the fringe of the dominant middle class values, and faced with the ever-present possibility of economic insecurity, they differ among themselves to the extent that they are affected by these factors. Some will remain relatively stable and unchanged throughout their life cycle, but others will vary, becoming more or less stable as they face changes in economic security and exposure to new values.

The greater disruption in working class families is probably related not only to the more precarious economic situation, but to the conditions and values making it difficult for the male and female to provide emotional support for each other as they encounter the rough spots.

The above discussion of working class problems should not obscure the fact that many working class families do achieve highly stable and satisfying marriages either in keeping with working class norms of highly segregated sex-roles or moving more in line with the middle class ideal of companionship and emotional support. Interpersonal skills and emotional commitments to a marital relationship vary within every socioeconomic position. However, our emphasis is on those social conditions and values *associated with social class,* which enhance or reduce the probability of marital success. Individual couples undoubtedly enter marriage with varying handicaps and advantages but their eventual success will depend on their skills in coping with the internal and external stresses which every marriage will encounter to some degree (Rapoport and Rapoport, 1965). The external stresses are probably more pressing the lower the socioeconomic position descends, where there are also fewer skills to cope with them. As job security increases, the external pressures remain but decrease in importance to the internal stresses, which appear as exposure to middle class norms gives rise to value conflict.[4]

Hurvitz (1964) sums up some of the major stresses and strains stemming from the job and the marital role expectations of husband and wife in the more secure segment of the working class. They are quite in keeping with the foregoing analysis.

[4] Rainwater (1965, pp. 321–29) reports that upper- and lower-middle class couples are much more likely to report adjustment problems in marriage than are working class couples. Working class couples, on the other hand, are more likely to report money problems.

Stresses from the Job. Even when current financial needs are being adequately met, the nature of the job produces certain anxieties and stresses. The major ones include the following:

1. The dependence upon a job which requires physical strength and skills makes the husband vulnerable to (a) technological changes which may eliminate his job, and (b) temporary loss of pay due to physical disabilities.
2. His marginal association with his employer makes him vulnerable to (a) temporary or permanent lay-offs, (b) strikes and other job disruptions, and (c) the general economic condition of the country —all of which are outside his control.
3. The lack of personal satisfaction and self-esteem gained from the job tends to make him seek affirmation of his masculinity through his family relationships.
4. Though he may feel that he should upgrade his skills or retrain himself as a cushion to changing technology, he lacks the energy after a day's work and the self-confidence to attempt additional training.
5. He is under the same pressure as other Americans to purchase a home, a late-model car, and modern household appliances. He is more likely to have to go into debt to purchase them, adding to the immediate dependency on the weekly paycheck. He has more to lose from temporary cessation of income, with only slightly greater ability to weather the loss than those in the less secure stratum of the working class.

Strains in the Marital Relationship. Marital strains in the secure segment of the working class are likely to differ from those in the middle class. The major sources of these strains follow.

1. His wife gains her greatest feeling of self-worth from her mother role. Her lack of education and restriction to home and family are likely to make her feel inadequate in relationships outside the family and cut off from many of her husband's activities. Her preoccupation with the children sometimes makes her husband feel that he was chosen as a means for her to achieve her goal of motherhood.
2. Although they are both likely to be interested in the development of their children, as income increases they tend to hold different values of how this should be done. This is not as likely to be true in the lower segment of the working class where neither spouse has been touched by the newer "developmental" approach to childrearing. In the more secure working class stratum the father is likely to believe, in keeping with more traditional methods, that "he helps his children grow by making them tough, teaching them to fight back, training them in physical stamina and endurance, and

teaching them to get ahead because they fear him." His wife, since she has greater contact with the mass media and middle class child-rearing values, is more likely to emphasize reasoning, comfort for their hurts, and to want them to "fulfill her expectations because they love her." The children are more likely to identify with the mother who is present, spends time with them, and is supportive, rather than with the occasionally present, more threatening father. He is, therefore, likely to feel inadequate and pushed out of the family relationships. His feeling of exclusion from the family is likely to reinforce his feelings of self-depreciation and lack of self-worth, increasing the irritations between himself and his wife.

3. He is likely to be able to express affection for his wife only in the sexual union. He tends to rank his role of sexual partner high while his wife ranks the sexual relationship relatively low in importance. Being rather uninvolved sexually, she may withhold response to show irritation, or participate as a reward or in exchange for favors desired. He may many times feel unappreciated and unrewarded by both his wife and children.

4. His feeling of inadequacy in the family as well as in the economic sphere leads him to express his authoritarian childrearing philosophy with his children, resulting in a family "hassle" with his wife on the side of the children. Her argument that his childrearing methods are like his father's which did not equip him to be successful is a telling one, and one he may be inclined to agree with, but unable to do anything about.

5. The factors operating to produce irritations and a negative self-concept in him are likely to keep him from providing any support for his wife's feeling of self-worth in her important wife and mother role. Feeling inadequate in the important male roles of bread-winner, sex partner, and father he can only preserve some feeling of masculinity by exerting his traditional authority and deprecating his wife's treatment of the children as not preparing them for the harsh world he knows.

The above sources of strain in the blue-collar marriage give us an indication of the sources of marital success. Success is likely to be achieved when the day-to-day interaction of the spouses enhances their self-concepts so that they are more able to cope with the external stresses and strains. Faced with feelings of inadequacy in outside relationships as well as an anxiety-provoking economic situation, the marital relationship can help furnish the elements of self-esteem necessary to sustain a continual expenditure of energy in a non-rewarding job. A male, appreciated for his efforts and enjoying his wife's genuine regard for his abilities (whatever they are) is more likely to gain the confidence needed to try new ways of coping with his economic problems. He is also more likely to be able to give her the appreciation and support she needs to ease the anxiety she feels in coping with her growing children, limited budgets, and household pressures. Relieved of some of her anxiety, she may be more able to resist criticism of her husband's differing views toward childrearing. As the spouses are able to support each other's feeling of self-worth, their relationships with the children have a heightened probability of building adequate self-concepts in them, thereby increasing the children's ability to cope with the economic world as adults.

As example of such a relationship in the lower-working class stratum is provided by Komarovsky (1964). The marriage she describes followed the traditional working class pattern of segregated sex roles and leisure time spent separately. The spouses each had had ten years of schooling, had been married eight years, and were expecting their fourth child. Both husband and wife (Mr. & Mrs. X) were subjected to taunts about being dumb as children, and both were somewhat sensitive about it. Komarovsky describes the relationship as follows:

'They sometimes called me a dumb Dora—it's on account of I can't talk sometimes. He bawls me out for minding what the others say and he says I'm not so dumb.' Her husband gives her a combination of support, protection and appreciation which makes her say fervently, 'Oh, he's the most!' He always compliments her when she cooks an especially good meal. His praise matters, she said, because unlike the in-laws who praise out of politeness, he doesn't say things he doesn't mean.

Mr. X in turn enjoys the deep respect of his wife:

I am the skipper of this marriage . . . when I got something to say, she listens. She don't sit there and wish I'd stop or be thinking about something else. Sometimes she'll be talking about the babies that aren't my work, but I listen to her.

And again:

"I understand her because I take the trouble to understand her."

The heightened ability to cope with economic limitations when the self-concepts are supported is illustrated by this same couple's delight over the recent purchase of a house with some help from their families. Mrs. X said:

I feel real happy and proud. . . . I had a lot to do with it, working between having babies and living cheaply and saving up . . . a couple of nights ago we were watching TV and the kids had gone to bed. We were feeling kind of good about the house and he just up and said he loved me (Komarovsky, 1962, pp. 174–76).

This marriage does not meet middle class standards of companionship or communication. Mr. X spends many evenings a week just walking, visiting with his brother, or in a tavern. He does not tell his wife where he is going or when he will be back. She doesn't expect it. She, on the other hand, has her deepest communication with her mother, sisters, sister-in-law, and girl friends. She fervently believes that women should stick together and men should stay by themselves because they just don't understand some things. Yet they are able, in their limited interaction, to provide for each other the support each needs for a feeling of self-worth which is not gained from the economic situation or from outside social groups. Families like this one are not immune to disruption from financial upsets, or from the intrusion of new values, but their mutually reinforcing relationship should heighten their ability to cope with external pressures. From all perspectives—the legal, the societal, and the individual —such families meet our criteria for success.

Sources of Strain in the Middle Class

Middle class persons escape the disruptive effects of extreme financial stress which affects many in the working class. They largely escape the barriers to communication imposed by low education, highly segregated sex roles, and anxiety about abilities to fulfill adult roles. Marriages are more stable in the middle classes, but this does not mean they suffer no stress. The strain is likely to be of a different nature and unlikely to be of the catastrophic variety that completely disrupts the relationship.

Higher Expectations for Marital Satisfaction. Stresses stemming from discrepancies between expectations and realizations are more likely in the middle classes than are strains from absolute deprivations of either money or communication. The greater exposure of the middle class to family norms emphasizing companionship, affection, and communication leads them to expect more from the marriage relationship. The wife who expects a high level of companionship from her husband is more likely to be dissatisfied than the wife who didn't expect much in the first place, regardless of the actual nature of the relationship. This seems especially true of the upper-middle class wife who may enjoy a great amount of companionship with her husband, yet be less satisfied than her lower-middle class counterpart who neither receives nor expects as much.

Greater Probability of Internal Value Conflict. The greater possibility of marriage between persons from different social class backgrounds increases the likelihood of value conflict between husband and wife in the middle classes. For example, consider the woman who has internalized the lower-middle class family-centered values in her family of orientation. She is sent to college where she meets and marries a promising young engineer from an upper-middle class background. Their extremely different concepts of the relationship between family and "career" is likely to heighten the dissatisfaction of both of them as he begins to "succeed." The added time he must devote to furthering his career may be interpreted by her as a lack of interest in his family, while he firmly believes that this is the way one shows devotion—by "succeeding for her." Although the marriage may never break up, the deep-seated value conflict is likely to create tension as well as feelings of being unappreciated and unloved. His emphasis on the importance of the family activities which enhance the career may be seen by her as shallow, unimportant, and detracting from the "real business" of creating a respectable, home-centered family. She feels he's not interested in the *family*—he feels she's not interested in *him!*

Greater Exposure to External Value Conflict. Both partners, on the other hand, may have grown up in the upper-working or lower-middle class and share the same values. Through education and continuous efforts they may achieve the "success" they both wanted. In this case the pressures for conforming to behavior appropriate to their new position may not only be difficult but lead to feelings of inadequacy in social relationships as well as anxiety about the kind of family life they are building. This represents consensus between husband and wife with conflict stemming from the outside social groups.

Not all who take the career route succeed. Those who fall short of their goals are especially likely to feel a sense of personal inadequacy, since the value system supporting the career orientation precludes the use of luck to explain failure as well as success. It takes an extremely strong relationship to keep feelings of personal inadequacy from introducing tension into the family.

Heightened Probability of Incompatible Demands. The increased demands for outside interests—community and school organizations, social activities, music lessons, dancing lessons, and other activities not seen as a necessary part of a child's education in lower status families multiply the potential conflicts from incompatible demands on a person's time. A father, for instance, cannot spend days at the office, evenings at meetings or "social–business" activities and still become vitally involved with his wife and children. A person cannot be in two places at once nor does he have an inexhaustible source of energy. When demands increase in one area, something else has to give. When *everything* is important, feelings of guilt and inadequacy over the things left undone mount.

In summary, the stresses and strains experienced in the middle classes are more likely to stem from: (1) both internal and external value conflicts; (2) high marital expectations which both enhance the possibility of success and increase the likelihood of dissatisfaction; (3) personal anxiety over the ability to "succeed"; and (4) high demands for outside community activity as well as for a "successful" family which may become incompatible expectations.

Sources of Stability in the Middle Class

On the other hand, the more education, the greater variety of experience, and the more secure economic position associated with the middle class provides greater facility in coping with the strains. The most important of these stabilizing influences are as follows:

1. The availability of outside activities aids in taking some of the demands off the family as the sole source for feelings of self-worth, especially for the woman.
2. The supply of funds even slightly above subsistence level allows an occasional relief from family demands. The husband who finds his wife tired and tense from an especially nerve-wracking day with several young children can say, "Come on, honey, let's find a baby sitter and go out to dinner tonight," only if he has a slight excess of money *and* notices her distress. Both the recognition of her feeling and the relaxation help take the strain off the marital relationship. The husband who notices the distress yet can do nothing about it because he lacks money is likely to experience a feeling of inadequacy himself and prefer to act as though he doesn't notice, thereby increasing his wife's unhappiness and assuring her that he doesn't care how she feels, even though this may be far from correct.
3. The higher educational level increases the verbal facility and personal resources these persons bring into the marital relationship. They are more likely to be able to talk and to have interests other than the segregated activities of the male and female to talk about.
4. They are more likely to be aware of alternative ways of solving problems and of the opportunities which exist in the community which can enhance their family life.

VARIATION IN ADAPTATION

The economic and social class positions structure the kind of pressures the family is likely to be exposed to. The norms and values one learned in his own family and the norms and values of the present social groups tend to structure the way in which the family attempts to cope with these pressures. The combination of husband–wife values and the way in which it fits with the values of the important social groups and with the external demands of the job and level of income create a variety of individual adaptations. The external situation and cluster of norms and values furnish the framework within which two people combine their love, their anger, their hopes, their fears, their personal assets and deficits to cope with the chain of events they encounter in their shared life. The result is a unique relationship between them—different in some respects from all others, yet resembling others in the prominent central themes emphasized in the relationship.

Variation in Central Themes

Cuber isolated five different themes which he found recurring in the marriages of people "successful" in the economic world (Cuber and Harroff, 1965, Chapter 3). None of the 270 marriages represented in this part of the analysis had been threatened by divorce. All had been married ten years or more. Most rated themselves as, at least, content. They were all faced with career demands but the personal relationships they developed in coping with the situation were quite different. The central themes he isolated were as follows:

1. *The conflict-habituated.* This relationship is characterized by a great deal of tension and conflict which is largely controlled. Specific areas of conflict are lacking but there is general disagreement about everything, yet the couples function well in the community and are managing to rear and educate children.

It's hard to know what we fight about. It's sometimes something I've said that she remembers differently, sometimes a decision—like what kind of car to buy or what to give the kids for Christmas. With regard to politics, and religion, and morals—oh boy! You know outside of the welfare of the kids—and that's just abstract—we don't really agree about anything . . . at different times we take opposite sides—not deliberately; it just comes out that way. . . .

Of course we don't settle any of the issues. It's sort of a matter of principle not to. Because somebody would have to give in then and lose face for the next encounter (Cuber and Harroff, 1965, pp. 45–46).

2. *The devitalized.* These people spend time entertaining together, planning and sharing activities with children, and participating in a variety of community activities. There is, however, a general feeling that they have lost something they had earlier in their relationship.

Judging by the way it was when we were first married—say the first five years or so—things are pretty matter-of-fact now—even dull. There are lots of outside things—you know, like Little League and the P.T.A. and the Swim Club, and even the company parties aren't always so bad. But I mean where Bob and I are concerned—if you followed us around, you'd wonder why we ever got married. We take each other for granted. We laugh at the same things sometimes, but we don't really laugh together the way we used to. . . .

You get children and other responsibilities. I have the home and Bob has a tremendous burden of responsibility at the office. You have to adjust to these things and we both try to gracefully (Cuber and Harroff, 1965, pp. 47–48).

3. *The passive-congenial.* These differ from the devitalized in that there is no disillusionment at having lost something that they once had. The relationship is comfortable, free from conflict, and contains common outside interests. They make few demands on each other for emotional involvement. It is a practical relationship, oriented toward outside interests.

We have both always tried to be calm and sensible about major life decisions, to think things out thoroughly and in perspective. Len and I knew each other from high school but didn't start to date until college. When he asked me to marry him, I took a long time to decide whether he was the right man for me and I went into his family background, because I wasn't just marrying him; I was choosing a father for my children. We decided together not to get married until he was established, so that we would not have to live in some little dingy apartment like some of our friends who got married right out of college. This prudence has stood us in good stead too. Life has moved ahead for us with remarkable orderliness and we are deeply grateful for the foresight we had (Cuber and Harroff, 1965, p. 51).

4. *The vital.* These people do the same things others do, but the involvement in the relationship is greater. There may be conflict, but when it occurs it is over something they think is important. They tend to settle their conflicts quickly and look for a solution rather than perpetuate them as in the conflict-habituated relationship.

I cheerfully, and that's putting it mildly, passed up two good promotions because one of them would have required some traveling and the other would have taken evening and weekend time—and that's when Pat and I *live*. The hours with her (after twenty-two years of marriage) are what I live for (Cuber and Harroff, 1965, p. 56).

Another couple states:

We've been married for over twenty years and the most enjoyable thing either of us does—well, outside of the intimate things—is to sit and talk by the hour.

The children respect this too. They don't invade our privacy any more than they can help—the same as we vacate the living room when Ellen brings in a date, she tries not to intrude on us. Being the specialized kind of lawyer he is, I can't share much of his work, but that doesn't bother either of us. The *big* part of our lives is completely mutual (Cuber and Harroff, 1965, p. 57).

5. *The total.* This relationship is much like the vital except that *all* aspects of life are shared and mutually reinforcing. There are no areas which are kept private and unshared. The demands for emotional involvement and companionship are extensive.

She keeps my files and scrapbooks up to date. I invariably take her with me to conferences around the world. Her femininity, easy charm and wit are valuable assets to me. I know it's conventional to say that a man's wife is responsible for his success and I also know that it's often not true. But in my case I gladly acknowledge that it's not only true, but she's indispensable to me. But she'd go along with me even if there was nothing for her to do because we just enjoy each other's company—deeply. You know, the best part of a vacation is not what we do, but we do it together. We plan it and reminisce about it and weave it into our work and other play all the time.

And from her side of the fence:

It seems to me that Bert exaggerates my help. It's not so much that I only want to help him; it's more that I want to do those things anyway. We do them together, even though we may not be in each other's presence at the time. I don't really know what I do for him and what I do for me (Cuber and Harroff, 1965, p. 59).

Cuber points out that the above relationships are not degrees of successful marriages. Most of the persons in all five kinds of relationships say they are content, if not happy. Neither are they representative of any marital cycle in which middle age necessarily brings a devitalized kind of relationship. They represent different kinds of adaptation to similar circumstances in which the people either by choice or chance have emphasized the personal aspect of the marital relationship over the utilitarian, or the utilitarian over the personal. They represent use of the relationship to release tension and hostility, to provide peace and escape from emotional involvement, or to provide close, emotional companionship. It is quite probable, of course, that marital relationships will shift from one type to another over time as economic circumstances, family responsibilities, changing interests, illnesses, accidents, and death weave an ever-changing backdrop against which the partners see each other in a different light—from a different angle—for better or for worse (if they are still looking!).

THE PRINCIPLE OF VALUE RELEVANCE

This chapter points up specifically the use of the principle of value relevance in the study of family relationships and family success. Stated simply, the principle of value relevance means that *the values people hold are relevant to their behavior and to the consequences of their behavior*. In other words what people believe, or desire, or expect influences how they act or react in specific situations. Many times the values are more important than reality factors in understanding human behavior and relationships. This book is organized around this principle, and the importance of value consensus and value conflict in understanding the variation in marital satisfaction will be referred to again and again. What may be reason for divorce for one couple may be the cement which holds the marriage together for another. The evaluation made of the marriage comes from the values concerning family life that the two partners hold and express in their interaction.

From this point of view, then, the success of a family, measured either by lack of separation or divorce or by the contentment of the members, is not the result of any one kind of marital relationship. Considering the variety of ways in which people divide the essential tasks associated with meeting everyday needs and the variation in the quality of interpersonal relationships, it is impossible to conclude that one pattern is superior to others for everyone and for all social positions. Each pattern has both strengths and strains. The deciding factor in success or failure is the degree to which the marital interaction fits the desires and expectations of the people within it and the degree to which it realistically copes with the external pressures impinging upon it.

Happy, successful families are found in all types of relationships and in all socioeconomic positions. Unsuccessful families are found in all social classes and in all types of relationships. The economic stability and higher levels of education found in the middle classes appear to make it easier to attain stable marriages in these strata. However, with the anxiety associated with pressing financial problems partially relieved, they are more likely to demand more of the relationship, with greater awareness of adjustment problems. Middle class couples may report as many

Table 4–1

Social Class and Difficulties Mentioned as Problems in Marriage *

	Problems of Living on Income, Budgeting, etc.	Serious Financial Problems	Adjustment Problems	Disruptive Adjustment Problems
Men				
Upper-middle (30)	17%	3%	33%	—
Lower-middle (30)	33	7	47	10%
Upper-lower (38)	24	37	16	13
Lower-lower (47)	21	45	9	21
Women				
Upper-middle (30)	33%	—	57%	—
Lower-middle (29)	31	7%	45	7%
Upper-lower (46)	39	26	30	7
Lower-lower (48)	22	33	13	38

* Combined data from tables presented in Rainwater, *Family Design: Marital Sexuality, Family Size, and Contraception* (Chicago: Aldine Publishing Co., 1965), pp. 323–25.

Numbers in parentheses represent bases from which percentages are computed.

problems but they tend to be of a different type and less disruptive than those experienced by the working class. These differences are pointed up by Rainwater. He differentiated between adjustment problems such as learning to understand each other, building mutually satisfying sexual relations, agreeing on what to do or how to do it—in other words learning to get along with each other—from the disruptive adjustment problems of staying away from home, drinking, unfaithfulness, and real incompatibility. In the financial area he differentiated between less serious problems of budgeting and living within an income from more serious problems involving unemployment, job instability, and financial disaster. The class differences shown in Table 4-1 show the varying emphases on certain kinds of problems in the several classes. Families face different problems of varying severity. The measure of success is not how well they conform to a particular type of marital relationship but how well their relationship copes with their unique set of problems imposed by both external pressures and their own personality needs.

SUMMARY

The rapid social changes occurring at different rates across our society have produced several different types of value conflict. These conflicts may occur: (1) in the societal norms themselves, so that conflicting values receive support at the same time; (2) between family values and those expressed in the part of society to which the family is attached; (3) between expectations for family life and the realization of those goals; and (4) between the values held by husband and wife, or between parents and children.

Social classes differ in terms of the types of stresses, strains, and strengths families are likely to encounter. The high anxiety concerning financial security heightens the probability of serious financial and disruptive adjustment problems in the lower classes. They are less likely to be disturbed by internal value conflicts because of their relative insulation from the sources of change in the society.

As the financial problems are alleviated and working class families move into middle class neighborhoods, stresses are more likely to occur from the intrusion of middle class values into the family value system.

In the middle class, value conflicts between husband and wife and between career and family demands are more likely, although greater financial security and higher education combine to lessen their severe disruptive effects. High marital expectations for happiness and success heighten the possibility of unrealized expectations.

At every class level and in every marital type are found successful and unsuccessful families. People bring different assets and deficits to the marriage relationship which combine to increase or decrease their abilities to realize their expectations. Rather than being related to any particular type of husband–wife relationship, marital success appears related to value consensus between husband and wife and their social groups, to the ability of the relationship to realize their expectations, and to the degree with which the partners are able to cope with the problems imposed on them by both external societal pressures and their own personality needs.

The external pressures stemming from social changes and social class position have been investigated in this part of the book. Part II will be devoted to the individuals—what they bring with them to the marriage relationship which will affect the demands they place upon the relationship as well as their ability to realize their expectations.

QUESTIONS AND PROJECTS

1. If you were asked to suggest ways to increase marital stability in the lower classes, what would you suggest? In the upper-middle class?

2. As far as your own marriage and family is concerned, would the quality of family life of people from other class positions make any difference? Why or why not?

3. Illustrate from your own experience each of the different kinds of value conflict discussed in this chapter. Try to explain how they occurred.

4. Which of Cuber and Harroff's central themes is more appealing to you as a model for marriage? Explain.

5. What are the conditions under which value conflicts between husband and wife are more likely to come into the open? Give some illustrations showing how this may happen.

6. Compare the different kinds of strain associated with working class and middle class marriages.

II

THE INDIVIDUAL

5

The Development
of a Sense of Self

By the time of marriage the individual is a complex organization of activity, beliefs, and feelings. He is a walking synthesis of his innate endowments, the reactions to and evaluations of his past experiences, and his relationships with numerous other individuals. He has developed a sense of who he is, where he has been, where he is going, and how important he is to himself and to others. For some, this *sense of identity* is well-developed and stable. Their various activities make sense in terms of their values and over-all pattern of their lives. They experience themselves as whole persons, with a fairly sure knowledge of what they will do in a variety of situations. For some, this sense of wholeness adds up to a positive self-evaluation. They think well of themselves and expect others to respond favorably to them. For others, it adds up to a sense of inadequacy. Their lives are very predictable from their point of view: "Nothing ever turns out right for me—I'm a born loser!" Some are not so sure of their identity. Their self-concepts vary from situation to situation. They are affected by every failure and every success, no matter how small.

Some persons need constant reassurance from others that they are worthwhile people; most need reassurance occasionally and in particular situations; all need to think well of themselves and to attempt to enhance their self-concepts. Some are successful in these attempts. Others seem to thwart themselves so their attempts to enhance their self-concepts continually result in failure.

The self-concept, then, has an impact on the kind of marriage relationship the individual wants, and the probability that he will be able to develop it. The marriage relationship, however, is the result of the interactions between *two* individuals—each with a self-concept, each with certain needs for reassurance, and each with habitual ways of attempting to enhance and stabilize his self-concept with varying degrees of success. In order to understand marital interactions, we must have some knowledge of how the self-concept is developed and how it influences behavior.

THE POTENTIAL FOR DEVELOPMENT

A sense of self is the essence of humanness, yet the newborn infant does not have it. His self-concept has to be developed slowly through repetitive interaction with others. He is born, however, with certain potentialities that allow this development to take place.

The human infant is endowed at birth with a capacity for producing, learning, using, and interpreting symbols. This allows the development of language, and the attachment of meaning to gestures, objects, and actions which enable him to develop and maintain complex interpersonal relationships. He has the capacity to order incoming stimuli in terms of some scheme of categorization and to generalize his knowledge about past situations to situations he has not yet experienced. As he develops this capacity, he does not need to react to each new situation as a unique experience but can put together many past experiences to allow him to define the new situation and predict what is expected of him and how others will respond to his actions. He is able to put himself in the place of someone else and view his own actions at the same time he is experiencing them subjectively. In other words, he has the ability to experience himself as both an *object* and as a *subject*. It is this capacity which allows him to develop inner controls over his behavior so that in time he need not have an authority figure present to control his actions.

These potentials are present at birth in the normal infant. They must be present for the qualities which distinguish the human from other animals to develop. Other characteristics such as sex, the limits on height, body build, coloring, facial features, limits on intelligence, tendencies for the development of certain diseases, and the potential for certain artistic or intellectual development are transmitted to the infant through inheritance. These are the ingredients which provide the means for him to develop a sense of self, unique to the human. They also provide some visible characteristics which will be evaluated by others in his society to give a basis for his developing self-concept. The process of genetic transmission will be discussed in the chapter on childbearing. At this point we are mainly concerned with what happens to the child from the moment of birth on.

The Impact of Society

The hereditary potentials are established at the time of conception. These potentials will not develop into human characteristics, however, unless there is an ongoing society to receive and nurture the newborn infant. The infant's development takes place according to nature's timetable and as influenced by three environments:

1. Physical
2. Cultural
3. Social

Physical Surroundings. *The physical environment* consists of various material elements and energies that at all times surround the human organism, influencing both development and behavior. Before birth it is made up of chemicals, temperatures, and other conditions within the mother. It is affected by such things as diet and emotion; and it, in turn, affects the growth rates, survival chances, and general health conditions of the child not yet born. After birth it consists of the many geographic factors—temperature, rainfall, sunshine, wind, soil, mineral resources, elevation, topography, and the like. During the prenatal stage this physical environment is the only one operating. In the postnatal period, however, there are competitive influences along with it—the social and the cultural.

Culture, particularly in the Western world, has developed nearly far enough to supersede geography in influence. To some extent man has learned how to control temperature, remove mountains, and in other ways harness the forces of nature to his advantage. Modern man is not nearly so dependent upon the elements as were his ancestors. Yet neither is he independent of them.[1]

Though the physical in recent years has been considered the least important of man's postnatal environments, it is rising in importance. It has become increasingly apparent that the technology which allowed control over much of the physical environment has also contributed to the pollution and depletion of that environment. The physical environment can no longer be seen as a constant, but as affected by man as he in turn is affected by it.

Whether man takes measures to reverse the polluting and depletion process or fails to reverse it, his cultural and social environments will change as he adapts to the physical conditions. Whether the earth is turned into a hothouse by the thickening layer of polluted air as some

---

[1] An interesting though sobering account of man's wrestle with nature, and his relative helplessness in the face of natural events, is given in George Stewart's novel based on the science of meteorology, *Storm*.

predict, or pressed toward another ice age, as others predict, or preserved
in its present condition by stemming the numerous activities contributing
to pollution, the way of life must change influencing man's development
and behavior.

Cultural Environment. The cultural environment is made up of the
multitude of man-made objects, customs, understandings, and skills that
one is born to accept. Culture, though not the same as society, is one of
society's products. It consists of all that is created by man in interaction,
deposited or retained by society, and passed down from generation to
generation.

Culture is sometimes defined as man's "social inheritance," for just as
individuals differ according to the kind of biological inheritance that is
theirs, so they also differ according to the kind of society into which they
are born. Someone born to live in the heart of New York City, for example, would have a far different social heritage, and therefore a different
personality, from someone on the upper reaches of the Amazon.

The culture provides meanings and evaluations of the genetically determined characteristics which have an impact on the self-concept. Sex
is one of the prominent characteristics with which the individual is born.
The culture provides differential evaluation, based on whether the infant
is male or female. A boy-child may be more highly valued and treated
quite differently from a girl-child. A child that is favored with physical
characteristics which are highly regarded in a particular culture will receive more positive responses from a variety of people than one who is
considered ugly. A fat child in one society may be considered beautiful,
and in another be called "fatty" and laughed at, with consequences for
his attitude toward self. A quick, inquisitive mind may win respect in
one society and be considered a nuisance in another. If redheads are
considered to be hotheads, then a redheaded child is likely to be subjected to teasing and repetitive interpretations of his anger which differ
from a blond or brunette. Thus, the cultural environment provides the
definitions of beauty and normality which give meaning to the inherited
characteristics; it provides the expectations for desirable personality traits
and appropriate behavior which guide the direction of the developing
potentials. An artistic boy, to give another example, may be encouraged
to develop his talents, with corresponding feelings of self-esteem in one
society; while in another he may be dubbed a "sissy" and teased because
of his lack of boyish traits, also with consequences for his self-concept.

Each family, however, has its own culture, selecting from the range of
available meanings and expectations. There may be general similarities
among families, but each develops a somewhat unique combination as
the personalities of the parents interact within a particular social context.

The level of income, type of housing, religious leanings, habits of inter-action, size of family, rituals surrounding meals, bedtime, celebrations, and so forth, all combine to form the family culture. As the infant grows, his view of the world, his place within it, and the value he places on himself begin to develop, all colored by the family culture.

Social Environment. The social environment comes from the presence of other human beings and one's interaction with them. Of primary im-portance is the social interaction which takes place in the "family of ori-entation." The family gets the infant first, when he is most pliable, keeps him the longest, and interacts with him more intensely than all other groups. A variety of things take place as a result of family interaction, all of which have an impact on the self-concept of the growing child.[2]

DEVELOPING A SENSE OF SELF

When the human infant is born he has no conception of the boundaries of his own body—he does not know where he ends and the bed or mother begins. Through his own flailings, grasping, biting, and pulling, he very slowly develops an awareness of his own bodily structure.[3] He flails his hands and hits the bars on his baby bed. He grasps the bar and the arm will no longer move. He makes contact with some part of his own body and grasps it in the same way. He may cry as he pinches his arm; yet continue to pinch. As his hands continue to explore, he finds his hair, his toes, his fingers, his eyes, ears, nose—all of his anatomy. As he comes in contact with them, he may pull, bite, scratch, or poke with cries of pain but no awareness that he is both the offender and the offended. It is close to the end of the first year before the child becomes able to distinguish between his body and the rest of the world.

Self-Awareness

Even after the infant learns the boundaries of his own body, he still does not have self-awareness. He assumes that all other persons are like himself, that both animals and inanimate objects are like people. If his doll's head breaks as it falls to the floor, he may think that his own head will do the same thing. If he hurts his knee, he may think that his moth-er's knee hurts, too. Even after several years, a parent may experience difficulty in getting a child to relate something in sufficient detail to

[2] For an excellent treatment of the effects of the sociocultural environment on the development of the self, see Edward Z. Dager (1964, pp. 746–77).

[3] The following discussion relies heavily on Edward Z. Dager (1964) and Alfred R. Lindesmith and Anselm L. Strauss (1956).

understand what he is talking about. The child may be just as exasperated, since he tends to think that what is in his mind is in his parent's mind also.

The acquisition of language is essential to the development of self-awareness. As he develops a set of labels to place on objects (himself and other people, as well as inanimate objects) he becomes able to distinguish himself from them. He learns that he is different from his mother and that his mother is different from his father.

From repeated interactions with the same persons, he experiences the evaluations they make of him. He absorbs feelings about himself which he gets from the way he is handled, the manner in which his needs are understood and met. Over and over, as a mother takes care of her infant, she transmits to him her feelings about him. The baby may not have been wanted; he may be seen as just an extra burden, another mouth to feed in an already over-crowded household. Although this mother may never tell her child that she didn't want him, we may expect it to come out in the harassed way in which she keeps him clean or leaves him dirty, in the hurried or disinterested way she feeds him enough or too little. Again and again, the child receives evaluations of himself in the general way he is treated. Since the child is unable to understand the circumstances which influence his treatment, he is likely to attach the reasons to himself—he is not worth her care and attention.

Even before the acquisition of language, the way in which the child's needs are met will develop in him some feelings about whether he is important enough to be cared for and whether he can trust other people to look after him. Erik Erikson suggests that this sense of trust or mistrust is the first thing the child acquires in his social development which provides a generalized basis for future development of the self-concept and kinds of relationships the child will be able to develop (Erikson, 1964).

As he grows he begins to understand the more complex evaluations made of himself in adult conversation. He hears his name repeated over and over by persons important to him. It is accompanied by other words, gestures, and voice inflections which give his name meaning. When his vocabulary is restricted, he can only pick up a few clues—"Billy, good boy!"—after he has eaten all his dinner or eliminated in the appropriate place. As his vocabulary becomes more complex he can carry on in his own imagination entire conversations concerning himself, *taking the role of the other* as well as himself. Through this process he learns to perceive himself as a person, with desires, feelings, ideas, and meanings which are his own. Since the evaluations he uses in becoming aware of himself come from a limited group of "others," his conception of himself is necessarily similar to the evaluations which those "others" hold of him. They are seldom exactly the same, however. The infant is not a sponge sapping up the evaluations made of him, in toto. He experiences strong impulses for continuing behaviors his parents have defined perhaps as bad. He may experience high anxiety as he argues with himself either before or after engaging in the forbidden act. The resulting appraisal he makes of himself will be colored by misinterpretations, anxiety, and past feelings about self and will not be exactly the same as the appraisal reflected to him by his parents. Repeated evaluative experiences result in a sense of self which develops slowly, then attempts to hold itself constant.

The Self-System

The human being develops a need to feel that he is living in an orderly and predictable world. Part of that order comes from the reassurance that others will reflect to him the same evaluation he makes of himself. He cannot define himself if he cannot predict what the responses of others to him will be. He is extremely dependent upon adults (usually his parents) for many years. If he cannot predict their responses to him he becomes highly anxious about their continuing love and support. Growing up is necessarily fraught with anxiety-provoking situations as he is torn between his own impulses and parental demands and as he is faced with unexpected evaluations and confusing situations.

Some frustration, anxiety, and internal arguments are necessary for the child to incorporate internal controls as a part of his sense of self. But too much anxiety is unbearable and immobilizing. For his own defense the child develops means for securing the necessary satisfactions while minimizing the accompanying anxiety. It is to serve this purpose that the self-system develops. The *self-system* is a process which selectively screens the incoming evaluations made of self, interprets them in the light of past feelings about self, and integrates these assessments with those already present in the self-concept. In this way, once there is a vague self-concept organized, the subsequent operation of the self-system will maximize the opportunities for reinforcement and minimize the opportunities for change especially since appraisals in contradiction to the self-concept are anxiety-producing.

Let us illustrate with two girls, one of whom has a self-concept which includes a very positive appraisal of her face and figure while the other considers herself plain and ill-proportioned. Although Plain Jane may want desperately to think she's beautiful, her self-system will tend to prevent any change in her self-concept in the same way that Pretty Kitty's will continue to reinforce her favorable concept. Both evaluations, by the way, may depart from the evaluation made by outsiders. Their self-systems will tend to reinforce their self-concepts in at least three major ways.

1. _Directing activity_. Since Plain Jane sees herself as unattractive she is quite likely to play down the importance of looks in her overt behavior and make little or no attempt to make herself attractive. By denying to herself its importance she cuts down the opportunity for receiving evaluations which might change her concept of her looks. She may avoid boy–girl situations to escape the pain of being ignored, or interact with males only on athletic or intellectual grounds. She cuts down her anxiety, but at the same time cuts down the opportunity for developing relationships which may truly deemphasize the importance of physical appearance or alter her concept of her looks.

Pretty Kitty will tend to do just the opposite. Thinking she is pretty, she is likely to spend time enhancing her attractiveness and call forth the attention which reinforces her self-concept. If she thinks this is her major asset, she is likely to seek out situations and activities where physical appearances are important to the neglect of other pursuits which may bring her greater satisfaction but also more anxiety.

2. _Screening incoming evaluations_. Not everyone responds to physical appearance in the same way. What one person sees as beautiful, another may consider plain, and another may not even see at all. Except in very extreme cases the self-images reflected by others will not be in total agreement. People vary in their attractiveness from day to day and from occasion to occasion. But, if physical attractiveness is important, one is likely to notice only the comments or gestures which are in agreement with the self-concept. Thus, Pretty Kitty is likely to be "selectively inattentive" to anything but positive evaluations just as Plain Jane will have her ears tuned for only the negative ones. Many mothers have probably experienced the frustration of trying to tell a teen-aged daughter that certain colors or styles look particularly unattractive on her, only to feel that they are talking to a post. "It's just as if she never heard a word I said." If the daughter is Pretty Kitty, she didn't hear or only heard the cushioning positive comments. If she is Plain Jane, she knew it all along —everything is unattractive on her so why bother.

3. _Influencing interpretation_. No one can respond directly to incoming stimuli. Stimuli must be interpreted before they have meaning. This can be called the second line of defense in the self-system. Not all contradictory reflections of self can be screened out, but those which get through can be interpreted in such a way that the self-concept is reinforced. Pretty Kitty may have to recognize occasional negative appraisals, but she can chalk them up to jealousy, lack of taste, or some other fault of the observer and discount them. Plain Jane can do the same thing by insisting that the positive appraisals come from persons who feel sorry for her, or are just being kind, or perhaps making fun of her.

They are likely to react to neutral situations differently also. Let's say they walk into a room. Two people glance up, then immediately begin a whispered conversation. Pretty Kitty may feel elated that they are commenting about her stunning appearance while Plain Jane is sure they are discussing her unbecoming hairdo. The people in question may have been discussing their plans for the next day, the weather, or politics; it makes no difference. The girls interpreted it for their own purposes. Since many of the situations we encounter day after day are of this neutral variety—having no reference to ourselves—we have ample grist for our reinforcement mill.

The intermingling of these three mechanisms in the *vicious circle* of the self-system can be seen in the case of a student who had begun to understand how her self-concept influenced her relationship with boys:

About the time a girl enters the fifth or sixth grade she begins to notice that boys are boys and she wants their attention. I was no exception. I began to see boys as a source of future dates and I wanted them to notice me. I couldn't imagine why they would notice me, though. I thought I was very unattractive. I was too big, ugly, and I inevitably had the wrong kind of clothes. I was so afraid that I would be laughed at that I never said anything to the boys I thought were really nice. I could only be natural with those I didn't like and considered undesirable [*directing activity*]. I *knew* my evaluation of myself was correct when the only ones who paid any attention to me were the ones I didn't like. They were the sloppy ones, the ones at the bottom of the class academically. None of the other girls would give them a second glance and when they paid attention to me I *knew* it was because the other girls had refused them [*interpreting behavior*]—I really felt on the bottom of the heap. It never occurred to me that I was ignoring all the others *myself* and just talking to the boys I didn't like.

I remember one incident—and there were many like it—when our music teacher in the eighth grade was trying to teach us social dancing—that was disastrous! When it was time for the boys to choose partners, I sat there panic stricken—certain I wouldn't be chosen. Some of them would start toward me, then change their minds and ask someone else. Sure enough I was about the last one chosen.

It was even worse when it was "ladies choice." I knew the boys I wanted to dance with wouldn't want to dance with me—so I didn't give them a second look. I went straight to the boys I didn't like, because I knew they were the only ones who might accept. And then I'd catch a look on their faces which told me they'd rather I hadn't asked them [*screening incoming stimuli*]. I really hit rock bottom.

I do have dates, now, in college. But, it's funny, it's always with boys I don't like. I don't know whether I still do the same thing I used to—or whether when a boy asks me for a date I decide he must be undesirable or he wouldn't have asked *me*.

The same mechanisms are available for the person who is convinced he is not very smart. The probability is fairly high that he will not perform up to his potential. However, he *may* work very hard in order to improve his self-concept and actually perform above average. Even so, he is likely to compare himself to those who do better, completely ignoring the majority who may not do as well. Forced to recognize his achievement through grades or some other recognition, he may insist that he was just lucky, the instructors were fooled, or the areas in which he excels do not require much intelligence. This was illustrated by a very intelligent college girl who had struggled with the idea that she was a dumbbell since she was a very small child. In her early school years her fears of appearing stupid had made her appear confused and halting in her class recitations. A speech impediment brought further laughter and jokes from her classmates which she attributed to the stupidity of what she had said as well as to the way she said it. She related one of the first experiences she had which should have aided in changing her academic self-concept:

> We had a final exam in our seventh grade history course, which was something we had not run into before. It was quite, difficult for us. When the exams were returned, I had an 82—the highest grade in the class! I was flabbergasted. For a few minutes I was the center of attention for the entire class—something I had never experienced before, except when they were laughing at me. It was a very pleasant experience. It occurred to me, for a moment, that maybe I wasn't as dumb as I thought. But then I noticed there was a B on the paper instead of an A. It seemed to me that the highest grade in the room should be an A. Then I *knew*—it was because I was the one who made it. A person with my lack of intelligence rarely, if ever, makes the highest grade on a test and when they do, by accident, it's not worth an A.

Changes in the Self-Concept

Although the self-system operates to maintain stability in the self-concept, changes can and do occur. There are periods during which the likelihood of self-concept change is greater than usual. These periods are characterized by a *loss of predictability and heightened anxiety*. Sometimes the periods are predictable because of the normal growth cycle and certain experiences shared by most people in our society. One of the first of these is exposure to the school system.

Starting to School. For many children in the United States this is the first important exposure to evaluations of themselves by persons other than family members. They undoubtedly hear a lot about school and about what they will have to do, and acquire numerous fanciful notions about teachers. It is hard for them to predict what will happen so we can expect their anxiety levels to be high. Their self-systems are operative but probably not too well-equipped to handle high anxiety. They must become open to new evaluations of their behavior by both teachers and classmates to again acquire the needed predictability. They are now being compared with others their own age by persons with little knowledge of their past experiences and behavioral habits. They are likely to be misinterpreted, to receive conflicting evaluations for similar behavior, and to be exposed to contradictory expectations for behavior. The child is forced to make sense out of a mass of stimuli with important consequences for his self-concept.

As he develops a changed concept of himself as a school child, his behavior is likely to become more predictable (his teacher and classmates will tend to expect certain behaviors), give the appropriate response when the behavior occurs, and thus support the new self-concept.

The expectations for predictable behavior and the controlling aspect of the expectations is well illustrated by the often heard comments: "Why, John, that's not like you at all!"; "Mary would never do a thing like that"; "Billy is always the trouble maker"; "Give us the answer, Betty, I know *you* did your homework"; "Don't bother asking her, she wouldn't do it"; "Who does he think he is, anyway, acting like that."

Adolescence. Probably the period of greatest change is during adolescence. At this time the rapid bodily changes force a reevaluation of physical appearance. When one emerges in a new body, the self-concept must change too. The evaluations of peers assume much greater importance as the awareness grows that one has an identity outside the family. Again, the expectations for behavior change, not always consistently. Behavior which was only recently approved is now looked upon as childish.

Different aspects of the self are likely to assume new importance. The evaluations made by the opposite sex take on new meaning. The bodily changes foretell the coming of "the man" and "the woman," and doubts concerning one's ability to fulfill these roles furnish new measures against which to measure the self. This period is probably characterized by the attempt to redefine oneself as a person rather than as an extension of the family. Anxieties, then, can be expected to be high and this stage in between the child and the adult is loaded with unpredictable situations. The adolescent does not really belong with the children and is not yet counted among the adults. It is hard to know when one should act like a child and when like an adult. The adult responses are not likely to be consistent either, since they must redefine themselves also in relationship with their almost grown children. The relationship between a parent and a ten-year-old son is not the same as the relationship between the parent and the same son who is sixteen. In a sense they must respond to each other as different people, evaluating each other from different perspectives with consequences for both of their self-concepts. These changes are not likely to be smooth and free from regression to former behaviors, expectations, and contradictory evaluations.

Contradictions are also highly probable between behavior considered appropriate for a teen-ager by adults and by other teen-agers. Values and behaviors are likely to be exposed to different evaluations. The teen-ager must reevaluate conflicting expectations, integrate them into his self-concept and emerge as a synthesis of his trials, errors, failures, and successes in a variety of relationships which have been important to him.

Changes in Groups. At any period of the growth cycle, a change in family or friendship group can bring about a change in the self-concept. Since stable groups aid in holding the self-concept constant, a change in these groups aids in bringing about change. Whenever one enters a new group in which he is unknown a certain amount of anxiety is inevitable. He cannot be sure just how his behavior will be evaluated, or what will be expected of him. If he is responded to differently than he has been in the past, he must either reevaluate his view of himself, throw his defense system into high gear to discount the new evaluations, or else he must withdraw.

Probably most people have had the experience while growing up of wanting to experiment with a "new self." They may comb their hair differently, walk differently, or talk differently only to be met with: "Who are you trying to be?"; "What's wrong with you, today?"; or "Come on, Jane, who're you trying to impress?" It is almost as if others are saying: "Get back where you belong, so I can predict your behavior, and know who I am in relation to you."

Some persons are quite conscious of this as they prepare to go to college, or move to a new town. One student expressed it this way:

I had grown faster than most of my classmates, and I was about 3 or 4 inches taller than the girls and most of the boys. I was teased about it, which made me feel more conspicuous. I never wanted anyone to know how I felt, so I laughed and joked right back when someone would ask, 'How's the weather up there?'—or 'It's a shame they won't let girls on the basketball team.'

When it was time to go away to college, I wanted to get far away—where none of my friends were going. I wanted a chance to stop being 'the clown,' and to start a new life. It wasn't as easy as I had thought, though, because I still had the tendency to act as crazy as ever whenever my height was mentioned.

Change of Status. As people continue to grow they change positions in the society. These new positions—or statuses—make demands on them for new behaviors and the acceptance of new responsibilities. They become husbands or wives, they become parents, and they must become engaged in an occupation. All these changes upset somewhat their predictability. They must learn new cues, construct a new system of order.

To do this they must let in new evaluations of self in terms of the new demands. As new ingredients are admitted, the concept of self changes.

Impact on Marriage

Since the self-concept is so influential in behavior and the interpretation of behavior, its effect on the marriage relationship is apparent. Some persons are only able to maintain an adequate self-concept by downgrading someone else. It is as if he says to himself, "I may not be worth much, but I'm better than you are." A spouse is a ready target for such a person, continually available to be used. Even if the person does not use his spouse in this way, he cannot provide support for someone else's self-concept if he must spend most of his energy in protecting his own.

The marital relationship is such an intimate relationship that interaction cannot help but affect the self-concepts of both partners. If the self-systems are such that a great deal of screening and reinterpretation of words and actions become routine, communication can become a comedy (or tragedy) of errors. The continual interaction necessary in a marriage provides constant evaluations of self in the important roles of breadwinner or homemaker, lover, companion, father, and mother. The need to feel a sense of self-worth is present in everyone, and the habitual ways one tries to maintain his self-esteem become part of the marital interaction. The kind of marriage relationship which develops reflects the impact these two people have on each other as they attempt to cope with everyday activities.

When one has an adequate self-concept, he is more able to accept and realistically evaluate criticism as well as praise. He can react more objectively to another person, can recognize and be concerned with another person's needs and feelings, and can trust another person with *his* needs and feelings. These characteristics are beneficial to any relationship and especially to the kind of marriage relationships considered desirable in middle class America. This is one of the ways in which it is correct to say that the kind of marriage partner one becomes is laid down in childhood. It is in the family of orientation that one begins to develop his self-concept and the characteristic means of enhancing and defending it. It undergoes change as he interacts with other groups in different situations, but even the change is influenced by the residue of feelings about self formed long ago.

SUMMARY

The human being is born with certain potentialities which allow the qualities we associate with humanness to develop. The potential transmitted through heredity is only developed in a human group, however. The group which has the first and most lasting impact on the developing infant is the family of orientation. It is here that he develops his self-awareness and begins to define himself as a person. The evaluations he makes of himself are strongly influenced by those that the family members (mainly his parents) make concerning him, but they are rarely exactly the same. These evaluations must be interpreted, synthesized, and integrated into a concept of self which will be continually tested, changed, and validated in subsequent situations and relationships.

The human develops a need for order and predictability. A loss of this predictability is associated with a rise in anxiety. The self-system develops to provide the order necessary to allow him to gratify his needs with a minimum of anxiety. This process provides continuity of the self-concept by: (1) directing activities into channels which are likely to emphasize strong points and draw attention away from felt weaknesses (at the same time it minimizes the opportunity for testing and changing the negative evaluations); (2) screening incoming stimuli so that one selects those evaluations which reinforce the self-concept and becomes inattentive to those which are contradictory; and (3) interpreting the stimuli which do enter awareness to give further reinforcement to the concept of self already held.

The self-system is rarely infallible, however, and changes do occur. These changes are most probable in situations where loss of predictability results in high anxiety. There is then the necessity to become cognizant of new evaluations of self in order to learn new expectations for behavior and construct a new system of predictability. The new ingredients are then available for integration with the older concept of self. These situations are more likely when the self is evaluated from new expectations such as beginning school, adolescence, changing social groups, and changing statuses.

At the time of marriage a self-system is in operation, functioning to stabilize the self-concept, enhance self-esteem, and influence behavior. It is an extremely important part of the marriage relationship. The interaction between the two self-concepts will influence the relationship. But since marriage is also an important change of status, the relationship will also influence both self-concepts.

QUESTIONS AND PROJECTS

1. Distinguish the physical, social, and cultural environments. Tell which of these you think is most important and give examples of the influence that it exerts upon the development of the individual.

2. Why is the family considered to be so important in the development of the self-concept even though the child begins very early to interact with people outside of it?

3. Illustrate from your own experience how the self-system operates to protect the sense of self. Be sure to include examples of all the ways the self-system operates.

4. Using your own experience, see if you can account for either a change in your self-concept or lack of change associated with adolescence, moving from one town to another or changing schools within the same town, or some other change which required you to interact with a different social group.

5. See if you can define "love" using self-concept terms. Are you satisfied with the definition? Why or why not?

6. Look back in Chapter 1 at the definition of a successful marriage. What key elements would have to be included in the interaction to make you define *your* marriage as successful? Can you see why interaction which would lead to satisfaction in one period of your life may not do so at another period? Explain.

7. Considering some of the suggestions being made for controlling pollution, what changes do you foresee in the physical environment which may have an impact on the self-concepts of future generations? On family relationships?

8. What changes in marriage and the family do you foresee if pollution continues unchecked?

6
Habits of Interaction

The mass of experiences the child has in the process of growth provides the ingredients which he uses to develop a sense of self. Since the experiences he has, for the most part, involves human relationships, he is at the same time acquiring habits of interpreting a variety of words, gestures, and behaviors. No word or gesture can be responded to until its meaning is first interpreted. The husband who comes home to find the table adorned with the best china and candles must attach a meaning to the scene before he can react. It means he forgot an anniversary, his wife is buttering him up for a new dress, or just that his wife felt especially festive or loving. His tendency to interpret it one way or another will affect his first words. "Oh mygosh, what day is this?" "O.K., what's this all about, what do you want now?" "What a wonderful surprise!" His reaction must then be interpreted by his wife. She must guess the meaning he put on her act by observing his reaction, requiring her to interpret his words.

Two persons can never communicate directly. Communication always involves interpretation, the impact on the self-concept, and the reaction which results.[1] This is portrayed graphically in Figure 6–1. The behaviors bounded by solid lines are the only ones which can be observed. Those bounded by dotted lines take place inside the person and are colored by the past experiences which have placed meaning on the observable act. The solid arrows trace the chain of interaction, while the dotted arrows show additional influences on the interpretation. It should be noted that the only crossing of the communication barrier between husband and wife occurs with *observable* behavior, whether verbal or nonverbal, intended or non-intended. The response to the observable behavior, however, is always in terms of the meaning it has to the *other*

[1] For an excellent discussion of the theory involved see R. D. Laird, H. Phillipson, and A. R. Lee (1966, Chapter 1.)

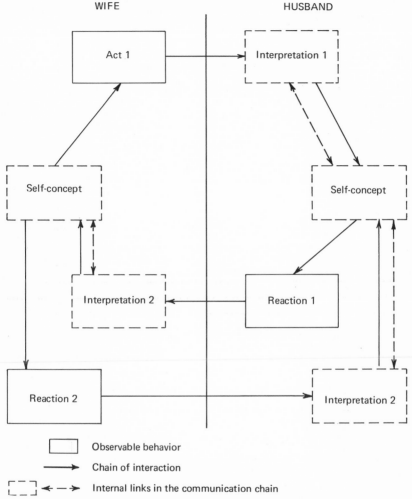

Fig. 6–1. Communication chain.

person, not the meaning it has to the actor. We can only guess the meaning it has for the other person as we observe his behavior, put ourselves in his place—take the role of the other—and interpret it in light of our own past experiences with this person or others similar to him.

The importance of these interpretations for future actions can readily be seen in the conversation of teen-agers as they begin their dating experience. "I wonder what he meant by that?" "How can I tell if she really likes me?" "If I do that, I wonder what he'll think I mean?" "But I don't want her to think that I . . ." and so on and on and on. The answers supplied to these questions will be partially related to the immediate relationship, partially related to similar relationships one has experienced in the past, and partially related to the habits of interpretation acquired in the process of building a sense of self.

HABIT SYSTEMS

The self-concept, as it develops, is always related to interpersonal situations. The individual *learns* that he is the kind of person who everyone likes; the kind of person who must fight to get what he wants; the kind of person others will try to flatter or cheat to gain their ends. All of these have implications for the individual's emerging habits of perceiving and interpreting the words and gestures of other people. They form his views of the world, of other men and women, and of his relationship to them.

Habits, used in this way, are not just repetitive routine actions such as brushing the teeth. Rather they imply a certain propulsive force which influences a person to behave in one way and not another. Habit implies that there is a special sensitivity to certain classes of stimuli, an acquired predisposition to react in certain ways to classes of behavior rather than simply to repeat a particular act (Waller and Hill, 1951, pp. 58–60). Thus, one person may have a strong tendency to react to any expressed opinion which differs from his own as an evaluation of his intelligence. No matter how his opinion is questioned, from "Do you *really* think it will rain tomorrow?" to "Nobody in his right mind would believe what you say!," his initial impulse is to feel that the other person doubts his word and is implying that he is stupid. He is likely to respond to a variety of situations containing this element as if he had been insulted. Another person, hearing the same kinds of statements, may have a strong tendency to write off the other person as being ill-informed, unable to comprehend his point of view, or a little "thick." Still another person may weigh each remark in its special context, including the kind of opinion, the personality of the other person, and the special circumstances. He may be sensitive only to certain areas of information. At any rate, the predispositions to interpret and to respond in certain ways are *habits* whether they are called into action once a day, once a year, or once in a lifetime.

The Combination of Habits

The combination of such habits and his evaluation of them give the individual a certain uniqueness and make him somewhat predictable. In a marital situation, the fit between the habits of the two spouses will either ease or endanger their adjustment and understanding of each other. Although many situations encountered in marriage will be new, they will still contain elements of habits which can be recombined.

Some of the habits a person acquires in the process of growing up are similar to those of many other persons. These are acquired in the day-to-day interaction with family members who are enacting habits shared by their social groups. Others will be quite unique—the result of the particular combination of values, norms, and habits expressed in the family and the individual's specific experiences within it. A few of these habits are of special importance in the marital relationship. These include the habitual meanings attached to sex, love, anger, illness, and controlling or being controlled. They include those gestures or words which are interpreted as expressing emotions such as anger, love, disgust, as well as the habitual reactions to them. They include habitual ways of coping with problems. They are developed at the same time that the self is developing and are an integral part of the self-concept. They are important enough to the marital relationship, however, that we will spend some time on the major factors influencing their development.

Social Context Influences

The child is born into a family which has already developed certain habits of communication. The parents have learned during their own growth processes certain consequences of anger, for example, and ways of expressing it. They have characteristic ways of showing love, hate, sadness, or happiness. They have learned to interpret, correctly or incorrectly, each other's actions. Since they are also part of the larger society, they have been influenced by the meaning attached to these actions by those groups in society with which they interact. Class and ethnic group differences have been found; for example, in the acceptability of the direct expression of anger, in the acceptance of affectionate interchanges between father and son or between brothers, in the expression of sexual attraction, the meaning of sex, and so forth. The child, then, will be exposed in his earliest experiences only to those meanings which have been attached to gestures in *his* social environment.

The social context will provide in general terms an ongoing culture which contains the meanings and interpretations of a variety of words, gestures, and actions. Particular occupational settings, for example, point up the importance of some characteristics and reduce the importance of others. It has been shown that persons working within these settings reflect in their childrearing values the demands made upon them in their work. Kohn (1966), to illustrate, found that fathers who worked in jobs where there was close supervision of their work chose obedience as an important characteristic to be developed in children much more often than fathers in jobs where there was loose supervision. The latter were more likely to choose self-direction or neither form of control as important in childrearing. Although this study was done in Italy, the results conformed to the class differences he found in an American sample (Kohn, 1959). Special pressures and emphases stemming from the social context will furnish, then, the broad guidelines for family interaction. Those meanings and reactions which are learned within the family are carried into other relationships outside the family. These meanings will be confirmed if the individual is interpreted correctly, helping to build a shared culture within the social context.

Thus, we have the ingredients for clear communication *within* a cultural group and for misinterpretation *between* cultural groups. An insulting phrase may indicate close friendship in one group and invite a fist in the mouth in another. What may elicit laughter in one group may bring forth disgust in another.

The Family Influence. Although the family will exhibit some of the habits shared by other families in similar social contexts, it will also develop a unique pattern. In the process of living day after day and coping with its unique set of problems, the family will develop a culture of its own. The child comes into this going concern and slowly absorbs the meanings of gestures, words, and inflections which are flowing all around him. What child does not learn to interpret the exact moment when his mother's voice inflection tells him that it is now time to act rather than play deaf?

Many of the interactions a child has in his family define acceptable and unacceptable *motives* for behavior (Gerth and Mills, 1953, Chapter 5). The way the parent responds to the child not only tells him whether the behavior is good or bad, but implicitly tells him what that behavior means as far as indicating his motive for behaving in that way. For example, a young child may pick up a pet kitten by two handfuls of fur, with accompanying yowls from the cat. Many mothers would stop the child, but the way in which they do it has implications for the meaning behind the act:

Stop it—You're deliberately hurting that cat—how can you be so mean?
No, no, that's not the way to pick up a kitten. I know you didn't mean to hurt it, but . . .
Let go of that kitten! Don't you care if you hurt it? You have no feelings for anything else, at all!
Don't hurt the cat—it will scratch you.

These differing interpretations of the motives behind the act, and reasons for not doing it again, are apparent in reactions to many behaviors, from the spilling of a glass of milk to kicking mother in the shins.

Since the adults in the family express their own habitual ways of inter-preting behavior in their interactions, the child's experiences are likely to be limited and repetitive. He develops his own habits in several different ways:

1. Observing the meaning attached to the behavior from the inter-action of other family members
2. Experiencing their responses to him when he behaves in a certain way
3. Identifying with the parent who reacts in a certain way
4. Discovering accidentally certain acceptable behaviors which allow him to satisfy his needs or desires.

In order to understand the processes by which the habits are acquired, we will illustrate with anger behavior.

The Development of Anger Habits

Probably no one escapes the effects of anger in his family experience. He either sees it being expressed among other family members, feels it himself toward parents or siblings, or has it directed toward him. Any relationship as intense as that between parent and child, which necessarily involves the frustration of someone's desires, is bound to produce some anger. This tells us that the parents also have had experience with it and have built up habitual ways of interpreting it, expressing it, and re-acting to it.

Giving Meaning to Anger.   The family develops a general atmosphere surrounding anger. In other words, anger takes on meaning for the whole family depending upon the meaning it has for the parents and the inter-action produced by the combination of meanings. For some people anger is a frightening thing. It makes them want to run away, to cry, or it throws them into a frenzy of attempts to placate the angry party. For others it is an invitation to fight back—angry words call forth angry words. Some begin to feel guilty, as if they were somehow the cause of every angry outburst. For others it is a normal expression or emotion causing neither flight, fight, nor guilt. They may find it amusing, frightening, or guilt-provoking depending upon the other person and the reasons for this particular episode. No matter what the meaning or reaction is, it is likely to be habitual in that the occurrence of anger will trigger an impulse to react in a certain way. The child, then, is likely to encounter a number of instances in which the repetitive interaction of family members will define anger for him.

Let us take a family group—mother, father, and small child. Mother and child are at home—mother is preparing dinner and the child is occupied with blocks or coloring books on the living room floor. Normally, Dad comes home in a good humor, picks up the child, tosses him in the air, and carries him with him to greet his wife. But on this particular day Dad has had a series of frustrating experiences—nothing has gone right for him since he broke his shoe lace as he dressed for work in the morning. He has had no opportunity all day to vent his feelings and they have been piling up. And now, just as he starts in the house, he trips over a toy car left on the front porch. This is the trigger and we can imagine him opening the front door, ignoring the happy smile of anticipation on his child's face, and giving vent to all his pent-up anger as he berates his wife for attempting to maim him.

We have just described a situation in which the child's predictability is upset; Daddy didn't perform as usual, the sound of his voice is disturbing, and the child needs to have someone tell him how threatening the situation is. He need not wait long, because Mother too, was caught off guard. She does not have enough information to explain the angry outburst, so she responds in terms of the generalized meaning anger has for her. She may become anxious, fearful, and dissolve into tears at (from her point of view) the unwarranted attack, or she may become angry herself, and rail back at him. Both responses have defined the situation to the child as threatening. His cries will probably add to the general commotion.

Another mother may see the same outburst as a release of emotion stemming from some other source, since she feels neither initial fear nor guilt when faced with anger. She may calmly wait for him to run out of steam so she can learn the reason for the explosion, or help him throw the situation into perspective. In this case the child may remain calmly interested or go back to his blocks. In either case, the mother's response is likely to be repetitive *since it is expressing the meaning which anger has for her.*

The father will also tend to react to anger in a characteristic way. The combination of the parents' reactions will tend to define the severity of threat to family relationships resulting from anger. The children growing up in the family will integrate this tone with other experiences with anger to form a generalized anger response.

Consider, for example, the following two exerpts from student papers concerning the atmosphere surrounding anger in their homes:

Case 1: Someone looking in our house would probably have seen a screaming fight which ended almost as soon as it started—often with much laughter from the observing members of the family. . . . It was a completely free setting for bursts of anger—physical or otherwise.

Case 2: For eleven years my mother tried to appease my father and keep things running smoothly—even bending backwards to counteract the effect of his anger on my sisters and me. If he became angry enough he would lash out at anything around him—which usually turned out to be me. Besides being afraid and resentful, I felt he was very unkind to my mother, as well. She finally decided it would be better for us if she divorced him.

It is obvious that these two students will have entirely different reactions to anger. One has learned that it is a momentary expression of emotion, meaning little as far as the stability of the relationship is concerned. No matter how violent the expression, it will soon pass. The other has learned it is a fearful, threatening thing—something which can wreck a relationship. They will take entirely different tolerance levels for anger with them into their marital relationships. Imagine for a moment what may occur if these two individuals happened to marry each other, or, in contrast, if each married someone who shared his meaning of anger. We can see that the family culture defining anger for the children in the three resulting families would be drastically different.

Learning To Interpret Angry Gestures. People express anger in different ways. Young children are exposed not to the full range of possible anger behavior, but only to the specific ways it is expressed in their families. They learn, then, what gestures, verbalizations, and circumstances forewarn them of parental anger, how far this anger is likely to go, how anxiety-provoking it will come to be and for how long, and whether or not they can or should do anything to forestall the development. Some expressions of anger everyone recognizes. The person turns red in the face, pounds the table, the wall, or the nearest other person, and screams his anger for all to hear. Other ways of expressing anger may not be so easily interpreted, however, and are understood only by those who have learned from long experience to "read" the particular expressions. "Oh, oh, I know what that frozen look means—watch out!" or "I can tell by the way he drove in the driveway," or "I wonder what Mom's mad about—she didn't say 'hello' when we came in."

Children become aware of parental ways of expressing anger. It is extremely important to the security provided by predictability that they learn to "read" their parents' early warning signs. Once learned—especially if coupled with anxiety feelings about anger—the signs become generalized so that these gestures warn of coming anger whenever they are encountered, no matter who it is! Many times it may not be an accurate interpretation, but the reactions to the gesture will be *as if* it meant anger, with consequences for the interaction.

Take, for example, a hypothetical young husband married only a short time. His mother always maintained stony silence when she was angry. As a child he would feel that somehow her anger was his fault, but he could never find out what she was angry about. He would feel a little anxious whenever his mother was silent for very long, whether she was angry or not. When he married it was not surprising that he was attracted to a girl who was quite outgoing—seldom silent for very long. One thing he never wanted in his marriage was a wife who expressed anger like his mother because he knew by experience that this left him ambiguously uncomfortable.

He had built up habits, however, which sensitized him to this behavior. One day he came home from work to find his usually exuberant wife strangely silent. There was nothing wrong with her, just a series of events during the day which had left her pensive, quiet, and unlike her usual self. Immediately he noticed the change and was ready with an interpretation by the time he took off his coat and headed back to the kitchen.

Husband: "What's the matter, honey?"
Wife: "Nothing."
Husband: "Come now, something's wrong. Have I made you angry?"
Wife: "Of course not, I'm not angry."

We can imagine a few moments of silence, while he tries to get interested in the evening news. But his habitual response is now in full swing and he tries again, and again, and again—until finally she slams down the coffee pot in her hand and says: "How many times do I have to tell you I'm not angry!" To which he quickly replies: "See there, you were mad. I knew it. You're just like my mother." His interpretation of her behavior is now reinforced and she feels frustrated, misunderstood, and angry. The turn that the interaction now takes will depend upon *her* habitual way of expressing the anger built up in her by *his* habitual interpretation of silence.

Learning To Express Anger.   A child has a model for the expression of anger in his parents. In the same way he identifies with other characteristics of the parent he can take on this characteristic also. If a parent expresses anger by pouting, by arguing, by shouting, or by other means, the child has been exposed to a way of expressing anger which works for the parent. But when a child expresses anger in the family situation, the parents must react. Sometimes the expression the parent uses is denied the child; then he must find some other way to relieve his angry feelings.

As he spontaneously explores different methods, the parents' habitual ways of interpreting certain actions as angry ones, and the meaning anger has for them, will provide acceptance for some ways and non-acceptance for others. The release of anger is satisfying in that it relieves the tension associated with the feeling. So the expression of anger in a way which does not bring additional punishment is reinforcing in itself. Once found it is likely to be repeated, thereby developing a habitual response to the feeling of anger. With the exception of violent expressions of anger which are likely to be disruptive to any relationship, the interaction between the spouses' habits of expressing, interpreting, and reacting to anger are probably more important to the stability of the relationship than any particular *way* of expressing it.

Intensity of Anger Feelings.   Certain childrearing experiences tend to heighten the intensity and the frequency of angry feelings over and beyond the specific learning of responses. For some persons, then, anger would comprise a minor part of any relationship, while for others it may be a major element. While the relationship between childrearing practices and aggression is very complex and inadequately understood, research findings do give some support to our discussion of the process by which these habits are learned. In reviewing the studies relating childhood discipline to aggression, Hoffman and Hoffman found evidence to support relationships between power assertive techniques of discipline (force, threat of force, deprivation, direct commands) used by hostile parents and (1) aggression in young children, (2) resistance to authority, and (3) power assertion to other children (1966, pp. 169–89).

There was evidence that consistent use of these techniques by both parents to curb open aggression eventually resulted in its inhibition but produced pro-social aggression (when a person has broken a rule, he should be punished for it) and self-aggression. The mechanisms by which these consequences are brought about were seen to be: (1) the hostile environment within which the power is used further frustrates the child and leads to a counter-aggressive anger reaction; (2) the model of aggressive behavior set by the aggressive parent shows the child how to be angry as well as implicitly sanctions it; (3) the aggressive parent is more likely than the non-aggressive parent to actually encourage aggressive behavior toward others (Hoffman and Hoffman, 1966, p. 189). In other words the parent who uses a good deal of physical punishment is also likely to insist that the child fight for his rights with others.

The family interactions can be seen, then, to influence the intensity of the anger feeling, to attach a meaning to anger, to develop a sensitivity to certain gestures or behaviors as being expressions of anger, and to sanction certain expressions of anger and inhibit others. By the time the individual reaches adulthood, the habits developed over the years are preset triggers, ready to influence future relationships—especially his own marital and family relationships.

Other Habit Systems

Habitual interpretations and responses are built up in numerous other areas in the same way that anger habits are developed. We develop sensitivities to the behaviors we are exposed to which remain ready to influence our reactions no matter how infrequently they are encountered.

A certain softness of voice, a show of interest or offer to help may be picked up immediately by one person—alert to any clue that another person is interested in him. It may readily be interpreted as an indication of love. Another person may not even notice the tone of voice or interest. If noticed, he may write it off as just a friendly gesture or an insincere attempt to win favor.

These habits of selecting and interpreting behaviors help to explain some of the bewilderment felt by the secretary who is sure her boss is in love with her, when he announces his engagement to someone else. What to him may have been "considerate boss" behavior was to her an expression of love. But this is only one illustration of innumerable life situations where clues are missed.

Ways of Coping.   Every child is faced with problems he must solve. He must deal with strong desires which cannot be immediately fulfilled. He must learn to gain some control over his parents—how to manipulate them to let him do what he wants, have what he wants, be what he wants. If siblings are present, he is continually confronted with situations in which he is pitted against a sister or brother or aligned with them to secure some common goal. He will not be successful all of the time—the parents are more powerful than he. But most children will be successful some of the time. Their failures and successes will encourage some ways of coping with difficult situations, and inhibit others. Since we are assuming that the parents are at least partially organized and predictable themselves, they will be vulnerable to some of the child's approaches to them and insensitive to others. Gaining the goal is immediate reinforcement for the means the child used to achieve it. Thus, he begins to build up a "bag of tricks," so to speak, which have served for him in the past. These operate as available behaviors which *may* be called into service when problems are faced in the future.

As people grow, the childish behaviors are replaced, hopefully, by more mature coping mechanisms. But in situations where the more mature methods fail and frustration mounts, the individual is likely to revert to those things which have worked for him in the past. Thus, the person who has failed to convince a spouse by rational means may resort to wheedling, to tantrums, to illness, to appeals to love (if you really love me you will . . .), to pulling in the reserves (Mary, Jim, Dorothy, Bob—everybody does the same thing), or to some other means of control. The ones he chooses will come from the habit patterns built up over time.

Parents, again, operate as models, displaying for the child ways of coping which are both successful and unsuccessful. The coping behaviors he will be exposed to in his early years will be limited to those in use by family members and his own accidental behaviors which are rewarded by success. The little girl, for example, may learn that she can get almost anything out of her father by becoming a lovable, charming baby, but that the same thing doesn't work with her mother. Her brother may learn that when he uses his sister's babyish tricks it brings instant disapproval from his father. He may find that mother is susceptible to a little soft soap, however. Thus, the "tricks" become filed under headings of *male, female, younger, older, same age*—ready to be called upon as the situation punches the correct key.

The foregoing discussion does not imply that the person cannot resist using the habitual behaviors or interpretations he has acquired in past relationships, although this may sometimes be the case. It means that his past experiences have restricted his perception of and reaction to a variety of situations which will color his future interactions. He may discover in new relationships that his habitual meanings do not apply and that his habitual responses are not appropriate. He *can* learn to recognize his habitual interpretations, attach new meanings to old gestures, and acquire different reactions. But the past habitual responses are still part of his experience, furnishing the ingredients he has at his command to make sense out of future unpredictable situations.

Everyone develops such habits. Some habits may be very conducive to satisfying personal relationships and constructive problem solving— others may not be. Some people may be rigidly controlled by habitual responses in a variety of situations. Others may be rather rigidly controlled in comparatively few areas of behavior and able to vary their perceptions and responses in the others. But all persons will have developed at least tendencies to perceive and respond in characteristic ways. The development of new habits in the marital situation will be discussed in a later chapter.

THE PRINCIPLE OF VALUE RELEVANCE

There are certain habitual ways of expressing anger, coping with problems, dealing with illness, and so on, that are disruptive to interpersonal relationships regardless of the persons or social groups involved. The person who expresses anger with such violence that he finally kills his wife has disrupted the marriage no matter how tolerant she had been of his violence. The person who attempts to solve his family problems by desertion has disrupted the relationship, although the evaluation of his actions may vary. Considering, however, the normal range of habits from which the majority of people will draw, the *fit* between the spouses' habits seems much more important to satisfaction with the relationship than any specific behaviors considered separately.[2]

If two people share many of the same meanings and if their habitual responses are interpreted as appropriate and appreciated, their communication is likely to be relatively uncluttered and satisfying. Even if they disagree, they are likely to know what it is they are disagreeing about. This is perhaps one of the reasons for the belief that people should select a marriage partner from roughly the same background as their own. The shared social context should at least heighten the probability that some of their habits are similar and that they have insights into those which are not—that they have a shared basis of understandings.

The Fit Between Habit Systems

The variability among families, however, and the individual's experiences within them would certainly not assure shared meanings even within the same social context. The habitual responses themselves, though heightening or lessening the probability of satisfactory relationships, are not as important as the fit between the habit systems of the spouses. A man, for instance, may have developed a sensitivity to overt shows of affection. Let us say he interprets any unasked-for caresses as an attempt to get something from him. The woman who spontaneously shows him affection is immediately tagged as a "gold-digger" out to "make a fool of him." Paired with a demonstrative, affectionate wife, the relationship may be very unsatisfactory. His rejection of her affectionate advances may make her feel that he doesn't love her, that he is naturally cold and distant, or that he is interested in someone else, depending on her interpretation of his behavior. They would have to discover the meaning the behavior has for each of them so it can be reevaluated in the new relationship, or run the risk of continued dissatisfaction and doubt. However, paired with someone not overtly demonstrative or one who expressed her affection in ways he was not sensitive to, this same man's habitual response would have no effect on the relationship one way or the other. Paired with someone who shared his mistrust of affectional display, the habit may be evaluated positively as indicating that he is a rational, mature male who is not susceptible to flattery. The important ingredient is the _fit_—not the specific behavior.

Some people may have developed habits so conducive to satisfying interpersonal relations that the range of persons with whom they could have a successful marriage is quite great. For others, it may be more important to find a suitable fit. Some may have to search long and hard for

[2] See John Scanzoni (1966) for a theoretical discussion of the consequences of different economic "fits."

the right fit, since they have a number of rigid habits which are so well engrained that it would be too arduous a task to bring them under control. Everyone has developed some habits of perception, interpretation, and reaction, however. The bearing they have on marriage is influenced by the combination of habits—the fit between the spouses—rather than by the specific habitual behavior.

It is not implied that the most satisfying relationships come from a combination of habits which are exactly the same, although in some cases this may be correct. Consider the man who reacts with panic at unpredictable situations. He expresses his panic by immediately telling everyone around him what to do, whether this is appropriate or not. After reacting this way he immediately is ashamed of his actions and feels he should have acted in a more manly manner. Married to a woman who agrees with his interpretation of his behavior completely, he has confirmation of his negative evaluation of himself—and before long may react to more and more situations in the same way. He may also begin to blame her for his behavior: "You get me confused—I can't think." Marriage to a woman who *misinterpreted* his panic behavior as meaning he was sure of himself and was taking command just as a man should may produce a much more satisfying relationship. The misinterpretation may influence his own evaluation of his actions and actually reduce the panic. Perhaps the often heard comment: "If you'd only try to understand me," really means, "If you'd only interpret my actions in a better light than I do."

One of the most important habit systems as far as male–female relationships are concerned is the interpretation of behavior as masculine or feminine. The next chapter will be devoted to the development of masculinity and femininity and the social changes taking place in their definition.

The habitual meanings and reactions which are of major importance in the male–female relationship become reinforced or adjusted during the dating period. During this period, the fit between habit patterns can be tried out and perhaps influence the development of the feelings of emotional attachment leading to marriage. This will be pursued in later chapters covering the mate selection process.

SUMMARY

As the child is developing a sense of self, he is also acquiring habits of perception, interpretation, and reaction which influence future relationships. Any interpersonal interaction involves selection of the clues which will be picked up, interpreted, and reacted to in terms of the meaning it all has for the reactor, rather than the *actual* meaning as assessed by the originator of the act or by any outside observer.

These habits are acquired initially in the family of orientation. Some of them will be shared by other persons in a similar social context, but others will be unique to the particular family. Habits imply a certain propulsive force which preconditions a person to be especially sensitive to certain classes of stimuli, and presses for a characteristic interpretation and response.

Habits are built up by: (1) being exposed to the interpretations and reactions repetitively expressed in familial interaction; (2) experiencing the meaning attached to one's own behavior through the responses of family members; (3) identifying with the habits of parents which are implicitly sanctioned because the parents repetitively use them; and (4) discovering behaviors which satisfy one's own needs and are not punished.

The combination of habits brought together in the marital relationship influence the communication, the interaction, the satisfaction with the relationship, and the development of a family culture which will pass meanings on to the children from the marriage. Rather than any particular habitual behaviors being related to satisfaction, it is the fit between the habit patterns of the spouses which is important.

QUESTIONS AND PROJECTS

1. Only a few examples of the development of habits were given in this chapter. See if you can think of some additional ones. Show how they might develop.

2. Picture some rather commonplace occurrences which may take place, such as your date is late and you must wait for him or her. Think of as many different ways of interpreting the action as you can. Ask some of your friends how they would interpret it. What things are likely to be involved in the interpretation you make in a particular situation?

3. Introduce some situation during class or in a group of friends. Ask for male–female or other differences among the responses. Can you explain them?

4. What kind of anger habits may prove most detrimental to a marriage relationship? Why? Can you think of a particular kind of marriage partner with whom these may not be detrimental at all? Explain.

5. In which areas of interaction in a dating relationship would the fit between habit patterns be most important for you? In a roommate relationship? In a marriage relationship? Note the similarities and differences in your responses to these three relationships and see if you can explain them.

7

Masculinity and Femininity

Perhaps one of the strongest habit systems developed concerns the interpretation of certain behaviors as being characteristically masculine or feminine. Certainly the most important factor around which the self-concept is organized is the sexual identity. One does not generally build a sense of self as a human being but rather as a male or female human being. Thus, the evaluations made of males and females in the culture become part of the ingredients man uses to construct his view of himself. He is born either male or female (a biological definition). But that categorization will subject him to a series of expectations and evaluations which will press him to acquire the socially designated traits associated with masculinity and femininity (a social definition).

Societies subject their members to different treatment depending upon their sex. They assign certain characteristics to them because of their sex. The beliefs built up about men and women in general sometimes subject one sex to anxieties and negative evaluations of self from which the other is freed. Occasionally, misconceptions about the opposite sex reduce the possibility of understanding and enhance the probability of misinterpretation of a specific member of the opposite sex. Since the complementary interaction between the sexes is the foundation of marriage, it seems appropriate to investigate the process by which they acquire socially imposed characterizations.

SIMILARITIES AND DIFFERENCES

Though different in some ways, men and women are also very much alike. They both belong to the same human species, are broadly motivated by the same sort of things, and live generally the same kind of lives. They

121

are, however, complementary to each other, which may occasionally make them see things from different perspectives. Persons on different ends of a two-man saw do not even see the same side of the tree; yet they are indispensable to each other in accomplishing their shared goal. They are not naturally antagonistic or competitive with each other, but they may learn to be so in the process of acquiring the skill and rhythm associated with their shared activity. So it is with man and woman—they are not naturally competitive or antagonistic just because they view the tree from different sides, but they may become so as they are subjected to anxieties in the process of acquiring the skills and characteristics defined as being masculine or feminine.

Acquiring Masculine or Feminine Traits

Learning the appropriate attitudes and behaviors associated with masculinity and femininity is part of the socialization process. The process begins with birth when the child is appropriately named. From then on the responses he gets from others will vary somewhat depending upon his sex.

Societies build stereotypes of the abilities, personality characteristics, interests, and modes of dress appropriate to each sex. The interest in labeling the sexual identity of babies in our society is perhaps reflected in the diaper covers adorned with ruffles or front zippers long before they serve any useful function. Babies' facial features are not distinguishable according to sex. Very early, however, the haircut and clothes make them readily identifiable as boys or girls. From the beginning, this labeling tends to call forth repetitive responses from others appropriate to the potential man or woman in the infant. The girl is urged toward feminine toys and games while the boy is confronted with more active, masculine-type toys. The girl is more likely to be cuddled while the boy is played with more roughly.

We do not have an exclusive set of characteristics associated with a single sex, however. The traits associated with masculinity and femininity vary along a continuum just as do the biologically determined traits of maleness and femaleness. But although some males are not as masculine as others, and some females are not as feminine as others, there are somewhat typical behavior patterns which have come to be associated with each sex. Males are expected to be more aggressive, dominant, independent, rugged, ambitious, sharpwitted, forceful, and adventurous; while women are supposed to be more passive, compliant, sensitive, softhearted, affectionate, warm, sympathetic, and kind (McKee and Sherriffs, 1960). We have, to a large extent, defined these sex-appropriate personality clusters in terms of the traditional division of labor in which the male is expected to occupy himself outside the home while the female is expected to occupy herself with childrearing and domestic affairs. In general, it appears that the more the division of labor is sex-based, the greater the differences ascribed to the two sexes.

The composition of the American family furnishes the adult models which the child can begin to emulate as he appropriately identifies himself with the same sex parent. There are continual pressures pushing the child toward acquiring these sex-typed behaviors from both inside and outside the family. In a society where the role of the sexes is clear-cut and few acceptable deviations are offered and where both sex-role models are visible and accessible to the child, the acquisition of appropriate characteristics and psychological orientations should be relatively easy. In our society, however, certain complications enter the picture providing sources of frustration and anxiety for both sexes but at different periods of development.

Early Identification.   In the urban middle class American family, the father is generally out of the home most of the day. The children, both boys and girls, are under the care of the mother. They receive from her the attention, care, and comfort which make them want to be near her and eventually to be like her (to identify with her) (Dager, 1964, p. 753). As the child grows he begins to imitate the activities of the mother; since she is with him more of the time, she is the one who is most likely to meet his immediate needs. To the child she appears to be the most powerful person in the family since she is likely to be the most constant source of discipline and rewards (Emmerich, 1959). These are the main characteristics consistently associated with strong identification—affection, visibility, and power.

The mother offers an appropriate sex-role model for the little girl but not for the little boy. The little girl can identify with her mother, take on her attitudes and behavior patterns, and receive approval. She can be a submissive, compliant child and receive approval. To some extent she can continue her submissive orientation throughout adulthood and still win approval. The little boy also can imitate his mother and win approval just like his sister for a while. At the point, however, when he begins to look like a boy rather than a baby, some anxiety is aroused in the parents if he continues to prefer feminine activities—if he does not give evidence of growing into a "real boy." Behavior that was approved earlier may now bring ambivalent or negative responses (Parsons, 1954). The little boy is encouraged to stop the behavior which has been rewarding to him, but is offered no substitute model. His father is out of the home much of the day and when he is there he is not involved in anything very important. The abstract nature of middle class occupations, toward which he is headed, makes the father's job incomprehensible to him.

Hartley (1959) suggests that the vagueness associated with the adult male role results in the appropriate sex-role behavior being defined negatively to the little boy, as something he should *not* do or be rather than defined positively as something he *should* do. Mainly he should not be like little girls—should not play with dolls, should not cry when hurt, should not be a "sissy." Lynn suggests that the male role is largely taught by *divergent feedback* rather than by positive example (Lynn, 1964). This kind of feedback means the child is given information that he is *not* giving a desired response. It suggests he should stop doing what he is doing but does not necessarily tell him what he should do in place of it. This results in much of the early male role consisting of *ungirl-like* behavior rather than positive boy behavior. He is still a child, however, and the child role itself contains some feminine characteristics. A child is to be obedient, compliant, affectionate, non-aggressive—all feminine traits. He is likely, then, to experience some difficulties in building a consistent self-concept which includes "good child" as well as "real boy."

The little girl has a different experience. Her mother serves as an appropriate model for sex role identification as well as for her future role of mother. She continues being rewarded for imitating her first object of identification—her mother. She knows what it means to be a "good child" and it is consistent with being a "good girl." She can, however, engage in boy-like behavior such as wearing jeans, playing ball, climbing trees without the same negative evaluations which the little boy suffers if he plays with dolls, wears skirts, or puts ribbons in his hair. There does not seem to be as much anxiety about her eventually becoming a woman as there is about her brother growing up to be a man. In other words, the little boy is punished for inappropriate sex-role behavior, with no ever-available model to furnish him with the appropriate behavior. The little girl is rewarded for the acquisition of appropriate sex-role behavior and not punished for inappropriate behavior. It is of little wonder, then, that by the time they enter school, the little girl is more secure in her role and more easily socialized into the school situation. Her predictability is much better concerning what behavior will be positively rewarded. The little boy is not so sure and becomes more concerned with avoiding girl-like behavior which he learns will win him disapproval from both adults and other children.

The Early School Years. Even if the young boy's parents have not exerted pressure on him to shift his identification from mother to father, the other children at school will punish him for continued feminine behavior—girls as well as boys. He is at a further disadvantage with the little girls, since they are about a year ahead of him in development at the start of school. Girls learn to read more easily and in general outperform the boy until about the fourth grade. No wonder little Johnny spends much of his time being obnoxious to the little girls who seem to excel, to be teacher's pets, to be clean and good, and whom he must *not* be like. It is not difficult to understand under these conditions why the words "bad boy" seem to be a more natural fit than "bad girl."

Evidence for the greater difficulty that the little boy experiences in achieving a masculine identity can be found in the much higher rate of psychological disturbances that occur among pre-puberty boys than girls (Lynn, 1961). The added difficulty confronting the little boy in the reduced visibility of the father as a role model seems supported by the finding that boys are more likely to identify with a stereotype of the male role than with the traits of their own father. Girls, however, are more likely to identify with the specific traits of the individual mother (Lynn, 1959).

Adolescence. As boys and girls grow, however, they begin to get a different view of the world. Both of them learn more of the father's actual position in the family, and to perceive that masculine traits are valued more highly than feminine traits in the society as a whole (Lynn, 1959). Furthermore, by the time the girl enters high school she has learned that in order for her to obtain the all-important mother role, she must be chosen by some man—one of those little boys she has looked down upon, who has tripped her, pulled her curls, and been a nuisance in the classroom. Now she must learn to appeal to him so he will choose her as his wife.

She begins to lose the consensus concerning the behavior which will win approval for herself. Her role becomes increasingly more ambiguous. The wife–mother role does not seem as prestigeful as it did when she was younger. There are still pressures upon her to excel academically, yet other people are not as interested in her choices of a career as they are in her brother's. The jobs open to her have a relatively low prestige. Her education has not prepared her for marriage which more and more seems to be the most "secure" choice. She may still be urged to prepare herself for an occupation but mainly as insurance in case she doesn't marry (is not chosen) or in case something happens to her husband. Her education is seen more as an ace in the hole in case the preferred wife–mother role does not work out.

The greater anxiety surrounding the female's sex-role identification during adolescence is substantiated by Lynn's finding that the male–female difference in psychological disturbances is sharply reduced as they grow older (Lynn, 1961). In other words, the males' disadvantage in rate of psychological disturbances in early childhood is slowly reduced as they move through their teen years. As they move toward maturity boys develop a poorer relative opinion of girls, and girls develop a better relative opinion of boys. Boys have a progressively better opinion of themselves and girls have a progressively poorer opinion of themselves (Smith, 1939).

More recent studies continue to give tangential support to this earlier conclusion. Rudy found in a study of ninth and tenth grade boys and girls in the metropolitan New York area that boys rate adjectives that are stereotyped as masculine as more desirable than girls rate those stereotyped as feminine (Rudy, 1968–1969). The girls were reluctant to assign many traits exclusively to males; they designated as exclusively masculine one-third fewer items than their male classmates. This same general tendency was found in a study of Purdue students in 1968 (Johnsen, 1969). Of 55 personality characteristics, 20 were seen as more descriptive of males by males. The females were in general agreement on 18 of them. Of these, only three were negatively evaluated (egocentric, blunt, and impatient). Twenty characteristics were seen to be predominantly associated with females by both men and women. Of these, half were negatively evaluated by both the men and the women (unpredictable, easily offended, illogical, fearful, artificial, insecure, moody, superficial, easily swayed and irritable). Although there was general agreement between the sexes on the assignment of characteristics, the tendency for females to refuse male exclusiveness on highly valued items was apparent. On seven of twelve traits most strongly associated with males by men, the women were significantly more likely to see them as not being sex-associated (leadership, rationality, ability to make decision, ability to handle money) or to evaluate them less highly than men (physical strength, adventurousness, aggressiveness).

The awareness of the differential status awarded males and females seems to affect the continued identification with masculinity and femininity. With increasing age, males become more firmly identified with the male role and females become less firmly identified with the female role (Lynn, 1959). The Purdue student study offers further evidence of this tendency among college women. Although the women were in agreement with the men in assigning negative characteristics to females, they were not likely to assign them to themselves. They appeared to be saying that, "Women have these negative traits, but I am not like them."

Another telling study supporting the devaluing of the female by college women is reported by Goldberg (1968). Six articles were chosen from the professional literature of six different professional fields which had been rated by 100 randomly selected college women as to the degree to which they associated the field with men or with women. Two (city planning and law) were strongly associated with men; two (dietetics and elementary school teaching) were strongly associated with women; and the remaining two (art history and linguistics) were not sex associated. Two sets of booklets were compiled. Each booklet contained all six articles. In one set three articles had female names as authors and three had male names. In the other set, the author's names were reversed, so that the article written, for example, by *John* T. McKay in the first set appeared under the name of *Joan* T. McKay in the second set. The women were instructed to read the articles in their booklet and rate the authors in terms of writing style, professional competence, professional status, and ability to sway the reader. No mention was made of the authors' sexes. Regardless of the author's occupational field, on almost all ratings the women consistently found an article more valuable and the author more competent when the article gave a male name as author. Out of 54 points at which comparisons could be made between the male and female authors, three were tied, seven favored the female, and 44 favored the male. Although the anti-female bias was strongest in those fields associated with men, the men were perceived as being superior even in dietetics and elementary school teaching. Since the articles were identical, with only the sex of the author changed, the tendency of college women to devalue professional contributions made by women is clear.

At any rate, it seems clear that by the time a sex-role identity has been achieved both sexes have experienced anxiety; have suffered at the hands of the opposite sex; but have achieved behavioral characteristics, attitudes, and beliefs which differ from each other.

Sex Differences

Differences in abilities, attitudes, personality traits, and behavioral patterns have been found between men and women. To what extent these differences are the result of socialization and to what extent they are influenced by biological factors is not adequately understood. But whatever the source, they form the sides of the tree from which the two sexes view each other as they attempt to cooperate in reaching the shared goals of selecting a mate and building a family. A partial list of these differences, as yet inadequately validated or understood, follows.

1. Though there is nothing in science to prove that either sex has more intelligence than the other, men seem to do better in mechanical, mathematical, and abstract reasoning tests, while women usually excel in tests based upon memory, language ability, artistic taste, and social awareness. Sometimes it is said that men are interested more in impersonal things, in facts as facts, and that women are primarily interested in personal

things, in people, in human relationships. Men appear to view things analytically while women are more likely to see things relative to the whole, or globally.

Comparisons of groups of boys and girls show wide within-sex variations in verbal and analytical abilities. In investigating the background factors associated with good verbal but poor mathematical abilities, Maccoby cited a variety of studies which suggest that early independence training, encouragement of self-assertiveness, and freedom to explore the environment at an early age are associated with ability in the math–science areas, while over-protectiveness, restrictiveness, and an intolerance of self-assertive behavior in the child are associated with good verbal and reading facilities but poor mathematical thinking (Maccoby, 1963).

Since broad differences in the childhood experiences of boys and girls in our society seem to parallel the differences in individual experiences associated with the development of these intellectual traits, it may well be that we consistently develop intellectual traits which fit the direction we encourage the sexes to go in adulthood. It may not be that girls are discouraged from entering fields like engineering solely because it is felt to be a man's occupation, but that they have been reared in a way that lessens the probability that they could excel in occupations requiring mathematical abilities.

2. Men are more aggressive than women. This is shown in their greater tendency to be pugnacious, to get in trouble with the law, and to pursue the opposite sex rather than be pursued. Women are more submissive and docile—more "domesticated." There is no question but that part of this difference is to be explained in biology by the genes and the hormones. But it is also highly probable that culture has had a lot to do with it. Denied until recently any real opportunity for open or aggressive maneuvering, woman has developed an art of being pursued and of getting her way indirectly and by subtle devices. This fact may also explain why women seem to have more insight into men than men have regarding women—they have had to study men more in order to better control them and adapt to them.

Part of this aggressiveness is seen in competitive behavior important for success in economic pursuits. The association of aggressiveness with masculinity and passivity with femininity is seen by Horner (1969) as affecting the unwillingness of the female to succeed even when she is undeniably capable.

In a study of undergraduate men and women, Horner found that over 65 per cent of the women evidenced a motive to avoid success compared to less than 10 per cent of the men. The women seemed to equate success (in this instance, top performance in medical school) with being unpopular, unmarriageable, and lonely, or with guilt and worry about not being a normal woman. A third group appeared to deny even the possibility of a woman being this successful. When the students were compared on achievement test performances when working alone and in competition with others, it was found that over two-thirds of the men and less than one-third of the women made better scores in the competitive situation than when working alone. The poorest performances by women were in competitive situations with men. This was especially true among women with high anxiety about success. Those who lacked this anxiety reacted like the men, performing better in competitive situations.

This form of aggressive behavior appears certainly related to concepts of masculinity and femininity which makes surpassing an opponent a source of pride for the male and a source of anxiety for the female—especially if the opponent is a male (Horner, 1969).

3. The sex drive of the male, in comparison with that of the female, is more constant, more easily aroused, and more physical. That of the female, though just as real, is more complex, more involved with affection and emotion, and, one might even say, more "spiritual." There are a number of facts which will bear out this generalization: It is the male who most often seeks premarital intimacy; female frigidity is many times more common than male impotence; husbands desire sexual intercourse more frequently on the average than do wives; male prostitution is an almost unheard-of phenomenon. Here again, part of the explanation lies in the different biological natures of the two sexes and part in the divergent cultural patterns to which the two are exposed.

4. Man is stronger physically, due partly to a larger and stronger bone and muscle structure by nature and partly to greater development through more exercise. Then, too, being free of the childbearing function, he is left with other advantages which he has often exploited. It is this greater physical power that has made it possible for man to define and control things pretty much in his own way. Thus the saying, "Woman is the weaker sex."

5. The woman's chances of survival are greater than the man's, both before and after birth. Woman outlives man an average of six or seven years, partly because man is exposed to greater hazards, it is true, but partly also because she has a tougher constitution. She is more resistant to disease, can seemingly endure pain more easily, and is not as plagued with hereditary defects. Feeble-mindedness, insanity, tuberculosis, and many other afflictions of this sort are more frequent with the male than with the female.

6. Judged by our standards of success (which in a man's world are largely man's standards) more men than women have achieved eminence in one way or another. It is true that most of our great statesmen, philosophers, scientists, artists, and literary figures of the past have been men,

and that in *Who's Who* listings today there is revealed the same imbalance between the sexes. But it must be remembered, first, that woman, because of childbearing and social discrimination, has not had the same opportunity to achieve as has man in a man's world, and second, that her achievements have been along different lines, in ways that bring little publicity or public recognition. As Bowman puts it:

. . . to say that women are inferior to men because there have been more male than female geniuses is absurd, because in fulfilling their traditional role women have had neither the need nor the opportunity for exhibiting the particular type of genius that men exhibit in science, invention, and the arts. It would be just as sensible to reverse the picture and say that men are inferior to women because throughout history men have been poorer mothers and homemakers (Bowman, 1954, p. 20).[1]

Man achieves eminence more regularly than woman, but he also fails life more frequently. We have observed how both mental deficiency and mental breakdown show higher incidence among males. It should now be pointed out that the male suicide rate is three or four times as high as the female, and that in the area of vice and crime males outdo females by an even greater margin.

Regarding the follies of the flesh, man can more accurately than woman be called the weaker sex. He seems both less able and less willing to control the sexual impulses. Someone has said that:

The weaker sex is the stronger sex because of the weakness of the stronger sex for the weaker sex.

It would seem, therefore, that man tends more toward the extreme and woman toward the mean so far as achievement and social adjustment are concerned. Just how much of this is natural and how much cultural no one knows, though it is probable that each of these factors has played its part.

7. Males and females appear to have different orientations toward the world as well as different orientations toward sex differences. A study by Seeley, Sim, and Loosley (1963, pp. 193–203), suggests that sex differences form the most fundamental cleavage in belief systems of the community. Women play down the differences between men and women while men play them up. Men seem to see the differences as an "impassable gulf to be accepted with good humored tolerance." Women are seen to be sentimental, non-logical, and incapable of the sustained efforts needed for accomplishments. They are so illogical they cannot even be shown the difference between the sexes and must be "handled" like children.

[1] Una Stannard (1970) presents an interesting argument supporting the idea that men rather than women have a maternal instinct and that the basis of sexual inequality is a long history of "womb-envy" among males.

The authors' study of 507 midwestern college students enrolled in sociology courses in the spring of 1967 tended to affirm some of these findings. Females were significantly more likely than males to think that neither sex has the easier time in life; that the sexes are equal in over-all native intelligence; that most women should *not* be satisfied with homemaking as a sufficient career; that family instability does not result from women being too independent and unwilling to stay home; and that part-time work outside the home is acceptable for a wife. Males, on the other hand, were more likely to claim a higher native intelligence; believe that women have an easier time in life; and affirm that wives should devote full time to homemaking.

Effect of Status Differential

These perceptions perhaps can be seen to be the result of the status differential in which the manly characteristics are afforded greater prestige than the womanly characteristics. Man, then, endeavors to hold on to the distinctions while woman wants to deny them. This cleavage itself may be of more importance to the lack of understanding between the sexes than any other. The more she succeeds at being feminine, the more she finds a negatively evaluated stereotype associated with her. If she tries to prove that she can think logically and rationally (which are positively evaluated functions) the more she is accused of "thinking like a man" and hence being masculine. Her frustration at being unable to break the "vicious circle" may make her more likely to react personally and take offense at statements not intended personally—thus continuing the stereotype that she is too emotional to be trusted in positions requiring objective, impersonal decisions.

To some extent the older she grows the more her experience parallels that of the little boy as he tried to acquire a masculine identity. To be feminine is to a large extent *not* to be masculine, but the masculine characteristics are more positively evaluated and offer the greatest rewards. She is punished for sex-inappropriate or masculine behavior which is highly valued in males but has no guidelines for the sex-appropriate behavior which will also win approval. She is told as she enters the economic world, for example, that she should not compete like a man (should not become masculinized). But to compete like a woman, stereotypically, is to be sly, underhanded, or to use inappropriate feminine wiles—all negatively evaluated. The guidelines for competing like a woman in a positively evaluated way are lacking. Small wonder she attempts to play down the differences between the sexes and to play up their shared human characteristics.

Even in the social sciences, which attract a larger proportion of women than the traditionally male-dominated physical sciences, the lack of successful feminine models is apparent. Alice Rossi has provided information on the attrition of women as one goes up the prestige ladder in academic rank in the field of sociology (Rossi, 1970). The study done in 1968–1969 was confined to universities with graduate programs and so eliminated the sociology departments in undergraduate colleges (see Figure 7–1).

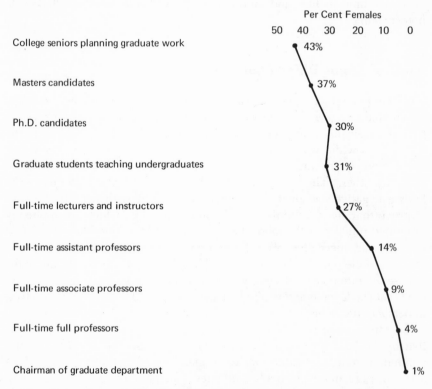

Fig. 7–1. Percentage of women in various status categories in sociology graduate schools. (Adapted from Rossi, 1970, p. 11.)

This gives some indication of the social context in which the young female aspirant for professional standing pursues her career. She is not likely to see many feminine models of successful academic achievement. Her male counterpart is exposed daily to successful models plus an academic structure which appears to offer numerous opportunities and a clear road to advancement once he completes his degree. She, however, may wonder where all the women degree holders go and see little place for her regardless of her performance as a student.

A Differentiated Equality

Perhaps it can be said that neither really is "the weaker sex"; that there are differences, specialization, but no general subordinations and super-ordinations so far as nature is concerned. While some males are superior to some females, the reverse can also be said; and these two facts tend to balance each other. There is equality in terms of general innate ability and worth. When it comes to the way society is organized, however, there are both differences and inequalities.

Equality does not require similarity. People can be dissimilar and still be on the same level. Nature made men and woman different as classes but did not make them unequal. Society then established divergent roles for the two sexes, corresponding roughly with the biological differentiations already established. But the social alignment between men and women somehow or other got tipped at the axis; it tended to become vertical in arrangement, with men having most of the advantage. Sex assumed status.

Recent developments have been away from stratification within marriage, and in the direction of partnerships. The older patriarchal family is yielding to an emerging democratic or equalitarian type. The newer assumption is that of a love relationship based upon a horizontal division of labor; it is the application of democracy to marriage.

Sex equality, therefore, means that neither men nor women are discriminated against because of their sex. They have somewhat different roles to play, both biological and cultural, but roles of equal dignity and opportunity. There are individual differences in ability and achievement, but the differences are not along sex lines. There can be a *differentiated equality* where opportunity is the same for all but where men and women are given certain divided functions, The sexes can be equal, each within its own sphere, without competition and hostility as the result.

CHANGING SEX ROLES

There is little need to labor the fact that in most cultures woman's social status has been significantly and consistently lower than man's. Suffice it to remind the reader that in some groups the husband has had the right of life and death over her; in others she could be beaten or abused almost at his will; and practically never, until recently, has woman been privileged to hold office or otherwise to participate in public affairs alongside man. She has been discriminated against politically, economically, socially, and morally.

This is not to say that woman's lot has always been an unfortunate or an unhappy one. There is a dignity about motherhood, a contentment to be found in homemaking. Men have very frequently loved their women, furthermore, and have been kind and considerate toward them—though with the power to be otherwise. What we are saying is that society has generally placed woman at a disadvantage, left her pretty much at the mercy of man, treated her as an inferior. Even kindness, if it is paternalistic and condescending, can be no real substitute for the kind of justice that is born of equality.

Emancipation of Woman

The recent trend, particularly in the Western world, has been toward an equalization of sex roles. Woman, in other words, is being emancipated, is becoming equal in the sense of having equal opportunity, free in the sense of having the prejudices and pressures that have been directed toward her gradually removed. She can now vote, has been able to in this country for approximately five decades. She can hold public office, though group opinion and childbearing responsibilities still work against it. One seldom sees a woman mayor, member of Congress, or other prominent public official. There are now several outstanding examples of women in public office, however, and the future is likely to bring increasing numbers of them. Women have made great inroads in the field of economic production and can now hold down just about any job, whether it be common labor or a clerical, business, or professional position, although barriers still exist among the most prestigeful and challenging positions.

Among other evidences of a trend toward sex equality are the recent removal of some of the discriminatory legal statutes, the large and growing enrollment of women in college, and the increasing amount of freedom females express in such things as dress, asking for dates, and proposing marriage.

It would be a mistake, nevertheless, to assume that social equality between the sexes has now been achieved. Woman has come a long way in the short span of one hundred years, but if equality is her goal she has not yet reached it. Public opinion keeps her out of some activities and handicaps her in others. She is the last to be hired by some employers and the first to be fired. Her rate of pay is frequently less than for man, even when her work performance is the same. She cannot be as free in asking for dates or in proposing marriage, and in cases involving sexual indiscretion she receives the greater condemnation. Family laws, while improving in some states, continue in others to discriminate against woman regarding property rights, place of residence, and the like. All in all, it would seem that this is still a man's world.

Periodically, over the last third of a century, there has been before Congress a proposal for an *Equal Rights Amendment*. It reads: "Equality of rights under the law shall not be denied or abridged by the United States or by any state on account of sex." Supporters of this amendment point to the obvious discriminations against women that exist in many state statutes and in common-law practice at present—not permitting women to work in certain occupations, or at night, or if they are married; setting female wage and salary levels lower than those for men; not letting the wife decide on her own domicile; giving the husband various discriminatory rights over the wife's earnings and property. They argue that legal equality established in this way would relieve woman of her present inferiority feelings and would give her a chance to develop and function in dignity and with justice. There are those who oppose the idea, too, as should be evident from the fact that the bill has been delayed in committee for over a decade. One reason for the proposal's not getting farther than it has may be that the majority of members of Congress are men. Opponents consist of both women and men, however, and they reason that women need certain protection under the law and that such an amendment, if passed, might cause women to neglect home and family all the more.

Different factions of the Women's Liberation Movement find themselves in disagreement over the Equal Rights Amendment. Certain groups, such as the National Organization for Women, believe that the amendment is a necessity for the achievement of equality. They further believe that state protective laws must be eliminated if sexual equality is to be achieved. Other groups oppose the amendment on the grounds that if it is passed the state protective laws would be declared unconstitutional and open the way for further exploitation of women workers. Before passage of the amendment they want to see the protective laws extended to men so that competition between them does not result in a lowering of working conditions for all.[2]

Legislation must wait upon shifts in ideology. Regardless of the arguments concerning the means of achieving it, public opinion is changing in support of sexual equality.

One concrete result of the change in public opinion was the passage of the Civil Rights Act of 1964 which included "sex" along with race,

---

[2] Joan Jordan (1970) gives a full explanation of the argument held by some members of the Women's Liberation Movement against passage of the Equal Rights Amendment.

color, religion, and national origin in its definition of grounds on which discrimination in employment was prohibited. This act also set up an Equal Employment Opportunity Commission before which complaints of discrimination could be brought. This legislation provided for a portion of the rights contained in the Equal Rights Amendment.

The Women's Liberation Movement

Recognition of the long history of sexual inequalities has resulted in a rebirth of women's liberation groups. There are a number of factions under the general Women's Liberation Movement which differ from each other in the scope of the changes they want as well as in the means they use to achieve them (Ellis, 1970).

The movement took form at the first national conference of the National Organization for Women (NOW) in 1967. A Bill of Rights was constructed which states the minimum demands with which all the groups would agree (Morgan, 1970). These demands include:

1. Equal rights under the law. For NOW this means passage of the Equal Rights Amendment. For others this is not acceptable until state protective laws for women are extended to all workers as mentioned previously.
2. Enforcement of the laws banning sex discrimination in employment.
3. Maternity-leave rights in employment and in social security benefits.
4. Revision of tax laws to permit the deduction of home and child-care expenses for working parents.
5. Child-care facilities for children from pre-school years through adolescence, as a community resource to be used by citizens from all income levels.
6. Equal and unsegregated education eliminating all discrimination and segregation by sex at all levels of education including colleges, graduate and professional schools, loans and fellowships, and federal and state training programs such as the Job Corps.
7. Equal job training opportunities for women in poverty with housing and family allowances on equal terms with men and a revision of welfare legislation and poverty programs which deny women dignity, privacy, and self-respect.
8. The right of women to control their own reproductive lives by removing laws limiting access to contraceptive information and devices, and repealing penal laws governing abortion.

The more conservative of the factions see the possibility of achieving their rights through legislative measures. Their major goals appear to be strengthening the family system while at the same time achieving economic and political equality for women.

The more radical factions see the present family system itself as one of the main deterrents to woman's equal status. They see woman's inferior status so rooted in the concepts of masculinity and femininity that the only way to achieve equality is to destroy the present man–woman relationship in marriage, seen as the product and perpetuator of the male supremacist culture.

The Male Viewpoint.   Some men support the viewpoint of the liberationists, seeing the concept of masculinity to be as confining and damaging to the development of the male as femininity is to the female.

Some have taken a different stand, writing off the movement as the cries of alienated women who are not feminine enough to attract or hold a man.   Others have taken an oppositionist stand, such as the founders of the Society for the Emancipation of the American Male (SEAM), formed in 1969.   This organization reportedly is dedicated to restoring the American patriarchy and returning the male to his rightful place as the head of the family (Ellis, 1970, pp. 176–85).

Lines appear to be drawn—at the extreme limits, at least.   To what extent these conflicting ideas have permeated the general public is not known at present.   The presence of the conflict in the culture probably heightens the anxiety as well as provides a stage for the expression of some of the hostility engendered in both sexes as they attempt to define themselves as masculine or feminine, however those terms are defined.

Recent Trends Toward Equality

Attainment of the goal of differentiated equality, where men and women complement each other socially and culturally as well as biologically, is proving to be rather difficult.   The task, as has been seen, is more than the establishment of equality; it is also one of reorganization, of role adjustment between the sexes.   Even equals can be disorganized in their relationships to each other.

Whatever the long-time results of the movement toward sex equality, the immediate effects are disorganizing.   We are in a period of transitional turmoil where values are confused and roles are in conflict.   In time, perhaps, society will find a way to have both equality and harmony at the same time.

At the present, however, there appears to be wide variation in the movement toward sexual equality, even among college students where the greatest consensus supporting equality would be expected.   Nor have all the changes in sex-role expectations over the last sixteen years been toward greater equality.   The previously mentioned study by the authors (see page 131) was designed primarily to discover the changes in attitudes toward sex-roles which have taken place among college students since the study was first done in 1951. The items remained identical over the years although the number of respondents rose from 88 in 1951 to 507 in 1967. On some items both males and females showed a sizable increase in percentage supporting more traditional norms. Over half of the men and almost 90 per cent of the women believe that girls should *not* be as free as boys in asking for dates and proposing marriage. Over fifty per cent of both sexes believed that swearing and telling dirty stories is worse for women than men. Both of these showed about a 10 per cent rise over the years. There was a minority—about one-fourth of the men and one-fifth of the women—whose chose the submissive over the equalitarian female as the most approved female type. Although the percentage was small it represented an increase since 1951. About ninety per cent of both sexes felt that masculine chivalries should be preserved—again an increase since the earlier study for both sexes.

As far as marriage roles were concerned the move toward a more traditional authority structure was unmistakable (see Table 7–1). Only one person chose the wife being at the head in either year.

Table 7–1

Which of the following authority patterns in the home do you most favor?

		1951	1967
Husband at the head	males	32%	74%
	females	41	72
Most capable at head	males	26	8
	females	3	5
Neither at the head	males	42	17
	females	56	23

Casting some doubts on whether or not males and females mean the same thing when they agree that the husband should be head of the house were the responses to an item about the most approved male type (see Table 7–2). The trend for the males is in keeping with the move toward male dominance in the home. The females however seem to be saying that the kind of male who is to be head of the house is one who shares his authority.

Also supporting the trend toward a more traditional division of labor were findings not presented in the tables given here. There was a heavier endorsement of the husband who helped "only occasionally when asked or when the need was great" than of the husband who helped his wife

Table 7–2

Which of the following male types has your greatest approval?

		1951	1967
The man who is aggressive and slightly egocentric	males	22%	42%
	females	34	29
The man who needs a wife he can lean on	males	0	6
	females	0	3
The man who both permits and expects half the responsibility to be with the wife	males	72	43
	females	66	59
Undecided	males	6	9
	females	0	9

"considerably and willingly." The females were about evenly divided between the two choices in 1967 while two-thirds of them chose the more helpful husband in 1951. The male trend was essentially the same.

Surprisingly though, this change was coupled with a shift toward more acceptance of the working wife (see Table 7–3).

Table 7–3

Which of the following wife types has your greatest approval?

		1951	1967
Devotes full time to home and family	males	70%	55%
	females	69	36
Works periodically and/or part-time outside the home	males	19	37
	females	19	50
Maintains full-time career outside the home	males	2	3
	females	3	5
Undecided	males	9	5
	females	9	9

The sexes were in essential agreement on this question in 1951. But in 1967 the women were much more likely to choose the part-time work role. This choice for the women was not related to their choice of husband role. From cross-tabulations not shown on these tables, it was found that those choosing part-time work were no more likely to choose a helpful husband than those preferring the full-time homemaker role. Seemingly, the desire for considerable help from the husband was not related to the need for that help. These two items were related for the men, but not in the expected direction. Males who desired the full-time wife were significantly more likely to endorse the helpful husband than were those who favored the working wife. Again, the choices were apparently not made according to logical fit between the husband and wife roles.

The partial acceptance of both types of husband–wife roles and the lack of logical fit between the choices in many cases give some evidence of cultural confusion in these expectations as we apparently move toward more equalitarian norms in some areas and traditional ones in others.

Effect of Marriage. The trends noted above were overwhelmingly influenced by single students. Marriage itself has an impact on role expectations. On some items, the married students in 1967 had more traditional views than single students (see Table 7-4). These items are mainly

Table 7–4

Percentage Agreeing That:

		Single *	Married
Males have the highest over-all native intelligence	males	40%	63%
	females	34	43
Husband should be head of the house	males	73	81
	females	73	79
Husband should be a little superior to wife in general intelligence and ability	males	46	56
	females	57	64
A husband should help considerably and willingly	males	60	38
	females	51	21

* The engaged students were left out to heighten the contrast.

concerned with the division of labor and power structure. Even though higher percentages of both males and females give traditional responses after marriage, there remains a fairly wide difference between them. They are closest together on the question of head of the house. Interestingly enough, however, they separate again on the approved male type (see Table 7-5).

Table 7–5

Choose as most approved male type:

		Single	Married
The male who both permits and expects half the responsibility to be with the wife	males	44%	53%
	females	57	79

On other items the gap between the sexes appears to grow larger after marriage. It must be remembered, however, that these married women were students. The potential conflict suggested by this study may apply only to marriages which bring together college educated husbands and wives. Remembering the limitation of this study, it seems safe to say that student husbands give more traditional responses and student wives give more equalitarian responses regarding work than single students (see Table 7–6).

Table 7–6

Percentage Agreeing That:

		Single	Married
A wife should work periodically or part-time outside the home	males	40%	19%
	females	51	57
Family instability results from women being too independent and unwilling to stay at home	males	38	56
	females	30	29
Most women should be satisfied with home-making as a sufficient career	males	42	53
	females	30	21
In hiring practices, males should have preference over females	males	57	66
	females	31	21

In keeping with these findings from 1967 are the results of a small study done by graduate students in a sociology class in December, 1969,[3] which attempted to discover the extent of support for Women's Liberation goals among Purdue University students. The non-random sample included 293 undergraduate and graduate students. The nature of the sample prohibits broad generalizations, but its consistency with relative positions of married and unmarried students in 1967 is reassuring. The questionnaire consisted of equal numbers of traditional and liberationist ideas. Responses were scored on a five-point scale of agreement with 1 representing the most traditional and 5 the most extreme liberation position.

The mean scores for the male and female groups showed a rather neutral position, neither strongly traditional nor strongly pro-liberation, though inclined slightly toward the latter. The relative positions of the single and married groups, however, reflect the same support of more traditional views by married men and more equalitarian views by married women. The most favorable opinions toward women's liberation were registered by married women (mean score = 3.88). Following them in support of liberationist ideas were single women with a mean score of

[3] The course was Christensen's "Men and Women in Modern Society" and the students responsible for the project were: Anthony Bruder, Ruth Fuchs, Ann Hoegemeyer, Gail Howlett, Cynthia McGrigg, and Rudeemon Ruangsiri.

3.40, and then single men with a mean score of 3.33. The group giving least support to the ideas of women's equal status were married men with a mean score of 3.02. Thus, marriage seems to *increase* woman's notion of sex equality but to *decrease* man's. If this study is at all representative of married college students in general a new area of conflict looms on the marital scene.

It seems that after marriage the male may want to restrict his wife more than he thought he would, while she is not as satisfied in being restricted as she thought she would be before marriage. The apparent conflict may arouse some guilt feelings in the wives about working, since, in 1967, almost 80 per cent of both husbands and wives felt that the husband's interests should be put first. Although the differences between the sexes appear to suggest a high probability that men and women with different ideas about their roles may meet and marry, there appears to be virtually no disagreement about the desirability of wives combining marriage with a full career. None of the married women and only four per cent of the single women in 1967 showed any desire for a full-time job or career.

Equality in the Economic World. A Gallup poll conducted in August, 1970, on a sample of 778 women appeared to support the position of those college men and women surveyed three years earlier. Among women who had gotten no farther than grade school, 78 per cent do not work outside the home, and 50 per cent of them do not want to do so. College women were more likely to work (43 per cent), but only 34 per cent of them were content not to work. At all educational levels, women who would like to work but do not preferred part-time jobs (*Trans-action*, 1970, p. 10). There are other indications that women either have no real desire to challenge the male dominance in the economic sphere or have been effectively discouraged from the attempt. Although the proportion of married women that are working has risen, only about one in three of those working today work full-time. The ratio of men to women receiving graduates degrees has increased since the 1940's and 1950's, so that the ratio is about the same as it was in the 1920's for Master's degrees, and earlier than that for the Ph.D. degree. In 1920, there was about one female Ph.D. to every five and one-half male Ph.D.'s. In 1960, the Ph.D. ratio was about one woman to every eight and one-half men and about one woman to every nine men in 1965. The same is true in female representation in the professions. From a peak in the 1930's, the percentage of professionals who are women declined in 1960 to about the same level it was in 1900 (Udry, 1966, pp. 39–43). The slight but persistent decline was still apparent in 1966 (Knudsen, 1969). There are, of course, more women in these fields now, but they have not increased at the same rate as the males. Women tend to predominate in the clerical, nursing, library, and teaching occupations. Even in these fields (with the exception of clerical positions) there has been a slight increase in the proportion of males entering them.

Although there has been a large increase in the number of women entering various professional categories since 1940, the percentage increase is considerably less than that of men; so that in 1966 the proportion of professional, technical, and kindred workers who were female was 37.9 per cent, compared to 41.6 per cent in 1940 (Knudsen, 1969). In 1969, 79 per cent of women workers were in clerical, sales, factory, service, and household jobs (Suelzle, 1970). In spite of the publicity given equal rights under the Civil Rights Act of 1964 the pay differential between full-time male and female employees actually widened from 1957 to 1969. Between these years the median earnings per year for female workers rose from $3,008 in 1957 to $4,457 in 1969. The median income for males during the same time span, however, rose over twice as much, from $4,713 in 1957 to $7,664 in 1969 (Suelzle, 1970).

With this apparent discrimination in the economic world, it is no wonder that, when asked, married women seem to view employment as an extension of their wife–mother roles—either to help out in periods of additional expense or simply for contacts with the world outside the family (Hartley, 1963). They are, with few exceptions, not working at careers but at jobs which give them few rewards—either in monetary or personal satisfaction. Whether this trend is a consequence of early socialization, or later social pressures steering them away from serious career commitments, or accurate appraisals of the barriers against them in the economic world, or limitations stemming from the reproductive function is not adequately understood.[4]

THE PRINCIPLE OF VALUE RELEVANCE

Whether the trend just noted is viewed as encouraging in that there seems to be a preservation of the traditional relationship between the sexes or discouraging in that women, for whatever reason, are not developing or utilizing their abilities and view themselves more negatively than males, will depend upon the value system supported by the culture and the values of individual readers. The prevailing cultural norms largely support the stereotypical personality clusters associated with masculinity and femininity. Both males and females tend to agree on their content, but there is variation both in the content and the strength of commitment to

[4] For a series of articles devoted to the numerous social and psychological pressures operating to hold down the aspirations of women see the special combined issue of *Trans-action*, entitled *The Amercian Woman*, 8 (November–December, 1970).

them. If a given marital pair support the stereotypical definitions, they will be more contented the closer their personalities conform to the stereotype. Where both parties depart from cultural expectations, then marital happiness will depend on their conformity to their own expectations, the fit between them, and the support they receive from their social groups.

The *paradigm of value conflict* becomes relevant here (see Chapter 4, page 71). Where both husband and wife agree on the sex-appropriate characteristics, and where these beliefs are shared by families and friendship groups, then the two partners would think well of themselves and each other to the extent that they possess the characteristics. If, however, the two people disagree on characteristics appropriate to the two sexes or are imbedded in a social group which defines masculinity and femininity differently from their conceptions, their daily interaction may become a continual source of self-doubt or spousal disapproval. The domestic, dependent woman paired with a male who sees her as possessing a valued feminine trait will never question the appropriateness of her behavior. If they move into a social group where the women are interested in community affairs and evidence a great amount of independence, both she and her husband may reevaluate her characteristics. She may begin to doubt the importance of her contributions and he may begin to be aware of her lack of certain characteristics which he never thought of before.

Whenever there is confusion or change in the characteristics associated with masculinity or femininity, the probability is heightened that persons will encounter situations which heighten their anxiety about their performance as males and females. Whatever the cultural definitions of masculinity and femininity, it seems obvious that for a person to think well of himself, the characteristics he develops in the process of acquiring a firm sex-appropriate identity must be valued by society and by the individuals with whom he interacts—most especially his spouse. Thus, the expression of the appropriate characteristics becomes rewarding in itself and aids in the maintenance of high self-esteem, reduction of hostility, and heightened cooperation between the sexes—all major components of stable marriages.

SUMMARY

The earliest classification made among human beings is made on the basis of gender. This classification gathers together relatively consistent groups of expectations which direct the developing individuals to differing sets of evaluations of behavior, depending upon their sex. Although nature makes the original distinctions, the socialization process develops them into masculine and feminine beings.

The combination of physiological differences, socially imposed expectations, and varying childrearing experiences results in observable behavioral and attitudinal differences between the sexes. There are also many areas of similarity, as well as wide within-sex variation. The acquisition of sex-appropriate behavior is fraught with anxiety for both sexes, although the greatest anxiety comes early in the male's development and during adolescence and beyond for the female.

Since masculinity and femininity are socially defined, changes over time occur in the definition in response to other changes in the society. A relatively low status for females has been supported by a long history, during which the physical superiority of the male and the dependency of the female during her reproductive period put her at a disadvantage. Long-range advances in technology have nullified, partially, the advantage accruing from physical strength and the disadvantages imposed by childbirth. Changes have occurred toward greater equality between the sexes, although the differential evaluation of masculine and feminine characteristics still leads the female to evaluate herself more negatively than the male, as they both grow to maturity.

Sex identification becomes highly important in the marriage relationship, where the male and female may see things from a slightly different perspective but must cooperate in reaching shared goals. The evaluation of themselves and each other will be at least partially influenced by the cultural evaluation made of masculinity and femininity. The main source of satisfaction or dissatisfaction in an individual marriage, however, will be the degree to which the spouses fulfill *each others'* expectations, rather than how well they conform to the societal stereotype.

QUESTIONS AND PROJECTS

1. Can women be equal with men without becoming masculine? Explain.

2. Considering the difficulties that are experienced by both sexes in acquiring masculine or feminine traits, what would you propose to make the process easier?

3. What are the major characteristics associated with masculinity today? Femininity? How do you think these definitions have changed in the last fifty or sixty years? As these ideas have changed, do you think a complementarity between the sexes has been maintained or are the concepts of masculinity and femininity becoming more alike?

4. It has been said that rather than women attempting to emulate men by entering the economic world, they should enhance their wife and mother roles by making them more creative and rewarding. Does this idea fit with the present worries about overpopulation? Explain your position.

5. Look at advertisements in magazines and commercials on television. Make a list of the things you see which seem to be defining masculinity and

femininity. Is there any consistency in the images being portrayed? What aspect of the male–female relationship seems to be emphasized in the images? Does there appear to be a difference in the way single and married men and women are portrayed?

6. How do you explain the growth of the Women's Liberation Movement? Is this a legitimate cause or just a way of expressing deep hostility toward men? Is the membership in these organizations largely composed of intelligent, able women who want equal opportunity to use their talents and skills or is it composed mainly of women who are failures in their attempts to win male attention? Do you see other motivations for involvement in this movement? Explain.

7. It has been suggested that some hostility toward the opposite sex is built up in the process of developing masculine and feminine roles. Can you think of some ways in which this hostility is expressed? How does this affect an individual male–female relationship?

III

PREMARITAL INTERACTION

8
Dating Patterns

The concept of self as male or female coupled with the habits of inter-action formed in the preadolescent years prepare the young person for entrance into the dating market. Experience in or exclusion from this popular game, however, will have an impact on his further development. It will alter or confirm his habits of interpreting and reacting to the op-posite sex, will aid in firming up his expectations for the kind of person he wants to marry, and will introduce new evaluations into his concept of self.

Experiences during this period will have these effects whether or not he has marriage in mind. In fact, dating, as it is used here, does not imply a serious commitment to mate selection. It refers only to the early friendship activities of young people whereby they seek to have fun in pairs. Its relationship to mate selection is about the same as that between window shopping and serious shopping for a particular item. One casually looks in the store windows with nothing definite in mind. He may see some appealing items, casually noting what things he may conceivably hope to buy, which ones are out of his reach, and which ones he wouldn't want if they were given to him. He casually establishes his ideas about what stores he will shop in when he's serious about buying. But in the process he may see something that catches his eye. He begins to think about getting enough money to buy it and before long he becomes ob-sessed with the idea. What started out as a casual window shopping trip ended up in a final purchase.

In the same way, dating must be considered as a first step in mate selection, regardless of the early intent of the relationship. It does, at some time, usually lead to more serious involvement, to engagement, and to marriage. The non-marital *intent* of the relationship, as well as its *in-fluence* on developing ideas about a future marital partner, can be observed in the following often heard comments of young people engaged in dating purely because of the fun, the social participation, and the status among peers that it offers:

"He's fun to date, but I'd hate to spend my life with a guy like that."

"Marry her? Not on your life—but she suits me fine, right now."

"You know, I don't think I'd mind spending my life with him—or somebody like him—I don't want to be tied down yet, though."

Those people who are available for dating also provide the field of eligibles from which the future mate will come. A man does not, in our society, hear about a girl with characteristics he desires, check on her family background, and then approach her father, credentials in hand, to bargain for her. He first must meet the girl, establish a casual relationship, and await further developments.

Dating, then, is part of the process of mate selection and has come under normative control, that is, the behavior is guided by norms which tell us what is or is not acceptable. Dating has become institutionalized (see Chapter 1) in our society and therefore is influenced by changes occurring in other parts of the society. It has not developed and changed in a vacuum but rather as an integral part of the changes which have affected our expectations for marriage.

CHANGES OVER TIME

Although many societies have ways for young people to interact, the dating system in the United States appears to be uniquely a twentieth-century American innovation. It differs from all other systems in its emphasis on the casual, non-committed, recreational relationship between a boy and a girl, which neither implies future marriage nor rules it out. It is appearing, however, in other societies which now are undergoing some of the same pressures the United States has experienced with its rapid expansion of the industrial system. Whether this is the result of contact with the American culture or a consequence of changes in the social structure accompanying industrialization is not known.

Before the twentieth century young people in the United States participated in social activities, but these were usually planned, chaperoned, and not oriented around paired relationships. The young man who asked permission to call on a young unmarried lady or to take her out was expected to have marriage in mind. If his attentiveness continued too long without the expected offer of marriage, the girl's father would become interested in his intentions. The "date" in this sense was a declaration that he was seriously interested in her as a future wife.

At about the turn of the century, however, a number of factors con-
verged to create the situation which spawned the dating institution as it
is known today. First, there was an increase in urbanization. As cities
grew the central values of individualism, freedom, and equality spread
more easily. It was more difficult for parents to supervise the young
peoples' activities since the cities provided more activities which were not
family centered. As the coeducational public school system was extended
through high school, it provided a meeting ground for adolescents where
they could arrange their own meetings out from under the watchful eyes
of parents. The first World War brought the femininist movement to a
peak. Although it did not involve a large proportion of the women, the
movement spread ideas about sexual equality and resulted in more freedom of movement for the female. All of these factors—the city, the public
high school, greater freedom for women, and ideas about sexual equality
—merged to produce the conditions for the development of an adolescent
sub-culture, from which the dating norms grew (Udry, 1966, pp. 108–10).

Functionally, dating can be seen to serve a purpose for mate selection
when the criteria for successful marriages are based more on interpersonal
relations than on skill in the performance of certain tasks. If skillful performance of certain tasks is the goal, as in the past, then older and wiser
heads are needed to be alert to essential characteristics without being
blinded by a pretty face or charming manners. But if individual happiness is the goal, then individual selection is necessary (or so it seems to
the individual). The greater emphasis on interpersonal relationships in
both marriage and the dating institution is an adaptation to changes in
the society, which have thrown the male and female into closer relationships at all ages and lessened the supervision and power of the family

From 1920 to World War II

Since the dating norms emerged from adolescent interaction as young
people sought recreation these norms would be expected to change as
young people discovered new ways to find satisfaction and meet common
needs. Since recreational needs and marital needs may not be the same,
the dating system at any one time may or may not be a constructive preparation for marriage, even though it functions as part of the mate selection
process.

Descriptions of the dating system from its inception in the 1920's to the
period following World War II, have stressed its competitive, exploitative,
and status-seeking nature. The emphasis at that time was on popularity,
determined by the frequency of dating, the number of different partners,
and the achievement of certain goals. The boy's goals were seen to be
the achievement of dates with the most popular girls and the obtaining

of sexual intimacy at the least cost. The girl's goals, on the other hand, were to attract a wide number of the most attractive boys and to have many dates involving large expenditures with minimum sexual surrender on her part.

From this picture, dating loomed as a battleground between the sexes, each partner offering less and demanding more than the other (Waller, 1938, p. 239, Gorer, 1948, pp. 104–12). This was the period of the long stag-lines, where a girl's popularity was measured by the number of "cut-ins" she had during a dance. The more popular she appeared, the more the other boys wanted to go out with her—success mushroomed. Obviously only a small number could be this popular, and they tended to attract most of the males. Some studies reported high schools in which 10 per cent of the girls were dated by 50 per cent of the dating boys (West, 1945, p. 195). A rather high proportion of high school students dated only rarely or not at all.

Changes Since World War II

Sociologists noted a change in the dating institution occurring at about the end of World War II (Erhmann, 1964, pp. 593–96). The extreme emphasis on popularity determined by the number of dating partners began to decline. The emphasis shifted to longer, more involved relationships. Steady dating began to be prevalent even among those newly arrived in the dating system. This largely replaced the random dating pattern characteristic of the earlier period, when steady dating announced the end of "playing the field" and the beginning of a serious relationship with marital ends in view.

Reasons for the change are not obvious, but perhaps it was an answer to the failure of the intensely competitive system to include a large enough portion of the adolescent population. The going-steady pattern, although negatively evaluated by parents, gave an entree to the social affairs which demanded partners, provided a sense of security in knowing there would be someone to go with, and relieved the pressure for competition once a steady was won. There is some evidence that in the 1950's a higher percentage of high school students dated, at least occasionally, than in the 1940's (Cameron and Kenkel, 1960).

As the norms have continued to develop, the "steady" relationship has taken on aspects of both the early casual relationship and the more involved steady one. There is evidence that those who have dated the largest number of partners during their dating experiences have also had more "steady" relationships. These relationships appear to be more personal although they lack a commitment to permanence. There is usually little intent on the part of either partner for the currently exclusive relationship to continue for a long period of time. Udry suggests that this kind of "dating game" uses all the gestures and language of courtship, but the players understand that it is only play (Udry, 1966, pp. 111–14). The object is to play the game well and to fall in love symbolically, with no obligations or commitments to the future. There are certain rules concerning who may play with whom, who initiates the play, and when it is permissible to call "foul." The object is ego-enhancement coming both from the satisfaction gained in the interaction itself and the gain in status from being seen playing with a high status partner. The more signs of involvement and displays of affection one can elicit from the partner, the greater the ego-enhancement (up to a point). The occurrence of coitus means the game is over. For the middle class girl, it generally means she has become too involved. In the lower classes it generally means, simply, that the girl lost. The game breaks down when both the partners become emotionally committed to each other—it then becomes courtship, with obligations to the partner and to the future of the relationship. Difficulties come about when one partner defines the situation as courtship and the other is still playing the "game."

PARTICIPATION IN DATING

Dating has become so widespread that socialization for dating begins very early. Young children are exposed to the fun and romance associated with it through teen-aged boy and girl dolls with their wardrobes of clothing for different events, their cars, and all the accessories for the dating game. The widespread influence of the dating pattern is perhaps reflected in the changes in heterosexual relationships of preadolescents. Broderick and Fowler report that studies done in the 1920's and 1930's without exception reported that friendship choices across sex lines dropped to almost zero in about the third or fourth grade and only began to rise slightly after the eighth grade. The typical twelve- or thirteen-year-old girl reportedly would not admit being attracted to a boy, though she may be interested at a distance. Boys of this age were reportedly either disinterested or actively antagonistic to girls (Broderick and Fowler, 1961). In the late 1950's, however, there appeared to be a sharp rise in boy–girl contacts in the younger years. About 50 per cent of fifth-grade children (10 and 11 years old) made at least one choice across sex lines when naming four of the children they liked best. Forty-five per cent of the boys and thirty-six per cent of the girls this age claimed to have had dating experiences. When asked if they had a sweetheart, 80 per cent of the boys and 94 per cent of the girls answered yes (Broderick and Fowler, 1961).

Choice of Dating Partner

As mentioned earlier, dating is defined as an uninvolved, opposite-sex relationship which is not consciously intended to lead to marriage, or at least is not expected to carry this meaning. Most young people say they date for fun—they want to enjoy it as an end in itself with "no strings attached," for awhile at least. They also see it as an opportunity to get out, to attend affairs that would be barred to them otherwise, and as a means of gaining status or being recognized, especially if the date is with someone who rates. Probably only a few have marriage in mind from the time they first start to date.

In the process of dating though, the interaction does contribute to the development of attitudes toward the opposite sex which will narrow down the field of eligibles from which they will finally choose. Some of these attitudes define the behavioral patterns which will exclude a person as a possible date and therefore mate, no matter how socially acceptable he is. Many of these come under the guise of general complaints about the opposite sex, suggesting that serious involvement will occur only with a person who is low on these negative traits.

Cross-sex Criticisms. Over the past several years the authors have asked students to prepare papers criticizing the opposite sex regarding traits and tendencies which were objectionable in both dating and courtship relationships. Illustrations of some of the more common comments follow.

As the man sees it:

There never seems to be any thought behind the actions of women, those of college age at least. They go blithely along, perfectly content as long as they have dates for everything. Anything that smacks of reality is avoided like the Black Plague. I perfectly agree that a girl should work a few years before marrying because I don't see how some of these coeds will ever be able to settle down long enough to manage a home.

· · ·

Too many girls, especially of teen age, think that just because you go out with them once or twice they have a life lease on you. They should realize that we are dating for companionship and without wanting to get serious so soon.

· · ·

Girls seem to enjoy competition—competition of two boys over her, that is. The idea that these two fellows will finally get to the point where they could cheerfully strangle each other is, of course, no concern to her.

· · ·

Every man knows that he can't make a general remark about women, to a woman, without getting a personal comeback of some sort. I can't understand why women seem to be always on the defensive. They act as if they were expecting a slight, or an attack, or an injustice.

. . .

I am of the opinion that it is woman's duty to society to be beautiful. If her main purpose on earth was to reproduce, I think God would have given her four legs, a glass door, a couple of internal racks, and in general designed her much on the same order as an incubator. Instead, he made her a work of art.

. . .

She displays her physical attractions in an obvious fashion, but pretends to be highly insulted that any man should think of her in such a "base" manner. She is adept in the ways of arousing the "animal" in man, yet she contrives to be quite hurt that he should "try to take advantage of her." Thus the man goes away bewildered and frustrated, while the woman retires confident and satisfied.

. . .

I dislike the necessity of making all the first moves on a date. I don't mind asking for the date, financing it, and furnishing the transportation, but I would appreciate a little cooperation when it comes to determining what is to be the activity of the evening. If the girl refuses to make suggestions, but insists on doing "whatever you want to do," how can a boy know the kinds of things she likes to do or will do of her own volition after marriage.

. . .

I believe a girl should watch her actions so as not to become boisterous or disgustingly silly. If she is this way, the fellows will soon begin to avoid her.

. . .

No man wants to be reformed. But also no man who loves a woman will refuse to correct his own shortcomings when he realizes that they are objectionable. However, the smart woman will use the subtle approach and let the man think he is bringing about the improvement of his own free will.

. . .

I object wholeheartedly to a girl who is *always* dainty. She can't go camping or on a weekend outing because there will be no electrical outlet for her hair dryer.

. . .

Girls who use too much makeup are not attractive to me. Makeup is a beauty aid and not beauty in itself.

. . .

It bothers me when a girl takes the lead in opening the car door, putting on her coat, and other little courtesies. If the girl wants the fellow to act like a gentleman she ought to give him time to do it. A girl who beats her date out of the car doesn't get the door opened for her.

As the woman sees it:

Fellows are too abrupt in their love making, taking it for granted that the girl's feelings are emotionally on the same plane as their own.

. . .

Men are too emotional. Biologically this is so, I suppose, and because of it we women are placed in a predicament. It isn't a pleasant thought that every time you go out with a boy you might be faced with a "battle royal."

. . .

Boys often calls girls "gold diggers." This is, to some extent, their own fault. They should let the girls know how much money there is to be spent on the current date. It is as embarrassing to the girl to order beyond the fellow's means as it is for the boy to have her do so. If he can only afford hamburgers why doesn't he say so? If the girl is the right sort at all, she will not hold it against him.

. . .

He wants you to be interested in the things he's interested in. He wants you to be good in any sport he's fond of, yet acts like a wounded puppy if you beat him at his own game. We can be liked as long as we allow the man to be certain that he's right on all debatable subjects. Prove him wrong and he'll pout the rest of the evening. Ask him what's the matter and he'll say, "Nothing."

. . .

Most men like to be babied. They'd never admit it, but they're all spoiled, overgrown boys.

. . .

Little courtesies on a date can almost make or break a girl's opinion of a fellow. Almost every boy I know could still stand a few pointers; little things such as taking off his hat when he comes into your house, being courteous and mannerly in front of your parents, helping you on with your wraps, and walking on the outside of the sidewalk. Men complain about the lack of femininity in modern women. Perhaps if these men treated women with more respect they would find that they more nearly lived up to their ideals.

. . .

I have little respect for a date who has not taken a moment or two to make himself look respectable for me. After all, I do it for him!

. . .

Guys have a way of taking a girl for granted after they have gone with her for awhile. When he begins assuming that I'll be there anytime he decides to call or drop in, my stubbornness takes over.

. . .

I find it confusing, frustrating, and irritating when males profess great love after knowing you a matter of hours, make an advance and upon being refused, proceed to get mad about it as if it were their right.

All of the above are comments of boys about girls, or girls about boys. Student *self-criticisms* have been equally revealing and along similar lines. Here are some typical comments, paraphrased:

"I am too shy, bashful, and self-conscious. I am awkward in the art of conversation."

"I am prone to worry excessively and to get moody."

"I am overly serious, jealous, and possessive."

"I am self-centered, acting egotistically, and flirting with or bragging about others while on a date."

"I am spoiled or have a bad disposition. My temper is quick. I make catty remarks."

That these comments are not unique is well supported by several studies. Evidently, a large proportion of each sex believes itself to be shy, ill-at-ease, self-conscious, and inadequate in dating situations. This is especially true in the early dating years (Williams, 1949; Christensen, 1952; Crist, 1953).

Typical Male—Female Patterns

As a follow-up on this earlier unstructured approach to dating behavior, Christensen constructed a questionnaire which was subsequently administered to nearly one thousand Purdue University students and also to several thousand high school students from throughout the United States.[1]

One part of the schedule presented a list of thirty objectionable dating traits, and students were asked to: (1) indicate which of the items they felt were more characteristic of males, and which of females; and (2) check, in the spirit of honest self-criticism, all items that represented outstanding problems in their own dating practices.

Since results from both the Purdue and the high school samples were strikingly similar, they will be summarized together. Figure 8–1 shows the relative strengths of different items in the Purdue sample, and how they fall into typical male and female patterns. It is based on responses from 674 Purdue University students and was calculated by subtracting from the largest number assigning an item to a particular sex the number assigning it to the opposite sex, and expressing this net figure as a percentage of all answers. The following facts concerning the results stand out.

1. Males and females are in close agreement as to how each sex is to be characterized. This is shown by the fact that on only a few items (three in the Purdue sample and two in the high school sample) did males and females disagree concerning where an item was to be assigned, and by the fact that intersex correlations on judgments were remarkably high

[1] The Purdue study was conducted during the spring of 1949. Completed schedules were returned from 933 students, 674 of whom (332 males and 342 females) were neither engaged nor married. Unless otherwise stated, reported generalizations will be for this single and unengaged part of the sample.

The high school study was conducted during the fall of 1950 as Poll Number 27 of the Purdue Opinion Panel (under the direction of H. H. Remmers of the Division of Educational Reference). Approximately 8,000 returns were received. However, analyses are based upon a smaller, but stratified and more representative sample of 2,500. Some of the findings have been previously published; see Harold T. Christensen (1952).

(.95 in the Purdue sample and .93 in the high school sample). Thus, by common consent, there is recognition that objectionable dating practices follow rather typical sex patterns.

2. Typically, males are considered to be less inhibited and more careless, thoughtless, disrespectful, sex-driven, and loud than are their partners in dating. By way of contrast, females are considered to be less natural and more touchy, status-conscious, unresponsive, sentimental, and flighty than are the boys and men they date. These general sex differences became very apparent in both studies.

3. Though agreement is high, there is nevertheless a tendency to project criticism or blame upon the opposite sex. This was true of both studies and it can be seen in the bar extensions of Figure 8–1. In the high school study, males were found to engage in cross-sex blame projection far more than were females.

In Figure 8–1 it is apparent that, with the exception of three items, male and female students agree on which types of conduct are most prevalent with each sex. Males are characterized as being more offensive in regard to such things as manners and intimacy, while females are characterized by a tendency toward artificiality and shallowness. Though each sex is willing to accept partially the patterns ascribed to it, there is a tendency toward projecting blame upon the opposite sex. "Acts nervous and rattled" was the only pattern which was accepted more than projected by both males and females, suggesting that both sexes feel self-conscious in the dating situation.

4. In general, for both studies, self-criticism tended to follow the respective patterns of the two sexes: males criticizing themselves more on items that are considered characteristic of male behavior and females on items considered characteristic of female behavior. Thus, introspective males felt themselves to be self-conscious and shy, weak in the social arts, overanxious for intimacy, etc.; while introspective females felt themselves to be self-conscious and shy, too cold emotionally, overly serious, and easy to offend, etc.

5. The statement that self-criticisms tend to follow same-sex criticisms needs to be qualified in one important respect. In the high school study, particularly, it was found that there are several items which females assign to the female pattern but do not accept to themselves; notably, "puts on airs," "stuck-up on dates," and "overmoney-minded." What they were saying in effect was "Yes, other women are like that, but not me." Apparently females, more than males, tend to project criticism upon other members of their own sex. Both sexes engage in some blame projection, but, typically, males upon females, and females upon other females. It would seem that each person, male or female, tends to rationalize his own behavior by projecting blame upon the "other woman"; she gets it from

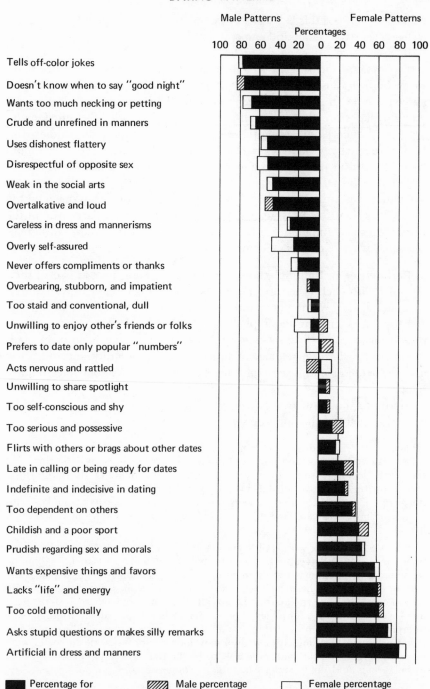

Fig. 8—1. Comparison of male and female patterns of objectionable dating behavior.

all sides. Perhaps this is because women, in a male-dominant culture, feel a strong sense of competition among themselves.

6. Special mention needs to be made of the trait originally labeled "self-conscious and shy, isn't calm or at ease, acts nervous and rattled." From both studies, this is the only item on which males and females disagreed in the direction of accepting it to their own sex; that is, males thought males are the more self-conscious, and females thought females are. Furthermore, in self-criticisms—and again from both studies—this is the item which both sexes checked most, by great odds. It should be evident from this that feeling inadequate, or ill-at-ease, in the dating situation is a rather common experience for both men and women. They may "put up a brave front" so as to conceal it, but deep down within themselves they feel nervous and unsure. This is particularly true in the early stages of dating. It can help just to know that the other person feels the same way. Confidence comes with practice.

Preferences in Date Selection.   The things young people like in their dealings with each other are the reverses of the complaints given above. In general, they want poise and self-confidence in place of being shy; courtesy and consideration in place of selfishness and egotism; respect and reserve in place of thrill-seeking intimacy; sincerity and honesty in place of superficial flattery; refinement to substitute for crudity and vulgarity; and cheerfulness and a sense of humor to substitute for touchiness and ill temper.

Here are the ways two college women and two college men describe what they want in the opposite sex:

Female 1. The ideal man is nice looking, although not necessarily handsome. He is well-groomed and very polite. In dating he states the time and the place definitely so as to leave no doubt in the mind of the girl. He is always on time. Above all, he does not pet until it is justified by their emotional relationship. He gladly meets the family, and he always complies with its restrictions. He can carry on an intelligent conversation without sounding like an encyclopedia.

Female 2. I think worlds of a guy who demands no more physically of me than I'm ready to give, with love. It makes me feel great to have him be considerate of me and really listen to me when I say something. It makes me feel especially feminine if he does unexpected little things like sending a note or a flower after we've quarreled. I really like to know where I stand with him—even if there's a girl back home. I'd rather know about it, than misinterpret the relationship. I think more of a guy who respects his parents, and is not ashamed to admit it. I really enjoy having him take me to spend time with his parents. I like him to be able to be happy, have a good time, yet able to be serious and enjoy serious intelligent conversation.

Male 1. What I want in a girl is easily put into words but not so easily found. She must be frank. She tells me the things she doesn't like about me and substitutes something for them that she does like. She must not flavor everything she says and does with premeditated femininity. Her habits and interests are on a level with mine. We get a kick out of being together. She feels that every date is important and makes a visible effort to prove it to me. We have fun. She is neat. Her appearance shows it. Her shoulders are straight. She stands as though she is proud of her figure. She is alive. She gives me a feeling of confidence that she will be able to adjust to taking care of a home, a family, and me, especially in cooking. She will remember that the seat of affection is the stomach, not the heart, and that many things other than food turn it sour. She honestly expects me to be courteous. She gives me every opportunity to be a gentleman. Not a manner-mad gentleman, but one that goes to the root of kindness, gentleness, and respect. She has succeeded in her family life. Her brothers and sisters love her. Her parents trust her. She is a good daughter and sister.

Male 2. I like a girl who makes me feel important, even in little things like expecting chivalry. I like her to say to me, "We'll do what you want," but when I ask her what she wants to do she'll tell me. After all it is a little upsetting when you ask a girl if she would like to get a coke and she answers, "Gee, I don't know." If she doesn't know, who does? She should have a word of encouragement for me when I feel low, but not overdo it. I want her to communicate with me honestly, and be very patient, especially with me. She needs to be warm, cuddly, and virtuous.

In the studies already referred to, students were also asked to rate a list of twenty-four items according to what they most liked in a date. High school students placed the following seven items first, listed in order of rank.

1. Is physically and mentally fit.
2. Is dependable, can be trusted.
3. Takes pride in looks and manners.
4. Is clean in speech and action.
5. Is pleasant and has sense of humor.
6. Is considerate of me and others.
7. Acts own age, is not childish.

The Purdue ratings are shown in Figure 8–2. Greatest emphasis by both sexes was given to pleasant disposition, which was further described in the schedule as "cheerful, agreeable, optimistic, sense of humor, good sport." Next in importance was the quality of being well-groomed and -mannered, meaning "clean, neat, wear clothes well, conventional, refined." Third preference was for sociability, where the date "meets people well, is able to mix well in most situations, is at home with the social arts." Other qualities regarded as extremely important for the date to possess are: emotional maturity, physical attractiveness, considerateness, and fitting the traditional role of masculinity (if a man) or femininity (if a woman). The ratings were based on responses from 674 Purdue University students.

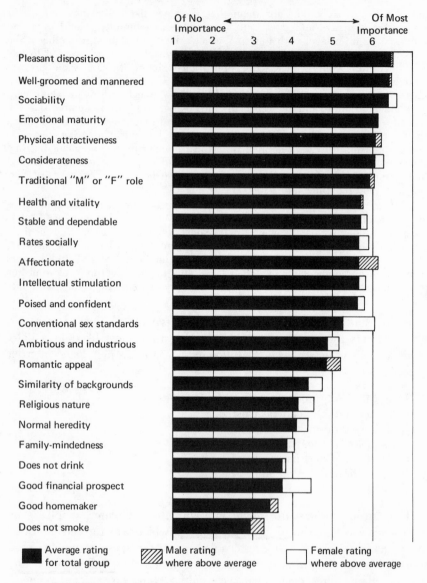

Fig. 8–2. Preference patterns in date selection.

Though phraseology was somewhat different in the Purdue from that in the high school study, it will be noted that results are at least broadly similar. Differences that do exist can be explained on the basis of the different age and experience levels of the two groups.

In both studies, males and females tended to agree rather well concerning what is important in a date; intersex correlations were high. But there were differences. When differences existed, males tended more to want a date who is affectionate, romantic (in the sense of emotional infatuation), and physically attractive, who does not smoke, and who offers promise of being a good homemaker. Females, in contrast, stressed more than males such things as conventional sex standards, good financial prospect, ambition and industriousness, religious nature, considerateness, and sociability (see Fig. 8-2).

There has been no recent research which is comparable to this assessment of preferences in dating partners. A similar study investigating characteristics desired in a prospective mate, however, does allow a comparison of responses in the years 1939, 1956, and 1967 (Hill, 1945; McGinnis, 1958; and Hudson and Henze, 1969). There has been amazing consistency in ranking of characteristics over the 28 year period. Out of 18 items, as evaluated by males, 3 remained in the same position and 11 moved only one position. Chastity declined from tenth to fifteenth place, while good looks rose from fourteenth to eleventh. Good cook and housekeeper rose from eighth to sixth place while good health fell from fifth to ninth. In all three studies the characteristics ranked one through four remained the same, although not in the same order. These were dependable character, mutual attraction, emotional stability, and pleasing disposition.

The same four characteristics were ranked in the top positions by females in 1967. However, mutual attraction and pleasing disposition were replaced by ambition-industriousness and desire for home and children in 1956. In 1939 the first four were emotional stability, dependable character, ambition-industriousness, and pleasing disposition. Chastity also declined from the point of view of females from tenth in 1939 to fifteenth in 1967. Education-intelligence rose from fourteenth in 1956 to seventh in 1967. Similar educational background rose from rank number 12 to number 9.

The consistency over time in criteria for selecting a mate is no assurance that the same consistency would be found in dating preferences, especially in the early period of dating. Perhaps, however, those personal characteristics which make a person of the opposite sex a good companion change relatively little over a period of thirty years.

Opinions Concerning Conduct

The high school study by Christensen included a few opinion items on dating conduct. This portion was replicated in 1961 to give some indication of change over the ten year period (Franklin and Remmers, 1961).

One item pertained to the question of which sex should take the initiative. Nearly half (48 per cent) of this national sample of boys felt that "it would be a good thing if girls could be as free as boys in asking for dates," compared with only about a fourth (27 per cent) of the girls who felt this way. For both sexes the percentage dropped in 1961, to 38 per cent of the boys and only 16 per cent of the girls who thought girls should have more freedom in asking for dates.

The difference between the sexes was more pronounced among 507 college students polled by the authors in 1967. In that study one-third of the males and only about one-twentieth of the females (5.4 per cent) thought equality between the sexes was a good thing as far as dating initiative is concerned. This suggests that large numbers of both sexes feel uneasy about approaching the opposite sex and that they would welcome having the other take the initiative. Most of the girls wanted to leave the asking prerogative with males, as it has been traditionally, though a large number of males would welcome a change. This gives support to our earlier findings regarding widespread feelings of dating shyness in both sexes.

Three questions directed to the high school samples dealt with physical intimacy. One of these asked if the first kiss should be delayed until after marriage. Almost no one (3 per cent in 1950 and 1 per cent in 1961) agreed that it should. The percent agreeing that it is all right for a couple to kiss on the first date rose from 51 per cent to 65 per cent for the boys and from 33 per cent to 50 per cent for the girls. The last question inquired if the students thought that intimate petting should be delayed unil after marriage. The per cent of the males agreeing with this statement (33 per cent) did not change over the ten-year period, while the percentage of females agreeing that petting should wait until after marriage went up slightly, from 66 to 77 per cent.

Opinions of College Students. Purdue samples were polled in 1951 and again in 1967 concerning the same behavior, but in slightly changed phraseology. The college students first were asked how they felt about casual necking in a dating relationship. Ninety-eight per cent of the males and ninety-seven per cent of the females approved. When asked about petting and sexual intercourse, this approval decreased consistently as the level of sexual activity increased and the commitment to the relationship decreased (see Figure 8–3). The only exception was among males, where a slightly larger percentage was likely to approve sexual intercourse in a dating relationship than in a love relationship prior to engagement. In every case males were more permissive than females, and college students more permissive than high school students.

From these and other studies, the conclusions appear clear that dating intimacy is less likely to be approved: (1) in the early stages of dating than during later courtship or engagement; (2) if it involves petting or intercourse rather than the lighter forms of necking; and (3) by females than males.

Figure 8–3 shows that both males and females at the college level have become more permissive since 1951 at every level of intimacy and type of relationship. The sharpest increase is in the males' approval of sexual intercourse in a love relationship before engagement. Males and females appear to be in greatest agreement concerning the approval of intimate petting during engagement and in increasing disagreement as the commitment to the relationship declines. It is obvious that the nature of the relationship has its greatest impact on females. 1951 data was based on responses from 88 Purdue University students; 1967 data was based on responses from 507 Purdue University students.

Implications for the "Going Steady" Pattern. The apparent association between strength of the commitment to the relationship and greater sexual permissiveness perhaps strikes at the root of parental objection to "going steady" relationships in high school (Poffenberger, 1965). Ehrmann discovered during the 1950's that the female's degree of physical intimacy actually experienced or considered acceptable varied directly with the intensity of familiarity and affection she felt toward the male. The male's varied *inversely* with the amount of commitment he felt to the relationship (Erhmann, 1959, p. 269). Essentially, the same thing was discovered by Schofield in his sample of English young people between the ages of 15 and 19 (Schofield, 1965, p. 62). There was only partial confirmation of this in our student sample in 1967, with a slightly higher percentage of males approving coitus in a dating relationship than in a love relationship. Unfortunately, data on the uninvolved dating relationship was not available for the 1951 study. There appears no doubt about the female's growing permissiveness as the relationship deepens, however.

On the other hand, Kirkendall (1961) found that the male's acceptance of responsibility in the sexual relationship and his movement away from a self-centered focus to a relationship-centered one was associated with deeper emotional involvement. If, then, parental worry about their daughters' "steady" relationships is centered around the fear of sexual exploitation, it appears that the female's greatest protection would be the emotional commitment of the male. This will be considered in more detail in the next chapter.

The dating game described by Udry (1966, pp. 111–14), the "rating and dating complex" described by Waller (1937), and the description of the American courtship pattern by Gorer (1948, pp. 104–12), all attest to the exploitative nature of the early dating situation. Dating was described by Waller as a dalliance relationship in which the members are interested primarily in thrill-seeking, experimentation, and exploitation.

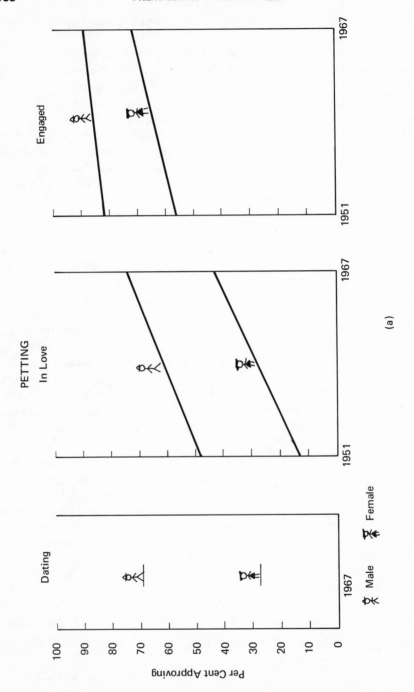

(a)

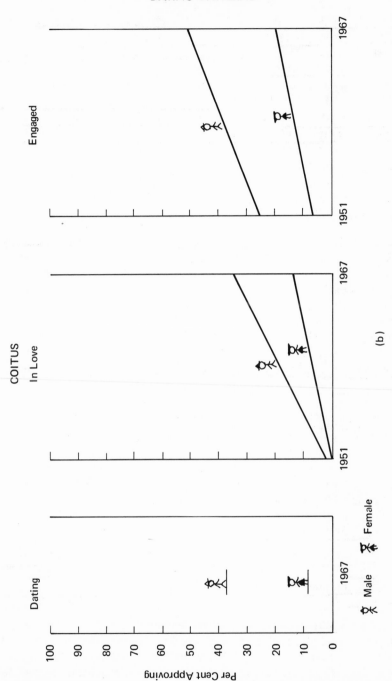

Fig. 8–3a and b. Approved intimacy according to type of relationship.

The "line," which is a conventionalized attempt to convince the other person that you care more than you do, was described as an accepted part of the game. The *principle of least interest* was used to explain the direction of exploitation. This principle simply means that the one least interested in the continuance of the relationship has the better chance of controlling and exploiting it. The principle of least interest is one facet of the *power-dependence relationship* which has relevance not only for the dating relationship but for family interaction as well. Since the relationship between power and dependency is of crucial importance in understanding the male–female relationship, we will consider it in some depth here.

The Power-Dependence Relationship

Power is to be understood as the *potential* for getting someone else to do what he or she would rather not do.[2] It does not necessarily mean that the power *will* be used to exploit; nevertheless the potential for such use is inherent in the relationship. A person may or may not want to exploit another, but whether he has the chance to do so depends upon the relationship. The person who consistently finds himself exploited by others is saying more about his perception of himself and the relationships than about the characters of the exploiters.

The power distribution in a relationship is related to the relative dependence of the two parties on the relationship. The power of Boy A over Girl B is equal to the dependency of Girl B on Boy A. Conversely, her power over him is equal to his dependency on her. They can be nearly equal in their dependency on each other, in which case they will have equal power. They may both feel relatively secure in the relationship, or equally insecure, but neither will be able to force the other to do anything he does not wish to do, without losing as much as he gains. It can be unequal in either direction, depending upon the amount of dependency in the relationship.

The relative dependency is related to two factors:

1. The emotional commitment each has to the goals controlled by the other.
2. The number of alternative sources each has for obtaining these goals.

John Jenkins may be a powerful dominant male who has gotten his own way in his family and with numerous others. He may see himself as the dominant partner in his relationship with Mary Martin. But if Mary Martin doesn't happen to admire these traits or is less committed to him

[2] This discussion leans heavily on Richard M. Emerson (1962).

than he is to her, John Jenkins' lion-like characteristics will melt into kitten-like docility where Mary is concerned. In fact, one of the things which makes him dependent upon her may be that she makes him feel powerful while they both do what she wants. Her power may not show until he tries to get her to do something she does not want to do.

The Power Structure in Dating.   The power structure is quite useful in understanding many early dating relationships. Most young people are rather highly motivated to date, some more so than others. Since each must have a partner to do so, the rudiments of a power structure are present. Let us assume that Betty wants very much to date. There are a number of activities at school which require dates if one is going to participate. Besides, her friends date and her self-concept is shaken if she cannot prove to herself that she can attract and hold the attention of a male. Al is the only boy who occasionally asks her out. He likes to date, too, but he has little trouble getting dates. He sometimes takes out Mary, and also Jane. He also is on the basketball team, which is an important source of his self-esteem.

The power structure begins to take shape. No matter how gentle and passive Al is, or how domineering Betty is, their relationship will be colored by the power structure. Al may find himself more assertive and Betty more passive in this than in other relationships. Because of their unequal dependence on each other for reaching certain desired goals, in this relationship Al is much more powerful than Betty. Al is not as emotionally committed as Betty to dating, per se, as a source of self-esteem. Furthermore, he has more alternative sources for obtaining dates.

If Al decides to exploit the situation, let us say through demanding more sexual intimacy than Betty wants to engage in, Betty is faced with a dilemma. Assume that Betty comes from a family which has instilled strong restrictive sex values in her. She also has a group of girl friends who feel the same way she does. If she gives in to Al's demands, she must reevaluate her self-concept; run the risk of the negative evaluation of her friends if they find out; but still she has not changed the power structure. In fact, she may be *more* dependent on the relationship, for Al now has information which she would not want known. If, on the other hand, she does not give in to his demands, she runs the risk of losing the relationship completely. Since the power structure doesn't change whether she meets his requests or not, she is still vulnerable to further demands from him.[3]

---

[3] An illustration of the effect of different motivations and involvements in the dating relationship is found in a study of the dating experiences of student nurses (Skipper and Nass, 1966).

Changing the Power Structure. If she is to be relieved of the pressure, her actions must change the power structure. By looking back at the two factors influencing the power structure, we see only four ways of altering the unbalanced structure:

1. *Increase Al's emotional commitment to goals mediated by Betty.* Obviously, since he is not going with her just to date, she would have to increase his interest in her in other ways. She improves her looks, redoes her hair, finds out what he's interested in and learns to talk about it, makes him feel important, and so forth. If his commitment to her increases, her power over him begins to increase—in other words she can refuse his requests and not be as afraid that the relationship will end.

2. *Decrease Betty's emotional investment in goals mediated by Al.* Betty can decide the pressure is not worth it—"All men are pigs, I'll devote my life to science." She may decide it's more fun being with her girl friends anyway, or find other ways of enhancing her prestige among her peers. To the extent that she reduces her interest in the activities Al opens for her, his control over her is reduced.

3. *Decrease Al's alternative sources.* To the extent that Betty becomes Al's only source of dates, her power increases. This appears harder for girls to manipulate than for boys. The male culture supports the respect of the other fellow's "property" much more than does the female culture. Boys seem much more likely to be able to secure their friends' cooperation in walling off a particular female than do girls with reference to boys. Since girls seem much more interested in dating during the adolescent years than boys, they are more competitive among themselves (Henry, 1963, pp. 154-69). She may, however, do some things, such as attempting to make the other girls angry at him so that they refuse to go out with him.

4. *Increase Betty's alternative sources.* Of course, if Betty is able to attract another boy friend, her dependency on Al decreases drastically along with his power over her. Whether the relationship breaks with either of Betty's moves—increasing her alternatives or decreasing her commitment—will depend on Al's reaction and the introduction of different goals to be achieved by the relationship. It will no longer be based solely on the goal of dating, per se.

Much of the high school dating behavior can be understood as a reaction to an intuitive awareness of the factors influencing the balance of power. Thus, we hear them cautioning each other to play "hard to get," "Don't let him know how much you like him," and "Don't be too anxious." It takes a great amount of trust in another person to be comfortable in a relationship where one feels deeply committed and yet powerless.

Effect on the Self-Concept. Since adolescent dating offers the first exposure to sex-paired relationships, it is an important contributor to the continued learning of sex-roles. Adolescents are now involved in learning to be boys or girls in relation to an age peer of the opposite sex. It's very difficult to practice, for example, some facets of being a girl if one has no boy to call forth the appropriate responses. One aspect of this relationship is the ability to maintain a power balance which gives both persons a sense of trust and security. Perhaps the need to test one's ability to gain a comfortable amount of power in a paired relationship explains partially the tendency of many adolescents to lose interest in a relationship once the other person becomes interested. When the other person shows interest, it is, in itself, an indication that one can attain some control. Since much early dating behavior is concerned with finding out about oneself rather than reflecting real feelings toward someone else, the other person is no longer attractive when one has found out what he needed to know about himself in this relationship. And so he moves on to another relationship to test himself with someone else. As he gains confidence in his ability to gain and maintain some control in a cross-sex power structure, he can then move away from the ego-centered focus of early dating to the pair-oriented focus characteristic of more mature paired relationships.

Varying degrees of success or failure in the dating system would be expected to have an effect on the self-concept, considering the importance placed on it in the adolescent sub-culture. It would have an effect not only on the feelings of self-confidence in relating to and understanding the opposite sex, but on the self-evaluation which occurs as one encounters new "significant others" or is denied access to them by being excluded from dating. By way of analogy, one never knows himself as a father unless he has reared a child. There is a vacancy in the reciprocal role, precluding the experiencing of demands for certain kinds of responses which can then be evaluated.

One student described the effect of her dating experience on her self-concept as follows:

It seems to me there are three main ways that casual dating or going steady can influence a person. First of all, the reactions of others play a big part. If friends are envious and tell you how lucky you are to be going with "Mr. Big" the feelings of pride and self-esteem are great. If, on the other hand, friends and family disapprove, feelings of anxiety and doubt are likely to appear. Secondly, the way the person reacts to you during the relationship definitely influences the way you feel about yourself. He can treat you like a queen, and make you feel like one; treat you like a piece of dirt and make you miserable. However he treats you, he's telling you how you appear relative to him. And thirdly the way you feel toward him influences your feelings about yourself. A person who truly feels she is in love with someone, feels somewhat of a different person than before she loved.

When I was in junior high school, my girl friends were beginning to date. They had boy–girl parties and although I was always invited, I never had a date. I felt so awkward, and out of place and usually ended up going home to cry. I really felt like a failure—no looks, no personality, nothing to offer.

Fortunately, we moved to another town and a bigger high school and things changed fast. It really took my first "steady" realationship when I was 15 to change my ideas about myself, though. It only lasted ten months but it taught me many things. Joel was an intelligent boy, and we talked about everything for hours and hours. I learned about him and myself at the same time. He always treated me with respect and consideration, and gradually I began to see myself as worthy of that kind of treatment.

When he broke off with me it was a crushing event. For awhile I went right back to feeling like a failure again. Finally, though, after the worst was over, it began to dawn on me that I was still the same person, but just because a boy liked me at one time was no reason for me to expect it to be permanent. I had to be alert and treat him with consideration, too, if I wanted the relationship to continue. I don't think I'll ever forget what I learned from Joel, even though I've gone steady several times since. I was very fortunate to start out with him.

The next boy I went steady with seemed to bring out all my bad characteristics. Bob took me nice places and I was afraid to break up again so I kept going with him for a year and a half. He was self-centered and inconsiderate and I began to be almost like him. My parents didn't like him, and I felt like I had to defend him. I began to have trouble at home and felt like a rebellious teenager. It extended to all kinds of things. I didn't like myself and yet didn't want to lose the security of a "steady." Even as unpleasant as this relationship sometimes was, I preferred it to dating around. I found I had to have the security of a close relationship.

The relationship I am in now combines all the best parts of the earlier ones. We plan to be married after graduation in June. He really treats me like I am a person of value. I can truly say, now, that I am glad I am the person I am. He not only treats me like a queen, as Joel did, but this time I love him back, not just because of the way he makes me feel, but because of what he is, and how he makes me want to treat him.

The above description is a clear tracing of the development of heterosexual relationships from an ego-centered focus to a pair-oriented focus as the self-concept becomes stabilized and secure. The description vividly points out the effect of the relationship on the self-concept. One wonders if the consequences could have been as satisfactory if all of this person's early relationships had emphasized the negative personality characteristics, thereby intensifying the family conflict and the defensive view of self in the male–female relationship.

Kinds of Dating Patterns

There is a need for studies of the consequences of different kinds of dating experiences on the marital relationship. Studies up to the present have been concerned chiefly with beginning time of dating, frequency of dating, number of partners, age of marriage, premarital pregnancy, and their relationship to divorce (Burchinal, 1964, pp. 629–30). There are both confusions and conflicts in the findings. Most agree that dating is generally functional for the socialization and developmental processes of the individual and as preparation for courtship and the kind of marriage favored in our American middle classes.

There is disagreement over the functionality of "steady dating" at early ages. On the one hand it is seen to limit the experience with many members of the opposite sex, which supposedly aids in an intelligent choice of a mate. It is said to lead to intimate relationships which may confront the young persons with emotional and sexual decisions that they are not mature enough to make. On the other hand, it is seen to provide the opportunity for communication and understanding between the sexes contributing to good socialization for marriage.

It has been shown that the tendency to go steady seems to be strong in at least three groups. First, there are those from higher socioeconomic classes who have American-born parents with high education. These adolescents appear to start dating early, date casually for awhile, go steady, then go back to casual dating. They are likely to have several steady relationships during their high school years. The second group is comprised of students who are from lower socioeconomic classes and have at least one foreign-born parent. These teen-agers start dating later but very quickly slip into a steady relationship and are not as likely to revert to casual dating (Lowrie, 1961). The third group is made up of those going steady in high school and actually expecting to be married soon after. For them the steady dating *is* courtship (Herman, 1955).

If the steady pattern does encourage earlier marriages, especially among the lower socioeconomic groups, then it is perhaps dysfunctional since the highest percentage of divorces appear in this group. But it is not known whether it is the steady pattern itself or the economic pressures and general lower class norms which produce both the early marriages and the high percentage of divorces.

It appears that for the first group going steady does not limit severely the experience with a number of different people. Herman (1955) found that of the 52 per cent who went steady in high school only about one-third thought about marriage before high school graduation. About two-thirds of those who had gone steady in high school, had had at least two such relationships. This was substantiated by Heiss (1960b) who added a further note to the differences between types of steady relationships. The relationship was more likely to be considered a serious one if the couple thought marriage was a possibility soon after high school. This resembles the window shopping trip mentioned earlier. If a boy sees a car he would like to have, and there is some possibility that by working after school and on Saturdays he could buy it, it looms more and more important to him and he devotes all his efforts to get it. But if he can see no way to get the money within the next five years, he may dream a little, but then move on to the next window.

Relationship to Marriage. It may be that the "steady" relationship, per se, is not the primary mover toward early marriage but rather its occurrence in a particular social context which supports norms for marriage soon after high school. In other words, if the steady relationship is defined as a short-term, recreational relationship with some degree of commitment between the two people, it may offer a greater opportunity for sex-role learning partially relieved of the competition and exploitation previously associated with the uncommitted casual relationship. The greater depth of communication possible in a prolonged paired relationship may be of value in developing the male–female communication and understanding valued in today's middle class marriage.

At the same time, however, the interpersonal intimacy and privacy beneficial to developing understanding of the opposite sex, may create emotional and sexual tensions increasingly difficult for young people to handle. They may encourage the development of feelings likely to lead to sexual involvement, premarital pregnancy, and/or too-hasty marriage at too young an age. Whether the "multiple-steady" pattern is beneficial in providing socialization for stable marriage or detrimental in encouraging "too-early" or "ill-considered" marriages probably varies across our society depending upon the social context in which it takes place.

Bell and Chaskes (1970) suggest that the multiple-steady pattern is, perhaps, related to experiencing premarital coitus. In a study of 205 college females, it was discovered that coeds who had gone steady three or more times were more likely to have had coital experience (46 per cent) than were coeds who had gone steady one or two times (22 per cent). The higher percentage of premarital intercourse associated with more numerous "steady" relationships, was also associated with a greater number of different boys dated. Girls who dated 21 or more different boys had higher percentages of premarital coitus (36 per cent) than those dating 20 or less (14 per cent). The data can be interpreted as showing that it is probably not the steady relationship itself, however, which encourages sexual involvement. Of all the coeds who had ever been engaged and ever had coital experience, 75 percent had their first experience while dating, only 6 per cent while going steady, and 19 per cent during engagement (Bell and Chaskes, 1970, p. 84).

THE PRINCIPLE OF VALUE RELEVANCE

A particular dating pattern is neither "good" nor "bad" in itself. Its "goodness" or "badness" depends on the evaluation made of the consequences which are likely to flow from a particular kind of relationship. A dating pattern does not create sexual values, it merely enhances or limits the opportunity for values to be tested. The pattern is enacted in a particular cultural climate which either negatively or positively evaluates premarital sexual involvement or early marriage. If the pattern invites this behavior which is then negatively evaluated, it is likely to be seen as bad and have negative consequences for the pair involved. In another situation the same behavior producing the same consequences may be seen as good and have positive consequences for the pair.

The steady pattern as it is developing probably does offer a greater opportunity for premature sexual involvement. It probably also allows a broader possibility for the development of male–female understanding than older dating forms. Perhaps it is impossible to develop one of these without including the other. Whether one or the other is emphasized however, will depend not upon the pattern but upon the values the individuals carry into it, the amount of protection and support offered by families as their youngsters enter the pattern, and the amount of consensus between the individuals in defining their commitments to the relationship.

SUMMARY

The dating system is a typically American innovation which developed during the present century from the coeducational public school system in a cultural climate stressing individualism, freedom, and equality. It has changed from its emphasis on random dating in the 1920's to the "going steady" pattern associated with recent years. Although the steady pattern appears to have different meanings and different consequences associated with social class and future aspirations, it is largely characterized by short commitments which are only expected to last as long as they are emotionally satisfying.

Early dating is described as potentially exploitative since it lacks a true commitment to the other person. It is seen as a relationship in which the partners play at love without actually meaning it. It can perhaps be seen as socialization for more serious involvements. The exploitative nature of early dating makes the power-dependency relationship important for understanding the interaction and consequences of the relationship.

Since adolescent dating offers the first exposure to a sex-paired relationship, it is an important contributor to the continued learning of sex-roles and the evaluation of self from the perspective of the opposite sex. The going steady relationship perhaps offers an opportunity for sex-role learning partially relieved of the competition and exploitation associated with the totally uncommitted casual date. At the same time it provides the privacy and interpersonal intimacy which may encourage sexual experience.

Whether this dating pattern is seen as "good" or "bad" depends upon the evaluation of its consequences in different social groups.

QUESTIONS AND PROJECTS

1. Discuss the advantages and disadvantages of the current dating patterns in high school. Can you suggest some changes in the dating system which would enhance the advantages and reduce the disadvantages inherent in it now?

2. If you were a high school counselor how would you counsel high school students about "steady" relationships? If you were a parent how would you react to your high school son or daughter going steady? Explain your position.

3. Analyze your present or a past relationship in terms of its power structure. Describe the behaviors which have been used to gain additional power in the relationship. What were the reactions of the other party?

4. Describe how the self-concepts may influence the power structure in a relationship.

5. Discuss the clues used to communicate the movement from a "dating game" to a more committed relationship. Is there agreement on the clues?

6. What do you think of the suggestion that the kind of relationship which may be the best preparation for marriage also heightens the probability of premature sexual involvement? What solutions can you suggest?

7. Some people have suggested that those people who do not date frequently probably will make the best marital partners. Give arguments to support this statement and arguments against it. What are the conditions under which it may be true? Under which it may be false?

9
Premarital Sex

It is on the sexual level that men and women interact most intimately. Relationships of this kind carry with them great feeling and far-reaching consequences. They can bring either happiness or misery, depending upon how well they are understood and used in the furtherance of human purposes.

Sex means more than the anatomical structures and physiological processes that have to do with mating and reproduction. It is all of that, but it is also a part of the emotions and the social processes. Sexual behavior is a very complex phenomenon relating to the whole of life; it is rooted in biology to be sure, but in psychology and sociology as well.

In filling out a campus questionnaire one college freshman is reported to have started as follows:

Age:	18
Religion:	None
Sex:	Yes

Though he was probably trying to be facetious, his answer on sex does illustrate some of the confusion and distortion so prevalent in this field today.

DEVELOPMENT OF SEXUAL PERSPECTIVE

To some persons sex is a mania; to others, a phobia. Some are obsessed with sex, finding little else to think about, or talk about, or participate in. Life for them becomes one continual process of erotic stimulation, of overindulgence and dissipation. Others are repulsed by sex, regarding it as evil, and living in constant fear or dread. For such people, life usually means either celibacy or frigidity—and frustration.

Many take a less extreme view. They regard sex as important; as a part of life to be accepted, controlled, enjoyed, and used constructively. For them, the sexual component becomes only a part of the total male–female relationship, a way of expressing and enhancing the emotional commitment rather than a way of proving one's power or something to be endured because of man's animalistic nature. These varying perspectives develop during the socialization process and reflect the place sex occupies in the total society as well as the attitudes toward it in the particular social context and family in which the individual grew.

Types of Sexual Behavior

Considered broadly, human sexual activity falls logically into three categories, according to whether the orientation is toward oneself (autosexuality), toward others of the same sex (homosexuality), or toward others of the opposite sex (heterosexuality).

Although descriptive of adult behavior, the three orientations can also be seen as stages in a very normal developmental process through which one finally reaches the heterosexual orientation associated with marriage.

1. *Autosexuality,* sometimes called *autoeroticism,* refers to sexual behavior that is oriented toward oneself. On the psychological plane its most common form is *narcissism,* the narcissistic individual being one who loves himself and is more or less incapable of directing his love interests toward another person. On the physical plane, *masturbation* or self-stimulation, often to the point of orgasm, is its most usual type. *Erotic dreams,* which frequently bring involuntary ejaculations to the normal adolescent male and which may bring orgasm to the female as well, should probably also be listed here.

2. *Homosexuality* describes the condition of love fixation on the same-sex level, male with male and female with female. It runs the gamut from ardent friendships to both crude and artful physical stimulations leading to orgasm. Variations are about as many and of the same kind as for heterosexual conduct, the chief difference being that in homosexuality the love object is of the same sex. Thus there is homosexual promiscuity, there are homosexual prostitutes, and there is homosexual incest.

3. *Heterosexuality* denotes love and sex responses between individuals of opposite sexes, males with females and females with males. By society at large this pattern is considered most normal. Not all heterosexual activity is within the mores, however. *Nonmarital sexual intercourse* includes the premarital, which takes place before marriage; the extramarital, which is during marriage but with someone other than the married mate; and the postmarital, which is sexual intercourse after divorce has taken place or during widowhood. Where sexual intercourse is for pay, the

term used is *prostitution;* where it is with a close blood relative such as a son, daughter, brother, or sister, the act is *incest;* where it is forced by the male it is called *rape.* Heterosexual stimulation short of intercourse is in this culture usually called *necking* when it involves just the lighter forms of kissing and embracing, and *petting* when there is some of the more intimate caressing and fondling. For before marriage, necking is about the only form that receives near universal approval. *Marital intercourse* is, of course, fully sanctioned by the group—except in cases of abuse.

The Orientations as Stages in Development

Psycho-sexual development in the individual may be thought of as occurring in three stages paralleling the three orientations just discussed.

The Autosexual Stage. All infants start from an autosexual orientation. The developmental process which, if successfully completed, will widen the focus on the self to include interest in and consideration for others, involves the development of a sexual concept of self along with the self-concept in other areas. If we interpret autosexuality broadly as an orientation it can be seen that one may engage in heterosexual activity and yet be interested only in his own desires, satisfactions, and motivations. As long as the sex object is considered a target only for one's own self-enhancement or satisfaction, the orientation is autosexual even if the behavior involves another person. This orientation is normal for young children and becomes part of the development of a mature sexual response.

The physical acts associated with the autosexual orientation come under evaluation, however, from the societal norms. For example, it was at one time claimed that masturbation led to insanity, weakened reproductive power, or caused other ailments of one sort or another. These claims are known now to be absolutely unfounded, the best medical opinion of the day being that masturbation results in no physical harm, except in extreme or violent instances. When disturbances do result, it is generally the result of the guilt, worry, or negative evaluation made of the act rather than the act itself.

Physical sexual responsiveness is developed also. It does not just appear because one has reached biological pubescence. Masturbation is seen to contribute to this development, when it does not fall under negative evaluations. It is normal with both sexes, but is more frequent with males than females. A certain amount is to be expected among children as they explore their bodies, and learn to define and accept their physical boundaries (see Chapter 5).

The Homosexual Stage. The homosexual stage is characterized by antagonisms toward the opposite sex, gang interests toward others of one's own sex, and strong friendships with, or even "crushes" on, selected persons of the same sex. At this level homosexual behavior is perfectly normal, and is but a passing stage for most boys and girls. Sullivan (1953, pp. 33–34, 248) suggests that the development of deep, same-sex friendships during the preadolescent period is extremely important in shifting away from the self-centeredness of early childhood. It becomes easier to shift interest from one's self if the other person is very like the self—same age and sex. It is easier to communicate with someone who sees things from the same perspective, has similar interests, and similar problems with parents and siblings.

The homosexual orientation may or may not involve physical sexual behavior. The relationship is the important aspect. If it does involve physical sexual acts, it is subject to the negative evaluations of our society. Where the family provides the framework for appropriate sex-role identification, this period gradually gives way to the heterosexual orientation associated with adolescence and adulthood. Occasionally, however, homosexual interests will become deeply implanted in the personality, and the person fails to make the heterosexual transition.

Too little is known concerning the causes. Nevertheless, professional opinion is that most homosexuality comes from social conditioning rather than biological nature (exceptions admitted), and that it relates to such things as these: overmothering a son so that he is kept emotionally dependent and attached, unable to shift his love interests to another woman; treating a girl as a boy, or a boy as a girl, so that these opposite roles become defined for the child as normal; overwarning the child against the opposite sex or in other ways discouraging or blocking his heterosexual adjustment. Sometimes an adolescent becomes introduced to the practice by seduction from someone more experienced or (and this is more common) by simply turning to homosexual love interests as an out when early heterosexual reachings are for one reason or another denied fruition. In any event, what happens is that the individual's love interests become fixated on the same sex level; he does not make the heterosexual transition and becomes homosexually habituated.

Other sexual aberrations—such as exhibitionism, voyeurism, fetishism, sadism, masochism, incest, and animal contacts—lie outside the scope of this book. Persons with special problems like these should seek professional help.

The Heterosexual Stage. The average person will move along quite naturally from the autosexual to the homosexual to the heterosexual stage of development without great difficulty or digression; the attainment of this latest stage should be regarded as a prerequisite for marriage.

This involves more than just a shift in object of sexual interest. It includes the orientation toward the total relationship. From this framework, a heterosexual orientation involves not only a *sexual* interest in the opposite sex but an interest which includes the *other person's* desires, satisfactions, and motivations as well as one's own. Our society is more successful in developing the physical heterosexual transition than in developing the total interpersonal heterosexual transition. Most persons have made the physical transition to heterosexuality by early adolescence, but it generally takes much longer to achieve the total interpersonal shift, if it is ever made.

Societal Influence on Sexual Values

The sex standard traditionally receiving the strongest support in our society has been the "double standard," which condones greater sexual freedom for the male than for the female. This was partially supported by beliefs of the biological differences between the sexes. Man was seen to have a stronger sex drive—woman was thought to have little or none! It was only in the early 1900's that the medical profession recognized that the average female was able to experience orgasm. Before that time, those females who did experience orgasm were thought to be abnormal. Since woman was not thought to have a sex drive, the only reason she would engage in sexual activity outside of marriage was seen to be because she was "immoral" or "bad." Although man's greater sex drive partially excused his behavior, all sex outside of marriage was still seen as evil.

In other words, because of the tie-in between a strong sex drive and masculinity, sexual activity with women who would allow it aided men in proving masculinity at the same time it created doubts about "character." This, together with the negative evaluations of female sexuality, has operated to produce some degree of sexual anxiety in most adults in our society.

Changing Sex Standards

Sex standards have been changing and although the direction of the change has been toward a single standard (judging both sexes equally), the shift is not yet complete. As a result, we have partial support for a variety of standards, ranging from the complete restriction of premarital coitus, per se, to specifying various kinds of relationships within which premarital coitus may be acceptable. Each standard has some supporters, but few can feel absolute confidence in the "rightness" of the one they support.

A study by Ira Reiss (1967, pp. 19–36) produced evidence of the variety of sex standards held simultaneously in our society. From the responses of students from both high school and college populations, plus a national sample of adults, he constructed four major standards with distinguishing sub-categories to cover the combinations of acceptable sexual behavior before marriage for each sex.[1]

I. Abstinence: Coitus not acceptable under any condition before marriage for either sex.
   A. Kissing with affection: The most intimate sexual behavior accepted for both males and females is kissing someone they feel strong affection for.
   B. Kissing without affection: Kissing, whether or not there is affection, is acceptable but nothing more intimate.
   C. Petting with affection: Petting is the most intimate behavior acceptable for both sexes, but only when there is strong affection.
   D. Petting without affection: Petting, whether or not there is affection is acceptable, but nothing more intimate.
II. Double standard: More permissive behavior accepted for one sex than the other.
   A. Orthodox: Males are allowed full sexual freedom; females are not.
   B. Transitional: Males are allowed full sexual freedom; females, only if in love or engaged.
   C. Reverse double standard: Logically, the reverse of the two double standards is possible, with the female being allowed greater sexual freedom than the male. Our society has no background to support these standards, however, and no study has found very many subscribing to them.
III. Permissiveness with affection: Premarital intercourse acceptable for both sexes if part of a stable affectionate relationship.
   A. Love: Love or engagement is a prerequisite for coitus.
   B. Affection: Strong affection is a sufficient prerequisite for coitus.
IV. Permissiveness without affection: Premarital coitus is acceptable for both sexes regardless of amount of affection.
   A. Orgiastic: Pleasure is the most important consideration.
   B. Sophisticated: Pleasure important, but precautions against veneral disease and/or pregnancy are of first importance.

The percentages of Reiss' student sample approving various types of premarital sexual behaviors are shown in Table 9–1. The greatest consensus occurs in the approval of kissing and petting under conditions of love and engagement. The rather sharp drop in percentages approving other behaviors indicates, at the very least, that there are differences of

[1] These categorizations are similar but more finely defined than those presented in Ehrmann (1959).

opinion among students concerning the conditions under which certain sexual behaviors are appropriate.

Table 9–1

Percentages Approving Each Type of Sexual Behavior for Males and Females

Behavior	Conditions	For Males	For Females
Kissing	Engaged	97.5	98.5
	Love	98.9	99.1
	Affection	97.2	97.8
	Any condition	64.2	55.2
Petting	Engaged	85.0	81.8
	Love	80.4	75.2
	Affection	67.0	56.7
	Any condition	34.3	18.0
Coitus	Engaged	52.2	44.0
	Love	47.6	38.7
	Affection	36.9	27.2
	Any condition	20.8	10.8

SOURCE: Ira L. Reiss, *The Social Context of Premarital Sexual Permissiveness* (New York: Holt, Rinehart & Winston, Inc., 1967). Adapted from Tables 2–9 and 2–10, pp. 30–31.

The higher percentages approving petting and coitus for males than for females give evidence that the double standard is still operating to some extent. It is clear, however, that for both sexes approval decreases as the behavior becomes more intimate and as the relationship indicates less commitment. This is the same tendency found with the Purdue sample discussed in the previous chapter.

SEXUAL BEHAVIOR

Sexual values are not the same thing as sexual behavior, although they are related. The most extensive study of sexual behavior was pioneered by Alfred C. Kinsey and his associates at the Institute for Sex Research at Indiana University. The work was begun in 1938, is still continuing, and is expected to continue for an indefinite period.[2] Although numerous criticisms have been leveled at the early volumes appearing from this research, the research findings do give us an indication of the changes oc-

[2] The summaries which follow are gleaned from various chapters and sections of two volumes concerning sexual behavior in males and in females (Kinsey *et al.*, 1948; 1953).

curring over time in premarital activity and point out some major male and female differences in sexual behavior and development.[3]

Intergenerational Trends

For males, Kinsey found almost no change over time. Except for lower-class males starting their sexual activities a little earlier, and college males engaging in a little more petting and doing it more openly than formerly, there have been no significant changes.

The same cannot be said for females, however. As a matter of fact, "decade of birth" proved to be one of the most significant factors explaining sexual variability among women. When females born prior to 1900 were compared with those born in subsequent decades, a significant trend was noted—in the direction of increasingly greater sexual activity and orgasm in the areas of masturbation, petting, and intercourse (both within and outside of marriage).

This lines up in a general way with Terman's earlier findings. By comparing older and younger generations as to per cent virgin at marriage, he found that premarital intercourse was rapidly on the increase for both sexes, but especially for the female; this meant both a changing of standards and a narrowing of the gap between male and female practices (Terman, 1938).

Thus the trend is one of convergence. There is more sexual activity today than formerly, especially for females. Males are still more sexually active than females—over-all, and in every category except petting—but differences are less now than they once were. This convergence in behavior is related to the growing emancipation of woman (see Chapter 7), it is being accomplished by increasing activity on the part of women rather than any decreasing of activity on the part of men. It seems probable, nevertheless, that the two lines will never meet completely, that women will never be as sexually active as men in all respects.

Life Cycle Patterns

Not only do males show substantially higher incidences and frequencies in sexual outlet, but they develop earlier and more rapidly along these lines than do females. According to Kinsey, each sex has a typical sexual cycle different from the other. The average male becomes sexually

[3] The major criticisms of Kinsey's work include the nonrandom nature of his samples; the impossibility of other researchers checking on the reliability of the results since the schedule guide was not made public; the over-emphasis on biological rather than psychological or sociological aspects of the subject; and the interpretations made of the data which in many cases went beyond the conclusions which could be supported by the findings.

active in early adolescence; reaches the peak of activity (measured by total orgasms per week) in late adolescence, or ages 16 to 20 (when he averages 3.4 outlets per week if he is single and 4.8 if he is married); and then tapers off gradually until old age, at which time his sexual activity may cease altogether. In contrast, the average female is not apt to be very active sexually during adolescence, though she will climb gradually to reach her peak in the late twenties and early thirties, after which she will maintain something of a plateau for a couple of decades, and then will decline again in the fifties and sixties. In terms of orgasm, the average female is never as sexually active as the average male, though she approaches it during middle and later life. But in terms of experience or participation in heterosexual acts, female percentages follow those of the male very closely (especially within marriage), since it is the male who determines the pattern.

Male–Female Comparisons

Kinsey has provided evidence which points to additional differences between the sexes. It has just been stated that sexual development comes earlier for males and that higher percentages of males participate in some sexual behavior.

Male activity also includes a greater variety of acts per person, reaches higher frequencies of experience in nearly every sexual outlet, and more often results in orgasm—as compared with females.

Females, as a group, show a much longer range and spread in sexual activity than do males. On the one hand, there are larger numbers of females than males who are totally uninterested and unresponsive sexually; and, on the other hand, there are a few females whose desires and capacities go beyond those of most males. Where the desire is insatiable it is known as *nymphomania*. This phenomenon is generally characterized by lack of orgasmic response and multiple partners.

The average female is less interested than males in physical sex as such. She can take it or leave it, depending upon how it lines up with her other interests. As a consequence, her sex life is usually more intermittent or discontinuous than that of males, and she is more easily distracted or diverted to other thoughts during the sex act. In contrast, the average male feels a sex drive that is more physical, urgent, and constant.

Closely related to the above is the finding that females are less influenced by psychosexual stimuli such as erotic literature, obscene art, and other forms of pornography. Furthermore, females do much less dreaming and fantasying about sex than do males; and they are much less likely to participate in such perversions as *exhibitionism* (sexual satisfaction from displaying one's own genitalia), or *voyeurism* (sexual satisfaction from observing others intimately, as do "Peeping Toms"). Since males are more conscious of these associated stimuli in our culture, they are more easily aroused sexually than are females.

Females are less promiscuous than males. For example, for those who participate in premarital intercourse, the average number of partners is fewer and the percentage confining their activity to the engaged person only is greater than for males. In Kinsey's data, nearly half of the female participants in premarital intercourse confined their activity to one person, and for many of these it was the engaged partner, with intercourse taking place shortly before marriage.

It almost goes without saying that there are numerous individual exceptions to all of this. We have been reporting here what seems to be average or typical. Though there are important differences between men and women, it must also be kept in mind that there are tremendous variations within each sex group and that there are margins of overlapping between the groups.

The general trends and major differences between the sexes reported first by Kinsey have received support from subsequent studies. However, the percentages engaging in various kinds of sexual activities at any particular time are less important than the conditions under which these acts take place or the consequences they have for future relationships. The actual extent of premarital intercourse is unknown, but there is some evidence concerning the social characteristics and attitudes of those likely to engage in it.

Effect of Values on Behavior

The dominant value system in a society produces a milieu which influences not only attitudes, but also behaviors. It also influences the reactions to behavior which are not in accord with beliefs. The influence of cultural values was tested by Christensen and Carpenter in 1960 using three cultural climates which vary in sexual permissiveness. They contrasted students from a Danish university, from a university in midwestern United States, and from a university of the intermountain region of the United States having a high percentage of Mormons in its student body (Christensen and Carpenter, 1962). It was assumed that the Mormon group represented the most extreme of the three on sexual restrictiveness. The midwestern group was expected to be somewhat more permissive yet still strongly influenced by restrictive norms. The Danish group on the other hand was assumed to represent the most permissive position, because of Denmark's long history of premarital permissiveness associated with committed relationships. The assumptions were tested with a ten-item permissiveness scale which validated the assumed differences between the groups. They arranged themselves along a continuum of permissiveness ranging from zero to ten, as shown in Figure 9–1. The percentages of students experiencing premarital coitus varied directly with the permissiveness of the value systems. The effect of the double standard was noted in the greater differences between males and females in the two American samples than in the Danish sample.

Although it is not apparent from Figure 9–1, in both American groups the percentage experiencing premarital coitus exceeded the percentage approving the behavior. The reverse was true of the Danish sample. It would be expected, then, that the consequences of premarital coitus

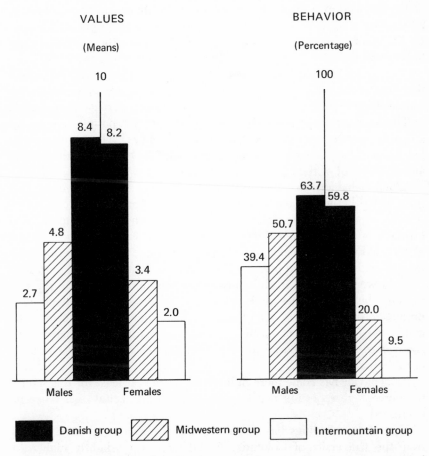

Fig. 9–1. Mean sexual permissiveness and percentage having premarital coital experience by sex and culture. (Adapted from Christensen and Carpenter, 1962.)

would differ between the cultures. This effect can be inferred from the finding that a much larger percentage of Danish students (males 72 per cent; females 73 per cent) reported pleasant reactions after first coital experience, than either the midwestern (males 45 per cent; females 35 per cent), or intermountain (males 33 per cent; females 14 per cent) groups. Values, then, affect not only behavior but the consequences of the behavior for the individual (Christensen and Carpenter, 1962).

This study was repeated in 1968, using the same measuring devices and comparable groups of students (Christensen and Gregg, 1970). On the whole the same differences were found but with an increase in permissiveness in all three samples. One hundred per cent of Danish males and females approved of premarital coitus in a committed relationship. In the midwestern sample, the percentage of females approving went up 20 per cent and males 8 per cent to 38 per cent and 55 per cent respectively. Interestingly enough, although 55 per cent of the males approved of premarital coitus, 75 per cent of them said they would prefer marrying someone who had not had previous coitus. This to some extent suggests that at least for some males the more permissive sex norms have a double standard foundation which comes into focus when marriage is mentioned.

The intermountain group also showed an increased permissiveness with again the greatest change occurring among females. They were still below the level of the midwestern group, with 24 per cent of the females and 38 per cent of the males reporting approval.

When behavior was investigated, the Danish group showed a clear relationship between values and behavior with about 95 per cent of each sex claiming coital experience. In each of the other two samples, coital experience was up for females but not for males. Fourteen per cent more of the midwestern females and 23 per cent more of the intermountain females had experienced premarital coitus in 1968 as compared with 1958.

Data were analyzed in the midwestern sample to investigate the relationship between values and behavior. Values appeared much more predictive of behavior in 1968 than in 1958. Eighty-two per cent of the males and 78 per cent of the females with premarital coitus had permissive values. This compared to 65 per cent of the males and 41 per cent of the females in 1958.

As behavior has come more in line with values, at least for this sample, the percentage reporting negative reactions to first coital experience has decreased.

Very similar findings have been reported by Kaats and Davis (1970) from the University of Colorado. Coital rates were slightly higher (41 per cent for females and 60 per cent for males) than in the midwestern sample discussed above. Males were more likely to express permissive norms than were the females. Further, males were likely to respond in

terms of a single permissive standard. The females, however, were likely
to respond more permissively for males than for themselves.

The double standard was in clear evidence when the responses were
in terms of the future spouse instead of males and females in general.
Among this highly permissive group of men, 45 per cent thought that
virginity was important in a future mate, while only 17 per cent thought
it important for themselves. The females showed a reverse trend, being
more likely to value virginity in themselves than in their future husbands.

Reiss (1967) also tested the relationship between values and behavior,
with results quite similar to Christensen's midwestern sample. With an
Iowa College sample he found that the current sex standard was highly
predictive of the most extreme sexual behavior the student was likely to
engage in. His study approaches from the other direction, however,
looking at the behavior of those holding a particular value. Figure 9–2

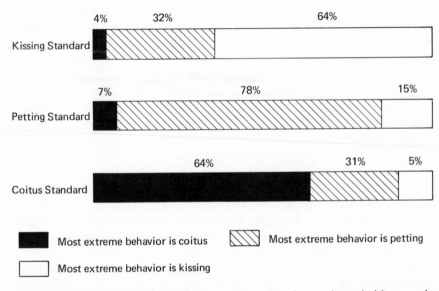

Fig. 9–2. Most extreme behavior engaged in by students holding each
sexual standard. (Adapted from Reiss, 1967, p. 117.)

shows that not all persons actually engage in behavior as permissive as
they believe is acceptable. Over one-third of those accepting premarital
coitus had not experienced it. This was mainly the result of lack of opportunity or approval of the behavior dependent on love or engagement,
which had not yet occurred. On the other hand over one-third of those
professing the non-accepability of any behavior beyond kissing had engaged in more intimate behavior.

Sex Differences in Value-Behavior Discrepancy. Engaging in behavior which exceeded the standard was more descriptive of females than males. Males who accepted either the kissing or petting standards were not as likely as females to engage in more intimate behavior (Reiss, 1967, pp. 116–17). This is undoubtedly related to the male role as initiator. If a man does not believe petting or intercourse is acceptable, he is not likely to initiate the behavior. The female, on the other hand, is much more likely to face the situation of a male pressing for behavior beyond the limits of her standards. Her standards, then, are much more likely to be tested in actual situations than the male's. She is more likely to slightly exceed her standards because of the press of a particular situation, a demanding partner, or her own emotional response. The effect of behavior which exceeds the standards on value change will be discussed later in this chapter.

The differences found among Reiss's respondents in both values and behavior, as well as the differences between the two American student groups studied by Christensen and Carpenter (and later by Christensen and Gregg) point up the variation in our own culture. One of the major factors in explaining this variation is the amount of exposure to groups supporting different norms. Probably one of the most important influences supporting traditional norms is the church. Although churches differ in their stand on sexual permissiveness, it is probably safe to assume that all churches in our society support some degree of sexual restraint before marriage.

Influence of Religion. Studies have been practically unanimous in showing a relationship between religiosity and premarital sex standards. If we assume that the churches have represented conservative standards concerning sexual morality, then it would be expected that a higher percentage of those coming under its influence would be non-permissive. Reiss's student sample supported this, as shown in Figure 9–3.

The relationship between church attendance and non-permissiveness is much stronger for whites than blacks, and for females than males. Sex differences are much stronger than racial differences when church attendance is low. However, when high church attendance becomes a factor, both the racial and sex differences are large. Reiss suggests that within the black culture, church attendance means something quite different than within the white culture. Historically, the restrictive sex norms stemming from early Christianity have had a much greater impact on the white culture than on the black culture (see Chapter 3). The traditional sex norms among blacks have been relatively permissive of premarital intercourse. This stems from the loose family structure associated with slavery. It may be hypothesized that as the black becomes more integrated into

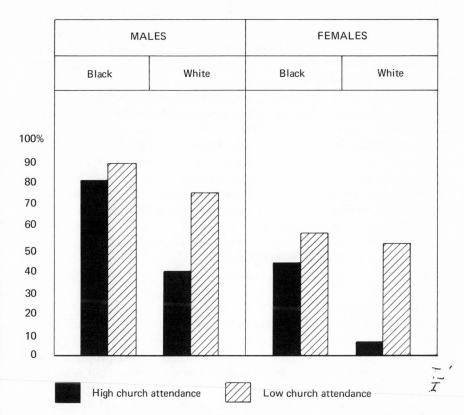

	MALES		FEMALES	
	Black	White	Black	White

Fig. 9–3. Percentage holding highly permissive sex attitudes according to race, sex, and church attendance. (Adapted from Reiss, 1967, Tables 3–2, p. 43.)

the dominant, middle class, white culture, he will also come under the influence of the more restrictive norms, if they remain strong.

The above discussion concerns attitudes only. There is evidence, however, that behavior as well is strongly related to religiosity. Kanin and Howard showed that premarital intercourse with intended spouse was strongly related to church attendance of the partners (Kanin and Howard, 1958). Where both partners were high church attenders, 28 per cent engaged in premarital coitus. When only one was a high church attender, the percentage rose to 48 per cent, and to 61 per cent when both were non-attenders.

Another study using unmarried college students showed an increase in coitus as church attendance declined (Scheck, 1967). For males, the percentages increased from 21 per cent of those who attended church three to four times monthly, to 41 per cent of those attending one or two times a month, to 49 per cent for those who attended less than once a month. The corresponding percentages for females were, respectively, 14, 26, and 38 per cent. This study, however, was restricted to sexual behavior in only one relationship, and was not concerned with the most intimate behavior ever experienced.

Although the above studies were based upon restricted samples (in one case, married persons and in the other, persons in love), the relationship between religiosity and premarital coitus is the same as that found by Kinsey in his much larger samples (Kinsey *et al.*, 1953, p. 304). Among women who had not married by age 35, the percentage engaging in coitus rose from 24 per cent to 55 per cent for Catholics, and from 30 per cent to 60 per cent for Protestants and Jews, as church attendance declined.

Exposure to religion, then, appears to be strongly related to both values and behavior in the sexual area. It is difficult to tell, however, whether it is the effect of religious values, per se, or whether certain highly conservative families are most likely to attend church, insist that their children attend, and also transmit restrictive norms.

Influence of the Family. From our earlier discussions of the development of the self and the learning of values (Chapter 5) we would expect that family values would be a strong influencing factor. Some writers have suggested that the sexual permissiveness of young people is essentially a rebellion against parental restrictiveness. Several studies do show differences between the generations, with the parental generation holding less permissive views (Reiss, 1967; Bell and Buerkle, 1961). It is difficult to tell whether this is an actual generational difference in sexual permissiveness or a difference in role perspective. Christensen and Carpenter's data show that when college men and women were asked about the degree of sexual permissiveness they would support for their daughters, they responded much more restrictively than for themselves (Carpenter, 1960, p. 98).

Reiss reported that only about one-third of his respondents saw themselves as differing from their mothers on sex standards. Most of these saw themselves as more permissive than the other two-thirds who saw themselves as holding standards resembling their mothers. However, about 79 per cent of the black males and 50 per cent of the white males who said their standards resembled their mothers' were highly permissive. Among the females who saw their standards as resembling their mothers' 40 per cent of the blacks and only 18 per cent of the whites were permissive. This suggests that, especially for males, permissive sex norms for many are not indications of rebelliousness but actually agreement with standards they perceive as being supported by their mothers (Reiss, 1967, pp. 130–

34). Needless to say, this does not mean that their mothers would necessarily agree that these are the standards they supported for their children. It may be that a parent transmits a different perception of his permissiveness to his children depending upon his own actual permissiveness as a young person, even though consciously attempting to teach restrictive norms. This would fit with the interactionist theory of the way in which values are transmitted, but unfortunately we have no studies which touch on this suggestion.

Influence of the Male–Female Relationship. The influences mentioned so far are those furnished by the person's social context of society, church, and family. These initial values are reinforced or changed as the young people move out of the family, form friendship groups, and have opportunity to interact with the opposite sex. Since the male culture seems to support much more permissive standards than the female culture, the female's permissiveness would be expected to increase as she has more interaction with males. In other words, her initial restrictive values are subjected to pressure for change as she comes in contact with the male's permissive standards and also as she develops an affectionate relationship with a male, heightening her own emotional response. This was supported by Reiss's data. The female's sexual permissiveness increased with the number of steady relationships, and also with the number of love relationships (Reiss, 1967, pp. 86–87).

Change in values seemed related also to the female's experience with behavior which exceeded her own standards. If, for example, she felt that only kissing was acceptable in an affectionate relationship but actually engaged in petting in one such relationship, she was likely to experience guilt. The guilt did not seem to halt the behavior, however. In only about one-fourth of the cases was the guilt-producing behavior stopped. Of the three-fourths who continued, about 90 per cent of them eventually came to accept the more permissive standard (Reiss, 1967, pp. 111–19).

The crucial factor producing increased permissiveness appears to be, then, the strength of the values inculcated within the family. If these values are not strong enough to prevent the more permissive behavior from ever occurring, under any condition, the probability is high that the standards will change as close interaction with the opposite sex continues. This is more true today than in the past, since the family no longer can so closely supervise the dating relationships of its teen-agers. The values are the main watchdogs of behavior.

It appears, then, that the steady dating pattern discussed earlier produces the situation within which pressures on the female for developing more permissive standards are high. Whether she actually changes appears related to the strength of the family values and the experience she has in the kind of relationships which heighten the probability that her behavior will at some time exceed her standards. Reiss states:

The key determinant of how permissive a female is sexually and what she will eventually accept, then, seems to involve her basic values, to the extent that these values must prevent certain sexual behavior from occurring if she is· to remain low on permissiveness, for three out of four females continue to engage in behavior that makes them feel guilty, and almost nine out of ten of these eventually come to accept it (Reiss, 1967, p. 113).

Whether the values prohibit behavior exceeding them depends partly on other things besides their strength. Although 89 per cent of the females in Kinsey's sample who had not engaged in premarital coitus said that moral considerations had been of primary importance, many of them also recognized other factors. About 45 per cent of them said that their own lack of sexual responsiveness was a contributing factor. In other words, as Kinsey suggests, it is easier not to sin if one has neither the physical nor psychological capacity to do so. The slower sexual development of the female probably aids many of them in living by restrictive standards. It probably also keeps them from understanding the more highly developed responses of their young male partners. Twenty-two per cent admitted abstaining because they had had no opportunity. Again, it is easier not to sin if there is no one to sin with. Fear of pregnancy was a factor for forty-four per cent of them. The same percentage cited fear of public opinion, which Kinsey was inclined to interpret as fear of engaging in an unfamiliar activity (Kinsey *et al.*, 1964).

Living up to restrictive standards, then, can mean many different things besides strong moral values. For some it means little more than that the opportunity has never arisen. For others, it means they are still sexually immature and have not recognized the problem. Some abstain, not from moral values, but for fear of reducing marriage chances, of becoming pregnant, or because of a fear of sex itself. But some are mature sexually, have had the opportunity, and have tested the strength of their values. Consequently, saying that women who abstain from premarital sex are morally stronger than those who don't may be misstating the situation.

More attention has been devoted to the reasons females abstain from premarital coitus than to the reasons males do. This reflects the traditional view of the male that he is continually sexually aroused and is controlled mainly by the female's resistance. According to Ehrmann's study of college males, the four reasons most frequently given for not going farther in sexual behavior varied according to the type of relationship, as well as according to the values of the male (see Table 9–2).

Although morals appeared among the top four reasons given for not going farther in all of the relationships, its percentage was only strong in

Table 9–2

Most Frequently Mentioned Reasons for Males Not Engaging
in More Intimate Sexual Behavior
(by type of relationship and sex standard)

	Relationship with Acquaintances				
	Conservative		Double Standard		Liberal
1	Respect for date	25%	Respect for date	35%	Date would not	45%
2	Timidity	24	Date would not	21	Respect for date	20
3	Date would not	22	Morals	19	Morals	10
4	Morals	16	Timidity	13	No opportunity	8

	Relationship with Friends				
	Conservative		Double Standard		Liberal
1	No desire	23%	Date would not	32%	Date would not	50%
2	Timidity	19	Respect for date	26	Respect for date	18
3	Respect for date	17	Morals	15	No opportunity	10
4	Morals	14	No opportunity	9	Morals	8
					No desire	8

	Relationship with Lovers				
	Conservative		Double Standard		Liberal
1	Respect for date	37%	Morals	45%	Date would not	47%
2	Morals	27	Respect for date	38	Respect for date	19
3	Date would not	18	Date would not	9	No opportunity	12
4	Fear	6	Fear	5	Morals	10
	Self-respect	6				

SOURCE: Adapted from Winston Ehrmann, *Premarital Dating Behavior* (New York: Holt, Rinehart & Winston, Inc., 1959), Table 6–4, p. 292. Reprinted by permission of Holt, Rinehart & Winston, Inc.

the relationship with lovers for double standard males. With acquaintances and friends it ran a poor third or fourth in every standard. The double standard males chose "respect for date" and "date would not" as the two most frequently given reasons for both acquaintances and friends, resembling the liberals. With lovers, though, "morals" took first place with "respect for date" second.

Among those with liberal standards the "date would not" was by far the most frequent reason in all three types of relationships, followed by "respect for date" as a poor second.

The conservative males were more likely to list "timidity" and "no desire" with friends. Only with lovers did "morals" enter the picture as a second to "respect for date" (Ehrmann, 1959, pp. 288–93).

The female's value system seems more important as a control mechanism with highly permissive males, and in uncommitted relationships with the double standard male. The conservative male, however, is more likely to feel that it is his own timidity and lack of desire which holds him back in uncommitted relationships and only becomes aware of his value system as a deterrent, in love relationships. Whether it is the value system affecting the timidity and desire or the other way around is not known.

The male is likely to become more permissive with age and with exposure to groups supporting more permissive standards than his own. He is less likely to be influenced by the number or type of opposite sex relationships. He is less likely to change standards than the female, but this is mainly because he tends to start out with more permissive standards.

CONSEQUENCES OF PREMARITAL SEXUAL BEHAVIOR

This discussion of the consequences of permissive sexual behavior is to be confined to the uncommitted relationship. We are not concerned, here, with petting or coitus during the engagement period and its effect on the marital relationship. This will be discussed in a later chapter.

The prevailing value system in the United States which still largely supports chastity before marriage, especially for the female, has its greatest impact on the casually dating couple. Casual dating implies lack of commitment, which opens the individuals to the possibility of exploitation by the other party. It also implies a relative lack of responsibility for the consequences of the behavior, heightening the probability of exposure to disease and unwanted pregnancies.

For these reasons, the greatest concern has been over the sexual behavior of young persons in the early stages of dating. Their immaturity probably makes it less likely that they have had sufficient experience to foresee the consequences, or to manage their own emotional responses. Thus, the concern is not only with premarital coitus but with the petting behavior which must be seen as a prelude to it.

The Petting Problem

Most of the recent evidence suggests that the greatest rise in permissive behavior has been in petting. As shown in Chapter 8, Figure 8–3, about twenty eight per cent of the Purdue sample of females, and seventy per cent of the males, approved intimate petting in a dating relationship. This is to be compared with the fifty-seven per cent of Reiss's student sample who said it was acceptable for females in a relationship where she felt affection for the partner and sixty-seven per cent who approved for the male in the same kind of relationship. Neither wording of the statement implied commitment to the relationship in terms of either love or engagement.

There is a school of thought which claims that premarital intimacy may actually be an aid to marital adjustment. The argument runs something like this: Frigidity and impotence are largely the products of sociocultural inhibitions. In order to control children and youth, we teach them that sex is wrong. Then, after twenty or more years of this kind of conditioning, we let marriage take place and expect them to be sexually adjustable —overnight. Kinsey's findings seem to support this contention for he reports a positive correlation between premarital petting and sexual adjustment in marriage.

Counterarguments are about as follows: (1) Granted that some non-petters may also be cold in marriage, there is no proof that the relationship is a causal one. The likely thing is that non-petting and frigidity are both the result of negative sex education, rather than one being the cause of the other. (2) Granted, also, that the transition into complete intimacy is more successful when it is gradual, there is nothing to show that *all* of the transition needs to come before the marriage ceremony. (3) Instead of aiding marital adjustment, in some cases premarital petting actually serves as a hindrance.

There is the possibility of habituation in response patterns, which means that a person (especially the female) who becomes accustomed to responding sexually and emotionally on the petting level may remain satisfied with that and find difficulty transferring to complete sexual intercourse in marriage. In this way intimate and continued petting can be a factor in the development of frigidity. There is, however, no empirical evidence either to support or to refute this. Then there is the factor of guilt feelings imposed by the culture.

Reiss presents evidence that petting behavior appears to produce more guilt feelings than either kissing or coitus when the behavior engaged in is at the same level as the standards. In other words, a boy or girl who thinks it is all right to pet is much more likely to feel guilty about petting than is the one who believes it is all right to have coitus and does so. This perhaps results from the in-between nature of petting. It may excite emotions which bring forth guilt when one feels that complete sexual gratification is wrong before engagement or marriage. It may also be that different levels of petting are subsumed under the same category, so that there are more cases of standards being exceeded within this category than the others.

The Progressive Nature of Intimacy Development. The acceptance of petting, and especially the age at which it is accepted is related to the eventual acceptance of coitus. Reiss's sample suggests that the average age of acceptance of petting by the female who will eventually accept premarital coitus is shortly after the sixteenth birthday. For the female who is not going to accept premarital coitus, at least before completion of college, the average age of acceptance is shortly before the eighteenth birthday. Only an extremely small number accepted coitus without the intervening step of petting. The girls who did, accepted kissing a full year younger (11.4 years average age) than those who moved through the intervening step of petting. Their average age of accepting coitus was shortly before the eighteenth birthday compared to shortly after the nineteenth birthday for those who moved through the petting stage (Reiss, 1967, p. 110).

The progressive nature of the growth toward permissiveness probably points to the difficulties encountered when two persons are involved in emotion-laden behavior which may be interpreted differently by them. A relatively light form of petting, acceptable to the female, may convey to the male that she is accessible for more intense involvement. Both are likely to feel angry or confused, experience a loss of trust in the opposite sex, and/or a negative evaluation of self as subsequent behavior makes their misinterpretations apparent.

Kirkpatrick and Kanin have reported on dating episodes involving male aggressiveness and female feelings of being offended. Their sample was 291 girls at a midwestern university. Of these, more than half said that they had been offended by some level of erotic intimacy, and more than one-fifth by forceful attempts at intercourse, during a single academic year. The majority of these episodes involved necking and petting above the waist, with petting below the waist coming next in frequency, and attempted intercourse last. Curiously, very few of these girls reported the offense to parents or other authorities. Most of them—though feeling angry, guilty, fearful, disgusted, or confused—simply kept it to themselves, or avoided the man and warned others about him. Their tendency to keep it to themselves increased to the extent of their involvement in some kind of sex play with the male prior to the offensive act. This was probably related to a belief that they had been partly to blame for the male's aggressive behavior (Kirkpatrick and Kanin, 1952).

Perhaps one of the main difficulties in a society which settles on petting as an accepted type of premarital activity is the placing of responsibility on young persons for controlling emotions and bodily responses which are at the same time stimulated and refused completion. Sexual control, if this is the goal of society, would seem to be easier to achieve if the restrictions were imposed before this level of stimulation and intimacy was reached. At an older age, with more experience, this difficulty may not be a factor.

Premarital Intercourse

Much of the reaction to premarital intercourse among teen-agers concerns the contribution of this behavior to several social problems: disease, unwanted pregnancy, and its consequences in abortion, marital disturbances, and divorce. These consequences are most pronounced within the uncommitted relationship, where responsibility for the other person is lacking.

Venereal Disease. Given present medical knowledge, this problem could be brought under control with adequate sex education *and* a sense of responsibility to others. The incidence of venereal disease was greatly reduced after World War II as a result of large-scale attention focused on it. Anxiety about it declined when the incidence decreased, and venereal disease was largely written off as a lower class problem. Recently, however, it has increased again, especially among the young members of our society.

Largely because of the stigma attached to venereal ailments, many who are infected never go to a physician and some physicians are persuaded to falsify the records. For these reasons the exact numbers who have these diseases are never known. It is known that syphilis involves several million of this country's population at any given time and that gonorrhea is at least twice as prevalent as is syphilis. Since many become cured, the incidence of persons ever infected would be considerably higher than for those infected at any one time.

Contagion is largely by means of the sex act. Promiscuous contacts can soon spread these diseases over a wide area and involve many people. Prostitution is particularly troublesome in this regard, for contacts there are both random and frequent. Though some have recommended periodic medical examinations of prostitutes as a control against disease, and though this would undoubtedly help somewhat, it could never be very effective for the reason that simple examinations cannot prove the absence of disease and that infection can take place and be spread far and wide between examinations.

Cures are possible in most cases if treatment is started early. Sulpha drugs and penicillin have in recent years proved to be extremely helpful against these diseases. But they are not always effective; there is no known "sure cure." In any event, prevention should prove to be the less expensive measure from whatever angle it is considered.

While prevention may be partially obtained through prophylaxis (the use of mechanical and chemical agents for the prevention of infection), this method is seldom certain and is effective only under conditions of utmost skill and care. Where sexual participants are uninformed, or are under the influence of alcohol, or are lazy or overconfident, they may fail to take the necessary precautions. It would seem, therefore, that the only really effective means would be the reduction of promiscuity and prostitution.

Recent medical studies suggest a relationship between age at beginning coitus, number of sexual partners, and the later development of cervical cancer. A group of 416 cancer patients was compared with a control group of the same number, matched on race, age, and religion. The results showed that twice as many patients as controls experienced first coitus at ages 15 to 17. Twice as many patients had multiple marriages and many more patients than controls had multiple sexual mates. Although medical explanations for the causes of this relationship are still being developed, the association between onset of coitus during the adolescent period, especially when there are multiple partners, and later appearance of cervical cancer is apparently strong (Rodkin, 1967).

Unwanted Pregnancy. The occurrence of pregnancy is one of the most disruptive consequences of premarital intercourse. The perfecting of birth control has made this a largely unnecessary consequence when the two people have adequate knowledge and feel a responsibility to each other. Information and/or use of the most reliable of these methods, however, is minimal among the very young and the uncommitted. The most reliable birth control methods are those employed by the female, which require the services of a physician (such as the diaphragm, intrauterine devices, and the "Pill"). Since our society still supports the standard of abstinence for the female, it becomes difficult for her to obtain these devices as an unmarried woman. For the birth control pills to be effective (if she is able to procure them) they must be taken regularly at specifically stated intervals. This assumes a measure of premeditation which does not appear to describe the sexual activity of adolescent females.

Although there are no data available to substantiate the prevalence of the phenomenon, in recent classroom discussions two reasons consistently appear for the non-use of contraceptives among many college females. The first of these is the embarrassment they anticipate feeling in requesting feminine contraceptives even though they are becoming increasingly easy to obtain. Secondly, and perhaps more importantly, it suggests to them that they are planning to engage in sexual intercourse which, from their point of view, removes the acceptability of the act. For many, premarital intercourse is only acceptable as a spontaneous extension of a feeling of love in a relatively close relationship. Shorn of its spontaneous nature it becomes unromantic, crude, mechanical, and unacceptable. Even after the initial contact, precautions against recurrences do not seem acceptable since each episode is expected to be spontaneous and unplanned.

If these feelings are prevalent, then we would not expect any substantial decrease in premarital conception to accompany an increase in effective contraceptive devices. This type of valuation by the female may represent a primary obstacle to effective contraception at the premarital level.

The male contraceptive—the condom—is reliable if used carefully and routinely. However, there is indication that the weaker the attachment of the male to the female, the higher the probability that he will take no precautions to prevent conception. He tends to feel that it is the female's responsibility (Kirkendall, 1961).

The unacceptability of anticipating sexual relations also appears to extend to some males. Although there does not appear to be as much agreement among males as among the females, the view is sometimes expressed in classroom discussions that if the male had contraceptives available it may appear to the female that he had planned the evening to include sexual intercourse or that he always had them available and was therefore promiscuous. To avoid either of these evaluations by the female, these males said they preferred to use nothing to prevent pregnancy.

One of the current objections to making female contraceptives easily available to unmarried women (even though it would reduce premarital pregnancy) is that this would appear to condone sexual intimacies before marriage. Yet male contraceptives have been available to the unmarried male for some time.[4] This undoubtedly is the result of the double standard which appears to condone irresponsibility on the part of the male while punishing the female for similar irresponsible behavior or for misplaced trust.

It is estimated that about one-sixth of all brides are pregnant at the time of marriage (Christensen, 1961). Although this estimate was made around 1960, there is no recent evidence to suggest that the percentage has changed. Considering that marriage is only one alternative to unwanted pregnancy, we can be reasonably sure that the advances in birth control knowledge have not reduced drastically the incidence of unwanted pregnancies. There are three alternative lines of action following unwanted pregnancy: (1) abortion, (2) illegitimate birth, and (3) marriage.

Abortion is of two kinds, spontaneous and induced. Induced abortion is likewise of two kinds, therapeutic and criminal. Spontaneous abortion is involuntary and cannot therefore be counted on as a way out from unwanted pregnancy. Therapeutic abortion is permitted by the various

[4] For a provocative discussion of this topic, see Birdwhistle (1968).

states in cases where the health or life of the mother is endangered by the pregnancy, but is usually surrounded by legal safeguards. Criminal abortion is so named because it violates state law.[5]

Since abortion is, for the most part, illegal it is difficult to provide statistics on its incidence. The Kinsey data, from a sample of 5,293 white, non-prison females showed that about 76 per cent of all premarital pregnancies ended in induced abortion. By far the majority of these were also criminal abortions. The high percentage ending in abortion gives some indication of the high anxiety associated with the problems of having a baby under conditions which are not socially approved. The percentage of Negro premarital pregnancies ending in abortion was much lower, for example. There is not the same social stigma applied to the unwed mother within the Negro sub-culture, again stemming from the historical background of the Negro family system (Gebhard et al., 1950, pp. 54–66, 158–62). This was true mainly of the lower class Negro population. As college education brought the single Negro woman in closer contact with the white culture, the percentage of induced abortions more closely resembled those of the whites.

Illegitimacy refers to birth outside of marriage. The problem is a serious one for both the unmarried mother and the illegitimate child. For the mother there is the dilemma as to whether to keep the child or offer it for adoption. If she keeps it, there are the problems of economic support and social stigma. She may be seriously handicapped so far as future marriage is concerned. For these reasons most unmarried mothers are inclined to give up their children. If this can be done early, as soon after birth as possible, there will be less of an emotional trauma, though for many the crisis is a serious one even then. Again, the Negro mother is much more likely to keep her child than is the white mother. The decision to keep or surrender the child is greatly influenced by the values of the sub-culture from which the mother comes and the amount of pressure she feels to conform to those values.[6] It follows that the individual consequences of the pregnancy and its resolution are strongly related to the mother's evaluation of her behavior from the standpoint of her own value system.

[5] As this book goes to press, abortion laws in several states are undergoing liberalization. Although variation in degree of liberalization exists, the general trend seems to be toward removing all restrictions beyond an agreement between a woman and her physician. These changes are occurring so rapidly that a listing of states with liberal abortion laws would probably be outdated even before publication. It can probably be predicted, however that for some time to come, there will be wide variation among the states concerning the legal status of abortion, unless abortion laws are judged to be unconstitutional by the Supreme Court. Lawsuits are now pending.

[6] For an excellent study of unwed mothers who elect illegitimacy as the alternative to marriage see Vincent (1961). For a discussion of Negro lower class norms concerning illegitimacy, see Rainwater (1967), pp. 172–216 and Hallowell (1969).

Illegitimacy has increased substantially in the United States and Table 9–3 shows the increase by age of mother from 1938 to 1963. The figures are based on reports by the Division of Vital Statistics and include projected estimates for 15 states where illegitimate births are not recorded. This probably results in an under-reporting of the white, older, and better educated females who are able to travel to one of these states for the births (Vincent, 1966b).

Table 9–3

Number and Rate of Illegitimate Births in 1938, 1957, and 1963 (by age of mother)

	Under 15	15–19	20–24	25–29	30–34	35–39	40 and over
Age of Unmarried Mother							
Number of Illegitimate Births							
1938	2,000	40,400	26,400	10,000	5,000	3,100	1,000
1957	4,600	76,400	60,500	29,800	18,000	9,400	2,800
1963	5,400	101,800	82,500	35,400	19,800	10,900	3,500
Rate of Illegitimacy (illegitimate births per 1,000 unmarried females)							
1938	0.3	7.5	9.2	6.8	4.8	3.4	1.1
1957	0.6	15.6	36.5	37.6	26.1	12.7	3.3
1963	0.6	15.3	39.9	49.4	33.7	16.1	4.3

SOURCE: Clark E. Vincent, "Teen-Age Unwed Mothers in American Society," *The Journal of Social Issues,* 22 (April, 1966), Table I, p. 26.

The concern over the rise in illegitimacy has been directed mainly toward the adolescent girl who is assumed to be the major contributor. Yet the greatest rise in *rate of illegitimacy* between 1938 and 1963 was in the 25 to 29 age group. The rate for that group rose 626 per cent compared to 104 per cent for the 15- to 19-year-olds. Between 1957 and 1963, the percentage increase in *rate* actually dropped 2 per cent for the younger group, but the *number* of illicit births increased 33 per cent. This difference in percentage increase between rate per 1,000 unmarried females and number of actual births results from the increase of teen-agers in our population as a consequence of the "baby boom" following World War II.

Although more recent figures showing illegitimacy rates by age of mother are not available, total numbers and rates are available for 1968. The total of about 259,300 illegitimate births for 1963 shown in Table

9–3 rose to an estimated 339,200 in 1968. In 1965 illegitimate births accounted for 7.7 per cent of all births. In 1968 they accounted for 9.7 per cent. Considered as the number of illegitimate births per 1,000 unmarried women between the ages of 15 and 44, the illegitimate birth rate rose from 23.4 in 1965 to 24.1 in 1968 (Bureau of the Census, 1970, p. 50).

According to the Kinsey data, the teen-agers were more likely than older women to choose the illegitimate birth solution to the problem of pregnancy out of wedlock. Even so, this alternative accounted for only 6.2 per cent of the premarital conceptions of Caucasian women under twenty. The percentage was higher for Negroes, especially among the lower educated women. The percentage of Negro out-of-wedlock conceptions ending in illegitimate births was about 27 per cent compared to 4.8 per cent for Causasians, all ages combined (Gebhard et al., 1950, pp. 77–161).

Hallowell's (1969) later study of unwed mothers in selected North Carolina counties revealed that 95 per cent of the Negro women compared to 62 per cent of the Caucasian women kept their illegitimate babies. The Negro women wɛre more likely to have been urged by family and friends to keep the baby.

The sample, it should be noted, consisted of women who were listed on birth certificates as mothers of illegitimate children. It, therefore, does not include those women who married before the birth of the baby, nor those who chose abortion as a way out of the unplanned pregnancy.

Almost three-fifths of the whites and three-quarters of the blacks were under 21 years of age. One-third of the whites and two-fifths of the blacks had completed less than the tenth grade in school. One half of the whites and two-thirds of the blacks were daughters of unskilled or semi-skilled workers, farm laborers, or sharecroppers. The sample is therefore limited in the number of cases from upper socioeconomic levels. Whether this represents an accurate distribution of the illegitimacy choice among the social classes or whether parents from higher socioeconomic levels are better able to circumvent the recording of illegitimacy on the birth certificates in local files is unknown.

Illegitimacy appears to have risen faster among Negroes than among Caucasians. In 1938, Negroes accounted for 53 per cent of all illegitimate births while in 1963, they accounted for 60 per cent. The increase probably reflects more accurate counting over the years rather than an actual rise, however. The proportion of all non-white, live births that were attended in a hospital or by a physician rose from 51 per cent in 1940 to 90 per cent in 1963, resulting in more complete records of illegitimacy (Vincent, 1966b).

Marriage as a solution accounts for under 20 per cent of all premarital pregnancies (Gebhard et al., 1950). This is most prevalent among those who had planned to be married eventually, but had to hurry up the wedding. In some cases, it is a means of forcing a wedding of which parents disapprove or in which the male appears reluctant. Termination in marriage is more common among the very young, perhaps because the parents exert more influence on the younger couple, and it is a way of avoiding some of the social stigma. It would be a mistake to assume that marriage following pregnancy is an ideal solution however. Frequently such a marriage will have two strikes against it at the start.

The following summary points are from Christensen's long-range study of a midwestern county, using a method he has come to designate as "record linkage." Though the generalizations are for one county only, it is believed that they may have general applicability for the country at large. The method consisted of matching individual couples across consecutive marriage, birth, and divorce records. In this way it was possible to measure the interval between marriage and birth of the first child, to isolate the short-interval cases which represent premarital pregnancy, and to determine how these phenomena relate to divorce and other factors. Since the method does not allow for either refusal or falsification in answering, it may be regarded as more reliable than either the questionnaire or the interview for getting at such intimate behavior as premarital pregnancy.[7]

Nearly 23 per cent of the couples had intervals to first birth of less than 266 days, the normal period of uterogestation. But some of this would be because of premature birth. When corrections were made for prematurity and other contingencies, it was estimated that approximately 20 per cent of all first births were premaritally conceived.

Most of the premaritally pregnant couples got married about two months after conception occurred, or as soon as it could be reliably diagnosed. Undoubtedly many of these were planning to marry anyway, but pregnancy had the effect of stepping up the wedding date. A few put off the wedding until shortly before the child was born—typical "shotgun marriages."

Premarital pregnancy was found to be associated with young age at marriage, a non-religious wedding, and an unskilled laboring occupation. It was also noted that premaritally pregnant couples, more than others, tended to falsify their ages in order to get married—a fact explained by their extreme youthfulness at the time they "got caught."

Significantly higher percentages of the premarital pregnancy cases end in divorce than the postmarital pregnancy cases. This is particularly true for the "shotgun" variety, those with extremely short intervals to first birth. The overall picture shows a consistent inverse relationship between divorce rate and interval from marriage to first birth, with divorce rate for the shortest interval group (0–139 days) being more than three times higher than for the longest interval group (532–1,819).

[7] Several journal articles reporting this research have appeared in print. See Christensen (1953a, 1953b), Christensen and Bowden (1953), Christensen and Meissner (1953), and Christensen and Rubenstein (1956). An extension of this study was made in 1964 with similar findings. See Christensen and Barber (1967).

It should be evident from the above that premarital pregnancy is frequently a divorce-producing factor. Couples who "get caught" are sometimes immature, ill-matched, and unprepared for marriage to start with. Furthermore, they might be resentful over being forced into a relationship, and hence determined to get out of it just as soon as they can. Even those more mature and prepared are apt to find themselves under some handicap because of the possible worry, guilt, blame, and stigma involved.

Again, the consequences of premarital pregnancy for marital stability will vary depending upon the values of the two people, the commitment they had to each other before the pregnancy occurred, their families, and the social groups within which they interact. As long as the dominant values of the society are largely disapproving, however, some negative consequences can be expected.

THE PRINCIPLE OF VALUE RELEVANCE

Increased sexual freedom has been heralded by some as a healthy, enlightened perspective on sex which is long overdue. By others it is seen as an extreme loss of morals which will end in the collapse of the family and society. These two positions can perhaps be seen as the end points on a continuum of values, all of which have strong adherents. Even persons sharing either extremely restrictive or extremely permissive values are likely to do so for different reasons.

It is impossible to assess the rightness or wrongness of sexual behavior without adopting a value position from which to assess it. Human sexual behavior, per se, is neither right nor wrong. It is a natural part of being human. It becomes right or wrong as it is subjected to norms and values, as meaning is attached to it. Once it has been evaluated in a society, however, the behavior has consequences for one's evaluation of self as well as his evaluation of the partner. So what may seem like individual decisions are always colored by the meanings one has absorbed while growing up in a particular society. The same act may have entirely different meanings and different consequences depending upon the values of the people involved *and* the norms of the supporting groups of which they are a part, which is graphically illustrated by Christensen's study of value-behavior discrepancies in three cultures mentioned earlier.

Value systems in our society range from complete restrictiveness, based on absolutistic ideas of right and wrong stemming from religious commandment, to complete permissiveness, based on the idea that sex is normal and necessary to man, whether married or not, and has no moral relevance. Between these extremes is found a variety of beliefs. There are those who believe in a situational morality, but further believe that the values of society should change to support greater sexual freedom for young people, and thereby reduce the negative emotional consequences. Close to the extreme permissive view which denies any moral relevance to sex and would remove all restrictions is the view that sex is fun and therefore good. The more of this fun a person has the freer and more complete he is (Rubin, 1965).

Although there have been major changes in the proportions of persons adhering to each of the value systems in recent years, all the values have been with us for some time and will probably continue to be with us. When there are conflicting value systems it becomes hard to predict the consequences of sexual behavior. The meaning of sex, and the consequences of sexual behavior for the individuals will be related to their particular belief systems, the ones supported by their closest social groups, and the prevailing values in the total society.

Kinsey, from his findings, supports this view of the differential consequences of premarital sexual behavior. He suggests that the psychological significance of any type of sexual activity very largely depends upon what the individual and his social group choose to make of it. He says:

The truth of this thesis is abundantly evidenced by our thousands of histories which among them, include every conceivable type of sexual behavior without subsequent psychological disturbance, while the same sort of behavior in other histories may bring shame, remorse, despair, desperation, and attempted suicide. The simplest matter can be built into an affair of gigantic proportions.

Failing to comprehend that their own attitudes and the social codes generate these disturbances, most persons identify them as direct evidence of the intrinsic wrongness or abnormality of the sexual act itself (Kinsey et al., 1953, p. 321).

Implication for Sex Education

Discussions of any of these value systems are likely to reify sex as behavior which is unrelated to other aspects of the person's life, personality, and relationship to others. This is a consequence of our long history of anxiety about it, as well as our fears that it is an all-powerful force that once unleashed will become uncontrollable.

This emphasis on sex, per se, and the belief that it is something wholly different from other kinds of behavior, has colored our whole approach to sex education. We have tended to see this as something totally removed from the rest of education, which assumes that the more completely a person understands a phenomenon the more control he is able to exert over it and the more he is able to use his knowledge for his own benefit and the benefit of others. The problem, from this point of view, becomes one of how to educate people to use *any* knowledge constructively, rather than using it to manipulate others for selfish interests. Part of this be-

comes the development of respect for other value systems, and an awareness that each value system contributes to the consequences of behavior
for the person who fully believes it.

Whatever the value system, whether it is restrictive or permissive, the
recognition that sexual behavior does reflect the individual's concept of
self and his orientation toward other people aids in removing the fears
that sexual awareness will lead to uncontrollable sexual involvements.
It is the combination of stimulating sexual curiosity in the culture and
cloaking it in mystery and secrecy in the family which contributes most
to preoccupation with it and irresponsible behavior.

Imagine the results if we attempted to instill values about the handling
of money by never mentioning it and keeping all relationships involving
its use secret, while vaguely alluding to the strong impulses which make
people want to have it and the power which its possession brings. Having
money and spending it would be presented as somehow related to being
grown up, but few grownups would talk about how you get it or how
you use it.

We can imagine TV shows in which a number of beautiful things are
displayed in front of a man. He looks at them, nods his head, and he
and the sales person walk away. The man puts his hand in his pocket,
pulls out something. Just as we are about to see what it is the lights
fade out, or the scene shifts! Perhaps we may see a woman beckoning
to a man. She begins to show him something in her purse. Just as he
gets excited about it and starts to take it, she slams the purse shut, and
walks away—laughing at his frustration or crying in her humiliation.

We can imagine the curiosity evoked in the child, living in a money-
based society, where there seems to be a conspiracy to keep him from
learning about it, at the same time he is constantly made aware of it. All
he knows is that from the way people act it is very important, maybe even
evil if you have it too early; but it is tantalizing, powerful, and someday
he's supposed to have some and be skilled in handling it. Certainly children reared like this would become progressively more anxious, curious,
and preoccupied with money as they approach adulthood. We can even
imagine them stealing it and secretly talking to their friends about it,
describing in minute detail how they got it, what money felt like, and so
on.

We would consider it ridiculous to train our children to handle money
like this. We aren't afraid that if we allow them to learn about money
they will become thieves. And yet this is very similar to the way we have
tended to treat sex, where the biological stimulus makes early guidance
and training even more important.

Because there are thieves, some of whom feel guilty about stealing,
we do not advocate changing the norms against theft; nor do we advocate

removing all the goods from the shelves to reduce temptation. We attempt to teach our children to be responsible for their own behavior in the midst of temptation and differing value systems.

The problem of sex education, then, becomes the larger problem of developing responsible human beings who can be tolerant of other people's values without having to become like them; who are confident of their own worth; who have an awareness and concern for the consequences of their behavior for themselves and for others; and who regard sex as a positive aspect of their humanness—neither the least nor the most important.

SUMMARY

Normally the individual develops through three stages of sexual interests known as the autosexual, the homosexual, and the heterosexual. As the individual is developing through these stages he is acquiring the values concerning sex and sexual behavior prevalent in the society and the family in which he grows.

Sex standards vary somewhat from culture to culture as well as among individuals within each culture. Variation among individuals is related to their exposure to groups supporting certain values. An individual's sex standards are strongly related to his premarital sexual behavior, as well as to the evaluation he makes of his own behavior.

When premarital sexual intercourse occurs in the uncommitted, adolescent relationship, it is likely to receive severe negative evaluations in our society. This is because of the greater probability of coitus in this relationship contributing to the social problems of disease, abortion, and unwanted pregnancies. Our simultaneous stimulation of sexual curiosity in the culture and cloaking it in mystery and secrecy in the family contributes to a preoccupation with sex and irresponsible behavior among some young people.

The variety of and conflict between value systems in our society will probably continue to produce anxiety and some negative consequences following from premarital sex behavior, regardless of its nature. Since sexual behavior is a reflection of an individual's orientation toward others as well as a reflection of his value system, sex education is seen to involve the development of responsible human beings who can be tolerant of other's values without having to become like them, are confident of their own worth, have a concern for others, and who regard sex as a positive aspect of their humanness.

QUESTIONS AND PROJECTS

1. What are some of the consequences of the range of sexual values existing in our society today? Which values do you think are most prevalent today among college males? College females? Parents of high school students? How would you account for the differences, if you think there are any?

2. Should a high school girl who becomes pregnant before she graduates be asked to leave school if she is unmarried? If she is married? If your answer is yes to either of these questions, when should she have to leave? Should she be allowed to come back after the baby is born? Defend your position.

3. How much sexual freedom do you think young people should have before marriage? Should the amount of freedom differ according to age? If so, how should it differ? Explain.

4. If sexual norms were completely permissive, do you think exploitation would increase? Decrease? Why?

5. Plan a panel discussion on the topic of abortion. See if you can account for the differences of opinion expressed during the discussion. If two people married with widely differing views on this subject, could you predict differences on other important values? Explain.

6. Venereal disease appears to be an increasing problem among high school as well as college students. What suggestions can you make concerning this situation? Why do you think the attitudes toward venereal disease tend to be more negative than toward mononucleosis or other infectious diseases? Would these attitudes be expected to change with the development of more permissive sex norms? Defend your position.

7. Discuss the proposition that increased drug use is a symptom of the same social conditions as increased sexual freedom. Build arguments for and against this proposition. What other relationships do you see between them, or do you see any connection?

8. Some people suggest that since a baby grows inside the female's body, she alone should be able to decide whether or not to have an abortion. What do you think of this view? Why?

10

Mate Selection

In the preceding two chapters we have discussed the dating systems and the problems of managing the sexual feelings in a casual dating relationship which also emphasizes affectional interaction. It was stressed that beginning dating is usually for fun and is frequently a prerequisite for participating in teen-age activities. If successful, it becomes an important source of ego-enhancement and contributes to the development of sex identity. The original intent is not usually to find a mate. The end result, however, of the long process set into motion by dating will be for most people in our society the selection of a marriage mate. In this chapter we will investigate this process of mate selection, the social pressures limiting and encouraging the process, and the factors related to the development of love and pair-unity.

THE SOCIAL RESTRICTIONS

Although there is a great deal of freedom in mate choice in the United States, there is also some order imposed. In many cultures mates are selected by family heads, with the marrying individuals having little or nothing to say about the process. Arrangements are frequently made while those to be married are still children, or, in some societies, even before they are born. Practical rather than romantic considerations are paramount, such as: "Will he be a good provider?"; "Will she be a good cook and housekeeper?"; "Will such a match be economically advantageous to the family?"; "Does the prospective mate come from a family with a good reputation, giving status value?" Sometimes a go-between or official matchmaker is employed to assist parents in the job of properly marrying off their children. This is the familistic way of doing things.

In contrast, our individualistic emphasis seems to imply an open market as far as mate selection is concerned. Theoretically it is possible for any two unrelated persons of the opposite sex to marry. There are, however, many barriers to this kind of freedom; legal, parental, and social controls exert themselves from the outside.

Legal Safeguards

Legal restrictions vary considerably from state to state. Common prohibitions are those against: (1) bigamy, where either of the parties is already married; (2) immaturity, where either is under legal age, usually 18 for the male and 16 for the female; (3) incest, where the prospective mate is first cousin or closer by blood; (4) mental defects, where there is evidence of insanity or feeble-mindedness; and (5) infection, where there is a communicable disease, especially syphilis or gonorrhea. These will be discussed again in a later chapter; here we simply note that these prohibitions exist and that they restrict one's freedom of choice.

Most of these legal safeguards seem highly desirable; though the legislation is so variable as to be confusing, is full of loopholes, and is not always enforced.

Parental Pressures

Although parents are not expected to intervene in the choice of a mate in our society, they do appear to have considerable influence. Over twenty-five years ago, Bates (1942) concluded that the majority of parents did make some attempt to influence their children in mate choice. Mothers attempted to influence children more than fathers, and daughters were subjected to the pressures more than sons. Although there are no recent studies to support these earlier findings, discussions with college students lead us to believe that little has changed during the generation which has passed since Bates's study.

Much of the parental influence is quite subtle and indirect. The parental values transmitted in family interaction implant many suggestions concerning desirable companions which may rule out numerous mate possibilities. Prolonged interaction with parents creates images of what an ideal mate should be. Many aspects of this concept come from pleasant, rewarding characteristics of one or both parents or from the desire to avoid the objectionable traits which caused unhappiness or pain. Studies concerning the influence of these *ideal-mate images* on mate choices are inconclusive. The evidence seems to suggest that the images change over time as the result of experience with the opposite sex. It is difficult to tell, even in the few studies which show a relationship, whether the resemblance between spouse and ideal mate occurred before the mate was selected or whether the ideal mate image was adjusted after selection had been made (Strauss, 1946, 1947; Udry, 1965).

The choice of neighborhood, schools, churches, and social groups certainly limits the opportunities the child has to form relationships which may lead to marriage. These limitations, generally imposed by parents, tend to form the field of eligibles, or the market-place wherein one may shop.

The Field of Eligibles

A person cannot choose a mate from the entire population, only from that part of the population to which he has access. Even some of these will be "off-limits" to him for all practical purposes because of social pressures from family and friends. There are several broad characteristics as well as considerations concerning accessibility which tend to mark off certain people for the kind of social interaction which may lead to mate selection.

Residential and Functional Propinquity. One of the major factors affecting the field of eligibles is nearness, or *propinquity*. This simply means that the opportunities for meeting other people are greater the closer we live to them—*residential propinquity*. The closer we live to them the more likely we are to frequent the same places, such as schools, churches, parks, and so forth. Thus, the opportunities for meeting, talking, dating, and the development of emotional involvements are greater among these people. Numerous studies have reported the high percentage of marriages among people who live within blocks of each other. Although many young girls may dream of the handsome, modern-day knight appearing on the scene from out of nowhere to carry her off, most will probably have to be content with marrying the boy from down the street.

Residential propinquity loses some of its influence in mate selection when other factors come into play. One of these is what we might call social or *functional propinquity*. When work or leisure time activities bring people together, some of these people are likely to become acquainted and to marry. As locality groupings give way to special interest and functional organizations in this day of rapid communication and transportation, it can be expected that people will more and more select their mates from among their social and occupational associates, regardless of how far apart the residences may happen to be. Marvin (1918), in an early study of Philadelphia marriages, found that men and women intermarried within the same occupation at a rate almost three times as high as could be expected from mere chance. Harris (1935) followed with a study of Allentown, Pennsylvania, and found that the older people are when they select a mate and the higher they are on the socioeconomic scale the less they are influenced by the factor of residential proximity. The chief reason for this seems to be that the older and higher-leveled individuals have more time and money to travel and to meet people from other areas.

Following these pioneer analyses there have been numerous recent studies on the problem of propinquity in mate selection and all lead to the same general conclusions: (1) mates tend to be chosen from among persons living close by; (2) this tendency is stronger in localities where the population is dense, among the lower educational, occupational, and income levels, and with those who are either quite young or quite old in age; and (3) as travel and communication facilities improve, functional association becomes increasingly more important than mere nearness in geographical residence.[1]

Unbalanced Sex Ratios.   Closely related to the matter of propinquity is the phenomenon of sex ratios. From the standpoint of marriage opportunity it does little good to be associated with a large group of people if they are all of one's own sex. Women have the advantage in groups showing a surplus of men, and men the advantage in groups where women are abundant, both because there are more to select from and because competition is less. The marriage rate is low whenever the sex ratio gets too far out of balance either way. Groves and Ogburn (1928, p. 193–219) have shown that women are more dependent upon a favorable sex ratio than are men, and that a ratio of about 120 men to 100 women favors a maximum marriage rate.

Endogamous Characteristics.   Not all of those persons whom we may be acquainted with will be available for further interaction. People tend to gravitate together in terms of broad social characteristics. The term endogamy refers to "in-group" marriages. Thus we find people tending to interact mainly with others from about the same social class, the same race, the same nationality, and the same broad religious grouping—Protestant, Catholic, or Jew. Propinquity explains part of this, but not all. Social groups within high schools, for example, tend to reflect the adult stratification system, even though there may be representation from several social classes and different races. They may cooperate and interact within the school structure but recreational activities and friendship groups will tend to form within the endogamous characteristics of social class and race.

[1] For an excellent critique of research on this problem, as well as a listing of previous research, see Kerckhoff (1956). For a more recent appraisal of this factor, see Catton and Smircich (1964).

There are no legal restrictions to enforce endogamous marriages in our society. The last legal barriers to interracial marriages were removed by a Supreme Court decision in 1967. There are informal pressures, however, which tend to enforce them. First, as the child grows within his family, he absorbs the values, the meanings of words and gestures, the preferences for dress, manners, speech, and actions associated with his social context. He is likely to be able to communicate more easily with others sharing his "way-of-life," to feel more comfortable with them, and to receive more predictable responses to his own behavior. Second, family and friends are likely to show some disapproval of relationships which depart too drastically from the in-group expectations. Since ego-enhancement is one of the gains from the early dating experience, friends' disapproval of the dating partner reduces the rewards. Unless there were already emotional commitments to the other personality, or a lack of alternative partners, the pressures are strong enough to produce a large measure of conformity to endogamous norms.

Interracial marriages face stronger informal barriers than any other departure from endogamous norms. The pairing which currently receives the greatest amount of attention is the black–white mating. While biologically there is no supportable reason for preventing these marriages, legally and socially they have encountered strong opposition. Until the recent Supreme Court ruling, eighteen states still had laws forbidding them. Consequently, the reporting of such marriages may not be accurate. A national estimate in 1965 placed the number at about 50,000, about one-third of one per cent of all marriages (Osmundson, 1965). Heer (1966) attempted to trace the trend of Negro–Caucasian marriages since 1953 in the only states which have made data available since 1950.[2] They appear to be increasing slightly in recent years. The pairing of black husband and white wife is more prevalent and rising faster than the white husband–black wife arrangement.

In earlier years it was thought that the Negro man–Caucasian woman pairing generally involved a Negro male of high social status paired with a low status Caucasian female. This no longer appears to be true, especially where education is concerned (Bernard, 1966). Amount of interracial marriage appears to vary with the relative status of the black and white populations in a community, degree of residential segregation, and the racial distribution in the area (Heer, 1966). It can be hypothesized, then, that as the factors limiting the field of eligibles change to include members of other races, the rate of intermarriage will increase. This is supported by Bernard's finding that the college-educated black man was

[2] The four states are California, Hawaii, Michigan, and Nebraska. California, however, has now passed legislation which prevents recording of race on marriage licenses.

much more likely to marry a white wife than lesser educated men (Bernard, 1966). It is on the college campus that shared interests, educational levels, and tolerance levels are more likely to increase the interaction between the races.

Even though the legal barriers have been removed prejudice and intolerance operate to hold down the proportion of these marriages. These same prejudices put pressure on the marriages after they take place. The problems of these and other interracial pairings will be discussed in more detail in a later chapter.

Interclass marriages do not suffer from the intense negative sanctions that interracial marriages do. They do not occur in large proportions because of the limitation of the field of eligibles. Many people have thought that these barriers have been breaking down in recent years because of the increase in mobility and the growth of large metropolitan high schools drawing from various residential areas. Dinitz, Banks, and Pasamanick (1960) provided some data on this with their study of 2,706 couples who obtained marriage licences in Columbus, Ohio, in the years 1933, 1939, 1949, and 1957–58. They found a growing tendency for marital partners to be selected from a wider range within the broad middle classes. There were fewer marriages from within exactly the same class, but also fewer combining widely different class backgrounds. Whether the decrease in marriages involving people from extremely different class backgrounds indicates increased social pressure against them or decreased interaction between young people of greatly different social classes as cities grow in population is not known.

Interreligious marriages come under attack from churches as well as families. It is difficult to tell just how prevalent they are, and to what extent they are increasing, if they are. Only two states record religious affiliation on the marriage license application. Religious affiliation at the time of application, however, gives no indication of the number of applicants who converted to the partner's religion before marrying.

Percentages of mixed marriages vary drastically from region to region and city to city depending on the distribution of the religion in the vicinity and the tightness of other controls which operate to enforce religious endogamy. For example, where there are close-knit ethnic groups associated with a religion the incidence of religious endogamy is high. Where there is a small proportion of a particular religious group in a community the intermarriage rate is likely to be high for that group; where the religious group is large, intermarriage for that group is proportionately low. This has to do with the field of eligibles. In a small group, the availability of marriage mates from the inside is limited. It appears that if the choice is between a mixed marriage or no marriage at all the mixture wins.

The relationship between religious endogamy and marital success will be discussed in detail later. The effect, of course, varies depending on the devoutness of the individuals and the extent of the religious gap separating them. However, the influence of endogamy in mate selection tends to hold down matings between the most devout, especially across the major boundaries of Protestant, Catholic, and Jew.

Endogamy on the College Campus.   Even on a college campus, where high education and distance from parental pressure is seen to break down some of the endogamous pressures, the influence is still apparent. In one study of college couples who were going steady or engaged, Kerckhoff and Davis (1962) found that in 87 per cent of them the couples were of the same religious groups (Protestant, Catholic, Jew). On a seven-point occupational classification system, the fathers of the man and woman were in the same category in 45 per cent of the cases, and in the same or adjacent category in 76 per cent of them.

Rogers and Havens (1960) found that pairings on a state college campus tended to correspond to the prestige ratings of the fraternities and sororities to which they belonged. The association grew stronger as the paired relationship changed from dating to engagement. Of the engaged men from high-prestige fraternities, 36 per cent were engaged to women in high-prestige sororities. Thirty-two per cent of the fiancées were from medium-prestige sororities; 14 per cent were non-affiliates or were not on the campus. Of the engaged men of low-prestige fraternities, none were engaged to women from either high or medium rated sororities. Forty-four per cent of them were evenly divided between women from low-prestige houses and non-affiliates. The rest were engaged to women not on the campus.

The effect of the endogamous characteristic of social status is apparent from this study as well as the approved direction of departure. This approved direction is substantiated by what is called the _mating gradient_ which refers to the tendency for men to marry down and women up. The approval of this kind of departure from endogamous norms can be seen in the differential evaluation generally made of relationships in which there is a wide disparity in family wealth. If it is a man from a poor family engaged to a wealthy girl, the tongues are likely to wag. "He must be marrying her for her money." "He's looking for an easy life." If it is the other way around, nods of approval are likely to follow the girl who "made a good match."

Endogamous characteristics tend to mark off the broad limits within which interaction can take place. But they do not explain why certain individuals tend to gravitate together within these boundaries.

PERSONAL CHARACTERISTICS

Homogamy

A recurring explanation for the next screening process in the selection of certain people out of the field of eligibles is the theory of *homogamy*— "like attracts like." There have been a number of studies which show a greater than chance tendency for persons to marry others similar to themselves in personal characteristics such as height, intelligence, age, and physical attractiveness. Thus, endogamy refers to mate selection in terms of similar social characteristics and homogamy refers to similarities in personal characteristics.

There is also some evidence that homogamy extends to personality characteristics in a broad sense. Murstein (1967b) discovered in a study of couples who were steadily dating that over a six month period those who felt they were progressing toward a permanent relationship were more likely to be similar in mental health adjustment (both non-neurotic or both neurotic) than those who had broken up or felt the relationship was deteriorating. The same researcher found that personality homogamy among couples who were going steady or engaged was significantly greater than between pairs randomly matched from the same sample. These were not actual similarities as measured by personality tests, however, but perceived similarities (Murstein, 1967a). These results were supported by a much larger, more complete study done by Trost (1967) in Sweden. Here, practically no support for actual homogamous matching was found but there was high support for perceived homogamy in interests, beliefs, and attitudes.

A number of studies provide evidence that similarity of interests, whether actual or perceived, encourages the continuance of a relationship. The evidence is fairly consistent that the most important factor as far as personality characteristics and attitudes are concerned is the perception of themselves as being similar. Whether the perception of the other as similar is the result of the interaction which is felt as rewarding or the result of external situations or experiences which increase the desires to become emotionally involved with someone at a particular time is not known. There are perhaps enough attitudes and beliefs which are not easily observable to allow the person who is (or wants to be) favorably impressed, to assume more similarity between the partners than actually exists.[3]

---

[3] For a superb comprehensive coverage of studies concerned with mate selection, see Jacobsohn and Matheny (1962).

Reciprocity

We probably interact with a number of people whom we may perceive as having interests and attitudes similar to our own. We still must explain why a person tends to select one of these and not others. A number of pairings can probably be explained in very simple terms:

> "She's the only one who ever acted like she wanted to go out with me."
> "He's the only one who asked me."
> "I was ready to get married and she was available."
> "We had to. She was pregnant."
> "I may not have had another chance."

Pairings for these reasons will upset any theory attempting to explain why who marries whom, based on personal or relationship factors alone.

The selection process is never one in which a person can choose *any person* from a group marked off by endogamous and homogamous characteristics. The influence of these factors is more easily understood when stated negatively. Interactional opportunities, social pressures, and internalized concepts of unacceptable characteristics in a spouse rule out the majority of potential mates. Among those left, the choice is restricted to those who reciprocate our attraction. So choice actually concerns a selection among those few who come within our limits of acceptability on social and personal characteristics, who also show enough of a sustained interest to allow a relationship to develop.

In view of the number of non-relationship variables which operate to throw two people together in the kind of context that presses them toward further involvement and eventual engagement, we perhaps should not expect to find strong empirical support for the theory explaining the final choice in relationship terms. And indeed we do not find strong support for it. There is, however, sufficient support to prevent its being rejected completely. This theory is phrased in terms of need complementarity between partners.

Theory of Complementary Needs

To this point there is general agreement that homogamous characteristics tend to sort people out and that the consequences of these similarities include ease of communication, fewer areas of conflict to be resolved, and reduced problems of adjustment. However, the final factor in welding two socially compatible people together is supposedly at the psychological level of personality fit in complementary terms. Robert Winch has pioneered this theory that at the level of individual motivation (the psychic in contrast to the social level) mates will be selected according to the principle of "maximum need gratification"; that is, from within their fields of eligibles individuals will tend to select those persons who best meet their own personality needs. He hypothesizes that the selection will be in the direction of persons whose need patterns are complementary rather than similar to ones' own. For example, a highly submissive person is more likely to be attracted to someone who is aggressive, and vice versa, than is either likely to be attracted to another of his own kind. Similarly, a person who likes to be protected and indulged will tend to pair up with someone who enjoys giving nurturance to others, and a person who has a need for self-abasement will tend to team up with someone who has a need for hostility expression, etc. These formulations constitute Winch's theory of complementary needs.

To test the theory, Winch and associates made careful and detailed statistical analyses of data from twenty-five Northwestern University undergraduates and their respective spouses. They expected to find complementary patterns that would express interspousal differences in both intensity (that is, one spouse would measure high and the other low on a scale of dominance) and in kind (one would measure high on dominance and the other high on deference). There have been several journal articles reporting on various aspects of this research, with the claim that the hypothesis tends to hold up.

Though conceding that their results are not as clear and compelling as might be wished, these researchers nevertheless show that a number (if not all) of their correlations do support the theory of complementary needs, and claim that there is nothing in their data to support the conflicting hypothesis of motivational similarity in the mates (Winch, 1955).

Other investigators, however, have presented contradictory findings. They suggest that even the clear discovery of complementary needs within marriage would not be a test of its operation in the selection process—that the marital interaction, itself, may develop complementary traits in the spouses which may or may not have been there before.

Value Consensus

Several recent studies provide evidence for examining the relationship between homogamy theories of interpersonal attraction and the heterogamy theory of complementary needs. Robert Coombs (1966) proposed that one of the reasons for the high associations found between homogamy and continuance of a relationship is the high degree of satisfaction produced by value consensus, and that value consensus is likely to be greater when people have had similar background experiences. When one attempts to communicate and his meaning is understood by the other person, he feels rewarded, is encouraged to talk about things he is interested in, and becomes attracted to the other person. If he is agreed with (similar values) he feels good about himself as well as the other person, and wishes to continue the relationship. If there are value conflicts which show up in the interaction, the person is likely to feel threatened when they appear, stay close to emotionally neutral topics in conversation, feel non-rewarded with little desire to see the person again. Coombs tested this in the initial stages of a relationship by using the participants in a computer-paired dance on a college campus. He discovered that those persons most satisfied with their partner reported that they communicated easily and that they also would like more dates with this person. Ease of communication was highly associated with the feeling that they were liked by the partner. Using only the few preferences provided for computer pairings, value consensus was found to be associated with both ease of communication and satisfaction with partner, especially for females. It appeared that in early selection, value consensus was more important for the female's continuing interest while the male was more preoccupied with physical appearance (Coombs and Kenkel, 1966).

Kerckhoff and Davis (1962) offered further support for the early effect of value consensus in their longitudinal study of couples. Measuring value consensus by the couple's agreement on items associated with family success, they found that consensus was associated with a move toward a more permanent relationship over a six month period only for those who had been going together less than 18 months. These investigators also measured need complementarity concerning desires for acting in a certain way and desires to have others act in a certain way toward one's self. They were concerned with the needs for closeness, control, and affection. Need complementarity was not a distinguishing factor between the couples who progressed and those who broke up of those who had gone together less than 18 months, but *was* related to progress toward more permanence for those who had been going together longer than that, especially for those long-term couples with low consensus. It appears, then, that value consensus plays a part in holding people together and perhaps in building some idealized perceptions of the other person. The longer they go together, however, the more likely is the interaction to break down some of the idealization, as they are exposed to more and more of the other's behavior.[4] Perhaps *then* the need complementarity enters in to provide satisfaction as idealization fades for those couples who progress toward engagement and marriage.

Although this theory needs much more testing, it again points to one

[4] Kerckhoff and Davis (1962) also found that those going together over 18 months were more likely to attribute negative characteristics to their partners than were those involved in shorter relationships. The short-term couples also assigned more negative characteristics on the second testing, six months after the first testing.

reason why we should not expect high associations between either consensus or need complementarity and mate selection. Couples marry at all stages of this interaction. Some marry in the early stages when consensus is expected to be high. Some marry when consensus may have faded, and been replaced by need complementarity. Some couples may exhibit both, since they are not mutually exclusive. Others may have committed so much time to the relationship and have developed a strong enough orientation toward marriage that doubts about the relationship are suppressed. They have neither consensus nor complementariness, but marry anyway. There is also the strong possibility that the large array of individual needs provides ample opportunity for similarity in some of them and complementarity in others, which vary drastically from couple to couple.

Goodman (1964), in a small study of 75 married couples at Michigan State University, offers evidence which clarifies further the possible operation of complementary needs. He found the personality needs of dominance, abasement, deference, nurturance, and succorance similar in couples who had high self-acceptance and complementary in couples who had low self-acceptance. Again, however, this was found among married couples and there is no way of telling whether the personality fit was an influence in mate selection or had developed during the marital interaction.

Individual Variation

There are indications that future research on this problem will give greater attention to individual variability and to the ways in which particular persons in specific situations can best be matched. If so, it may be found that some couples gain greater harmony when they are similar in most respects, others when they are complementary in most respects, and still others when they are similar in some ways and complementary in others. Perhaps more important than either similarity or complementariness, per se, is the way in which the couple's personalities are matched according to their own needs and the particular social circumstances in which they find themselves. This is not to throw out general principles, but only to emphasize that generalizations must always be qualified when applied to specific cases and situations.

Practically everyone is agreed that there is a tendency for mates to be selected within broad eligibility categories such as same race, same religion, same social class, etc.; and that when the spouses are endogamous in these respects they may have fewer adjustments to make and hence better chances for success in marriage. Yet there are exceptions. As has been shown, certain persons ignore these barriers and at least some of those who do so are able to escape the potential handicaps. These are those who either live where there is little prejudice or are themselves unconventional and highly adaptable, or more likely both. So much depends upon the values of the culture and the persons involved.

It used to be that the culture was relatively homogeneous and demanding on the individual; sex roles were prescribed and there was little room for confusion over what a husband or a wife was supposed to do and what the marriage relationship should be like. Now, however, the culture is much more heterogeneous and permissive, which means that the individual is apt to meet a wider variety of the opposite sex than formerly; that he is more free to marry whomever he wants; but that he is less sure of how he should behave toward the one he marries. What was formerly set up within the culture is now left more to the individual.

This shift in emphasis may mean greater opportunity for compatible relationships but it also gives more responsibility to the individual and more importance to the problem of personality matching. At the academic level we need more research to discover the various workable and unworkable trait combinations. At the personal level we need more self-insights, together with greater understanding of the opposite sex and of the findings of science to use as guides in the mate-selecting process.

THE LOVE PERSPECTIVE

Whatever the social and psychological processes are by which people select each other for marriage mates, it is relatively simple from the personal perspective: We met—we fell in love—we married! At some point between "we met" and "we married," the two people are expected to define themselves as being in love. So we must turn our attention to the meaning of love and some theories concerning its development.

Meaning of Love

In our society love and marriage are very much interrelated and are generally thought of together. Simply and broadly defined, love is any sentiment of attachment that is centered on any person or thing. It is a pleasurable feeling, in other words, and it is directed toward and derived from some object.

The love object might be entirely nonmaterial, as when we say that one loves some standard, principle, or cause that he shows a strong devotion for; he can love democracy, for example, or peace, or the Christian church. Similarly it can be said that one loves a certain type of activity such as swimming, reading, or listening to musical concerts. Again, the love object might be material though nonhuman, as when we say that one loves ice cream, or new hats, or horses. Finally, the love object might be a human personality. There are many varieties of this latter also: there is self-love; there are filial and parental loves; there are friendships everywhere, regardless of age, sex, or social relationships; and there is the sweetheart love of courtship and marriage. Broadly considered, love exists whenever and wherever people obtain satisfactions from the objects and the activities that attract them.

It is to the narrower usage of the term, to sweetheart love, that attention is now being turned. Though love is of many types, it is only that one which relates to marriage that will concern us here.

Common Fallacies.   A frequent fallacy is to regard love as an irrational force, mystically and mysteriously operating to shape man's destiny. It has been said, for example, that *"love is blind."* Though the development of love probably involves "blindness" to parts of a person's personality and behavior, and "super sight" in seeing some things which aren't there, the continuance of that love comes more from knowing, understanding, and accepting the other person as he *is* rather than transforming him into something he *isn't*.

It has also been claimed that everyone has a "one-and-only," a *soulmate*, who is waiting and searching for him, just as he is seeking in return. Part of this belief is that people are "meant for each other," predestined to get together; and that unless one finds the right person—the one intended—he can be only partially happy.

Some say, for instance, that you are only half a person until you find the other half meant for you. This may be partly correct; but, given an equal start, there are very likely any number from the opposite sex who could provide that other half. If the one chosen does not provide that sense of completeness, the blame would have to be placed somewhere besides in the fates.

Our position is that love is more likely to develop through intelligent choosing rather than from any mysterious *searching* or *intuitive reaching* for signs.

Another notion is that people *fall in love*, suddenly and completely, whenever the right person comes along. People talk about *love at first sight*. They say that "when love strikes, you will know it." The main problem with this is that when one feels the pulse racing, the knees shaking, the spine tingling, he has to wait to see if it heralds the onset of the "flu" or the onset of "love." There may be strong attraction or the *beginning of love* at first sight, but that is all.

Whether that beginning will ever develop into "the real thing" will take time and testing to determine. Love is a process, not a static fact;

we grow in love, not fall into it. Many have thought that they were in love at first sight, only to change their minds after taking another and a closer look. On the other hand, many have thought that they didn't particularly care for the one they were going with, only to find themselves coming to love this person after a time of close association.

Sometimes, too, people hold to the mistaken idea that "love is all that matters," that if a man and woman are madly in love they should be willing to give up everything else in order to have each other; that if they are in love and marry, they cannot but be eternally happy regardless of everything else.

If love is the result of a relationship, then whatever affects that relationship can affect love. Rational considerations of the external pressures which will affect the relationship will give love itself a better chance of maturing and enduring. Emotional love needs to be tested, strengthened, and protected by the intellect.

Love, like other growing things, needs more than occasional care and attention. Once developed, it does not remain the same if ignored. Subjected to too much stress, strain, and arid soil too early, it withers and dies. In a partially protected environment, with continual pruning, feeding, and watering, it grows into a sturdy plant, able to endure more stress, strain, and longer arid periods. "Love conquers all" is likely to appear more true when there are not a great number of things to conquer.

Students of marriage and family very commonly group all these mistaken notions concerning love under the term *romantic fallacy.* The fallacy lies not in the acceptance of romance as an element in love (for certainly every relationship needs some demonstration of affection to serve as a social lubricant, if nothing else), but rather in the belief that romantic love is just about everything that needs to be considered in choosing a mate or in making a happy union.

Component Elements. We have seen some of the things that genuine love *is not.* It is not a mystic force that strikes without warning and can be recognized at once every time it hits. Though it is more emotional than rational, there is reason for thinking that it can be understood and even strengthened by the rational process.

There are, of course, many kinds and degrees of love between men and women. There is *narcissistic love,* where the lover is basically self-centered and exploitative; there is *infatuation,* sometimes defined as a swift attraction which is superficial and untested. From the romantic fallacy, this term is applied to past relationships which were once defined as love— thus protecting the idea that true love occurs only once and is undying. There is *romantic love,* where the emphasis is upon physical attraction and sentimental notions; there is *sexual lust,* where physical desire is paramount and other love elements are largely absent; there is *platonic love,* where the couple derives almost its sole satisfaction from its pattern of intellectual friendship; and there is *conjugal love,* where all of the elements necessary for the building and the strengthening of the marriage relationship are present.

What are the ingredients of an enduring conjugal love? They may be classified into three broad groupings:

1. *Physiological,* which includes all kinds of bodily and sexual attractions
2. *Psychological,* which includes the various sentimental and affectional feelings
3. *Sociological,* which includes the many adjustments which make the man and woman companionable and interdependent

Conjugal love means sexual attraction, but it is more than that; it also means affectional warmth, but it is more than that; and it likewise means interdependence, trust, and companionship, but it is more than that too. Each of these elements adds strength to the others. If any one of them is absent, love is weakened.

Generally speaking, men, more than women, have tended to overemphasize the physical aspects of love in their concern for sexual satisfaction; women, more than men, have tended to overemphasize the sentimental aspects of love in their concern for romantic glamour; and both sexes have tended to *underemphasize* the sociological or adjustment aspects of the love relationship—at least before the wedding.

But, though it is possible to separate the ingredients for purposes of analysis, one should also know that conjugal love is a *generalized response* cutting across many levels of feeling and interaction. Actually, it is a very complex phenomenon made up of various images, ideas, drives, and emotional states, all grouped together and fixed upon some person through experience.

Another way of viewing mature conjugal love is in terms of its developmental stages or processes. Considered thus, its principal elements or ingredients are as follows:

Love = Needing + Adjusting + Trusting + Giving

This means that it will start out by meeting the particular needs of the particular personalities involved, through selective matching; that it will grow by association and adaptation, leading to greater and greater interdependence and trust; and that it will be sustained by an attitude of otherness and helpfulness, where each person is able to go beyond himself and to be primarily concerned about the welfare and the happiness of the other. This latter is sometimes referred to as *outgoing love,* in contrast to the ⟨ingoing⟩ type where others are loved, not for their own sake, but for how they can be used by the person doing the loving.

Developmental Processes

When the doubts, anxieties, and distrusts which have been associated with early dating (see Chapter 8) are remembered, we may wonder how any relationship manages to get beyond this stage to begin to develop the trust and acceptance associated with love. Obviously, not all couples who move into courtship and later into marriage do overcome these feelings. The doubts and mistrusts may continue throughout the marriage. But it is possible for them to be overcome. In fact, Waller suggested many years ago that in a relatively equal power structure, the anxieties and attempts to get the other person to commit himself in the "dating game" can contribute to moving them along toward a deeper commitment (Waller, 1937). If each has about the same bargaining power and they continue their relationship until some emotional involvement occurs, then the relationship changes. One or the other or both are likely to be unsure of the true nature of the other's feelings, afraid he is being led on, but hoping he is wrong. Tension builds until one or the other brings it to a head, which results either in breaking the relationship or redefining it at a deeper level. The person accused of "leading the other on" may be surprised at his own denial and expression of love that results (Leslie, 1967, pp. 359–60). But at that time the relationship is redefined and the interaction between them is likely to be somewhat different. The deeper commitment opens the way for more serious conversation, allowing each a more complete view of the other. It also increases their responsibility to each other and aids in the redefinition of themselves as a pair. Reiss has suggested a theory of the development of love in keeping with these ideas.

The Wheel Theory of Love Development. Reiss (1960) suggests that the possibility of two people continuing a relationship until emotional involvement begins to occur is enhanced if there is *rapport* between them. Rapport refers to the feeling of being able to communicate and feel understood. In other words there is a feeling that they are looking through the same "knot hole." They may disagree about the action taking place on the field, but at least they are looking at the same "game."

The ease of talking and the feeling of being understood lead them to talk about things which mean something to them—things they may not divulge to someone else. As they exchange ideas, past experiences, and feelings they enlarge their areas of understanding (or shared culture) and increase the feeling of rapport, inviting deeper *self-revelation*. If this is felt to be satisfying they are likely to want to spend more time together. As they are together more and more they begin to build a pattern of *mutual habits*. That is, they develop rewarding habits of interaction which cannot be completed unless they are both present—they talk on the telephone at a particular time each evening—they have special places they walk—there is a certain song that always brings the same exchange of words or gestures—there are more and more sentences which do not have to be completed. All of these create periods during the day or week when they look forward to meeting, or experience a feeling of loss if the other is gone. If these habits are mutually rewarding they are likely to be satisfying some of their personality *needs*. Having one's needs met makes one feel good, more satisfied, and complete. There is a feeling of warmth toward the person who makes us feel this way, and a desire to spend more time with him. Thus, rapport is increased and the wheel turns inviting more openness and fewer defenses (see Figure 10–1).

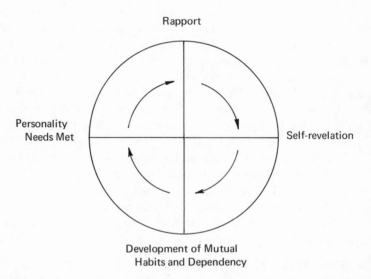

Fig. 10–1. The Wheel Theory of Love Development. (Adapted from Reiss, 1960.)

Recent attempts to test the way in which relationships develop offer some support to the relationship between self-revelation, the self-concept, and a naturally rewarding experience (Murstein, 1970; Worthy *et al.*, 1969).

The evidence supports the notion that the more one person is attracted to another the more he discloses his private world to that person. Such disclosures are rewarding to the listener since they show he is seen to be worthy of receiving intimate information, thereby raising his self-esteem. Reciprocation is also encouraged at about the same level of intimacy

(Worthy *et al.*, 1969). As this process continues, the two people should develop a better understanding of each other and greater liking as a sense of acceptance grows. In support of this idea, Murstein has reported evidence that couples who show good courtship progress over a six-month period are able to make more accurate predictions of the partner's self and ideal-self than couples with poor courtship progress. Furthermore, they show greater congruence between their conceptions of ideal spouse and perceptions of the partner than those couples making poor courtship progress (Murstein, 1970, p. 472).

Decline of the Love Feeling. Obviously, the wheel can unwind as well as wind. At any point in time, the self-revelation may bare feelings or aspirations that are totally misunderstood or introduce points of conflict over deeply felt goals and values. Sometimes it is discovered that previously revealed feelings are used to hurt or control. The introduction of these doubts or rebuffs into the interaction reduces the feeling of rapport, leaves unsatisfied some of the needs formerly met in the relationship, causes the defenses to close as trust is questioned, and perhaps reduces the desire for continuance of the relationship. There is a gradual loss of interest in the other person as the warmth and emotional involvement cools. Occasionally, the breaking of the mutual habits reduces the time spent together where it is possible for self-revelation to take place and continue to enlarge the shared culture within which the couple can communicate. This may occur when the couple is separated geographically for a long period of time. Their separate experiences may change their ideas and values enough so that they can no longer communicate and feel understood by the other person who has not been subjected to the same influences.[5]

This is a relatively common experience of college students who leave someone behind in the hometown, or who attend different colleges. If there is enough commitment to the relationship, they may start the wheel turning again; but it may take a great deal of conversation to exchange enough of the unshared experiences to rebuild the feeling of rapport. One student who was engaged to a girl on a different campus remarked that, on the occasional week ends when they could be together, they were just getting to the point where they could talk to each other again when it was time to part. It is easy to see that, without other kinds of pressures holding this couple together, the unsatisfying aspects of the relationship, under stress of separation, could eventually result in their redefining themselves as having never "really been in love."

[5] Separation during courtship is one of the most frequent reasons given for breaking engagements. See Landis and Landis (1963, p. 230).

Content of Self-Revelation. The level of material included in the self-revelation varies drastically from couple to couple. The number of twists of the wheel necessary to produce the love feeling varies from individual to individual. The amount of intimacy in divulging feelings and experiences necessary for one person to feel secure, understood, and loved may be extremely threatening to another, who needs some degree of distance and privacy to feel secure. This tends to be associated with both sex and education. The more highly developed the verbal skills and the more aware one is of one's own feelings (both associated with higher education), the more likely he is to desire deep communication with a loved one. The socialization process of the female, being largely geared to the development of interpersonal competence, is more likely to create needs for communication in her than in the male. Therefore, the marriage counselor is often faced with the complaints of a wife that: "We never talk, he never tells me anything, I feel closed out. We just live together; we aren't married!" The husband, confronted with this complaint is likely to say: "What does she mean we never talk? We talk all the time—about the kids' clothes, where or when we are going out to dinner, who we're going to have over, her hair, the house, and on and on and on. What more does she want?" What for the husband is too much chatter is for his wife too superficial and lacks self-revelation. There are, then, no criteria for determining how many twists of the wheel will result in a feeling of love. The crucial factor is that the level of revelation and degree of mutual dependency is sufficient for both parties to feel tied to and supported by the relationship rather than threatened by it.

Difference Between Friendship and Love. A careful look at the components of love development, as presented by Reiss, suggests that these may describe deep friendships as well as opposite-sex love relationships. Perhaps one of the big differences between these two types of relationships is that in the romantic relationship sexual feelings are included in the self-revelation and mutual-dependency stages.

Many love relations start as friendships in which the attraction between them is the solution of mutual problems—sometimes problems involving other love relationships. As they discuss their problems there may be much revealing of themselves, their fears, doubts, anxieties. Their mutual understanding and growing trust may then begin to include feelings of sexual attraction toward each other, redefining the friendship as a love relationship. Bolton (1961) suggests that this may be a crucial condition for the development of love where one or both parties are inhibited or fearful of a lasting involvement in a male–female relationship. The focus on external problem-solving such as parental conflicts, school difficulties, and so on, provides the atmosphere for a build-up of trust and dependency which sets up the conditions for love to be recognized and gradually to include the sexual component.

The other important distinguishing factors between friendship and romantic attachment include the future planning for marriage and family as well as the permanent commitment, both of which are lacking in friendships. Friendships are expected to last as long as circumstances make them mutually satisfying while romantic love is expected to last forever!

External Influences. A recognition of the winding and unwinding of the feeling of love alerts us to the effect of external influences in holding a relationship together or pulling it apart. Part of the process is the periodic redefinition of the two people in relationship to each other. The feeling of love is quite likely to rise, fall, or rock along on an even keel for a while as they are exposed to new experiences and outside pressures. They are likely at some time along the way to begin to define themselves as a pair—thus the "steady shirts," the exchange of symbols which formalizes for themselves and others this new definition of the two individuals as a pair. If it is an approved relationship, then families and friends provide the expectations for its continuance which put an additional responsibility on the pair to stay together. As friends and families reinforce the new pair identity, the relationship tends to be supported over the normal "low spots" of the love feelings.

Although these outside pressures support many "good" relationships and keep them from succumbing to normal stresses and strains, they may also cause confusion and hold together relationships which have ceased to be mutually rewarding. College students occasionally express doubts about continuing a relationship with someone who has remained behind in the hometown. While on the campus, they feel that there is nothing holding them together; the love has died. But when they return home they hear so many references to the two of them as a pair, or receive so many expressions of dismay if they suggest things are not the same, that they question their doubts. One student, faced with such a situation put in this way:

I let it slip at home that I wasn't as interested in Ron as I used to be. It seemed like all I heard after that were comments like, "Oh no, not you and Ron—what a shame! You two were just made for each other." "Poor Ron, what will he do without you!" "This is just a lover's quarrel, you'll be back together." Before long I was even wondering if they could see something I couldn't see. I began to think that if everyone else thought we were so right for each other, there must be something wrong with me! But now I'm back on campus and I know it won't work, but how will I ever get out of it?

Some people, obviously don't get out of such a situation—some because of social pressures, some because it is too anxiety-provoking to redefine oneself as a single person again rather than as part of a "team," and others because the desires for marriage are so great that they override the doubts about the other person.

The Conditions for Love Developing

We can see that a number of different things come together to aid in the development of a love relationship. First, there is some feeling of rapport or attraction which encourages the two people to continue interacting. Second, there is the opportunity for exposing certain things about the self which are understood or appreciated by the other. Third, there is a feeling that the growing dependency and interaction satisfies some of the personality needs one has. These may be complementary in Winch's terms or they may be homogamous in that the personalities are much alike and enhance their mutual enjoyment of similar activities, or they may be satisfying a temporary need for recognition. The opportunities must arise, however, for these satisfactions to be discovered and appreciated. Since external circumstances probably accentuate different needs at different times, we may be attracted to one type of person at one period and another type later on. This is more likely to occur during adolescence when the self-concept is undergoing rapid change. Fourth, there is the matter of social pressure which reinforces the definition of the two people as a pair. Even strong negative evaluation of a particular pair may reinforce their dependence on each other, so that they feel it is the "two of them" against the world. Without the negative evaluation or the particular needs which meshed for the two of them at a particular time they may not have defined themselves as "in love." Lastly, there is the assumption that the two persons have matured enough to be capable of turning their attention away from themselves to be concerned about the happiness and welfare of someone else.

Considering these conditions for love it can be seen that two people may meet at a particular time under certain circumstances and find themselves "falling in love." The same two people may meet at another time under different conditions and hardly give each other a second glance. It can perhaps also be seen that marriage does not guarantee that love will remain, even though the marriage remains intact. Marriage enhances the opportunities for interaction which can be used to keep love alive and growing. It also enlarges the possibilities for interaction which can endanger the feeling of rapport, trust, understanding, and self-esteem.

Ambivalence in Love

It is apparent that love, viewed in these terms, can be directed toward more than one person. Depending upon the content of the interaction it can be directed toward a number of different people, but in different ways and in different degrees. Presumably there will be one of the opposite sex that each will come to love best, not because of any supposed predestination but because of better matching and/or more complete and intense communication, trust, and adjustment.

Love does not assume that everything about the other person is liked or that there are no conflicts, arguments, or angy outbursts. It is, in fact, quite normal to both like and dislike the same person—liking him in respect to some things and disliking him in respect to others. This contradiction (and sometimes fluctuation) between love and hate of the same person is referred to technically as *ambivalence*. The problem is one of weighing the loves against the hates to determine if the "net love" is sufficient to provide the trust necessary to allow love to continue growing. If the dislikes cause one to use the self-revelations of the other to humiliate, control, or enhance his own self-concept at the other's expense, trust wavers and love is likely to suffer. The husband who jokingly lays bare to friends his wife's privately confided feelings has undermined the trust which made the confidence possible.

Recognition and Measurement. An important question that nearly everyone faces at one time or another before marriage is this: "How can I know I am in love?" Sometimes the question is asked when there are several of the opposite sex that a person cares for and there is difficulty in making up one's mind. At other times it is asked when the choice has been narrowed down to one person, but there are doubts and contradictory emotions concerning that one.

The first prerequisite in recognizing love is to know its true meaning and nature. We have tried to explain love as the natural involvement of personalities, one with another. Instead of being a mysterious and uncontrollable force, as some believe, it is a normal unity based upon interdependence, and it grows out of need fulfillment, habits of association, and achievements in adjustment.

The question, then, is not just, "Am I in love?" but "What *kind* of love?" and "How *much*?"

Although there is no formula by which one can be absolutely certain, there are ways in which love can be tested and most doubts removed. It must be remembered, however, that doubting is normal and does not mean the absence of love. So long as people are imperfect there will be doubts in their dealings with each other, and so long as adjustments are necessary there will be misunderstandings and conflicts in the process; but neither of these, if mild, need interfere with love. It is only with a few that feelings of absolute certainty precede marriage, and with many of them the reason is romantic illusion and the result is post-marriage disillusionment. Better it is to be realistic, considering all angles before taking the plunge. If the following questions can be answered affirmatively, it is reasonably sure that one is on the right track:

Do you think and plan in terms of we?

Do you try to make your partner happy; are you proud of him (or her) in public?

Do you enjoy being together, talking together, working together?

Do you stimulate, but not antagonize, each other in conversation?

Are you interested in essentially the same things; do you have the same ideals and purposes?

Do you know each other well enough to be sure that your love is for the person and not the glamour?

Are you able to be agreeable most of the time and to settle your differences constructively; does each quarrel end with a better adjustment?

Do you protect each other's self-revelations so that confidences are never used to enhance one partner at the expense of the other?

Have you made your growing relationship a matter of both study and effort?

IMPORTANCE OF LOVE TO THE NUCLEAR FAMILY

Love, of course, is not necessary to the stability of a family system. Stability can be maintained by loyalties, obligations, mutual economic benefits, and commitment to family. These constraints on family dissolution are more likely to be found where the extended family is the most important unit. They are more prevalent where the family is rooted to one piece of ground and the newly married couple becomes part of the larger family system. This is not to say that love doesn't exist in the extended family system, only that it is not essential to family stability.

In our society, however, the newly married couple is expected to move away from both parental families. It is considered a hardship on the new relationship if economic conditions make it necessary for them to live with either set of parents. They must establish their own routine and make their own adjustments to each other without benefit or hindrance of an established household. All old ties must be broken sufficiently to allow the new nuclear unit to form. In this kind of family system, love aids in binding the new couple together while they break their ties and make their initial adjustments to each other (Goode, 1965, p. 39). Love provides the mutual dependency which aids in the resocialization of both partners which takes place as they refocus their lives to include the other. As the mutual dependency of family members on each other for economic survival is reduced, dependency on each other for emotional satisfaction increases. Love becomes one of the primary satisfactions desired in marriage.

Increased Emphasis on Love

There are a number of trends in our society at present which, if continued, suggest that love will become an important basis for marriage for a larger proportion of our population. The current efforts to make the relationship between the family and the economic system more secure should reduce the number of families in which the economic function takes precedence over emotional maintenance. As our society grows, becomes more complex, and moves into the "computer age," the feelings of depersonalization are likely to become more widespread. The family function of restoring the feelings of self-worth and affirming the identities of its members is likely to assume greater importance. Part of supporting these identities is the opportunity for openly communicating, confirming, and having accepted our human feelings of love, hate, anger, doubts, fears, and triumphs. It may become much more important in the future for our families to develop these skills and pass them on to their children.

The importance of interpersonal skills has been recognized in a few large industries in recent years (Poppy, 1968). It remains to be seen whether these "rehumanized" relationships are compatible with the goals of large industries. They are compatible with families, however, especially where love, which equalizes the power structure, is the basis of the relationship. It is important to remember, however, that this is love defined in a special way: not the romantic notion which implies the fairy book concept of never-ending bliss, but a tough, realistic ability to mutually express, accept, and affirm all the human yearnings, feelings, failings, sorrows, joys, and ecstasies.

This is admittedly an idealistic conception of one way our family system may develop. There are indications that many of our young people are seeking this kind of relationship. Whether they succeed or not will be influenced not only by their own skills and effort but by the future development of society itself. From all indications at the moment, though, love, however defined and experienced, will continue to be an important part of the mate selection process for a large proportion of our population.

THE PRINCIPLE OF VALUE RELEVANCE

The principle of value relevance becomes important at all stages of the mate selection process. The selection of a mate from the same or differ-

ent race, religion, or social class is influenced largely by the values of the
two individuals concerning the importance of these factors, as well as pressures from the social groups with which they are in contact. Some will
have values so strong that they will preclude even the early interaction
which, under favorable conditions, may lead to the development of a deep
relationship. Others may become involved in initial interaction, but when
they become serious they re-evaluate the importance of endogamous factors or succumb to pressures from family and friends and break off the
relationship. Still others may have values which make endogamous characteristics completely unimportant or actually make persons from dissimilar groups seem especially attractive.

The definition of when one is in love, or even whether love outweighs
factors such as ambition, financial security, good looks, or domestic abilities, will depend upon the meaning that marriage has for the people involved. Certainly, expectations for the type of relationship which will be
defined as love vary from individual to individual. Rather than there
being any one kind or level of feeling associated with "true" love, the
definition will depend upon whether the relationship meets the needs and
expectations of the individual. From this viewpoint it would not be expected that any one theory of love or of mate selection would explain all
relationships which end in marriage.

SUMMARY

In the United States today, mate selection is more a matter of individual choice than at most other times in history or places in the world.
However, order is introduced into the mate selection process so that who
marries whom is not left completely to the young people.

Certain conditions serve to influence and limit one's choice of a marital
partner: legislation pertaining to marriage; indirect and direct pressure
from parents and friends; residential and functional propinquity; the
norms of endogamy, which press one to select from within his own race,
ethnic group, religion, and social class; and the balance of the sex-ratio
in one's geographical location and age grouping. These limitations tend
to form the "field of eligibles" from which the individual choice will be
made. Very few have a wide choice even from among the field of eligibles. Since it is not only a matter of choosing but of being chosen, the
choice is from among those few who show interest in maintaining a relationship.

Final selection in terms of love is the norm in our society. Studies
designed to discover whether love and mate selection are more likely to
occur between people sharing similar personality traits or complementary

ones have been largely inconclusive. Probably both are operative but in different ways and to different degrees, depending upon the strength of the self-concepts and the personality needs most apparent during the time the relationship is developing.

Present trends in the society suggest that love will become more important for a larger proportion of our population in the future. This is not a romantic idea of love, however, but a realistic ability to mutually express, accept, and reaffirm the self-concepts of the individuals involved.

QUESTIONS AND PROJECTS

1. Do you have any suggestions as to the best or optimum age for young people to start dating? To start going steady? To get married? What are your reasons?

2. Should a high school girl who gets married during her senior year be asked to leave school? A high school boy? Discuss pro and con.

3. There are certain legal restrictions on who may marry whom. What is your opinion concerning legal restrictions of any kind? Should there be more or less than exist now? State reasons for your answer.

4. List the informal pressures which tend to enforce endogamous marriages. Can you think of other ways these are enforced besides those mentioned in the text? Do you think these pressures are stronger from the family or from peers? Explain.

5. Discuss the pros and cons of interracial dating. Of interracial marriages.

6. Discuss the pros and cons of interreligious dating. Of interreligious marriage.

7. Recognizing the effects of social pressures on the field of eligibles, construct your own theory of individual selection out of the field of eligibles. If you say the deciding factor is love, then explain what influences a person to love one person and not another when both may have many similar admirable qualities.

8. Apply the wheel theory of love development to one of your own relationships—either a love relationship or friendship with a member of either sex. Can you explain either a break-up or a deeper relationship in these terms? Do you think it is an adequate model to explain the development of love? Explain.

9. Discuss the relationship between commitment and love. Can one exist without the other? Explain. Which is most important for marriage? Defend your position.

10. Can a person love two individuals equally well (a) at different times, implying that love can occur more than once? (b) At the same time, implying that love does not center on one object? Discuss.

11

Engagement

Engagement for most persons is the last step in a long progression of deepening commitments leading to marriage. It is the final chance for changing one's mind without legal procedures. The old "breach of promise" suit which viewed engagement as a binding promise to marry has virtually disappeared. A broken engagement is no longer seen as disgraceful but as fortunate that the mistake was discovered before marriage. A broken engagement is not accomplished easily, however, for at every step of the progression—casual dating, going steady, informal understanding, and finally engagement—more and more pressures converge on the pair to make it harder and harder to break up.

FUNCTION OF THE PUBLIC COMMITMENT

For many the actual engagement is merely the formalization of an understanding which has grown privately between them. Sometimes the progress of the private understanding is announced by the exchange of symbols, each carrying a slightly different meaning.

On a college campus, for example, the process may be broken into a progression of steps such as lavaliering (the male presents the female with a necklace bearing his fraternity insignia), pinning (presentation of the fraternity pin to the female) and engagement. The more complicated the process becomes, however, the higher the probability of misinterpreting the steps. "Lavaliering," for some, means an engagement to be pinned, for others it means only the assurance of a date. Some males consider it a way of tempting the girl to assume deeper feeling than really exists to gain sexual advantage. Some females find it is a convenient way to keeping track of her victories, like notches on a gun or scalps on a belt.

238

"One of my fraternity brothers has seven lavaliers out—one in every port, so to speak."

"Lavaliering is a college version of the exchange of high-school class rings."

"It really is an engagement to be pinned. It does involve an emotional commitment."

Pinning also has different meanings. It occasionally is a way of gaining prestige from being "pinned to a high status house." It is a serious commitment for some, a way of seeing if they want to become engaged. For some it is considered the same as engagement. No difficulty is involved if both parties agree on the degree of commitment and the limitations involved. Whatever the meaning, however, it is likely to carry a public announcement of the pairing. Many campus newspapers carry a pinning column which keeps all aware of the current condition of the dating market—which ones have been taken out of circulation, which have recently reentered through de-pinning, and so on.

Off the campuses an additional step between the high school ring and engagement is likely to be a sweetheart ring. Whatever the actual meaning of the symbols, however, the public announcement contained in the exchanges serves to alert the family and friends to the progress of the relationship. It forces a redefinition and provides support for their developing definition of themselves as a pair. It invites more serious thought about the future of the relationship, a deeper investigation of their goals, values, and emotions toward each other without the degree of commitment involved in an engagement.

The engagement, whether private or public, is the only one of the steps clearly declaring the intent to marry. A couple may privately have an understanding and their friends may have been told about it, but the public announcement is the step which brings full social pressure to bear on holding the couple together, and focuses their attention on their plans for the future. The public commitment allows the individuals to begin seriously to make plans with some relief from the insecurity involved with a private understanding. Although engagement does not remove all doubts and anxieties about the marriage actually taking place someday, it does provide comfort in that both parties have publicly committed themselves to it. It may also bring discomfort as the relationship with the partner's family takes on new facets.

RELATIONSHIP BETWEEN ENGAGEMENT AND MARITAL SUCCESS

Several studies have shown a relationship between successful engagement and marital adjustment. It is difficult to know whether this indicates that a successful engagement contributes to marital adjustment or only indicates that those persons most likely to go through an engagement period prior to marriage possess other characteristics which are associated with marital stability. There are several factors associated with both engagement and marital stability which support the latter interpretation:

1. Engagement is more likely to be found among the higher socioeconomic positions where marriages are more stable anyway.

2. Engagement is likely to indicate a relationship of longer duration also associated with marriage stability. The "no-engagement" group is more likely to contain those who marry on short acquaintanceship or who hurry the wedding because of unexpected pregnancy, military service, or some other pending separation which would put an added burden on marital adjustment. This, of course, does not mean that these reasons predominate among those who do not go through the engagement stage; it means only that those who do marry quickly for reasons such as these are more likely to skip the formal engagement.

3. Engagement is likely to indicate at least surface acceptance of the relationship by family and friends. The no-engagement group is obviously more likely to contain those who experience opposition from families which forces either elopement or concealment of the seriousness of the relationship until they are ready to marry. Approval of the marriage by family and friends is also associated with marital stability.

It may be, then, that the relationship between engagement and marital adjustment appears mainly because other characteristics positively associated with marital stability are more likely to be found among those who go through an engagement period than among those who do not. Theoretically, however, we can suggest some reasons why engagements may be causally related to future marital adjustments.

Testing the Relationship

Although most couples probably do not see engagement as a further testing period, it probably functions in this way. At engagement the decision to marry has already been made, it is not seen as an invitation to further trials. However, as Udry (1966, p. 260) puts it, the agreement on plans to marry encourages the couple to overtly begin to look at each other as prospective spouses. This change in perspective is likely to call attention to things in the other which never mattered before.

Planning for the future forces them to consider problems and to discover values, tastes, and habits of interaction that were not part of their earlier relationship. Decisions which must be made cause them to be specific about things which may have been discussed only in generalities before.

Habits of Perception, Interpretation, and Reaction. Some of the habitual ways of interacting which will be extremely important in marriage may have been largely absent in the earlier relationship, as it was mainly oriented around recreation and leisure time. The handsome, fun-loving, carefree boy friend may be interpreted quite differently when it is found that this is a habitual reaction to anything requiring decisions and planning. What was endearing in a playmate may be interpreted as irresponsibility and weakness in a future spouse. The petulant expressions of jealousy which may have been flattering coming occasionally from a girl friend may be stifling when it is discovered during engagement that she reacts with anger and jealousy if her fiance does not devote all of his time and attention to her. The strong, decisive male who appeared so masculine as he made all of the decisions in the dating relationship may take on an entirely new look when this is extended to wedding planning, house furnishing, and money budgeting.

On the other hand, the habits of interaction as they are displayed in the new situation of coping with problems of the coming marriage may be found to be even more satisfying than was expected. The engagement period, however, is very likely to uncover hitherto hidden aspects of their habitual ways of reacting to stress and strain, enabling them to begin developing interaction patterns which will carry over into marriage.

Adjusting Value Differences. Many young couples have discussed values and tastes in generalities before they get to the point of engagement. If there were easy ways to discover differences of importance to them, they probably never made it to the engagement stage. But agreeing in general terms and agreeing on the specifics of application are two different phenomena, for here we begin dealing with different meanings of the same words. In planning a wedding for instance, both may agree that they want a simple wedding. He may be astounded to discover that a "simple wedding" for her means five attendants and a guest list of several hundred. They may both be astounded when her mother adds two more attendants and expands the list by another hundred or so. At this time they may be caught up in weighing the relative importance of family loyalty, their own independence and control, their social obligations, and their personal preferences.

At every step along the way toward the marriage ceremony, there are decisions to be made—about the wedding, the guests, the invitations, whether or not there will be reception and what kind, arrangements for housing and household equipment, decisions about jobs perhaps, whether or not they can afford a honeymoon and, if so, how much can they afford, where to go, arrangements for packing and transportation, arrangements for medical examinations and the license, arrangements for the minister if there is to be a church wedding, and innumerable other details. The complexity varies depending upon the elaborateness of the wedding. But some decision-making and planning accompanies even the simplest of ceremonies.

If there is a large group of friends and family members there are likely to be parties and showers leading right up to the night before the wedding, placing demands on the time the individuals can spend together.[1] All of this is likely to increase the tension between the partners and force not only recognition of differences but, hopefully, ways of coping with them while preserving their affectional relationship.

As one student put it after going through such a situation:

By the time the wedding was over I felt like telling my new mother-in-law I never wanted to see her again. If Jane and I survived the last month of our engagement, we should be able to survive anything.

Stress and Strain During Engagement

The stress and strain associated with engagement was discovered by Burgess and Wallin (1953, pp. 244–71) to be a very common and normal experience. Of their sample of one thousand engaged couples, more than one-fourth of the partners (28.1 per cent) disagreed between themselves in five or more areas of their relationship; over one-half (51.5 per cent) disagreed in from one to four areas; less than one-fifth (18.5 per cent) "almost always" agreed in all areas; and only about one out of fifty (1.7 per cent) reported that they always agreed in all areas. Disagreements were least frequent in the area of dating and most frequent over issues having to do with family or friends. In between these two extremes were the following problems, listed in descending order of agreement: demonstration of affection, arrangements for the marriage, religious matters, table manners, matters of recreation, matters of conventionality, philosophy of life, and money matters.

Perhaps another reason for the high frequency of disagreements in engagement is the partial loss of "posing" that accompanies the less committed relationship to some extent. Heiss (1962) found some evidence that the female especially loses some of her adherence to the norms of male dominance under the protection of a committed relationship. Using a measure of traditionalism to separate the sample into low and high traditional groups, he found that non-traditional females were more likely to behave in a traditional way concerning male dominance in a casual relationship than they were in an engaged situation. Engaged persons (both

[1] See Philip Slater (1961) for a superb description of the function of these rituals.

male and female) were more likely to hold non-traditional values than were the casual daters. This perhaps indicates a change in the power structure once the male is emotionally committed to the female, which allows her to voice views during engagement that she would keep to herself earlier for fear of losing the male. Thus, more awareness of disagreements would be expected as more honest opinions and attitudes are exchanged.

Broken Engagements

As stated earlier even though engagement usually means that the two people have already decided to marry, the period does seem to operate as a further testing ground for the relationship whether or not it is intended to be. Not all engagements end in marriage. According to Burgess and Wallin, at least a third of the men and half of the women who marry have had one or more broken engagements. At the time of their study 24 per cent of the men and 36 per cent of the women reported engagements that had been previously broken, and an additional 15 per cent broke with each other subsequent to this time. In comparison with those having only one engagement, engagement-breakers were found: (1) to have less confidence and show less affection in the relationship; (2) to have had a shorter acquaintance, a shorter engagement, and to have spent fewer hours together per week; (3) to have experienced parental opposition or disapproval over the engagement; (4) to have wide cultural differences, as indicated by interfaith mixtures and lack of agreement over activities to be engaged in together; and (5) to have basic personality clashes, with engagement-breakers being more argumentative and wanting to be on the go all the time rather than staying home (Burgess and Wallin, 1953, pp. 272–302).

Probably most of these were broken not because of a rational decision that future marriage with this person would be unsuccessful, but because the satisfactions derived from the current relationship declined for at least one of the members. This can perhaps be seen as a consequence of a change in the way the relationship makes one feel as new, more practical facts are added to it.

In this sense, engagements can be viewed as a *dress rehearsal* for marriage—not in the sense that all the problems of marriage can be solved during engagements but that the ability of these people to continue to provide satisfactions for each other when faced with differences of opinion, tensions, and problems is tested.

A successful engagement does not guarantee a successful marriage, but an unsuccessful engagement should at least warn the couple that they can expect the same kind of problems in marriage. The marriage ceremony does not change the couple's ability to cooperate and reinforce each other's feeling of self-esteem; it merely opens the door to a wider variety of activities in which cooperation and emotional support will be needed.

SEXUAL BEHAVIOR

One area of disagreement most likely to arise during engagement is the nature and depth of the sexual relationship. Although there is a growing tendency for both males and females to accept engagement as sufficient protection for coitus, there is still ample room for disagreement. There is also individual indecision concerning the behavior on the part of many.

In the spring of 1968, the authors polled about 200 college juniors and seniors on their premarital attitudes. Reiss's scale of sexual permissiveness (see Chapter 8) was used. Of these students, 73 per cent of the women and 69 per cent of the men were either going steady, had an informal understanding to be married, were engaged, or married. Thus, well over two-thirds of them were in relationships which would be expected to heighten their sexual permissiveness. This probably accounts partly for the greater permissiveness of this sample compared to the Purdue sample reported in Figure 8–3. Another difference between the two studies is in the categorization of responses. The earlier study had only three response categories—approve, disapprove, undecided. The 1968 study had a six-point response pattern registering degrees of approval or disapproval. Apparently if a respondent has any reservations about premarital sex, he is more likely to check disapprove when no opportunity is given to register his reservations. The "strongly approve" category, taken alone, is quite comparable to the "approve" category in the earlier study. As well as asking the students about their own attitudes concerning the appropriateness of premarital coitus for males and for females separately, we asked them to predict the responses of most males and most females to the same items. Thus we have not only the actual responses of each sex but their perceptions of the norms of each sex (see Figure 11–1).

Male–Female Differences

There was little difference between actual approval for males and for females. Only two per cent more men and five per cent more women approved coitus during engagement for males than approved for females. In fact this was true for coitus when in love and when there was strong affection also. As in other studies, the per cent approving premarital coitus dropped at each lesser degree of commitment, but the difference between approving for males and for females was negligible. A slight indication of the double standard was found in the response to approval

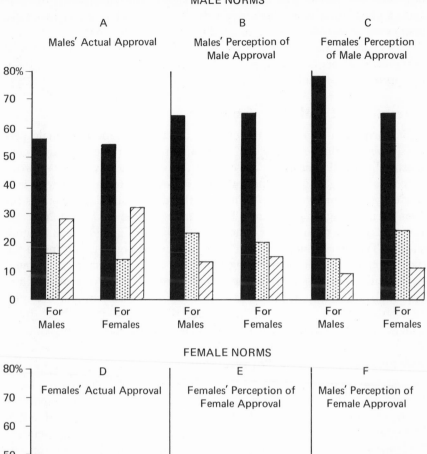

MALE NORMS

A
Males' Actual Approval

B
Males' Perception of
Male Approval

C
Females' Perception
of Male Approval

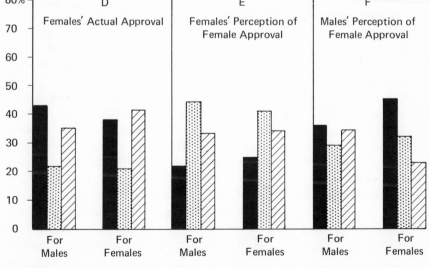

FEMALE NORMS

D
Females' Actual Approval

E
Females' Perception of
Female Approval

F
Males' Perception of
Female Approval

Strong or medium
approval

Slight approval or
disapproval

Strong or medium
disapproval

Fig. 11–1. Comparison of actual and perceived approval of coitus during engagement for males and females.

of coitus when there is no affection (not shown in Figure 11–1), but this was minimal for those who approved. Fourteen per cent of the males responded with either strong or medium approval for males, while only five per cent approved to the same extent for females. At the other end of the scale, 61 per cent disapproved for males, while three-fourths of them disapproved for females.

Perceptions of Male Permissiveness

Segment C in Figure 11–1 shows the females' perception of male permissiveness during engagement. It is apparent that there is high consensus about male norms. A large majority think that most males approve of coitus during engagement for both males and females. There is a tendency for some women to think that the double standard operates for men even during engagement. The men also agree that most men approve of coitus during engagement for both sexes (segment B, Figure 11–1). The perceptions were accurate but just barely so according to the men's actual responses concerning their own attitudes shown in Segment A. Slightly over one-half of them registered either strong or medium approval. Obviously, the male is seen as being highly permissive during engagement. It is, therefore, interesting that almost one-half of these college males are ambivalent or have strong reservations about it.

Perceptions of Female Permissiveness

The high consensus associated with perception of male norms disappeared when the students tried to predict the permissiveness of most females. Women were likely to think that other females would either strongly disapprove or be undecided about coitus during engagement for both males and females (segment E, Figure 11–1). The men, on the other hand, tended to see them as either undecided or approving the female's engaging in coitus during engagement. They were split about evenly in thinking she approved, disapproved, or was undecided concerning the male (segment F, Figure 11–1). It is small wonder that no consensus appeared in the perception of female behavior since the women are obviously in greater disagreement than the males in their actual responses concerning their own attitudes as shown in Segment D. It is apparent that many women see themselves as more permissive than most other women. In general, they see themselves as having strong opinions one way or the other but tend to think that other women are undecided.

Value Conflict

The opportunities for value conflict appear great when we compare the total range of the actual responses of each sex *for themselves:*

	Males	Females
Strong disapproval	17.9%	31.2%
Medium disapproval	10.5	9.4
Slight disapproval	9.5	8.3
Slight approval	6.3	12.5
Medium approval	17.9	21.9
Strong approval	37.9	16.7
	100.00%	100.00%

The actual disagreement among women coupled with their perception of most women as being relatively restrictive or undecided gives us some indication of why women seem to suffer from guilt feelings more than men.[2] Although the per cent of permissive women was almost as great as the per cent of permissive men, the men were likely to see most other men as supporting their position, while at most half of the permissive women thought their position was supported by other women. If we recall the value conflict paradigm of Chapter 4, we will remember that the situation producing the most harmonious relationship was the one in which there was pair-agreement *and* support of these norms in the social groups. Just slightly over 20 per cent of the women would be expected to think they had general support of permissive behavior from other women. It probably also tells us why women are less likely to talk about their sexual experiences than men, since they would be more likely to anticipate disapproval. Thus, they are less exposed to relief from their guilt feelings even from other women who would approve.

Further indication of this perception of the differing permissiveness of the sexes can be found in the Purdue responses to a question about the tendency of males and females to exaggerate the extent of their sexual experiences when talking to others of the same sex. Over two-thirds of the women agreed that most women do *not* do this and that most men *do*. Almost 80 per cent of the men agreed that men exaggerate their sexual experiences when talking to other men. They were not sure what women do—57 per cent of them were undecided.

Relationship to Marital Success

Many persons look for scientific proof through research that premarital intercourse is either favorable or unfavorable for subsequent marital adjustment. The results of studies, to date, are not likely to remove the doubts or reinforce the positions of either those "for" or "against." Without further evidence, there is little in science to aid in making personal

[2] Several studies have supported this sex difference in guilt feeling. See Reiss (1967, pp. 118–19), Kinsey *et al.* (1953 p. 332), and Burgess and Wallin (1953, p. 375).

decisions of this sort—except the strong suggestion that difficulties arise from violating one's own value position, whatever that may be—though it is quite possible that future research will throw some light on the problem.

It should be clear from previous discussions of the place of values in the evelution and subsequent consequences of any behavior for the persons involved that an easy answer concerning the relationship between premarital intercourse, per se, and marital happiness is not available. The literature is literally sprinkled with arguments pro and con, but these reflect different value positions rather than empirical evidence (Mace, 1961; Guyon, 1961; Kirkendall, 1960; Poffenberger, 1960).

The early studies of marital adjustment generally supported a small negative relationship between premarital intercourse and marital adjustment or happiness. In the late 1920's Hamilton (1929) and Davis (1929) both reported that marriages were more successful where the wife had had no premarital sexual relationships. In the 1930's, Terman (1938, pp. 324–25), in a study of 792 husband–wife pairs, found greater marital happiness among those who were without premarital intercourse experience. However where relations were with future spouse alone, the correlations were not significant, and he warned against reading causation into the findings.

In the forties, Locke (1951, pp. 133–39, 156) found larger percentages of happily married couples as opposed to divorced couples reporting no premarital relations (especially men reporting no intercourse with persons other than present spouse) and reporting no belief, knowledge, or suspicion that the mate had had intercourse with others before marriage. At about the same period, Burgess and Wallin (1953, pp. 353–90), in a longitudinal analysis of engaged and married couples, found higher adjustment scores in engagement and in marriage for those who had not experienced premarital intercourse. The relatively small relationship however, prompted them to agree with Terman (1938, p. 329) that the ". . . relatively small prediction weights warranted by our data on sex experience prior to marriage are in striking contrast with the importance attached by moralists to premarital chastity."

Relationship to Marital Sex

When the relationship was between premarital intercourse and the wife's orgasmic capacity in marriage, the relationship was different. Both Burgess and Wallin and Kinsey found that frequency of marital orgasm was related to premarital sexual experience. Burgess and Wallin (1953, pp. 362–63) discovered that the lowest frequencies of marital orgasm were within the group who had had no premarital experience. Those who had sexual relations only with their future spouse had somewhat higher frequencies, while the highest frequencies were among those with sexual experience with their future husbands as well as others. Kinsey (1953, pp. 386–88) added a further dimension while agreeing with the Burgess and Wallin findings. Premarital coitus was positively related to marital orgasm only if the premarital experience resulted in orgasm. Otherwise, those with premarital experience were less likely to have reached orgasm with their husbands than those who had had no premarital experience. Whether this represents a selective factor at work in that those with greater sexual responsiveness are more likely to respond orgasmically both before and after marriage or indicates a negative effect of an unsuccessful premarital experience on subsequent marital sex is unknown. Whatever the reason, the findings are complex enough to be of small comfort to the individual looking for guidance.

It is wise to remember that the marital adjustment scores used in the above studies probably operate to give more conventional people higher scores. So when the norms support chastity, the more conventional people will adhere to them and also receive higher scores. If this is the case, more recent studies may show different results.

In the 1950's Kanin and Howard (1958) studied the effects of premarital intercourse on adjustment during the honeymoon period. They found that those women who had been having intercourse with their husbands prior to marriage were: (1) less likely to have taken a honeymoon trip; (2) more likely to report satisfactory sex relations on their wedding night (71 per cent to 47 per cent); and (3) more likely to report their over-all marital sex experiences as satisfying (87 per cent to 32 per cent). Among those who reported problems during the honeymoon, however, three-fourths of the wives with premarital experiences reported sexual difficulties compared to 43 per cent of those without. The seeming contradictions between the higher report of difficulties as well as higher over-all satisfaction was explained by Kanin and Howard as the probable result of the higher expectation the experienced women had for marital sex. When the wives were asked about the influence of the premarital experience on marital sex, 58 per cent of those with premarital coital experience reported it was beneficial, while 42 per cent said it had not helped.

Also in the fifties, Kirkendall (1961, pp. 199–200) analyzed the relationships of 200 college males. He could come to no general conclusions about the effect of sexual intercourse, per se, on the relationship. He was only able to conclude that some couples had built relationships of devotion and mutual respect. Of these, some were relatively free of inhibitions about sex. Where this combination exists, sexual intercourse can occur "without damage" to the relationship. He used "without damage" rather than strengthen because it was his opinion that the relationships which were not damaged were already so strong that intercourse did not have much to offer toward strengthening them.

Effect of Current Values

Kirkendall's conclusion points to the effects of current values, suggesting that where values are restrictive it takes a strong relationship and two relatively autonomous people to withstand the negative effects of deviating from them.

One recent study attempted to test the relationship between premarital coitus and *predicted* marital and sexual adjustment (Shope and Broderick, 1967). This study compared three groups of single college women on predicted marital happiness. One group was comprised of 80 virginal girls; the second group of 40 girls had had coitus over 15 times in the last two months *without* orgasmic response; the third group of 40 girls had had equivalent sexual experiences *with* orgasmic response. The virginal group differed from the non-virginal ones on only three of the twelve sub-sections of the marital prediction inventory used. On these sub-sections and on the over-all predicted adjustment scores the virgins were significantly higher than the non-virgins. The differences between the orgasmic and non-orgasmic groups were not significant even for predicted sexual adjustment. The authors suggest that the major factors explaining the relationships between virginity and later adjustment appeared to be conventionality and personal stability. This, again, is probably telling us only that conventional people are more likely to live within the norms (or report that they do) before as well as after marriage, and that these norms are still supporting (especially for women) chastity before marriage.

The advice offered by Kinsey and his associates in the 1940's is about as definitive as any that can be gleaned today from more recent research.

The clinician might very well advise the individual who is strongly convinced that coitus before marriage is morally wrong to hesitate about having such experience, for she is more likely to be emotionally disturbed by it (Kinsey, 1953, p. 320).

Here again we see application of the principle of value relevance.

LEGAL REQUIREMENTS

There are certain legal regulations pertaining to marriage which must be faced before engagement can end with a wedding. Some of these put restrictions upon the act of getting married; others specify the respective rights of husbands and wives; while still others deal with requirements and procedures for dissolving the union. Though there is some uniformity, there is also a great diversity in the legal provisions of the various states. As part of preparation for marriage, every engaged person needs to become familiar with the major features of marriage and family laws in general, and with those of his own state in particular. Following is a brief nine-point summary.

1. All states provide that marriage shall be preceded by a license, performed by an authorized officiant, and that it shall be duly reported and recorded. Marriage, in other words, is regarded as a *civil contract* to be handled by definite legal machinery. Minor exceptions to this are found in nearly half the states, where recognition is given to *common-law marriage*. Such a marriage is one in which there has been no license or wedding, but in which the man and woman have been living together as husband and wife and have been accepted as such by the community. Recognition of such a union as a legal marriage is usually established only after the matter is brought into court. These conditions must be established before the common law marriage is validated: (a) the couple has lived together and presented themselves to the community as husband and wife; (b) they possess marriageability (they meet the legal requirements for marriage); and (c) they had made known their intent to marry at some future date. Usually the last is the most difficult to prove. The general trend in all states appears to be toward non-recognition of these marriages.

Common law marriages mainly appear in lower socioeconomic groups because of their convenience without a long-range commitment, or as a result of mistaking the marriage license for the marriage certificate. Sometimes they result from matings which violate state regulations, such as interracial marriages in those states which, until recently, had laws prohibiting them.

2. All states forbid *bigamy*, or the marriage of persons who are already married.

3. All states prohibit marriages of close blood relatives: brother and sister, parent and child, grandparent and grandchild, aunt and nephew, and uncle and niece. Such matings are branded as *incestuous*. Many of the states carry these prohibitions even farther than those listed above; over half, for example, rule out marriages between first cousins. Almost as many forbid the marriage of a stepchild with a stepparent.

4. *Minimum age* specifications are universal among the states, though the standards are so low in some that it is occasionally still legal for girls to marry as young as twelve or thirteen and boys as young as fourteen or fifteen. The legislative trend is toward a raising of these age limits. The most common present requirements are that the male must be eighteen

and the female sixteen, provided that they have the consent of parents or guardians, or twenty-one and eighteen, respectively, if they do not have consent.

5. There are a variety of provisions intended to insure *accountability and capability* on the part of those who marry. Most states prohibit the marriage of persons who are either feeble-minded or insane, and about a third extended the restriction to those that are epileptic. Undoubtedly there are eugenic reasons in back of such laws, as well as the attempt to see that those who contract for marriage are able to understand the situation and to give intelligent consent. In addition many states specify that there must be mutual consent, with both parties being in a normal state of mind and with neither acting under threat or duress. Some states require that the husband must be capable of rendering support.

6. Marriage is frequently forbidden in cases where either party is afflicted with a *communicable disease*. Only a few states, however, have clauses general enough to cover all transmissible diseases. In some states tuberculosis is named as a disqualifying factor. But it is with respect to the venereal diseases that most of the health legislation pertaining to marriage is written. At the present time approximately forty-seven states have laws requiring premarital blood tests for the veneral diseases, although many of these apply to syphilis only, and in a few states only the male is required to be examined. In most instances it is provided that a marriage license will be denied where the disease is found to be present in an infectious or transmissible stage.

7. Over two-thirds of the states require a *waiting period* between the time the couple applies for a license and the time the ceremony can be performed. In most cases the wait is between the application and the issuance of the license, though in some states it comes after the license but before the marriage. The most common length of waiting required is five days; the next most common, three days. The purpose of these laws is to stop hasty, ill-considered, and, in some cases, illegal, marriages—by giving advance notice in case anyone wants to object and by allowing the couple a little more time to think it over. Popenoe found that in one year's time in the city of Los Angeles, more than a thousand couples who applied for marriage never came back three days later to secure their licenses (Popenoe and Johnson, 1953, p. 183). Sometimes these laws are referred to as "gin marriage laws," for they tend to prevent impetuous marriages that are being motivated by gin, or the moon, or such.

8. States differ rather widely in their provisions regarding the *legal rights of husbands and wives.* In general, wives are still at a disadvantage, though the trend is definitely in the direction of greater equality. Some states give the husband almost complete control over the family purse, including what the wife earns. Sometimes, too, the husband is privileged

with certain discriminatory rights over the wife's property. In most states it is the husband's prerogative to decide on the place of residence.

In other words, in case of disagreement about place of residence, if the husband provides a dwelling for his family and his wife does not follow him within a designated length of time, she is guilty of desertion.[3]

9. All states provide for the *dissolution of marriage* through one means or another. This may be done legally by annulment, separation, or divorce. *Annulment* is the court's declaration that the marriage was never legal in the first place, that it didn't actually exist, due to some misrepresentation or circumvention of the law. Most states make provisions for annulment. Someone must instigate the court action, in this case. These are called *voidable* marriages in that they can be voided if legal attention is called to them. Others, however, are *void* from the beginning and do not require court action. This applies mainly to cases of bigamy and marriages performed by someone other than an authorized person. At the time the violation is discovered, the marriage is void requiring no court action. It is as though the ceremony never took place. The important distinction is that marriages may be discovered to be void even after the death of one of the partners, but no marriage may be voided after death. This sometimes has consequences for inheritance and the naming of heirs. The other legal means of dissolving marriage—separation and divorce—will be discussed in a later chapter.

THE WEDDING

Meeting the legal requirements (acknowledged through the issuance of a marriage license) clears the way for engagements to end in marriage. The custom of requiring some sort of ceremony to designate entrance into marriage has been almost universal; details have differed, but the essence of the practice has been, and is, quite general. Except for common-law marriage, where recognized, this same generalization holds for the United States today. All marriage laws in this country set up requirements for a license, for a ceremony, and for a public recording of the act.

Public recognition of the change in roles to husband and wife endows the couple with all the privileges and responsibilities of marriage. Supposedly, the more public and solemn the ceremony, the more the participants are impressed with the importance of the responsibilities they are taking on themselves, and the less the likelihood that they will take them lightly.

[3] For an interesting treatment of the legalities involved see Harriet F. Pilpel and Theodora Savin (1952).

Statistically speaking, this appears to be correct. One study of "Gretna Green" marriages (so-called as a carryover from an early practice of English youths crossing the border to Gretna Green, Scotland, because the local blacksmith could legally marry any couple, using his anvil as an altar) found that in 10,000 marriages involving Philadelphia couples there was a significantly higher divorce rate for those going out of the city to be married in nearby communities with less restrictive marriage laws (Kephart and Strohm, 1952).

Marriage may be regarded both as a _civil contract_ and as a _religious sacrament_. Legally considered it is a contract authorized and controlled by the state. Yet millions consider it as a sacrament, sanctioned and supervised by the church. In this country marriage may be solemnized by either a civil or a religious officiant—not just anyone, of course, but those authorized according to state law.

The majority of marriages are initiated by a religious ceremony, and studies have long shown that these are the ones most likely to succeed. There are probably reasons other than the impressiveness and public nature of the ceremony which contribute to their greater stability. Civil ceremonies are more likely to include the secret marriages and elopements, which many times signal parental disapproval, premarital pregnancy, hasty decisions, and extremely young age. They are more likely to involve interfaith unions and probably those previously married (Christensen and Barber, 1967). All of these factors are associated with greater marital disruption.

Although the greater solemnity and impressiveness of religious ceremonies may contribute to a higher commitment to the marriage, the major factors associated with marital success are to be found in what the people make of their relationship within their own peculiar framework of social supports and conflicts.

THE PRINCIPLE OF VALUE RELEVANCE

Whether or not an engagement is seen as an important step in the process leading toward marriage undoubtedly varies from individual to individual and group to group. For some it may be considered an entirely unnecessary bow to tradition—after all, if we know we intend to marry, who else matters? For others, however, the reluctance of the other person to go through the formalities of an engagement may indicate to them a less than full commitment to the relationship or perhaps even, from the girl's point of view, the man's unwillingness to spend money for a ring. Even if the two individuals agree that an engagement is not necessary, the evaluation from friends and family may cause occasional doubts about one's own or the partner's commitment.

The principle of value relevance perhaps becomes more important in accounting for the relationship between engagement interaction and marital success. The numerous decisions which must be made increase the probability of discovering differences in values which may not have been apparent before. Whether or not the discovery of deep value conflicts results in a broken engagement is also influenced by the meaning attached to it. One person may see a broken engagement as an indicator of personal failure, evidence that one is really unlovable, another may view it as proof that people (especially those of the opposite sex) cannot be depended upon. Others, however, may see it as a lucky thing that they discovered their differences before marriage.

The sexual relationship is another point at which the principle of value relevance becomes important. The conflicting and inconclusive findings from studies of the consequences of premarital intercourse on marital success appear to support the idea that coitus, itself, is not the most important determining factor but the way in which its occurrence or nonoccurrence influences the individuals' views of themselves, their partners, and their relationship. This will encompass not only their values but the values of the people whom they consider important.

SUMMARY

Engagement serves the function of public announcement of the commitment of two people to each other. It invites a redefinition of the relationship by family and friends which presses the couple to begin perceiving each other as future spouses, in addition to leisure time companions and lovers. It adds a new dimension to the relationship by bringing realistic problems to be solved as plans are made for the wedding and the beginning of married life together. It becomes a dress rehearsal for marriage as the wedding preparation and waiting period produce tensions and conflicts which draw attention to habits of perception, interpretations, and reaction largely lacking from the relationship when it was oriented mainly around leisure time activities.

Engagement heightens the problem of premarital sexual involvement. It is the period in which approval of premarital intercourse has had its largest increase. Yet studies still show a wide range of attitudes about it, with women less likely to approve than men. The range of attitudes and the perceptions of differential support for permissiveness between males and females are likely to result in greater disturbances in the female as a consequence of premarital coitus.

Studies of the relationship between premarital intercourse and marital success are complex and inconclusive. They appear to support the generalization that consequences will depend mainly on the consistency between the values and behavior of the persons involved as well as the attitudes of their social groups.

Meeting the legal regulations on marriage clears the way for engagement to end in the wedding ceremony. The two persons are then formally recognized as endowed with all the rights and responsibilities accompanying marriage. What happens to their relationship after that will be the result of their combined assets, deficits, personal commitments, and effort within a social context containing varying amounts of conflict, challenge, and support.

QUESTIONS AND PROJECTS

1. Some people today say that the legal ties of marriage are stultifying—that many times they force people to stay together when the relationship is no longer rewarding. Thus, they suggest that living together without the legal ties is a better answer because then they know they stay together because they want to. What elements do you think this *partial* commitment to permanence would introduce into the relationship? How do you think these elements might influence the development of the relationship? The power structure? Openness of communication? Can you imagine situations in which the same kind of obligations to an unhappy relationship may develop in these unstructured relationships? Discuss the pros and cons of this kind of relationship.

2. How do you feel about parents' support of married children in college? If married, how much help would you personally expect or be willing to accept? Give reasons. Similarly, discuss the pros and cons of a wife putting her husband through school. Of a husband putting his wife through.

3. How do you feel about parents' support of married children when they are not in college? Under what conditions would you expect or be willing to accept help from parents?

4. What are the conventions on your campus for showing the level of commitment of a relationship? Are they generally understood to have the same meaning? Does the use of the convention (pinning or whatever) tend to change the nature of the relationship? Explain.

5. Are there any serious incidents in your past which you would not care to tell your fiance(é)? What type of incidents, if any, do you feel he or she would be justified in withholding from you? Explain.

6. It has been argued that there is no reason for an engagement to be as long today as formerly, due to the greater freedom which allows young people to know each other in a shorter period of time. Do you agree? How long do you think an average engagement should be today? Is there need for an engagement at all? Discuss.

7. How much sexual intimacy do you think should be expected during engagement? Make a list of the pros and another of the cons of complete sexual intimacy during engagement. When you compare the lists what are your "net" conclusions?

8. If the premarital examination revealed that your fiance(é) had a bad heart condition and could not be expected to live over three or four years, would you go ahead with the wedding? Why or why not? If it were a condition like blindness which was inevitable and incapacitating but not fatal, what then? What if you were the one so afflicted? In a similar way discuss what you would do if you had been married a year and were faced with either of these situations?

9. If knowledge were developed to the point that it were possible to tell which personality traits, values, and goals were compatible and which were not so that computer matching of marriage mates were feasible, would you consult such an agency to find a mate? Would you subject yourself and the person whom you were planning to marry to computer matching to obtain your probability of marital success? Why or why not?

IV

MARITAL
INTERACTION

12

Husband–Wife Roles

The marriage ceremony punctuates the severance of old family ties and the formation of a new family group. It legitimates the adult status of the couple and paves the way for the development of intimacy patterns associated with the husband–wife relationship.

THE HONEYMOON PERIOD

The culturally prescribed "honeymoon" immediately following the wedding stresses the development of intimacy roles freed of the tasks associated with "setting-up housekeeping." The honeymoon is seen as a recreational period, with no obligations to other social roles. But its focus on intimacy is stressed by the usual expectations that the couple will take a trip alone, keep their destination and time schedules secret, and spend the period getting to know each other sexually and emotionally. For the first time they have the privilege to legitimately register at a hotel as a couple, sharing the same room as husband and wife.

Even though there are seemingly no specific tasks associated with this period, general expectations do appear in the cultural definitions of what a honeymoon is supposed to be like. The honeymoon is seen as a blissful state in which the pair is supposed to enjoy each other's exclusive company ecstatically for a period of time during which there is nothing to distract them except non-demanding pleasurable activities. It is something the new husband is expected to organize and present to his wife. He is now to be in full charge of arrangements immediately following the wedding ceremony about which he may have had little to say. It is seen as a state of suspended life where the *only* demands are for love-making and enjoyment.

261

Tasks of the Honeymoon

From the pair's point of view these expectations themselves impose tasks. Their recognition of their new role relationship sometimes has unexpected results. Two persons who have known each other for some time with no difficulties in conversation may suddenly find themselves in a hotel room, or sitting across the table from each other, with nothing to say.

Rapoport and Rapoport (1964) suggest that there are four major tasks specific to and highlighted by the honeymoon period.

Dealing with One's Own Feelings about Sexual Competence. This involves, for many, a review of their feelings about intimate sexual relations. Even if there have been sexual relations prior to marriage, they are now occurring under different conditions. The association of this task with the honeymoon, however, is perhaps one of the reasons that couples who have been sexually intimate before marriage are less likely to go on a honeymoon trip.

Many young couples are concerned about their sexual abilities. Women appear more concerned about the pain of intercourse, whether they will be able to satisfy their husbands, and whether their husbands will be patient and gentle with them. Men's fears seem to be mainly with their ability to be potent with their wives. For both sexes there are anxieties about the effect on their self-concepts of this new experience in intimacy with another person. There are the associated problems of the place of sex in married life, the use or non-use of contraceptives, and the obvious overtones of how important sex is in the feelings of one toward the other.

Dealing with Feelings of Privacy and Intimacy. The honeymoon brings many couples together for the first time under conditions which accentuate their feelings about privacy in dressing and undressing and sharing a bathroom and bed with someone of the opposite sex. The intimacy needs include the amount of close association one wants with another. One young couple may find the long hours together particularly enjoyable, while another couple may feel uncomfortable and begin looking for activities or other people to relieve the dependence on each other. Some couples may be divided, so that one wants more time to be together and the other appears to be looking for excuses to avoid being alone together. These differences may not be seen so quickly where the honeymoon trip is skipped and other obligations, such as job or studies, provide spaces within the togetherness.

Dealing with Each Other's Sexual Needs and Feelings. This is an interpersonal task which brings together the individual tasks of dealing with the separate feelings and attitudes about sexual relations. This is the task of dealing with *each other's* needs and feelings, exploring ways of overcoming fears or anxieties, and mutually developing ways of enhancing the satisfactions. This perhaps begins to lay the basis for ways of coping with other areas in which the pair may find differences in needs, attitudes, and anxieties.

Beginning the Redefinition of Themselves as a Married Pair. The honeymoon provides a restricted range of activities which allows them to begin to cooperate "a little at a time," rather than being faced with the problem of cooperation over the whole range of activities which will confront them when they pick up the "threads of life" again after returning. It involves the task of breaking the past pattern of seeing themselves as individuals and redefining themselves as a married pair. Even the hotel clerks and others they come in contact with provide support for this redefinition by the liberal usage of "Mr. and Mrs.," since they have not known the newly married pair as individuals but only in their marital identity.

The shared experience of harmony and cooperation, if achieved, is seen to provide a basis for widening the cultural base within which they can share and cooperate in the more complex activities awaiting them. The Rapoports suggest that the degree of harmony the couple achieve in the management of the honeymoon sets an emotional tone by the end of the period which may form the basis for a set of stereotypes of each other and the relationship. These stereotypes color both expectations concerning future interaction and images of each other, far into the marriage.

THE EARLY STAGE OF MARRIAGE

When the newly married couple pick up the threads of day to day living, either after the honeymoon trip or immediately following the ceremony, they are faced with the age-old task confronting any two people attempting to coordinate their activities when certain things have to be done. In this sense it adds a new dimension to the honeymoon relationship. Even two men on a camping trip together for the first time or two women attempting to prepare a meal together are likely to have difficulties until they become somewhat accustomed to each other's ways of doing things—that is, until they come to some agreement about who is going to do what, when, and how. This involves predictability—learning to anticipate and to interpret the actions, gestures, and words of each other. Marriage represents a major status change. It calls for a host of new behaviors, new perspectives, and responsibilities. This is why marriage itself is said to change people. It forces a new range of behavior which will be continually evaluated in interaction with the spouse. It is the expectation for certain behavior from a person because he is now a husband or a wife that we collect together under the terms "husband role" and "wife role." These are reciprocal roles. Whenever you speak of one, you are automatically speaking of the other. A man can not be a husband, unless he has a wife. He is either a bachelor, a divorcee, or a widower if he is not currently paired with a wife.

Roles involve the expectations for privileges as well as obligations. The privileges accruing to a man because he is a husband become the obligations of his wife. Conversely, his obligations become her privileges. The idea of roles involves something more than what *should* be done, it implies *how* it should be done, and implies a hierarchy of the elements of the role—such as which things are more important, and which should be sacrificed if there is a conflict between them. For example, two people may agree that a husband should kiss his wife every morning. For one it implies a passionate kiss and for the other a perfunctory "good morning" peck; for one it takes precedence over the burning toast, and for the other, it doesn't. Obviously, early development of and satisfaction with roles is enhanced if the two people have similar concepts of the roles they are developing.

Development of Roles

The intensity of the problems of the early development of marital roles varies, depending on the amount of agreement between the ideas the two partners have formulated about married life and about the opposite sex. It varies depending upon the kind of relationship they have had prior to marriage, the strength of the commitment they have had to each other, and their ability to communicate. All of this is as true of the two men on a camping trip as of marriage. If the two men camping find that they must stay hungry a while longer because both were cleaning fish and neither started the fire, they can organize their future activities with the division of labor clearly understood. If they cannot reach agreement, they can maintain separate camps or go home.

Marriage, however, is something more for most people than just cooperating to get the jobs done. For many people it is the closest and most important interpersonal relationship they will ever have. The spouse's evaluation becomes exceedingly important as a source of self-esteem and as reassurance that one is still loved. The person one marries is highly important to the feelings about self. The more wonderful the spouse appears, the more wonderful you must be because he or she chose you. Thus, the little things one discovers about the other in the process of living together can cause doubts, misgivings, joy—all connected to the feelings about self. The roles, then, are being developed in the midst of a highly emotional relationship. The evaluations implicit in every interaction between the spouses are highlighted and important for feelings about self, which cannot now be completely separated from feelings about the spouse. Thus, the young wife who finds that her new husband leaves his clothes along a trail from the front door to the bedroom is likely to react immediately in terms of what this says about his feeling toward her. "He thinks I'm here just to pick up after him." "He doesn't want a wife, he wants a maid." "He thinks he's too important to be bothered with picking up his own clothes, he thinks my time isn't important." Then she remembers the permanence of the relationship. "I will *not* spend my life being his slave." "I'm going to stop this right now." And she begins looking for a counter attack to break him of his habit. Her refusal to pick up his clothes, in turn, may be interpreted by him as a lack of her love for him. "If she really loved me, she wouldn't mind picking up my clothes, she would want to do things for me." It becomes hard to be rational about who does what, when "who does what" is enmeshed in "who cares about whom," and how much.

The same string of clothes in another case may not even be noticed. It is seen as the way husbands are and the role of the wife includes picking up their clothes. Or in yet another the euphoria of the early days of marriage turns the clothes into endearing piles of "his things," which she lovingly picks up—beautiful evidence that they are really married! Of course, this may wear off after a while with new interpretations being made of the same behavior, but at least it has helped the early adjustments.

Differences in Role Expectations

Couples vary greatly in the degree to which they encounter differences of opinion regarding marital roles early in the marriage. Couples who come from similar family backgrounds, have similar habits of neatness, and have developed a close relationship over a relatively long period of time may have very few adjustments to make. Their major problems may concern learning to perform the agreed upon roles and vary according to their tolerance for low budgets, burned stew, and overdrawn checking accounts. This doesn't say they'll be any happier over the long run, only that they will have fewer difficulties in developing their early marital roles than couples from widely different family backgrounds who married after a short courtship under a summer moon.

Influence of Past Experiences. Everyone builds up ideas of what marriage will be like. As one grows up in a family, he is exposed to a particular married pair—his parents. For awhile this is accepted as the only way for husbands and wives to act—notice the heat with which children playing house will argue: "That's *not* the way you are supposed to do it. Mothers act *this* way!" This use of the word "mother" alerts us to something else about the early learning of husband–wife roles. The perception is a distorted one. The child views his parents' interaction as mother and father, not as husband and wife. The child is not exposed to the nuances of meanings shared between husband and wife. For many, especially in the white middle and upper classes, all aspects of the sexual relationship are carefully hidden from the child's view. He finds it hard to believe that his mother and father are really sexual beings—even when the idea is finally forced upon him by a growing knowledge of the reproductive process.

Some get a view of nearly everything except the conflict, which is kept away from the children. Some see the conflict but miss the smoothing out that occurs when Mom and Dad are alone. Some get a distorted view of what they see by hearing a one-sided account from one parent or the other. These perceptions, whether happy or unhappy, are likely to carry with them some deep feelings of what is right, wrong, good, or bad in marriage relationships. They are also likely to create some areas of sensitivity to certain emotional expressions, gestures, and behavior.

As children grow they are exposed to their friends' families, TV, movies, and books. They begin to evaluate their parents' marriage. They fantasy how their own will be, either patterned after or as a reaction against their view of their parents' marriage. More realistically, the fantasies contain some "good" elements of their parents' marriage, supply what has been missing in their relationships with parents, and contain over-reactions to the "bad" aspects of the parental marriage, with a liberal sprinkling of romantic ideas gleaned from various sources. The younger the people are at time of marriage, the more likely it is that their ideas are influenced by these unrealistic fantasies.

Influence of Fantasies. Whatever the source of the fantasies, every one is likely to have developed some very clear ideas about certain aspects of their future marriages. Classroom discussions indicate the strength of some of these convictions, as well as the variation among ideas:

I will never let my wife work. I want her waiting for me every day when I come home.

I will never become the dull, home-body my mother is.

I'll tell you one thing, we will never have TV dinners in my house. If a man is going to work, he's got to have home-cooked, wholesome food, not artificial slop!

My wife is going to serve my breakfast every morning on a table with a clean tablecloth and fresh flowers on it. She'll have on a pretty house dress and apron, and have the morning paper folded by my plate.

I think it's ridiculous to get up and cook breakfast for your husband if all he's going to do is read the morning paper over his coffee. He should certainly be able to make coffee and toast bread.

My dad always brought Mother a cup of coffee before she got out of bed in the mornings. I thought that was so sweet. My husband will do the same thing when I'm married.

The opportunities for these kinds of conflicting expectations come not only from highly unrealistic ideas about marriage, but from the actual existence of many different kinds of marriage relationships. It used to be that prospective mates knew fairly well what society expected of them and what their roles were to be. When they married they were likely to have clear ideas of what to expect and their expectations were likely to agree. Today, prospective mates are no less likely to have clear ideas about what to expect, but are much more likely to find that their expectations differ.

Many of these preconceptions will disappear after marriage. They will be replaced by satisfying interactions that were never anticipated before marriage. They remain, however, as points for comparison when things are not going well, or even when they are. It's difficult for a real person to act exactly like a fantasied one, especially if he doesn't know about the fantasy! Even if the fantasy involves how one is going to perform one's own role, it is difficult. The girl who before marriage envisioned herself looking fresh and crisp while lovingly cooking pancakes for her husband's breakfast may be quite unprepared for the difficulties involved in getting herself or her husband up in time. She was not expecting the frantic dash to the kitchen, in her bathrobe, to get the pancakes ready. She didn't foresee burning the first batch because she was too busy setting the table, fixing juice, and coffee. Her fantasy never included her new husband saying, as he gulped his juice: "I'll be late if I stop to eat. Why didn't you wake me up earlier?" Nor was she ready for the peck on the cheek, as he said: "You look terrible in the morning. Couldn't you manage to comb your hair?"

The tears attest to the wide discrepancy between her fantasied vision of herself and the actual situation. Now if she manages to get closer to her dream, it looks like it's because of his complaints rather than because she wanted to do this for him of her own free will. The husband who watches her become more adept at her role and then jokes to friends, "My wife was a mess at breakfast before I straightened her out," is probably in for a series of subtle counter attacks if not open rebellion.

Influence of Intense Interaction. The intimacy of marital interaction, the anxiety attached to learning new roles and the discovery of small incompatible habits (the bright canary who chirps cheerfully upon getting out of bed can bring homicidal thoughts to the befuddled brain of the morning sphinx) may cause not just adjustment to reality, but a swing in the opposite direction from idealization. Hobart (1958) found strong evidence that there was a change from underestimating the amount of actual disagreement between oneself and one's fiance, during engagement, to overestimating it in early marriage. He found the pattern stronger for men, especially where there had been high romanticism prior to marriage. He called this perception of greater disagreement a measure of disillusionment, since it was not related to an actual change in pair agreement between engagement and marriage. The areas showing the highest disillusionment (perception of greater disagreement) for both males and females were marital roles, having children, in-law relations, values on neatness, savings, money, and attitudes toward divorce. Additional areas for males, but not females, were personal freedom, sex and affection, economic roles, and religion.

The jolt sometimes associated with putting ideas into practice in early marriage is reflected in the percentage of those who contemplated separation. Landis and Johannis both studied college couples married two to three years. Landis found that one-fifth of his sample, married two years in 1948, had considered separation (Landis, 1948). Johannis (1956) discovered that one-third of his sample of student marriages had considered separation by the end of the third year—this, in marriages involving highly educated spouses, which is normally associated with low actual divorce rates.

Influence of the Power Structure. The loss of societal consensus about marital roles has tended to result in the early part of marriage being a period in which husband and wife maneuver and struggle for positions of advantage and control. This is probably more apparent the more insecure the people, but if the relationship between power and dependency is remembered, it can be seen that it has something to do with reassurance that the other is committed to the relationship.

If the norms support complete control as being in the hands of the husband, then the wife need not interpret her exclusion from decision making as his lack of consideration of her wishes, or his lack of respect for her judgment. She abides by his decisions because she is a wife, not because she is a particular kind of woman. Normative support legitimizes the delegation of power to one person as the accepted _authority pattern_. One abides by it because he steps into the appropriate role. An employee, for example, doesn't feel unloved by his boss because his boss does not consult him about company policy. He is not supposed to; it has nothing to do with the two men as people but with their employment statuses. When the authority structure within marriage is largely lacking, as in our society today, the distribution of power *does* say something about the relationship, at least to the participants. Thus the often heard complaint from wives that, "It makes no difference what I think or say, my husband goes right ahead as if I weren't there," probably expresses the feeling that the husband doesn't care enough about her to be influenced by her. This may be correct, but it may be just as likely that he sees this as part of the culturally determined husband role (authority) while she sees it as part of their personally derived relationship (power).

This relationship between the ability to influence and emotional dependency is one of the factors which introduces tension, tears, and anger into role conflicts that would seem to someone peering in the window to be easily resolved.

Effect on the Self-Concept. Perceiving ourselves as the kind of person we want to be and being perceived as that kind of person by others is a major factor in maintaining a positive self-concept. Evaluations of role behavior are likely to be made in terms of the whole person rather than in terms of specific behavior. We convey to each other our approval or disapproval in a number of ways, both intentional and unintentional. This is, perhaps, one of the reasons that marriages which are homogamous or hypergamous (husband higher) according to social class background are seen to be more satisfactory than hypogamous (husband lower) marriages (Kephart, 1954b). Where husband and wife share the same expectations for standard of living (homogamous) or if the husband's expectations are higher than the wife's (hypergamous), then the satisfaction with the global situation is more likely to produce interaction which reinforces the positive aspects of their self-concepts, without any effort.[1]

Consider the wife who has higher aspirations than the husband. He has a job which interests him and takes about as much time and energy as he wants to invest. He is satisfied with their current standard of living. She, on the other hand, finds her self-esteem suffering because of her husband's underachievement (from her perspective), because of the current standard of living which is beneath her expectations, and because she sees no hope for improvement in the long run. Her dissatisfaction is likely to find its way into numerous complaints about him as a husband or as a man. As he becomes aware of her negative evaluation, his self-esteem suffers and he interprets more and more of her remarks as "digs at him." He will be very likely to retaliate in anger or withdraw, either of which will be threats to her self-concept as a wife. And so the cycle continues.

On the other hand, if his aspirations are higher than hers, his level of achievement and resultant standard of living are likely to enhance both

[1] For an excellent theoretical discussion of this idea see John A. Scanzoni (1966).

of their self-concepts. Her appreciation of his contribution serves to bolster his self-esteem, and he can be expected to retaliate in kind. Just by normal interaction, the fortuitous fit between their values enhances the probability that they will make each other feel like better people. This direction of differences would not produce these results if they differ on the importance of family time. If she feels that too much effort goes into the career at the expense of the family, her self-concept can suffer ("He thinks more of his job than of me"), with consequences for his self-esteem as she fails to appreciate his economic contributions. In other words, she does not see him as the same "success" that he sees himself.

The sense of defeat associated with another person not seeing the same thing in us that we value and see in ourselves is a global kind of feeling. It may be difficult to describe, but it makes us look for things to criticize in the person who contributes to the feeling, or look for things which will lessen the time of interaction with them. Thus we sometimes hear people say:

"I don't know what it is. Even when she does everything right, it's wrong."

or

"I can't put my finger on it, he's a good husband, I shouldn't complain. He just irritates me, and I act like a shrew!"

And on the other hand:

"Well, I could list all sorts of things he doesn't do that husbands should, but I wouldn't trade him. He makes me feel so glad to be me."

Levels of Role Expectations

There may be a variety of reasons which could account for the differences in the above examples. To begin with, some may be accounted for by differences in strength of the self-concept. Some persons may have such a low opinion of themselves that they are incapable of giving support to another or of taking the support which is offered. Others, however, find themselves in unsatisfactory relationships because the external situation is so precarious and threatening to the self-concept that even a good marital relationship cannot withstand the pressure. These are things pushing in from the outside as a result of personality difficulties or societal failures about which the relationship can do little. On the other hand, some of these result from differences in marital role expectations. These can occur at different levels (Dyer, 1962).

The Cultural Level. Since the couple has come from different families (representing different sub-cultures), they may have formed different ideas about generalized husband and wife roles as well as different hierarchies of important areas of interaction and different values about the goals of marriage.

The Habitual Level.   They have developed idiosyncratic ways of dressing or keeping house, reactions to tension, expressions of anger. If these habits irritate the marital partner or conflict with expectations of the marital role, difficulties may arise even though the two of them agree at the cultural level. They may both believe that a husband should be calm, strong, secure, and even-tempered. But habitual ways of expressing anger through shouting, fist slamming, or icy silence, may make it virtually impossible for him to do what both think he should do.

The Expectation Level.   They may agree on the general ideas of marital roles, but have different ideas about how they should be carried out. They may both agree that the wife is responsible for housework, for example, but disagree on standards of neatness; agree that there should be equal authority but disagree on what areas, or on who is more equal.

The Behavioral Level.   The fact that two people agree on what each should do doesn't mean they will do it. They may both agree that a husband and wife should share their leisure, but there is no leisure time, or he prefers golfing with the boys to golfing with her. He agrees a husband should spend leisure time with his wife, but he doesn't do it. She agrees a wife should bake homemade cakes and pies; but she doesn't like to, so can't find the time. Conflicting expectations enter in. A couple agrees that a husband *should* "get ahead" economically; that he *should* spend a great deal of time with his wife; that he *should* take his sons fishing and participate in little league activities; that he *should* be active in community affairs; that he *should* be a handy man around the house and take an interest in the yard. Translating all of these into behavior is an impossibility, even if they agree that a husband *should not* take time out to sleep.

The Personality Level.   Aside from the tasks and affectional expectations associated with roles, each partner usually has expectations for what each should *be* as a person. Of course, this is related to the role aspects but is more likely to become a catch-all explanation for disagreement. Negative evaluations of the other as a person are much harder to undo than negative evaluations of his role behavior. It is easier to resolve a conflict between role expectations for handling money than to undo the wife's feeling that her husband is stingy, overbearing, stubborn, and unconcerned about her needs. If the conflict is defined as a defect in the other's personality, then it is likely to become a global evaluation distorting other perceptions of him. On the other hand, if it is defined merely as a role conflict there remains hope that his ideas may change.

The Interpretation Level. Differences may occur in interpretation of the same behavior. What to one may seem like becoming a "dull homebody" may to the other seem like "settling down to domesticity." What to one is efficient, rational planning may to the other be cold, unfeeling stubbornness. What to one is a healthy expression of feelings may to the other seem a childish display of emotions.

It may seem that the above listing of possible sources of conflict dooms any couple to a dismal life of hurt, misunderstanding, and misery. Fortunately, it is not necessary for people to agree on everything to be happy. A marriage in which there is complete agreement would undoubtedly be suffocatingly boring. Stumbling upon areas of disagreement can be as stimulating and exhilarating as the sudden finding that you feel exactly the same about something. Irritating habits can, in an otherwise satisfactory relationship, become treasured trademarks of the mate. In a growing relationship where confidence in the love and respect of the partner has taken away the need for a power struggle, the earlier gnawing anger can give way to warmth and affection as, for example, one views the bathroom still cluttered with jars, bottles, hose, and curlers, in spite of the fights over them.

Although not all of the differences in role expectations would be eliminated if there were societal consensus, at least the complexity would be reduced if there were general agreement about them. On the one hand, the partial approval of several different types of marital roles introduces confusion in the individual relationship. At the same time it enhances the opportunity for the development of marital roles which express the desires and personalities of the individual couple. The ability to make use of the opportunities afforded by lack of consensus is increased by an understanding of the cultural definitions of marital roles and their relationship to interpersonal interaction.

CULTURAL DEFINITIONS OF MARITAL ROLES

Kirkpatrick (1963, pp. 168–69) has attempted to extract the essence out of three logically different types of husband–wife roles. They differ in terms of the primary focus of the relationship and the authority structure implicit in them. They can be seen as a historical development but with the last one appearing and receiving support before the first one has disappeared.

They are not attempts to describe any one marriage, for a given marriage may combine parts of each. Each marriage will probably lean closer to one than to the other with a general value orientation influencing the feelings of satisfaction.

Neither is it to be expected that marriages will be characterized by the same marital type all the way through the life cycle. Life circumstances, changes in occupation, and even geographical changes may subtly change the emphasis from one to another. This method of analyzing marital relationships accentuates the wide differences among satisfactory relationships; stresses the fluid character of marriage; and alerts us to the numerous points of conflict and dissatisfaction which are in the cultural ambiguities surrounding marital roles.

Marital Role Types

As stated at the beginning of this chapter a role is composed of both obligations and privileges. Therefore, it always assumes a reciprocal relationship—the obligations of the wife being the privileges of the husband. From the essential obligations defining the husband–wife roles which go together, we can imagine the character of the relationship in many areas of activity. It is also well to remember that a role is not the same as an interpersonal relationship. There can be varying degrees of love and communication in any of the three types. The types stress different aspects of the roles as the pivot points of the relationship, however.

A careful inspection of those roles shown in Figure 12–1 suggests tremendous differences in the orientation toward marriage, major emphasis in the relationship, and consequences for marital interaction and decision making. The expectations for marital roles and the kind of interaction implicit in them create entirely different "marriage flavors," so to speak. For instance, it is well to remember that children can be present in any of the role relationships. The place they occupy and the resulting parent–child relationships can be expected to be different, however, depending upon the husband–wife role. It is also well to remember that these are ideal types—extracting the essential elements from the different emphases represented by the roles. No *real* marriages would ever be composed of just these elements. Most are composites, but many can be characterized as emphasizing one group of expectations over another, and some can be characterized by an overloading of either obligations or privileges from several roles.

The Traditional. The traditional roles probably still serve as the basis for the division of labor and the general authority structure in most families today. They are characterized by a high segregation of interests and activities. The husband is concerned with his main obligation of protecting and supporting his family. The wife's main obligations involve the

TRADITIONAL ROLES

Obligations of Wife–Mother	*Obligations of Husband–Father*
1. Having and rearing children	1. Loyalty to the mother of his children
2. Making a home	2. Providing economic security and protection
3. Rendering domestic service	3. Allowing a certain amount of domestic authority
4. Loyal subordination of self to economic interests of husband	4. Making major decisions
5. Acceptance of a dependent social and economic status	5. Sentimental gratitude and respect for wife because of her devotion to family
6. Tolerance of a limited range of activities	6. Providing alimony in case of divorce

COMPANION ROLES

Obligations of Wife	*Obligations of Husband*
1. Preservation of beauty	1. Providing admiration and chivalrous attention to wife
2. Providing ego support and erotic satisfaction to husband	2. Giving wife a romantic emotional response
3. Cultivating social contacts which are advantageous to husband	3. Providing funds beyond support for dress and recreation
4. Maintenance of intellectual alertness	4. Providing leisure for social and educational activities
5. Providing relief from boredom	5. Sharing leisure with wife

PARTNER ROLES

Obligations of Wife	*Obligations of Husband*
1. Economic contribution in relation to earning ability	1. Economic contribution in relation to earning ability
2. Responsibility for support of children	2. Responsibility for support of children
3. Sharing of domestic service	3. Sharing of domestic service
4. Sharing of legal responsibilities	4. Sharing of legal responsibilities
5. Willingness to dispense with any appeal to chivalry	5. Acceptance of wife's equal status (socially, morally, financially)
6. Equal responsibility to maintain family status by career success	6. Acceptance of wife's equal voice in deciding place of residence
7. Renouncing alimony except in case of dependent children	7. Acceptance of wife's equal voice in decision making

Fig. 12–1. Comparison of three cultural types of husband–wife roles. (Adapted from Kirkpatrick, 1963, pp. 168–69.)

bearing and rearing of children and the household tasks. If they were not able to produce children, it would be seen as a tragedy. Sexual relations are for the purpose of reproduction, not primarily for the enjoyment of the spouses.

Their separate activities would not be likely to produce great understanding of each other's worlds, especially since one of the wife's obligations is to restrict her activities and interests to the family. And herein is the logic for the right of alimony. This is the little woman who has "given the best years of her life" to the family—has had no way to learn to make a living for herself. So in return for this "obligation" she has the "privilege" (husband's obligation) of alimony in case the marriage breaks up.

There are no obligations on the part of the husband to include the wife in recreational or leisure time activities. She would not be expected to "understand" the technicalities of his work or be able to discuss books, politics, or sports with him because her interests are *expected* to be confined to the family. In these roles, the stereotypes of masculinity and femininity would be expected to be very strong, forming around the specialized areas of interests and activities. This is also the basis for the authority structure. The husband is the one with the outside contacts— he is the only one *expected* to understand the economic world, so it logically follows that he is the only one equipped to make decisions concerning money and the family's economic interest. Many possible conflicts of interests are solved by the roles. This is the wife who says to her husband when he announces that he has decided to take another job across the country, "Anything you think is best, dear. When shall I start packing?"

In return for her devotion to family, she is entitled to his loyalty and sentimental gratitude. It doesn't matter that her "hair has turned to silver," or that her "hands are wrinkled and red"; he is still expected to remain faithful and grateful because she has "worked her fingers to the bone" for him and *his* children. Marital stability is written into the role. It is not contingent upon continued mutual attraction and satisfaction, which is part of the companion type of marriage role.

The Companion.   In the companion roles, economic security and "success" are taken for granted. The essential aspects concern the interpersonal relationship, which brings the wife into the husband's career as a junior partner in charge of social contacts and emotional support. It is based on the glamorous aspects of masculinity and femininity. The traditional wife meets her husband when he comes in from work with his slippers and newspaper which he reads while she prepares supper. The "companion" meets hers with the lights low, soft music, and a refreshing drink—ready to relieve him of the day's frustrations.

Stimulation, both intellectual and sexual, is an important element of this role relationship. In order for the wife to be able to meet these obligations, she must have response from her husband. No one can continue to be sexually stimulating to a "cold fish." She has to have rewards for looking pretty, keeping up with the latest books, politics, and her husband's career needs (husband's obligations number 1, 2, and 5 in Figure 12–1). She also cannot be expected to do this without funds, or at the same time she is taking care of several little children and doing all the housework without help—thus the privilege of funds for dress and leisure time (obligations of husband role). This focus on glamour is also one of the reasons that gray hair and dish-water hands are more frightening to this woman than to the traditional wife. She has supposedly given up little for her family, and must depend on continual attraction for marital stability rather than loyalty. Children are not essential to this role. If present, their interests and needs are secondary to the husband and his career.

The authority structure is not so apparent in the companion roles as in the traditional roles. The wife has some contact with the outside world and is a contributor to her husband's "success." If her husband comes home with the news that he is taking another job in a different city, he is likely to be met not with, "Anything you say, dear"; but with "Are the opportunities for advancement better? Is it a better job? Is there a salary raise?" Only after questions of the relevance of the move to career success are satisfied is she likely to throw herself wholeheartedly into preparations.

These are the couples who do things together. They maintain the chivalrous manners associated with the romantic acceptance of the inequality of the sexes at the same time the female is viewed as an asset. She is not expected to equal the male in instrumental accomplishments. The companion roles have been part of leisure time culture in many societies, though perhaps more often associated with the "mistress" than with the "wife."

The Partner. These roles emphasize the equality of the sexes, and deny that a division of labor along sex lines is either necessary or desirable. The major distinguishing factor is that the wife is attached to the economic world in the same way the husband is attached to it in the other two roles. This is not just an extension of the traditional role for the wife, but an acceptance of a share of the breadwinner obligation. The authority structure is equalitarian, and many potential conflicts which have solutions written into the other two roles must be solved on the basis of individual circumstances and bargaining.

Consider, for example, the husband announcing that "the company" wants him to move to Carlton Corners. The traditional wife is obligated to abide by his decision; the "companion" is obliged to move once the economic advantages are ascertained. The "partner" says, "But what about my law practice? Do we stand to lose more than we gain? We'd better talk this over seriously before deciding!"

Since she is taking over part of the breadwinner obligation, he is expected to take over part of the household responsibility. It may be difficult to come to an agreement which makes both partners feel they have a fair share of the privileges, since there are few guidelines and the division of labor is not contained in the role as it is still loosely defined.

Overlapping of Roles

Parts of all of these roles have approval from some parts of our society. Many people expect parts of each of them to be incorporated in their own marriages. Over the life cycle, the emphasis is likely to change, so that during the existence of the marriage all three may have a turn as the pivot point of the relationship, though at different times. The inconsistency, ambiguity, and marginal support for all of them can cause difficulties in a number of ways.

1. *Socialized for one role, called upon to play another.* Since families differ in the extent to which they emphasize one role over another, children grow up with different ideas of the *right* role. A girl may be socialized well for the traditional role, for example, and find herself in a marriage and social setting which calls for a "companion."

2. *Disagreement between husband and wife.* A husband and wife from different family backgrounds may have completely different ideas about the husband–wife roles. Each may be a "good spouse" from his own perspective yet fail to receive the expected rewards from the mate.

3. *Choosing for one role, evaluating from another.* It is quite likely that many middle class men and women choose marriage partners with the companion role in mind, as a result of the romantic elements in the dating system. Many of them, however, begin after marriage to evaluate their spouses in terms of the major elements of the traditional role. The very thing that attracted them to the spouse may be seen as inappropriate after marriage.

4. *Inconsistency in expectations.* Sometimes a person expects an overdose of privileges from several of the roles, without expecting to pick up the corresponding obligations. This can lead to an intolerable situation for the spouse who cannot possibly live up to the expectations. For example, the man who expects his wife to look after several little children,

do all the housework and laundry alone, cook and bake everyday as his mother used to do (obligations of the traditional role), and at the same time be ready to sit and talk to him when he comes home, look like she has been in the beauty parlor all day, keep up with the latest in news, books, and community affairs, be a gracious, relaxed hostess as she entertains his friends at dinner, and then be an enthusiastic sex partner when the guests leave (obligations of the companion role), can only be disappointed that all his expectations are not met. His wife will either feel resentful, rebellious, inferior as a wife and mother, or frightfully tired. The problem is that they are all legitimate parts of *some* wife role, and she may feel as badly about complaining as she does about complying.

5. *Personality incompatible with role*. Although roles are usually discussed as expectations for behavior which need only be understood to be enacted, some are more compatible with a particular personality than another. A competitive, dominant male may find it very hard to preserve his feelings of masculinity in a partner relationship, which logically requires an equalitarian relationship with his wife. Some men, reared in traditional homes, feel a severe threat to their masculinity if forced to do housework. They may, at the same time, see the logical consistency in helping at home if their wives are working. They end in a "damned if you do, and damned if you don't" situation as far as their own self-concept is concerned. On the other hand, men reared in equalitarian homes, or those who enjoy cooking or the companionship afforded by cooperating in the housework, may find their greatest satisfaction in the same role which is anathema to other men.

This points up an additional factor about marital roles. They are never just the agreed upon arrangement by husbands and wives. They are influenced by the press of external circumstances such as job pressure, illness, growth stage of children, and prevalent pattern in family and friendship groups. The role we are pressed into performing has an impact on the relationship, the concept of self, and the perception of the partner. The changes in environment which force role changes can sometimes explain differences in marital happiness at specific points in the marriage. If a couple is aware of the effect that certain roles have on their relationship, they are better able to resist the social pressures which press toward a role relationship which is not compatible with their personalities or values.

CHANGES IN ROLES

For some people the marital roles may stay fairly steady throughout the marriage. Both of the spouses may come from the same kind of family, continue to live in the same community, maintain a stable set of friendship and extended family relationships, stay at approximately the same occupational level, and find their roles compatible with their personalities. They will probably change little over their lifetime and be highly resistant to any ideas such as marital roles or role conflict as a source of marital discord. As far as they are concerned people don't get along because they don't try, are irresponsible, lazy, or unlucky.

Fewer and fewer people today have this kind of predictable existence. For most, changes in the life cycle, moves from one place to another, job changes, and changes in friendship groups will bring about changes in the marital roles.

Changes in the Family Life Cycle

A family is born, grows, withers, and dies just as an individual does. Current trends support a succession of marital roles for a rising percentage of marriages. Many young people marry and combine some of the romantic elements of the companion role with elements of the partner role, as both partners work until the birth of the first child.

The newness of the situation and the "honeymoon glow" may take the edge off the cooperation in household tasks for the male. The newness of the traditional role may make the wife take on an added share of the household tasks even though she may work as many hours away from home as her husband. As part of a study the authors conducted at Purdue, college students were asked to respond to an item: "Even if a woman works, the housework and children are still her responsibility." Sixty-seven per cent of the males and 85 per cent of the females agreed. In response to the item: "After a man works all day, he shouldn't be expected to help his wife at home" only 20 per cent of the males agreed, as compared with 27 per cent of the females. At least, at this age and before marriage, the glow of helpfulness associated with the expectations for marriage would seem to hold down conflict in combining these two roles, especially for college educated couples.

This combination is perhaps partly aided by the anticipation of it as only a temporary situation. Most of the wives will quit work, if finances permit it, at the birth of the first child and stay at home as long as there are young children in the home. During this period, the necessity of taking care of young children will tend to make the traditional role more prominent. For middle class couples, the expectations seem to combine elements from the companion with the traditional focus. Lower class couples are more likely to remain essentially in the traditional relationship throughout marriage, even though the wife may work. The power structure varies, depending on the competence with which the husband meets the breadwinner role (Blood and Wolfe, 1960, pp. 40–41).

As the children grow and take up less of the mother's time, other elements of the companion role may become important. This, of course, will be highly related to the type of occupation and stage of the husband's career.[2]

Finally, when all the children are in high school or have finished school the trend is for more and more wives to reenter the work force, thus completing the circle, ending their productive lives back where they started in the partner role.

Inconsistency in Expectations.   Since these changes occur partly as a result of the ebb and flow of pressures from the outside, it is very easy for both partners to hold on to the privileges of the past role while expecting to add the privileges of the new one.   The shift from partner to traditional occurring with the birth of the first child is likely to hit the wife hardest.   Many husbands look forward to the privileges accompanying this role and a loss of the obligations of sharing housework and authority associated with the partner role while they both worked immediately after marriage.   Anticipating their wives being at home all day, they look forward to the one-sided domestic service and home cooked meals ready when they come home, which are logical obligations of her traditional role.

The wife may look forward to it, too, as she expects the new baby. She may expect his continued help around the house because he loves her, not because it was his obligation in the partner role; expect the same voice in the handling of money and other decisions which her sharing of the breadwinner role entitled her to; expect to enlarge her social contacts since she will no longer have the time demands of working; and at the same time have the added delight of being a mother.   She is likely to find that instead of this happening, her husband's help around the house drops off and her power in decision making decreases—both of which were privileges of the partner role (obligations of the partner husband).[3]   She may find that she is not only cut off from her contacts at work but that the added burden and demands of a new child also restrict her social activities.[4]   Leisure and funds for social activities are privileges from the companion role, while the restriction of outside activities is an obligation of the traditional role.

[2] An example of this combination is to be found in J. R. Seeley, R. A. Sim, and E. W. Loosley (1963, Chapter 7).

[3] Blood and Wolfe (1960) show that the husband's participation in housework drops considerably between the honeymoon period and the period when preschool children are in the home; it also drops considerably when the wife stops working (pp. 62, 71).

[4] One estimate suggests that for a full-time housewife, the work load jumps from 50 to 94 hours a week when a baby is added (Blood and Wolfe, 1960, p. 43).

Probably both husband and wife, especially in the middle class, expect some of the privileges of the companion role only to find that the available funds and leisure time for carrying on this role have disappeared with the loss of the second paycheck and the demands of the baby.

The same kind of inconsistencies may be present in the shift to other roles as the family grows and the needs change. As people become uncomfortable in certain parts of one role, it is very easy to look forward to the privileges that seem to accompany the next shift without realizing that obligations go along with it.

Inconsistency in Evaluation. Sometimes changes occur suddenly associated with geographical moves. Parts of the country vary in the approval accorded the different roles. Approval varies according to social class and degree of urbanization of an area. The most approved form in a social group has an effect on the couples participating in that group. This is because it alerts the couple to new ways of interacting which may seem desirable to one or both of them. Although they may see the privileges of someone else's role relationship, they cannot so readily see the obligations which go along with these privileges.

For example, consider a couple with both from small towns in the Midwest. They marry and live in a small town on the fringe of a large city where he is employed as an engineer with a large company. Let us assume that their backgrounds and present neighborhood groups support the traditional relationship. As they have children and he advances in his company we can expect a high degree of satisfaction with the marriage. She is restricted in her interests; he appreciates her domestic abilities and her devotion to the family; friends and families give recognition and approval. She is proud of her husband's achievements and the approval that her friends' husbands appear to give him for his knowledge of his job and "masculine" interests about which she knows little.

His "success" in his job wins him a promotion and a move to one of the company's plants in an East coast suburb. His advancement in the company coupled with the move to this particular area will very probably bring them into a setting where the companion role is in full swing. As they interact with others in the new setting, they are likely to become aware of the new elements in this role which were missing from the traditional roles. As he becomes aware of the range of interests prevalent among the companion wives, he wants his wife to look more fashionable, to talk about something besides the children—to make a better impression. He now begins to look at her through the eyes of the new role, evaluating her on things that were never important before. He is not likely to realize that for her to develop this role, he must provide funds, leisure time, and emotional response to her behavior—assume the obligations of the companion husband. Neither is he likely to realize that he will have to give up some of her devotion to the family that was also satisfying.

She may well do the same thing. Noticing the privileges the companion wives receive in terms of more chivalrous and attentive treatment from their husbands, she may conclude either that she is stupid or that her husband doesn't love her as he used to. Since they are now evaluating from the standpoints of different roles, they are not as likely to receive the rewards for good performance of the old ones. They can at this point realize that the roles have changed, adjust to the new ones, or learn to protect the old ones from the outside pressures if they are happier with them. If they do not recognize the impact of the roles or fail to find the new roles satisfying, the probability is high that they will accuse each other of "changing," of "losing interest" or "of being insincere." It is much harder to handle marital problems if they have been defined as personality difficulties or as "falling out of love," than if they are defined as role problems. The former strikes hard at the feelings about self, while the latter focuses attention on performance difficulties.

On the other hand, moves such as the one described above may result in a happier relationship than ever before. The new demands may be very compatible with aspects of the personalities that had not been tapped with the older relationship. They may find the new evaluations of self which accompany demands for different kinds of interaction very satisfying, especially if both recognize that as new obligations and privileges are added, some of the older ones disappear. No one can meet all the demands of all the roles at the same time.

THE PRINCIPLE OF VALUE RELEVANCE

The question of which marital role is "best" or which produces the most happiness cannot be answered in any absolutistic sense. That role relationship is best which is most compatible with the personalities and expectations of the partners and is most appropriate for the particular part of the family life cycle, the unique circumstances, and the economic and social pressures that the marriage is experiencing. There may be periods when the circumstances press for a type of role relationship which is disturbing to one or both partners. The interpersonal relationship can provide support and satisfaction in spite of incompatible role demands if the couple perceives that the situation may be temporary or that the distress comes from legitimate role demands rather than from the insensitivity, selfishness, and irrational demands of the spouse.

Rigidly holding to a particular role type because it is "right," whether or not it is appropriate to the situation, can create stress. The husband, for example, who insists that his wife must not work, even though she wants to and financial problems are pressing, can make the financial problems seem larger, as well as make himself appear like a stubborn, selfish spouse.

Applying the value relevance paradigm presented in Chapter 4, we can see that satisfaction in a particular role relationship is related to many other things than just the personal preferences of the individuals. Role relationships which may impose severe stress at one point in the life cycle may be very rewarding in another. One which brings satisfaction in one social context may bring doubts and conflict in another. A type of relationship which seems very appropriate in a particular situation may bring blame and recriminations when there is disagreement between husband and wife.

A relationship which brings great happiness to one couple may bring misery to another in the same situation! Rather than there being one type of role relationship suitable for a particular couple throughout life, or a particular relationship suitable to all couples under a particular circumstance, it appears that the "right" one is the one that allows them to coordinate their activities: to meet the particular goals they have in such a way that their necessary activities enhance their feelings about themselves. If this arrangement deviates greatly from the expectations of their families and friends they will have to provide additional support for each other in their unique roles. For example, the couple who finds it more appropriate for the husband to stay home and take care of the house and family while his wife provides financial support will find it especially hard in our society to protect their feelings of self-esteem. They will need a more complete and supportive communication system to keep their relationship satisfying and intact than couples in a more accepted relationship.

SUMMARY

Part of the adjustment necessary in marriage involves the definition of the marital roles each will assume. Every role assumes a reciprocal role that is in interaction with it. Roles are organized in terms of obligations and privileges associated with a certain position. Thus the privileges belonging to a wife become the obligations of her husband and her obligations become his privileges. The way in which these privileges and obligations are combined produce a certain "flavor" to the marriage relationship which distinguishes it in both goals and interaction from another marriage with a different combination of obligations and privileges.

Difficulties occur when two people, because of their background and past experiences, have different expectations for the husband and wife roles. Since being the kind of husband or wife one wants to be and being treated by the spouse in the way one desires has an impact on the self-concept, role conflicts are many times interpreted as personality conflicts, which makes them difficult to resolve.

Conflicts or disagreements can occur at several levels: the cultural, the habitual, the expectation, the behavioral, the personality, and the interpretation levels. People may agree or disagree at any or all levels. At the cultural level, three completely different roles are in evidence in our society at the same time—the traditional role, the companion role, and the partner role. Each contains implications for the authority structure, the division of labor, the major goals of the relationship, and the resolution of certain common conflicts.

No marriage is seen to be an exact duplicate of any particular type but combines different elements from each. Since societal pressures, past experiences, and personality characteristics combine to create pressures for one type over another, difficulties may arise from husband and/or wife: being socialized for one role and forced to play another, choosing one and evaluating from another, having a personality incompatible with the role called for, exhibiting inconsistencies in the matching of obligations with the appropriate privileges, or disagreeing with each other on expectations for marital roles.

The resolution of role conflicts is made more difficult when they are perceived as personality conflicts or as a lack of love in the relationship. It becomes important then to be able to distinguish between the two.

There is no "right" or "best" marital role for every one or in every situation. The right role relationship depends upon the values and personalities of the individuals, the demands of the particular situation, and the expectations of the families and friends. The greater the discrepancy between the partners' expectations, or between the couple and their supporting social groups, the more important communication becomes for preserving the relationship.

QUESTIONS AND PROJECTS

1. Why is it important for the newly married couple to develop a pair identity? What do you think this indicates?

2. Do you think looking at marriage as a role relationship helps or hinders preparation for marriage? Explain. Would roles develop when two people live together even if they are not married? Why or why not?

3. Describe the role relationship which you would most prefer to have in your marriage. Look at your description to see if the obligations and privileges

are fairly evenly matched. Think carefully about the major tasks involved in managing a home and family. Are they all included in your role description? Why do you think this is the way you would like things to be?

4. Why is it disquieting to have someone react to something special you have done for them as if it were something you were expected to do? Relate this to marital interaction when the two spouses have different role expectations.

5. Which of the roles discussed in the text do you think would be most predictive of marital success? Defend your position.

6. Look at each of the role relationships described just as it is given. Do not add anything to it. State your objections to each of them. Now put together the elements from each of them that you would think you would have to have in your marriage to be reasonably satisfied. Is there anything missing? Explain. Did the obligations of husband and wife stay evenly matched? If not, logically explain your rearrangement.

7. Do you think a couple could come to sufficient agreement about marital roles before marriage to eliminate role conflict in marriage? Discuss.

8. What is the relationship between love and roles? Does love make a role relationship unnecessary? Explain.

9. Think about all of the supporting values for family life and male–female relationships associated with each of these roles. Which one, if any, could you absolutely not live with as a major orientation? Why? Do you think marriage itself may change your ideas? Discuss.

10. If you were in a situation which pressed for a certain kind of role relationship which you and your spouse did not enjoy, what could you do to keep it from harming your over-all relationship? What if your spouse enjoyed it and you did not?

13

Communication and Conflict Resolution

Early role adjustment is only one of the tasks confronting newly married couples. They must learn to communicate their desires, their feelings, and their daily schedules so that they can coordinate their activities. They must learn to handle the conflicts which arise in such a way that the least damage is done to themselves or the relationship. Only a portion of these tasks comes under the heading of marital roles.

COMMUNICATION

Communication is essential to any continuing human relationship, whether or not there are words spoken. The nature of the communication can produce disagreements where none exist, or it can smooth out potentially disruptive conflicts even before they become recognized. People differ in the quality as well as the quantity of communication, but it is an ever-present part of every marital relationship as the couples face certain inevitable facts of marriage. These facts of marriage are facts of life for single people too, but marriage means that there is always the same person available to blame for the frustration and worries which accompany day-to-day living.

Inevitable Facts of Marriage

Every marriage faces the prospect of a certain amount of boredom. No matter how much two people love each other they occasionally will grow tired of looking at each other—the same face across the breakfast

286

table morning after morning after morning, the same clichés, the same conversations. These provide predictability, but so much predictability can become exceedingly tiresome. For some, the boredom is fleeting. Something happens or they deliberately upset the routine and stimulate their interest again. For some, boredom characterizes rather long periods, punctuated by quickened interests and renewed attachments of variable duration. For others, it characterizes the whole of marriage. Most of the exhilarating experiences and stimulating conversations occur outside the marriage. But whether brief or of long duration, every marriage, if it lasts more than a year or two, will experience boredom.

All marriages will face frustrating day-to-day experiences. The furnace won't work, the washing machine breaks, the promised job doesn't materialize, Junior drops his jelly bread on the newly mopped floor, there is no clean shirt, John is late for dinner, the car won't start, and on and on. These kinds of things happen to the unmarried person too, but they happen to him alone. These are inevitable irritants for everyone, but the unmarried person is not likely to pick on the *same* person each time as the target of blame. The married person is! He not only endures his own frustrations but those of his spouse too, which he gets second hand. No marriage will escape them. They are likely to be more numerous in the young marriage, where inexperience, small children, and financial problems heighten the probability of their occurrence.

Every marriage will occasionally face conflict. It is almost impossible to conceive of a marriage relationship which involves no disagreements or conflicts. The numerous decisions which have to be made, the disappointments, frustrations, and adjustments will inevitably lead at some time or another to the frozen look, the hurtful word, the angry shout, or perhaps the violent blow. But whether muted or thunderous, conflict will enter into every relationship. Some people learn to handle their conflicts so easily and well that it seems they have none. But if there *are* actually none we would suspect one extremely insecure or fearful partner. The conflict would still be there—just forced underground.

Every marriage will face some of the inevitable factors of living—illness, accident, job-loss, success, disappointment, joy, birth, and death. Any of them can bring major readjustments. Some couples face these inevitable facts of living and feel that they have been a support to each other through them. Life has been made easier because they were married to each other. As they look back they remember the high spots, feel they have grown closer together because of their shared sorrows, joys, and conflicts. Others look back and see mainly the low spots. They have not grown closer but more distant. Their conflicts have driven them further apart, so that they seem to live on separate islands in the house they share.

Differences Between Happy and Unhappy Marriages

The difference between happy and unhappy marriages appears not to be so much that happily married people have no problems and unhappily married ones do, but that they have different kinds of problems, and the unhappily married have more of them. Matthews and Mihanovich (1963) provided evidence in support of this. Although their sample had some bias in that it concerned only Catholic couples who perhaps have more constraints on marriage disruption than a more representative group its representativeness in other social characteristics compared favorably with the major studies of marriage. Out of 1,004 respondents, about two-thirds were happily married and one-third unhappy as judged by a scale of 21 questions concerning the marital happiness of self and spouse. Of 364 marital problems, 30 failed to distinguish statistically between happy and unhappy marriages. The median number of problems per married person was 19, but 85 per cent of the unhappily married and only 28 per cent of the happily married reported more than this. It was also discovered that happiness is not related to the resolution of problems over time. One hundred and fifty of one hundred and ninety problems tested were as likely to be present at any period of married life. Some people learn to live with their problems and others don't.

The most important finding, for our purposes, was that the *kind* of problems differed between the groups. The unhappily married were much more likely to report problems reflecting neglect and lack of affection, understanding, appreciation, and companionship. The authors went on to say about the unhappy group:

Worse, their self respect is attacked, for their mate magnifies their fault, makes them feel worthless, belittles their efforts and makes false accusations (Matthews and Mihanovich, 1963, p. 302).

This seems to indicate that the unhappily married react to frustrations and disagreements by attacking the self-concept of the mate to a greater extent than the happily married. There is always the question in a study of this kind as to whether the unhappiness makes people perceive that many things are wrong or whether the misunderstanding and rejection precipitates the unhappiness. The causal sequence cannot be established, but it seems reasonable to assume that, once generalized unhappiness with the spouse becomes part of the interaction, it will tend to generate further defensive behavior and greater unhappiness.

Blood and Wolfe have given further indication of the damage done by personal attacks in marriage. They found that by far the kind of disagreement most related to marital unhappiness concerned what they called "personality clashes." Broken down, these seem to involve mainly the same type of complaints mentioned above—differing tastes, irritating personal habits, temperamental quirks, and criticisms of the other's skills. They noted:

Personal attacks hurt the ego too much to be easily repaired or easily forgiven. The damage they do lives after them to haunt attacker and victim alike. If any particular disagreements are symptomatic of crippling stresses in marriage, personality conflicts are the ones (Blood and Wolfe, 1960, p. 250).

It is obvious that they were talking as much about the kind of reaction given to any disagreement, as they were to true personality clashes. The critical or negative response to disagreement becomes a personality assessment and lingers as an area of disagreement itself. This becomes clearer from their analysis of the husbands' responses to their wives telling them about their bad days. The authors stated:

Confronted with a drowning ego, some husbands do nothing. As if that weren't cruel enough, others answer her cries with the cavalier comment that she couldn't possibly be in trouble. Worse yet are those who criticize her inability to swim and tell her she deserves to drown anyway because she is so dumb (Blood and Wolfe, 1960, p. 209).

and

Marriage is an interactive process of action and reaction in vicious or beneficent cycles. Responsive husbands produce satisfied wives. But a wife who encounters only negative responses to her overtures will eventually either leave the field of battle through divorce or call a cease-fire by living alone in the same house with an unutilized husband. The human spirit cannot stand being caught in a vicious cycle forever (Blood and Wolfe, 1960, p. 203).

The complaints showing the greatest difference between happy and unhappy respondents in the Matthews and Mihanovich study was "Don't think alike on many things." Fifty per cent of the unhappy compared to eleven per cent of the happy reported this as describing their marriages. The next most discriminating item was "Mate has little insight into my feelings" (40 per cent compared to 6 per cent). This can be interpreted in different ways. It may mean that there are actually greater differences between the unhappy spouses in values, concepts of the husband–wife roles, attitudes, and interests and that the differences lower the capacity or desire to understand the other's point of view. But it also can mean that there is so little communication between them that they have not built a common culture of shared experience and feelings; there may be little insight because the unhappy spouse has not provided any clues for the partner to develop understanding. It is of interest to note that the same percentage (40 per cent) which reported "Mate has little insight into my feelings" also reported that "I keep things to myself (Matthews and Mihanovich, 1963)." If a person does not like some aspect of the relationship but continues to engage in it without communicating his unhappiness, the mate has no way of knowing of the discontent. When challenged on this in a marriage counseling situation, many will respond: "Why talk about it; it wouldn't make any difference anyway." This may be correct, but to assume it is correct without trying is assuming that the other doesn't care, or is too stubborn or self-centered to change. This assessment of the other cannot help but influence the interaction.

Problems in Communication

People communicate even if they are silent. Silence in various contexts, at particular points in a conversation means different things—and it means different things to different people. It is not possible to cease communication, so the need is not just for communication of any kind but for communication which is mutually understood and says what the people intend it to say.

A child develops certain codes of communicating as he is growing up in his family. He is likely to be understood by family members because he learned the code from them. The differences in communication patterns are subtle and he is likely to assume that all codes are alike, that every one else means the same thing he does by a pause, a phrase, or a silence. It is the business of early marriage to learn to decipher each other's codes.

Since we are not always alerted to the subtle differences, we may go through life feeling misunderstood, brushed off, or convinced that we or our spouses are callous, insensitive people. As Richard Rabkin put it: ". . . husband and wife are constantly decoding with two different decoders." When this results in difficulties, they do not generally see it as a communication problem. They are more likely to chalk it up to personality conflicts (Rabkin, 1967).

What for instance does the question, "Where are the fingernail clippers?" imply? There are a number of different meanings hidden in this question, each requiring a different answer. The meanings vary according to the mode of communication prevalent in a particular family and cannot be picked up in the inflection. A few of the possibilities follow.

1. "Where are the fingernail clippers?" may be only a simple question requiring a simple answer: "In the top, right-hand dresser drawer," or "I don't know."

2. It may imply a polite request for the other to get them, which might be easily refused if not convenient. An appropriate response would be: "In the dresser drawer, but I can't get them for you right now," or "I don't know. If you can't find them, I'll help you look when I finish this."

3. It may, however, contain a command to bring them, which cannot easily be refused. The only acceptable response becomes the appearance of the nail-clippers.

4. It may mean that one has already looked, and the clippers are not where they are supposed to be. It may further imply that the other has failed to put them back. Interpreted in this way, it is likely to get a defensive response such as: "I haven't had them. You were the last one with them. What did *you* do with them?"

The way the question is meant and the way it is interpreted will be related to the codes so well learned in the families of orientation that it is difficult to conceive that it could be interpreted any other way. But consider the interaction and impact on feelings resulting from different combinations of the meanings.

A husband asks his wife: "Where are the fingernail clippers?" In his family it was a simple inquiry (interpretation #1). His wife is washing dishes. She stops, dries her hands, brings him the nail clippers. To herself (interpretation #3) she thinks:

He expects me to drop everything and wait on him! He could see I was busy. There he sits, doing nothing, yet I've got to stop and get him the nail clippers!"

She will probably convey her displeasure in the way she gives them to him, triggering an interaction something like this:

Husband: Thanks. (Pause) What's wrong?
Wife: You could see I was busy. Why didn't you get them yourself?
Husband: I didn't ask you to get them!
Wife: You most certainly did. I heard you.
Husband (to himself): Did I? I thought I just asked where they were.

He begins to wonder if he really had been that inconsiderate or if his wife is being unreasonable or is angry about something else. The way he interprets her reaction will color his response—and so on and on and on. This throws some light on the rather common situation in which a couple find themselves sniping at each other, feeling bitter and unhappy but unable to remember what it was that started the argument. The other person appears to be irrational, as reflected in the words of a bewildered husband:

I made a simple comment and she blew her cool. Don't ask me what set her off! Who knows? I don't think she knows either.

From this discussion it is easy to see why couples sometimes show wide discrepancies between *actual* marital role agreement and *perceived* marital role agreement. Both of the above partners could actually respond with equalitarian expectations; but the wife would probably perceive her husband as expecting her to wait on him and to respond immediately to his requests, even though he doesn't actually expect this. It is obvious that there could be times when this husband would perceive himself as being a tolerant, patient person at the same time his wife was reacting to him as a self-centered, demanding man. Each may feel misunderstood, imposed upon, and unappreciated.

One perceptive wife found an amusing way to bring into the open different interpretations of questions such as the above. Not sure what her husband meant, and recognizing her own feelings of resentment in responding, she began to reply to any question about the whereabouts of anything with a good humored, "Under the bed." Her good humor and the obvious inappropriateness of the response would prompt an open discussion of what was actually implied, and her interpretation of the question. Soon, any question concerning where things were became a source of amusement to both of them rather than a source of resentment. If there was any question in either of their minds about the other's meaning, "under the bed" became a warning of pending misunderstanding.

There are some recurring problems in communication which are almost certain to produce misunderstanding. A few of these follow.

1. To the extent that a person has built up unshakable ideas about what members of the opposite sex are like, what they mean, or how they feel when they laugh, frown, cry, or speak certain words, he is likely to assume that he readily understands the spouse when she (he) acts or speaks in a certain way. Entire conversations can occur with oneself this way, even though the words are being directed to another person. This can be very frustrating to a person trying to make himself understood and occasions the often heard complaint: "It does no good to talk to him, he never listens." One can only begin to be sure he has understood another person after he has repeated the meaning he attached to the words or gestures and has it reaffirmed by the other person.

2. Another problem confronted in communication is the assumption that people are logically consistent in their feelings and behaviors. Because a man likes the same breakfast menu day after day with no deviation does not mean he doesn't enjoy wide variety at dinner. Because he likes his wife to be comfortably conservative in her dress doesn't mean he won't appreciate mini-skirts on someone else or maybe even on her at certain times. The key to understanding is not through logical deduction but finding out what prompts the illogical, non-rational behavior and feelings.

3. The search for who is right or intelligent and who is wrong or stupid produces another problem to open communication. The response, "How could you be so stupid," to a confession of mistaken judgment or an irrational feeling is a good way to dampen the enthusiasm for further disclosure. It forces the other person to defend himself, to search for the

logic behind his action which can be manufactured if it isn't there. Neither person is likely to find out how the other really feels. They have just shored up the defenses behind which they can attack.[1]

The communication process is aided more by a genuine expression of one's own reaction and feeling than by a judgment of the other's behavior. The response, "I feel like throwing something at you when you do that," prompts a question as to what it is that disturbs you; while, "Any third grader could keep a check book better than you," prompts defensive countercharges and anger. Such a comment is fairly certain not to uncover the difficulty or allow explorations of ways to avoid the disturbing behavior in the future.

4. It probably goes without saying that the honesty necessary for good communication is hampered by behavior that one wants to hide from the spouse. The need to keep the spouse from finding out that one is having an extra-marital affair, or is playing the horses with the grocery money, or that the last baby was fathered by someone else, is likely to cut off communication in many areas for fear that something will slip. Feeling that one must always be on guard many times makes one hate the person he must lie to, even though there is no rational reason for it.

A discussion of honesty in spousal communication has some hidden pitfalls. Some people interpret this as license to say whatever is on one's mind to the spouse, saying only the hurtful things and then accusing the spouse of not wanting "honesty" when he or she responds with anger. The angry response is just as *honest* as the honest comment which provoked it. Understanding comes when the honesty extends to why one *wanted* to hurt and why the other *felt* angry.

Barriers to Communication. Other barriers to communication have been discussed by Komarovsky (1964, Chapter 7) as a result of her study of blue-collar marriages. Although the following four barriers were discovered in blue-collar relationships, the generalizations are probably applicable wherever the conditions exist, no matter what the class position of the spouses.

Differentiation in interests of the sexes. To the extent that there is little convergence of interests of the spouses, the range of subjects they can talk about will be narrowed. When this is reinforced by stereotypes about men and women the reason for attempting to share interests is gone. The general feelings reflected by many of Komarovsky's illustrations of the effects of stereotypical thinking can be seen in the following (paraphrased):

There's no point in talking to her about that, women don't understand.

---

[1] The above discussion borrows heavily from Harper (1958).

or in this comment:

Men are all alike. They want to eat, have some sex, and sleep. They don't
listen when their wives talk, and don't talk to their wives. They talk up a
storm when they get together though.

Neither spouse can be an audience for the other, because there is no
overlapping of interests. Each finds the other boring.

Blood and Wolfe, for example, found that the wife's satisfaction with
companionship went up with the number of areas in which decision making was shared. It rose with the frequency with which the husband talked
about his work and with the number of organizations to which they both
belonged. It was greater where the spouses were equal in education and
had attended college (Blood and Wolfe, 1960, pp. 151, 152, 163, 164,
170–71). All of these seem to be describing situations in which there is
a higher probability of shared interests.

Nature of husband's job. The monotonous nature of the husband's job
in the blue-collar world produces little to talk about. He is likely to
want to forget about it at home. Dissatisfaction with one's work is not
restricted to the working class, however. Wherever this is true, some
barrier is likely to appear. If a husband does not want to talk about
what happens to him, his wife has no way of developing any insight into
his world or how it may affect his feelings about himself.

The same effect is produced in certain highly technical positions, where
the husband may want to talk about his work but it is so abstract that
he cannot communicate it to his wife who is not trained in the same field.
This whole area of communication may be blocked, not because they
want it that way, but because of the technical nature of the job. A wife
in this situation expressed her frustration in these words:

When I'm with him and some of his friends from work, I feel like a perfect
dunce. When he gets excited over something he's working on, I know he'd
like to talk about it, but he gives up when he realizes I don't understand a bit
of it.

Some jobs necessitating secrecy about the work erect the same barriers.
It becomes hard even to talk about the people one works with if there is
the constant need to be on guard lest secret information slip into the
conversation.

Impoverishment of life. In some marriages there may be few barriers
to communication if there was something to talk about. There may be
so few stimuli in the person's life that there is nothing of interest to share.
If this has been characteristic of the whole life, there is likely to be a
stunting of personal development, a lack of skill in expressing one's opinions, or little inner awareness of feelings or reactions.

One aging woman client, virtually cut off from friends and previous activities because of the paralysis of her husband, put it quite well:

We just sit and look at each other. We've said all there is to say. No one comes in, he can't go anywhere, doesn't want me to leave him, and won't watch TV. After we've said good morning and what we have to say to get him dressed and fed, that's it. You have to do something or see somebody to have something to talk about, and we don't do either one.

Personality problems. Some persons, for a variety of psychological reasons, find any close relationship threatening. They do not disclose anything about themselves because they fear the other person may use it against them or "throw it up to them." They are happier in a marriage relationship which puts few emotional demands on them—where the main focus is on the marital roles with little demand for a close interpersonal relationship. Paired with someone like themselves, they have little need for communication except to coordinate their activities.

Relation to Marital Happiness

Obviously, good communication will not guarantee a happy relationship. As some couples understand each other more completely they may come to realize that they have such wide differences in values and perspectives that they cannot reach their separate goals together. Understanding does not guarantee either approval or agreement. The wife who finally understands that her husband really has no scruples about how he earns the money for his family may be more unhappy than when she thought he was just showing bad judgment or was misinformed. The husband who discovers his wife is truly self-centered and cares nothing for him or the children is not likely to be happier than when he misinterpreted her actions.

Rollins and Feldman (1970) provide some evidence of the relationship between different measures of marital satisfaction throughout the stages of the family life cycle. Two of these measures appear to relate to the feelings resulting from communication. One question asked for the frequency of laughing together, having a stimulating conversation, calmly discussing something, or working together on some project. These were viewed together as "positive companionship." The second measure asked about the frequency of negative feelings following interaction with the spouse. These were described as feelings of being misunderstood, not needed, or resentful, all of which give an indication of dissatisfaction with communication. Figure 13–1 shows a rather slight positive relationship between frequency of positive companionship and satisfaction with present stage of the life cycle until the "launching" stage which spans the period from when the first child leaves until the last child leaves. As

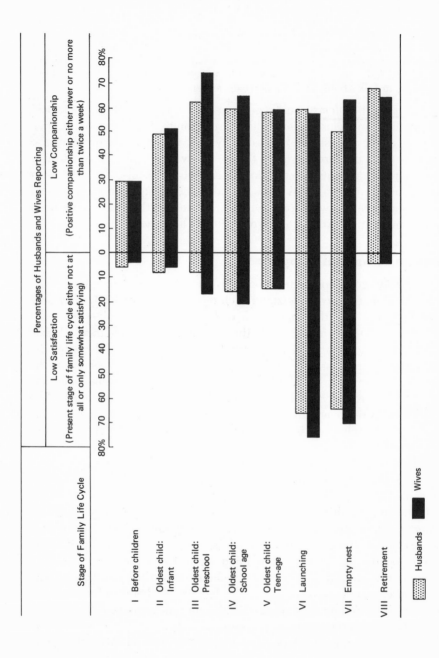

Fig. 13–1. Comparison of husbands and wives in positive companionship and satisfaction with stage in the life cycle. (Adapted from Rollins and Feldman, 1970, Tables 2 and 3, p. 24.)

frequency of husbands and wives reporting positive companionship only once or twice a week or less increases, the percentage reporting that the present stage of the life cycle is only "somewhat satisfying" or "not satisfying at all" also increases.

This is specially true of wives. The increase in dissatisfaction from early marriage to the period when preschool children are in the home is at a much slower pace than the decrease in positive communication, however. There is an increase in the reporting of more frequent companionship when the oldest child is of school age, which remains fairly stable throughout the remainder of the life cycle. Dissatisfaction, however, increases tremendously during the "launching" and "empty nest" stages with little apparent fluctuation in companionship. Evidently interests in children or careers serves to counter the effect of low communication until the middle years when children leave.

When negative consequences of husband–wife interaction are viewed, however, the relationship to marital satisfaction appears stronger (see Figure 13–2). As the percentage of wives, especially, reporting negative feelings that result from interaction with husband "once or twice" a month or more increases, the percentage reporting the marriage is going well "all the time" decreases. The percentage of wives reporting negative feelings greatly exceeds that of the husbands during the period when young children are in the home.

It is interesting to note from Figures 13–1 and 13–2 that during retirement lower percentages of both husbands and wives report negative feelings. Positive companionship does not increase, yet marital satisfaction appears to be more prevalent during retirement than at any period except for the pre-childbearing stage. The relationship between positive and negative communication and satisfaction with the marriage relationship appears to vary over the life cycle.

Several studies indicate that, in general, satisfaction with communication is associated with marital satisfaction. Leslie Navran (1967) found a strong association between marital communication and marital happiness. He concluded that happily married couples differed from unhappy ones in that they:

1. Talk to each other more
2. Convey the feeling that they understand what is being said to them
3. Have a wider range of interests open to them
4. Preserve communication channels and keep them open
5. Show more sensitivity to each other's feelings
6. Make more frequent use of words which have a private meaning for them
7. Make more use of non-verbal communication

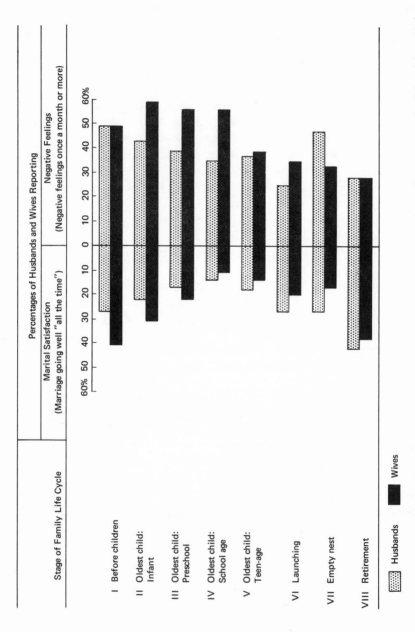

Fig. 13–2. Comparison of husbands and wives on two measures of marital satisfaction over the life cycle. (Adapted from Rollins and Feldman, 1970, Tables 2 and 3, p. 24.)

Importance of Perceived Agreement. Along with findings that good communication is associated with marital happiness are some others which qualify this somewhat. Several studies show a relationship between marital satisfaction and spousal agreement on role expectations and/or perceptions of self. Ort, for example, found that marital satisfaction was associated with the perception that the spouse's role performance agreed with the other's role expectations (Ort, 1950). In a more recent study Hawkins and Johnsen (1969) found the same thing, with the added finding that *perceived consensus* on role expectations was highly correlated with marital satisfaction ($r = .72$). In other words, as long as a person thought the spouse agreed with him on marital role expectations he was likely to report the marriage as a happy one, whether or not there was actual agreement.

Stuckert and Luckey both discovered in different studies that accurate perception seems more important for the wife than for the husband. Studying role expectations, Stuckert (1963) found that in the early part of marriage actual role similarity was related to the husbands' marital happiness but not the wife's. If there was role disagreement and the husband was *unaware* of it and thought his marriage was typical of others he was very likely to rate his marriage as happy. If the wife, however, accurately perceived her husband's role expectations, she was likely to be satisfied whether or not there was agreement between them. If she was not perceptive, then she was more likely to be happy if their role expectations agreed.

Luckey (1960) came to somewhat the same conclusions studying the perceptions of self and spouse. If the wife perceived her husband as he perceived himself, the marriage was likely to be a happy one. The relationship did not hold for the husband's perceptions. It made little difference to happiness whether or not he saw his wife as she saw herself.

These findings seem to indicate that if there is consensus between the partners it strengthens the relationship to find out it is there. If, however, there is not consensus, the husband is happier if he doesn't know it, while the wife is happier if she does. It would seem then to be more important in early marriage for the husband to disclose things about himself rather than the other way around. This is probably due to the cultural expectations that the wife will adjust more in marriage than the husband. It helps, then, if she knows what he expects, and she can find satisfaction in knowing she is being the kind of wife her husband wants.

Selective Communication

Marital satisfaction has been shown to be related to good communication. Just what constitutes "good" communication is not well-known.

These findings come from assessments of the feelings which result from communication, so good communication produces the perception that there is a feeling of understanding, of caring, and of appreciation. This obviously does not mean that everything one feels is communicated at the moment one feels it.

The wife who is busily trying to prepare dinner while holding a crying baby in a kitchen which is piled high with dirty dishes (because the plumbing stopped up and the sink is full of dirty water) is not likely to accept gracefully the most tactfully worded feelings of her husband that it makes him angry to come home to such a mess. She is likely not to care how he feels at the moment. In other words, her needs are so great that she is not able to be concerned about his. The ability to withhold certain reactions is related to both commitment to the relationship and awareness of the other's ability to accept the reactions.

If one is aware of an extremely sensitive area in the partner, it does little good to continue to refer to it, especially if nothing can be done about it. The wife who continues to lament the low earning capacity of her husband when he is working as hard as he can does not create understanding with her communication. The husband who openly and continuously displays his annoyance with the short stature of his wife, when she obviously cannot grow to please him, does not endear himself to her with his open communication of feelings. Probably what most people view as good communication is selective communication which provides a feeling of helpful concern and understanding, as much by what is left unsaid as by what is said.

Certainly the early marriage relationship is not helped by the husband giving "honest" appraisals of his young wife's attempts at cooking. His gallant efforts to smile and nod approvingly while he chews the rubbery meat does more for the relationship than communication of his "honest" reaction of nausea. What he is really communicating, which she perceives, is that "We both know this isn't very good, but I know you tried and I love you for it, so we'll both pretend." He has actually communicated more honestly and completely by pretending than by giving a frank opinion of the food.

The beneficial results of selective communication are perhaps supported by the finding that college educated wives are more likely than others to selectively tell their husbands their problems (Blood and Wolfe, 1960, p. 194). They are likely to give as their reason for not telling him all of their problems the feeling that they should not bother him, while lesser educated wives are more likely to tell or not tell according to their own mood or their anticipation of whether their husbands will react negatively. College educated wives are also more likely to be highly satisfied with the understanding they get from their husbands and to report greater over-all satisfaction in their marriages (Blood and Wolfe, 1960, p. 216). Hence, one communicates understanding, affection, and concern for the other by *not* communicating some of the unhappy or unfavorable feelings, while at the same time communicating enough happy or favorable feelings to build an atmosphere of acceptance strong enough to withstand those negative reactions which *must* be communicated.

Abortive Communication.   Some verbal exchanges which masquerade under the heading of communicating information are not that at all but a communication of resentment or a desire to lash out. For example, the car keys are lost and neither spouse can find them. She knows and he knows that she had them last. When he says to her "You had them last," he's telling her nothing—they both already know that. What he may be trying to say is that he's angry and he wants her to know it. She probably already knows that, too. Or what he may mean is, "I'm glad you did something wrong so I can blame you just as you blamed me yesterday for forgetting to stop by the store." If this is what he means and he says it —the communication lines are open for her to see what she had to do with his response to the lost keys. "You had them last" communicates nothing and does not aid future encounters. Most people talk—not many really communicate.

The nature of marriage is such that there are bound to be periods when one spouse must put aside his own needs to come to the support of a hard-pressed partner; when their goals and desires meet head on in conflict; when frustrations and disappointments make them question the value of the marriage itself. The over-all evaluation of the marriage at any one time, however, will be the result of a general weighing of these low spots against the pleasant and stimulating periods; and the extent to which the communication, whatever its nature, has enabled them to build a shared culture within which to understand each other and still find each other interesting.

The fear which keeps many people from communicating adequately is the knowledge that the understanding that gives the greatest satisfaction is also the same understanding that allows the greatest hurt. The more one person understands another, the more effective are the weapons he is capable of bringing to a conflict.

CONFLICT

The conflict pattern which develops in a marriage will be partially related to the habits of conflict the spouses bring with them, partially the result of the way the two habit systems fit together, and partially the result of their tolerance for conflict.

Conflict comes in many forms. Generally it assumes that there is a difference of opinion, and some maneuvering occurs to get one or both persons to move to a more congenial position. The conflict can be as small as one person wanting to read a book and the other wanting to talk. The maneuvers may be alternate wheedling, playful pestering, and coaxing, until the book goes to the floor amid laughter. Conflict was there, but it was resolved with such ease that neither would define it as such. The same situation, however, may take on the appearance of conflict, even with the same maneuvers, if the reaction of the book reader is different. "Stop bothering me. I am going to read this book, and nothing you can do will stop me." The "reader" has now taken a position; he has told the "player" that he will not be moved from his position and that they have not interpreted the playful gestures in the same way.

Resolution may or may not occur at this point, depending upon how the "player" reacts to the obvious rebuff and display of power. If the "reader" goes on reading and the "player" sighs and gives up the play, the conflict is resolved, but with some lingering awareness that a conflict of interests exists between them. If the "player" interprets the rebuff as a rejection of self and an invitation to fight, the conflict may continue, ending in accusations of lack of interest or lack of love. Again, depending on the "reader's" reactions to the latest maneuver, the conflict may be resolved with reassurances of love, apologies, and a forgotten book, or continue with the accused "reader" storming out of the house after throwing the book at the "player." At this point, if not before, both partners are aware there has been a conflict, but they may be quite hazy over why it occurred and how it grew.[2]

In the example just given, conflict was present from the beginning; but whether the spouses perceived it as conflict was related to the ease of its resolution. Conflict is easy to detect when there are sharp words or blows, but it tends to go unnoticed if resolution is quick and painless. The intensity of conflict may not be as closely related to the sharpness of the differences as it is to the habitual ways of resolving them. If the methods of resolution avoid throwing the conflict into a power struggle or attacks against the self-concept, then intense conflict is not likely to occur.

This is difficult to do in the early part of marriage, however, when anxieties about self and the relationship as well as inexperience with the habit patterns of the mate are likely to heighten the importance of their differences. The nature of the power structure itself is one of the things being defined in the new relationship (see Chapter 8 for a review of the elements in the power dependence relationship). The difficulties in de-

---

[2] An interesting analysis of the "moves" and "counter moves" present in the bargaining which takes place in the resolution of marital conflict can be found in Jessie Bernard (1964).

fining and developing the marital roles produce frustrations which are likely to heighten the sensitivities to slights and to minor differences in habits and opinions.

Types of Conflict

Conflict can appear in either overt or covert forms. It can be out in the open, so to speak, or underground so that neither knows that hostility is the motivation for certain actions.

Overt Conflict. Folsom has developed a typology of overt conflict. He distinguishes between acute, progressive, and habituated forms (Folsum, 1943, p. 447; Leslie, 1967, p. 471–79). *Acute conflict* is seen to be most characteristic of early marriage and of subsequent situations which introduce new elements, heighten anxieties, and present undefined problems to the relationship. It accompanies the formation of mutual habits out of individual ones when irritating habits, misinterpretations, and personal insecurities combine to threaten the euphoria associated with engagement or prior adjustments.

This type of conflict is characterized by intense emotional involvement and explosive hostility. For the moment, each party seems more intent on doing damage to the other than in resolving the conflict or preserving the relationship. Given a relatively high tolerance level for conflict on the part of both partners, the release of the negative feelings can result in apologies and affectionate "making up" which soothes the hurts, until the build up of unmet expectations and bruised self-concepts mounts to another "blow-up." If the tolerance levels are unequal, the smoothing over may be more difficult. If both partners have low tolerance levels acute conflict may not be so likely, with hostility going underground. A student of one of the authors' gave this account of the acute conflict in her marriage, rightly connecting it to personality differences, differences in habits and background, and the newness of the relationship.

By nature Ralph is rather quiet. He is slow speaking, easy-going, and not generally very organized or orderly. I, on the other hand, am a nervous, quick-thinking, fast-acting sort of person. In addition, you could say my motto is "A place for everything and everything in its place." Not that I'm fanatic about neatness, but I cannot stand messiness for very long. And when something needs to be done, I want it done quickly, efficiently, and "just. so." It should be quite obvious that these personality differences, especially when coupled with differences in religion, family, and regional backgrounds, can contribute to much conflict, and they do.

Much of it centers around interpretation, or I should say misinterpretation. For example, if Ralph would rather read than talk, I am prone to think he's annoyed with me, while it may only be that he's interested in what he's reading (at least, that's what he says.) If I give him what I consider a helpful hint about his project-of-the-moment, he thinks I'm criticizing or that I believe my way is the only way.

Partly, the conflict comes from insecurity. Our marriage is a new one and we are still probing many areas of life together. We seem afraid to completely let down our defenses. I suppose that each of us is afraid the other may be furnished with ammunition for future arguments.

Another difference is the way we react to arguments. For me, when the apologies are made, the affair is finished, I seldom even remember much of the argument's viciousness. Sometimes I even forget what it was about. Ralph, on the other hand, is not accustomed to arguing. The least little bit of criticism seems to make an indelible mark on him. He can't forget, it seems, even when he wants to. I almost enjoy the excitement of an argument, but he loathes it.

It appears fairly certain that the kind of remarks classified as "the least little bit of criticism" differs between these two people. A high tolerance for conflict allows her to classify as small those criticisms which, to him, are extremely damaging. Their problem, as with others, will be to round off the jagged edges which wound each other before the damaging effects of the conflict destroy the foundations of the relationship.

If couples do not learn rather early in the marriage to resolve, at least partially, conflicts resulting from their differing family backgrounds and habits, the conflict may begin to turn into what Folsom labels *progressive conflict*. Each acute conflict is likely to leave a residue of hurt feelings and perhaps some apprehension about discussing certain areas of disagreement in the future. As the residue grows larger and the number of tabooed areas increases, interaction may be fraught with tensions reduced only by greater and greater estrangement. They may stabilize over time by avoidance or gravitate toward separation or divorce. They may, however, achieve working arrangements in most areas leaving only a few conflicts which tend to recur over and over. The emotional involvement may decline even in these arguments and result in what Folsom calls *habituated conflict*.

Habituated conflict differs from acute conflict in that it is less explosive and is restricted to certain recurring behaviors. It may even be rather satisfying because of the predictability furnished by the same heated reaction and the feeling that one knows exactly how the spouse will react to certain behaviors. It differs from progressive conflict in that it does not get worse or creep from area to area.

Depending upon the needs for tension outlets and tolerance levels, habituated conflict may be sentimentalized and become part of the spice or stimulation in a relationship. The affection in the words of a husband who knows exactly how to "set his wife off," is quite apparent:

When things get a little dull, I just pull the right switch, and off she goes. She's cute when she's angry. Of course, I know how to shut her off again, too. She knows I'm doing it half of the time, but it doesn't seem to make any difference. Off she goes, anyway!

Sometimes a point of conflict is sustained consciously by a vague awareness that it serves a purpose. Occasionally an irritating habit is defended by words such as the following:

If he didn't have that to fuss about, he'd find something else. He needs to let off steam occasionally and it doesn't bother me, so why change? He screams about it, but it really makes him feel good to think he's so much smarter than I am about such things.

These are part of the little illusions about self that married partners help each other maintain. Only when conflicts lead to hurt feelings are the illusions likely to be shattered, leading to battered self-concepts, bitterness, and retaliation or withdrawal (Leslie, 1967, pp. 471–72).

Covert Conflict.   When conflict occurs in obvious areas or is accompanied by either verbal or physical combat, it is fairly easily recognized. One spouse or the other, however, may be unable to express his anger openly. The power structure may be such that one person always loses any open contest or is afraid to oppose the other openly. When this happens and anger is present, it is likely to go underground, perhaps unrecognized as conflict by either spouse.

Covert conflict is difficult to observe because, by definition, it is hidden or disguised. The main source of evidence of this kind of conflict comes from the clinical studies of whole families, where the complex interaction has produced disturbance in one of the members (see Handel, 1967, Part VI). It can perhaps he assumed that covert conflict exists in many families to a lesser degree. Its expression or accompanying disturbance can generally be attributed to causes other than covert conflict, however. The problem in identifying it lies in the obvious fact that the same behaviors *can* be the result of organic problems, of personal likes and dislikes, or of personality misfits.

Some sexual problems fall under this heading. Since a denial of sexual responsiveness is a threat to the self-concept of the other person, what better way to attack without appearing to do so? The underlying hostility is sometimes expressed by constant fatigue, ironings which have to be done late at night, absorption in the late, late show on TV, or a book, or the work-shop, or many other things which appear so commonplace that an accusation of avoidance can be countered with an accusation of inconsiderateness of the other's interests or heavy work load.

It sometimes appears in the form of illness which can produce guilt in the person who even begins to suspect the underlying hostility. Illness can prevent one spouse from performing the obligations associated with his role, putting a heavy burden on the partner. On the other hand, protective solicitation toward an ill spouse—keeping him an invalid and totally dependent even when medical opinions attest to the need for activity and resumed outside interests—can accomplish the purpose of undermining his self-concept and confidence while masquerading as the devotion of a loving spouse.

At a less intense level but equally destructive to contentment are the refusals to participate in activities the spouse enjoys because of the press of other demands, personal dislikes, or sundry other reasons for non-participation. The problem is that there are also real, non-hostile reasons for non-participation. They can always appear non-hostile. But if the non-participation is recurring and covers a wide range of the spouse's interests even though the same activities were enjoyed before marriage, covert hostility can be suspected.

When hostility goes underground, it is hard to recognize and harder to resolve since the source of the hostility is hidden. Covert hostility hits hard at the other's self-concept forcing the defenses up, which reduces the probability of productive communication. This appears to be a statement in favor of overt conflict, so that the feelings and differences can be recognized and dealt with. Whether overt or covert, however, continuous conflict is likely to cool the ardor of the most devoted pair.

Areas of Conflict

There is a general myth in our society that conflict is associated with the early years of marriage and that, after adjustments are made, the couple will live happily ever after. Although this has some basis in fact considering the high percentage of divorces which occur in the early years of marriage, it obscures the changing nature of the marriage relationship over time. Each change in the life cycle is likely to produce new areas of interaction, which include the possibility of new conflicts of values, attitudes, and behavior.

Problems Related to Life Cycle. Blood and Wolfe (1960, p. 247) give an indication of the influence of the stage in the life cycle on types of problems reported by wives. Recreational interests are more likely to be a problem for those who have the leisure time for recreation—those in the first years of marriage before children appear and those who never have children. As young children enter the picture, money problems become more prevalent and disagreements about children begin to appear. As the children grow, disagreements about them become more prevalent, reaching a peak when the children are adolescents, as do money problems. Only 7 per cent of those with preadolescent children and 10 per cent of those with adolescent children reported no disagreements at all. This can be compared to the 15 per cent of the honeymooners and 31 per cent of the childless couples who said they were free of disagreements. Personality problems were more prevalent among honeymooners and those with grown children. This perhaps emphasizes the adjustments to a new relationship occurring in the honeymoon stage and the readjustment necessary when the loss of children again focuses their attention on each other.

Problems Related to Social Class.   Kinds of marital problems differ according to social class as well as stage of the life cycle. Rainwater (1965, pp. 322–28) provides information on the prevalence of varying kinds of money and relationship problems among different social class positions and between Negroes and whites. From Figure 13–3 it can be seen that the interpersonal adjustment problems are more prevalent among the higher socioeconomic groups where companionship and communication are a valued part of marriage. They are especially prevalent among upper-middle class wives. The same pattern is repeated among Negroes, with the higher status Negroes perceiving more problems of adjustment than lower status Negroes.

When the problems concern disruptive relationship difficulties, such as drinking, gambling, staying out late, and irresponsibility, the reverse pattern is seen for both races—the lower the socioeconomic level the higher the frequency of these more serious problems, especially for wives.

The same contrasting patterns appear when money problems are separated according to their severity (see Figure 13–4). In the middle classes, where an adequate supply of funds is assumed, there is more likely to be an awareness of budget problems. They have some excess of money to argue over. Budget problems are not so prevalent among the lower class, but serious financial problems involving chronic unemployment, lay-offs, and insufficient funds affect a much higher percentage of people in this class than in the middle class. It seems fairly clear that middle class people will have difficulty in completely understanding the severe threats to the lower class marriages stemming from their tenuous attachment to the economic system.

Problems Related to Conjugal Role Type.   Among lower class couples, the type of marital role relationship appears related to the seriousness of the problems. Rainwater (1965, Chapter 2) divided the couples in his sample according to conjugal role type. His "highly-segregated" category is roughly equivalent to our "wife-and-mother role" described in the previous chapter. The separation of tasks along traditional lines cuts down the pair interaction as well as communication and sharing of interests. At the other extreme is Rainwater's "joint" type which involves high involvement in each other's tasks, a valuing of communication, and a sharing of interests. A third type, the "intermediate" is a mixture of the other

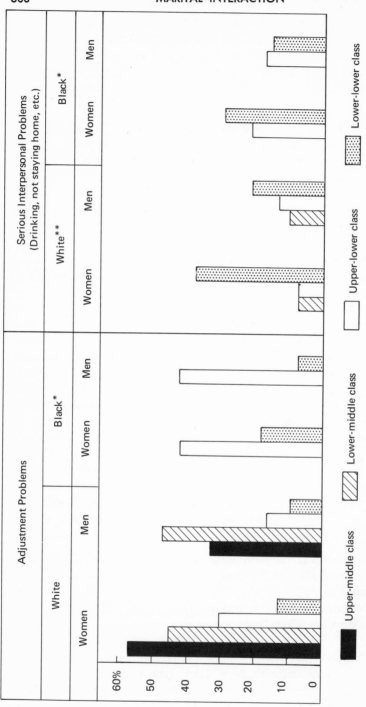

*There were no black middle class respondents.
**No upper-middle class men or women reported problems of this type.

Upper-middle class   Lower-middle class

Upper-lower class   Lower-lower class

Fig. 13–3. Comparison of severity of problems reported by white and black respondents at different social class levels. (Adapted from Rainwater, 1965, Table A–9, p. 323.)

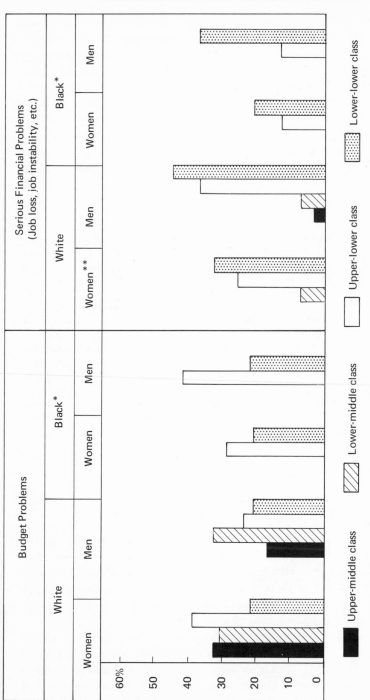

*There were no black middle class respondents.
**No upper-middle class women reported problems of this type.

Fig. 13–4. Comparison of severity of financial problems reported by white and black respondents at different social class levels. (Adapted from Rainwater, 1965, Table A–10, p. 325.)

two, involving some segregation and some areas of shared activities. When the lower class couples were separated according to conjugal role type, Rainwater found that the joint and intermediate types were much more likely to report minor personal adjustment problems (64 per cent) than were the highly segregated couples (13 per cent).

The highly segregated on the other hand were much more likely to report severe relationship problems (41 per cent) than were the joint and intermediate couples (11 per cent). The same was true concerning money problems, with the segregated types much more likely to report serious financial problems (56 per cent to 27 per cent) (Rainwater, 1965, p. 327).

That the segregated conjugal role relationship may be both cause and effect of the more serious marital problems plaguing it is clearly suggested by Rainwater:

. . . it is clear that couples in the more segregated relationships are more likely to have serious problems of economic insecurity and instability, and not only because such couples are more often of the lower-lower class. To some extent, these problems are an expression of the life style characteristic of the group; that is, both segregated role-organization and economic insecurity are part of the lower class life situation. But in addition, some financial problems arise out of the segregated relationship: husband and wife do not consult each other and plan together; each acts separately, and they over-spend and accumulate debts, which, in turn, can lead to loss of the husband's job when his employer is asked to garnishee his wages. More commonly, poverty and economic insecurity deepen the separation of husband and wife by lessening the respect of the wife for the husband and encouraging the husband to pursue his own interests as compensation for his sad lot in life and as a way of defending himself against feelings of impotence as a man and as provider for his family (Rainwater, 1965, p. 328).

RESOLUTION OF CONFLICT

From the above discussion, it is probably already apparent that the ways in which conflict can be resolved are related to the causes of the conflict and to the kind of marital relationship in which it takes place. Some conflicts tend to disappear by themselves, especially those associated with life cycle changes. Obviously, disagreements about how to spend one's leisure disappear if there is no leisure time. Disagreements about how to "potty train" children disappear after the child is "potty trained."

Perhaps one of the reasons that older married couples report fewer disagreements than younger ones is that many of their sources of conflict have disappeared, not that the basic issues have all been resolved (Blood and Wolfe, 1960, p. 245). Sex is no longer such a frequent source of either pleasure or disappointment; children, once a source of both conflict and satisfaction, have left home; income demands have decreased so that the money problems are not so serious.

It does not appear, however, that satisfaction goes up as the sources of conflict disappear. Blood and Wolfe (1960, pp. 264–65) also report a decrease in marital satisfaction the greater the number of years married and with each stage of the family life cycle. Older couples no longer report many conflicts, perhaps either because they no longer interact so intensely over such a wide range of activities or because they have ceased to communicate—neither disagreeing nor agreeing about anything. It may not mean that they understand each other better or have grown more tolerant, only that they have lost interest. The contradiction between this study and the Rollins and Feldman (1970) study reported earlier probably lies in the measures of satisfaction. The Blood and Wolfe study included satisfaction with communication in the over-all measure of satisfaction.

By Changes Outside the Relationship

Some conflicts cannot be resolved within the marital relationship alone. The most supportive relationship can do little about the severe economic deprivation facing families in which the husband cannot get and keep a job. The family, by just being there, is a constant reminder to all family members of his failure. Before the relationship can function to cope effectively with day to day problems, the economic strife must be relieved in a way that preserves the self-esteem of the persons involved.

Some conflicts can be resolved by changing the external environment. Where there is consensus between the couple but conflict with outside groups, such as familial or friendship groups, the easiest way to resolve the conflict is to reduce the amount of contact with the conflicting values. Many couples report a decrease in marital conflict when a move takes them away from daily contact with one or both sets of in-laws. Others discover that certain friendship groups heighten marital disturbance and harmony is restored with decreased contact with them. Sometimes certain jobs create extreme pressures, such as those which require a great deal of travel or unpredictable hours. Several studies indicate a higher level of marital happiness among occupational groups which allow a great amount of stability in the husband's home life.[3] Many times if it is possible to change the job marital conflicts decrease. The willingness to do this, of course, shows a commitment to the marriage which in itself appears to be beneficial for conflict resolution.

By Changes Within the Relationship

Some conflicts can be resolved by *compromise*, that is, each person moves a little so that each feels he has not done all the giving in. This

[3] For an extensive review of these studies see George Levinger (1965, pp. 19–28).

generally requires a knowledge of what it is that is bothering and assumes some communication. It sometimes amounts to a trade off: "You stop hanging your hose on the towel rack, and I'll stop putting out my cigarettes in my coffee cup." "We'll spend Christmas with your family and Thanksgiving with mine." Sometimes, each relaxes his expectations slightly so a mutually agreeable solution can be reached. This kind of solution assumes a relatively balanced power structure and the ability to communicate rationally about the conflict.

Conflicts are also resolved by *accommodation*. The greatest difference between compromise and accommodation is that, in the latter, one person does all the moving. One spouse may decide its not worth the effort and merely lives with the disturbing element. There are no further attempts to change the spouse, and no resentment remains—it's better to ignore the toothpaste tube squeezed in the middle or buy two tubes (His and Hers) than to continue to fight. In other words, harmony is seen to be more important than the area of disagreement.

Occasionally, over time, one partner actually is convinced that the other's ideas or ways of doing something are better. If the conflict has not been thrown into a power struggle so that one can change without losing face, the conflict disappears. Communication, good humor, and understanding aids this kind of resolution.

Most marriages are probably characterized by a number of accommodating moves, where each partner gradually ceases to be upset by certain habits or attitudes of the other. They become part of the unique personality pattern of the other and are either stoically or humorously accepted or become sentimentalized.

Some conflicts are resolved by *avoidance*. An impasse is recognized; and, rather than continue the conflict, the couple tacitly agrees to avoid the area. This is sometimes reflected in a teen-ager's caution to a girl or boy friend he is bringing home for the first time, "Whatever you do, don't mention race relations. Mom and Dad will be at each other the rest of the night."

If these are not areas requiring interaction, most marriages can probably support one or two of them. If they are important areas of interaction though, an avoidance resolution will probably cut off communication in other areas as well. "Walking on tip toes" around certain areas can produce a great amount of tension for fear the tabooed areas will be opened inadvertently.

It takes cooperation between the two spouses to maintain this resolution. If one spouse habitually responds to conflict by avoidance and the other wants to "talk things out," another area of conflict is added to the first. The latter may be more difficult to deal with—conflict over how to resolve conflicts.

Some conflicts are resolved by *hostility*. The particular conflict is re-solved, but the way it was resolved was so painful to one of the partners that the resentment goes underground to appear in other areas. This is probably more likely in one-sided power structures where the more power-ful spouse forces the other to give in.

THE PRINCIPLE OF VALUE RELEVANCE

The pattern of conflict resolution finally adopted in a family will be greatly influenced by the patterns of conflict resolution operative in the two families of orientation and the fit between them. Some people come to marriage with a readiness to get all their feelings out in the open. They feel that a few harsh words are a small price to pay for the air-clearing function of a good argument. They feel stimulated and carry nothing over to the next encounter. Others come unable to verbalize feelings, threatened by the least swell on their sea of tranquility. Still others are ready to do battle with any weapon at hand to win any and all contests—no matter how unimportant the issue. They are unable to give in even once, for fear they will lose every future encounter. Others fear open, direct encounters, preferring the subtle approach. They try to foresee the conflict before it appears, and manipulate the outcome. Others scurry, hurrying to do the bidding of the partner for fear that anger may be di-rected toward them. In this instance, avoidance of conflict itself is more important than any issue.

Obviously, the pattern of conflict recognition and solution will vary, depending not only on the spouses' habitual patterns but on the fit be-tween them. Two people sharing the same habits may be blissfully happy or reside in an armed camp, depending on the habits they share. People with different habits may fit together well or hit head on in their attempts to resolve difficulties. It becomes impossible, then, to say which method of conflict resolution is best for all couples. One wife, for example, may only be convinced her husband cares about her when he becomes angry enough to blacken her eye. Another, meeting the same treatment, will file for divorce the next day. So the acceptable method is influenced, not only by the habitual patterns of responding to conflict, but by the inter-pretations of what is legitimate behavior on the part of the spouse.

These interpretations are influenced by the cultural setting in which one grew, by one's individual experiences within it, and by the norms of the social context in which the marriage takes place. It may have been legitimate to use knives, fists, or frying pans on an erring mate in a previ-ous environment. But if the couple now lives in a more restrained setting, the mate who becomes violent will have little support from the new social groups. Old behavior takes on new meaning, with different consequences under a different set of norms.

The pattern of resolution varies with the relative commitment of the two people to the relationship. If the association between commitment to the relationship and power is remembered, it seems apparent that the person most committed will be under constraint to adjust his mode of response to the expectations of the least committed. Since power structures sometimes change over the life cycle of a family, methods which serve to resolve conflicts at one period may cease to serve at another. The husband who is able to resolve conflict by firmly putting his foot down in an early part of the marriage, may find the rug pulled from under the foot if the power stucture shifts later on. Whether it *is* pulled or not will probably be related to the amount of ego-deflation this wife suffered when the power structure supported the husband's mode of conflict resolution.

Whatever the method of resolution, it is more likely to be successful and to reduce future conflict if it is mutually acceptable to the two people and does not attack the important sources of self-esteem of the spouses. Attacks on the self-esteem can only lead to resentment, withdrawal, or counterattack.

SUMMARY

All marriages face certain inevitable facts of life which will certainly produce feelings of frustration and conflict at some point along the way. The difference between unhappy and happy marriages is not so much that happily married people have no problems and the unhappily married do but that they have different kinds of problems and the unhappily married have more of them. The kinds of problems encountered by unhappy marriages may be more serious and disruptive, but the way the spouses attempt to handle them appears to be different also. Unhappily married spouses are more likely to report problems reflecting neglect, lack of affection, lack of understanding, lack of appreciation, and lack of companionship. They are more likely to attack each other's self-concepts, magnify faults, and make each other feel worthless.

There may actually be greater differences in values, habits, and attitudes among unhappily married pairs, but it is also possible that communication between them is such that it cuts down the opportunity for understanding the other's point of view. Patterns of communication are developed in childhood, with words, phrases, inflections, and silences meaning different things to different people. One of the problems in early marriage is to learn to decipher the communication code of the spouse.

Problems in communication arise from a variety of sources, including: (1) the preconceptions built up about the opposite sex which lead one to assume that his way of interpreting the spouse's words or gestures is always correct; (2) assumptions that a person's feelings and behaviors are logically consistent; (3) the search for who is right and who is wrong; (4) desire or need to hide something from the spouse; (5) wide differences in the interests of the sexes; (6) the nature of the husband's job; (7) the impoverishment of life; and (8) personality problems.

Good communication does not guarantee a happy marriage. The kind of communication associated with happy married people seems to imply a selectivity. More than unhappy couples, the happy ones appear to: (1) talk to each other more; (2) convey the feeling that they understand what is being said; (3) have a wider range of interest open to them; (4) preserve communication channels and keep them open; (5) show more sensitivity to each other's feelings; (6) make more frequent use of words with a private meaning; and (7) make more use of non-verbal communication.

Conflict in some form is probably inevitable in marriage. It may constitute an insignificant part of the relationship or become the major focus of interaction. The amount of conflict is probably not as important as the type of conflict which characterizes the relationship. Overt conflict can be acute, progressive, or habituated. The acute form is more highly associated with early marriage and any period in which drastic changes result in undefined areas of behavior. Progressive conflict is characterized by a build-up of hurt feelings and resentments from past quarrels, which may result in greater and greater estrangement between the pair if they remain together. Habituated conflict becomes a regular part of the relationship and is less explosive and more restricted than either the acute or the progressive. Covert conflict is probably the most difficult to observe and the most destructive, since it is hidden from view and masquerades under many behaviors. The type of conflict which predominates in a marriage will be related not only to the extent of husband–wife differences but to their personality needs, tolerance levels, and modes of resolving previous conflicts.

Some conflicts can only be resolved by changes in the social structure, which result in greater support for the self-esteem of husband or wife.

Interactional types of conflict resolution include compromise, accommodation, avoidance, and hostility expressed in another area. Since habitual ways of resolving conflict are brought into marriage, the resulting mode will be influenced by the fit between the respective habits, the interpretation made of it by supportive social groups, and the power structure of the marriage. Whatever the method of resolution, it is more likely to be successful and to reduce future conflict if it is mutually acceptable to the people involved and does not attack the self-esteem of the spouses.

QUESTIONS AND PROJECTS

1. Look carefully at one of your own existing relationships. What barriers to communication exist? What contributes to these barriers? Would you want to do away with them if you could? Why or why not? Are there things the other person says or talks about that you would like to stop? Explain.

2. Do you agree that "selective communication" is what most people mean when they say "good communication"? Explain.

3. Is it possible to have a satisfactory marriage with little communication between the partners? Explain. When you apply the principle of value relevance, what level of communication appears to be more conducive to marital happiness?

4. Do you think it would be possible for a couple to resolve all their conflicts during the first few years of marriage? Discuss.

5. Would it be possible for a couple to have value conflicts which do not harm the relationship? Explain.

6. Explain the most usual social class differences in types of marital conflict.

7. Do you think the ways of resolving conflict may differ according to type or area of conflict being resolved? Explain. Use personal examples to make your discussion clear.

8. Analyze your own reaction to different types of conflict. What are your habitual ways of attempting to resolve conflict? How did they develop? Does your position in the power-dependency aspect of the relationship make a difference? Explain.

14
The Sexual Relationship

The sexual relationship in marriage cannot be separated from other areas of marital interaction. Although an important one, it is only one of the many areas in which husband and wife must communicate and cooperate to reach their desired goals. While sexual maladjustment usually accompanies other marital difficulties and precedes divorces it is as much an effect of these other troubles as it is a cause. Sexual difficulties can appear in a marriage, however, when other aspects of the relationship are quite satisfying. This is especially true in a society where cultural norms are changing, where discussion of sex has traditionally been clothed in secrecy, and where it has been draped with ignorance and feelings of guilt.

THE SOCIAL CONTEXT

Whenever norms are changing in a society, it can be predicted that there will be a number of people unprepared for incorporating the newer norms into their behavior. It can also be assumed that there will be people subscribing to all or part of the newer norms who are in contact with persons who still adhere closely to older ones. The opportunity for misunderstanding, feelings of inadequacy, and guilt is enhanced when changing expectations and new information upset strongly held beliefs of right, wrong, good, and bad. This is essentially what has been happening in the sexual area within marriage (as well as in the premarital period, discussed earlier).

Within marriage the decline of Puritanical ideas on sex has brought new obligations and new privileges to the husband–wife roles which many of those marrying have not been prepared for, either socially, psychologically, or intellectually.

If the norms, reinforced by medical opinion, lead both men and women to believe that the female has no sex drive and that the modest, decent woman submits to her husband only to please him, and, except for the desire of children, prefers to leave sex out of her life, then neither she nor her husband would be upset that she is unresponsive. As long as she submitted, her unresponsiveness would not reflect on either them or their relationship. Given this viewpoint, we would not expect non-enjoyment of sex to be strongly associated with marital dissatisfaction. The spouses, it is true, may be missing a part of the relationship which could be mutually rewarding. But if they do not know the potential exists, they will not blame each other or feel guilt because it is absent.

As the definitions of sex as "dirty," "evil," and "degrading" began to disappear and it became recognized that the human female not only possessed sexual desire but also was capable of fully enjoying it, new norms concerning marital sex began to appear. Many of the "How to do it" manuals appearing in the late 1930's and the 1940's stressed the male's techniques in aiding his wife to achieve satisfaction. Perhaps inadvertently norms began to develop which placed responsibility on the husband for his wife's gratification. The new normative structure focused attention on the sexual relationship as a major part of marriage. If satisfaction was not attained (measured by orgasmic response) then someone was at fault. The husband might feel guilty, or inadequate, or blame his wife for being frigid. She might also feel inadequate or guilty because her lack of response made her husband unhappy, or she might blame her husband for being inconsiderate and for not thinking of her needs.

The effect of the norms on the definition of a situation as a problem is illustrated by Vincent (1956) in what he calls the "tyranny of the majority norm." A husband and wife who have been relatively satisfied with their sexual relationship may suddenly decide they have a problem when they learn that other couples of their approximate age have intercourse more often than they do, or that other wives achieve orgasm a greater proportion of the time. One of the difficulties is that norms are different in various parts of the society.

Social Context Differences

As in marital roles, the lower classes appear to lag behind the middle and upper-middle classes in conformity to newer norms. This is probably due to the lower level of educational exposure as well as to the greater association with extended families reinforcing older norms. Rainwater (1965, Chapter 3) vividly showed the impact of the newer norms on husbands at different class levels through the differences in percentage indicating that mutual gratification was an important part of satisfactory sex relations. He found that not only was social class a distinguishing factor but so also was religion. The proportion of husbands replying that the wife's responsiveness was of importance to them varied from 85 per cent of the middle and upper-lower class Protestants to 46 per cent of the Catholics from the same class levels, to a low of 37 per cent of those in the lower-lower class (Rainwater, 1965, p. 104).

Effect of Education. Masters and Johnson (1966b, p. 202) found an even greater difference among husbands according to education. While 82 per cent of the college males expressed concern with their partner's satisfaction, only 14 per cent of those who had had no college education did so. Consequently, fears about sexual performance were more prevalent among the higher educated males. Those without college experience were more likely to feel that, while it was a woman's privilege to achieve satisfaction if she could, it was not the concern or responsibility of the male to help her achieve it. This same attitude was expressed by Rainwater's lower class respondents (1965, p. 106). Part of the reasoning behind the statements seemed to reflect older ideas about the sexuality of women.

"I think with a woman it's mostly just to satisfy her husband and then she's happy."
"Actually a woman is not as interested in sex as a man is."

As far as the women were concerned, the husband's concern appeared to increase the wife's satisfaction. It may be, however, that exposure to the norms emphasizing the importance of a wife's being responsive made middle class wives more hesitant to report lack of gratification. Whatever the cause, Table 14–1 shows a strong relationship between social

Table 14–1

Wife's Gratification in Sexual Relations

	Very Positive	Positive	Negative– Rejective
Middle class (58)	50%	36%	14%
Upper-lower class (68)	53	16	31
Lower-lower class (69)	20	26	54

SOURCE: Adapted from Lee Rainwater, *Family Design: Marital Sexuality, Family Size, and Contraception* (Chicago: Aldine Publishing Co., 1965), Table 3–5, p. 68. Numbers in parentheses represent bases from which percentages are computed.

class and negative evaluations of marital sex. Only fourteen per cent of the middle class women, compared to 54 per cent of lower-lower class women, held negative attitudes toward sex relations.

Effect of Marital Role Type.   The role relationship in the lower class marriage was highly related to the wife's evaluation of sex. In the more traditional, segregated relationships, 68 per cent of the wives reported negative reactions compared to 32 per cent of the wives in less segregated marital roles. The males' lack of concern, as well as perhaps their views on female sexuality, were illustrated by the tendency of husbands in segregated roles to overestimate their wives' satisfaction. Fifty-one per cent of these husbands overestimated their wives' sexual satisfaction, compared to 21 per cent of the husbands in intermediate role relationships. None of the upper-middle class husbands did so, all of whom were in more equalitarian role relationships (Rainwater, 1965, p. 71). These findings not only tell us something about the effect of the social context on exposure to newer norms concerning marital sex but also point out the close relationship between communication, satisfaction with sex, and the rest of the marital interaction. Even though sexual satisfaction appears higher for middle class couples, still about 50 per cent of these wives report less than highly positive reactions.

Effect of Religiosity.   Wallin and Clark (1964), in a study of 770 middle class husbands and wives, show a rather complex relationship between sexual enjoyment and marital satisfaction for women. If low sexual enjoyment was paired with low sex desires and high religiosity, the relationship of sexual gratification to marital satisfaction was much lower than if low sex enjoyment was paired with high sex desire and low religiosity. This was true in early marriage as well as in the middle years (Wallin, 1957). The same did not hold for husbands; the relationship between their sexual enjoyment and marital satisfaction was much more direct and not influenced by religiosity. This again suggests the effect of norms on the importance of sex in marital satisfaction, especially for women. It seems safe to assume that the more exposure to religion and to traditional sex norms which deemphasize the importance of sex, the less important is sex for marital satisfaction.

Male–Female Differences

The difference between men and women in the importance of sex in marriage is probably more complicated than it appears, however. The male culture has supported the enjoyment of sex as a physical act in which success is more related to the techniques than to the quality of the relationship in which it takes place. The female culture has supported the enjoyment of sex as a culmination of a close feeling of affection and oneness, regardless of the success of the individual physical act. This may influence the male to use the sexual relationship as an indicator of the total marriage. If his wife comes to bed with him and is responsive, all is well. The female on the other hand is perhaps more likely to use the general tone of the rest of the marriage for evaluating the sexual relationship. If all is well in the rest of the marriage, then she is more likely to regard the sexual relationship as satisfactory, whether or not she obtains full satisfaction (Leslie, 1967, p. 504).

There is, however, a wide variation among both men and women (especially in the middle class) in the extent to which they are influenced by the male and female cultures. Some men will be closer to the female perspective and some women closer to the male point of view. Their points of view will influence their expectations for marital sex, their sensitivities to each other, and the importance placed on it in their perceptions of marital happiness.

PHYSIOLOGICAL ASPECTS

There has been much ignorance associated with male and female sexuality, largely as a result of restrictive norms which have reduced objective investigation of it. When any behavior is clothed in secrecy, the opportunities for false ideas and fantasied images, both monstrous and utopian, are greatly increased. This is especially true for females, who are normally more "protected" from sexual information than males.

One of the difficulties encountered by some young women in marital sex comes from the over-idealized ideas of the bell-ringing, cloud-floating experience she will have on her wedding night. If she has this idea she is likely to be disappointed. Kinsey's data show that in the first year of marriage one in four wives failed to achieve orgasm. Another one out of every four achieved orgasm less than half the time (Kinsey, 1953, p. 408). Although the percentage usually achieving orgasm increased with the length of the marriage, it never exceeded 50 per cent. Some women build up fears about the pain they think may accompany the first encounter, and others do not know what to expect. The percentage having these kinds of fears and anxieties can be expected to drop as more permissive pre-marital norms allow greater communication and preparation for full sexual involvement earlier in marriage, but the drop is not likely to be fast enough to eliminate the problem for some years to come.

Males also suffer from misinformation or misconceptions about the female. This is understandable since even the so-called authorities have been confused. Female sexuality, until very recently, has been interpreted mainly from the point of view of male sexuality, accentuating either differences or similarities, many of which do not exist. Many of these misconceptions have been cleared up by the intensive laboratory studies of the human sexual response by Masters and Johnson. Through long and careful study of the sexual responses of 694 men and women, they have provided factual information about the physiological aspects of the sexual response which should clear up much misunderstanding (Masters and Johnson, 1966b).

The Sexual Response Cycle

Normally, in a complete sexual response, both males and females go through a series of four phases. The first is the *excitement phase*, indicated by the erection of the male penis and the moistening of the female vagina with a lubricating secretion. Both of these reactions may occur within a few seconds of stimulation for both sexes. Excitement may begin from actual stimulation of the male penis and female clitoris, from sexually stimulating sights, thoughts, and/or caresses. As stimulation continues, swelling occurs in the clitoris glans and breasts of the female, and in both sexes there is an increased pulse rate, blood pressure, and tension in both voluntary and involuntary muscles.

As stimulation is maintained and tension continues to build, the excitement phase gradually gives way to the *plateau phase*. During this stage, the intensity of feeling increases. In the female, swelling continues in the breasts and area surrounding the vaginal opening. In both sexes, heightening tension engages the entire body, accompanied by increased breathing rate, until tension is released in the brief, explosive contractions associated with the *orgasmic phase*. The orgasm brings the ejaculation of semen for the male and various muscular reactions throughout the body for both sexes. Immediately following orgasm during the *resolution phase* the male's penis and the female's breasts and vaginal area return to their unstimulated state. The pulse rate, blood pressure, and breathing rate more slowly return to normal (Masters and Johnson, 1966b, pp. 55–58).

A recognition of these phases and the male–female differences within them explains the differences in men's and women's reaction to non-orgasmic completion of the sex act. Once the excitement period produces full erection, the male is very likely to feel uncomfortable and irritable if orgasm does not occur. If he reaches the plateau phase, orgasm will almost certainly occur. The *major* changes in the female's body, however, occur during the plateau phase. The excitement phase merely indicates she is beginning to respond. For a variety of reasons, she may enjoy the closeness and love-making yet not respond with physiological changes in her body—even to the point of the first excitement phase. Unlike the male, she can carry through her part of the sex act even if sexual excitement is lacking. Nor is sexual excitement necessary for her to conceive. If the physiological changes do not occur, however, she will not attain orgasm. The non-occurrence of orgasm does not generally produce in her feelings of discomfort or irritation if she has not reached a point in the sexual cycle which produces physiological changes. Even if she reaches the plateau phase, orgasm still may not occur if stimulation is not maintained. If orgasm does not occur after she reaches this point in the sexual cycle, however, the resolution phase is prolonged, which may bring feelings of fullness, discomfort, and irritability.

Individual Variation

Masters and Johnson point out what has been known by clinicians and suggested by interview-type studies for some time: The normal variation among individuals is immense. Tremendous variations exist in the level of sexual tension, in the tolerance for sexual stimulation, and in the intensity of the sexual response. Although previous studies indicate that most males have greater interest in sex and desire higher frequencies of sexual contact than females, there is much variation when a particular male is compared with a particular female, which is what interests most marital couples.

The tolerance for sexual stimulation varies not only between individuals, but for the same individual from day to day depending on numerous factors other than sexual adequacy. This seems especially true of females who are more likely to be influenced by external situations than males. If she is expecting to hear a baby cry, or anticipates any other interruptions, the female is not as likely to be responsive. If she is fatigued, preoccupied, feels unloved, or just generally below par physically, she may be temporarily unresponsive. If she has just been through an evening of argument with her husband, she is not likely to respond enthusiastically to his attempt to make up by a sexual overture. For him, this may be his way of assuring himself that the argument was superficial, and assuring her that he loves her. For her, it is likely to be taken as proof that he *doesn't* love her, and that sex is his primary concern (Vincent, 1956, p. 360). Her response to him, given this common misinterpretation, is very likely to be interpreted by him as her attempt to "get even" with him for things he may have said in the heat of the argument. Although both may want to make up, their different perceptions of the "time for sex" are likely to produce two rigid bodies about to fall off opposite sides of the bed. If she had understood that his request for coitus was a request for love, or if he had understood that she needed a making up period first, the unresponsiveness and subsequent unhappiness need not have occurred.

Intensity of the sexual response varies greatly—all within a normal range of perfectly satisfying relations. The time required to complete a full sexual response cycle varies from individual to individual and within the same individual from time to time. To expect two people to always

match on desires, speed of sexual arousal, and phases of the sexual response cycle seems a completely unrealistic expectation. Even trying to
achieve this may result in such conscious restraints on the more demanding partner and feelings of guilt and inadequacy on the less demanding
one, that the joy and love stemming from spontaneous expression is damp-
ened. More important than attempting to manipulate time schedules and
techniques mechanically is the transmission to the partner of the feeling
of affection, of tenderness, and of a regard for him (her) as a person. If
these are transmitted and understood, mistakes in techniques and timing
and occasional failures and inadequacies readily become lost in the satisfaction with the total relationship.

Aging

As people grow older, their sexual interest declines. This is more
likely to occur when the earlier relationship was unsatisfactory. As a
husband grows tired of a wife's lack of responsiveness his interest in marital sex declines. If it has been largely a routine kind of experience for
them, the interest lags as other demands on their time appear.

Although sexual activity does slow with advancing age, just as one
walks more slowly or trades hand ball for chess, the drastic decline in
interest experienced by many is the result of factors other than the aging
process. For some women, the menopausal period is a signal that sexual
desires should be gone. For those who have merely "put up" with sex
previously, it offers an excuse for further disinterest. Masters and Johnson show, however, that the healthy, aging female is physiologically capable of sexual response, with "no time limit drawn by advancing years"
(Brecher, 1966, pp. 246-47). Her response cycle lengthens and the intensity of reaction decreases; but the capacity is still there, especially if
she has had regular stimulation in an active sex life earlier.

The male shows more of a wane in sexual responsiveness after fifty.
Particularly after sixty, erection takes much longer and his responses decrease. However, it is possible for his capacity for sexual expression to
be extended beyond the seventy- and eighty-year age level. The major
contributing factor seems to be regularity of sexual expression earlier, and
a sexually stimulating environment within marriage.[1] The factors associated with loss of responsiveness in older males fall into six categories:

1. Monotony of a repetitious sexual relationship (usually translated
   into boredom with the wife)
2. Preoccupation with career or economic pursuits
3. Mental or physical fatigue

[1] For a review of these findings as well as other studies concerned with sexuality
after marriage, see Isadore Rubin (1966, pp. 251-66).

4. Overindulgence in food or drink
5. Physical or mental infirmities of either husband or wife
6. Fear of failure (Rubin, 1966, p. 261).

The major deterrent as far as older women are concerned seems to be the lack of a male partner. It would seem that while the young male is concerned with increasing the responsiveness of the female to match his own, the older male becomes increasingly dependent on the female to stimulate and maintain his continued sexual expressions. If the female has had a positive interest in sex at earlier ages, many factors collect together at around 50 which may increase her interest and enjoyment. She no longer needs to fear pregnancy; she has resolved most of the problems concerned with childrearing; and demands on her time may be greatly reduced. Whether the declining years offer an opportunity for more relaxed, enjoyable sex relations as the couple begins to withdraw from active participation in society depends mainly on the quality of sexual expression throughout the whole marital history and the awareness of the different effects of aging on the two sexes.

Marital sex seemingly can be a cementing force, easing tension in other areas and providing assurance of mutual affection throughout the life cycle, or it can become the battle ground upon which such painful wounds to the self-esteem are inflicted that both withdraw from the field into their private worlds.

MAJOR SEXUAL DISTURBANCES

The causes of sexual disturbances are many and varied. They can stem from individual attitudes of fear, anxiety, and aversion. They can arise from individual physiological problems. But most of them arise from the interaction between the couple and the circumstances surrounding them. Whatever the cause, the end result is likely to be labeled *impotence* or *frigidity*, depending upon which partner is seen to have the greatest difficulty.

Impotence

Impotence refers to the lack of adequate sexual response in the male. Medically speaking, this refers to his inability to achieve or maintain a full erection, or to his inability to ejaculate in the process of intercourse. The term is sometimes applied to premature ejaculation, in which ejaculation occurs before, during, or immediately after entry into the female vagina.

Causes of Impotence. A minority of the cases of impotence are physiological, requiring medical attention. But far and away the vast majority have a social psychological basis. It is common for the healthy young male to be troubled with temporary impotence or premature ejaculation until he has gained experience. As he gains self-confidence the problem disappears. The "fear of failure," however, many times induced by an occasional early failure, may cause him to have serious doubts about his own masculinity which further reduces the probability of success, turning his fear into a self-fulfilling prophecy.

At any point in the marital relationship the male may have a temporary loss of desire or a temporary period of impotence because of worry, preoccupation with business matters, fear of pregnancy, feelings of inadequacy, or guilt. As the sources for these feelings are reduced, adequacy returns. The main difficulty here, again, is the *fear* of impotency. The need to prove his masculinity coupled with the doubt that he will be able to do so reduces his chance of success. Rubin states that "few factors play as important a part in bringing about impotence as does the fear of failure" (Rubin, 1966, p. 264; Hastings, 1966; Masters and Johnson, 1966a).

Situational impotence is sometimes the result of external circumstances or the response of the wife. For example, awareness of a noise which indicates a possible invasion of privacy may cause him to lose his erection. The perception of his wife as uninterested or preoccupied with something else may have the same result. A derogatory remark or an ill-timed question about the gas bill may be enough to make him unable to carry the act through to completion (Hastings, 1966). Consistent behavior of this kind may cause a male to become impotent with his wife but not with another female who is more receptive and less threatening. Obviously, impotence problems like this can only be improved by improving the relationship between husband and wife.

Since the majority of impotence problems stem from the "fear of failure," an understanding of the situations which can induce temporary difficulties enables both husband and wife to resist placing undue importance either on the early attempts at intercourse or on periodic inadequacies. A recognition that completed intercourse need not be the end of all sexual play takes the responsibility off the male for proving his competence every time he feels like expressing his love for his wife. The false association of masculinity with high sex desires, easily triggered into active sexual performance under any conditions, is responsible for many painful periods of self-doubt among males in our society. Since rebuilding self-confidence is the basis for most therapy in treating these cases, the role of an understanding, interested, and knowledgeable wife in both preventing and "curing" impotency problems is obvious.

Frigidity

There is more confusion over the word *frigidity* than the word impotence. It applies to sexual inadequacies in the female; but since her part in sexual relations is different from the male's, the assessment of female sexual inadequacy is more difficult and is more likely to be made relative to individual definitions of the "adequate" response. The label of frigidity, therefore, may be applied to many diffierent types of female non-response.

A male who thinks his wife should achieve orgasm at every encounter may label her "frigid" if she does so only 50 per cent of the time, while another man who expects little response from his wife may find the same response level quite adequate.

A wife who is non-responsive to her husband because of his personal habits of cleanliness, his lack of concern, or her negative feelings toward him may be quite responsive to another male, or perhaps even to her husband under more favorable circumstances. Sometimes women who are emotionally responsive and able to complete the sex act but do not respond orgasmically are labeled frigid. Failure to achieve coital orgasm is not in and of itself an indication of frigidity. Medically speaking, frigidity applies only to the inability to respond *at all* to effective stimulation, or to the inability to participate in the completion of the act (Masters and Johnson, 1966a, pp. 213–14).

In the same way that the term impotent affects the self-concept of the male, the term frigid does psychological damage to the female—since it focuses attention on her lack of sexuality as a female, rather than on the conditions within which the unresponsiveness may occur. Since cases of *true* frigidity are relatively rare, this discussion will involve the more common usage of the term—female unresponsiveness whether emotional or orgasmic.

Causes of Frigidity. As commonly defined, frigidity is a more common occurrence than impotence. There are, at least, six reasons for this.

1. Our cultural norms concerning the sexuality of males and females make it more likely that any sexual disturbance in marriage will be seen as a result of the female's lack of sexual interest rather than as a result of the particular male–female relationship. It is assumed she would be as unresponsive in any relationship as she is in this one.

2. The prohibitions against premarital sex hit hardest at the female. The methods sometimes used by parents and others to assure her virginity are likely to result in guilt over her normal sexual feelings and fantasies, fear of the male's sexuality, and ignorance of her own body and its responses.

3. She is likely to have a lower level of sexual desires than the male at the point they enter marriage and therefore feel, at least some of the time, that she is unresponsive. Her husband, led to believe that his desires are more normal than hers, is likely to interpret their different levels of desire as an inadequacy on her part rather than normal differences in sexual development and interest.

4. Since everyone varies from day to day and week to week in the strength of their sexual tensions, one is bound to be more interested and responsive sometimes than others. The male is normally expected to be the initiator of sexual expressions. It is to be expected, then, that he is more likely to initiate love-making when *he* feels a heightened sexual tension. It would indeed be remarkable if the ebb and flow of their sexual desires were perfectly synchronized. This would mean that they must both be tired at the same time, worried at the same time, catch cold at the same time, have insomnia at the same time, and be amorously aroused at the same time. Since the timing of initiation is more likely to be established by the husband than the wife, it seems reasonable to expect that she would appear to be unresponsive more often than he, even given the same basic sexual tension level. The equivalent situation may be one in which the husband was labeled *dyspeptic* if he was not ready to eat heartily when and only when his wife decided to cook, whether this was six times a day, six times a week, or once every six months. Males naturally would exhibit a higher frequency of the disturbance than females, given this definition of dyspepsia.

As our norms change and encourage the female to play the role of the initiator more often, the increased times when the male will be unable to respond may heighten the use of the term *impotent* and lower the use of the term *frigid*. As this happens, the female will have to learn to take responsibility for the arousal of the male, and realize that full orgasmic response on his part is not the only criterion for evaluating his sexual responsiveness. If she does not develop this capacity as she takes the role of the initiator, the consequences for the male may be far more devastating than the present consequences for the female.

5. Since pressing sexual needs are, at present, less likely to be a problem for the female than the male, she is probably more likely to express in the sexual area hostility stemming from the total relationship. She is also more prone to withhold responsiveness as a way of making her unhappiness felt. She is less likely to be responsive, even if she would like to be, if lingering feelings of resentment or hurt feelings cloud the relationship. Her behavior might be labeled sexually inadequate when it is actually an instance of relationship inadequacy.

6. Because of the close association between sexual adequacy and masculinity it may be more difficult for her to communicate to her husband

that her responsiveness might improve if he approached her differently or if the foreplay were different or more prolonged. Since she is supposed to be inexperienced, she can be enlightened by him with no loss of self-esteem. The same is not true of some husbands, especially those who feel they are highly experienced or insecure in their masculinity. She remains unresponsive because she cannot bring herself to tell him of her desires.

The above discussion treats mainly the cultural reasons for a higher prevalence of frigidity than impotence; certainly these influences do not affect all women nor all men. But when individual cases of female sexual inadequacy occur, many of the disturbances can be seen to stem in part from one or more of these cultural influences.

As with males, a minority of the cases of frigidity among females have a physiological base. Any prolonged pain or discomfort during intercourse suggests the need for a physcial examination. Most of these can be cleared fairly easily with minor surgery, physical therapy, or hormone treatment. The majority of the "causes," however, fall into three categories, although more than one may be operative in any single case:

1. The sexual attitudes of both marital partners
2. Total relationship between the marital pair
3. Fear of pregnancy

Fear of pregnancy is the easiest to prevent if there is agreement between the partners about birth control, if there is adequate information about reliable methods, and if there is cooperation between the two of them to increase the reliability of any method compatible with their religious beliefs. Disagreement or lack of cooperation on any of these suggests problems other than sexual ones which will need resolving first.

Problems Stemming from Sexual Attitudes

Under the heading of sexual attitudes of both marital partners come several problems of varying degrees of complexity. Perhaps the easiest of these to resolve are those attitudes which so restrict the "normal" range of sexual behavior that satisfaction of individual needs and variation are precluded. Sometimes all that is needed is increased awareness that experimentation, spontaneity, and playfulness are an acceptable part of the sexual union—that the only rules of the game are those developed by the two players in their own "playpen." Some people approach marital sex as serious business, governed by strict ideas of "normal" and "abnormal," "human" and "animal." If this satisfies them both, there is absolutely nothing wrong with it. But if one spouse has needs that are definitely not being met within the rules of their game, then it can be reassuring for them to discover that people play by a wide variety of rules, all within the normal, human range.

Sometimes female unresponsiveness is the result of a husband's attitude toward sex. If he sees sex as mainly a male prerogative, with the wife only performing a duty of submission, he is not likely to produce the climate within which she can respond. This is likely to contribute to premature ejaculation on his part as well as unresponsiveness on hers. Again, if this is acceptable to both of them, there is *no* problem since what is "premature" to one couple may not be to another. There are no outside standards which can be applied to a particular couple to judge the adequacy of *their* sexual relationship. If *they* assess it as satisfactory—it is satisfactory. Problems occur when both assess it as unsatisfactory, or one does and the other doesn't.

Female unresponsiveness sometimes is the result of early negative attitudes toward sex or ideas about "nice women" being those who respond passively, having few sexual desires. She is likely not to be aware of her own bodily responses and therefore cannot communicate them to her husband. It does no good to ask her to communicate her desires—she has nothing to say! Some women are afraid to let their feelings have free expression for fear they will be embarrassed by a full response. These women, probably more than most others, need patient, gentle husbands who can project both security and affection to them while assuring them of the normality of full sexual involvement.

Problems Stemming from the Relationship

Some non-responsiveness comes neither from attitudes toward sex nor from lack of adequate information or preparation. Rather it comes from a difference in level of sexual desires between the partners. When this is not recognized as a real difference between them, the highly motivated partner may feel personally rejected, while the less motivated one feels resentful of "excessive demands" (Masters and Johnson, 1966a). Personally interpreted in this way it can only lead to wider differences in their sexual desires. If, however, they are able to recognize the differences as being "real" variations in levels of desire, a more cooperative atmosphere and attempts at adjustment may actually decrease the differences between them.

Few sexual problems are solely sex problems, however. Both males and females are extremely vulnerable to rebuffs in this area. They are generally seen as rejections of the total self, rather than just sexual incompatibility. Since this vulnerability is perhaps intuitively known, the sexual area becomes the focal point for releasing negative feelings leaking from other areas of interaction. As this happens, the loss of self-esteem occurring in the sexual area leaks back into the relationship, creating a vicious cycle of unhappiness.

Perhaps more important in the sexual area than in any other is the effect of the spouses upon each other. If they are able to transmit a complete acceptance (of their bodies as well as of their personalities) and a deep regard for each other as people, the sexual relationship is likely to be satisfying regardless of the frequency of intercourse or the orgasmic capability of either of them.

A regard for another person is shown not only by the way he is received, but in the way one presents oneself to him. Careful attention to his sensitivities regarding appearance, odor, sounds, and modesty is an indication that he is a person worthy of being considered. Willingness to communicate one's own desires and sensitivities is indication that the other person is trusted and is seen as both considerate and cooperative. This, of course, applies to other areas as well as the sexual one. But here, more than in any other, there is the opportunity to experience the joy and release which comes from the free spontaneous acceptance of one human being by another. When arbitrary norms, rigid ideas of right and wrong, or standards of adequacy enter in, the spontaneity suffers.

SEXUAL ADJUSTMENT

As with every aspect of the marriage relationship, sexual adjustment usually takes a little time and requires the accompaniment of love and cooperative effort. Here are four quotations from the Burgess and Wallin interviews. The first illustrates how some husbands feel guilty when their wife isn't responding; the second shows how some wives feign response in order to please their husband; and the last two show how time and compromise enter into the adjustment:

Husband. I have a sense of guilt when I have relations with her and feel she does not enjoy them as much as I do. The fact that she's not getting orgasms takes the pleasure of intercourse away from me.

· · ·

Wife. My husband definitely has the stronger sexual desire, but this doesn't make for difficulty. He has accepted this like he accepts everything. After we had been married a while I told him I was receiving a great satisfaction from intercourse just not to make him miserable.

· · ·

Husband. One of the biggest adjustments we had to make was in sex urge. Naturally we had to compromise. I would not put that as a difficult adjustment to make. I think I have a great deal more sex drive than my wife and that involved compromising, if you want to call it that. That was mainly in frequency of intercourse.

Wife. Sex was difficult the first several months. It took a year or so to adjust itself. It was mostly the difference in frequency of desire. It wouldn't have made any difference if sex were taken out of marriage when I first got married. Now I would miss it. My change in attitude came as a result of experience (Burgess and Wallin, 1953, pp. 667, 671, 672, 682).

Though the roots of frigidity and impotence frequently reach back into the experiences of premarriage, there is much that husband and wife can do to forestall or overcome the problem. If there is already an inadequacy, they can strive for a reconditioning, using professional help when necessary, and engaging in mutual assistance. They can be careful to see that conditions surrounding the act are kept harmonious, aesthetic, and restful. They can study the needs and reactions of each other and adapt to them. Husbands can be more considerate and romantic, for example, and wives can come to be more interested and active than they sometimes are in the physical act. Gone are the days when it was thought normal for husbands to satisfy themselves selfishly and at will, and for wives to be merely dutiful though devoid of desire. Sex has come to be seen as a mutual experience in which mutual participation and responsibility is expected.

The Overall Relationship

Mutuality in sex is more a matter of attitude than it is technique. While we would not belittle the value of knowledge and skill as applied to intercourse, it seems clear that these alone are not enough. Where husband and wife are mature personally and are well mated psychologically and socially, they will tend to adjust better sexually and to overlook any minor maladjustments that may be experienced in the process. The opposite is also true; immature and poorly matched mates find greater difficulty in reaching sexual harmony and are less tolerant of each other in their difficulties. Conversely, sexual adjustment contributes to harmony in other segments of the marriage relationship, and incompatibility in sex only adds to incompatibility in other things. Sex, then, is both cause and effect.

Not all sex problems can be solved by adjustment to each other's needs —and it seems obvious from the foregoing discussion that not all sex problems can be resolved by concentration on them. They are too closely woven into the whole fabric of the marriage. In view of this it seems safe to conclude: (1) that the stress which present-day culture puts on the importance of orgasm in the female may be overdone, since sexual adjustment may derive from other factors as well; and (2) that the current stress placed on the importance of sex in marriage may be overdone, since marital success is dependent upon many factors, only one of which is the sexual. Though sexual responsiveness makes marital adjustment easier, it is quite possible for a spouse—especially the wife—to feel sexually adjusted and happy in the marriage even when relatively unresponsive. It is the total relationship that counts most.

Kinsey recognized this, and pointed to perhaps the main distinguishing factor between the varying effects of sexual incompatibility on the outcome of the marriage.

Sexual adjustments are not the only problems involved in marriage, and often they are not even the most important factors in marital adjustments. A preliminary examination of the six thousand marital histories in the present study, and of nearly three thousand divorce histories, suggests that there may be nothing more important in a marriage than a determination that it shall persist. With such a determination, individuals force themselves to adjust and to accept situations which would seem sufficient grounds for a break-up if the continuation of the marriage were not the prime objective.

Nevertheless, sexual maladjustments contribute in perhaps three-quarters of the upper-level marriages that end in separation or divorce, and in some smaller percentage of the lower-level marriages that break up. Where the sexual adjustments are poor, marriages are maintained with difficulty. It takes a considerable amount of idealism and determination to keep a marriage together when the sexual adjustments are not right. Sexual factors are, in consequence, very important in a marriage (Kinsey, 1948, p. 544).

Commitment to the Marriage

The commitment to the marriage as a factor in sexual adjustment is further substantiated by Kephart's (1954a) study of persons seeking divorces in Philadelphia. He found that persons citing sexual complaints as the reason for divorce were divorced sooner after the wedding than those citing other reasons. The typical complaint of males was that the wife showed too little interest in sex relations, and of the females that the husband either desired sex relations too often or that he desired "abnormal" sex practices. We have already seen that this difference in level of desire is a common male–female difference, and that the definition of "abnormal" can change if one attempts to widen his knowledge of the various definitions of "normality" operative in different segments of our society. It seems apparent then that in at least some of these early divorces, the commitment to the marriage was insufficient to produce either a climate of tolerance, efforts to understand the attitudes of the partner, or willingness to extend oneself to accommodate to another's needs.

Sexual behavior, as has been said before, is not isolated behavior. The same personality traits which contribute to satisfactory sexual adjustments are apparent in other interactions and can be observed before marriage. Rigidity of thought, a demanding or hostile orientation toward the opposite sex, inability to compromise, the use of other people for personal advantage, little regard for another's feelings, inability to give and receive affection, all give evidence of the kind of person who will make a poor marriage mate in many areas—sex being only one of them.

Other Sexual Outlets

When adjustments fail, or as a way of taking pressure off the sexual relationship, other sexual outlets are sometimes substituted for marital sex. For males whose sexual urges are quite strong the commonest of these is masturbation. At lower educational levels about 30 to 40 per cent of the married men engage in masturbation at some time. Among college educated married men about 70 per cent do so (Kinsey *et al.*, 1948, pp. 273–77). This is probably related not only to the greater recognition of masturbation as an acceptable outlet by the educated but to their greater concern with their wives' sexual desires and responsiveness.

The variation in sexual interest among women according to education is indicated by an increase in masturbation from lower to higher educational levels. The gradual loss of sexual inhibitions and increased interest with age is shown by a rise from about 30 per cent of married college women (age 21–25) to 48 per cent of married women with graduate training (age 41–45) using masturbation as a substitute outlet (Kinsey, 1953, p. 181).

Not all substitute outlets preserve the sexual exclusiveness of the marriage relationship. Extra-marital relations are almost as widespread as masturbation. Variations are found according to educational level. Among males with little formal education the highest incidence is at the younger age levels and the incidence decreases gradually with age. College educated men, however, show a reverse trend. Only about 15 to 20 per cent are involved at younger ages, but the percentage steadily increases until slightly over one in four are involved by age 50 (Kinsey, 1948, p. 587).

College educated women are just as likely to be involved in extra-marital sexual relations by age 40 as are their husbands. Only 10 per cent of them are involved by age 25. The percentage increases to about 26 per cent at age 35, to a high of 31 per cent at age 40. Less educated women are slightly more likely to be involved at younger ages but do not increase at the same rate as college educated women. About 24 per cent of them have had extra-marital relations by age 40 (Kinsey, 1953, pp. 439–40).

Effect of Infidelity

Relatively little is known about the effect of infidelity on the marriage. Obviously, it depends partially on the situation surrounding its occurrence, whether or not the spouse knows about it, and the reason for the infidelity. Kinsey (1953, p. 433) suggests that the sexual affairs of the women in his sample frequently led to difficulties when their husbands found out about it. Whether marital dissatisfaction was present before or only after the affair was not ascertained. One study suggests that a major difference between those who participate in extra-marital affairs and those who do not is in the strength of their consciences rather than in the degree of dissatisfaction with the marriage (Neubeck and Schletzer, 1962).

The effect of infidelity on the relationship undoubtedly varies depending on the values of the persons involved, their perception of the seriousness of the encounter, and their perception of the reason for it. Perhaps one cause among upper-middle class couples is the gradual erosion of the total relationship as the husband becomes more and more involved in career interests and his wife becomes more and more involved with children and community affairs. As they continue to change as the result of their separate experiences, the probability of finding someone in their own sphere of activity who provides a better "audience" for their communication is heightened. The new relationships may develop slowly with little awareness that it is gradually replacing a larger and larger part of the marriage relationship.[2]

THE PRINCIPLE OF VALUE RELEVANCE

In no other area of interaction do values and expectations play such an important part as they do in the area of sex. There are such wide variations in perceptions of normality, in values of good and bad, in levels of sexual desire, and expectations for adequate response that no outside authority can lay down workable standards of adequacy or normality.

Whether or not a couple achieves what they see as good sex adjustment will depend not on frequency of intercourse, length of time spent in foreplay, per cent of the time the wife experiences orgasm, or any other arbitrary listing of physiological or esthetic conditions. It will depend on the fit between the expectations of the two spouses, the fit between their expectations and their actual relationship, the degree to which they can exclude other's expectations as a measure of their own relationship, and the amount of mutual security and affection they are able to transmit to each other in expressing and satisfying their sexual natures.

[2] For an excellent discussion of the developmental aspect of a marriage relationship see Nelson N. Foote (1963, pp. 13–21).

SUMMARY

The sexual relationship in marriage cannot be separated from other areas of marital interaction. Any area of interaction in which there are changing expectations for behavior can be expected to produce difficulty. This is as true of sexual relations as of any other area of interaction. We might expect a decrease in the incidence of sexual problems if the newer permissive norms reduce the amount of guilt and negative evaluations associated with normal sexuality.

Athough tremendous social class differences appear in concepts of male and female sexuality and expectations for marital sex, the newer middle class norms will probably seep through all class levels. These norms emphasize mutual gratification of both partners and focus on the female orgasm as an indicator of success. Although this focus has lead to greater fulfillment in many marriages, it has had the unanticipated consequences of creating some anxieties in the male concerning his sexual capabilities and has created some self-doubts and guilt feelings in the female who fails to respond. The norms have perhaps begun to work as standards against which to measure performance as well as to provide the freedom from restrictive ideas which hampered free expression during an earlier period.

The sexual maladjustments manifesting themselves as impotence and frigidity, though occasionally the result of physiological problems, are largely the result of social psychological factors. The main contributors are misunderstanding of common male–female differences, lack of adequate information, restrictive or negative attitudes toward sex, widely divergent attitudes between husband and wife, unrealistic expectations for sexual relations, wide discrepancies between tension levels of husband and wife, and disturbances in other parts of the relationship. Far and away the greatest contributor to male impotence is "fear of inadequacy." The main factors contributing to adjustments and satisfaction in the sexual area are the feelings of acceptance and regard for each other as people. If these feelings are transmitted, then the sexual relations are likely to reinforce other areas in the marriage, regardless of the way in which they are carried out or the success of the act as judged by any outside authorities.

There are no arbitrary rules for achieving adequate sex relations. Success will depend upon the fit between the expectations of the spouses; the fit between expectations and their actual relationship; the degree to which they can exclude outside criteria as a measure of their own relationship, and the amount of mutual security and affection they are able to transmit to each other in all areas of the marriage.

QUESTIONS AND PROJECTS

1. From discussions in this and earlier chapters, make a list of the various ways in which males and females differ in terms of sexual behavior and response. How can an understanding of these differences aid in marital adjustment?

2. "Marriage is more than love and love is more than sex." Give evidence to either support or refute this statement.

3. Some people are saying that the sexual relationship confined to one person goes against man's sexual nature and thus puts an added burden on monogamous marriage. Discuss the pros and cons of this issue. Do you think monogamous marriage could survive sexual freedom for both mates? Give the reasons for your opinion. How would you react to infidelity on the part of either you or your spouse in your marriage?

4. Considering the social trends in sexual attitudes, premarital sexual behavior, and contraception, would you predict a decrease or increase in marital problems in the sexual area? A change in kinds of sexual problems? Support your answers.

5. If sex education becomes more widespread, do you think the sexual relationship will become more or less important to marital satisfaction? Why?

6. It has been said that the educated, middle class man has more fears about his sexual adequacy than lesser educated men. Explain this difference. Is this a necessary consequence of these factors? Discuss.

7. Why is frigidity more prevalent than impotence? Give as many reasons as you can think of. Do you think there may be a change in this in the near future? Explain.

8. What solutions are possible in a marital situation when there are differences in sexual desire between the spouses? Consider the inequality of desire in both directions. What solutions do you think would be more conducive to marital satisfaction? Why?

15

The Economic Relationship

In a commercial culture such as ours, where economic self-sufficiency is gone and dollar values tend to be uppermost, we can expect that family members will be concerned over the amount of income and how it will be spent. The economic relationship, broadly viewed, is central to the life style of the family. It is probably safe to say that, for most males in our society, this relationship is central to the feeling of self-worth. The wide variation in husband–wife roles, discussed in Chapter 12, does not include a variation in the breadwinner role of the husband. The wife may aid him in meeting the obligation, but the major responsibility remains his. The amount of income and the way it is spent proclaims for all the world to see his relative success or failure in this all-important role.

RANGE OF PROBLEMS

Problems stemming from the economic relationship cover a wide range. They involve the actual level of income as well as the perceptions of its adequacy. They include possible conflicts over the decisions which have to be made concerning how much is to be spent for what, when, and by whom. Tangential to these problems, and influential in their solution, is the satisfaction with the source of income; for example, the prestige of the job, the relative success within it, the degree of encroachment on other aspects of the marriage, such as companionship, and whether it comes only from the husband's job or from the combined incomes of husband and wife.

Underlying all these areas of possible conflict are the values defining the meaning of money, its importance relative to other things, the mean-

338

ing of cash or credit buying, and the expectations for the authority structure in the family. All of these values have been undergoing change in
our society. As in other areas when social change is occurring not all
segments of the society change at the same pace, and the probability of
two people marrying who have absorbed different values increases. When
these underlying values are in conflict, the two people are quite likely to
encounter difficulties, not only in coping with the everyday problems of
money management, but in their evaluations of the adequacy of their
level of living.

Level of Income

The level of income considered adequate varies depending upon the
standard of living. The *level of income* refers to the actual income one
has at a particular time. The *standard of living*, however, refers to the
expectations one has for income and the ways in which it will be expended
to provide acceptable living conditions. The standard of living is a set
of internalized values varying according to what one has been accustomed
to in his childhood, what his neighbors and friends appear to possess at
the moment, and the actual demands for expeditures at a particular period.

Certainly there is a lower limit of income adequacy upon which most
people would agree. There is disagreement concerning the exact point
at which an income is considered inadequate to support a family of a
certain size. Only when family members are continually hungry, do not
have enough clothes to keep them warm, enough beds to sleep on, or a
house which can be heated and contains the minimum requirements for
sanitation, is there general agreement that the lower limit has been
reached.

Effect of Poverty. Well before this point is reached, however, lack
of sufficient income has an effect on family life. Evidence is being rapidly
compiled to show the debilitating effect on family life of sub-standard
housing, malnutrition, and constricted lives. The constant fear, anxiety,
and hopelessness present in these homes leave little energy or motivation
for developing satisfying family relationships. Level of income, obviously,
is not the only reason for the higher family disruption rates among the
very poor, but relief from constant deprivation is a necessary foundation
upon which stable relationships may be developed. Not only do hunger,
illness, and overcrowded conditions make people more quarrelsome, but
the constricted life experiences reduce the chances for modifying the
transmission of self-defeating behavior patterns (Chilman, 1968a; Rainwater, 1967; and Rainwater and Yancy, 1967).

Many indices of instability collect together at extremely low levels of
income including higher rates of illegitimacy, school dropouts, juvenile

delinquency, crime, disease, death, desertion, separation, and divorce. Although these things occur at higher income levels also, they are not likely to occur so frequently that they become part of the life experience of most of the children as they grow up. When one is surrounded with these evidences of failure in the adult world, one is likely to be filled with fear or anger and drained of hope and dreams of anything better in his own future.

Above the poverty level however, differences of opinion abound concerning the definition of an "adequate" level of living. The differences become even more pronounced when the discussion centers around those things considered necessary in one's *own* life. The designation of things as either luxuries or necessities is an expression of one's standard of living, one's hierarchy of values, and one's concept of self. To a large extent, it is not the amount of income so much as the realization of discrepancy between one's standard and one's level of living that causes conflict.

Changes During the Life Cycle. Whether the income is actually inadequate or only appears to be so, the end result is a concern over money problems. A general comment is that if there were more money there would be fewer arguments. This is, of course, partially realistic. If people have an inexhaustible supply of funds, everyone's desires can be satisfied at the same time. Not as many decisions have to be made about whether to buy this or that. But most families do not have an inexhaustible supply. Furthermore, as money becomes more plentiful the desires for spending it are likely to increase. As income rises, the standard of living increases. The family is likely to want a more expensive home, in a better neighborhood, with better furniture, more expensive clothes, a better car, and so on. The level of living appears to have a hard time keeping up with the standard for many people.

The type of problem encountered changes as the level of income increases. As income rises, the problems are more likely to concern what to buy, when, and how to divide the expenditures among savings, investments, necessities, and luxuries, rather than catastrophic problems of job loss, loss of furniture or car due to non-payment of installments, inability to pay the rent or buy food (see under social class differences in Chapter 3).

There are certain periods of the life cycle where expenses can be expected to increase, resulting in either an actual or perceived inadequate level of income. Blood and Wolfe (1960, p. 247) show that during these periods a higher percentage of couples report conflicts over money. Few newly married couples report money problems, especially if they are both working. Even though each of them may have relatively low wages, their combined incomes are high in comparison to their expenses.

When children come, however, the picture changes rapidly. There is not only an increase in expenses but a reduced income with the loss of the wife's wages. Disagreements over money jump to the highest point of any period during the life cycle when the family is composed completely of preschool children. Lansing and Morgan (1955) report that many families go into debt at this time and experience a decreased satisfaction with their level of living. This is probably more true when the wife's income previously had been used for current expenses, thereby raising the expectations.

Although children's expenses increase as they grow older, so, generally, does the income of the family so that the percentage of couples reporting money problems remains about the same from the time children are pre-adolescent until the post parental period, when there is a slight decline.

Source of Income

About as important for marital harmony as level of income is the source of the income. The prestige or satisfaction associated with some jobs may make people content with a level of income which would be considered inadequate in another occupation.

In a comparison of dissolved and intact marriages, Scanzoni (1968) attempted to assess the importance for marital stability of the wife's satisfaction with the husband's job. Among the dissolved marriages in which the husband was manually employed, 92 per cent of the wives reported dissatisfaction with the former husband's job. This compared to 27 per cent of the comparable wives in intact marriages. Apparently this had little to do with the actual level of income, since the mean actual income of the dissolved group was slightly higher than that of the intact group. The major reason given for dissatisfaction was that the job was not the kind that could provide either the prestige or the life style desired by the wife. Among those with non-manual jobs, 63 per cent of the divorced wives were reportedly dissatisfied with their husbands' jobs compared to 21 per cent of the wives in intact marriages. The reason for dissatisfaction was different, however. Most of the divorced wives complained that the husband spent so much time with his occupational role that his family roles were slighted.

The occupation, then, can introduce conflict in at least two ways: (1) it can fail to provide the expected status or level of living desired; or (2) it can consume so much time and energy that the wife feels neglected or deprived of expected interaction with her husband. This may have little to do with the *actual* rewards or demands of the job, but rests instead with the discrepancy between the wife's expectations and the reality of her own situation.

The Working Wife. Whether the income derives only from the husband's occupation or from the combined employment of husband and wife has an impact on satisfaction with the economic relationship. Most women today will work at some time during their marriage. That this is an increasing phenomenon is illustrated by Blood and Wolfe's study (1960, p. 103) of Detroit area marriages in the late 1950's. They discovered that 78 per cent of the wives who were married between 1947 and 1955 were working or had worked at some time since their marriage. Only 39 per cent of the wives married before 1913 had worked at any time after marriage.

Studies of the impact on marital satisfaction of the wife working have been largely inconclusive. It appears that the wife's work pattern, per se, has little impact on marital satisfaction. However, when the analysis is taken a step further to include her husband's evaluation of her working, a different picture appears.

Gianopulos and Mitchell (1957) were among the first to consider the relationship between husband's evaluation of his wife's working and marital harmony. They discovered that marital disagreement was much higher in marriages where the wife worked and the husband disapproved than in marriages where the wife either did not work outside the home or worked with the husband's approval.

Ivan Nye (1963a) presented similar findings. The husband's approval of the wife's employment status was related to good marital adjustment whether she was working or staying at home. The non-employed wife whose husband wanted her to work reported poor marital adjustment to about the same extent as the employed wife whose husband wanted her to stay at home.

Scanzoni (1968) offered further evidence supporting the importance to marriage of the meaning that a wife's working has for the husband. He found that, among the manually employed divorced husbands, 81 per cent disapproved of their wives working as compared to 50 per cent of the manually employed husbands in intact marriages. Fifty per cent of the divorced, non-manually employed husbands disapproved compared to 28 per cent of them in intact marriages.

The reasons for disapproval among the divorced husbands centered around the impact his wife's working had on his concept of himself as a responsible male. The wife working was considered a threat to his feelings of masculinity and was taken to mean that he was not capable of meeting the needs of the family. The reasons given for working by the divorced wives did appear to connote criticism of the husband. The manual wives were likely to state that they worked in order to obtain things for themselves and children which their husbands were not able to provide. The non-manual wives were more likely to say they were working to occupy their time since their husbands were so busy.

Within intact marriages, the basic reasons wives gave for working were similar to those of the divorced wives—for extra money or for enjoyment. The interpretations made of this by the husbands were different, however. These husbands were not likely to see the working wife as a threat to the husband role. They were likely to approve as long as she wanted to work and the children were adequately cared for. They either were more satisfied with their own performances or were receiving approval for their performances from their wives in daily interaction so that the wife's working was not interpreted as expressing dissatisfaction with the husband.

Additional information comes from the most extensive study to date of the effect of the wife's work pattern on marital satisfaction (Orden and Bradburn, 1969). A national sample of both husbands and wives was interviewed. The working wives were separated according to whether or not they would work regardless of the need for money. Those who would work anyway were seen to be working by choice, the others for necessity. This factor made a startling difference on the marital relationship. Marital relationships were as satisfying (and more so, in some cases) when the wife was working by choice as when she was at home full-time. Marital dissatisfaction was associated with either the husband or wife perceiving her working by necessity when she would have preferred being at home. It may be that the marital satisfaction scores of the stay-at-home wife were depressed because of the inclusion of wives who would have preferred to work. This distinction was not made, however, so it could not be assessed.

Again we see that it is not the wife working, per se, which contributes to marital disharmony but the meaning her working has for both husband and wife. It can be quite easily seen how these meanings are translated into everyday interaction. Let us consider a husband and wife with different expectations for an "adequate" standard of living. The husband is satisfied with his job and the level of living it provides. The wife, however, is dissatisfied, feeling that she and the children are being deprived of things she considers necessities. We can imagine that numerous recurring interactions will convey her displeasure to her husband such as the times she mentions Junior's needing new shoes because she had to buy such cheap ones that they are already falling apart, or the way she points out things they need but will probably never be able to afford. Her husband cannot fail to get her message, with resulting feelings of inadequacy and resentment because he does not receive expected rewards for providing what he sees as an "adequate" income. When this wife goes to work, both spouses are likely to be resentful—she, because she feels she has to work to make up for her husband's failure, and he, because he perceives this as an open declaration of her evaluation of him as inadequate. The ensuing interaction when they both come home from work in the evening can do little but reinforce the resentments. He will probably be more alert to the inconveniences stemming from her not being at home. If he complains about them, she is likely to defend herself by blaming him for her having to work.

The contribution of differential expectations for level of living to the wife's dissatisfaction with husband's job and husband's disapproval of wife working is perhaps supported from Scanzoni's (1968) additional finding that 61 per cent of the divorced wives married downward from their fathers' occupational level. This was true of only 15 per cent of the intact marriages. These differences in occupational background suggest that many of the wives in the dissolved marriages would expect more of their husbands in the way of occupational attainment than their husbands expect of themselves.

The intact marriages, on the other hand were more likely to be characterized by husband–wife similarity in father's occupational level (59 per cent compared to 20 per cent in divorced group), and also educational attainment (54 per cent compared to only 15 per cent of the dissolved marriages). Both of the findings suggest a higher probability that husbands and wives from the intact marriages would share more occupational values than the husbands and wives from the divorced group.

The Changing Authority Structure

Problems over money would obviously be decreased if there were clear normative support for an authority structure which placed responsibility for money management squarely on the shoulders of one of the partners. Arguments would decrease, although not necessarily individual unhappiness over the way it was expended. The main problems then would be with the personal abilities and responsibility of the person in charge.

This is largely the way things were in the past, when the traditional husband–wife roles were firmly supported by our economic system (see Chapter 12). Since the husband was supposedly the only one with financial experience and contact with the economic world it was logical that final decisions would rest with him. With the growth of equality between the sexes, higher education for women, and the growing work experience of most women, logic no longer supports the unquestioned right of the husband to make these decisions alone. Conflicts, then, can no longer be resolved so easily by calling upon the authority structure to legitimate the husband's final authority.

The way in which money is handled, and conflicts resolved, is likely to have a greater impact on the self-concepts of the individuals involved than ever before. If a husband fails to consider his wife's opinions he is no longer so apt to be interpreted as merely fulfilling the role of responsible husband but as being stubborn, or thinking her opinions are worthless, or as not loving her.

The Power Structure

Especially in the middle class, norms appear to support a fairly equal authority structure which makes the interpersonal power structure more important. Some decisions are considered largely the husband's concern, such as the car and his job, while others are seen to be within the wife's department, such as food and household expenditures (Blood and Wolfe, 1960, p. 21). The balance of power in the family appears related to the personal and social characteristics that the individuals bring with them to the marriage and the changes which occur thereafter. Blood and Wolfe have found that the husband's power in decision making fluctuates with his income, his prestige in the community, his education relative to that of his wife, and the stage in the family life cycle. All of these would then be expected to play a part in the power structure concerning money management.

Effect of Occupational Status. Measured by the number of everyday decisions made by the husband alone, the wife alone, or both together, concerning their jobs, car buying, life insurance, vacation plans, housing, medical care, and food, the power of the husband goes up consistently with the prestige of his occupation, with his income, and with his social status (Blood and Wolfe, 1960, pp. 30–33). What this appears to mean is that, as he contributes more to the family status, his power in the family increases. His power, however, seldom reaches the absolute decision making authority associated with the older patriarchal norms. It mainly means that as the husband achieves more prestige in the community, the wife makes fewer of these decisions alone.

This relationship, however, is altered when both husband and wife work. When the wife is employed the decision making power of the husband is decreased (Blood and Wolfe, 1960, pp. 40–41). Again, this does not mean that as wives work they become dominant in making decisions. It means that the spouses are likely to make more decisions together than if she does not work. The greater skills and experience that working gives her continues to affect the power structure even after she ceases to work. Her power in decision making is directly related to number of years worked, whether or not she is presently employed.

Effect of Education.   The relative educational attainments of husbands and wives also affect the balance of power. The husband's power increases to the extent that he exceeds his wife in educational attainments. The comparative education of the spouses influences decision making at all occupational levels, so that high status husbands who exceed their wives in education have much more say in decision making than the equally high status husbands who have the same or less education than their wives. This again seems to suggest that decision making depends at least partially on the skills the partners bring to the marriage with them (Blood and Wolfe, 1960, pp. 37–38).

Effect of Organizational Membership.   Membership in community organizations is likewise related to the balance of power. The husband's power is reduced to the extent that his wife is more actively involved in community organizations than he is. This may be another way of saying that more active people belong to more organizations and are also more active in family decision making. It is probably further evidence, however, that when no strong norms support a particular authority structure, the balance of power is affected by the relative experience, knowledge, and resources of the marital partners. As the power structure develops and changes, however, with new experiences and circumstances, it may be *evaluated* from concepts of masculinity–femininity and ideas of equality or dominance absorbed from one's family orientation, one's peers, or other reference sources—with consequences for one's concept of self.

Satisfaction with Balance of Power.   Satisfaction with decision making processes in the marriage relationship is influenced by one's expectations of the husband–wife roles as well as by personality factors including dominance–submission, need for order and predictability, and tolerance for conflict. In general, however, expectations for companionship and freedom of expression in marriage appear to be widespread enough to produce a relationship between equality in the power structure and the wife's satisfaction with companionship and love.

Blood and Wolfe (1960, pp. 164, 226–28, 256) found that the wife's satisfaction with companionship and love increased with the number of decisions shared by husband and wife. Satisfaction with love and the total marital relationship was higher with two factors which appeared to increase equality in the power structure—equal age and equal educational attainments.

Scanzoni (1968) provides evidence of the relationship between inequality in decision making and marital breakup. About 70 per cent of the wives from dissolved marriages reported that their husbands made most of the decisions either before or after discussing the issue with the wife. Only about 30 per cent of the wives from intact marriages reported this pattern of decision making, the rest reported that they usually decided together. The divorced wives were very similar to the still married wives in percentage reporting that they were willing to compromise in resolving conflicts. They differed drastically, however, in the percentage reporting that their husbands were also willing to compromise. Twelve percent of divorced wives compared to 65 per cent of the still married wives reported this willingness of their husbands to compromise disputes over money.

Obviously, we cannot take these reports as actual descriptions of the marital interactions in either group of wives. What these findings do tell us, perhaps, is that the divorced wives are more likely to perceive the power structure in their marriages as being one-sided while the still married wives see it in more equalitarian terms. The actual percentage of decisions made by either spouse alone is not so important as is the perception that the power structure reflects the importance of each person to the other and that each is a worthwhile individual with something to contribute.

It becomes impossible, then, to say what way of handling money would be "best" for any individual marriage. A dole system, in which the husband handles all the money and gives it to family members as he sees fit, may work well for the family in which the wife was brought up to expect this and sees it as the husband's role. It may also work well when the way this is done reflects an appreciation of the wife's contributions and importance as an individual. It will probably only bring resentment and conflict, however, if it is interpreted as a display of power or an evaluation of the wife as incapable or inferior.

In the same way a *wife-allowance* or a *husband-allowance* system will work for some and not for others, depending upon the protection for the self-concepts included in the way it is implemented and carried out. A husband, for instance who has difficulty managing money may willingly turn it over to his more capable wife for management, provided the arrangement does not reflect on his worth as a person.

A *joint bank account,* which is becoming more popular as a method of handling funds in the marriage, seems to carry the implication of equal worth and equal responsibility. This system, however, will only work if both partners are in essential agreement on when and for what they will spend money.

Any system can be either efficient, inefficient, satisfying, or dissatisfying, depending upon the way it meets the expectations and needs of the two spouses. Essential in working out a satisfactory arrangement is an awareness of the meaning that money and its management has for each partner.

MEANING OF MONEY

Underlying the everyday decisions about money is the meaning that money has for the individual. A sufficient amount of money can mean security, added control over one's life, independence, or power. It can be saved, converted into other forms of security, spent in a variety of ways, given away, lost, or increased. By the time a person is old enough to consider marriage, he has probably had many experiences with the lack of money as well as with the spending of it. He has undoubtedly developed some feelings of anxiety about it and has developed some concept of self related to it. He *feels differently about himself* as he is in debt, as he watches a savings grow, as he is able to treat or entertain his friends, as he must forego certain pleasures or necessities because he is broke, as he buys new clothes or must wear the old ones, as he buys a new car, as he is dependent on someone else for his funds, or as he is financially independent.

Not everyone feels the same about himself in each of these circumstances. The individual develops these feelings in the process of growing up in a family which expressed certain values and anxieties about money management and usage in its everyday interactions. Values about money, however, are also influenced by norms and anxieties generated in the society, as many people share experiences stemming from changes occurring in the economic system—inflation, depression, stability, expansion, large-scale unemployment, and so forth.

Changes in the Society

Since the 1930's, the meaning of money has changed drastically in the society as a whole. Much of this has come about as the result of the growth of the insurance industry and the welfare programs of the government which were a direct consequence of the Great Depression.

Before the growth of these programs, money in the form of savings or easily converted securities meant security. Savings "for a rainy day" meant being able to meet unexpected emergencies such as fire losses, illness, or accident. It meant security for one's old age, or made the difference between children going to college or going to work. If one wanted to purchase a home, a large down-payment was required before a mortgage for the rest could be secured. This meant saving. The values supported by the society followed the Benjamin Franklin philosophy of a "penny saved is a penny earned." Credit was something one used only in the direst necessity—furthermore, it was difficult to get. The prudent man prepared for the future and he taught his children to do the same.

The encouragement of saving continued during World War II even though the economic system was expanding, employment was high, and incomes were rising. The industrial expansion was geared toward war materials and the production of civilian goods was low. The reasons for saving, however, were changing. Saving was a by-product of aiding the war effort—through the purchase of government bonds.

At the end of World War II, the industrial system was geared for mass production, the market for civilian goods was large, money was available, and the United States was committed to an ever-expanding industrial base. Production techniques developed during the war were turned to the manufacture of civilian goods, and the necessary element needed to keep the wheels turning was the willingness of the consumer to spend rather than save. Benjamin Franklin and his "rainy days" were being laid to rest, to be replaced by an "enjoy it now, since you can't take it with you" philosophy.

For many families and the children growing up in them, a number of things came together to affect the value changes concerning the meaning of money. Many parents who had themselves felt deprived as children during the depression wanted their children to have the things they had missed. Steadily rising wages allowed them to indulge both themselves and their children.

The rapid growth of the insurance industry was taking the sting out of emergencies such as illness, accident, and death for many people. Industrial employment with growing health and retirement plans was beginning to be seen as a lifelong ticket to security. A good job and steady income was as valuable as money in the bank. With security made not so much a personal as a social responsibility, money became the means to buying a better life in the here and now.

With the aid of the mass media and the advertising industry, a "better life" began to be pictured as one including the luxury items being produced to enhance both the home and the individuals within it. Along with the change from "preparing for the future" to "enhancing the present" came the easy way to do it—installment-plan buying. At first applying only to large expensive items, it has now been extended to normal department store purchases, vacation trips, "happy cash," and almost anything one can think of to buy.

Impact on Individual Values. As in other areas, when societal values are changing they do not affect all segments of the society at the same time. Individual families have different economic experiences and, depending upon the values held, react to them differently. One father, for example, as a result of depression experiences, will bend his efforts to teaching his children the value of money, of thrift, of savings so that they may better prepare for "rainy days sure to come." Another, with similar experiences, will teach his children to enjoy what they have while they have it, for "tomorrow it may be gone." While both sets of children may be exposed to the general cultural values, they will react to them differently depending upon the meaning of money which has been instilled in them in their own families. Not every one has experienced the general rise in income level; not everyone participates in the increased protection offered by insurance and retirement plans. Different feelings of trust or distrust of the system and differing moral values impinging on the newer meanings of money throw forth a number of different values all at the same time. The probability is high that people who carry quite different values concerning money will meet and marry. Since money is related to a feeling of security no matter how it is used, there are likely to be anxieties attached to its management.

One attempt to analyze the economic value systems operating among a group of married college students found support for five different values concerning money (Price, 1968).

Status. Money is seen mainly as a way of purchasing status and prestige. This would characterize the type of person who always wants to pick up the dinner check, have the expensive car, house, and clothes. His feelings of self-worth may be dependent upon presenting an extravagant image to the world.

Security. Money is valued for itself as a symbol of security. A savings account may be extremely important to such a person, regardless of whether or not the interest paid is as much as he could get through investments. Seeing money earmarked for time payments even before it is earned may produce extreme anxiety for a person holding these values.

Self-actualization. Money itself is seen as unimportant. Its importance is related to how it helps a person fulfill himself—what it contributes to his life. Money, though unimportant in itself, is nevertheless necessary to self-fulfillment. Records or a valued piece of art may be more important than an expensive car, but all take money. Investing or saving for future security when it interferes with today's fulfillment may seem to be stinginess to a person who wants to "live" rather than just "exist." Today's college students occasionally express themselves like this: "My parents have saved all their lives for their old age. They never went on a vacation or bought the little luxuries that would have made life more pleasant. Now that they've retired they don't know how to spend it. That's not for me, money is to enjoy, not hoard."

Self-indulgence. Money is for satisfying immediate urgent desires. No justification is needed for spending except that one has a strong desire for something. This is the value system appealed to by manufacturers to produce "impulse buying." A person characterized by this orientation to money wreaks havoc with budgets, since the urge to satisfy immediate desires overrides plans for the future. Importance is placed on the here, the now, and the self. This tends to be characteristic of children and adolescents but is also carried into adulthood by many people.

Faith. Money is nothing to worry about. It will take care of itself. This orientation is more related to the difficulty of obtaining it than how it should be spent, although there should be some relationship between the two. A person who is unconcerned about where the money is coming from has few built-in restrictions on his spending. He probably suffers little anxiety from mounting bills—"Something will turn up—we'll have the money when we need it." Imagine what feelings this attitude in a husband or wife would provoke in the spouse who saw money as security.

Probably no person is characterized entirely by only one of these value systems. It is more realistic to think of a person as leaning toward one but also influenced by some of the others. The particular combination a person holds to would influence the amount of anxiety he experienced about money, his decisions about what are necessities and what are luxuries, the amount of anxiety associated with debts, and his general feelings of satisfaction and security associated with the total financial management.

If two people marry and share similar value orientations toward money, few conflicts would be expected. They might argue over tastes or selections, but would be in essential agreement about how and when to spend, save, or invest. Of course, two people could share the same value orientation and have little conflict over money, but with financial disaster as the result (for example, two people sharing the value orientations of "faith" and "self-indulgence").

Some awareness of one's own and the spouse's values about money aids in developing ways of handling it which reduce each person's anxieties and increase his satisfaction. A little money carried around in the wallet for occasionally giving in to the urgent desire may make the self-indulgent person more willing to go along, in general, with the saving program of the security-minded person. The realization of the importance of purchasing some prestige items for the self-concept of a status conscious spouse may make it easier for him to skimp on other items in order to splurge on one which obviously means so much to him. Seemingly illogical reactions to money questions sometimes appear quite rational when the value orientation prompting the behavior is known. Budgets which take into account the meaning that money has for the two people are more likely to work than those which are arbitrarily imposed either from an outside source or from the value position of just one of the partners.

Objective Meaning of Money

In the final analysis, money means the difference between food on the table and going hungry, between shoes on the feet or going barefoot, between paying one's bills or being sued for non-payment. Reg rdless of the fit or conflict between money values, a certain realistic fi between income and expenditures is at the base of the economic relationship.

Some financial problems stem from the inability to provide sufficient funds—where the income is so low that even the most idealistic of couples would become hungry. Other problems stem from an inability to manage the money one has. Problems such as these may result partially from discrepancies between one's standard of living and the realistic level one can afford to pay for. They may just as easily result from a failure or inability to plan for unexpected expenditures or from a gradual accumulation of small debts which ultimately combine into a staggering financial burden. The growth of easy credit plans has undoubtedly increased problems of over-extended spending. The extent of problems like these is suggested by several bankruptcy studies.

Bankruptcies have almost tripled in the last 10 to 12 years. The increase has been due mainly to individual bankruptcies which comprise about 90 per cent of the total petitions filed. According to these studies, bankrupts were men in their early to mid-thirties and younger. Although all occupational groups were represented, the blue-collar occupations were over-represented. The debts which precipitated the bankruptcies were mainly loans from bank or loan companies, and bills for clothing, department store merchandise, and medical bills. The principle cause of the financial distress was the gradual accumulation of an overwhelming load of debt on which they had been unable to meet payments. The breakdown seemed to result from a combination of inadequate incomes, insufficient insurance or savings to cover unexpected contingencies, and expenditures which were excessive in relation to income (Hermann, 1966).

We can be reasonably sure that as the number of individual bankruptcies increases so does the number of families in serious financial difficulty who do not resort to bankruptcy. The effects of bankruptcy on the self-concept, and the evaluations of other family members, would be expected to vary, depending on the values held by the individuals involved. For some it will be a turning point in their financial management; for others it may be a humiliating experience which will leave marks on the family relationships for many years to come. Whatever the results, it will not be the consequence of the bankruptcy, per se, but the meaning that bankruptcy has for all involved.

THE PRINCIPLE OF VALUE RELEVANCE

The principle of value relevance is perhaps more visible in money problems than in any other area of marital interaction, especially when one rises above the poverty level and assumes some skill in practical money management. The amount of financial security necessary to produce an "adequate" level of living varies according to the expectations of the spouses, and the groups with which they interact. Satisfaction with economic achievement is related more to the fit between level and standard of living than to any arbitrary amount of income or set of living conditions.

As far as authority structure is concerned, it becomes impossible to say which method of assigning responsibility produces the most satisfactory relationship. The evaluation of the particular arrangement and resulting amount of satisfaction will vary, depending upon the expectations of the spouses and the meaning the particular method has for their concepts of self. Of much greater importance than the particular method is the consensus between husband and wife concerning the meaning of money, the way it will be handled, and definition of an "adequate" level of living.

The same can be said for the husband's occupation and the working wife. It is not the type of occupation or the wife working, per se, which heightens or lowers marital satisfaction. It is the meaning placed upon them from the value systems of the spouses and the consequences the resulting interactions have on their concepts of self and each other.

SUMMARY

Problems stemming from the economic relationship cover a wide range. They include actual level of income, perception of its adequacy, source of income, and decisions over how much is to be spent for what, when, and by whom.

Underlying all of these areas of possible conflict are the values defining the meaning of money, its importance relative to other things, the meaning of cash or credit buying, and the expectations for the authority structure in the family. All of these values have been undergoing change in our society. As in other areas, when social change is occurring the probability of marriage between two people who have absorbed different values increases. When underlying values are in conflict, the difficulty in coping with everyday problems increases.

Income so low that it is impossible to meet minimum requirements for housing, food, and clothing has a debilitating effect on family life. This can be seen in the higher disruption rates as well as in the tendency for children from these families to reproduce the self-defeating pattern in their own adult lives.

Above the poverty level, however, money problems fluctuate through the life cycle with the highest incidence during the early part of the child-rearing period. This is likely to be the greatest period of financial shock when suddenly rising costs coincide with loss of the wife's paycheck. Expectations for level of living have to be scaled down—with resulting feelings of deprivation.

Many different values concerning the meaning of money are in our society at the same time. Money can be seen as providing status, security, self-fulfillment, or self-indulgence. It can be seen as something hard to get or as nothing to worry about. All of these furnish different perceptions of necessities and luxuries, as well as different anxiety levels about the way money is used. Within certain practical limitations, satisfaction with the economic relationship will be more related to degree of value consensus between marital partners than to any particular way in which money is earned and managed.

QUESTIONS AND PROJECTS

1. To what extent and under what conditions would you like to work after marriage (if female), or to have your wife work (if male)? If your spouse viewed it differently how far would you be willing to compromise in his or her direction? Discuss.

2. What are the conditions under which the wife working is most likely to be conducive to marital satisfaction? To marital dissatisfaction? Why do you think this would be true?

3. Consider the situation of a husband who did not want his wife to work, married to a wife who wanted to work. Which do you think would be most disturbing to the marital relationship—her working against her husband's wishes or staying at home against her wishes?

4. Prepare a paper from other sources on the advantages and disadvantages of a wife working when there are no children. When there are children of various ages.

5. If a wife works should she deliberately attempt to keep from making more money than her husband even if she were able to? Why or why not?

6. Discuss the reasons for money problems being the most prevalent of all marital problems. Would you predict an increase or decrease of money problems in the next generation of marriages? Explain.

7. Describe the "meanings of money" given in this chapter by illustrating ways in which they would be expressed in behavior. Are there any others that you have noticed in yourself or others? If so, describe them.

8. Which combination(s) of meanings of money do you think would be most conducive to marital satisfaction? Most disruptive? Explain.

9. What does money mean to you? Are there any meanings attached to money that you think you could not live with? Is this a trait of a person that would influence the feeling of love before marriage? After marriage?

10. Discuss the difference between the authority structure and the power structure in resolving money conflicts. Do you think there should be a final authority concerning money in the family? Who should it be? Discuss.

16

The In-Law Relationship

Marriage marks the beginning of a new exclusive relationship, requiring the development of new roles vis-à-vis each other. It also marks the beginning of new roles with the spouse's family, without marking the termination of old roles developed through the years with one's own parents and siblings. As new role relationships are taken on, the old ones are altered somewhat but in most instances are not severed completely. When a girl marries, for example, she becomes not only a wife to her new husband, but also a daughter-in-law to his parents, a sister-in-law to his siblings, and a married daughter to her own parents. Each of these roles is subject to the expectations of all participants. There is the possibility, for example, of two sets of parents and of a husband and wife all having different ideas of how the newly married woman should relate to her husband, her in-laws, and her own parents. It may be next to impossible to meet all the expectations, especially if they result in her being expected to be in three different places at the same time.

It is small wonder then that in-law troubles are a rather common source of marital tension, especially during the early years following the wedding. Marriage means a reshuffling of family patterns which takes time and requires a certain amount of intelligence and effort on the part of both parents and children. Parents have the problem of releasing their child after years of care and supervision. Newly married couples have the problems of establishing a new family relationship without completely severing the old one.

ROLE READJUSTMENT

Many in-law problems can be explained by the role readjustments necessary in the new relationships. The anxieties and needs of the two

356

generations are likely to be different and many times in conflict with each other.

The Older Generation

Mothers appear to have more difficulty than fathers in readjusting their roles. It is generally they who have had most to do with the rearing of children. They have been more intimately interested in the affairs of the children, and perhaps even up to the day of the wedding have been consulted on the numerous arrangements. For a mother, the marriage of her child may signal the end of her all-important place in her son's or daughter's life. Especially if there are no more children at home and few interests outside the family, she may feel a great need to see herself as still needed and important to her married child. As she attempts to hold on to her role, the continued interest and advice giving, appropriate such a short time before, may be interpreted by the newlyweds as meddling or attempting to dominate. This was the most typical complaint in Duvall's (1954) study of 5,000 men and women.

The role she moves into as a result of her child's marriage is not an appealing one by societal definition. The ever-present mother-in-law jokes probably do not help to build happy anticipation for the position. These jokes tend to picture her as a critical, trouble-making busybody, perhaps expressing in humor some of the feelings of guilt and jealousy in a relationship between two people, one of whom has replaced the other as an important love object in the life of a person important to them both. The potential rivalry in this relationship is recognized in more than three-fifths of the world's societies by taboos on the meeting of a man and his mother-in-law (Schlein, 1962). Although our society has no actual taboos, the anxieties concerned with redefining important relationships enhance the probability of hurt feelings, resentments, and criticisms.

Fathers are not as likely to undergo such a severe role adjustment. They are generally not as involved in the childrearing process or as interested in the children's everyday activities. Furthermore, they are still involved in their jobs at the time their children are likely to marry, and the marriage does not alter their primary role of breadwinner in the same way it alters the primary mother role of their wives. There is not then the same need in them to be involved in their married child's life. They will suffer their most extreme role readjustment later on when they retire.

A man is likely to enjoy the attention he may receive from a young woman, as he approaches middle age. The daughter-in-law relationship allows him perhaps some vicarious feelings of renewed youth as he identifies with his son in his new marriage. This is easier for males to do than for females who are more likely to be reminded of their loss of youth and sexual appeal in comparison to their daughter. The overattention of the father-in-law can occasionally introduce conflict too, although it doesn't appear to be a common problem. One young newly married college woman explained it this way:

It's embarrassing when we go to see Jack's parents. His father is so attentive and affectionate that he acts more like a suitor than a father-in-law. It doesn't help my relationship with my mother-in-law either, and I dont blame her—he treats her like she was there only to wait on me. I wish he would just act his age and be a father-in-law, things would be easier all around.

The Younger Generation

The newly married couple have some role adjustments of their own to make. If they have been quite dependent on their parents up to the time of marriage, they may feel a strong need to break these ties and assert their independence but at the same time feel some reluctance to let go. To the extent that they feel this conflict, they may react violently to any perceived threat to their independence. What from the parental point of view is normal interest may seem from the newlywed's perspective to be prying or interference.

In our middle class society, there is generally a desire to develop dependence on the marital partner. It is expected that married mates will share secrets with each other rather than with parents. If there have been close parental ties it sometimes becomes hard not to use the parent for moral support when conflicts appear in the marital union. When this happens the other spouse is likely to feel threatened and think that the parent is more important or more respected than he is. The more precarious the development of the marital roles, the more threatening the continual parental contacts may become.

The new wife is attempting to learn her domestic role in a goldfish bowl, so to speak. Her successes and failures are many times open for all to see—how she keeps house, how she cooks, how her husband's clothes look, and so forth. Since these chores are generally thought to take little practice, she is likely to be compared to women who have been in the role for twenty years or more—her own mother and her husband's. Since her mother-in-law helped develop her husband's expectations and tastes, evaluations of the new wife's role are likely to be in comparison to her mother-in-law, whose ways of cooking and keeping house may differ drastically from those she learned from her own mother. In other words, her new role is visible and is subject to comparison with two other women who have had much practice in developing theirs. Each may want to give her advice, and if the advice conflicts, she endangers at least one relationship no matter which way she turns.

The husband role is of a different kind. The primary aspect of it is that of breadwinner. He performs this role away from the watchful eyes of parents. They only see the consequences of it in the way he maintains himself and his wife. It is usually assumed that it will take him many years to reach the peak of his performance, so he is not as likely to be compared to the older men who have been in the role longer. He is not as likely to come under critical comparisons or be exposed to advice on how to do his job, as is his wife. This is one reason for in-law problems being more exclusively feminine conflicts.

The Feminine Pattern in In-Law Problems

In-law friction is more typically a feminine than a masculine pattern. Duvall (1954, p. 187), for example, found that many more complaints came from the female than from the male side. Furthermore, more sisters-in-law were blamed for causing trouble than were brothers-in-law, and more mothers-in-law than fathers-in-law. And again, in cases of mother-in-law difficulty, it was more frequently the husband's mother who proved troublesome to the wife than the wife's to the husband.

There are several reasons for this, some of which have already been mentioned.

1. The role adjustments are more extensive for the females than the males in both generations.
2. The family roles tend to be more central to the self-concepts of women and thereby more anxiety-provoking as they are being developed and as they disappear.
3. The visibility of the wife role opens her to comparisons mainly with her mother-in-law, whose advice and continued concern about her son may be interpreted as criticism of the new wife.
4. The wife and mother-in-law are more likely to compete for the attention of the husband–son than are husband and father-in-law for the attention of the wife–daughter. This is due in part to the greater emotional attachment between mother and child than between father and child.
5. There is likely to be a more dependent relationship between mother and daughter than the other parent–child combination at the time of marriage. When the daughter has not resolved this emotional dependency at the time of marriage, she is likely to turn to her mother more than to her new husband, endangering the development of the marital relationship.
6. The females are more likely to be the transmitters of family culture. As a family culture develops it is likely to be solidified through rituals: foods for special occasions, childrearing practices, religious observances, and so forth. These take on a certain feeling of right-

ness. Since it is the wife who is more intimately involved in establishing these for the new family, she is likely to continue the practices observed in her family. If these rituals differ greatly from her husband's family culture, she is likely to come under criticism from her mother-in-law who may see both her son and grandchildren deprived of significant experiences. "I feel so sorry for my grandchildren. Their mother insists on opening the Christmas gifts on Christmas Eve. They miss all the excitement of seeing the toys Santa left under the tree on Christmas morning. I know Paul misses it, too. He used to love Christmas so—the way we did it, of course."

7. Leslie (1967, p. 321) proposes another reason for the higher incidence of female in-law conflict. He suggests that the greater power enjoyed by the male in our society makes it less likely that his mother-in-law will express her criticisms openly to him. He has the power to move his family to another location where there would be no contacts at all, if the relationship becomes too uncomfortable. He is probably also less reluctant to force an open break with either family than his wife would be. It may be reasonable to assume that his wife receives not only her share of the in-law conflict but a goodly portion of his, which can be more easily expressed to her.

The feminine nature of in-law problems has been supported by most studies. One exception to this is provided by a study of married male students and their wives at Purdue University (Switzer, 1966). Although the mother-in-law was more likely than the father-in-law to be seen as troublesome, she was also more likely to be seen as helpful. The father-in-law was more likely to be reported as having no effect on the new marriage. As can be seen in Figure 16–1, forty-nine per cent rated him this way as opposed to only 34 per cent who said the mother-in-law has no effect. Mothers, then, from the perspective of both the sons and daughters seem to be more involved for either good or ill. In the same vein (not shown in the graph), the wives were much more likely to say they loved their mothers-in-law (58 per cent) than were the husbands (38 per cent). Wives were no more likely than their husbands to say they disliked them (9 per cent in both cases). This is in direct conflict with other studies which show considerable more dislike of mothers-in-law by wives than by husbands (see Wallin, 1954).

In the Purdue study, husbands were just as likely as their wives to have high in-law difficulty scores, which again runs counter to the findings of most research. These differences perhaps can be explained by the marginal position of the student husband. He may be more likely to feel the resentment of his wife's parents as she works to help him get through school. As they try to help out with occasional clothing or luxury items, he is more likely to interpret it as a criticism of his inability to support his wife than is a husband who is working in a job rather than

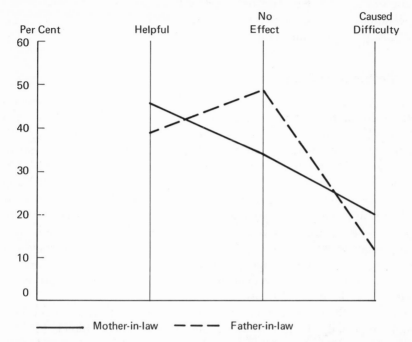

Fig. 16–1. Married college students' perception of effect of parents-in-law on marriage. (Adapted from Switzer, 1966, Table 2, p. 39.)

toward a degree.[1] On the other hand, the wife's in-laws are likely to feel grateful to her for helping their son finish school, thereby reducing the friction between them. Whether this pattern continues after the couple leaves school and the male becomes established in his occupation is not known.

VALUE CONFLICT

If the in-law problems stem mainly from role readjustments, they would be expected to disappear as all persons become more secure in their new roles. To some extent, however, the achievement of satisfactory role adjustments is dependent on the similarity of the family cultures. The in-law relationships involve many of the same problems surrounding any meshing of individual habit systems into a new system composed of shared meanings and interpretations. In order to meet the expectations of others as well as one's own needs it is first necessary to understand what the ex-

[1] Gratitude is expressed to E. J. Kanin for private communication from his files of student papers concerning the problems of student husbands.

pectations are, what certain behavior and expressions mean, and which expectations can realistically be met and which ones must be changed. This involves communication.

The Problem of Communication

The more similar the family cultures are which are being brought together, the more likely it is that the people involved can talk to each other and be understood. If they have all absorbed similar ideas of etiquette, of expectations for family relationships, of help patterns, and of values and interpretations of behavior, there should be little difficulty in developing the new roles. The main obstacles would be immaturities and personality factors. This perhaps accounts for the findings that in-law problems are more numerous and harder to resolve in marriages which cross class, religious, and ethnic group lines than in those which are more endogamous (Sussman, 1951). In these marriages, the misunderstandings stemming from different concepts of the husband–wife roles as well as child–parent roles would be expected to slow down the role adjustments necessary in the new relationships.

One or both sets of parents are likely to remain aloof from the new couple, especially if the mixed marriage was opposed (Blood, 1969, p. 100). This calls forth a different kind of complaint from the newlyweds than the most common one of "interfering," or "meddling." Duvall (1954, p. 289) found this complaint the second most prevalent—the in-law is seen as distant, indifferent, and thoughtless. The complaint that the in-law is either too meddling or too distant can be a correct assessment of the behavior of the in-law. It may also be only a difference in the ways of expressing interest or emotions which get misinterpreted by someone with a different system of habits.

The beneficial results of thinking one understands and can communicate with a parent-in-law is shown in Switzer's (1966, pp. 85–101) study of college marriages. He measured the perceived similarity between the mother and mother-in-law using a personality check list. Among those who reported a love feeling for the mother, there appeared a strong relationship between love feelings for the mother-in-law and high similarity of the mother-in-law to the mother. Where there was high similarity, 63 per cent reported love for the mother-in-law, and 58 per cent reported little or no mother-in-law difficulty. On the other hand, only 32 per cent of those who perceived the mother-in-law as greatly different from the loved mother reported loving the mother-in-law and only 17 per cent reported little or no mother-in-law difficulty.

Although similarity was measured on personality characteristics, it probably can be assumed that similarities of expectations, ways of expressing oneself, and general life style contributed to the personality assessments.

Although differences in background do not necessarily produce in-law problems, the adjustments would probably take longer and require more effort than in those situations where one "felt at home" in the spouses' family from the beginning.

The Problem of Feeling Included

One of the problems of building in-law relationships is that of feeling like an "insider" rather than an "outsider." Many times hurt feelings and resentments build up from misinterpreting the ways of expressing emotions in a family. Some families are characterized by open, hearty, back slapping, and bear-hugging kinds of welcoming behavior. When a member returns to the fold, the whole family rushes to the welcome, all talking at once. The homecoming may call for an immediate loading of the table, where all gather round to eat, drink, and bring each other up to date on the happenings of family, friends, and neighbors. Other families may be no less glad to see a homecoming member, but act in a much more formal, reserved way. There may be little bodily contact beyond a brief hand holding or peck on the cheek. The all-talk-at-once effervescence of the first family may be replaced in this one by a polite, quiet, one-at-a-time conversation which to them shows respect for each member's contribution. They may eventually cover all the same topics but in an entirely different way.

Imagine now a son from the first family marrying a daughter from the second. Each wants to feel accepted and loved by the other family. When they visit the husband's family, the wife may not be able to join in the hearty welcome, no matter how much she may want to. Her reserved behavior may be misinterpreted by his family—"She doesn't like us. She acts like she thinks she's better than we are." When in *his* family environment, even her husband is likely to look at her through the eyes of his family, seeing her from a different perspective and accusing her of not liking his parents. She is apt to feel hurt, misunderstood, and resentful.

When they next go to her house, he may feel that they treat him like a guest rather than a family member—that they are cold, distant, and do not accept him. When he complains to his wife about his feeling of being excluded, he's likely to get a, "Oh for Heaven's sakes, of course they like you, they just don't fall all over you like your family." And now we may have each defending his own family and accusing the other of not trying to get along with them. The visits may get farther and farther apart, with feelings of guilt, resentment, and rejection all around.

Even in the most benign of circumstances, there may be a period of time before the new in-law feels like a family member. Family histories contain many shared experiences. A feeling of oneness is enhanced by reference to these experiences when all the family members relive the memories and emotions associated with them. These are seldom fully communicated in words. Usually some word or situation triggers an association with the previous event. Perhaps at the same instant several family members will ask, "Do you remember when . . . ?" That is all it takes for everyone to remember, to relive, and to begin reminding each other of specific events with incomplete phrases, gestures, and laughter. Everyone remembers, that is, except the new in-law, who cannot join in and feels pointedly his position as outsider. Some family members may notice his discomfort and attempt to fill him in on the left-out pieces of information. But it is almost impossible to communicate the whole situation in its context. The story is likely to fall flat and end with an inept phrase such as—"Well you had to be there to understand!" The new in-law feels more left out than ever.

It takes time, shared experience, and much conversation recounting past experiences to allow a common culture to develop which includes the new family member. The diagram describing the development of love presented in Chapter 10 (Figure 10-1) can be used to describe the development of love between in-laws as well as between a man and a woman. The initial feeling of rapport would be expected to be greater if the family cultures are similar, if there has been a long courtship with prolonged interaction within the two families, if the marriage has the approval of the family, and if all the persons involved are emotionally secure and mature enough to recognize that love for a spouse and a parent are two different emotions and each can exist without endangering the other.

If rapport is easy between the new in-law and other family members, visits are likely to be fairly frequent. Mutual aid situations are likely to develop, and rituals appear around holiday and special occasion celebrations. Some families get together ritualistically every week for church services or Sunday dinner. Others get together mainly for special holidays or birthdays. The ritualistic aspect of the visitation pattern aids in producing a shared family culture which increases a sense of belonging and continuity over time (Blood, 1969, pp. 262–64).

Time Allocations

Even under the best of circumstances, certain realistic problems of equal distribution of time can create tensions. If both spouses have parents who expect holidays to be spent with them, certain conflicts are sure to appear. It is impossible for any family to be in two places at once, especially when the places are in different cities. When competition for leisure time also includes friendship groups as well as two family groups, the choices which must be made can result in feelings of guilt, resentment, or jealousy even when the spouses have no conflict between themselves. If each spouse has close ties with his own family the conflicts over time allocation are likely to be even more severe.

Sometimes the allocation of time is thrown into a power struggle between husband and wife. One young couple argued vehemently whenever they visited the hometown where both sets of parents lived. The arguments ranged from which house they would visit first, through which one they would spend the night in, to which one they would visit last before leaving. This was labeled an in-law problem since it would, of course, have been alleviated if one set of parents had not existed. But one would expect that in a situation like this, the in-laws had only provided an easy battleground on which to fight; if the in-laws ceased to exist, another area of conflict would probably take its place. If there is already resentment and tension between the couple, from whatever source, the allocation of time between families can become very difficult.

CHANGES OVER THE LIFE CYCLE

In-law problems are certainly not inevitable. Ways of adjusting and meeting the needs and expectations of both generations will have to be worked out but most families evidently do not see in-laws as a source of serious conflict. Although percentages vary depending upon the sample being interviewed, rarely do more than one-third of any sample report difficulties. In general, the difficulties are more pronounced in the early years of marriage and among those who marry at young ages (Blood and Wolfe, 1960, pp. 247–48). This would be expected from the discussion of major sources of friction. The younger the spouses are at marriage the greater would be the probability that they had not broken the dependency relationship with the mother. Parents would be more likely to see the young couple as needing their advice and help, and the young couple may feel more anxiety over perceived threats to their tenuous feeling of independence.

Greater difficulty would be expected during the early years because of the role readjustments required. As these are made, the perception of the in-laws as trouble-makers should decrease. The number reporting problems should decrease over the years, however, whether or not role readjustments are satisfactorily achieved.

Reduced Contact

If the relationships are not satisfying, contact is probably reduced either by cutting down the time spent with the troublesome family or reducing contact almost completely by moving to another part of the country. Some couples do this at the time of marriage, anticipating in-law problems if they remain geographically close. Characteristic of attempts to avoid trouble before it appears, is this student's statement:

Linda doesn't know it, but I'm going to take the job offer which is the farthest away from her mother. The only way I could get along with her is to never see her.

Coming of Children

Also, as children enter the picture parents-in-law become grandparents. Although this may open up new areas of conflict, children can, in many cases, provide a common focal point of interest for the two generations. New opportunities for aid appear if the grandparents live near enough to offer help during childbirth and to function occasionally as baby sitters. If they enjoy this new role and are not made to feel imposed upon, the shared experiences with the third generation broaden the base of communication and understanding between the first two. The second generation begins to understand and appreciate more fully the perspective of the first generation as they become parents themselves. To the extent, however, that there are great differences in ideas about childrearing between the parental families, or great differences in religious affiliations or degree of devoutness, the coming of children may increase rather than decrease the in-law conflict. If, however, some respect for each other as mature individuals has been developed before children come, conflicts over childrearing methods are less likely to appear.

Aging

As all the generations continue to age, some in-law problems will disappear because of the death of the parents. As old age reinforces the dependence of parents on their married children, the problems encountered are not quite as likely to be labeled "in-law problems." They are now the problems of caring for aged parents, no matter which set of parents is involved. The problems may become more financial and custodial in nature and involve difficulties between siblings in establishing responsibility.

THE PRINCIPLE OF VALUE RELEVANCE

What is interpreted as "good" in-law relationships will vary from family to family. For some families, good in-laws are scarce in-laws. There is little desire to build or maintain close intergenerational relationships. This may be entirely satisfactory to all concerned. Both sets of parents as well as the married children may have such a wide variety of interests or friendships that family connections are secondary.

Some couples may develop close ties with only one parental family. This may also be satisfactory to everyone, with no feelings of resentment or jealousy. Others may want and be able to maintain relatively close ties with both in-law families, but with fairly ritualized ways of maintaining equality. Still others may only feel that in-law relationships are good if there is frequent interaction, with much sharing of confidences, work, problems, and leisure time. No matter what pattern of interaction develops, it may be interpreted as satisfactory as long as all concerned agree that this is the way things should be.

Difficulties arise not from any particular kind of relationship but from disagreements about what the pattern should be. The disagreement may be between the generations, with the younger generation so valuing their privacy and independence that even minimal desires for continued inclusion on the part of the parental pairs are interpreted as meddling or attempted control. The conflict may go the other way, with a parental pair enjoying their new freedom from family responsibility and avoiding a continual involvement desired by the married child. In this case the parent may be seen as too distant or disinterested. Some hurts or resentments are almost inevitable, not as a result of a particular behavior pattern but because the expectations differ.

The lack of fit may occur between the spouses. One spouse may desire continual close family involvement while the other values privacy and independence. The resultant problems stem not from the nature of the interaction but from the lack of fit between the expectations. No matter how understanding the families, the conflicting goals of the spouses cannot both be met in the same pattern of interaction. The result is likely to be labeled "in-law problems" however. As long as the conflict is blamed on meddling in-laws, overdependency of one spouse on his parents, or rejection of his parents by the other spouse, a harmonious solution is not likely to be reached. When the conflict is seen as stemming from differences in strength of desire for *any* family interaction, it is easier to find a compromise than if one must protect either himself or his parents from blame.

Good in-law relationships would, then, be more likely to exist when the spouses and both families agree on the amount and depth of the inter-generational involvement. Conversely, the greatest conflict would be expected when the spouses disagree and each position is reinforced by his own parents.

SUMMARY

Marriage marks not only the beginning of new roles between the husband and wife but the beginning of new roles with the parents and siblings-in-law and readjustments of older parent–child roles. Difficulties in developing the new role relationships are likely to be perceived as in-law problems, especially when the marriage occurs at a very young age.

In-law problems are most likely to be feminine problems. This results from several sources: (1) the greater emotional involvement of the mother in the childrearing process; (2) the greater importance of the family for the woman's self-concept; (3) the greater visibility of the wife's role, opening her performance to comparison with women who have had practice in the role for twenty years or more; (4) the need of the younger generation to break the emotional dependency relationship with the mother; (5) the expectation of trouble with the mother-in-law, supported by image-making jokes in our society.

The role readjustments are achieved more quickly when the marriage was approved and the two family cultures are similar. Not only are the expectations for the new relationships likely to be similar but communication is easier when words, gestures, and behaviors generally have the same meanings. Marriages combining different religions, races, and ethnic groups are more likely to encounter in-law problems than endogamous ones.

One problem facing most new spouses is that of becoming included in the in-law family. Sometimes this happens before marriage in situations where the courtship was long and offered the opportunity to visit in both homes. Whether it occurs before or after marriage, the problem is one of building a shared culture within which all can communicate and feel understood.

In-law problems tend to be concentrated in the early part of marriage. Tensions decline as role readjustments are achieved and as one becomes more familiar with the culture of the spouse's family. As grandchildren enter the picture, the two generations are likely to find a new area of interest they share. If the relationships are not satisfying, contact with the families may be curtailed or almost eliminated by geographical moves.

As the years go by in-law problems may be terminated by the death of the parents or by the changed nature of the relationships as parents age.

The kind of intergenerational interaction which is perceived as "good" or "troublesome" varies from family to family. Far more important to intergenerational harmony than any specific type of relationship is the agreement among family members on the type, amount, and depth of the interaction.

QUESTIONS AND PROJECTS

1. Why are in-law problems greatest among those who marry young? Greatest in the early years of marriage? Greatest with mothers-in-law? Greatest when related families are living in the same house? Discuss.

2. "The best way to maintain good in-law relationships is to live a thousand miles away." What is your opinion of this statement? Would it apply to your parents as well as to the parents of your future spouse? Do you think you will feel the same way when you are the parent-in-law? Explain.

3. Look back at the wheel theory of love development discussed in Chapter 10. What are the implications of this for developing satisfying in-law relationships?

4. Give all the reasons for in-law difficulties you can think of which are not related to personality conflicts. What solutions can you think of for these problems?

5. Why does the arrival of children tend to reduce in-law problems? Under what conditions would the problems tend to increase? Be sure to include in your explanation the contributions of both generations to possible increase and decrease of problems.

6. What is the responsibility of married sons to their aging parents? Of married daughters? Under what conditions should aged or ill parents be brought into the younger generation's home? Do you think differences of opinion on this between the spouses would cause much difficulty? Explain.

7. How much interaction would you like with your family after marriage? With your spouse's family? Do you think differences of opinion between the spouses concerning this would cause much difficulty? Explain.

17

Special Problems
in Mixed Marriages

There are certain social characteristics which tend to be associated with differences in important values concerning aspirations, concepts of masculinity–femininity, family roles, preferences for ways of spending leisure time, and ideas about the importance of the individual. The most important of the characteristics are social class, religion, and race. We would expect that marriages across these lines would present some special problems in establishing a new family culture.

SOME BACKGROUND CONSIDERATIONS

The kinds of problems encountered vary according to the nature of the mixed marriage. There appear to be three different sources from which most problems stem. The intensity and scope of the problems in an individual mixed marriage will be related to the degree to which the marriage involves these sources of strain: social pressures, cultural gap, and selectivity in mate choice.

Social Pressures

The influence of the norms in reducing the percentage of marriages across these lines was discussed in Chapter 10. Since the preferred pattern appears to be endogamous marriages (marriages within one's own social class, religion, and race), it can be expected that marriages which

370

violate the expectations will come under more social pressure than those which conform to them. Mixed religious marriages are less likely to have the wholehearted approval of minister, family, and friends than are intrafaith marriages, for example. Interracial marriages are likely to come under even greater pressure than are the interfaith marriages.

Although in the individual case the amount of pressure varies, as a group these marriages are more likely to experience the special problem of combatting negative evaluations while attempting to build a positive image of their relationship. When everyone is pulling with you it is easier to develop supportive relationships and to withstand hardships than when there are either reservations or an active opposition to the new marriage.

Cultural Gap

Mixed marriages are also likely to indicate differences in cultural background so that value conflict between husband and wife is more probable. Most marriages will occasionally experience value conflicts between spouses, between parents and children, and/or between one or both spouses and the in-laws. It would be surprising, indeed, if all family members were so similar that they always saw things from the same perspective and valued the same goals—both in the same hierarchy of importance. Such a situation, if it ever existed, would perhaps produce harmony—but also boredom.

Some values, however, form the nucleus of a cultural base. They are important elements in the self-concept and provide a major source for a person's sense of identity. The person who says with pride, "I am Italian-American, Catholic, and the best bricklayer in town," is not only identifying himself but saying to all who care to hear that he has a certain group of values which provide him with a perspective from which to observe, evaluate, and react to many different things. Generally, this man will be married to an Italian-American, Catholic woman who sees bricklaying as a good occupation. They will have friends who are Italian-American, Catholic, and who pursue similar occupations. They will share many values, aspirations, prejudices, and ways of expressing their anger, their joys, and their sorrows. They may differ on a number of things, but their broad orientations toward life will be understandable to each other and provide a shared cultural base within which differences can be either fought over, accepted, or resolved.

Within this shared culture, the husband and wife may grow to love each other more and more; or they may grow to hate each other, and eventually break up their marriage. If conflict exists in these shared-culture (endogamous) marriages, it is not likely to be a conflict of basic values, but of personalities, from the external pressures they are unable to cope with, from failure to fulfill expectations both spouses fundamentally agree upon, or as a result of the shared values themselves being ill-suited for successful family life.

When mixed marriages combine people from vastly different cultural backgrounds, they are still subject to the same kinds of conflict as the endogamous couple. But in addition they may perceive the external pressures differently, hold different expectations, and differ in their concepts of successful family life. All of these differences, stemming from a cultural gap between them, make it more difficult to build a shared culture within which they can cope with everyday problems.

Selectivity

As mentioned above, there are social pressures influencing people to marry within their own cultural groups. These are probably strong enough to produce some selectivity among those who marry out. Even though the sociologist can establish differences in values according to social class position, religious affiliation, racial and ethnic group membership, there is also wide within-group variation. There are differences in degree to which an individual person has identified with a particular group and absorbed its values. One person's unique experience and reaction to his particular family culture may make him more similar to someone from a different social context than he is to people from his own background. The Jewish female who is highly emancipated from her own family and religion, for example, may be more compatible in many ways with a Unitarian Gentile male than with an Orthodox Jewish male.

The selectivity among those who enter mixed marriages perhaps operates to bring together couples who are less identified with their own cultural background and are more mature so that the potential cultural gap is reduced and their ability to cope with their differences is increased. It also tends to bring together those who are less influenced by the social norms and perhaps less affected by the social pressures against them. On the other hand, it may bring together some who are acting out rebellious feelings against family or society in general, who may be less able to find satisfaction in any marital relationship, let alone one which combines negative social pressures with a cultural gap between spouses.

The interplay among social pressures, the potential cultural gap, and the selectivity process probably produces wide differences in probability for success for any given mixed marriage. The relative influence of each of these on different kinds of cross-class, interfaith, and interracial marriages will be discussed below.

INTERCLASS MARRIAGES

Marriages in the extreme class positions (upper-upper and lower-lower) are very likely to combine persons from the same class. Most of the interclass marriages occur across adjacent occupational strata within the broad middle and working classes. Few studies have been specifically directed toward the effect of class differences on marital adjustment. Several suggest that *similar family backgrounds* are conducive to marital success, and presumably the probability of family similarity would be greater if the social class backgrounds were similar.

At least one study presents evidence that the greater the difference between socioeconomic position of the spouses at the time of marriage, the lower the percentage of spouses with good marital adjustment scores (Roth and Peck, 1951). This was not a test of social class *background* differences however, since a number of the respondents were socially mobile compared to the socioeconomic position of their parents. College education appeared to be the main way of achieving the mobility, since this was mainly a college educated sample. College education itself instills new values and shakes up old ones. In cases of upward mobility it may be that marriage to a person in the new class position is more conducive to satisfaction than similarity of backgrounds. From a value framework, it would be expected that it is the similarity of values *at the time the marriage interaction is taking place* which is important to marital success, no matter when the values were acquired.

Direction of the Difference

Not all mixtures would even theoretically be expected to lead to trouble. Some mixtures may combine conflicting expectations for marital roles in such a way that both partners find the actual situation better than they dared hope. Nearly all studies show that middle class marriages are more satisfactory to the persons involved and more stable than lower class marriages. The stability of society in the middle and upper class strata contributes considerably to this difference. It would be expected, then, that the marriage of a lower class woman to a middle class man would increase *her* marital satisfaction, even though it may lower his. There is practically no research which bears on the relationship between the direction of the cross-class marriage and marital satisfaction. Considering the class differences in family values and stability, however, we can hypothesize the effect of the direction.

Since it is the man who establishes the family's position in society through his occupation, the woman marrying up into the middle class marries into a more stable economic position more supportive of marital success. The middle class woman who marries down into a lower class position, however, moves into a less stable condition (see Udry, 1966, pp. 326–28). This is considering only the social stability contributed by the more secure occupations in the middle class and has reference to the *current* socioeconomic position of the male rather than his background. When the relationship is considered, the marriage and family norms supported in the middle class appear more advantageous to the female than those associated with the lower classes. Where both partners have absorbed the expectations associated with their respective social class backgrounds, the combination of middle class man and lower class woman would seem more advantageous than the other way around. The ideas of equality between husband and wife, the attitudes toward marital sex, the substitution of verbal manipulation for physical violence, expectations for mutual sharing of leisure time, all would provide a more satisfying marital experience than the lower class woman would expect.

On the other hand, if the middle class expectations are carried by the woman into marriage with a lower class man, she is almost sure to get less than she expected as far as status, companionship, and sexual consideration are concerned. This generalization would only be expected to hold if the class-associated norms were still strongly held at the time of marriage.

Effect of Education. Education as one indicator of social class is also associated with marital success. The more education one has, whether male or female, the greater the probability of marital satisfaction. This finding is consistent across many studies. Theoretically one would expect that the more equal the spouses are in educational level, the more satisfying would be the relationships. Communication should be easier and interests more similar.

Research tends to support the conclusion that marital satisfaction is higher when the spouses are roughly of the same educational level (Blood and Wolfe, 1960, p. 256). Many studies, however, show that marital stability (lack of divorce) and marital satisfaction both go up with the educational level of the person one marries. From this it may be conjectured that marriage to a more highly educated spouse improves one's own probability of happiness, although it may decrease that of the more highly educated spouse from what he may have expected from marriage to one of equal education.[1]

Again the direction of the difference is *seen to be* important by many

---

[1] Komarovsky's study (1964) of working class marriages provides some indication that high school education of one of the spouses improves communication and companionship in the marriage.

college students, even though there is little evidence to support its *actual* importance for this group. The authors' Purdue studies have consistently shown that the majority of student respondents think that spouses should be of equal educational achievement. Where there is a difference desired, however, the direction overwhelmingly favors the husband having more education. Support for the husband's feelings of masculinity appears to be the reason for the anxiety of many students about departures from equality of the kind where the wife has more education.

Education, however, does not produce similar values in all who are exposed to it. This is quite evident from the variation in student responses to ideas of masculinity, femininity, marital roles, premarital sex, and so on. One college educated student with a liberal humanitarian value system married to another with a value system supporting personal success at any cost, may have as severe a value conflict at the base of their relationship as any combination of extremely different educational levels.

Once formed, cross-class marriages are not likely to experience great social pressure except perhaps from the families. They are not usually visible and therefore are not likely to be noticed by new friends and acquaintances. The cultural gap is probably more important in these marriages than the social pressure. To what extent selectivity may mitigate the effect of the cultural differences is not known.

INTERFAITH MARRIAGES

Interfaith marriages heighten the probability of a cultural gap between the spouses. Depending upon what religions are combined, they may also be subject to strong social pressures long after the marriage has been consummated. The extent of the value differences and amount of social pressure would be expected to be related to the severity of marital problems. Unfortunately, there is little research which has investigated these aspects of the interfaith marriage. From the value relevance framework, however, we can hypothesize that marital conflict stemming from an interfaith mixture would be more severe:

1. The deeper the commitment of each spouse to his own religion
2. The wider the discrepancy between the belief systems, and the more areas of behavior these beliefs affect
3. The stronger the support of the parental families for the separate religious affiliations of the spouses
4. The more frequent and close the interaction between the spouses and their parental families who support the separate religions

5. The more the religious affiliation is associated with personal and family identity, that is, the more the assertion, "I am a Catholic" or "I am a Jew" implies a definition of one's self, one's family, and one's heritage rather than just one's beliefs or one's church membership

6. To the extent that there have been no other family members involved in a successful mixed marriage

At least theoretically it is impossible to say that interfaith marriages, per se, are either bad or good for marital satisfaction. It depends upon what is being mixed and how easily the separate elements can become homogenized. If two people are only minimally identified with their separate religions, if the beliefs are not far apart to begin with, and if the families have no emotional stake in the child continuing in the same religion, there should be little trouble resulting from the mixed marriage. These couples may become increasingly more indifferent to any religious participation. They may both choose the church affiliation of the spouse with the strongest commitment, or agree on a third church in which both feel comfortable, which is geographically convenient, or to which some of their friends belong. In any case it is no longer a mixed marriage.

In cases where the spouses may have disassociated themselves from religious beliefs to which their families are still strongly attached, the major problems may be in-law difficulties, especially when children enter the picture. Even though these couples may resolve their conflicts between themselves, the continual disapproval of the parental families may cause feelings of doubt, divided loyalty, and dissatisfaction. Many devout parents interpret the child's desertion of their faith as a repudiation of them also, adding yet another element to the intergenerational conflict.

Characteristics of the Intermarried

Selectivity in choice of mate appears to keep many couples with the greatest potential for cultural gap in religious beliefs from marrying in the first place. Several studies show that those who contract interfaith marriages are likely to be older than usual at the time of marriage, are emancipated from their families, have families which were not strongly religious, and report rather tenuous ties with their families when young (Burchinal and Chancellor, 1962; Heiss, 1960a). All of these characteristics describe a population within which the pressure from parental families would be decreased and religion would not be of primary importance.

There are other characteristics, however, which would suggest a higher potential for marital problems whether or not religion was an issue. The intermarried include, along with a higher percentage of older couples, a higher percentage of the very young at time of marriage. These are more likely to involve the disapproval of parents as much because of young age as because of the religious intermarriage. They perhaps include some rebellious youths who marry *because* of parental disapproval.

Some are not choices but the result of unexpected developments in the relationship. Interfaith marriages appear to include a higher proportion of premarital pregnancies than do intrafaith marriages (Blood, 1969, p. 74; Christensen and Barber, 1967). Premarital pregnancy has already been shown to be related to marital disruption.

Some authors have suggested other motives for intermarriage which would spell trouble for a marital relationship no matter who the partner was (see Blood, 1969, pp. 74–76). Among these are: (1) self-hate, in which an individual has a psychological need to degrade himself by marrying someone he perceives as inferior; (2) rebellion against the parents, in which the marriage is undertaken more to hurt the parents than because of an emotional attachment to the mate; and (3) rebellion against society, in which dismay over prejudices in one's own group leads the individual to proclaim his liberalism by marrying a member of the minority group discriminated against.[2]

Evidence of these motives for interfaith marriages come mainly from clinical studies, so there is no way of estimating their frequency. Motives for marriage such as these would put strains on any marital relationship, regardless of the religious affiliation of the spouses.

Many of the interfaith marriages, however, are the result of an emotional relationship developing between two people before the religious question became an issue. They just enjoy each other's company without intending to "fall in love." After the emotional attachment develops, it is easier to discount the importance of the difference in religious beliefs. For some of these, the religious difference will make no difference; for some, it may only become a tender spot in the relationship that they gently avoid touching; for some, it will introduce occasional conflict while children are being reared; but for others, it will become a major irritant which affects many of their evaluations of each other.

Catholic–Protestant Marriage

The relationship between interfaith marriage and divorce has been thoroughly investigated by many researchers, with inconclusive results. Only two states routinely record the religious affiliation of marriage license applicants.[3] Studies outside these states, then, must rely on samples which

[2] For illustrations of a variety of personal motivations for intermarriages see Albert I. Gordon (1966).

[3] Iowa and Indiana.

may or may not adequately represent any given population. Results tend to vary according to method of sampling and geographical location, but all show a slightly higher divorce rate for the intermarried.

Burchinal and Chancellor (1963) have provided perhaps the most definitive study to date of interfaith divorce rates using data from the whole state of Iowa. Their data were taken from marriage and divorce records between the years 1953 and 1959. Marriage survival rates for the inter- and intrafaith marriages range from 77.6 for the Catholic mixed marriage to 96.2 for the Catholic–Catholic marriage. Some mixed Protestant marriages showed a higher survival rate than some homogamous Protestant marriages.

The survival rates of marriages of Catholics combined with specific Protestant denominations provide some support for one of our hypotheses stated earlier in this chapter: Problems will be greater the wider the discrepancy between belief systems. Figure 17–1 shows that the survival

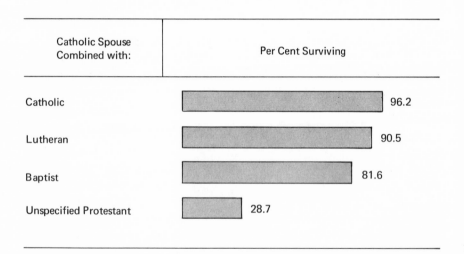

Fig. 17–1. Marriage survival rates of selected mixtures involving Catholics. (Adapted from Burchinal and Chancellor, 1963, Table 5, p. 360.)

rate dropped only about 5 per cent from the Catholic–Catholic high of 96.2 to the Catholic–Lutheran combination—both "high church" orientations. It dropped 14 per cent when the Catholic was combined with a Baptist—a "low church" orientation; and 67 per cent when the combination was between a Catholic and one who belonged to no church at all (unspecified Protestant). The survival rate for this mixture was only 28.7. The differences in belief system are no doubt much greater between a

Catholic and one who is not religiously oriented at all than between any combination of persons both of whom have some religious orientation albeit different ones.

Table 17–1 shows a comparison of survival rates of the intermarried with those of the intramarried for three status positions when the bride

Table 17–1

Selected Marriage Survival Rates by Religious Type, Husband Status, and Age of Bride

Religious Type	Age of Bride	Per Cent Surviving		
		Husband Status		
		High	Middle	Low
Both Catholic	over 20	99.4	97.6	95.5
	under 20	97.2	92.6	88.3
Both Protestant	over 20	96.3	92.0	83.1
	under 20	93.2	81.5	68.1
Catholic–Protestant	over 20	91.0	86.1	77.6
	under 20	85.5	71.2	60.3

SOURCE: Adapted from Burchinal and Chancellor, "Survival Rates Among Religiously Homogamous and Interreligious Marriages," *Social Forces* 41 (May, 1963), Table 2, p. 357.

is either over or under twenty years of age. There is relatively little difference in rate among those marriages where the husband is of a high status, whether or not the marriage is religiously mixed or whether the bride is over or under twenty. If one compares the survival rates across the status categories, it becomes apparent that stability decreases much more rapidly for marriages involving the younger brides as status of husband declines, regardless of religious mixture. When a low status husband is combined with a wife under twenty in a Catholic–Protestant marriage, for example, the survival rate drops to 60.3 per cent from a high of 95.5 per cent for the homogamous Catholic marriage involving a bride over twenty. The comparable difference for the middle status position is 26.4 per cent compared to only 13.9 per cent among the high status couples. Evidently, for those vulnerable couples involving low status husbands and teen-age brides the religious difference is likely to be just one of too many problems with which they have to cope.

Divorce rates are probably not a good indicator of conflict stemming from religious differences. Some of the characteristics of the intermarried suggest that religion would be of small importance, others indicate hazardous marriages on other grounds. Some devout couples who may be expected to have the greatest difficulty from the religious difference may keep the marriage intact solely because both their churches condemn divorce. Divorce rates tell us little of the variation in marital satisfaction associated with religious mixtures. Again, the results of studies attempting to trace this relationship are inconclusive. From our beginning hypotheses we would expect them to be. It is not the intermarriage, per se, which would cause the difficulty but the extent to which the intermarriage indicates a wide discrepancy in strongly held value systems, different group identifications, customs, rituals, and the degree to which the parental families prolong and reinforce the potential for conflict between the spouses. Research to date has not specifically investigated these factors.

Jewish–Gentile Mixtures

Jewish–Gentile marriages meet more overt resistance on the whole than other interfaith mixtures. This is especially true of the Jewish community which sees intermarriage as a threat to Jewish identity. Actually there are relatively few of these marriages, although there is a wide geographical variation in percentage of Jews who intermarry (Blood, 1969, p. 86). The predictions that Jews would intermarry at a greatly accelerated pace as ritualistic observances of Jewish tradition and customs declined have not materialized (Gordon, 1966, pp. 174–203). There has been an increase but it appears to be a modest and gradual one.

The Jewish–Gentile mixture, in general, combines not only differences in religious beliefs, but differences in food rituals, Holy Days, and many other areas of behavior. The Jewish religion is to a notable extent a family religion and an affirmation of Jewish identity as well as of beliefs. The reaction of the Jewish family, then, to the intermarriage of their children is likely to be extreme, since marriage to a non-Jew is likely to be taken as a rejection of the family and the Jewish community—as well as rejection of the norms against intermarriage (Mayer, 1961).

The marriages which do take place seem to be mainly among those who have already departed from many of the Orthodox Jewish traditions. Gordon suggests that there is a negative correlation between the observance of Jewish ritual and practices, identification with the Synagogue, and the degree of intermarriage (Gordon, 1966, p. 207). To the extent that this disassociation from Jewish tradition describes the Jewish partner, marital conflict stemming from the religious difference should decrease. There is evidence, however, that Jewish–Gentile marriages are somewhat more hazardous than the Catholic–Protestant mixture (Blood, 1969, p. 87; Zimmerman and Cervantes, 1960, pp. 153–54).

Effect of Prejudice. The Jewish–Gentile intermarriage introduces a new element to the interfaith mixture. In some parts of our society prejudice and discrimination exist against the Jew. Although an intermarriage does not change this for the male, it may change the experiences of the female. A Jewish woman married to a Gentile man may lose her identification as a Jew as she takes a Gentile name. If she desires she can become absorbed in the Gentile world and thereby remove herself and her children from whatever discrimination exists. The situation is reversed for the Gentile woman as she takes the name of her Jewish husband. She may find herself and her children targets of discrimination for which her Gentile background had not prepared her.

This possible consequence of intermarriage is not the result of value conflict between the spouses but the result of prejudices in our society. The effect of prejudice on the marriage of course varies, depending upon the part of the society in which the couple settles and the amount of discrimination that exists there.

INTERRACIAL MARRIAGES

Interracial marriages come under stronger normative control than any of the other mixtures. There are, consequently, fewer of them and they are under more severe social pressure than either the interclass or interreligious marriages. One of the reasons for the greater pressure is that they are more visible than other mixtures. The racial characteristics are easily identifiable and existing prejudices make one alert to these infractions against the norms of racial endogamy.

Interracial marriages may not indicate widely different value systems unless they also combine interclass or interfaith mixtures. Black–white values, for example, are thought to be quite similar when the social class backgrounds are the same.

Negro–Caucasian Marriages

Even though the value systems may be similar when the Negro–Caucasian marriage is endogamous in class and religion, personal identification with race is likely to be quite strong and racial prejudice may then result in difficulties. Parental pressure against the marriage is generally quite severe, especially from the white family. Pressure from the black family tends to be negative, but acceptance has been more easily achieved for the white spouse by the black family than the other way around. This may not remain the case as a more positive racial identity develops among blacks.

The discrimination to which the black person is subjected becomes more intense following a marriage to a white spouse in many parts of our society. The white spouse becomes black as far as community participation and discrimination are concerned. Many mixed couples learn to use the differential treatment of the races to their own advantage. The black spouse will take the car to be repaired because he is not as likely to have the bill padded by the mechanic as is a white person. The white spouse will make the contacts for housing because he is likely to be shown a wider selection of more desirable homes or apartments (Larsson, 1965).

The effect of discrimination on the marital interaction will depend upon the maturity of the partners and the strength of the relationship. It is sometimes difficult not to blame the spouse when job loss, housing discrimination, the turning away of friends and perhaps family follow marriage to that person. Either spouse is likely to feel guilty and responsible for the suffering of the other, with varying consequences for the interaction.

Children from Negro–Caucasian marriages may have difficulty in establishing a racial identity. In most cases, however, they are absorbed into the black community and tend to identify themselves as racially Negro.

Stability. Because of the long history of legal prohibition in some states of these marriages, and restrictions in others against recording race on marriage licenses, statistics on their stability have been largely lacking. In only three states—Hawaii, Michigan, and Nebraska—is there any official published record of Negro–Caucasian marriages (Heer, 1966). Although it is generally thought that the divorce rate is higher among them, there is little evidence to either support or to refute this assumption.

Non-white marriages are less stable than white marriages even at the same educational and occupational levels. Since the highest percentage of non-whites are black, the instability undoubtedly is related to his more precarious integration into the economic system and the discrimination to which he is exposed. The mixed marriage shares this social milieu and discrimination pattern with the intra-black marriage. The consequences for the marriage are probably much more related to the social pressures against them than to anything intrinsic to the mixture.

From a few rather small studies of marital relationships in racially mixed marriages there is evidence that many of them involve religious mixtures as well (Barnett, 1969). Earlier studies suggested that they also involved social class differences but more recent studies seem to support similar class backgrounds (Heer, 1966). To the extent, however, that value conflict may be introduced by differing backgrounds we would expect the resulting marital disturbance to be more the result of this factor than of the racial differences.

There appears to be an increase in Negro–Caucasian marriages at the higher educational level. This would be expected since integration on college campuses allows interracial dating to occur. Stability and satisfaction from these marriages should in time come to resemble the pattern of other marriages combining spouses of equal, high educational attainment. To the extent that the educational attainment moves them into social groups where discrimination is at a minimum, marital satisfaction should vary in terms of factors other than race.

Oriental–Caucasian Marriages

Oriental–Caucasian marriages have in the past come under social pressures on the West Coast much as Negro–Caucasian marriages have in the South and Midwest. It was only in the late 1940's that legal restrictions were lifted against them in California. These mixtures involve sub-cultural differences to a much greater extent than black–white marriages. Ideas of marital roles and the male–female relationship differ greatly. They are also likely to involve religious differences, food differences, and perhaps language differences. A study in Chicago of the marriage relationships of American servicemen and Japanese war brides, however, indicates that these are quite stable and satisfying marriages (Strauss, 1954). It would be expected that marriages combining Oriental women with American men would be more satisfying than the other way around. The American man would gain a more attentive and dutiful wife than he would have expected from American norms and the Oriental woman more freedom and equality of treatment than she would have expected from Oriental norms. Each should be pleased with the direction of their differences.

Further support for the importance of the direction of the difference comes from studies in Hawaii where intermarriages are much more acceptable than in other states. Cheng and Yamamura (1957) found that marriages between a Caucasian woman and non-Caucasian man were much more likely to end in divorce (49.3 divorces per 100 marriages) than were marriages between a Caucasian man and Oriental woman (27.4 divorces per 100 marriages).

A later study confirmed these findings. Lind (1964) found that the divorce rate went as high as 57.5 per cent when a Japanese man was paired with a Caucasian woman and dropped to 20.1 per cent when the combination was between a Caucasian man and a Puerto Rican woman. In fact this latter mixture produced a lower divorce rate than intramarriages for both Caucasians and Puerto Ricans. The Spanish cultures represented by Puerto Ricans resemble the Orientals in supporting submissive and family-dominated roles for women.

Conditions Intensifying Stress

The conflicts and satisfactions stemming from interracial marriages are much more complex than our negative sanctions against them would have us believe. Although empirical evidence concerning the extent and kind of marital disturbance in interracial marriages is sparse, it is possible to hypothesize the conditions which would intensify the stress. Strain from social pressures and discrimination should be more severe: (1) the more visible the mixture; (2) the stronger the social norms against the mixture; and (3) the greater the resistance of parental families to the mixture.

Stress from value conflict should be intensified: (1) to the extent that the racial differences imply differences in language, religion, traditions, and family values; (2) to the degree that the direction of the value differences keep the individuals from realizing expected satisfactions from the marital relationship; and (3) the more frequent and necessary are interactions with families supporting the cultural differences.

Some intermarriages will involve few of these conditions. Others will combine many of them. The more of these conditions a particular marriage combines, the stronger the marriage relationship will have to be to withstand the pressures. The kind of problem more likely to become part of the marital interaction of each type of mixture is presented below.

		Social Pressure		
Type of Mixture	Cultural Gap	Family	Prejudice	Selectivity
Interclass	x°			
Interreligious				
Mixed Protestant	x			
Catholic–Protestant	x	x		x
Jewish–Gentile	x	x	x	x
Interracial				
Negro–Caucasian		x	x	x
Oriental–Caucasian	x°	x		

° Direction of difference important.

OTHER NON-NORMATIVE MARRIAGES

The effect of departures from normative expectations on the marital relationship can be more easily seen from departures which have little to do with class, religion, or racial identities. We have some general norms governing the matching of marital partners which suggest that the husband should be taller, slightly older, and physically stronger than his wife. When matings depart drastically from these expectations, we do not merely note the deviation, but generally impute something to the relationship because the physical characteristics upset our expectations.

When we see a small, slightly built man married to a tall, heavy woman, we are likely to make some evaluation about the power structure in the relationship. When we see a young man married to a much older woman we are inclined to impugn the motives of the young man and the sanity of the older woman. The same is true of a young woman married to a much older man—"She's waiting for him to die, and she won't have long to wait"—"How can he fool himself into thinking she cares for him?" Probably every adult in our society, including those who depart from them, is aware of these general expectations.

Pair Identity

One of the processes at work in early marriage is that of building a *pair identification*—that is, building a concept of the marital pair as a unit in much the same way an individual builds a concept of self. This is built within the relationship itself to the degree that each person redefines himself relative to his spouse and shifts his orientation from a single one to a paired one. Thus, as this change occurs, he less often says "*my* car," "*my* house," or "*I* am going to do thus and so," and more often refers to "*our* car," "*our* house," "*we* are going to do thus and so."

Part of the input used to develop this pair image comes from the evaluations of others. To the extent that a couple fits the normative expectations of their particular social context, the evalutions should reinforce the idea that they are an "ideal couple." Their friends and acquaintances would be likely to assume that the total relationship also fits the normative expectations and reflect this to them. They would not then be forced to try to counteract negative evaluations either for themselves or for others.

When there are departures, however, the evaluations are more likely to reflect assumptions about the power structure of the relationship. These may be mainly humorous comments, but they still convey the assumption being made and have an effect on the developing pair identity. Neutral comments are more likely to be interpreted as pair evaluations. The man who refuses an invitation to a "stag" party, for example, may receive the comment, "Wife won't let you come, huh?" If he is not sensitive to this reference to his power position in the relationship he is not likely to take it as a serious evaluation. He may laugh or agree: "Yeah, that's right, she can't live even a night without me." If, however, he thinks it may be a serious evaluation he may react angrily, resentfully, or in some way attempt to deny the evaluation. Whatever he does, the reflected evaluation of his marriage relationship will influence the way he interprets the interaction between himself and his wife. He may interpret even the smallest suggestion from her as an attempt to control, and react violently against it or accept it as proof that he really is weak and sub-

missive. The reflected evaluations in this way affect the development of
the habits of interaction and the pair concept. The effects may vary, but
the relationship has been affected. The husband in such a case may become a tyrant, ruling his wife absolutely, or he may become a "Mr. Milque-
toast." He may have become neither of these in a different relationship
which does not call forth such assumptions.

Not all non-normative marriages are equally affected. Some are non-
normative in ways that are not visible and so do not call forth the evaluations in repetitive interactions. In others, the spouses have self-concepts
which are not sensitive to the assumptions about the relationship and
therefore do not react defensively. The external intrusions into the relationship are there, nevertheless, carrying the potential for influencing the
development of the pair concept.

The same processes operating in the visible non-normative marriage
operate in the other mixed marriages to the extent that the mixture is not
approved and is visible. The assumptions may include the nature of the
relationship, motivations for marriage, and personalities of the spouses.
To the extent that the assumptions are repetitive and known to the spouses
they have the potential for affecting the interaction and the evaluation of
that interaction.

THE PRINCIPLE OF VALUE RELEVANCE

The importance of values in the success of mixed marriages is easily
seen. It is not the mixture, per se, which causes difficulty; it is the extent
to which the mixture indicates that the spouses hold different values which
are important to them. The difficulties faced by participants in a mixed
marriage also vary, according to the degree to which the marriage is in
conflict with strong values held by the social groups within which they
must interact. A black–white marriage, for example, will, in general,
experience fewer difficulties if it is imbedded in the entertainment world,
or in a highly educated, liberal academic setting, than if it is located in a
middle class neighborhood in one of the states of the deep South.

Mixed marriages are no more static than other marital arrangements.
The degree of satisfaction may vary through the life cycle as new experiences reveal unforeseen areas of conflict or consensus. This is true of every
marriage, but the number and quality of potential conflict areas change
with the similarity and dissimilarity of social contexts in which the individuals were reared.

The mixture of characteristics such as race, nationality, ethnic group,
and religion merely heightens the probability that the social context differences will have produced individuals who differ in values. The value

differences may range from the very broad perceptions of the world—man's place in it and the meaning of life itself—to the more specific habits of communication, orderliness, and food preparation. The degree of success will depend in part upon the depth and range of the differences, in part on the experiences which bring the differences to light, in part on the strength of the emotional commitment between the spouses, and in part on their ability to cope with the differences in such a way that the self-concepts of each are supported.

SUMMARY

Among the special problems more likely to confront interclass, interfaith, interracial, and other non-normative marriages in building a new, shared family culture are adverse social pressures and a cultural gap between spouses. These may be either alleviated or made more difficult by the selectivity process, whereby those who resist the pressure against mixed marriages have special qualities to start with that will either aid or hinder their coping with the situation.

Many of the values associated with social class, religion, and race involve basic orientations toward the world, one's place within it, the relationship between the sexes, and expectations for family interaction. When a mixed marriage indicates that the spouses do, indeed, hold different perceptions at this basic level, the probability of conflict, misunderstanding, and marital disruption increases.

Some mixtures may be beneficial or not, depending upon the direction of the mixture. Although there is little evidence to either support or refute it, a combination in which the different values provide more than each person had expected from a marital relationship may prove highly satisfactory—an Oriental female married to an American male, for example.

Individual adherence to values associated with a particular social group varies tremendously, however. Theoretically, it would be expected that stress in a mixed marriage would increase to the extent that the mixture indicates large differences in language, beliefs, traditions, and value systems, to the extent that these differences prevent the individual from realizing the satisfaction he expected from marriage, and to the extent that there is strong resistance of the parental families to the mixture. Social pressure should be greater the stronger the norms are against the intermarriage and the more visible the mixture.

Non-normative marriages which are readily visible tend to call forth imputations about the motivation for marriage as well as about the relationship itself—such as the short man married to the large woman being thought of as "hen-pecked." To the degree that these imputations are repetitive and known to the spouses they have the potential for affecting the interaction and evaluation of that interaction.

The degree of satisfaction found in mixed marriages will depend in part on the depth and range of value differences, in part on the experiences which bring the differences to light, in part on the strength of the emotional commitment between the spouses, and in part on their ability to cope with the differences in such a way that the self-concepts of each are supported.

QUESTIONS AND PROJECTS

1. What are the conditions seen to heighten the stress associated with mixed marriages? What kinds of mixtures do you think would involve more of these conditions? Explain.

2. Do you think interclass marriages will increase or decrease in the next twenty-five years? Interfaith marriages? Interracial marriages? Discuss.

3. Do you think mixed marriages which occur now will be more, or less, satisfactory than those occurring in the last twenty-five years? Discuss.

4. Consider the solutions to an interfaith marriage such as both going to his own church, neither going to any church, and so on. Which solution do you think would be most conducive to reducing conflict? Under what conditions would this solution be most likely to work?

5. Considering the interclass, interfaith, and interracial mixtures, in which ones do you think the direction of the mixture (example: husband Oriental, wife Caucasian; or wife Oriental, husband Caucasian) would make a difference? Discuss.

6. What other mixtures, such as political or geographical mixtures, do you think may have the potential of heightening stress in a marriage? Discuss.

7. Do you think love could develop between two people holding opposing political beliefs? Opposite views toward racial questions? What conditions may be conducive to this? What conditions operate against it? Do you think opposing beliefs like these would make any difference after marriage? Why or why not?

8. Make a list of non-normative marriages other than those mentioned in this chapter. Show how the relationships may be affected by social pressures. What kinds of things differentiate between those affected and those not affected by these pressures?

9. Discuss the relationship between pair identity and the self-concept.

18
Childbearing

Childbearing is a part of the marital interaction process at some time for most couples in our society. It enters that interaction as a result of accident or intent. It may appear unexpectedly and unwanted, as at a time of particular financial stress or when it interrupts plans for education, career, or just the enjoyment of the husband–wife relationship. It may enter unexpectedly causing some readjustments of goals, but for the most part is welcomed. It may be entirely expected, welcomed, and occur after careful planning and waiting. For some the desired child does not appear when wanted and there is a long period of anxious waiting before the first conception. For others, it does not come at all, again either by intent or because of some impairment of the reproductive functions.

There is considerable evidence that the effect of childbearing on marital adjustment is related to the ability to control the birth process so that the desired number of children arrive when they are wanted (Christensen, 1968). Perhaps this is just an extension of other findings that a feeling of having control over one's life is associated with better adjustment in general.

VALUES CONCERNING FAMILY SIZE

Individual attitudes concerning the number of children one wants are influenced partially by social norms. During the 1940's the ideal family was seen by most Americans to contain two children. By 1955 this ideal family had increased to four children. This desired number held steady, for the most part, throughout most of the 1960's (Freedman et al., 1959; Whelpton et al., 1966).

A mid-1960 study conducted by the authors showed that college students also were more likely to desire four children in their future families than any other number. The modal response for both males and females of the 513 students in the sample was four. Thirty-two per cent of the males and 33 per cent of the females chose that number. Three children came a close second (30 per cent and 29 per cent, respectively) and two children came next (22 per cent and 15 per cent) in their choices. Relatively few wanted either fewer than two or more than four children.

Changing Social Norms

During the late 1960's and early 1970's there has developed an increasingly strong public concern over the depletion and pollution of our natural resources and a recognition of the crucial role played by over-population in this so-called "environmental crisis" (Ehrlich, 1968). It is pointed out that at present growth rates by the year 2000 the world's present 3.5 billion people will increase to around 6 billion and the 200 million plus population of the United States will expand to about 300 million, with corresponding expansion in future centuries—unless population growth is checked. Population is seen as being already out of balance with resources, with the prospect for the future looking grim indeed. Some social analysts regard control of population as the most important item on the agenda for man's survival. As a consequence, strong movements for "zero population growth" have developed and for promotion of a "two-child family" norm. (Zero growth will require that the national average of children per family be brought down to approximately 2.3.) Many Americans today seem to be adopting these notions, as reflected in very recent declines in the birth rate.

Birth rate is not only a social problem in the broad sense, but it is also a factor that affects family size, and this in turn may affect the adjustment patterns of husbands and wives. As the desired number of children decreases, it might be expected that the spouses of large families may sense some discomfort in being out of line.

Family Size and Marital Adjustment

The influence of the social norms on satisfaction with one's own family size can perhaps be seen by the conflicting results from studies of the relationship between family size and marital adjustment. Lang (1932) found that in the early years of marriage those without children were the happiest, and after five years those with one or two were happier than those without any or more than two. In 1939, Burgess and Cottrell found that those with none or one child were better adjusted than those with two or more. In 1960, Blood and Wolfe (1960) found that women with three children were happier than those with fewer or more. These differences may reflect differences in samples tested or measures of adjustment used, but in view of the changes in ideal family size from the 1930's to the 1960's, the differences partially may be reflecting satisfaction from conforming to social norms. In the 1930's one could feel satisfied if childbearing was put off or if the number was held to one or two, but in the 1950's the social norms seemed to press young couples to begin their families early and not to stop at one and preferably not at two (Campbell, 1968).

Christensen and Philbrick (1952) clarified the relationship between family size and marital adjustment using a sample of married college students in the early 1960's. They found that on the whole marital adjustment went down as family size went up. This relationship held, however, only up to two children (couples with three or more children were too few in number to permit reliable comparisons); and it was noted that the negative relationship may have resulted in large part from the stresses and strains of parenthood during college attendance. When adjustment scores were compared with number desired *eventually* the relationship was a positive one, up to four children. Significantly lower marital adjustment scores were found for parents with unplanned children as compared with the all-planned group. The authors concluded that marital adjustment increases according to the ability of the couple to control fertility in line with their desires for a certain number of children.

The changes in ideal family size are reflected in the statistical changes that have taken place in childbearing. In the 1920's, those college educated women who were at the peak ages of reproduction completed their families with an average of 1.4 children per woman. One-third were childless. Twenty-four per cent more had only one child. College women who were at the peak age of childbearing in the 1950's had nearly three children per woman. Only about 11 per cent were childless. The same trend was evident for high school graduates but was less extreme. The average number of children increased from 1.8 to about 3, and childlessness was decreased from 24 per cent to 8 per cent (Campbell, 1968, p. 202).

Factors Influencing Individual Desires

Individual desires for children are influenced by other values as well. If a woman has many interests outside the family she is not as likely to want as large a family as the woman with interests more narrowly domestic. Rainwater (1965, p. 191) found that only 21 per cent of married women who were oriented to outside interests and to the companion wife role desired a large family, as compared to 72 per cent of those who were solely oriented to children and home.

The pressures of the social environment are also important factors on the desires for children as well as the timing of the first birth. Many couples report increasing pressure from friends and families if they wait "too long." Parents begin to long for grandchildren. Friends who are parents talk about how much the childless couple is missing. They may be discreetly or not so discreetly asked about their family plans.

Sometimes a childless wife begins to feel that she has little in common with her friends who have recently become mothers. She and her husband may have been in complete agreement that they would wait to begin their family until he finished college, or until they had a savings account built up. But confronted with continual conversation about babies and the "joys" of motherhood she may feel a sudden strong rise of her "maternal instincts" and begin to feel that she is being deprived of her "natural role" of motherhood. Her husband may be totally confused by what to him is an irrational, emotional reversal of values. They may both be surprised how quickly the "maternal instincts" subside if a move, a job, or new childless friends reduce this contact with the group of new mothers.

The number of children desired may change according to the sex of the children already born. It is generally thought that the ideal family should have both sexes represented. The college students polled by the authors seemed to indicate a strong preference for more boys than girls if an odd number of chlidren were desired, and a sex balance if an even number was chosen. A couple may desire three children until all three turn out to be girls, then increase the number wanted, hoping for a boy. There seems to be a tendency to stop the family with the preferred sex if both sexes are already represented. By stopping the family with a child that represents the desired sex, parents can, with luck, increase the proportion of the kind preferred. For example, if males are preferred and a family of three or four children desired, parents will be likely to stop with the third child if it is a boy but try again if it is a girl. Winston (1932) first suggested this phenomenon when he found a disproportionately high sex ratio among the last children of completed families, indicating a male preference and the possible use of birth control as a selective device. It does not determine what the sex of any particular child shall be, of course, but it may be used to exert some control over the sex proportion in the family and in the population.

Since the fit between desired and actual number of children as well as satisfaction with the spacing of them, seems more important to marital adjustment than any specific number or age distribution of children, it would appear to be beneficial that the husband and wife agree. There are practically no studies which show the effect on marital satisfaction if husband and wife disagree that they have too many or too few children. There are, however, indications that husband–wife agreement and communication are important in effectively controlling their family size.

FAMILY PLANNING

Family planning involves the ability to prevent the conception of children when they are not wanted and to have them when they are wanted. Since the collective decisions and behaviors of millions of individual couples have a profound effect on the society, the ability to effectively control births is of concern to everyone. As knowledge, technological advances, and public interest in this area have grown, Planned Parenthood clinics have mushroomed. These clinics have as their main goals the dissemination of information about the effects of overpopulation on the society, as well as the effects of over-reproduction within the individual family. They are concerned with aiding some couples to overcome sterility so they may have the children they desire and in aiding other couples to limit the number of children and to space them as desired.

The Control of Pregnancy

Until recent times, man has exercised little voluntary control over either family size or the general growth of population. Nature's controls have operated, in that high birth rates were usually accompanied by high death rates. In addition, some societies practiced infanticide (the killing of infants soon after birth) or resorted to crude means of inducing abortion. Though voluntary, both abortion and infanticide are means of holding down the population by inducing death after conception has taken place. As knowledge about reproduction has grown, however, it has become increasingly possible to interfere with this process by preventing the conception from occurring in the first place. The different methods used for birth control interrupt the reproductive cycle at different points— all prior to conception.

Conception. Life begins with the uniting of a sperm and an egg (ovum). This union usually takes place in one of the Fallopian tubes, after which the fertilized egg enters the uterus and attaches itself to the wall. Growth takes place by multiple cell division. Approximately nine months later the child is ready to be born.

The timing of conception is controlled primarily by the physiology of the female. Sperms can be released by the normal adult male at almost any time, while the releasing of an egg (ovulation) by the female is auto-

matic and happens only once each month. Furthermore, upwards of
200,000,000 sperms are released in each ejaculation (any one of which is
good for fertilization), while normally only one egg is involved in each
ovulation. This means that conception can only occur at, or about, the
time of ovulation.

Ovulation most generally takes place midway in the menstrual cycle.
Since the cycle usually runs about twenty-eight days, this would place
ovulation at approximately the fourteenth day from the beginning of each
preceding menstrual period. Sexual intercourse which takes place within
twenty-four, or even forty-eight, hours either before or after ovulation is
most likely to result in conception.

The "safe period" from the standpoint of birth control is just before
and just after menstruation. However, since women vary and are often
irregular in their menstrual patterns, it is not always possible to predict
the time of ovulation; hence the "safe period" may not be very safe. There
is no exact knowledge as to how long a sperm or an egg can survive in
the reproductive tract after it has been released. Medical opinion allows
about twenty-four hours for the egg to survive and nearly twice that long
for the sperm, though this latter estimate is less definite. Since less is
known concerning the length of time that a sperm can survive, the time
preceding ovulation is less "safe" than is the time following it.

Non-contraceptive Controls. Every method of birth control interferes
at some point with the process of conception by either non-contraceptive
or contraceptive methods. The non-contraceptive methods of birth control are those which rely solely upon personal controls over the sex act
in order to reduce the probability that the sperm will make contact with
the ovum. These include *abstinence*, which is of course the most reliable
if least acceptable of all the means of preventing pregnancy; the *rhythm
method*, which employs abstinence at that time of the month when the
female is most likely to conceive; and *coitus interruptus*, in which the
male withdraws before ejaculation so that the sperm are released outside
the woman's body. All of these call for self-control in either beginning
or completing the sex act.

When self-control alone is involved, reliability of the method for preventing conception declines. The rhythm method not only involves self-
control but a reliance on the "safe period" being safe, which is many times
questionable.

These are the only methods approved by the Catholic Church, with
the exception of the *douche*—especially viewed with approval when used
for "sanitary" rather than birth control purposes. The douche involves
rinsing the vagina with water or solutions containing disinfectants immediately after intercourse. This supposedly interferes with conception,

not by keeping the sperm from entering, but by washing them away before contact with the ovum can be made. The extremely short time period required for the sperm to enter the uterus, however, makes this a highly ineffective control.

Contraceptive Controls. The mechanical or chemical devices which interfere with conception without interfering with the timing or completion of the sex act can be categorized as: (1) those which prevent the male sperm from entering either the vagina or the uterus of the female; (2) those which produce a lethal environment for the male sperm; (3) those which prevent the female from ovulating; and (4) those which prevent the fertilized ovum from imbedding itself in the wall of the uterus.

The most widely known contraceptive device which prevents the sperm from entering the female is the *condom*. It is a male contraceptive in that the male must take the responsibility for placing the condom (a sheath usually made of rubber) over the erect penis before entering. The sperm are released into the sheath rather than into the female.

The contraceptive devices which prevent the sperm from entering the uterus after they are released in the vagina are female contraceptives; that is, it is the female who takes the responsibility for their use. These include the *diaphragm* and the *cervical cap* which place a mechanical barrier over the opening of the cervix and thus prevent the sperm from entering. Both devices require the services of a physician. The diaphragm is to be used with a spermacidal jelly which destroys any sperm that may pass the barrier. It may be routinely inserted and must remain in place at least eight hours after coitus, therefore its use need not detract from the emotional or physical satisfaction of the love making.

Cervical caps are inserted by the physician and remain in place until removed by the physician. Periodic checks for infection or irritation are necessary. Not all women can use them and not all physicians recommend them.

Various spermacidal *jellies, creams, foams, tablets*, and *suppositories* are designed to be used alone. These are available over the counter, without prescription. They are intended to interfere with the conception process by immobilizing or destroying the sperm. Effectiveness depends partly on the timing of the application so that sufficient time is allowed for coverage and not so much time elapses that the chemical action is dissipated. These vary considerably in effectiveness. Johnson and Masters (1962) found that some of these contraceptive materials failed to distribute themselves evenly and that effectiveness was questionable with some women and under certain conditions.

The newer *oral contraceptives* operate to prevent ovulation in the female. Indications are that this method of controlling pregnancy is growing rapidly, especially among the younger and better educated women (Ryder and Westoff, 1966). They are 100 per cent effective when taken according to direction (Behrman and Gosling, 1966, pp. 403–404). Since there are side effects for some women and research and improvement are still underway, it is extremely important that they be prescribed by and taken under the supervision of a physician. It is absolutely essential that "the pill" be taken every day for the prescribed number of days or ovulation may occur. They do not lower the fertility of the woman when use is discontinued. In fact, they are sometimes used therapeutically to heighten the probability of pregnancy occurring in some cases of subfecundity. Since they also have the effect of regulating the menstrual cycle, they may aid in more effective use of the rhythm method.

Advances in technology have reintroduced the use of intrauterine devices (IUD's) which had been discontinued earlier because of dangerous side effects. This method consists of an object, made in a variety of shapes, inserted into the uterus by a physician. Although the precise mechanism by which this prevents pregnancy is not known, it appears to prevent the fertilized ovum from implanting itself in the uterine wall for further development. Once inserted it may be left in until pregnancy is desired. When removed the ability to conceive is not impaired. The main drawbacks to this method are that it is generally not recommended for women who have not had at least one pregnancy; occasionally the object is expelled without the woman's knowledge; and it sometimes causes pain during menstruation, especially when first placed. Although not 100 per cent effective, it is almost as reliable as the oral contraceptives and removes the necessity of remembering to take a pill every day.

Effectiveness of Family Planning

Studies indicate that almost 90 per cent of the married people in the United States approve of family planning (Chilman, 1968). In 1960, the second Growth of American Families Study showed that about 81 per cent of this national sample of 2,713 married white women were using or had used some form of birth control (Campbell, 1968). Most of the couples who had never used any birth control methods were below normal in their capacity to reproduce. Only 4 per cent of the couples were able to have more children and also said they had not used some form of birth control and did not intend to in the future. In spite of this widespread use of birth control, 60 per cent of the women with one or more children reported either that they had had some pregnancies earlier than they intended or had had more pregnancies than they or their husbands wanted (Campbell, 1968, p. 205).

Birth control mechanisms differ in their effectiveness and in the degree to which they invite human error. The couples who use them differ in their attitudes toward birth control, their confidence in their ability to control, their understanding of the devices and how they work, and in their ability to cooperate with and trust each other in family planning.

Use of Most Efficient Methods. The most efficient methods of birth control would be those which reduce the probability of both technological failure and human failure. Those methods which require self-control or interruption of the sex act can be expected to introduce more human failure, no matter how technologically sound the method itself. When these methods are combined with an indifferent attitude toward family planning or a lack of confidence in being able to effectively control pregnancy, the human failure becomes even more probable. Several factors appear to combine to make these least effective methods more prevalent in the lower classes.

There is little accurate knowledge in the lower classes about the process of conception. Because of this the methods which visibly prevent the male sperm from entering the female's body, or which immediately wash them out, seem more sensible than the more sophisticated methods. This, then, makes the condom, withdrawal, and the douche especially prominent among the lower class. These methods also fit psychologically with the antisex attitudes of many lower class women. The feelings of "dirtiness" or even revulsion associated with coming in contact with the male semen are allayed somewhat by having the condom intervening and by douching immediately afterwards. It also reaffirms their idea that sex is for the man's pleasure and so contraception should be his responsibility (Rainwater, 1960, pp. 125–66).

Used consistently and carefully the condom should be effective; however, the consistency varies with the husband's motivations for planning and his displeasure with the method. Many men complain that it interferes with their pleasure, or say that it may break anyway and that it doesn't hurt to "take a chance" every once in a while. One study in 1960 of low income urban families found that the main reasons for "accidents" while using birth control methods were, in order of frequency of response, "took a chance," "disliked the method," and "failure of the method" (Chilman, 1968, p. 216).

Other reasons for the prevalence of the least reliable methods in the lower class include the ease of obtaining them, the widespread knowledge about them, and their inexpensiveness (it costs nothing but self-control to withdraw before ejaculation or to douche immediately afterward). When methods other than douching, the condom, and withdrawal are used they are likely to be ones which are sold over the counter without pre-

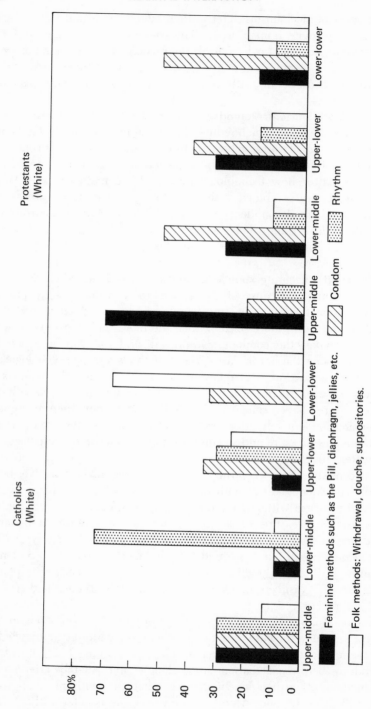

Fig. 18–1. Social class and religious influence on contraceptive choice. (Adapted from Rainwater, 1965, Table 7–7, p. 218.)

scriptions which have been heard about from families or friends. The cost of the physician's services and lack of knowledge about the cost of the methods he prescribes makes these more reliable methods practically inaccessible to lower income families.

Rainwater (1965), from his in-depth interviews with 409 men and women in 257 different marriages, has reported the influence that social class and religion have upon contraceptive choice. Figure 18–1 shows that among lower-lower class Catholics and Protestants alike the great majority rely on the condom, withdrawal, or the douche. Only among upper-middle class Protestants are the most reliable feminine techniques the preferred methods. Among Catholics, the rhythm method is the most prevalent one only in the lower-middle class. Upper-lower class blacks (not shown in the graph) resemble the upper-lower class white Protestants, with 80 per cent of them relying on either feminine methods or the condom. Lower-lower class blacks are more likely than either Catholic or Protestant lower-lower class whites to use feminine techniques and less likely to use the condom. They fall between the other two groups in use of withdrawal and douche.

Confidence in Ability To Plan. One factor in motivating people to inquire about more reliable methods of control from physicians or free Family Planning Clinics is their attitude toward the possibility of successful planning. Rainwater (1965) distinguished three different orientations toward family planning. He found one group optimistic and self-assured in their ability to exert control over the size of their family. A second group was hopeful but less confident in the methods and more bothered by the prospect of "accident." A third group was quite fatalistic about it. They did not think anything would help so there was little use in trying. They went through the motions of using some method but were inconsistent in its use because they were not convinced it would work for them. There was again a social class and religious influence on these attitudes, with middle class Protestants being the most sure and lower-lower class whites and blacks being the most fatalistic regardless of religious affiliation (see Table 18–1).

Fatalistic attitudes toward success seem to be imbedded in a general feeling that one has little control over his life, coupled with lack of knowledge of the process of conception and how the various methods of control interfere with the process. When this is combined with a negative attitude toward sex, the reluctance of the female to take responsibility or to use the more effective feminine techniques which require her to touch her own genitals further reduces the probability of active, successful planning.

Table 18–1

Percentage of Attitude Toward Likelihood of Success in Limiting Family to Desired Size

	Planful and Self-Assured	Hopeful— But Unsure	Passive and Fatalistic
Middle Class Protestants	63	37	—
Middle Class Catholics	23	63	14
Upper-lower Class (white and Negro)	18	58	24
Lower-lower Class (white and Negro)	5	32	63

SOURCE: Reprinted from Rainwater, *Family Design: Marital Sexuality, Family Size and Contraception* (Chicago: Aldine Publishing Co., 1965), p. 201, Table 7–1.

Earlier it was shown that the type of marital role relationship was related to satisfaction with the sexual relationship (see Chapter 14). Now it appears that effective family planning is related to both sexual satisfaction and type of role relationship. Rainwater (1965, p. 240) found that three-fourths of lower class whites and blacks who were very positive toward sexual relations were also effectively controlling their family size after the birth of the last wanted child. Only 40 per cent of those with negative views toward sex were successfully engaging in contraceptive practices. It was also found that of those in a joint or intermediate role relationship where sexual satisfaction was highest 64 per cent used the feminine type contraceptives compared to 27 per cent of those in highly segregated role relationships, in which negative views toward sex were more prevalent (Rainwater, 1965, p. 225). All of those in joint relationships were effectively limiting their family after the last wanted child while only 26 per cent of those in highly segregated relationships were effective (Rainwater, 1965, p. 231). These factors of sexual satisfaction and joint marital role relationships appear to combine to make discussion about family planning easier, so that a method which is agreeable to both partners can be conscientiously practiced.

Effect of Husband–Wife Attitudes. With the exclusion of those contraceptive methods which provide little or no protection against conception the effectiveness of the practices appears much more related to the attitudes of the users toward them than to the technical efficiency of the method. When husband and wife disagree on either the number of children wanted or on the method of family planning used, the efficiency of any method is likely to go down. Confidence in a particular method implies trust in the partner who is responsible for the precautions. This becomes more important the less conspicuous the method and probably reaches its peak with the use of the oral contraceptives. Rainwater (1965, p. 202) speaks of one woman who had contrived to have three "accidents" to have the five children she wanted instead of the two her husband wanted.

Effective family planning appears related to mutual enjoyment of sexual relations, a joint or intermediate role relationship which implies some sharing of interests and family goals between the spouses, and good communication. Whether the effectiveness of family planning is a consequence of or a contributing factor to sexual satisfaction is difficult to determine. Certainly anxiety about pregnancy can be expected to reduce the enjoyment of sexual relations, especially if this is accompanied by distrust of the partner. It is quite easy to make an association between "he (she) doesn't respect my wishes about having more children" and "he (she) doesn't care about me." This is especially true of the lower class wife who is likely to interpret her husband's sporadic or non-use of the condom as "selfishness" and lack of concern about her, as long as his pleasure is not interfered with.

On the other hand negative feelings toward sex itself reduces the probability of open discussion and cooperation in using effective methods consistently and efficiently. For the woman it reduces her concern in seeking a method which would be acceptable to her husband, since she would rather cut down the frequency of contact than make it "safe."

Effective planning, no matter what methods used, appears to be a consequence of positive sexual attitudes, a mutual regard for each other's feelings and desires, open communication, and an agreement on family planning goals (Rainwater, 1960, pp. 125-30). On the other hand, effective planning probably heightens the couple's feeling of control over their lives, enhances sexual enjoyment and their confidence in each other, and increases the probability that the children will be a welcome addition to the family.

Involuntary Sterility

Some couples experience the reverse of the limitation problems discussed above. They want children but fail to conceive. The 1955 Growth of American Families Study showed that nearly one-third of the couples were below normal in their ability to reproduce. About 10 per cent were sterile, however, because of sterilization operations on the husband or wife either as a contraceptive measure or for other medical reasons (Freedman et al., 1959). An additional 7 per cent were classified as probably sterile and unlikely to have children, while 12 per cent were expected to have some difficulty in producing children.

Formerly there was the belief that involuntary childlessness was always the fault of the wife; in many earlier societies, barrenness was sufficient grounds for a husband to secure a divorce. But it is now known that in at least one-third of all cases the sterile condition is with the male. Actually, with the majority of cases involving difficult conception there is something which needs correction in both husband and wife.

Sterility may result from one or more of many conditions. In the female there is likely to be a blocking of the Fallopian tubes or of the cervix; or the uterus may be out of place; or the ovaries may not be functioning properly. In the male there may be a blocking of the sperm duct; or the sperm count may be below normal; or the testicles may be impaired and producing an inferior quality of sperm. Sterility can be the result of an earlier infection, such as mumps in the male and gonorrhea in either sex. In rare instances sterility stems from an absence, underdevelopment, or malformation of some part of the reproductive system of one of the mates. Poor health, either physical or mental, is known to lessen the probability of conception.

Physicians and clinicians dealing with this problem report success in about one-half of the cases that come to them. There is little doubt but that even this record will be bettered through future advances in medical science. Sometimes conception is made possible by means of surgery; sometimes through hormone treatment; sometimes as a result of changes in the timing and technique of sexual intercourse. It frequently happens that a presumably sterile couple will conceive after mental tensions have been relaxed, or after the general physical condition of one or both has been improved. Certainly all sterility is not absolute. Many cases are on the borderline and can be corrected by a relatively slight alteration of mental and physical conditions. As evidence of this, note the fact that adopting couples frequently find that they have conceived a child of their own some time after they had given up and adopted a child. The changed family situation released mental tensions and improved general health sufficiently to tip the balance in the direction of fertility.

Alternatives to Childlessness

Childlessness is, at this writing, not considered a desirable state by very many couples. The Family Growth Study showed that 96 per cent of the childless couples married 15 years or longer were classified as below normal in their ability to reproduce (Freedman, 1959, pp. 21–26). It can perhaps be assumed that childlessness, for most of them, was not the result of personal preference. Permanent childlessness is not the only possibility for couples who cannot conceive. There are at least two other alternatives—artificial insemination and adoption.

Artificial Insemination. If sterility cannot be overcome, and if husband and wife have no scruples against it, one alternative to childlessness in some cases is artificial insemination. This technique is most useful in cases where the difficulty in conception results from an inadequate sperm count or some problem in the sperm reaching the wife's uterus. By the use of a syringe, the physician will place some of the sperms from a male donor at the mouth of the wife's uterus, near the time she is expected to ovulate. Thus there can be normal pregnancy and childbirth, though the husband may not be the biological father. If the husband's sperms are adequate, however, they will be used. Otherwise an anonymous donor will be sought, usually a medical student or intern who is of superior endowment and whose inheritable characteristics are somewhat similar to those of the husband. Sometimes the donor's semen is mixed with that of the husband so that there will be at least a chance that the husband becomes the father.

This solution to childlessness is growing, although it continues to call forth opposition. One study in 1959, using college students, reported that close to fifty per cent of the students had not heard of it. A majority of them, however, found it acceptable if the husband's semen was used. The percentage approving the practice dropped sharply if an outside donor was the source of the semen (Vernon and Broadway, 1959). It is estimated, however, that tens of thousands of persons in the United States have been born by this procedure. It is reported that artificial insemination results in conception even faster than the five-month period that is required for the average married couple who cease contraceptive usage in order to have a child (Behrman and Gosling, 1966).

Opposition continues, nevertheless, and there are a number of social and legal problems connected with the practice which have not as yet been solved. One of these has to do with the legitimacy of the child. Some physicians urge the artificially impregnated mother to change doctors prior to the birth of the child, so that the physician who delivers will not know what has happened and will therefore make the birth records show the husband as the legitimate father.

The few cases which have reached the courts have been largely divorce cases in which custody or child support were in question. The legal issue remains unclear. The moral issue continues to be debated. The answer is unequivocal as far as the Catholic church is concerned. It is seen as immoral regardless of the marital status of the woman and regardless of who the donor is, including the husband (Udry, 1966, p. 478).

Adoption. With the moral and social issues associated with artificial insemination, many couples prefer adoption, even when artificial insemination is medically feasible for them. Until the mid 1960's, adoption was a long drawn out experience. The demand from couples who wanted to adopt far exceeded the supply of illegitimate and orphaned children available. The restrictions on adoptive parents concerning age, health, income, and the insistence on matching child and adoptive parents on a number of characteristics were in keeping with the oversupply of prospective parents. Both the long wait and lengthy investigations encouraged the development of a "black market" in babies, which was both expensive and legally risky.

The medical advances in treating sterility and the increase in numbers of illegitimate children, however, have reversed the supply and demand picture, resulting in changes in the way adoption is regarded. A few states have even begun allowing single persons to adopt children, reasoning that it is better for a child to have one parent than none at all. Required income levels have been reduced. Requirements that the adoptive mother not work outside the home have been relaxed. The compatible matching of characteristics has been redefined so that it has become possible for a couple to adopt a child with racial characteristics different from their own. Still, in general, care is taken in these cases to assure that the personalities of adoptive parents are stable and that their motivations for adopting a racially different child are healthy ones.

Many of these changes have come about because of the increase in Negro and racially mixed children among those available for adoption. A more tolerant climate for interracial adoption was probably encouraged by the activity of both church and secular groups to promote the adoption by American parents of Korean War orphans.

Adoption and the parent–adopted child relationship can be as satisfying as the parent–natural-child relationship. The parent–child love grows through interaction after birth even when the child is genetically one's own. Giving birth does not automatically result in love for the child. When both parents accept the idea of adoption, when the baby is adopted at infancy through a reliable agency, which assures that the legal release has been obtained from the natural mother and protects against either the natural or adoptive parent discovering the identity of the other, the feelings of love and belonging should be no different than for a natural child.

With the greater ease of adoption, many parents find it possible to space their children according to both age and sex with greater ease and accuracy than parents producing their own children. What the child will become depends more on what happens after birth than before. Some people claim there is less risk in adopting a child than in having one of your own, since babies with known genetic inadequacies, or who are in any way defective at birth, are not available for adoption, at least not without the adoptive parents knowing of the defect and deciding to share whatever difficulties it will present to the child.

THE PROCESS OF BIRTH

Once conception has taken place the heredity of the organism is established. Although knowledge is developing rapidly in the field of genetics which may eventually result in the ability to predictably control certain consequences of the genetic structure, the genetically controlled characteristics of the infant will be the result of the combination of genes carried by the parents.

Principles of Genetics

No two persons are at any time exactly alike. Neither nature nor nurture is capable, seemingly, of making exact duplicates. Each situation is unique. Variability is the only constant.

Peoples related by blood are more nearly alike than are those unrelated. Variability is therefore partially offset by continuity and similarity. In nature, each of the species tends to reproduce its kind, never exactly, but always approximately. The force making for long-range variabilities in biological organisms is called evolution. The force making for similarities in lines of descent is called heredity. *Genetics* is the science of them both.

In addition to the body cells, every normal individual carries within him certain *germ cells* (sperms in the male and eggs, or ova, in the female) which become active at the time of puberty and upon which reproduction and heredity depend. Within each germ cell there are twenty-three pairs of stringlike objects called *chromosomes,* and within or upon each chromosome there are numerous protein bodies called *genes.* It is these genes that determine the various inherited traits of the individual—hair color, nose shape, body build, mental level, and the like. The genes are originally in pairs, but each pair separates as the chromosomes split longitudinally at the time of cell division prior to fertilization.

There are both *dominant* and *recessive* attributes in the genes; those that are dominant always show up in the offspring, but the recessive traits appear only when they are matched with similar recessive traits from another germ cell. This, together with the facts of multiple gene combination at the time of cell division and chance sperm selection at the time of fertilization, explains how children in a family can be so different from their parents and from one another. The number of combinations that genes can take in forming the new offspring is almost infinite. By carrying traits recessively, parents of similar tendencies can pass on to their children characteristics which were not apparent in themselves. It should be clear from this that one's heredity depends primarily upon the kind of genes present in both parents and the particular gene combination that happens to result from the processes of cell division and fertilization.

Another factor in biological variability is what geneticists call *mutation*. Sudden changes occasionally occur within the internal structures of the germ cells which affect heredity and which breed true. Exact causes of mutations are not known, nor are their results predictable. It is known that new traits are set up in this way, however, and that these tend to perpetuate themselves from generation to generation.

Changes in genetic structure can occur as the result of certain drugs. Discovery of alteration of the genes as a result of LSD usage has led to speculation about the consequences for offspring. As yet, conclusive evidence is not available concerning the permanence of the genetic alteration or its effect on reproduction.

Sex Determination

One of the twenty-three pairs of chromosomes in the human germ cell has to do with sex determination. Geneticists represent this in the female with the symbol XX and in the male with XY. During cell division these pairs split. If an X sperm then unites with the egg during the process of fertilization, the result will be XX, or female; from a Y sperm an XY cell, or male, will be produced. It will be seen from this that the sex of the child is determined through the father, not the mother. Let it be clear, however, that there is no willful determination on the part of either father or mother; though the determining factors lie within man's nature, they are presently beyond his control.

Recently, however, research has been reported on predetermining the sex of the child. It has been discovered that the degree of acidity in the female's vagina affects the Y-carrying sperm differently from the X-carrying sperm. The degree of acidity varies throughout the monthly cycle of the female in a regular way. Therefore, if fertilization takes place when the acidity is high a girl is more likely to result. If fertilization occurs when the vaginal environment is alkaline, a boy is the more probable result. How accurate the prescribed procedures will be is not reliably known at this writing, but the attention presently drawn to this way of predetermining the sex of the child will undoubtedly furnish some evidence of its reliability in the near future (Rorvik and Shettles, 1970).

Predetermining sex is of great interest as far as population control is concerned. It is suggested, for example, that if people could control the sex of their children, they may have fewer children, as discussed earlier in this chapter. Just as important a concern is the effect on the sex ratio over time.

Life begins with a preponderance of males. There are at least 120 males conceived to every 100 females (some believe this ratio to be as high as 150 or more males to every 100 females). Reasons for such a large male surplus are not entirely known, though it is thought that sperms containing characteristics for maleness are a little lighter in weight or are otherwise more agile, so that they travel faster than do sperms with female-determining characteristics and thus more frequently reach the egg first. Support is given to this theory by the fact that Y chromosomes are known to be somewhat smaller in size, which should make the sperms containing them lighter in weight than are the sperms carying X chromosomes. Recent research has provided evidence supporting this difference in agility (Rorvik and Shettles, 1970).

Genes located on the sex chromosomes sometimes produce what is known as sex-linkage. Thus, color blindness and hemophilia, where they exist in heredity, are known to be carried recessively by females but occasionally to skip generations and to show up only in males.

The Sex Ratio. Although in the sex ratio at birth males exceed females the male surplus is considerably lower than at the time of conception. It remains fairly constant at about 105 or 106 male to every 100 female live births. The explanation for this lower proportion of males at birth than at conception is the higher prenatal death rate of males.

Comparisons in live birth male–female ratios reveal both variation from group to group and fluctuation from time to time. But differences are usually small. The following facts seem significant: (1) the Negro ratio is below that of Caucasians; (2) births from young parents show higher sex ratios than those from parents who are older; and (3) live birth sex ratios go up during and following war.

Since there has been little real research on the subject, we can only speculate as to why these differences exist. There is good reason for believing, however, that the major factor is variation in the stillbirth rate, which, as has been seen, affects males more than females. Negroes have more stillbirths per family than do Caucasians because of their lower economic level, and this higher rate probably eliminates male embryos in greater proportion than it does female ones, thereby reducing the sex ratio of live births. So too, young parents, being usually the most healthy and fit, have fewer stillbirths and hence produce higher sex ratios in their children. Similarly, wartime means more marriages, parenthood at a younger age, and therefore fewer stillbirths and higher sex ratios in the offspring. Whether in the future improved prenatal care and increasing ability to predetermine the sex of the child will raise the sex ratio at birth remains to be seen.

Multiple Conceptions

Twinning is a tendency that seems to be inherited, although the laws by which it operates are not completely understood. Twins are of two kinds, *identical* and *fraternal*. Identical twins come from one egg which has been fertilized by one sperm. A dividing or splitting of the egg takes place after fertilization. That is why identical twins are so much alike; the same genes go into the making of them both. Fraternal twins, on the other hand, may be as different as ordinary brothers and sisters. They are often of opposite sexes, while identical twins must be either both males or both females. Fraternal twins result from the fertilization of two different eggs by two different sperms. Multiple births of a higher order, such as triplets, quadruplets, and quintuplets, may be of either the identical or the fraternal variety.

There is an inverse relationship between the number of children born from a given confinement and the frequency of such confinements. Among births in the United States from 1960 to 1966 twins occurred about once out of every 100 confinements. With this frequency of twins, the probability of triplets is about one in every 10,000, and quadruplets about one is every 1,000,000 (Metropolitan Life, 1969).

There is some indication that the use of oral contraceptives heightens the probability of multiple births. If this is the case, there should be a noticeable increase in the frequency of twins in the next decade or so among educated white women where the use of the pill is most prevalent.

Multiple conception varies according to both age and race. The probability of its occurring is least likely with mothers under age twenty and most likely with mothers aged thirty-five through thirty-nine. Non-white mothers outdo white mothers, having one and one-fourth times as many twins, one and three-fourths times as many triplets, and almost four times as many quadruplets (Metropolitan Life, 1954).

The Rh Factor

Special attention has been given to the so-called Rh factor in human blood types, so named because of its discovery in Rhesus monkeys. Approximately 85 per cent of the white population is known to possess this factor; these are labeled Rh-positive. The remaining 15 per cent is rh-negative. The factor is hereditary, with Rh-positive dominant over rh-negative. Complications can develop when the wife is rh-negative and the husband Rh-positive, which happens in about one out of every dozen marriages. In such cases the fetus is apt to be Rh-positive (will definitely be if the father is homozygous, Rh Rh, and may be if he is heterozygous, Rh rh). Antigens from an Rh-positive fetus will sometimes pass into the blood stream of the rh-negative mother. This takes place rather rarely, however. When it does happen, antibodies are produced in the mother's blood, which can pass back into the blood stream of the fetus, combine with the Rh-positive cells there, and destroy them. The condition is characterized by anemia and is known as *erythroblastosis fetalis* or hemolytic disease. It frequently causes stillbirth. Most of those born alive are now saved by means of rh-negative blood transfusions.

Fortunately the antibodies produced in the mother's blood accumulate slowly, and as a consequence the first child of a marriage is usually not affected—unless previously there has been an aborted pregnancy or unless the mother has at some time had an Rh-positive blood transfusion. The possibility of a child's developing this disease increases with each succeeding pregnancy. It is estimated that only about one out of every thirty or forty children of rh-negative women are affected by the hemolytic conditions.

Medical developments now make it possible to control the consequences of the Rh-positive–rh-negative mating after the first pregnancy. As prenatal medical attention is extended in the society, the incidence of this phenomenon should decrease.

Indicators of Pregnancy

Usual early signs of pregnancy are the missing of a menstrual period, an increasing fullness and tenderness of the breasts, a feeling of nausea known as "morning sickness," and a greater frequency of urination. But none of these is absolute proof of pregnancy; each may be the result of other causes. If several of them occur together, however, it is a fairly good sign that pregnancy is under way.

Greater certainty is obtained through the physician's examination. This will not ordinarily take place until about two months have elapsed from the last menstrual period, for it is not until then that the positive signs become evident. If pregnancy is present the doctor will then notice certain changes in the vaginal lining, in the cervix, and elsewhere.

Sometimes it is important to know sooner whether a woman is pregnant, without waiting for two months for the appearance of positive signs. To meet this need, there have been developed a number of tests whereby pregnancy can be determined with almost 100 per cent accuracy a few days after the missing of a menstrual period. Urine from the female is injected in a mouse (Aschheim-Zondek test), or a rabbit (Friedman test), or a toad (Hon-Morris test). If the woman is pregnant there will be a reaction set up within the animal which can be easily recognized.

Development During Pregnancy

The fertilized egg implants itself on the wall of the uterus about seven or eight days following fertilization. Already it has commenced to grow through a process of cell division. Continued growth in the same manner brings about an enlargement in size and a differentiation of body structures. The embryo, as this new life is at first called, receives its food and disposes of its wastes through the umbilical cord, which, in turn, reaches to the placenta attached to the wall of the uterus. There is no direct connection between the blood streams of mother and embryo; foods and wastes merely filter through the walls of the two separate systems of blood vessels within the placenta. Growth will necessarily follow the pattern laid down by heredity. Once conception has taken place there can be no altering of sex, eye color, intellectual capacity, or anything else which has been dictated by the genes. Though prenatal environment is important from the standpoint of the baby's survival chances, there is no way by which a mother can influence or condition her unborn child along specific lines.

The stages of prenatal growth follow a regular pattern. At first the embryo is scarcely distinguishable from those of other life forms. By the end of two months it will have grown to a little over an inch in length and most of its body features will be formed. After this it is called a fetus and subsequent changes will have to do principally with an increase in size. By about the middle of pregnancy the heartbeat will have become strong enough for the doctor to hear it through a stethoscope and movements will have become vigorous enough for the mother to feel them. If birth takes place during the first seven months the child's chances for survival are rather small. These chances increase as the time of delivery approaches the date for normal termination of pregnancy. The normal period of human pregnancy is usually figured as 280 days (40 weeks). This is counting from the beginning of the last menstrual period. Since conception cannot take place until ovulation, it follows that the actual length of pregnancy is about two weeks shorter than this, or approximately 266 days. If the exact date of conception is known, the probable time of delivery can be determined rather simply by adding 266 days. A more usual method is to add seven days to the beginning of the last menstruation and then subtract three months. For example, if the first day of the last menstrual period were June 15, adding seven days and subtracting three months gives March 22 as the estimated date of confinement. These predicted dates are approximations; there is nothing abnormal in a pregnancy's running a few days under or over the expected time.

Birth

After pregnancy has run its course, the fetus is expelled from the mother's body and is then ready to begin a new phase of development, this time as a child. The process by which birth takes place is known as labor.

Labor begins with rhythmic contractions of the uterus accompanied by a gradual dilation of the cervix so that the baby can come through. These contractions involve a certain amount of discomfort and are known as "labor pains." They start out rather mildly and widely spaced, but increase in intensity and frequency as the labor proceeds. The length of labor varies with individuals. First births (averaging about sixteen hours) generally take longer than subsequent ones. After dilation has become complete, uterine contractions grow more severe so as to force the infant through the cervix and the vagina and into the outer world. It usually arrives head first. Almost immediately it starts to cry—and breathe. The doctor then cuts and fastens the umbilical cord. Within a few minutes the placenta (afterbirth) is also expelled. Birth is over. The mother's uterus now starts to contract and the muscles supporting it commence to return to their original positions.

There are three stages of labor, as described above. (1) The first and longest stage involves the contractions of the uterus and the dilation of the cervix. (2) This is followed by the relatively rapid passage of the child through the vaginal canal; and finally, a few minutes later, (3) the expulsion of the afterbirth.

Some doctors believe that the pain of childbirth is due almost entirely to fear. Women in our culture expect it to hurt so they enter labor tense; if they could relax, the cervix would have a better chance of dilating and the birth process would be easy. Such doctors follow the pioneer work of Grantley Dick Read, and the technique they advocate is known as *natural childbirth* (Read, 1944).

Though the claim that absence from fear can remove *all* pain from childbirth might be open to question, there is little doubt that the general theory has merit. Medical men are agreed that it is the women who are relatively calm and who cooperate who have the easiest time in delivery. There is need, therefore, to educate women toward acceptance of childbirth as a normal process. With improved knowledge and facilities for handling maternity cases, there should be less cause for fear today than in earlier times. If requested, most doctors will administer anesthesia during childbirth for the relief of pain. The practice has become rather general, though it remains controversial.

HUSBAND–WIFE RELATIONSHIP DURING PREGNANCY

The reactions of the wife to her pregnancy are related to the reactions of her husband, and vice versa. If both husband and wife want the baby, the adjustments to the idea of pregnancy are likely to be minimal and produce a euphoria in the relationship. In one study of the first pregnancies of 212 student wives, 47 per cent reported a change in their husband's attitudes toward them. Of these, 94 per cent said their husbands had become more thoughtful, considerate, and helpful (Landis and Poffenberger, 1950). Those who had not wanted the pregnancy suffered more feelings of unhappiness and emotional upset during the first three months of pregnancy than those who had wanted to become pregnant (Poffenberger *et al.*, 1952). The differences disappeared by the second trimester, however.

Fears associated with childbirth, worries about the normality of the baby, and anxieties about approaching an unknown situation produce a need for reassurance and support from the husband in a large percentage of cases. This is especially true during the first pregnancy. Where the husbands can provide this support, wives tend to feel better understood and not so alone in the new experience.

Although pregnancy is a normal state, some women tend to view it as an illness and a reason to be excused from routine duties and they worry about their changing bodies. This reaction appears strongest among women who are unhappy and insecure in their marriage, experience conflict between the pregnancy and other values such as desires for a home and furniture, or resent having to leave their job (Rosengreen, 1961).

Even a woman who sees pregnancy as a perfectly normal occurrence and who enjoys each new sensation as she is aware of the development within her is likely to grow tired of waiting before the pregnancy is over. She is likely to become impatient with the increasing difficulty of performing normal tasks and become quite sensitive to joking comments from her husband that she would "look better in a tent." Since she is probably feeling that she bears the brunt of the responsibility and discomfort in this "family affair," her husband's lack of interest or understanding is likely to leave her feeling lonely and martyred. With his support, however, the anticipation of the coming birth is more likely to overweigh the discomfort.

The Sexual Relationship

The effect of pregnancy on the sexual relationship appears to be different for the first pregnancy from that for subsequent ones. Most women having their first baby report a decrease in sexual interest and responsiveness during the first three months of pregnancy. Very few of those who have had previous babies report any change (Brecher, 1966, pp. 90–91). This difference is perhaps occasioned by the strangeness of the experience for those who are pregnant for the first time, coupled with some unwarranted fear that the fetus might be hurt. In cases where chronic fatigue, nausea, and other symptoms of early pregnancy are present, sexual interest appears to decrease whether this is a first pregnancy or not.

The second three-month period, however, seems almost universally marked by increased sexual interest, compared not only to the first three months but to the pre-pregnancy period. Sexual responsiveness during the last three months tends to decline gradually. Some women report that their husbands also lose interest, either because of the physical changes in the wife or fear of hurting either their wife or the baby. Many physicians restrict sexual intercourse at some time during the last three months, some for the full time and others for just the last month.

Masters and Johnson also interviewed husbands with pregnant wives. Only about one-third of the husbands said they understood the reasons and agreed with and honored the sexual restrictions before the baby's birth. Nearly a third said they did not understand or questioned whether the physician had actually said it—suspecting that their wives made it up to avoid intercourse (Brecher, 1966, p. 93). Ideas such as this would be expected to have negative repercussions in the marital relationship.

Medical restrictions on sexual activity before birth are mainly rooted in a lack of information about the effect of intercourse on causing premature births, injuring the baby, or heightening the probability of infection. Since all of these results can happen in select cases, physicians have tended to "play it safe" and restrict the activity for all. As more knowledge is available from studies such as those of Masters and Johnson, it may become possible for physicians to make recommendations tailored to the individual case. Until then, however, it appears that it would be helpful for husbands to know that this is generally a restriction imposed by most physicians rather than an attempt by their wives to reduce sexual activity (Brecher, 1966, p. 93).

Most physicians also forbid sexual intercourse until six weeks after the baby's birth, which is the usual time for the first checkup. In some women, however, strong sexual interests reappear two or three weeks after the birth. For most it seems to reappear within two months. The early return of sexual interest seems associated with breast feeding the baby. Breast feeding aids an earlier return of the uterus to its normal size and position (Brecher, 1966, p. 90).

Many women who breast feed their babies report strong sexual stimulation when the baby nurses. This sometimes causes deep feelings of guilt and is the reason for some mothers deciding not to breast feed subsequent children. Sexual stimulation during nursing is an absolutely normal reaction and appears occasioned by the release of a hormone during breast feeding which is associated with hastening the return of the uterus to normalcy. An understanding of this phenomenon by both husband and wife can remove the unnecessary guilt feelings occasioned by the long rejection of sex in our cultural history (Brecher, 1966, p. 92).

Pregnancy does put some temporary stumbling blocks in the way of the sexual relationship. But the more the two people understand the necessary restrictions and the woman's decline in interest resulting from fatigue, discomfort, and prolonged healing after birth, the more easily can they accept the interruptions and find ways of accommodating to the situation. If there is a good sexual relationship before pregnancy, open communication, understanding, and concern for each other's feelings, the adjustments to this period can reaffirm the total relationship, rather than producing frustration, doubt, and spousal blame.

THE PRINCIPLE OF VALUE RELEVANCE

Values and the agreement between husband and wife play an extremely important part in making the childbearing period one which increases marital satisfaction. As has been mentioned earlier marital adjustment appears to be at least partially related to the ability of the couple to control fertility in line with their desires. Part of this control comes from agreement between husband and wife on number and spacing, as well as the means for limiting conception. The attitudes of the parents toward each other, toward sex, and toward the methods used to limit conception appear to be more related to the effectiveness of the practice than its technical efficiency except for those methods which provide little or no protection regardless of how meticulously used.

If both spouses share the feeling that it is morally wrong to use mechanical or chemical methods of birth control, and at the same time desire to limit their family and have a commitment to each other, they are more likely to be able to use the methods open to them efficiently. They are likely to seek medical advice on ways to make the rhythm method more reliable, for example, and less likely to resent the restrictions this method places on their spontaneous desires. Their shared values may also make them less likely to resent the "accident" that may result.

If, however, they both feel that there is little one can do ("it's all fate anyway") then the willingness to "take a chance" goes up, as well as the unwillingness to seek information or restrict sexual activity in accord with the fertile period.

If husband and wife have different attitudes—one thinks it is morally wrong to use mechanical methods and the other does not, or one thinks "it's all fate" and the other believes in rational control—efficiency can be expected to go down. The frustration of at least one partner would go up, and "accidents" would be more likely to result in spousal blame and resentment.

When pregnancy occurs, the attitudes of both spouses appear to play a part in reducing the amount of anxiety and discomfort associated with pregnancy and birth. The meaning the baby has for the spouses as well as for their respective families appears to influence the effect the pregnancy and new baby has on the marital relationship.

Pregnancy does interfere with the sexual relationship, but as far as lasting effects on the marital relationship are concerned, it is the way the interference is interpreted which is more important than the disruption itself.

SUMMARY

Individual values concerning the number and spacing of children are influenced by social norms, individual interests, stage in the life cycle, pressures from family and friends, and sex of children already born. The fit between the desired and actual number of children as well as satisfaction with the spacing of them seem more important to marital satisfaction than any specific number or age and sex distribution.

The concept of family planning has received wide public interest as technological knowledge of birth control methods has increased. Family planning involves the ability to have children when the couple desires, as well as the ability to limit the number one has. Techniques for meeting both problems have improved drastically in recent years.

Birth control measures differ among themselves in the point at which they attempt to interfere with the process of reproduction. Whatever the method used, effective family planning appears related to mutual enjoyment of sexual relations, a marital role relationship which allows the sharing of interests and family goals, and good communications between the spouses.

Some couples experience the reverse kind of problem. They want children but fail to conceive. There are two alternatives to involuntary sterility—artificial insemination and adoption. Because of the legal and moral issues in artificial insemination, some couples prefer adoption. Adoption procedures have become less restrictive as a result of changing attitudes toward it, the increased success in overcoming sterility, and the increased numbers of illegitimate births. Since the parent–child love grows through interaction after birth rather than through the birth process itself, the feelings of love and belonging should not differ between the natural and the adopted child.

The normal period of human pregnancy is roughly 266 days. During this time, the changes in the woman's body as well as the psychological effects of pregnancy introduce some changes in the marital relationship. Women experiencing their first pregnancies tend to report a decrease in sexual interest during the first three months of pregnancy. That this is partially due to the strangeness of the experience is supported by the finding that most women in subsequent pregancies report no change.

Almost universally the second three-month period is characterized by an increase in sexual interest and activity. There is generally a decline in interest during the last three months, helped along by restrictions on sexual activity imposed by most physicians. These restrictions are generally continued until six weeks after birth. Pregnancy does put some obstacles in the way of the sexual relationship. But if there is a good relationship before the pregnancy, open communication, understanding, and a concern for each other's feelings, the adjustment to the period can reaffirm their total relationship rather than cause frustration, doubt, and blame.

QUESTIONS AND PROJECTS

1. Describe the social factors influencing individual desires for family size. What is the ideal family size being suggested today by the mass media? What are the ways, if any, in which this ideal is being transmitted.

2. The percentage of childless couples has been dropping in very recent years. What do you predict will happen to this trend within the next ten to fifteen years? Why?

3. Discuss the pros and cons of making voluntary sterilization available to any couple who wants it for purposes of birth control.

4. Discuss the factors associated with the effective use of contraceptives. Show how these may be related to marital satisfaction.

5. Take a student poll on ideas about abortion as a solution to contraceptive failure. Note the reasons given for both opposing and supporting points of view. Would these conflicting ideas be easily compromised? Discuss the possible consequences in a marriage where the husband and wife hold opposing views.

6. Have a class discussion on the use of artificial insemination as a solution to involuntary sterility. Note the reasons given for both opposing and supporting points of view. What values seem to be in conflict when there is disagreement?

7. The adoption of interracial babies by intraracial couples appears to be growing. What is your opinion of this trend? Would you be willing to adopt an interracial baby? Is there any combination of races you would not accept? What factors might influence your decision? Explain your point of view.

8. Describe the normal process of birth—starting with conception, continuing through pregnancy, and ending with childbirth.

9. Consider the effects of pregnancy on the sexual relationship and discuss the possible implications of premarital pregnancy on the developing marital relationship.

V

FAMILY
INTERACTION

19

Childrearing

The foregoing discussions of the individual's socialization process which provides him with the concept of self, of others, of marriage, and with the habits of perception and reaction which will influence his marital and family interactions now come full circle. In Chapters 5, 6, and 7 the development of the child was discussed from the child's point of view as he grew up in his family of orientation. Now the perspective is from the role of the parent in his family of procreation.

It has been shown how the interaction of parents and other family members affects the developing values and personality of the child. The child also affects the parents, however—their self-concepts, their marital relationship, and the over-all family climate.

PARENTHOOD AS CRISIS

Before the first baby comes, generally within the first two to three years of marriage, husband and wife have developed habits of interaction which involve only the two of them.[1] From the treatment of the wheel theory of love development in Chapter 10, it will be recalled that the development of mutual habits is one of the main components in sustaining the feeling of love. The addition of any third member disrupts these habits, whether the addition is a mother-in-law, an insurance salesman, or a new baby.

[1] The study of births by Westoff *et al.* (1961, pp. 117, 120) showed half the first births within the first eighteen months and three-fourths within the first thirty months of marriage. An earlier study showed the average number of months before first birth to be 23 for Catholics and 27 for Protestants (Freedman *et al.*, 1959, p. 279).

The First Baby

The new baby is probably the most disruptive of all intruders for several reasons. He is an unsocialized third party who is unaware of the time schedule of his new family, is totally insensitive to their occasional needs for uninterrupted privacy, or sleep, and who loudly makes known his slightest discomfort or needs. From the moment of entry into the family he is capable of altering the power structure between his parents. This is not because he enters into their interaction by any activity of his own, but because he is there to be used by one or the other to sway the balance—"You can't play the TV so loudly any more, you'll wake up the baby." The spouse who may have resisted all previous efforts of the mate to get the sound on the TV lowered, now has two on the other side, even though one of them has voiced no opinion on the subject.

The new baby is very apt to interfere with the normal routine in many ways completely unanticipated by his new parents. The expectations of what it will be like to have a new baby are evidently fairly unrealistic and romanticized. The mass media, especially in advertisements for baby merchandise, present a glamorous picture of motherhood. The fantasy of a sweet clean little angel, smiling or sleeping in his baby bed as Mother and Dad beam at him, arms entwined, is far removed from the actual experience of caring for an infant hour after hour after hour. This may be the first experience for many people of having a demanding job, from which one may not go home and rest—rather like being at the battlefront with no replacements in sight.

Studies of the reaction of parents all support the existence of a crisis period in the marriage following the birth of the first child. The studies taken together seem to suggest that there is a period of early elation over the new baby which begins to wear off after four to six weeks (Feldman, 1967). Hobbs (1965), for example, found that only 13 per cent of his sample reported moderate to severe crisis, with the remainder classified as experiencing slight crisis. LeMasters (1957), investigating at a much later period after the birth, found that 83 per cent of his sample reported readjustments severe enough to be classified as a "severe" or "extensive" crisis. Dyer (1963), replicating LeMasters' study, found 53 per cent reporting severe or extensive crisis. The feelings of the mother associated with the first child included chronic fatigue, loss of sleep, restriction of activities and reduction of social contacts, loss of income from outside employment, increased washing and ironing, guilt over not being a "better" mother, the continuous nature of the job of caring for an infant, worry over appearance, and decline of housekeeping efficiency. The fathers complained about economic pressures, worry about another pregnancy, reduced social life, the wife's decline in sexual interest, and general disenchantment (LeMasters, 1957). All investigators tend to agree, however, that for most couples the crises are successfully resolved within a relatively short time.

It is rather easy to see how feelings of guilt and anxiety can appear during this time, especially for those who have high aspirations for being good parents. If a woman has pictured herself as a loving, calm mother, always understanding and meeting her child's needs, she may understandably be dismayed at her own occasional feelings of mayhem when she cannot find out what is wrong with a crying baby. The more tired she becomes, the more impatient she gets, and when she finally roughly puts the baby back in bed "to cry it out" she may be overwhelmed with shame as she catches a look of bewilderment or disapproval on her husband's face, or even sees her own face in the mirror. This was not the picture she had of herself as a mother!

It is neither possible nor desirable for a parent to be always calm, loving, and accepting no matter what feelings the child is calling forth. Ambivalence (both liking and disliking the same person) seems to be a very natural part of family interaction (Kirkpatrick, 1963, pp. 239ff). It may take new parents a while to realize this and to build more realistic images, rearrange their interaction to make room for their husband–wife roles amid the demands of the mother–father roles, and again reach an equilibrium in the new three-person family.

Subsequent Children

As other children enter the family group, the parent crisis is not likely to be so severe. They now know what it is like to have a new baby in the house and so shock is reduced. They have readjusted their relationship to include one other member, and the second does not cause such an overhaul of family interactional habits.

The second child may produce a crisis for the first-born, however. The triad of mother–father–child may have made the first child the focal point of attention. At least he was the only contender for their attention. He may, at times, have competed with Mother for Daddy's attention, with Daddy for Mother's attention, or with the TV or guests for their combined attention. But once that was done he did not have to share the rewards. With the advent of a sibling, however, he must learn to share the coveted parental favors.

Each new child changes the structure of the family group. A three-person group is inherently different from a two-, four-, five-, or six-member group. Family interaction is characterized by shifting coalitions between family members. Thus, mother and daughter may join forces to get father to "give in" to her desires for a new party-dress; mother and father may join forces to assure that daughter comes straight home after the party; father and son may join forces to win mother over to his playing football.

The shifting of coalitions adds to the vitality of family life and may add to the cohesiveness of the total family by preventing any one pattern from becoming rigid and divisive (see Caplow, 1968, pp. 62–113). When coalitions are rigid over time, such as the mother and son united against the father, serious obstacles may be introduced into the child's identification process, sex-role learning, and ability to form satisfying relationships in adulthood.

Because of the changing structure of the family with the introduction of additional children, as well as from other sources such as geographical moves, more stable or instable economic status, and the increasing child-rearing experience of the parents, no two children in the same family experience exactly the same set of parents, nor do they have exactly the same sociocultural environment. The childrearing methods which produce the desired results with one child may not have the same effect on another, not only because of differences in the children's genetic structures, but because the meaning of the same parental act may be completely different for the two children.

The number of children in a family, the spacing between them, and the sex distribution all contribute to the results of the socialization process. The larger the family, for example, the more authoritarian the power structure appears to be, the more the group is emphasized over the individual, and the more important siblings are in personality development (Bossard and Sanger, 1952). It appears obvious that the more children there are and the closer they are together, the less intense and frequent would be the parent–child interaction. The amount of interaction with parents and the effect of family size would also be different for the older children than for the younger ones, for the family does not generally become big all at once, but grows from a small one, through a medium-sized one, to a large one.

Where there are other children in the family, the parent–individual child interaction generally has an audience of other children whose reactions become part of the experience for all. The complexity introduced by the multiplicity of family role relationships, the variety of values which influence the goals of childrearing, the methods by which the goals should be achieved, and the evaluations made of numerous child behaviors precludes any one-to-one relationship between childrearing methods and any particular personality traits.[2] Sewell (1952), for example, found little statistical support for any relationship between early patterns of feeding,

[2] There have been attempts to associate childrearing methods with the personality of the mother, however. See, for example, Robert R. Sears, Eleanor E. Maccoby, and Harry Levin (1957).

weaning, bowel and bladder training, and the personality structure of the child. He concluded that perhaps more important than specific practices is the over-all personal–social situation in which these practices find expression, including the attitudes and behavior of the mother.

THE GOALS OF PARENTHOOD

Childrearing is never carried out in a vacuum or as the sole activity of parents. It is continually going on but enmeshed in many other activities and interests. It is happening whether or not the parents are consciously applying themselves to the task. Most parents have goals in mind that they would like to achieve—short-term goals as well as long-range ones— some specific and some rather vague. Some goals are specifically determined by the culture in which one lives, some are the result of the reaction to one's own childrearing experiences, others are not recognized perhaps, but are just achieved in the process of family living.

There are some tasks parents must to some extent carry out if the child is to survive and be acceptable to his society. These have been listed by Clausen (1968) as:

1. Nurturing the child, at least to the extent of meeting physical needs.
2. Training the child to meet his physiological needs (food, elimination, sleep) in ways which suit the habits of the parents and which will eventually conform to cultural standards.
3. Teaching and providing opportunities for practice of motor skills, language, technical skills of dressing, feeding himself, recognizing and negotiating danger spots to insure safety.
4. Orienting the child to his immediate world of family, community, and society.
5. Transmitting cultural goals and values, and motivating the child toward them so that he develops a sense of right and wrong and becomes able to establish his own goals.
6. Training and practice in interpersonal skills, so that he becomes responsive to the feelings of others.
7. Controlling the child's behaviors, correcting, guiding, and interpreting his actions and reactions so that the child becomes able to control and evaluate his own behavior.

Most of these are taken for granted in the concept of a "good" parent which also includes ideas about how the training should be done, the age by which the child should have acquired certain skills, how the "correcting" should be carried out, and what the end product should look like in the "good" child.

Cultural Influences

There are historical trends in the concepts of good parent and good child just as in the concept of a good marital relationship. In order to develop techniques for achieving childrearing goals (however they are specifically defined) there must be some general concept of the nature of the child. These ideas about the nature of the child and the methods appropriate to mold him into a good child and eventually a good adult change as changes occur in religious beliefs, in scientific knowledge, and in the economic and educational institutions.

During the nineteenth century, the nature of the child was seen as willful and sinful. These "evil" tendencies had to be brought under control by strong discipline and punishment for wrongdoing if he was to grow into a responsible adult with a strong character (Sears *et al.*, 1957, p. 310; Miller and Swanson, 1959, Chapter 1). The good child was seen and not heard, was obedient, and showed respect for his elders. Outbursts of anger toward the parent, sexual curiosity, and attention-getting behavior were not acceptable.

From the turn of the century until about 1930, basic assumptions about the nature of the child began to be questioned, notably through the work of Sigmund Freud and John Dewey. In the early 1940's the combined effects of the Freudian-oriented clinical studies relating children's disturbances to their mothers' childrearing practices, the broad social changes taking place, and the educational theories of John Dewey resulted in new concepts of the nature of the child and "good" adult, as well as a reversal of recommended practices. The period from 1940 to 1950 was characterized by an emphasis on permissiveness (Wolfenstein, 1951; Stendler, 1950). The child was no longer a small-sized adult. He was not inherently violent, aggressive, and willful but made so by parents who frustrated him and denied him freedom of expression and understanding. The emphasis was no longer on early conformity or instant obedience. The hard working, well-disciplined adult was dethroned by the happy, well-adjusted man as the "ideal adult" to be developed by good parents.

During the 1950's and continuing until the present, the child guidance literature has reflected a clarification of permissive childrearing, evidently in response to what was considered too extreme a position. Now permissiveness is presented not as implying a lack of control or guidance but as involving a different definition of the "good" child and new techniques for achieving this goal.

The child is now seen as having a "right" to express his opinions and feelings of anger and frustration. Sexual curiosity is seen as natural; and open, frank sex education viewed as necessary for producing a mature, constructive sexual adjustment. Allowing the child to develop his own set of internal standards by questioning the rules he is to follow as well as the judgment of his elders is seen as the way to mold an independent, responsible, well-adjusted adult. It is considered more important that he understand the reasons for restrictions on behavior than merely to conform to them. Strictness and punishment are replaced by tolerance and understanding of immature behavior and by encouragement of more mature forms (Johnsen, 1966).

It is not correct that the newer norms have replaced the older more restrictive ones. Rather, they exist side by side, each receiving support and each being blamed for contributing to juvenile delinquency, laxity of morals, decline of respect for the law, heightened aggressive behavior, and so forth. Conflict over the "correct" way to rear children is found among educators, legislators, judges, and individual parents. One of the sources of the conflict may well be that different concepts of the good child are held by different groups and maybe even by the same person at different times under varying circumstances.

Individual Family Goals

Since cultural norms and values concerning the good child and methods of molding him have been undergoing change, it is understandable that individual families differ in the way they rear their children and the way they evaluate their behavior. Melvin Kohn, for example, found that middle class mothers were likely to name happiness, consideration, and self-control as the most important traits to be developed in children, while lower class mothers tended to name neatness, cleanliness, and obedience (Kohn, 1959). He also found a difference in the way parents responded to their children's misbehavior, with a middle class mother being more likely to respond to the motivation she perceived as prompting the behavior than a lower class mother, who was likely to respond to the disruptive character of the behavior itself (Kohn, 1963). Thus, the middle class mother would be likely to punish for a broken lamp if it were broken in anger while the lower class mother would be more likely to punish if the lamp breaking caused a commotion when she was already irritated, regardless of the reason for the breakage.

Parents may differ between themselves about the proper disciplinary methods as well as the ultimate goals they hope to achieve. Depending upon their own treatment during childhood they have absorbed ideas about the nature of the child, concepts of the "good boy" and "good girl" at all stages of growth, as well as ideas about the personality traits, habits, and goals they want to instill in their children. Most of these concepts are probably rather deeply instilled and express themselves mainly in the interpretations they make of the child's behavior and the response they think should be made.

Imagine a family in which the mother and father are agreed that they want their children to be polite and mannerly when they have guests. One evening neighbors have dropped in and the adults are talking in the living room when their ten-year-old son comes in to listen. They are talking about a recent sports event and the son says excitedly: "That's like the game I saw at school last week, the score was all tied up, and . . ." His father, seeing this as an impolite interruption of adult conversation says: "That's enough, son, you can tell us about it later."

Son: But, Dad, I . . .
Dad: I said that's enough. Now either be quiet and listen or go to your your room.

His mother, seeing this as an expression of her son's interest in the conversation and as good practice in developing sociability, enters the conversation at this time: "Why don't you let him talk, he'll never learn to talk to adults if you keep shutting him off?"

Dad: He is just trying to get attention and the Smiths are not interested in his school's ballgame.
Mother: You make him feel like he's not wanted.
Dad: He's got to learn not to interrupt.
Mother: He wasn't interrupting, he was joining the conversation.

These parents, and others like them, will have great difficulty in agreeing on specific methods of childrearing because they really do not want the same child. They are unlikely to argue this point, however. They are more likely to argue about the techniques of discipline and to blame each other for the failure of all of them to produce a "good" child.

PARENT–CHILD RELATIONSHIP

From studies of the parent–child relationship it appears that the specific methods of discipline are not as important as is the need for the total configuration of family climate and interpersonal interaction to provide the child with a nurturant, predictable, and status-giving set of interactions. Repetitive, consistent interactions which provide an orderly, warm environment allow the child greater opportunity for developing a positive self-concept, with internalized controls on his behavior.

From a review of the studies of parent–child relationships, Dager (1964) has set forth some generalized, tentative conclusions concerning the effect of parental behaviors on the personality of the child. He suggests that:

Permissive (not extreme) and democratic parent–child interaction appears to be associated with children who demonstrate self-confidence, initiative, independence, creativity, and cooperation.

Restrictive or over-protective parent–child interaction is associated with children who are withdrawn, submissive, and dependent.

Rejection by parent(s) is associated with children who are aggressive.

Punishment by parent(s) is associated with children who are aggressive.

These conclusions deal with a consistent group of interactions which transmit to the child certain evaluations of himself within the context of the family group. They do not apply to the single instance of rejection or punishment, for example, but to the case where the continuing relationship is characterized in this way.

Effect on Development of Self

Theoretically, Dager suggests that either extreme permissiveness or extreme restrictiveness inhibits the development of a sense of self. Extreme permissiveness can be interpreted by the child as rejection or indifference. The lack of predictability in an extremely permissive environment prevents him from defining himself in relation to other members of the family, and eventually, we may presume, in relation to the total society. He perhaps loses the self-enhancing experiences of knowing he has learned to control behavior of which his parents disapprove or learned to master a skill of which they heartily approve. In other words, it may appear to him that what he does or does not do is of small value to them because *he* is unimportant to them.

Extreme restrictiveness, on the other hand, makes the developing self of the child merely an extension of the parent, leaving the child little status or independence. Again, his security in the family may appear to lie not in developing a sense of identity of his own, but in being able to predict and comply with the parents' wishes.

Extreme punishment does not appear to inhibit the development of a sense of self, but leads to a negative definition of the self. The child may begin to feel that he can do nothing right, which eventually results in aggressive behavior in an attempt to gain some measure of status (Dager, 1964, pp. 766–67).

These parent–child environments are the result of several factors including the personalities of the parents, the marital relationship, the norms prevalent in the family's particular social context, and the general values defining the nature of the child and of the "good" child which the parents have absorbed from their own socialization process. The environment created in the family will aid or hinder the child's ability to cope with the special problems which confront him as he progresses through the stages of physical and social development.

STAGES IN PERSONAL GROWTH

Development follows a similar, though not identical, pattern in each child. Variations are explained by such factors as sex, intelligence, and socioeconomic opportunity. Girls develop more rapidly than do boys. Bright children develop at a faster rate than do dull children. Those who are well stay ahead in development of those who are undernourished or sickly. In addition, each child has his own timetable of development which in some respects may be unique. Yet there is enough uniformity to establish general patterns.

There is to be a dual scheme of classification in the discussion to follow. Brief descriptions of five periods in postnatal development will be given: infancy, early childhood, late childhood, adolescence, and adulthood. Superimposed upon this time sequence are listed eight developmental stages in the growth of a healthy personality. This latter is adapted from the work of Erik H. Erikson (1950, pp. 6–25), prepared for and presented to the Midcentury White House Conference on Children and Youth.

Infancy

This period, extending from birth until about age one, is characterized by rapid growth and decreasing helplessness. After losing a little weight during the first few days of life, the infant again starts to gain, and by the end of the first year it will have about trebled the birth weight. This is a rate of growth more rapid than at any future time of life. The infant also gains a gradual control over the muscles of his body. He starts to smile and to raise his head a little at about the age of one month. By approximately five months he can roll over; six or seven months, sit up; seven or eight months, crawl; eight or nine months, pull himself up to things; nine or ten months, walk with support; ten or eleven months, stand alone; and eleven to thirteen months, take his first steps without help. The first tooth is likely to appear when the infant is six to eight months old. By one year the child has learned to imitate a number of things; he may play peek-a-boo, or wave "bye-bye," or say "da-da."

Of primary importance during this first stage of life is the building of (1) *a sense of trust*. This develops more or less naturally through the everyday experiences of being cared for and of exploring the world round-about and finding it dependable. Being fed when hungry, changed when wet, and all the time comforted with a tender mother love; finding objects in the same place each time or in the same shape when grasped or held; recognizing consistent actions and reactions on the part of those it sees—these are the kinds of things that make the infant feel safe, secure, and trusting. Denied them he is likely to feel confused, become distrustful, and have difficulty moving to the next task which confronts him in early childhood.

Early Childhood

The period from age one up to about age six, when the child is ready to start school, is known as early childhood. During this time the child gains greater control over his body and its processes. He learns to feed himself and to put his clothes on and take them off. After a few bumps he becomes more sure-footed in his walking and running. Bowel and bladder control are usually mastered during the second year, except perhaps for the nights. Also during this year the child learns to speak; by two he is able to assemble simple words into short sentences. A little later he starts to ask all sorts of questions and to beg for nursery rhymes and bedtime stories.

Early childhood is a period of great curiosity, imitation, and exploration. Children at this time are continually getting into things or trying things out. Lacking experience and judgment, they are likely to take chances which put themselves and others in danger—such as running into a busy street without looking or striking matches without taking proper precautions.

For approximately two years following infancy the child's chief task is that of acquiring (2) *a sense of autonomy.* He comes to assert himself, to feel important as a person, and to be self-reliant. This development must usually wait upon the earlier sense of trust, for unless the child can feel secure he will not dare to risk standing on his own. The new independence of this period is sometimes baffling to parents. Some will welcome the change as an indication the child is growing up. Others will not—wanting to keep the feeling that the baby is totally dependent on them. Still others may feel rejected because the child no longer wants to be cuddled or held so close.

The child has a need, however, for firmness from the parents in keeping him from harm as he learns what he may and may not touch, where he may and may not explore. He also has a need for help in developing confidence in "standing on his own feet." The self-assertions of this period will either turn into normal feelings of adequacy or into feelings of doubt and shame, depending upon how they are handled.

Following trust and autonomy in development is (3) *a sense of initiative.* The four- and five-year-old child wants to do more than just assert himself; he wants to find out what kind of person he is or can become. This is an extremely creative period. During it the child is likely to intrude himself into the activities of others, to engage in an unusual amount of imagination, and to dream up and try out things which are beyond his present abilities. If unduly discouraged he may develop deep feelings of guilt. If properly guided the child will come to distinguish reality from fantasy, though keeping enough of the latter to remain creative and enterprising.

It is believed that these first three stages are of utmost importance in setting the foundation for future development. The amount of trust, autonomy, and initiative the child has developed will influence the way he presents himself to others as he starts to school and the way others respond to him. The exclusive control of the family, if it ever existed, is now at an end as he enters the period of late childhood. The family still remains vitally important, however, as it aids or hinders the accomplishment of new tasks associated with maturing.

Late Childhood

This period extends approximately from age six through age twelve; it roughly parallels grade-school attendance. Sometimes it is referred to as "The Gang Age." It is characterized by rapid learning and by a strong desire for companionship with those of one's own sex, coupled with antagonisms toward the opposite sex. The influence of associates upon one another is great at this time. Learning proceeds at a new pace, because of added stimulation from the classroom. It is now that the child first learns to read; with reading, a whole new world of knowledge and interests opens up.

Paramount in the child's development during late childhood is the acquiring of (4) *a sense of accomplishment.* He will now give up his earlier preoccupation with fantasy and will become interested in real things, in jobs to be done and how to do them. This is a period of steady growth on just about every front. If all goes will, the child will become much more understanding and skillful in tasks performed; he will learn the meaning of fair play and of cooperation in relation to others; and he will acquire the attitudes necessary for responsible citizenship. Chief dangers lie in either underchallenging the child during this stage of growth, so that he loses interest and becomes bored, or in overchallenging him, so that he becomes discouraged and develops feelings of inferiority.

Adolescence

Adolescence begins with the onset of puberty, which is about age twelve or thirteen for the girl and thirteen or fourteen for the boy. It ends at about age twenty-one, the time of legal maturity. Puberty brings with it certain body changes: with the girl, menstruation starts, the breasts commence to enlarge, and hair develops in the armpits and at the pubic region; with the boy, nocturnal emissions make their appearance, the voice deepens, facial hair becomes more prominent, and hair develops in the armpits and at the pubic region. In both sexes physical growth takes place rather rapidly. Generally, also, there will appear such symptoms as loss of appetite, indigestion, headaches, fatigue, insomnia, and skin disorders accompanied by daydreaming, restlessness, moodiness, and irritability.

Early adolescence is known as the awkward age; new and strange changes are taking place within the body which the youth is not quite sure of, or in control of, and which build up a feeling of self-consciousness. For a while, therefore, the teen-ager is apt to pull within himself, to draw away from the crowd. In time he gains control of his body and builds up a new self-confidence. It is then that he starts to assert his individuality by showing off and rebelling against adult authority. Attractions for the opposite sex gain new strength and are surrounded by the glamor of romance. Love affairs tend to be intermittent, separated by periods of disillusionment. Decisions concerning school, work, and one's future are likely to consume a large amount of mental and emotional energy. The adolescent boy or girl is no longer a child and not yet an adult; he is in transition between the two. It is from this fact that most of his problems are to be explained.

Important to development at this stage is (5) *a sense of identity.* The adolescent boy or girl is apt to question previous certainties and to seek new meanings for life and new clarifications of his own place in the scheme of things. It is commonplace for the adolescent to be confused by his own physiological changes and by the multiplicity of conflicting choices which face him as an emerging adult member of society. Such questions as career choice, social status, eventual success, and his relationship to parents and other authority figures loom large in his mind. His tendency at this time to cling to his peer groups and to overemphasize uniformity in dress, behavior, and ideas is to be explained as an attempt to find security in the midst of contradiction and uncertainty. It is essential that he comes to "find himself," so to speak, to establish a new integration after emancipation from earlier ties.

After identity comes (6) *a sense of intimacy*—with others and with one's self. Unless the adolescent is first sure of himself (of his identity) he will tend to shy away from close interaction and introspection. Yet "boys and girls late in adolescence usually have need for a kind of fusion with the essence of other people and for a communion with their own inner resources" (Erikson, 1950, p. 22). Dating in early adolescence serves mainly as a means to explore others' reactions and in this way define one's own role or identity. In later adolescence, however, there comes a greater need for mental, emotional, and physical intimacy as personality expressions in their own rights. Whether or not he is able to achieve satisfying intimate relationships will depend partly on his success in coping with earlier developmental tasks. To the extent that he has not developed some degree of trust, autonomy, and initiative he is not likely to be able to build an intimate relationship with others. Unless he has developed some sense of identity and self-worth he will be unable to turn his attention away from himself. He may have dates and "love affairs" but the intimacy will not be mutual since he will have little interest in understanding someone else.

Although the accomplishment of this task is dependent on the partial resolution of the earlier ones, it is also an influential factor for further maturity.

Intergenerational Conflict. It is during adolescence that communication is likely to be most difficult between the generations. This is partly because the adolescent is consumed with his own problems of developing a sense of identity apart from his family. He must disengage himself, so to speak, to find out who he is without them. He must prove to himself that he can be independent, but dependency is comfortable, too. He may lack the necessary knowledge, experience, and finances to be truly independent so he attempts to artificially establish it by attempting to overthrow or by rebelling against prior authority—as if by doing away with it he wins independence by default.

Since he is also attempting to establish a feeling of intimacy with the opposite sex, he may feel that to do this he must deny the feeling of intimacy with his parents, although this feeling (love for parents) is the groundwork upon which his success in achieving adult intimacy is built. In other words, he is likely to be caught between powerful pulls which he does not understand. If parents do not understand them either, there can develop much tension and conflict in the parent–child interaction.

For parents who are unprepared, this phase of their childrearing experience can be difficult indeed. They will have grown accustomed to having their children look up to them as persons who know everything and can do everything. But now, somewhat suddenly, they find themselves being challenged, criticized, or even defied. It is something like the father whose early adolescent son called him at the office saying, "Hello, who is this?" The father, recognizing the voice, answered, "I am the smartest man in the world," after which the son hesitated, mumbled, "Pardon me, I got the wrong number," and quickly hung up. The point is that adolescent children commonly come to regard their parents for awhile as "wrong numbers," and for parents this is no joke.

Yet this pulling away is both inevitable and desirable. This is the only way that the child can mature into a responsible adult capable of making

his own decisions as a citizen and as a husband or wife. There are fundamental differences between youth and age which are likely to be highlighted during this period. Youth is full of energy and is out to conquer
the world which is opening up before it; having neither experience nor
possessions, it is willing to turn things over, to take a chance. Age, on
the other hand, has less energy at its command and less time for a new
start; having invested a large portion of a lifetime in status quo, it is less
willing to see things changed. Youth has nothing to lose and perhaps
much to gain by change; age has nothing to gain and perhaps much to
lose. Therefore, youth tends to be radical and age conservative.

Another factor tending to throw the present and oncoming generations
out of gear with respect to each other is the fact of social change itself.
Society never stands still, so that with each generation there are new ways
of doing things. Unless the older generation is willing and able to continuously alter its deep-seated ways of thinking and behaving, it runs the
danger of being branded as "old fogies" and of considering the younger
generation as "upstarts."

Intergenerational conflicts tend to concentrate within the family. This
is because of the intimate and somewhat continuous manner in which
two or more generations are thrown together there. Also, it frequently
happens that adolescence in children comes along at about the same time
as the climacteric in parents. Since each of these life-changes is accompanied by problems of its own, their coincidental occurrence can often
mean a doubling up of the tensions of family relationships.

In spite of the normal tensions and potential dangers outlined above,
it is entirely possible for parents and their adolescent children to thoroughly
enjoy each other. This, however, will depend upon the approach, both
before and during the adolescent period. If the child hasn't been permitted to grow up and the parents still try to hold on too closely, naturally
there will be trouble. But if the approach has been positive and if the
controls have been internalized within the child, there will then be a
common basis for mutual understanding, respect, and satisfaction. The
adolescent period needn't be unusually difficult; it can even be fun.

The main job parents have is to work themselves out of a job. It is
that of teaching self-reliance, so that the children gradually learn to make
their own decisions, to stand responsible for their own behavior, and in
time to achieve an integrity and creativity in their own right. After parents have succeeded in "weaning" their adolescent children so that these
youngsters emerge as independent, responsible individuals, their job is
done.

When this has been successfully done so that the child no longer needs
the parents to stay in the parental role, new relationships can develop between them and the child has entered adulthood.

Adulthood

Adulthood, beginning in the early twenties and extending until the end of life, covers a span of approximately fifty years. It can be subdivided, of course, and in later chapters we will have occasion to look at different portions of it separately. Here we can note that in general the period is characterized by less rapid learning and the acceptance of mature responsibilities, such as those or marriage, parenthood, jobs, and citizenship.

Frequently starting in adolescence, but not reaching full development until adulthood, is what Erikson spoke of as (7) *the parental sense*. By this he meant broadly that one becomes interested in productivity and creativity, but specifically that he becomes interested in nourishing and nurturing children, as a community trust rather than a selfish indulgence. Failure to develop this sense of parenthood leaves one self-absorbed and self-indulgent, lacking in a social or humanitarian point of view.

Finally, in normal development there comes (8) *a sense of integrity*. In Erikson's words, "Integrity thus means a new and different love of one's parents, free of the wish that they should have been different, and an acceptance of the fact that one's own life is one's own responsibility" (Erikson, 1950, p. 24). At this point the individual has completed his own value system and is able to operate in his own right, with initiative yet with responsibility. Without this sense of integrity, adults are apt to feel disappointed with life and, in extreme cases, full of despair.

It goes without saying that not everyone successfully copes with the personal development tasks associated with the physical growth stages. Successful coping is enhanced, however, when a child has parents who understand the growth process, who are able to build a mutual sense of trust and respect between themselves and their children, and have enough integrity of their own to be able to provide controls and guidance as well as to allow freedom and independence in terms of the child's needs rather than their own. In other words, parents who have reached psychological adulthood are better able to rear children to psychological adulthood.

SPECIAL PROBLEMS

The discussion above has dealt with intact families in which both mother and father are present. Since both parents are important for the development of proper sex identities for both boys and girls, those cases in which one parent is gone permanently or for long periods of time, or in which interaction with one or both parents is reduced become special problems.

The One-Parent Family

Although the one-parent family can be headed by either a male or a female, by far the most prevalent pattern is the father-absent household. It has been estimated that in the urban "slum" areas, from 25 to 40 per cent of the households follow this female-based pattern (W. B. Miller, 1959).

Father Absence. The absence of the father leaves a vacancy in one of the roles in the expected family constellation. Theoretically it would be expected that if there is no adequate masculine substitute the opportunity for learning appropriate sex roles is lessened for both sexes. The mother becomes the sole source of affection, power, and visibility—the most important factors associated with identification. Thus, both boys and girls develop a more intense identification with her when the father is not present. This is more appropriate for the girls. But even girls are put at a disadvantage, for normally the father–daughter relationship provides initial practice in the male–female relationship as well as rewards for appropriate feminine behavior which may affect her later adjustments in dating and marriage.

Studies of the effects of father absence tend to show that the early consequences are more devastating for boys. One study of the conditions under which young boys are more likely to make the normal shift from a feminine to masculine identification shows that boys with strong masculine identifications are more likely to see their fathers as nurturant, punitive, and powerful (Mussen and Distler, 1968). This finding suggests that if the father is not available for rather intensive interaction, the son's masculine identification is impaired. Evidence from comparisons of boys from father-present and father-absent homes supports this view. Boys without fathers tend to be more infantile, dependent, and to show more conflict in their sex identification than boys with their fathers present (Lynn and Sawyer, 1959; Tiller, 1957; Winch, 1962).

The absence of the father not only removes one of the primary role relationships in producing sex identification for both sexes but appears to change the nature of the mother–child relationship also. She is, of course, relied on more by the child since there is no alternative, but she also tends to become more over-protective and concerned about her children (Lynn and Sawyer, 1959; Tiller, 1957). Thus, some of the consequences of over-protection perhaps intensify the effects of father absence. Fatherless children tend to have unsatisfactory peer group relations and to feel insecure and inferior more than children with two parents (Green and Beall, 1962).

Disturbances in masculine sex identification do not always manifest themselves in overt feminine behavior. As the boy grows and is confronted with other boys, male teachers, and the cultural definition of masculinity, he is more likely than boys with adequate fathering to develop a defensive masculinity with a wholesale acceptance of the culturally prescribed traits. This seems especially prominent in the lower socioeconomic segments of the society (W. B. Miller, 1958).

The Sometimes Father. The fact that the father role is occupied does not necessarily mean that the father is available for interaction. The commuting father who leaves for the office before the children are up and returns late at night is not available for visible contact except perhaps on weekends. The preoccupied father may be physically present but psychologically absent. The abdication of the father role is more visible in the lower class family, but may be fairly prevalent in the career-oriented, upper-middle class family. The external demands on the father's time and energy may be just as effective in removing the upper-middle class father from interaction with his children as is the lack of family involvement among lower class fathers.

There is practically no research concerned with the effects of the psychologically-absent but physically-present father on the development of children (See Bronfenbrenner, 1969 and Tiller, 1967). It may be that the unavailability of a physically present father may produce more feelings of rejection and frustration in the child than the physically-absent father. On the other hand if the father is "successful" by societal standards and admired in the community, the child may attempt to identify with the image of the father transmitted to him by the mother. In other words, a "phantom father" may be constructed by the child, built on evaluations of him coming from the mother and others in the community. Theoretically, it can be expected that the lack of consistent, involved interaction with either parent or adequate substitutes, would effect the development of sex identification and the internalization of parental values. Empirical substantiation of the effects of psychological absence will have to await future research.

The Working Mother. The consequences of the absent or the sometimes father on the child's development may perhaps be duplicated in the working mother, to the extent that her working removes her physically or psychologically from interaction with her children.

It is of course not necessary for either parent to be in continual interaction with the child for him to develop adequate sex identification and internal controls. Some absence may be desirable. The parent who is "excessively" present and protective does not allow the child to develop a separate sense of self, or create any need for the child to internalize a set of inner controls. On the other hand, the parent who is "excessively" absent is not visible enough for the child to be aware of parental values, let alone internalize them as inner controls. The major problem for research seems to be in defining what is "excessive" in either presence or absence.

The studies attempting to define the relationship between the working mother and effect on children have been contradictory and inconclusive. That this should be so is apparent. The category of working mother takes in a wide variety of work patterns, reasons for working, attitudes toward work, and age of child when the mother is working. It includes all kinds of arrangements for child care from grandmothers, aunts, and babysitters to day-nurseries or to no adequate supervision at all. We have not concerned ourselves with the effect of the "working father" because it is assumed that he works for one reason—to provide for his family. The same is not true of working mothers. Her working may be interpreted as rejection of motherhood, as being necessary for financial reasons, as expressing her interests, because of boredom, or for any number of other reasons.

She may enjoy it or hate it, as may the working father, with repercussions on the parent–child relationship. She may feel she is being asked to do too much without adequate appreciation of her efforts, as may the working father, with implications for familial interactions. The social context in which the work takes place and the impact it has on the self-concepts of all involved will influence the quality of the parent–child relationship, as well as the quantity of interaction. This is true for both the working father and working mother. But since the mother has for so long been seen as the most important parent as far as child development in the early years is concerned, more concern has been shown for her absence. It is assumed that the father will be away working, so the attention has been focused on the variability provided by the mother's habits, since the phenomenon of maternal employment is relatively new, especially to the middle class scene.

Although the research in this area is largely inconclusive, it appears that the mother working affects sons and daughters differently. Several studies suggest that when the working mother has negative attitudes toward her work, her grade-school children tend to be more assertive and aggressive toward her and their peers and have less impulse control in general than children of non-working mothers. Boys are likely to be more dependent. When she has positive attitudes toward her work, her children are likely to have less initiative and be less aggressive than children with non-working mothers. Regardless of attitude toward work, children with working mothers are likely to perform less well in school and have less effective ways of reacting to frustration than children with non-working mothers (Hoffman, 1961). The differences between the children from working and non-working mothers are not large, but there is some consistency in the findings that sons of working mothers, in particular, are more dependent, obedient, less self-reliant, less sociable, and more likely to seek succorance from adults than those of non-working mothers (Siegel et al., 1963). Whether these are seen as positive or negative traits in grade-school boys will depend upon the value system of the parents.[3] By the time adolescence is reached, part-time employment of the mother seems to have a favorable effect (Douvan, 1963; Nye, 1952, 1963b; Peterson, 1961). The effect, however, appears to differ depending upon the socioeconomic position as well as upon the work pattern of the father. Bronfenbrenner gathered data on the relationship between what he called "saliency," or the extent to which a parent was actively present in the child's world, and personality development. As far as responsibility was concerned he found that the effect of parental absence on the child varied according to sex of the child and the amount of time the remaining parent was in the home (Hartley, 1963). When the same-sex parent was present in the home a good deal of the time, the child of either sex was rated above average in responsibility. When the same-sex parent was absent much of the time and the opposite-sex parent was present much of the time, the child was rated low in responsibility. This would seem to suggest that our prevalent family system in which the father is at work much of the time and the mother is at home promotes greater responsibility in girls than in boys.

When both parents were absent much of the time the responsibility development was low for both sexes. When the same-sex parent was gone much of the time and the opposite sex parent was present only an intermediate amount of time, the highest responsibility rating of all was obtained. Thus, if a father's occupation keeps him away from home for long hours, his son's development of responsibility is likely to suffer when his mother is home most of the time, or when she is away much of the time. It climbs to its highest point, however, if she is away an intermediate amount of time, such as in part-time employment or in community activities.

The child, then, seems affected by the total configuration of the relative presence or absence of both parents, their orientation toward the work that takes them away, and the impact that the work has on the parental self-concepts. Hartley (1963) suggests that if the assumption of psychologists is correct that one can give to others only what one has as part of his self, the mother's increased feelings of self-fulfillment and personal freedom should decrease the amount of crippling maternal possessiveness. The same can probably be said for fathers—although our unwarranted assumption that middle and upper-middle class men have a great amount

[3] For a review of studies on maternal employment, see Lois W. Hoffman (1963).

of freedom of choice and receive self-fulfillment in their work has kept us from asking the same questions about the connection between their working experience and the development of the child that we have asked about mothers.

It is well to remember that a mother can be a non-working mother and still be out of the home when her children are there. A working-mother may have her work days arranged so that she is gone for seven or eight hours but still be at home when the children go to school in the morning and when they come home in the afternoon.

Non-Interaction

Bronfenbrenner (1969) speculates that urban and suburban living have created a situation in which the school-aged child is not home much of the time, and when he is there he is not in interaction with grownups. He leaves home early in the morning on a school bus, and may not return until late in the afternoon. His father probably leaves before he does in the morning and arrives home much later after an hour or so of commuting.

His mother may or may not be at home when he arrives. If she is not working she may be out because of community obligations. If she is there she may be involved in dinner preparation, leaving the child to the company of other children or the TV. Where parents are absent physically or psychologically for long periods of time, the peer group takes over as the greatest influence on developing values. These values, unless under adult control, are likely in American society to emphasize aggressive, anti-social behavior (Bronfenbrenner, 1969, p. 530).

The continual physical presence of the parent, then, would seem less important than the quality and intensity of interaction with the adult representatives of society. Where the societal structure itself imposes segregation of age groupings, family interactions become more important as an insulator against anti-social or irresponsible behavior.

THE PRINCIPLE OF VALUE RELEVANCE

People desire different things in their children. Some want children who are conforming, quiet, conscientious, and easily influenced. Some want children who are lively, aggressive, bold, and independent. Some who want girls like the former, may want boys like the latter. Some may want children when they are young to be quiet, obedient, and conforming but to grow into individualistic, aggressive, and independent adolescents.

People not only differ in their ideas of the children they want, they differ in their ideas about what it takes to develop these traits. The ideas people have about desirable traits in children and their own responsibility in developing them will influence the way they interpret the children's behavior, and whether they encourage or rebuff it.

If both parents have the same concepts of what they want in their children and similar ideas about how to achieve it, the result for the child is likely to be a relatively consistent, predictable world. If other families with whom he is in contact do things much the same way, he is likely to see this as the way "parents are supposed to treat children," and accept it as inevitable. What the parents do, what they encourage and inhibit, and the ability of the child to meet their expectations will have consequences for his developing personality, but the expectations are likely to be clear, with few opportunities for confusions, ambiguities, and frustrations stemming from not knowing what to do to win approval. This does not mean that the child will always conform but there is likely to be a rather clear behavior–consequence relationship.

This amount of consistency between parents and supporting groups is not very probable today, however. Conflicts can exist at various levels— between mother and father; between mother and father and supporting family members, such as grandparents; between the family and outside authorities, such as the school; between the family and the child's peer group. Because of the variability in childrearing values and concepts of the "good" child or adolescent existing in the society at the same time, there is an increased probability that every child will at some time receive conflicting evaluations of the same behavior. It is perhaps more important today than previously that the family provides a consistent value framework within which the child can organize his developing self-concept and more easily put conflicting evaluations in perspective.

All methods of childrearing, short of some extreme forms of permissiveness, restrictiveness, and punitiveness, have produced productive, responsible, well-adjusted adults as well as non-productive, irresponsible, and mal-adjusted adults. The key factors are to be found not so much in the techniques used but in the extent to which the interaction between family members provides consistency in response. This aids the child in developing a sense of self which defines him as a person of worth, who knows and is willing to accept the consequences of his behavior. A person who develops this kind of feeling about himself is able to use his abilities, whatever they are, for the benefit of himself and others. This family environment is more likely to be achieved when the parents are in basic agreement on their concepts of the nature of the child and on their expectations for "good" child behavior.

Even so, there may be occasional disagreements on the methods of achieving certain behaviors. They are, however, more easily resolved if the basic values are in agreement.

SUMMARY

Not only do parents affect the development of children, the children affect the parents. The first baby occasions such a reorganization of the husband–wife role relations that it has been called the first crisis in marriage. Most parents manage to adjust to the addition of the third party within several months.

Subsequent children are not as likely to produce crisis reactions, but each new child changes the structure of the family group. Family interaction is characterized by shifting coalitions between family members. Each additional member expands the possible combinations, with consequences in the complexity of the power structure.

Childrearing is a continuous process which goes on hour after hour, whether or not the parents are consciously involved in the task. It tends to have some continuity to it since the evaluations of and responses to the child are influenced by deeply held ideas about the intrinsic nature of children, concepts of the "good" child, and ideas about how one transforms the "natural" child into the "good" child.

Since 1900 there has been considerable change in our culture concerning all three of these aspects of childrearing—the intrinsic nature of the child, concepts of the good child, and methods of discipline. The change has not replaced older ideas with newer ones, but has resulted in the simultaneous existence of conflicting ideas about childrearing in the society. Social class differences, for example, have been found not only in the goals of childrearing but in responses to similar child behavior.

Studies tend to indicate that the specific method of childrearing is not so important as is the requirement that the total configuration of family climate and interpersonal interaction provide the child with a nurturant, predictable, and status-giving set of interactions. A positive self-concept, with internalized controls on behavior, seems associated with repetitive, consistent interactions which provide a warm, orderly environment. These environments are the result of several factors including the personalities of the parents, the marital relationship, the norms prevalent in the family's social context, and the general values defining the nature of the child and the "good" child, absorbed by the parents from their own socialization experiences.

Special problems in childrearing are produced by the one-parent family, whether it results from the complete absence of one parent, prolonged absence because of work, or psychological absence because of preoccupation. Although the studies are selective and therefore inconclusive the important factor appears to be the total configuration of relative availability for interaction of both parents rather than just the physical absence of one.

Bronfenbrenner speculates that the pattern developing in urban and suburban areas is one of decreased adult–child interaction, even though the family may be intact and the mother not employed. He suggests that TV and peer relationships both in and out of school may be becoming more important influences on developing values than are adults. These values, unless under adult control, are likely to emphasize aggressive, anti-social behavior. Although always important, perhaps meaningful family interaction is more important now than ever before, as the structure of society reduces the amount of contact between children and the adult representatives of society.

QUESTIONS AND PROJECTS

1. Some people have claimed that "a good way to save a disintegrating marriage is to have a child." What do you think? Is your answer to this question different after reading this chapter than it was before? Explain why or why not.

2. What are some ways a couple may guard against the crisis period associated with the first child?

3. If you had older brothers and sisters, describe the differences which occurred in the family "climate" as each left home. Can you explain the changes if any.

4. Describe the typical stages of child development from infancy through to adulthood. Why is an understanding of the maturation process important to successful parenthood? Discuss.

5. Give the reasons for the prevalence of intergenerational conflict during adolescence. What could be done to reduce it? Would it be a good idea to reduce it to zero? Why or why not?

6. Give reasons for the frequency of parental conflict over childrearing. If parents seem to agree on childrearing during early childhood, is this a guarantee they will still agree during adolescence? Why or why not?

7. Using other sources, prepare a paper on the effect of father absence on the development of children in the family. Are there differences in the effect of the physically absent father and the psychologically absent father? Discuss.

8. Prepare a paper on the effects of the working mother on the development of children in the family. Can you draw any conclusions about the differential effects of physical absence and psychological absence? Discuss.

9. Discuss possible interrelationships among several current social trends in our society, such as: (1) the rising juvenile delinquency rate; (2) rising demands for women's rights as exemplified by the Women's Liberation groups; (3) the fears of overpopulation; (4) the rising incidence of student violence in the public schools. What suggestions can you make for family roles which may aid in alleviating the problems seen to be related to these trends?

10. Describe your ideal son and daughter at the age of five; the age of twelve; the age of sixteen; the age of twenty; the age of thirty. Does the ideal at one age seem to be socializing for the ideal at the next? Be honest in your descriptions. Do not deliberately construct them so that they are logically

consistent. Discuss these ideal images with your friends. Are there many differences between your ideas and theirs? What things account for the differences, if any?

11. What are your ideas about the nature of a child? Do your ideas agree with those of your friends? What are the implications of this for ideas about childrearing?

12. Describe the power structure in your own family, including the coalitions and conditions under which these form and shift.

20

Postparenthood
and the Aged

Normally, every family runs through a cycle—commencing with marriage, continuing through various stages of parenthood, and ending with the death of the mates. Families have both beginnings and ends, and within that range, periods of both expansion and contraction. The 1948 National Conference on Family Life considered seven stages: early marriage and the expectant family; the child-bearing family; the preschool family; the school-age family; the family with teen-agers; the family as a launching center; and the family in later years. This scheme, though recognizing prechild and postchild periods within the cycle, gives major attention to parenthood.

The growth and decline in the family cycle suggests that just as each new child changes the structure of family interaction, each child moving out of the family has an impact on the remaining relationships. A second son who has enjoyed a fairly accepting attitude from his father because his older brother has taken the brunt of the father's irritations and demands may find that life is not nearly so comfortable when the eldest son goes off to school, gets a job, marries, or moves away. The target of the father's irritation and demands may move from child to child until the last one leaves, when it is turned toward his wife—or the family dog.

On the other hand, previous sources of conflict may entirely disappear as the child who was the focal point moves out of daily interaction. At any rate the family interaction changes as the children leave one by one, as the sex composition of the family changes, and as the number of available coalitions decreases. The youngest child may have a long experience as an *only* child, if there was a wide gap in ages between the last two

446

children. The coming, the growing, and the going creates an ever changing pattern of family interactions with consequences for the self-concepts of all.

THE FAMILY AS A LAUNCHING CENTER

At about the time of legal maturity children commence leaving home, getting married, and starting families of their own. The parental family is the launching center. It serves as a place of preparation prior to the parting, and it stands by ready to help in case of an emergency following the separation.

The most traditional launching pattern has been that of getting the daughter married and the son set up in some kind of job or occupation. But parents are interested in whom the son marries also, though they have less responsibility there and are not concerned so directly or so extensively in the wedding preparations. Furthermore, with the equalizing of sex roles, more and more girls plan for employment in addition to marriage. Parental attempts to dictate either the occupation or the marital choice to a son or daughter frequently result in resentment and rebellion. Guidance in these matters is important, but it had better come somewhat subtly or by invitation. The major task of parenthood is to transfer responsibility. It is foolish for parents to continue to feel responsible for adult children who themselves have become responsible. Transferring responsibility is sometimes difficult, whether one is retiring from an active parental role or an active occupational role or any other role. It is especially difficult when the role is imbedded in deep emotional bonds and feelings of self-worth.

Readjustment of Parents

In a previous chapter we discussed the problem of establishing new roles in the marriage and with in-laws in the midst of redefining old roles carried forward from the family of orientation. Now the focus is on the other side of the picture, on the readjustment of the parents. The *young* couple is looking toward the future to a new life of expanding relationships. The *older* couple is experiencing a decreasing set of important relationships, with frequent feelings of emptiness and loneliness at the loss. *They* are the ones being replaced as an important part of their child's life. Theirs is the problem of filling the gap rather than one of allocating time to the many demands for evidence of continued affection.

As mentioned earlier, this readjustment is more difficult for the wife than for the husband. It also varies depending on whether the child leaving home is the first of several children or the last to leave. Adjustments, of course, come with each departure, but the most devastating comes when the wife defines the situation as one in which she has lost her reason for living because the children no longer need her. Some women will never feel this. They either have never derived the major source of their self-esteem from the mother role or they have gradually replaced it with other activities during their children's teen years.

Not only does the emancipation of children from their parents contribute to a more successful marriage, but the emancipation of the parents from their children appears to contribute to a more successful middle age. This does not mean complete severance of the emotional attachments but that the attachments become warm relationships between adults who respect each other's independence while remaining interested in their well-being.

MARITAL ADJUSTMENT IN THE MIDDLE AND LATER YEARS

For the vast majority of parents, the time will come when all of the children are gone and the mother and father again become primarily husband and wife. The proportion of time spent in this postparental period of the family cycle (frequently referred to as the "empty nest" stage) has been increasing, due both to the lowering of the age of marriage and increased life expectancy. A husband aged 25 and a wife aged 22 in 1912 had less than a one out of two chance of both being alive when the wife reached age 60. This would be only about five years after the last child was launched. Their chances were only two out of five that they would both survive an additional five years! Today, a husband aged 25 and a wife aged 22 have better than a two out of three chance of both living until the wife reaches age 60—about eight years after the marriage of the last child. Their chance of surviving together another five years is better than one out of two (Metropolitan Life, 1968, p. 10). Looked at another way, if they live to launch their last child (average age of husband, 54; wife, 52) the white husband can look forward, on the average, to 20 more years of life, while the white wife can look forward to 25 more years. The life expectancy at these ages is slightly lower for non-whites—18 years for the husband and 22 years for the wife (Metropolitan Life, 1967, p. 9).

In 1890 the average woman was a widow before her last child was launched, by 1950 she could expect her marriage to endure another 14 years after the last child left home (Glick, 1947, 1955). For two out of five couples married in 1968 the remaining time of joint survival will be extended to 18 years, and for 1 out of 4, to 23 years or more. For many couples, then, close to one-third of their time together will be spent after the childrearing period is over.

Variation in Adjustment Patterns

Since postparental marriage is a relatively new phenomenon, there is not a great deal of empirical information about it. What information there is gives varying pictures of married life in the later years. Evidence from the earlier studies tended to show that satisfaction in these years was associated with the ability to find substitute activities to fill the vacancy left by children. Rose (1955), for example, found life satisfactions to be highest for those middle-aged women who experienced close family relationships and who cheerfully accepted their homemaking chores, but who also supplemented these family activities with paying jobs outside the home, participation in community programs, and relatively frequent evenings out with the husband.

After the launching of children, most couples experience an increase in joint activities, both within and outside the home. Sussman (1955) has shown that at this stage of the family cycle parents begin to spend more time together conversing, listening to the radio, watching television, playing games, entertaining friends, doing housework, making home repairs, taking trips, dining out, and attending clubs, movies, or concerts. Furthermore, with the children off their hands, many couples now turn to major undertakings long planned for, such as remodeling the house, acquiring a summer cottage, or taking an extended vacation. They can do these things because they have more time and usually more money. Even more important, however, is the fact that they must now fend for themselves, turn to each other for support, and set up substitute activities for those that formerly centered around children. Wives expressed these needs more frequently than did their husbands. Adjustment patterns were two: some couples welcomed their new-found freedom and anxiously turned to hobbies or activities that they had been held back on previously; others were able to continue close relationships with the married child and his family—through helping out with shopping, sewing, baby-sitting, house-building, and the like—and these couples had little time or desire for substitute activities of a nonfamilial variety.

These studies suggest that the freedom from childrearing responsibility offers a renewed opportunity for husband–wife interaction, fewer financial demands and therefore more money available for luxuries, and more free time for individual interests.

Another view of marriage in the later years, however, suggests that it is a time of loneliness and estrangement between husbands and wives who have for so long been mother and father that they can no longer find enjoyment in each other. They may have more time to pursue their own interests but they have no interests except in their children who have little time for them. Several adjustments are seen to come together at this time to make the marriage relationship difficult. Both sexes undergo the climacteric—changes in the hormonal balance—with varying psychological consequences. It is also the time when men must recognize the extent to which they will realize their occupational goals. Along with this are the fears of waning sexual capacity, discussed in Chapter 14. These things coming together are seen to make the adjustments of the empty nest period more difficult. It may be seen to be not only empty of children but empty of all meaningful interaction.

Evidence of Declining Satisfaction

There is some evidence to support the picture of declining marital satisfaction in the middle years. Pineo (1961), in a follow-up study of marriages after twenty years, described a general drop in marital satisfaction and adjustment from the earlier years. There was less intimacy, less confiding, and less reciprocal settlement of disagreements. More persons reported loneliness although personal adjustment did not decline over the years.

Blood and Wolfe investigated changes over the family cycle in several aspects of marital interaction. Over the years there is a decrease in the frequency wives turn to their husbands with their troubles (1960, pp. 191–92). Wives become less satisfied with love and in general less satisfied with their marriages (pp. 232, 264). There is likely to be less sharing of tasks between husband and wife as children come, grow, and leave home (p. 70; Hill, 1965, p. 128). It appears that there is a general tendency for them to live more separate lives as time goes by. Somewhat contradictory to this, however, is the slight upswing in satisfaction with companionship and husband's understanding in the postparental years (Blood and Wolfe, 1960, pp. 156, 217). Whether this means that the amount of companionship and understanding of the husband increases as they are no longer distracted by children, or that the wife has scaled down her expectations, is not known.

A later study of lower- and upper-middle class postparental couples in Kansas City, Missouri, gives a less dismal view of the middle years and also shows the variation among couples (Deutscher, 1964). A couple who had a great deal to share in their marriage while children were present would not be likely to cease sharing just because their children had left. On the other hand, a marriage which had been characterized by boredom or conflict would not be expected to change miraculously in the postparental stage. Certain habitual ways of interacting would be expected to continue to characterize the marriage.

Although Deutscher's (1964) sample was small, the depth of his interviews provides insight into the satisfactions and dissatisfactions experienced by the couples who were between the ages of 40 and 65, had had from one to four children, all of whom had been launched. Close to one-half of these couples rated the present period of their life as "better" than preceding stages. About one-third said it was "as good." The rest were either undecided about the evaluation or definitely thought it was "as bad" or "worse" than earlier periods of their marriages.[1]

Typical Satisfactions

Typical satisfactions were expressed such as: the relief from the financial responsibility of children, freedom from excessive housework and the feeling of being tied down, and freedom to be oneself rather than a model for the children. Some mentioned a decrease in nervousness and irritability and generally more enjoyment of each other's company. Among the difficulties encountered by those who did not see it as a satisfying period were problems associated with the menopause and other disabilities accompanying aging; the definition of oneself as a failure either in occupational or childrearing terms; and the inability to fill the vacancy left by the departing children (Deutscher, 1964).

Another study (Rollins and Feldman, 1970) of 799 middle class couples suggests that there is a gradual decrease in satisfaction from the period when the oldest child is an infant to the launching period when only about nine per cent of the respondents report that this stage of the life cycle is "very satisfying." There is then a dramatic increase in satisfaction during retirement (see Figure 20-1).

GRANDPARENTHOOD

One of the changes which helps to fill the gap in the postparental period is the advent of grandchildren. Most parents look forward to this after their children are married. However some find it difficult to define themselves as old enough to be "Grandma" or "Grandpa." The problem is not in accepting the grandchildren but in accepting themselves in the new role with its connotation of aging. Indicative of this paradox in assuming the grandparent role is the often heard quip, "I don't mind being a grandfather, but I hate the idea of being married to a grandmother."

The coming of grandchildren introduces a new focus of interest and new ways in which the grandparents can contribute to the second generation.

[1] This rather euphoric view of the postparental period does not appear to go beyond the age of 60. In a study of couples aged 60–80, only 2 per cent looked upon this later period as the happiest of their lives (Jacob Tuckman and Irving Lorge, 1954).

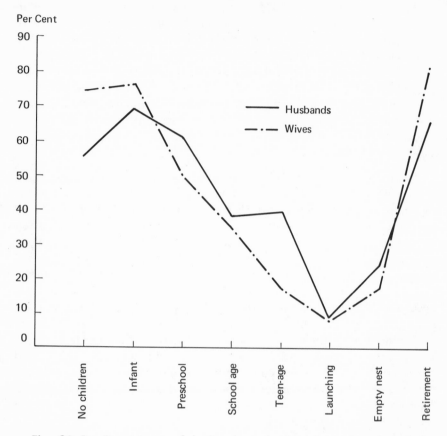

Fig. 20–1. Percentages of husbands and wives in each stage of the family life cycle reporting present stage as "very satisfying." (Adapted from Rollins and Feldman, 1970, Figure 4, p. 26.)

A study of more than 700 old people in a midwestern community revealed that 24 per cent of the grandparents and 4 per cent of the great-grandparents at least occasionally assumed the role of baby tender. Most of these avoided turning this role into a full-time job, however; they enjoyed their grandchildren for short periods but felt the need to go back to peace and quiet for the long stretches. Nevertheless, of the few who took regular care of children while parents worked, some were able to derive personal pride and pleasure from it, as shown in the following quotation.

I think them that has lots of interests live longer. . . . Right now I could live with my daughter, live a lady's life and not lift a hand but I don't want to. . . . I always have to keep busy. I'm here to take care of the children because they need a home. My daughter-in-law works and I think the children need someone around all of the time—the granddaughter who is 19 needs me and my 11-year-old grandson needs more time than his working mother can give him (Albrecht, 1954b, p. 201).

Von Hentig (1946) has shown how the modern grandmother often plays a vital and effective role in family survival. Though not generally accepted as an active member of the group, she is always "standing ready in emergency, especially when there is a gap to be filled and missing members of intermediary generations have to be replaced." Here are typical situations into which she fits: providing shelter for divorcees, caring for illegitimate or neglected grandchildren, receiving children and grandchildren into her home when apartments cannot be found or when the man is out of work.

Cavan (1956) decries the modern tendency to reject old people, and argues that closer relationships among generational levels would be of benefit to all concerned: to the aging parents by supplying their emotional and affectional needs; to the adult child by supportive aids of various kinds; and to the grandchild by building a sense of family continuity. Regarding this last point, she says:

> Grandparents are often called upon in emergencies, but there are many ways in which grandparents can make a continuing contribution. When affection and protective care of children are as much emphasized as at present, grandparents may provide additional security to children. The inclusion of grandparents in the circle of loving and beloved adults may also prevent too exclusive a relationship from developing between parents and children. Grandparents can also give children a sense of the continuity and unity of family life and some knowledge of their own family history. Mobility has tended to destroy historical contacts and knowledge. Grandparents carry with them in memory and sometimes in documents the past history of the family, which they have received from their parents and grandparents. The memory of a grandparent may span 150 years of family history (Cavan, 1956, p. 327).

Changing Grandparent Roles

One of the changes following the quickening of the early part of the family cycle is the earlier age at which parents become grandparents. If both mother and daughter, for example, have babies at the median age of first birth (age 22), the mother will become a grandmother age 44. Since this is a median, many will become grandmothers well before this age.

The increasing prevalence of more youthful grandparents would be expected to be accompanied by changes in acceptance of the role and the way it is played. Neugarten and Weinstein (1964) have provided data concerning variation in grandparenting as well as variation in satisfaction with the role. The majority of grandparents in their sample found only comfort, satisfaction, and pleasure in being grandparents (59 per cent).

Approximately one-third, however, expressed discomfort or disappointment in their roles. This was slightly more prevalent among grandmothers (33 per cent) than among grandfathers (29 per cent).

There were five distinct styles of grandparenting which emerged. The most prevalent for both grandmothers (31 per cent) and grandfathers (33 per cent) was the *formal*. These grandparents are characterized by doing what they consider proper for grandparents to do. They like to provide special treats and occasionally provide a baby-sitting service. They maintain a clear distinction between parenting and grandparenting. They are careful not to offer childrearing advice, and leave parenting to the parents. This style was more characteristic of grandparents over age 65 (59 per cent) than of the younger ones (31 per cent).

The second most prevalent style for grandmothers (29 per cent), but not for grandfathers (24 per cent), was the *fun-seeker*. This role is characterized by informality and playfulness. The grandchildren are seen as a source of leisure activity or as self-indulgence. Lines of authority—with either the grandchild or his parents—are irrelevant. The goal of the relationship is fun for both grandchild and grandparent. This style was more popular among grandparents under age 65 (37 per cent) than among the older group.

The *distant figure* style was the second most prevalent for grandfathers (29 per cent) but was third in prevalence for grandmothers (19 per cent). This describes the grandparent who appears on Christmas and birthdays, but rarely in between. In this study the distance was not geographically imposed since they lived in the same metropolitan area. This style appeared to be associated with difficulties in redefining the self as a grandparent, strained relations with the son or daughter-in-law, or concentration on other activities in the community or occupational world. This style was also more characteristic of younger grandparents (32 per cent) than older ones (21 per cent).

The other two styles occurred infrequently. The *surrogate parent* was found only among grandmothers and occurs at the request of the young parents to help out with childcare while the mother works. The *reservoir of family wisdom* describes an authoritarian role, in which the grandparent is the dispenser of special skills or resources. Both the parents and grandchildren display a submissive attitude toward the grandparent. Only four per cent of the grandfathers and even fewer grandmothers followed this style.

The fun seeker and the distant figure styles characterized over two-thirds of the younger grandparents. Both styles de-emphasize service, authority, and responsibility associated with grandparenting. One emphasizes an equalitarian, pleasure seeking utilization of leisure time, and the other the role of a benevolent, non-involved, special occasion, gift-giver (Neugarten and Weinstein, 1964). Whether these styles will continue to grow and eventually replace the more traditional authoritarian, nurturant, and service aspects of grandparenting, or are just characteristic of relatively young grandparents is not known, at present. Whatever their future, their development probably results from a more active involvement in non-familial activities associated with relatively youthful middle class grandparents.

THE AGING PROCESS

It is common practice to call people old who have passed a certain birthday, say the sixtieth or sixty-fifth. The age used to mark old age tends to change with the age of the person doing the categorizing, however. It is not uncommon for high school students to see their parents as "practically ancient." Within four or five years they may perceive them as amazingly rejuvenated.

It is a mistake to assume that oldness commences with any given chronological age. The process of growing old does not apply itself with equal speed to every person. Some individuals become feeble and dependent even before sixty, while others remain active and able to take care of themselves long after seventy. Furthermore, culture has something to do with it—by either providing socially respected roles for the aged, as has been true in some times and places, or by artificially restricting the activities of older people, as is largely true today in our own culture.

Considered in this light, it is possible to describe four general characteristics of the aging process. Each of these is to be understood as applying more to the later than to the middle years, and as starting earlier and developing farther with some individuals than with others.

1. There is a decline of physical health and vigor, which lets one know that the body is gradually wearing out. The skin becomes more wrinkled; the bones more brittle; joints stiffen; the hair turns gray or the head bald; hearing ability diminishes; the eyes grow less able to accommodate themselves according to distance; motor coordination declines; reproductive capacities decrease; chronic illness often sets in.

2. There is a similar slackening of mental ability. This starts long before the period of old age, however, as is shown by the fact that intelligence test scores are highest at about the end of the second decade of life, declining gradually thereafter. Old people generally learn more slowly, grasp new material with greater difficulty, show greater mental fatigue, and remember less easily than do the young.

3. There is a shift of social role in the direction of less participation and greater dependence. Part of this is due to the decline of physical and

mental powers within the individual and part to cultural prescriptions. Older individuals have more leisure time but are less active in community afiairs; they have fewer companionable relationships either within the home or on the outside; they are less likely to be employed and more likely to be dependent upon others for support.

4. There is a greater tendency to worry, to lose interest in life, and to be generally less happy. Feelings of nervousness, of inadequacy, and of being unwanted are common. Old people tend to be more religious than those of the younger ages. They also tend to be more cautious and conservative. It seems likely that both of these are results, primarily, of the insecurity that surrounds old age in our culture.

Economic Response to Increasing Numbers of Aged

One consequence of the increasing proportion of young people in the society, at the same time the number of older people is increasing, is a shifting pattern of production and consumption. Although the market among older people is increasing, they do not spend as much money or have as great a recurring need for replacement as the younger members of the population. Thus, while more and more stores are catering to the teen-agers and newly married population, the older people have to look harder for items geared to their needs and tastes. Some stores make no bones about their desires to cater to the young, actively discouraging their older clientele because of the "depressing atmosphere created by too many old people in the store."

Although many communities have begun to plan along the lines of recreation and housing for the elderly, they are perhaps more interested in the young. Young people are more likely to cause trouble if they are not actively engaged during their leisure hours. The separate interests and activities associated with the different age groups have resulted in the growth of age-segregated housing units. More and more we see apartment complexes which rent only to childless couples between the ages of 21 and 35. Others rent exclusively to those between 35 and 50, with children. Some are exclusively for single persons below age 35, while still others rent or sell only to those beyond the age of 50, with no children. Some even put an education requirement in addition to the age criterion, renting only to those with more than two years of college education. Even public housing seems to be moving toward segregating the elderly. Whether this trend is motivated by the desire to create a more congenial environment for the elderly or to remove them from public view of the young is open to question.

Retirement to elderly communities or housing projects with activities centered around Senior Citizen's Clubs or Golden Age Clubs perhaps hastens the identification of oneself as old. At least some research has given evidence that identification with old age is associated with maladjustment (Phillips, 1957).

At any rate the increasing number of elderly persons, plus the lack of useful roles for them in the society, will increase the burden of supporting them. Their increasing influence in the political arena will probably be reflected in political platforms catering to them and more public funds being expended for their welfare. The tendency of people to become progressively alienated from all social activities, however, probably gives the elderly less of a political voice than their numbers would indicate.

We are already seeing a tremendous increase in retirement homes, nursing homes, and church and public supported homes for the aged. This is a direct reflection of the problem created by increasing numbers of persons who need occasional or constant help in meeting their daily needs. That the cost of these facilities is not always within the budgets of those who need them most, hardly requires saying. Institutional care was meeting the needs of less than 800,000 of the aged in 1962. However, this number will undoubtedly go up as the long range effects of Medicare, Social Security, and other retirement plans are felt in rising incomes among the aged of the future.

Of the 19.3 million people 65 years of age and over in 1970, about 9.4 million were in husband–wife families (Bureau of the Census, 1970, p. 281). The vast majority were living independently of their children. Five million of those never—or no longer—married in 1962 were heading their own households, with 55 per cent of the women and 65 per cent of men living alone. Almost three million were living in the homes of relatives, usually with the family of a son or daughter (Tibbitts, 1965, pp. 1–11). About 25 per cent of the total population 65 and over resided with one or more adult children in 1962 either in their own households or in the household of the adult child. Tibbitts (1965, p. 7) suggests that this is probably a higher proportion than at any other time in our history, in spite of our norms which support the generations living apart. Data for 1970 were not yet available at this writing.

Intergenerational Interaction

The extended life span has increased the probability that a recent postparental pair will be called upon to aid the new marriages of their children at the same time they are aiding their own aging parents. Hill (1965, pp. 123–26) describes the parental family as occupying a kind of patron status in relation to the generations on either side of it. They perceive themselves as giving more than they receive in financial aid, emotional gratification, household management, and childcare. The married-child generation perceives itself as both giving and receiving. They receive more financial aid and childcare help but give emotional gratification, household management help, and care during illness to the older generations. The grandparent generation is the high receiver in all areas of interdependency.

The perception of intergenerational interaction differs between the generations. The parental generation is more likely to perceive themselves and their children as a close family group than is the adult-child generation. Interestingly enough, the adult-child generation is much more likely to see themselves and their children as forming a close family than to see the relationship with their parents this way (Streib, 1965). This undoubtedly shows the movement of the center of focus from the parents to the children as marriage forms a new family. That the parents would like to maintain closeness with their grown up children is indicated by the much higher proportion of parents who say they would like more interaction with their children than children who want more interaction with their parents. This difference in perspective is again shown in the overwhelming proportion of parents who say that ties of affection are much more important than financial help in intergenerational interaction. The adult child is more likely to say that both are equally important (Streib, 1965, pp. 471–72).

Most studies show that although visitation patterns may not come up to parental expectations, a high frequency of intergeneration interaction does take place (Streib, 1958, p. 51). To some degree for most people (especially for those with low incomes) the aging process tends to reverse the roles between parent and child. The parent becomes progressively more dependent on his children for emotional, physical, and financial support as the years take their toll (Glasser and Glasser, 1962). In this reversal, what may have been termed child neglect in the earlier period turns into parent neglect in the later period.

Albrecht (1954a) in a study of people over 75 in a town of 7,000 persons found that 15 per cent showed this role reversal, distance, or neglect. The other 85 per cent maintained some independence or still assumed responsibility for some members of the second generation. At advanced ages some loss of independence is almost inescapable, but the degree to which reversal occurs depends upon financial level, health, and the quality of the previous relationship with children.

The inescapable loss of independence is better accepted if everyone recognizes that self-respect depends partly on being considered useful and responsible—for the aged as well as for the young. Being patronized at any age is detrimental to the concept of self.

Death, of course, is the ultimate end of life. If it comes with dignity at the close of a full and useful life, those who survive gain strength and dignity from the experience. And so it is with families. Family ties strong enough to nurture and guide the young, and elastic enough to rejoice in the independence of the mature, should be resilient enough to support the self-respect of the aged.

But families need societal support. If the society provides no rewarding social roles for the aging, families cannot provide a feeling of self-respect. It is a paradox that many service organizations seek volunteer workers among those who have the least amount of time to give and shun those with the most time—the older volunteer. There is evidence that many of them would welcome the opportunity to be of service (Tibbitts, 1965, p. 11). It seems we have not yet become adjusted to the fact that many people are mentally and physically able for a number of years after they reach mandatory retirement from the economic world. Until we do, we can expect a toll among the self-respect of older citizens, guilt feelings among their adult children torn between responsibilities to three generations, and a resulting strain upon the relationships.

THE PRINCIPLE OF VALUE RELEVANCE

What is considered a satisfactory adjustment in the postparental period varies according to marital patterns considered "good" in the earlier years and according to the expectations for what life "should" hold for the aging person. Some people will feel lonely and rejected with the same amount of contact with family members which makes others feel wanted and loved. More than any specific amount of generational interaction being related to satisfaction, it is the meaning placed on what interaction there is and the way the interaction fits the expectation of the family members involved.

The same is true of the marriage relationship in the later years. Some couples will be perfectly content with decreased interaction and segregated lives as they gradually alienate themselves from society or redefine themselves in roles other than family ones. Some aging couples may find life more meaningful as they confine themselves to relationships with others their own age in retirement homes or communities. This same arrangement for others may signal the end of their useful lives and provide the final evidence that their families no longer want to be bothered by them.

Above the extreme levels of isolation or poverty, satisfaction in the later years is related not to any particular type of marital role relationship, amount of family interaction, or amount of income. It is more related to the feelings of self-worth the aging couple is able to maintain. The kinds of interaction, activity, or amount of income which contribute to these feelings will vary among individuals according to their own evaluations of themselves and the evaluations made of them by their supporting groups. Some people define themselves in terms of possessions, skills, or positions which are bound to decrease with age. For others, the sense of worth is related to characteristics which are not so vulnerable to the passage of time. As in early periods of the life cycle, satisfaction can be expected to increase to the extent that the continual relationships reinforce for the aging persons positive self-concepts which are in keeping with their current social environments. As long as society as a whole withholds constructive social roles from the aged, regardless of mental or physical ability, we can expect that feelings of self-worth and satisfaction will deteriorate with advancing age for most people in our society.

SUMMARY

As children begin to leave home, the family structure undergoes change with each departure, just as it did during its growth period with each new addition. As the launching period draws to a close, the parents are faced with re-emphasizing the husband–wife relationship. This adjustment is more difficult for the wife than for the husband, since her self-esteem is more likely to have been anchored in the mother role.

The proportion of the life cycle spent in the postparental period has been increasing in the past fifty years, due to the lowering of the age at marriage and increased life expectancy. Evidence seems to show that satisfaction in these middle years is associated with the ability to find substitute activities to fill the vacancy left by children. There appears to be tremendous variation in individual abilities to build satisfying marital relationships after children have been launched. Several studies show a decline in marital satisfaction, a greater segregation of activities, but a slight increase in companionship. Other studies show a high percentage reporting their marriages "better" or "as good" as in the preceding phases.

Grandparenthood enters the life experience of most postparental couples and offers a new source of activity and interest for some. This is not true of all, however, since a relatively high percentage of grandparents maintain a distant role relationship with their grandchildren. This role, along with the "fun-seeker" grandparent role, seems more characteristic of relatively young grandparents. It was suggested that the emerging grandparent role is devoid of either responsibility or authority, furnishing mainly a leisure time activity or a "holiday" role with little interaction at other times.

The postparental period may last until old age begins to require new adjustments. Retirement from active life requires a new definition of self with no rewarding social role in which to anchor it. For many this means a loss of dignity and increased dependence on the adult children. There is evidence that intergenerational interaction does occur frequently, but that the older generation tends to desire more interaction with their children than their children desire with them.

Some degree of dependency is inevitable, especially if financial or health difficulties are present. The inescapable loss of independence is better accepted, however, if all are aware that self-respect is partly dependent on being considered useful and responsible. Families can help the adjustment to old age, but probably what is needed most are socially rewarding roles for the elderly which can utilize their skills and time and provide them with a sense of usefulness.

QUESTIONS AND PROJECTS

1. What other changes, social and familial, usually take place at about the same time to complicate the problem of the climacteric? Discuss.

2. A student said: "When people get older they are just naturally unhappy, so they should not be allowed to live with their children and clutter up their families, too." What do you think of this statement? When grandparents live in the home is there greater unhappiness all around? Explain.

3. When older people are unhappy is it their own fault or society's? Will self-effort solve the problem? Discuss.

4. Give ways you think society or the culture could change to make old age more satisfying. Are any of these under way?

5. What useful family functions may grandparents still perform? To what extent should grandparents be permitted to give advice about childrearing? To indulge or spoil their grandchildren?

6. What are the likely social consequences of an aging population? Which do you consider desirable? Which undesirable? Discuss.

7. Assuming good health and financial independence, about how long would you like to live? Point out conditions that could change your mind, indicating how and why.

8. Discuss the pros and cons of arbitrary retirement rules. What social changes are needed to make retirement easier? What can the individual do to aid his own adjustment?

21

Separation, Divorce, and Widowhood

Not all families progress through the complete cycle to the final dissolution through death. Some are disrupted suddenly at various points along the way by desertion, separation, or divorce. The most obvious and convincing evidence of failure in family relationships is where husband and wife cease to live together. This, of course, does not mean that those who stay together are necessarily happy or even satisfied with the arrangement, but it probably does mean that the "pulls" toward the continuance of the relationship are greater than the "pulls" toward disruption.

MARITAL DISRUPTION

The relative stability of any marriage is the result of a balance between the internal attractions drawing the individuals toward the relationship, the external supports for the marriage, and the external attractions pulling the individuals away from the marriage (Levinger, 1965). See Figure 21–1.

Internal Attractions

Some marriages are so satisfying to the individuals involved that the existence or non-existence of external supports are of little importance. They stay married because the internal personal rewards of the relationship overweigh any potential external attractions.

Other marriages are also stabilized by internal attractions, but not necessarily by personal attachments. The status and level of living may

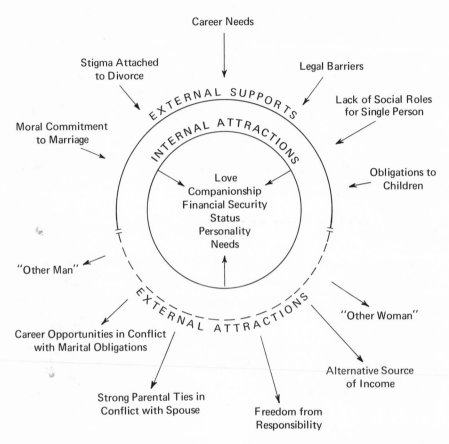

Fig. 21–1. Factors contributing to marital stability balance. (Adapted from Levinger, 1970.) Levinger uses the term "social barriers" to describe the factors we call external supports.

be much higher in the marriage than it could possibly be outside. This position may characterize many upper-middle class women. They could not hope to provide the same kind of life for themselves alone that their husbands provide for them. Only if the unhappiness of the relationship begins to outweigh both the economic rewards and the external supports does dissolution become a possible solution. For their husbands, the convenience of having someone take care of the daily details of living; the assets to his career of a socially gracious wife; or just the benefits of having a home may overcome the emotional deficits of the relationship itself. If an alternative source for emotional gratification presents itself, however, it may well be only the weight of the external supports which prevents disintegration.

Some marriages, however, may have such a delicate balance between internal attraction and external supports that the accidental appearance of an alternative source for financial security or emotional gratification may tilt the balance toward marital disruption. In other words, the external supports provide just enough pressure for stability to keep down awareness of the lack of meaningful internal attractions but not enough to hold the marriage together if the "emptiness" is recognized. The sudden appearance of an alternate source of support or satisfaction may be enough to make one of the partners question the value of the existing marriage.

External Supports for the Marriage

The external supports stabilizing a relationship may be moral ones, in that strong beliefs that divorce is "wrong" furnish enough pressure to make the marriage partners rationalize their present unhappy situation as being all that can be expected from marriage. Other external supports include the stigma still to some extent applied to divorce, the lack of social roles available to a single adult in our society, the need to show that one has a "successful" family life to aid in the furtherance of a career, and the idea that two parents, even unhappy ones, are better for children than only one. Goode (1966) labels this family which merely resides in the same physical location but provides no emotionally satisfying connections with one another the "empty-shell" family. It presents the external appearance of a family group but there is nothing to sustain the members in the family interaction.

External Attractions

The factors drawing both investment of time and emotion away from the marriage include the proverbial "other woman" or "other man." They also include things like concentration on a career to the detriment of the marriage and family relationship. Sometimes the attachment to parents who disapprove of the spouse-in-law or who continue to attract the primary loyalty of the married son or daughter may tip the scales toward marital disruption.

Especially in the lower socioeconomic strata of the society, the guilt and feelings of inadequacy accompanying failure in the provider role may make desertion seem more rewarding than the continual pressure of familial responsibilities. Current welfare practices which provide support for a wife and children only if the husband–father is ill, injured, or absent may actually overcome all external supports as well as the internal attractions for the unemployed man who cannot provide for his family's daily needs.

Family stability is not an all or none concept. Each family can be seen as embodying a balance of factors contributing to and against the continuance of the relationship. Some socioeconomic statuses, occupations, and social group affiliations provide a strong bulwark against desertion, separation, or divorce regardless of the internal rewards from family life. Others provide support, but the strongest factor contributing to continuance is found in the internal satisfactions. Still others provide few external supports and present many opportunities for external attractions, such as the entertainment world. Among these marriages, the strength of the internal attractions becomes the sole bulwark of marital stability.

As our society takes a more lenient view toward divorce, and as both men and women enlarge their spheres of interaction outside the family, the ability to develop and maintain emotionally rewarding marital relationships will probably become more and more important as the main stabilizing factor in marriage. In other words, we may have to learn to develop "full-shell" families or find that they are easily "cracked." [1]

Separation

About 2.7 million persons, or approximately 2 per cent of the adult population were living in a state of separation due to marital discord in 1969. Over half of these separated persons have either deserted or agreed informally to live apart. Such practices are sometimes referred to as "the poor man's divorce." The rest have gone through formal court proceedings to obtain legal separations, sometimes called "separate maintenance," or "separation from bed and board," or "limited divorce." Separation, legally sanctioned, is in operation in only about half the states. It permits (indeed requires) the mates to live apart, but while remaining married— that is, without the right of marrying anyone else.

Proceedings for obtaining legal separation, in the states that provide for it, are similar to those for divorce. Some of the laws are now being changed to provide that, after a specified length of time, legal separation can become grounds for absolute divorce.

Separation sometimes ends with a reconciliation, at other times with a final divorce decree, but in many instances it is neither and so the arrangement becomes permanent. It is not known how many fall into each of these categories.

In many ways, the consequences of separation are similar to those of divorce. There are likely to be torn emotions and disturbed behavior patterns. In addition, desertion is apt to carry with it even greater feel-

[1] The usage of "full-shell" as an extension of Goode's analysis of the "empty-shell" comes from George Levinger (1965), p. 20.

ings of humiliation and problems of economic dependency. In addition also, legal separation puts the husband and wife at a particular disadvantage by leaving them unsettled, in a state of *marital suspension*—in a way they are neither married nor unmarried, for although they do not live together they cannot marry anyone else.

Wives are more likely to bring suit for legal separation than husbands. In fact, in some states, such as Pennsylvania, only wives are legally permitted to bring suit. Thus, it is a mechanism by which a wife is freed from an unbearable situation while retaining the right to financial support for herself and children (Kephart, 1964, p. 955). Sometimes the legal separation is a substitute for divorce, such as in the case of church restrictions against absolute divorce.

Legal separations account for only a small amount of family dissolution. Probably the most extensive type of separation results from desertion. In this case, there is no provision made for the family that is left, and the intent of the escaping spouse is to "get lost." Most deserters return and many are repeaters, suggesting that desertion may often be a holiday from family obligations (Goode, 1966, p. 512). However, desertion is a legal ground for divorce in virtually all states (Kephart, 1964, p. 953).

Divorce

Divorce is the final dissolution, leaving both spouses legally free to enter another marriage contract. Church restrictions against remarriage may, of course, override this freedom in individual cases. Since domestic relations law is a state matter rather than a federal one, tremendous differences in grounds for divorce exist from state to state.

The variety of grounds recognized across the states include such things as drunkenness, impotence, vagrancy, conviction of a crime, drug addiction, incest, epilepsy, venereal disease, non-support, and so on. By far the highest percentage of divorce uses two grounds—cruelty and desertion. Cruelty is called by different terms in various states, such as "mental suffering," "cruel and barbarous treatment," "indignities," but, however named, it has become a catchall phrase which many times means "incompatibility." Kephart suggests that about two-thirds of the divorces are granted using this legal ground. Only New Mexico and Oklahoma actually include a ground called "incompatibility."

Until very recently, there was only one communality in the more than 40 different grounds for divorce in existence in the United States—adultery. Even here there was one partial exception—Texas recognizes only the wife's infidelity as reason for divorce (Kephart, 1964, p. 953). This common ground no longer exists, however. Beginning in January, 1970, California dispensed with adultery as well as other traditional grounds for divorce which require one spouse to prove the other is at fault for breaking up the marriage. Only two grounds are now recognized—"incurable insanity" and "irreconcilable differences." This major reform in California divorce laws recognizes that marital disruption may be the fault of both partners or their interaction with each other rather than always the result of a guilty party creating an intolerable situation for a blameless spouse. The word "divorce" is even eliminated. The new decree is called "dissolution of marriage."

Desertion is the legal ground for about 30 per cent of the divorces. States vary in the length of time the spouse must be absent before the desertion ground may be used, from six months to five years. Absence itself is not enough, however, in those states which hold to the view that blame must be placed on one of the spouses. The complaining spouse must show that the other spouse had no just cause for leaving. If the husband deserts and it can be shown that the wife failed to perform her housekeeping duties, or, in some states, refused her husband sexual relations, it is considered that the husband had just cause for leaving and the divorce may not be granted. In most cases, however, the husband does not appear to defend himself, the wife presents herself as a dutiful and blameless spouse, and the divorce is routinely granted.

Actual Reasons for Divorce. Since the legal grounds for divorce are provided by the state in which the couple resides, it is apparent that the actual reasons may not correspond to the legal ground used. Levinger (1966) analyzed the records of 600 divorce applicants from the Counseling Department of the Domestic Relations Court in greater Cleveland, Ohio. All these divorcing couples had children under 14 years of age. He found that among wives from lower socioeconomic positions the major actual complaints were physical abuse, financial problems, drinking, neglect of home or children, and vague complaints such as jealousy, suspicion, untruthfulness and so on—all grouped under mental cruelty.

Middle class wives also complained of mental cruelty and neglect of home and children but were significantly more likely to complain of infidelity, lack of love, and the husband's excessive demands than were their lower class counterparts.

The husbands did not make as many complaints as their wives. The complaints they did voice concerned mental cruelty, in-law problems, neglect of home and children, and sexual incompatibility. Lower class husbands were significantly more likely than middle class husbands to complain of their wives infidelity, while middle class husbands complained more about "lack of love."

Problems such as these make themselves felt at all stages of the marriage, but the highest frequency of divorce is found in the first two to three years. Since it takes some time to go through the legal process of divorce, it is evident that a number of couples decide very quickly that they do not want to stay together. There is indication from some states that divorce after the twenty-fifth year of marriage may be increasing. However, reliable statistics are difficult to obtain from all states. In those furnishing statistics, the median duration of marriage at divorce was about about 7.5 years in 1963 (Plateris, 1967).

Avoidance of Divorce. Divorce is sometimes thought to be the only solution to an unbearable relationship. It frees the spouse and children from a situation which may be damaging to the entire family. New relationships can be made which may again build stable family units. Many times, however, time apart and a realization of the emotional and practical "costs" of marital breakup are enough to make the couple renew their efforts at reconciliation.

Sometimes divorce occurs when it was never intended. In the heat of an argument one spouse threatens divorce, expecting the other to "give in." But the reaction of the other spouse boomerangs, he walks out or dares the other to carry through with the threat. Communication is cut off and they can see no other way out without "losing face" or thinking they will lose so much power that they will be at the other's mercy (see Bernard, 1956).

These are the cases which may be most easily reconciled by an enforced "cooling off" period or by outside help from family courts or marriage counselors. The concept of a family court, which handles all family problems such as divorce, legal separation, adoption, desertion and nonsupport, neglect, custody, delinquency, and intrafamily conflict or behavioral problems is being tried in several states. The family court brings together the services of social workers, psychiatrists, marriage counselors, probation officers, and nurses in the attempt to aid the troubled families in resolving their problems. The idea here is not to affix blame on a "guilty" party but to investigate all elements in the difficulty and the resources for meeting it, in an effort to strengthen the family ties.

In a few states, counseling is mandatory for all divorce applicants before final granting of the decree. In others it is optional except for those involving minor children. In others it is purely voluntary. Kephart (1964, p. 956) states that these courts have not, as yet, produced statistics to show that the percentage of marriages "salvaged" is any greater than the percentage who withdrew the application without outside help. This lack is partially accounted for by the scarcity of funds for adequate staffing or for follow-up research which can provide evidence concerning the effectiveness of the program. The major problem appears to be that these courts are generally introduced on a trial basis with low funding until they prove themselves. The lack of funds for providing complete service reduces the efficiency of the court, thus making it more difficult to achieve the results or evidence of the results which may bring needed funds. Since the present court system contributes little to the complete understanding of the depth or nature of family problems of which divorce application is a symptom, it is to be hoped that adequately funded experimentation with new ways of dealing with the problem will appear in the future.

Death

While divorce may mean a prolonged period of discontent and perhaps preparation for the disruption through separation preceding the divorce, the death of a partner may come suddenly and interrupt the happy as well as the unhappy union.

In 1967 there were close to eleven million widowed persons in the United States. This figure includes those who were widowed at the time of the census count. It does not include widowed persons who had remarried. Close to nine million of those in the widowed state were women. The ratio of widows to widowers is about 4 to 1 currently, and is expected to continue rising. In 1940 the ratio was 2 to 1, in 1960 it was 3½ to 1 (Berardo, 1968). Widowhood is more likely to strike women and is likely to continue longer for them. There are three reasons for this: (1) females outlive males about seven years on the average; (2) females are likely to marry males who are two or three years older than themselves; and (3) after widowhood females are less likely to remarry than are males. Thus women are more likely to become widowed than men, to become widowed younger, and to live as widows longer.

Widowhood is most likely to strike the elderly and therefore carry with it the economic problems of the aging. It is likely to be less of a problem for the male than for the female, or at least to change things less for him. If his wife dies before he has retired, he can continue with his job, although he may have additional expenses and inconveniences if there are young children to be cared for.

The widow, however, loses the economic rewards from her deceased husband's job. She may be forced to seek employment from which she can expect significantly less income while at the same time her expenses for child care go up. She is, however, more likely to be the recipient of insurance payments. Women are the beneficiaries of about 80 per cent of all life insurance policies. A survey of all widows 55 years old or older made in 1964 showed that almost two-thirds of the husbands left a total of assets including savings, cash, insurance, value of the home and other assets, of less than $10,000 to their families. Forty-four per cent left less than $5,000. Almost three-fourths of the husbands owned less than $5,000 in life insurance at the time of death and another 20 per cent owned less than $10,000. Many of the widows had to use what insurance they received to pay funeral expenses, medical bills, taxes, mortgages and so on, leaving little left for daily expenses. The median income of the wives in the year preceding the survey was less than $2,000 (Berardo, 1968).

CONSEQUENCES FOR CHILDREN

The traditional view of the traumatic effect of family disruption on the personalities of children has led many observers to support the view that when at all possible, parents should stay together if only to provide an intact home for the child. As research has continued in this area, the traditional view has been challenged and the complex relationship between broken homes and their effect on children has begun to be spelled out.

Divorce and Separation

Children of the divorced are frequently forced into a life of tension and strain. Their affections are torn between the two parents, who are in conflict. If the court decrees that they are to spend some time with each parent, as is often done, they may be made the buffer to that conflict, the victim of jealousy and hate. Being young and immature they do not understand. Conflict comes to be normal in their way of life. No wonder that these children have a higher than average chance of becoming divorced themselves later on.

However, when parents stay together solely for the sake of the children, the result is not always a happy family environment, but one torn with conflict. Whether this is better or worse for the child's adjustment was investigated by Ivan Nye (1957). For all the criteria of adjustment used, the child from the happy unbroken home was favored. When the comparison, however, was between the *broken* home and *unhappy, unbroken* home, adolescents in broken homes showed less psychosomatic illness, less delinquent behavior, and better adjustment to parents than did children from unbroken, unhappy homes. They did not differ significantly in respect to adjustment in school, church, or delinquent companions. Little difference was observed between children in homes where the parent had remarried and those where the mother was a "solo" parent. In the parent–child relationship the adjustment was superior for "solo" mothers, perhaps indicating that some problems are encountered in adjusting to a new parent after the child has experienced an exclusive relationship with the mother after the first marriage had been dissolved. Of course, the favorable readjustment of the child after marital disintegration will depend on the ability of the remaining parent and substitute parent, if any, to bear the responsibilities of parenthood either in remarriage or alone (Nye, 1957, p. 361).

Comparative Effects. Rosenberg (1965) has thrown light on the differences between different types of broken homes in comparison with intact families. He found that a lower percentage of adolescents from divorced parents had high self-esteem than adolescents in intact families or in homes broken by separation or death. Those in separated families were just as likely as those from divorced parents to have *low* self-esteem, however. Children from divorced homes were more likely to have a higher number of psychosomatic symptoms than those in the other categories. In light of Nye's findings, we would expect the differences to be even greater if children of divorce were compared to children of only happy, intact families. This difference in psychosomatic symptoms was more extreme than differences in self-esteem perhaps indicating that divorce tends to heighten the anxiety level of the children involved. The adverse effect of divorce was more noticeable among Catholic and Jewish children than among Protestants. There was no difference according to religion in the effect of death of a parent, so apparently the greater social pressure against divorce in Catholic or Jewish groups produced more of a trauma in the child when divorce did occur.

The interaction between the mother's age and the child's age at the time of divorce appeared to be a crucial factor as far as the child's self-esteem was concerned. If mother and child were both relatively young at the time of divorce (mother 23 years or less and child 6 years or less), only 22 per cent of the adolescents registered high self-esteem compared to 42 per cent of the adolescents who experienced the divorce of their parents when both mother and child were older. This percentage is close to the percentage of children with high self-esteem in intact families (45 per cent).

The same relationship between age of mother at time of disruption and negative effect on the child held for families broken by death of the father. The younger the mother at the time of the father's death, the greater the impact on the child. If the mother was still relatively young at the time the child was an adolescent (37 or younger), no matter when death occurred, only 15 per cent of the adolescents had high self-esteem, compared to 48 per cent of those with mothers aged 48 or over. These findings are apparently focusing on the mother's ability to cope with the problems associated with both divorce or widowhood and to provide a secure environment for the child. The more insecure, anxious, irritable, and frustrated she feels under the circumstances the less likely it is that she would be able to meet the needs of her children. It appears that the younger she is the less likely she is able to handle the strain.

Landis (1960) has provided evidence that the child's reaction to divorce is more traumatic if the home had been seen as happy before the divorce occurred. Thus the impact on the child appears to vary with a number of factors: (1) the child's perception of the happiness of the family prior to divorce; (2) age of the child and the mother; (3) strength of the norms against divorce in the social groups of which the family is a part; and (4) the ability of the remaining parent to aid the child in coping with his anxieties and to provide a secure environment.

Consequences of Remarriage

It has already been stated that as far as delinquent behavior, school adjustment, or delinquent companions were concerned, little difference was found between the children of "solo" mothers and remarried mothers. Differences in adjustments to parents, however, tended to favor the "solo" mother arrangement. Rosenberg (1965) investigated the differences in self-esteem and psychosomatic symptoms between children whose parents remarried after divorce or death and those whose parents remained single. He found that the children whose divorced mother remarried had lower self-esteem and more psychosomatic symptoms than those whose mother did not remarry (almost all the children of divorce remained with the mother) (Rosenberg, 1965, pp. 98–102).

The same was true of children of a widowed parent. If the surviving parent did not remarry, the self-esteem and distribution of psychosomatic symptoms was no different from the children of intact families. If the parent did remarry the child was more likely to have low self-esteem and higher anxiety reflected in psychosomatic symptoms. It appears, then, that remarriage puts additional strains on the readjustment of the child regardless of the cause of the family disruption. The acquisition of a stepmother appeared slightly more disturbing than the addition of a step-father in the case of death of the natural parent.

Again the age of the child at the time of divorce or death appeared to have something to do with the effect of remarriage. If the child was 3 years of age or younger, remarriage made no difference—the child was not likely to have high self-esteem regardless. At older ages, however, remarriage had a marked relationship to low self-esteem. At age 10 or above there was no difference in self-esteem distribution between the children from broken families and those from intact families if the remaining parent had not remarried. The percentage with low self-esteem increased 15 per cent, however, *with* remarriage (from 26 to 41 per cent).

This seems to indicate that the longer the child has lived in an intact family the harder it is for him to adjust to a new one. Although not tested in this study, it can perhaps be assumed that the longer the mother and child live alone between the disruption and remarriage, the more devastating to the self-concept would be the mother's shift of attention to a new spouse and perhaps to stepchildren who may enter the picture.

These older children may frequently regard the *stepparent* as a stranger and intruder. Sometimes they will have objected to their parent's remarrying and will deliberately try to break up the match. The parent, in turn, is likely to feel competing loyalties between his children and the new mate. The problem of discipline comes in, with the parent's often feeling that the new mate is being unkind or harsh with his children. If there are children from both sides by previous marriage, or from the new marriage too, the problem is further complicated by a tendency toward favoritism. Even when there is no favoritism, certain happenings may be interpreted that way. Little mannerisms or habits of the children can prove to be quite annoying to a stepparent.

The finding that about 32 per cent of the children have high self-esteem at any age, even when the mother remarries, is indication that the potential negative effects are not inevitable. Parents and stepparents can become aware of the special needs and feelings of children who have undergone the experience of losing one parent and then losing the exclusive attention of the other one to a new parent. If they are willing to work together to provide a supportive and secure environment while the child makes his adjustments and eventually accepts the new situation, the difficulties can be eased. Many remarriages are more successful than the earlier ones for both spouses and the children involved. At least from the mothers' perspectives, remarriage tends to make them think that their children's lives have been improved in comparison to the first marriage (Goode, 1956, pp. 329–30). Further research is needed to continue to define the conditions under which this is more likely to be a correct impression.

PROBLEMS OF LIVING WITHOUT A MATE

The adjustment problems associated with the period following separation, divorce, or death of a spouse include the one of learning to live without a mate. Others have this problem not because of marital breakup but because they never married. Some of the problems are the same; but others are different, since the permanently unmarried person does not have the task of untwining his life from that of another. The permanently unmarried will be considered here as a special case of living alone.

The Permanently Unmarried

In 1969, about 8 per cent of the males and 5 per cent of the females aged 30 through 54 had never married. Some of these will eventually marry. Glick (1968) suggests that of all young adults in 1960, probably all but three or four per cent will eventually marry. Of the six million unmarried men over 35 and women over 30 in 1960, about five per cent were in religious orders and about ten per cent of the men and five per cent of the women were involuntarily confined in institutions (over one-half in mental hospitals). Living conditions for these people were controlled. It is the remainder who are unmarried either by choice or lack of opportunity in whom we are interested. Norms supporting marriage are extremely strong in our society, although there is some movement toward accepting the unmarried state as normal and removing the stigma formerly associated with it.

Characteristics of the Never-Married. Martinson (1955) has suggested that the person who delays or rejects marriage may frequently be better adjusted than the one who marries early out of need for emotional support. He studied 59 matched pairs of single and married girls, and found the single girls to have had better personal, social, and academic adjustment at an earlier period during high school. The married girls were the ones most likely to have lacked self-reliance, to have manifested withdrawal tendencies, to have engaged in antisocial conduct, to have done poorly in school, etc.—showing greater ego deficiences among them. The conclusion: "It may be that it is the immature or not-so-well adjusted person for whom marriage has its strongest appeal."

Another suggestion is that marriage tends to be selective in the direction of personality *means,* leaving unmarried many of those who possess the *extremes.* If this view holds, we would expect to find disproportionate numbers of both the adjusted and the unadjusted, and both the talented and the untalented, among the permanently unmarried—since the least able might be eliminated from marriage through competition and the most able might have least need for marriage and might feel that marriage would compete with other things they may want to do. This latter is especially true for the very talented female. Though the theory needs further testing, there is some evidence to support it. Klemer (1954), in studying personality factors which differentiate single from married women, based on a sample of thirty matched pairs, found that the single women showed greater proportions with *both* high and low self-esteem. Incidentally, he also found that the single women had had less culturally approved interaction with men during the age period of sixteen to twenty-five years, and had had more "obligations" at age twenty-five which had interfered with their getting married.

There is a strong probability that unmarried men and women differ from each other in regard to quality. In an earlier chapter we referred to the commonly observed tendency of men to marry beneath themselves in the areas of age, education, general socioeconomic status, and very possibly with reference to physical and emotional aspects of the personality. Folsom (1943) has used the term *mating gradient* to describe the tendency, claiming that it "would seem to leave an unmarried residue on the upper rungs of the female social ladder and on the lower rungs of the male ladder."

This point finds reinforcement in the fact that women who do not go beyond the sixth grade in school are more likely to marry than those who graduate from college.

Apparently it is the more able and career-minded of the females that go on for higher education, and in going on they reduce their marriage chances, both by becoming older and by becoming too intellectual for the dominance-loving male. We should add parenthetically, however, that though marriage after college graduation becomes slightly less likely for the girl, this does not apply while she is in school; the college campus has proved itself to be an extremely productive laboratory for mate selection. Furthermore, as studies reveal, college marriages, when they do take place, are less likely to end in divorce than are noncollege marriages.

Reasons for Staying Single.   Some people remain permanently unmarried by choice, others as a result of circumstances. Major types are as follows. (1) Certain individuals are denied the right to marry by society. These are those who fail to meet the minimum requirements of the marriage statutes or who are under long-range custodial care in institutions. (2) Sometimes people remain single in the spirit of self-sacrifice and because of defects in heredity, health, ability, or character. These are likely to feel inadequate to the marriage situation—incapable of a normal sex life or of anything else that goes with marriage and family. (3) In certain cultures there are individuals who remain single out of devotion to a cause. A good example of this is religious celibacy, as in Roman Catholicism. (4) There are some who are basically unresponsive to heterosexual love. These include the exclusively homosexual person who for a variety of reasons (as yet not clearly understood) is emotionally and sexually attracted to one of the same sex. Although many homosexuals may make relatively permanent relationships resembling the heterosexual marriage, they are unmarried in our present legal sense but may have few of the problems of living alone faced by other types of the never-

homos

married. Others are unresponsive to heterosexual love because of auto-eroticism, strong parent fixations, or conditioning against marriage. (5) Then there are those who see marriage as something that is competing with other desires, and who consider the price too great; they are reluctant to give up their independence or to accept this new responsibility. Men (more than women) sometimes seek arrangements whereby they can have sexual satisfaction without the obligation of marriage. Women (more than men) sometimes find love and marriage interests interfering with their plans for an education and career. (6) Finally, there are persons who never marry through lack of adequate opportunity.

This last point requires further elaboration. It seems likely that the majority of those who remain single do so out of circumstances rather than desire. This is especially true with the female, for she is less free in making advances. Yet choice is relative to the values and standards which people hold. Many of those who have gone through life alone could have married had they been willing to lower their sights and had they done it in time. But who is there to say which is better—no marriage, or marriage to an undesirable person? Judgment in such matters must be left to the people concerned. It is true, however, that single people as they get along in years frequently feel regret over having passed up earlier opportunities.

One's chances for marriage decrease with age. The middle-aged female is at a particular disadvantage, for men generally choose someone younger than themselves. Furthermore, the older men are when they marry, the greater is the age difference between them and the ones they marry. For this reason, older girls frequently get skipped and left out. By waiting too long—because of career interests, or extreme standards, or immaturity and indecision—young people sometimes let the opportunity slip away. Not only is the marriage market smaller as they get older, but they also become more set in their ways and harder to please.

Marriage opportunity is contingent upon situations which permit people to meet and associate with adequate numbers of the opposite sex. If the residential sex ratio is unfavorable, or if occupational activities keep the sexes apart, or if the culturally provided contacts are so formal or superficial as to make it hard for men and women really to get acquainted, marriage becomes difficult.

Sometimes people remain single because they are not able to attract a mate. It may be that they are immature, neurotic, or unmannered in personality; that they give evidence of being selfish and overindependent; that they are too shy to be sociable or even friendly; that they appear overanxious or aggressive (especially the girl); or that they are unprepared for the responsibilities of marriage.

It is unfortunate, however, that the stigma of personal failure is so often applied to all spinsterhood, regardless of the causes or factors involved. Unmarried women are frequently made to feel that they are inferior or at fault. Actually, the condition may be due to choice, or to circumstances that are largely beyond the person's control.

It appears, however, that more positive evaluations are beginning to be made of the unmarried female. The coinage of terms to replace "spinster" and "old maid" such as "bachelor girl" or "career woman" connotes a less critical appraisal and perhaps a growing awareness of the *choice* of the single life by some.

Problems of Adjustment

As has been pointed out throughout this book, everyone is continually faced with problems of adjustment whether he lives within a family structure or not. To some extent the special problems encountered by the single person, whether he is single because of choice, divorce, or death of a spouse, come about because of our pair-organized society. Society is organized in favor of the pair. Many social events are planned for couples, and frequently the partnerless person is either not invited or is made to feel out of place. As a consequence there is the temptation to stay at home more than one should and to become a social recluse.

Sexual adjustment is another difficult problem to be faced by the single person. This will vary, of course, according to the age at which the single life begins. For some, such as the permanently unmarried, it is a continuing problem. For the divorced or widowed, the single life may begin early so that they resemble the never-married. It may even be more of a problem if they have become accustomed to a regular and satisfying relationship. For others, the disruption may occur so late that sexual desires have declined in the over-all hierarchy of important needs.

The partnerless person is denied any culturally approved means of expressing his sexual desires. Some succeed in rechanneling the drive and in finding substitute satisfactions along other lines. Others give themselves to a certain amount of overt sexual expression, regardless of society's disapproval. Undoubtedly the largest number of these engage in occasional masturbatory practices, with heterosexual stimulation coming next, and then homosexual contacts.

Although these problems are common to all who live alone, there are differences depending upon the route by which one reached the single state.

The Never-Married. The never-married person, unlike the divorced or widowed, has never had the experience of living with a mate or having children of their own. (We are excluding here the small percentage of unmarried mothers who keep their children and maintain a series of relationships with non-permanent pseudo-husbands.) They vary in the degree to which they see their unmarried state as a personal failure, the failure of a cruel and unjust world, or as a blockage of the attainment of their most cherished dreams. The severity of adjustment is greater for some than others simply because people view it differently and have different goals and personality needs. Many women experience their greatest loss in being denied motherhood and deprived of the opportunity to associate with and care for little children. Others miss most the companionship of a marriage partner. Frequently it is all of these.

Note the following self-analysis of a forty-year-old college woman:

> Like most normal girls, it was my utmost desire to have a husband, some children, and a home of my own. I have always been the home type, rather than a social climber. I love children very much and the sight of a sweet, clean little youngster will bring a lump to my throat faster than anything else. To be deprived of all this has been difficult.
>
> Perhaps the thing which has been the hardest for me to face, and the thing I have cried myself to sleep over more than anything else, is the lack of love of both children and a companion. I have been fortunate in living near enough to married members of my family who have been kind to me in letting me share a little of their children's love. Realizing the pitfalls of this type of thing, I have tried to guard myself against interfering in any way or spoiling the children
>
> There are many, many times when loneliness overtakes a single person. There are places to go and types of recreation to participate in designed for couples only, or where society frowns upon the single woman's going alone. This need not be missed too much if she makes up her mind to the fact, and centers her interests on the kinds of activities that can be enjoyed alone or in the company of other girls.
>
> Sometimes an unmarried girl gets to feeling that she is queer or without special charm. It is the way people regard marriage and the things they are apt to say that make her feel that way.
>
> Not wanting this disappointment in life to make me the cynical "old maid" which society knows so well, I have tried to adjust and to make my work of primary importance. The thing which I desire most now is to be able to do my work in a pleasing and creditable manner. I want to live a useful life and to have the health and strength necessary for taking care of myself without becoming a burden to anyone (from the authors' files).

Though not entirely typical, this case illustrates some of the problems common to many women who fail to marry: there is a strong sense of loss at the lack of children and companionship; there is a feeling of social inconvenience in not being able to participate as freely in group functions; and there is a sensitiveness to being classed as peculiar or inferior. Adjustment, however, is reasonably complete and satisfactory; she has come to accept the situation and to rechannel her drives mainly in the direction of work activities.

Recent changes in adoption procedures may give some unmarried women and men the opportunity to be parents, which has been denied them in the past. If the practice continues, it may increase the number of women who choose to remain unmarried.

Until recently, the single person has faced inadequate living conditions unless he or she was in a relatively high income bracket. The need now is becoming recognized, with housing units being built for single persons only which include recreational facilities and central dining, reading, and conversation areas that facilitate social interaction. These are mainly oriented toward the young single person. However, there also are indications that the needs of the older single person are being recognized in specially designed housing units.

If our society, hopefully, begins to accept and make room for those who never marry, many unhappy marriages may be avoided. Some individuals are temperamentally more suited to a life alone than to marriage. Some have all-consuming interests which are highly beneficial to society but detrimental to a marriage. Some prefer to remain single and are happier that way. Some of these people do marry as a result of social pressure and then make both themselves and their spouses miserable.

The Widowed.   The widowed individual experiences most of the same problems as the permanently unmarried, plus a few extra. There are the same inconveniences attached to attendance at social functions. There is the same loneliness resulting from a lack of intimate companionship. There is the same sexual tension bound in by cultural restrictions. The difference is that while the single person must learn to do without certain things, the widowed person has to give up things to which he or she has become accustomed; the one is required to adjust and the other to readjust. It is frequently more of a crisis to have to give up what one has known than never to have known it in the first place.

But there are at least two advantages the widowed has over the never married: (1) he is not stigmatized or made to feel inferior or abnormal; and (2) he has the satisfaction of memories, and perhaps children, to help in the adjustment. This is especially true of women.

It is likely that the majority of women would prefer widowhood to spinsterhood if they had to choose. During World War II one of the writers asked several large groups of college women to express themselves on this point; more than 90 per cent said that they would rather be widows—which, incidentally, helps explain the high marriage rate of that time.

Generally, widowhood presents less of a crisis if it comes in old age than if it strikes the family during an earlier phase of the cycle. Aging mates will usually have realized the high probability of one of them dying first and will have made at least partial preparation. Furthermore, their sexual needs will have diminished by that time, which means less of a problem there. Even so, the loss of a mate by death is seldom easy. After a lifetime together there will inevitably be deep and lasting feelings of loneliness. If financial preparation has been incomplete, there may be the added problem of dependency. Then, too, adjustment at this stage of life is frequently complicated by the piling up of crises; failing health, retirement, and widowhood all come at about the same time, which makes each problem all the more difficult.

Young widowhood is complicated by the fact that it usually comes suddenly and catches the surviving mate unprepared. The following account from a woman who lost her husband fifteen years ago, during the early years of their marriage, suggests some of the difficulties:

The shock of losing my husband when we were both so full of plans for the future, our son just a year old, and life seeming so good, could well be compared with a shipwreck. Life seemed very empty for the first few months and my thinking was all mixed up. Yet I knew that I must go on, face the future bravely, make a living for myself and son. New plans had to be made. If friends had not insisted on my taking more time for major decisions, I am sure things could have been worse.

It was the companionship of my husband that I missed most of all. There was no one left to advise and counsel with, to show interest and encouragement over my accomplishments, to share my intimate joys and sorrows. Friends have compensated a great deal, but none can ever take the place of a married companion. Social activities had to change. This was not too serious in my case, since I could always find congenial people to go places with— picnics, shows, musicals. Dances and parties calling for partners had to be dropped. The problem of supporting a family was a more serious one. It is still a man's world, I find, and women who are often better qualified than men receive less pay and much less recognition. But in spite of these difficulties, one has only to look around to see others in much worse circumstances. To feel sorry for oneself is unforgivable, I think. It is much easier to be cheerful and friendly (from the authors' files).

Readjustment requires the alteration of fundamental habit patterns. Marriage will have made the mates interdependent in a number of ways; they will have become accustomed to each other, habituated to a way of life. Death changes all this and leaves the surviving partner numb and bewildered for a while, feeling as if he or she is only half there. Little habits of eating, sleeping, dressing, conversing—to say nothing of the more fundamental habits of sex and ego support—all have to be changed. There are also disturbances in patterns of group participation which frequently require the making of new friends and reducing and adjusting one's social activities to those events which are permissible for the unattached. Habit reorganization is never easy and is frequently very painful. It means the mastering of frustrations resulting from blocked drives. It requires the focusing of consciousness upon just about everything that one does, for much of one's activity for a time will be new and unchanneled.

Readjustment during widowhood is in one sense made easier, and in another more difficult, by the fact of death. The widowed individual often finds support in memories of the past life. This is more than is possessed by those who never marry. It is also more than divorced persons have to help them readjust, for their recollections are more likely to be those of frustration and defeat. Yet, to have a loved one die is an extremely traumatic experience. Generally speaking, the closer the marital adjustment, and the more sudden and unexpected the death, the greater is the immediate crisis.

Waller (1938, pp. 491–522, 580–88) compares the death of a loved one with an amputation. The following brief analysis of the mourning process is adapted from his discussion. (1) The primary source of bereavement is "the conflict between wish forces, which refuse to give up the object, and reality, which demands that it shall be given up. . . ." (2) In the early stages of the process there are a number of protective mechanisms within the self which serve to shield it against the loss. There is a numbing effect incident to the catastrophe. The person is unable to realize fully what has happened. He struggles against reality, refusing to believe or accept the situation. He has "bereavement dreams" which tend to preserve the illusion; sometimes, in his waking hours, he is convinced that it is only a dream. His memory tends to be undependable and highly selective. At first he may have difficulty in thinking clearly about the deceased person at all; in time he is likely to forget past unpleasantness and to construct within his mind an idealized picture of the departed. (3) Mourning serves a socially useful function. Attention and sympathy focused upon the mourner tend to bring ego support at a time when part of him seems to have been taken away. By self-absorption, the mind is less likely to dwell upon the loss. In time the self can be freed (or nearly so) from the former love object and made capable of attaching itself to another. Mourning provides a needed transition into an acceptance of the newer reality. When pretentious or overextended, however, its purposes may become perverted. (4) As much as anything else, adjustment requires a lapse of time. It is largely automatic. Though personal attitudes and the assistance of friends are undoubtedly helpful, each widow or widower must still go through the rather painful processes of love and habit reorientation. With the first shock there is likely to be the feeling that one doesn't care to go on, that life is meaningless; one may have to force oneself to respond. For a while the personality may be quite disorganized.

But then, in time, reality becomes accepted, habits change, new interests appear, and life becomes normal again. This means the attainment of a new life organization. When it happens, adjustment is complete.

Since death is inevitable, one might expect more preparation for it than is usually the case. A few husbands and wives are spared widowhood by dying simultaneously (though this is rare and usually accidental); some others escape by way of divorce (though if they remarry they may yet be widowed); and half of those remaining never become widows or widowers because they die before their mates do. Widowhood is common enough, nevertheless, and the problems involved grave enough to warrant very serious attention. There needs to be more preparation ahead of time—psychologically, so the happening will be less of a shock, and economically, so that the survivors can be self-supporting and have a better chance to readjust. One type of financial preparation consists of savings, annuities, and insurance. Another is for the wife to include some kind of job training in her premarriage experience, as "insurance" against such an emergency. Married mates need to discuss death as a possibility, and to lay plans for such an eventuality.

The Divorced.   Certain of the problems which we have been discussing are common to all who live without a mate—whether they be unmarried, widowed, or divorced. One is the problem of loneliness and lack of affection. Another is the problem of social inconveniences within a society that is geared to the marriage pair. On top of these, however, the divorced person is generally presented with a few others: in common with the one who is widowed, he has the task of reorganizing his love life, rechanneling his habit patterns, and re-establishing himself with social groups; in common with the one who never marries, he is faced with a certain amount of social disapproval or stigma connected with the status; and, in addition to these, he has had to experience all of the disillusionments and hurts that go with a lost love.

Waller (1930) has compared the divorce situation with bereavement, pointing out symptoms and processes common to both—early feelings of shock and numbness at the loss, the persistence of old habit patterns, the need for gradual readjustment, and so on. But he went on to say that readjustment after divorce is made all the more difficult by the absence of culturally approved patterns. There are certain socially sanctioned means of working out problems when a mate has died, yet there are practically no approved means for the painful task of readjusting after a marriage has "died." As a result, the divorcee is held in a certain amount of scorn and is left with roles that are both undefined and contradictory. Though this observation is undoubtedly correct, it is probably less true than at the time Waller wrote it about four decades ago. Divorce is coming to be accepted within the folkways.

Goode (1956, pp. 12–15, 208–16), however, has pointed out that certain structural differences in the reactions to death and divorce leave the divorced person in a more ambiguous role as he attempts to adjust. Death carries with it the ethical imperatives for family and friends to cluster around the surviving member and offer emotional and economic support. Although such support may be forthcoming in the case of divorce, it cannot be counted upon. It will depend on the direction of the blame, the amount of approval of the divorce, and how friendly the friends are to the other spouse. Although both extended families are expected to help in case of the death of a spouse, it is not clear where the responsibilities lie in cases of divorce. There are few customs concerning what one is supposed to do after divorce.

Insurance benefits and reduced cost of living for the remaining spouse may ease the financial problem in widowhood. In the case of divorce, the two spouses separate, and at least one of them must set up a new dwelling. Two households must now be maintained on the same income as before, with the additional cost of legal fees.

The deceased spouse is buried, to be recreated in the memory of the survivor and perhaps idealized, but never in this life to be interacted with again. The divorced spouses may *have* to meet or talk to discuss mutual concerns of the children. Visitation privileges generally mean that the spouses cannot avoid knowing something about each other's present life through the children's accounts of their visits. So, although in some ways the ex-spouse may be considered "dead," he does not stay "buried" so that final adjustment can be made.

When a spouse dies, the remaining spouse is expected to grieve and to mourn the loved one. Friends and family expect this and can provide support and sympathy. It is not clear what the divorced person is supposed to feel. Relief? Grief? Anger? Self-pity? Joy? It is, therefore, difficult for one's friends to know how to approach the divorced person.

Winch (1963, pp. 732–34) suggests that the actual feelings after divorce differ, depending on a number of factors surrounding the disruption. The feelings of the remaining person would be expected to vary from relief and a feeling of accomplishment to feelings of rejection, martyrdom, guilt, or tragedy depending upon whether or not he wanted the departing spouse to leave; whether or not he perceived the departing spouse as wanting to leave; and whether or not he felt responsible for the other's leaving. Certainly the emotional disturbance and difficulty in adjustment would be less if one felt mainly relief than if one felt a great deal of guilt, hostility toward the departed spouse, or that the whole thing was a tragic mistake.

Goode (1956) has analyzed the adjustments of 425 divorced mothers living in the Detroit area. Among his many findings are that the majority of these divorcees claimed not to have lost their community standing and established friendships (in contrast to the situation with earlier generations), believed that divorce with its problems is *preferable* to unhappy marriage with its problems, and felt that their children were actually *better off* than in a marriage of conflict.

Though not universal, the following reactions to the divorce experience are nevertheless rather common. (1) There will frequently be a feeling of shock, accompanied by self-pity and projected blame. The divorcee tries to rationalize the situation and to show an outward bravado as a cover-up for inward disturbances. Thus the real emotional problems may lack adequate ventilation. (2) There is usually a feeling of restlessness resulting from disturbed habits and confused roles. As a result, the divorced person often tries to increase his or her social activities. Friends and relatives may help in establishing new contacts. (3) Not infrequently the divorced person will go through a period of unconventional behavior, trying to drown his sorrow in drink or to compensate for his loss by degrading sex (Waller, 1930, p. 56). (4) It is not uncommon for divorced individuals to experience ambivalent attitudes toward the former spouse; they may want revenge and feel affection both at the same time. Sometimes husband and wife continue with sexual intercourse for a time after they have been divorced. Occasionally they will remarry each other.

In spite of these many difficulties, divorce is sometimes preferable to staying married. If the mates remain basically incompatible after serious and extended efforts to get along, there is little point in extending the misery.

But divorce is no panacea. It, too, requires adjustments—which in most ways are more difficult than those of the married state. There are but two alternatives worth considering: learning to live alone and marrying again. We have already discussed the former.

REMARRIAGE

Today, slightly over one out of every five marriages is a remarriage, and at least one out of every eight married persons has been married more than once. Furthermore, there is evidence that the rate of remarriage is increasing, reflecting both an increasing divorce rate and a growing acceptance of remarriage for the divorcee. It was estimated in 1957 that about two-thirds of the divorced women and three-fourths of the divorced men would eventually remarry (Glick, 1957). With the remarried group constituting an expanding proportion of the total, it can be predicted that interest and attention regarding this phase of the family phenomenon will grow.[2]

The majority of those who remarry do so only once; that is, they enter a second marriage but not a third. It is to be noted, however, that some 2 or 3 per cent of all marriages each year are contracted by persons entering their third or subsequent marriage. This is evidence of what has been called "sequential polygamy," where a person has several mates in succession rather than at one time.

The rate of remarriage is higher for the divorced person than for the widowed. One reason is that people sometimes get a divorce for the very purpose of marrying another who is already selected. Too, the divorcee is generally more anxious to break with the past and to demonstrate by remarriage that there is nothing wrong with him or her; this is a reaction against the inference of failure. Then there is the matter of marriage opportunity; divorce generally takes place at an earlier age than widowhood, which leaves the person with greater bargaining power and more time to work out another match. Also, children sometimes interfere with one's chances for remarriage, and the divorcee—because of being younger and married for a shorter length of time—is not so likely to have as many. There is evidence that the tendency to remarry varies inversely with the number of children. It has been estimated that the chances of eventual marriage are 50 per cent greater for the divorcee who is thirty years old than they are for the widow of the same age. And both the divorcee and widow are more likely to marry than is the never-married woman of this age. This is true at younger ages also. During the age period 20–24, the divorced woman is twice as likely to remarry as is the single woman (Carter, Glick, and Lewit, 1955, p. 170).

Success of Remarriages

Virtually all research on the subject shows higher divorce rates for remarriages than for first mariages. About one-third in 1958, 28 per cent in 1960 and about 25 per cent in 1965 of all divorcing persons had been involved in a previous marriage (see Appendix). So although there has been a slight decline in the divorce rate of the remarried they are still overrepresented in the divorcing population. The divorce probability goes up drastically with the number of times the person has remarried. Very probably this is because more of those who remarry are divorce-prone to start with; that is, they have immature or neurotic personalities. When this type of person remarries, he usually has no better chance of succeeding the second time than the first. Some people marry to escape

[2] The first book on this subject appeared as recently as 1956. See Jessie Bernard (1956). For a statistical treatment see the Appendix at the end of this text.

problems which they were not able to solve during courtship, then divorce to escape the deeper entanglements which enveloped them during marriage, and remarry to escape the still greater problems that can pile up after a divorce—when the real problem all the time is within themselves.

With divorce coming to be more generally accepted, however, it is possible that the divorcee group is including more and more well-adjusted individuals who failed largely because of poor matching or extreme circumstances surrounding the prior experience. There is little reason to think that this type of person would be too much handicapped in a second of subsequent marriage. Yet it is highly probable that the divorced group still contains more than its share of neurotic individuals.

Though there are no reliable data by which we can compare the relative success of widowed and divorced persons in remarriage, it seems reasonable to assume that failure is greater among divorcees. A higher percentage of the widows and widowers will have been happily married prior to the crisis, and hence a lower percentage will possess warped or neurotic tendencies in their personalities. By way of comparison, more of the divorcees will be embittered over the marriage experience and more of them will have unstable personality tendencies—which may be either a cause of the crisis, or a result, or both.

At any rate, once remarried, the same factors will be at work in the marriage as have been discussed throughout this book. The relative success or failure will be influenced by the fit between the habit systems of the partners, the extent to which they are able to enhance each other's feelings of self-esteem, the feelings of reward and satisfaction each gets from the relationship, the social factors operating to keep the marriage together, and the external attractions operating to pull it apart.

THE PRINCIPLE OF VALUE RELEVANCE

The prevailing value systems of the culture, the supporting social groups, and the individuals involved influence the decision to divorce or separate, and the consequences of these actions for all the family members.

Where divorce is condoned in the society—seen to be preferable to an unhappy situation by the individuals and the social groups with which they interact—it becomes a ready solution to marital problems. On the other hand, if commitment to marriage is viewed as more important than individual happiness, divorce is seen as a last resort. Even the definition of problems as unresolvable varies depending upon the relative importance attached to marriage permanence and individual happiness. Problems which to one couple may appear insurmountable and adequate justification for divorce to another couple may appear troublesome but more acceptable than the larger problem of divorce. They may either decide to live with the problems or work harder to resolve them within the marriage.

If, however, divorce is condoned as better than an unsatisfactory marriage, the consequences of divorce on the individuals involved may be lessened. They are not as likely to suffer from feelings of guilt, defeat, or resentment as are those for whom divorce is seen as the last resort after all efforts to reconcile differences have failed. Then blame must be placed, as reflected in the divorce laws in most states.

Consequences for children have already been shown to vary depending upon the evaluation of divorce prevalent in their religious groups. The meaning of divorce for their parents should have an even more pronounced effect.

Marital disruption is probably always disturbing, but the extent of the disturbance for all family members is at least partially related to the meaning attached to divorce itself.

It is probably quite accurate to say that strong feelings against divorce in a society holds down the divorce rate, but when divorce does occur its consequences are likely to be severe and lasting. When a society has permissive norms concerning divorce, the divorce rate undoubtedly goes up, but the consequences of divorce are lessened and adjustments to either a single life or new relationships are easier. Which condition is seen as "best" varies according to the values concerning the intrinsic importance of family permanence relative to the importance of the individuals within that society.

SUMMARY

Not all families progress through the complete family life cycle to old age and eventual dissolution through death. Some are disrupted suddenly by desertion, separation, or divorce. These are the extremes of instability, but many families who do not go this far nevertheless teeter on the edge, balanced precariously between the internal attractions or social pressures holding them together and the external factors pulling them apart. Those for whom the balance has tilted sufficiently to end in separation or divorce share with the permanently unmarried and the widowed the problem of living without a mate. Although the different routes by which unmarried persons reached the solitary state result in some unique problems, they also come together in common ones, as shown in the following chart.

Though living without a mate is seldom easy, there are cases in which it is preferable to other alternatives. In the case of widowhood, there is, of course, no real choice. But eventualities can be prepared for, and later adjusted to.

Problems	Unmarried	Widowed	Divorced
Social stigma	x[1]		x[1]
Social inconvenience	x	x	x
Isolation and loneliness	x	x	x
Sexual tensions	x	x	x
Financial need		x[2]	x[2]
Sense of loss		x[3]	x[3]
Sense of failure	x		x
Absence of parental satisfactions	x		
Need for habit reorganization		x	x

[1] More with females than males; less today than formerly.
[2] Especially great when there are young children present.
[3] Bereavement for the widowed; disillusionment for the divorced.

Most of those who lose a mate remarry. This tendency is stronger with divorced than widowed persons, with males than females, and is greater now than formerly. More remarriages than first marriages end in divorce, which probably is because the remarrying group is to some extent weighted with divorce-prone individuals. However, with divorce more accepted today, this observation is less true than it used to be. Increasing numbers of reasonably normal and mature persons are now getting divorced and then remarrying—with success.

QUESTIONS AND PROJECTS

1. Describe the attractions and supports for marital stability discussed in this chapter. Look back at the descriptions of central themes found by Cuber and Harroff in Chapter 4. Describe the variation in types of attractions and barriers which seem to hold these marriages together.

2. Do you agree with the adage: "It's better to have loved and lost than never to have loved at all?" Applying this thought to marriage, would you say it is better to have married and failed than never to have married at all?

3. Some persons deliberately choose against marriage. List any reason which you think might produce such a choice. Do you think one can be as happy without marriage as with it? Defend your position.

4. What advantages do men have over women in staying single? In getting married? In remarrying after widowhood or divorce? How do these differences vary with age? What accounts for these advantages?

5. With the sex-ratio of male to female becoming lower with advancing age what social changes do you suggest? Consider questions such as: Why should a woman be denied pregnancy and legal motherhood if she desires it just because she is unmarried? Would polygyny be an acceptable answer to the decreased sex-ratio? At any age or just after the reproductive period? Should communal groups of the permanently unmarried be encouraged? Defend your position on each of these and suggest other alternatives.

6. Compare the problems of living alone for the never-married, the widowed, and the divorced? How are they similar and how are they dissimilar

in respect to: (1) numbers and trends in the population; (2) problems of adjustment; (3) economic problems; (4) advantages and disadvantages; (5) typical modes of reaction, adjustment, and maladjustment.

7. If a couple have children but are unhappily married, would it be better to divorce or to stay together until the children are grown? Look at the question from the point of view of both parents and the children. Give evidence to support your answer.

8. Should laws be revised so that marriages may be more easily obtained, even though the number of divorces would probably go up?

9. Suppose the marriage laws were strengthened so that it was more difficult to get married? What consequences do you think this would have? Why?

10. If you were able to strengthen the marriage laws in order to attempt to reduce the divorce rate, what new restrictions would you include? Why?

VI

CONCLUSION

22

The Challenge
of the Future

The preceding chapters of this book have all attempted to draw attention to the relationship between family roles and activities and the social structure with which they are intrinsically bound. We have looked at the major areas of family concern and discovered that the changes occurring in these activities over time can be related to changes in other activities and institutions—the economic, the educational, the religious, and the political. It has been pointed out that the famliy is both a conservative and an adaptive institution. Through the long socialization period of the child, the family implants moral values, habits of perceiving and interpreting himself and others, and expectations for relationships which hold the past family patterns over the generations. As the family motivates its members to participate in the activities of the larger society, however, they face demands for changed behavior patterns and come under the influence of conflicting value systems. As families attempt to hold on to satisfying habits and values of the past and at the same time participate in the society of the present, certain adaptations in family roles and activities occur. The family is largely on the receiving end of social pressures, yielding, adjusting, and changing as society changes. Although forced to adapt in order to survive, it exerts influence on the future and the direction of societal change through influencing the personalities, expectations, and values of its children.

We have not only looked at the global changes occurring in the family institution, but we have seen that the changes in the economic, educational, religious, and political systems have not affected all families to the same extent or in the same way. Thus, we have simultaneously supported in the society different values concerning the family, different expectations for the male–female relationship, the husband–wife roles, and the parent–child roles. We have seen how this heightens the probability of value conflict within the culture itself, within the individual, between the individual family and the society, and between husband and wife, parent and child.

The direction in which the family changes, the types and intensity of problems it is likely to encounter, and the satisfaction and support it can offer its members, are influenced greatly by the changes going on in the total society. Speculations about both of these must be based on the direction of changes which have occurred in the past. We will, then, review briefly the major trends which have had an impact in shaping the family today.

MAJOR SOCIAL TRENDS AFFECTING THE FAMILY

It would be impossible to list all of the factors influencing the family. They are too numerous and intertwined to be individually spelled out. There appear to be four basic social trends, however, which seem to be central to all social changes taking place today and which have had a profound impact on the structure of the family (Christensen, 1970).

The Technological Revolution

As discussed in Chapter 2 the discoveries and inventions of the last two hundred years have had a tremendous impact on man's whole way of life, including his family life. The shift from an agricultural to an urbanized, industrialized society which accompanied the technological revolution has resulted in the weakening of kinship ties, the rise of the nuclear family, an accelerated emphasis on the individual, a reduced differentiation between and segregation of sex roles, a decline of the patriarchal authority structure, and a rise in equalitarian family relationships. All of these are not necessary consequences of a shift from an agricultural to an industrial society, but in the special context of the American scene this shift has opened the way for these changes.

The technological revolution is not over but continues to contribute to the material culture at an ever increasing pace. As new innovations alter man's behavior patterns the consequences reach deep into his value systems, altering his expectations of himself, of others, and of his relationship to his environment.

The Population Revolution

Just as the material culture has expanded, so too has the population. This population explosion has had more drastic repercussions in other parts of the world than in America, but even here the consequences of a rising population and concern over it have had a major impact on the American family. There were 76 million people in the United States in 1900, somewhat over 200 million now, and the estimates predict 300 million or more by the year 2000 (Thomlinson, 1965).

This revolution is related to the technological revolution, since the major causes are improvements in diets, sanitation, and medicine which have drastically decreased the death rates. The added longevity has resulted in changes in the family life cycle, increasing the childless years a married couple spends together (see Chapter 20).

Although there has been an interest in ways of limiting birth for centuries, concern over the rapid increase in population has concentrated efforts on perfecting convenient and reliable contraceptives. A consequence has been reduced family size and the general acceptance of the value of family planning. A partial listing of the effects of decreased family size might include: a rise in the level of living; fewer restrictions on the wife working, or on geographical mobility, or perhaps on divorce; smaller dwelling units; less sibling interaction; more emphasis on the individual; and greater educational advantages for children.

Consequences of the rising population, even given the lowered birth rates, are the problems of congestion, over-crowding in the urban areas, pollution, and reduced familial interaction as travel from work to suburban dwellings consumes more and more time.

The effects of this revolution are not over. The advances in knowledge which produced more effective contraceptives have also contributed to an increase in knowledge about the complete reproductive cycle opening the way to more and more control. The consequences of these innovations may have an even more profound impact on the family than effective contraception.

The Democratic Revolution

The whole American experiment can be seen as a democratic revolution which has inevitably seeped into family life as other changes have made it possible. Gradually but relentlessly the democratic ideals have overturned the patriarchal family structure of yesteryear, but have not yet fully replaced it with a workable authority structure that provides both necessary control, direction, and individual voice in the decision. The continual eruption of this problem in the total society is reflected in the family. The family is an integral part of this revolution, supplying citizens who can operate in and maintain a democratic society. It is both affected by this movement in the society and affects its eventual outcome by the way it adapts to the challenge.

The emancipation of both women and children is part of this revolution. Consequences of their greater freedom have affected family roles, increased expectations for personal happiness in marriage, and put heavy pressures on the family to be flexible at the same time it is providing stable and continuous support for changing individual needs.

The Secular Revolution

There has been a strong trend toward materialism and secularism in the society. In the past, strong religious beliefs supplied a braking effect to family change. Family roles, the relationship of male to female, the authority structure in the family, the importance of reproduction all had divine support from religious teachings. As these took on "intrinsic rightness" the resistance to social pressure for change was reinforced. This support has largely disappeared, however, as the churches have been caught up in the cross pressures and in part have become agents of change themselves. The interest shown in some churches in discussing the pros and cons of premarital sex, for example, shows the effects of secularization as well as democratization. Perhaps an authoritarian church is not supported by a democratic society anymore than is an authoritarian family.

Whether this change, along with the others mentioned, is viewed negatively or positively will depend upon the values of the individual. It can perhaps be expected that, as this trend continues, the braking effect of the religious institution will be decreased and the adaptation of the family to social pressures for change will be swifter and more varied. This is to say that, as the central religious values receive less absolute support from *all* denominations, the direction adaptations take will reflect the increased emphasis on the individual, with less restriction from absolutistic ideas of "right" and "wrong" supported by the religious institution. From one point of view this may result in a more creative, flexible, and satisfying family relationship. From another, it may result in a tremendous increase in value conflict as the multiplicity of roles reduces consensus on what marriage and family life "should" be.

The basic trends just mentioned can be expected to continue or at least to contribute to debate and conflict over the direction in which they seem to be taking us. This debate can be seen in the variation of speculations made by sociologists concerning the direction of social changes and their impact on the family. Since all of these trends are subject to evaluation and reaction at any time, it is impossible to anticipate all of society's changes or their consequences. It is not surprising that these speculations about the future family do not agree. We will consider some of them here while keeping in mind that unexpected changes may take us in new directions not conceived of by anyone at present. What actually happens will be the result of millions of individual responses to changes in the society which force adaptations in family life or offer new goals for the individual.

PROJECTIONS INTO THE FUTURE

Parke and Glick (1967) have projected recent statistical trends to forecast what we may expect to happen between now and 1985 if present trends continue. They see the percentage of teen-age marriages continuing the decline registered in recent years. Twenty-three per cent of the women who were 30–34 years old in 1966 married before they were eighteen, whereas only 15 per cent of the women 18 or 19 years old in 1966 married before age eighteen. The percentage of males marrying before twenty has been stable at about 18 per cent over the same period. The percentage of males marrying before age eighteen has never been higher than 4 per cent (Parke and Glick, 1967, p. 251).

This downtrend in very early marriages among women may be partially the result of the changing sex-ratio in the marriageable ages. The "marriage squeeze," that is, the over-supply of women relative to the men in the next highest age bracket, will either result in a higher proportion of unmarried women or a lessening of the age gap between marital partners (see Appendix). If the latter occurs, and there is slight evidence that this will be the trend, the joint survival rate of married pairs will be increased, reducing the number of widows in the population.

If the economic level of the population continues to rise and is extended to cover a widening proportion of the population, marriages should become more stable. Marital stability is greater among the economically secure. As more of the population realizes this security, coupled with the decline of teen-age marriages, two of the highest risk groups as far as desertion and divorce are concerned should be reduced (Parke and Glick, 1967, pp. 253–54).

But, there are other trends which lead one to question this prediction of greater marital stability. Changes have been and continue to take place which make it less necessary to marry. The loosening of the sexual restrictions before marriage make it less likely that the unmarried person is condemned to a life of either celibacy or loveless sex with a variety of accidentally available partners. Widening educational and occupational opportunities for women make it unlikely that marriage will be seen as her only approved goal. The availability of pre-cooked foods, no-iron shirts, and household appliances make it less necessary that men have wives for these domestic services. In other words, marriage now does not serve the utilitarian functions that it did in earlier years; and it is likely to continue to be less and less necessary for these reasons, especially with the increase of housing designed especially with the needs of the single person in mind. Yet, more and more people are marrying and the projection is that the proportion of those ever-married will continue to increase. They are evidently marrying for other reasons—companionship, emotional security, and an enhancement of personal satisfaction. These reasons for marriage, and the growing acceptance of divorce, may result in an increased divorce rate—especially as a better quality of marriage relationships raises the standards for marital success.

We have already found that marital stability (the absence of desertion, separation, and divorce) tells us little of the quality of family relationships in the stable families. If quality becomes of primary importance then stability will depend not so much on the external pressures supporting "staying together" for appearance's sake, for the children, or because it is the accepted thing to do, but on the ability of the members to make continuation of the marriage intrinsically rewarding. In other words, people will have to develop this awareness of human relationships and learn to live together in such a way that they enhance each other's lives.

Decline of External Control

The social control stemming from continual association with extended family members, friends, and neighbors will perhaps continue to decline with increased geographical mobility. The close association with unchanging groups over time reinforces the commitment to marriage, since one's reputation in loyalty, trustworthiness, and fidelity are also at stake. Close scrutiny by the circle of friends and family members not only holds down transgressions but puts pressure on the individuals to cleave to the marriage even if it becomes emotionally unrewarding.

Continuous shifting of geographical locality not only lessens the external controls but increases the number of readjustments the family members must make and lessens the support from these groups during times of stress (Hobart, 1963).

Increase in External Pulls

Hobart (1963) sees an increase in non-family, non-church, and non-neighborhood friendships for both the male and female—relationships made through voluntary associations, school, or work. With more and more women entering the work world, the opportunity for these relationships to be cross-sex ones increases the threat to the marriage bond. While males have been the ones most vulnerable to these external pulls, the greater activities of females outside of the family increases their vulnerability. Hobart sees this as having at least two consequences: (1) the increased probability of developing more human potential in the society as people are exposed to a wider range of personalities, values, and activities; and (2) the increased probability that relationships, work, or activities outside the family may loosen the marriage bond.

Another of the external pulls, mentioned in the last chapter, is the valuation of achievement and success to the point that it interferes with family values. Hobart (1963, p. 407) sees this as a pervasive value conflict in our society. The family depends upon and symbolizes the values of "knowing, caring, and unconditionally committing oneself." These values are in conflict with the values of individual achievement and success. The valuing of *things* over *people* is a common resolution of the conflict. When this is the resolution, the children are likely to be socialized with an anxious need to be materially successful as a prerequisite to being accepted or considered worthy. When conflict occurs between family loyalty and career success, the career often wins. From Hobart's point of view, the future of the family depends on which way this value conflict is resolved.

Ascendence of Human Values

Hobart believes there are indications that the value conflict will be resolved in favor of the human values of knowing, caring, and loving. It is suggested that a society of scarcity must encourage efficiency and productivity if it is going to rise above a poverty level. This emphasis discourages human values. But once poverty is conquered, the opportunity for turning attention to human values is opened. The direction of energies toward development of human potential is seen not only as possible but functional by diverting energies away from production in a society where *over-production* is a greater threat to the economic system than *under-production*.

He suggests then that the family, with a more flexible structure which can be tailored to the individual needs of its members, will likely flourish. The increased mobility involving numerous changes in friendships will increase the commitment to the only stable, secure, emotionally satisfying interpersonal relationship remaining—marriage. As the commitment grows, more time will be spent developing the kinds of marriage relationships which stabilize the sense of self-worth and satisfy personality needs so that more people would be able to *use things* and *love people*—rather than the other way around as Eric Fromm suggests that we do now (Hobart, 1963).

Another Point of View

The foregoing view is countered by Edwards (1967). He takes issue with the concept that increased geographical mobility is necessarily in opposition to family solidarity. Many of the adjustments which must be made as the result of moves are advantageous. Relief from the social pressures for a particular family form may allow considerable freedom for developing family forms more tailored to individual desires. The decrease of group support over crisis periods has not been demonstrated to accompany mobility—spatial distance does not necessarily imply emotional distance or lack of support and aid when needed.

Edwards also argues against the notion that greater involvement in economic and associational activities by wives exerts a greater external pull away from the family. His viewpoint is that higher education and economic opportunities for women involve them more deeply in the structuring of the family, as well as in the economic activities.

The threat to the marital bonds presented by cross-sex contact in voluntary associations is also discounted. The bisexual nature of many associations increases the opportunity for joint husband–wife activities, thus decreasing the polarization resulting from single sex organizational memberships. The complexity of organizational membership prevents a definitive appraisal of its effect on marital solidarity, but there is perhaps as much evidence to support its integrative consequence as its disruptive consequence on the family.

However, the widening of economic opportunities for the woman may well open for her an acceptable alternative to marriage. Edwards suggests that she is already imbued with the value of economic success and when she fully realizes economic equality, economic support as a reason for the attractiveness of marriage will decline for the most able women. She may still seek marriage eventually, but not because of economic necessity. There is already some evidence that marriage is more desirable for men than for women. Women, for example, are less likely to remarry after divorce or widowhood than men. This is not all because of differences in opportunity since the sex difference in remarriage is especially noticeable among women who are *economically secure* (Edward, 1967, pp. 509–10; Bernard, 1956, pp. 55, 62–63). In other words, those divorced or widowed women who are economically independent are less likely to remarry than are those without adequate economic means. We either must assume that women with money are less attractive than women without, or that their motivation for remarriage is decreased if the economic need is removed. If the latter assumption is correct, then, as the economic necessity of marriage at all lessens, Edwards sees a decline in the marriage rate and a shift in the reason for marriage—especially for women. Fewer marriages will be entered because of habit or from necessity.

Edwards, then, comes to the same conclusion as Hobart in expecting the affective behavior of family relations to become more important, but does not share his optimism in seeing a supremacy of human values over economic ones take place. An emphasis on human values in marriage involves mutual sacrifice and sharing and an awareness of and desire to meet the emotional needs of those we value. Current trends appear to suggest that our marriages today are primarily utilitarian in nature, with the partners primarily interested in what each, himself, derives from the relationship (Cuber and Harroff, 1965; Pineo, 1961).

Edwards relates this to the pervasive effect of our economic emphasis which makes us mainly reward-seeking organisms. We learn to expect rewards for everything we do, and if rewards are not forthcoming we cease to "do." The early dating situation, he suggests, intensifies the reward-seeking behavior in the male–female relationship and serves as a training ground for the husband–wife relationship. Low commitment, as we have seen earlier, heightens control over a relationship so that the one with the least commitment can extract more rewards. As more and more people grow up with the reward-seeking orientation, Edwards argues, they perhaps will learn that commitment reduces rewards and therefore will avoid it.

Perhaps we see indications of this among those young people who say that marriage is outmoded because it ties people together who no longer love each other. They want to feel that they stay together freely because of the emotional bond with no strings attached. This may be another way of saying that they want everything they do rewarded, and if the rewards are not immediately forthcoming they want to be free to move on to a better bargain. Commitment is to be avoided because it connotes loss of control and perhaps a reduction of rewards.

Edwards sees a heightened interdependence between the family and the economic sphere. As we continue to seek both economic rewards from integration with large organizations and highly individualistic and affectional rewards from marriage and family relationships, marriages of the future will be based more on reason and rational considerations than on impulse or habit and will develop much more variability in structure as the meeting of individual needs is adapted to the demands of the economic system.

From this point of view, it appears that each individual family in the future will be even more of an experiment in living than it is today. It will be even less likely that the parental marriage structure will serve as an adequate training ground for the marital roles of the offspring. The future then offers the opportunity for either unprecedented freedom in tailoring relationships to fit the needs of the individuals or mounting conflict, anxiety, and instability as individuals are unable to cope with the lack of family structure.

If Edwards is correct in his suggestion that reward-seeking behavior will become even more prevalent as the twin values of economic success and individualism are equally held, the implications for socialization are immense. The parent-role in socialization is not instantly rewarding. As discussed in an earlier chapter, socialization or the development of self does not take place without some frustration and anxiety being created in the child. The child does not thank the parent for doing this, yet he does not mature socially or emotionally if it is not done. Parents must wait a long time for their child to grow up. Only then can they tell if their efforts will be crowned with success. This does not seem to fit with universal needs for immediate rewards or approval.

Is the Family Outmoded?

Among the few social thinkers who believe that the family has outlived its usefulness is Barrington Moore (1969). He suggests that in our present society, children, when young, are burdens on their parents; and parents, when old, are burdens on their children. Furthermore the expectations that one should love his family members just because he was born into the group imposes guilt feelings and encourages exploitation of one family member by another. The education of women has made them unable to accept the drudgery of housework and child care without damage to their personalities. He suggests that the family is no longer adapted to modern society and will eventually be replaced by more efficient institutions of child care.

In the view of Margaret Mead (1966) the family is not outmoded but is in trouble. One of the reasons for this is the expectation that it meet emotional needs of the adult members and that it also remain permanent in order to meet the emotional and social needs of children. She suggests a marriage in two stages. The first would be primarily a sexual relationship without children. This "marriage" could be easily discarded if it did not work out. The second stage, if the first proved successful, would allow the bearing of children and would be permanent—very difficult to dissolve. Others have suggested a third step, after the children are reared, at which time the marriage again could be easily terminated.

Depending upon one's point of view and the future resolution of the conflict between humanistic and economic values, one may look to the future with either hope or despair. What happens will be the result of millions of individual adaptations to pressures coming from changes in the economic, religious, educational, and political institutions. These adaptations are forced by the changing nature of the society, but the nature of the adaptations also shapes the direction of future institutional changes. Each individual family has a hand in shaping the future.

Questions Posed by Biological Discoveries

The rapid growth of the biological sciences, especially in the area of human reproduction, will undoubtedly pose some dilemmas for families of the future. Control of the sex of the child is already at hand, with seemingly a high degree of accuracy. Although the procedure is extremely new at this writing it is said to result in producing the desired sex in 80 to 85 per cent of the cases. Since precise instructions for controlling the sex of the unborn child through timing of sexual intercourse has appeared in popular magazines, dissemination of the procedure for control can be expected to be rapid (*Look*, April 21, 1970). Given the slight preference for male children in our society, the opportunity for choice may have a profound influence on the sex-ratio, with implications for the power relationship between the sexes as well as future marriage rates.

Since there is evidence that many families have more children than they actually desire in an attempt to obtain the desired number of both boys and girls, the ability to choose the sex of the offspring may lower the birth rate and thereby be an aid in population control. On the other hand, over one generation the slight preference for males may relieve the "marriage squeeze" enabling a higher percentage of women to find mates, producing more marriages and thereby increasing the population rapidly even if the number of children in each family stabilizes at a lower figure. The short-term and long-term consequences of sex-determination may be quite different.

Transplantation of the fertilized ovum into another woman for the nine months gestation period may also become possible. Thus, a woman who because of health reasons may be unable to carry a child through the full term of pregnancy could hire a substitute to carry it for her. It would also enable career women and their husbands to have children who carry their genetic traits without having to interrupt their careers because of pregnancy or childbirth. A new job opportunity for women who wished to work and stay home at the same time would be created—"baby sitter" for the unborn child. Legal problems in this situation may become quite complex: who is the "natural mother"—the one who conceived the baby or the one from whom it was delivered? [1]

Interference with the genetic structure is also in the future. The obvious advantages in reducing the transmission of defects encourages research in this area. However, knowledge gained for these purposes becomes available for alteration of "normal" traits, perhaps to the specifi-

---

[1] See *Life's* Science Editor (1969) and accompanying Louis Harris poll for a resumé of the biological discoveries dealing with reproduction and the willingness of American men and women to accept them. See also Meyer F. Nimkoff (1962) and "Man into Superman" in *Time* (1971).

cation of the parents. If one lets the imagination run wild, he may en-
vision the day when a woman enters a physician's office, hands him a list
of physical characteristics (with her husband's signature, notarized, of
course) which they want in a son who is to be delivered within the next
fifteen months. A whole new area for conflict between husband and wife
will certainly appear, as they argue about the sex composition of their
family, their preferences for blondes, brunettes, redheads, skin coloring,
physical builds, eye coloring, nose shapes, and so on. Imagine the hostility a child may feel toward parents who ordered for him a physical
appearance which he doesn't like, or who failed to alter genetic traits seen
as unattractive.

This amount of control is, of course, a long way away—if it ever comes
—but its implications for the future of the family and society are immense.
Who will decide what genetic alterations are legal? Who will decide how
much control the individual may have over the sex composition of his
family? Or as population problems become more acute, who may have
how many children?

If one can order certain characteristics in his unborn child much as he
specifies the upholstery for a new chair, what will be the legal position of
the parent if for some reason the child does not fit the specifications? Will
economic values prevail so that the parents can refuse to accept the child?
Will he be able to bring suit against the physician? Will family values
prevail so that the child is still considered part of the family whether or
not the sex or physical characteristics meet specifications? The effect on
the family will not come from the scientific developments, per se, but
from the interplay of values influencing the incorporation of the advances
into the lives of millions of families.

We have experienced the tremendous effects of industrialization, urbanization, and automation on family structure and human relationships.
From some points of view, the most influential of all in altering the meaning of the family will be the biological revolution, especially as it concerns
reproduction and mortality. But looming in the future is the revolution in
space exploration. Its influence on the future of the family must be at
this time purely fanciful.

Influence of the Space Age

When the first man set foot on the moon his first words were, "One
small step for a man, one giant step for mankind." We might add to this
"and a fateful step for the family." It is of course impossible to tell how
space exploration will effect the future of the family but we can spell out
some of the dilemmas it will pose and suggest some possible adaptations.
Already analogies are being made between our planet and a spaceship in

order to awaken people to the need to conserve our consumables. We will here, however, confine our imaginations to families personally connected with the space technology, without considering its effect on families throughout the society.

In the beginning, the space exploration crews will probably be composed largely of young, intelligent, healthy men, especially as the time of space expeditions lengthens to one, five, or ten years. These will be men in the prime reproductive years of their lives. The final resistance to full acceptance of the sperm banks (storing in the frozen state the male sperm) may crumble as a way is sought to have a family while husband and wife are separated by two or three light years. Week-end trips are out, but his sperm may be left behind for use on a pre-arranged schedule. Reproduction may continue in his absence but completely separated from the emotional bond of the sexual relationship. This situation completely reverses the traditional position of the sexes as far as sexual freedom is concerned. The long period away from home in an all-male environment out in space puts severe restrictions on the male's freedom to be unfaithful but leaves the female with unmet needs and the freedom and opportunity to meet them at the same time she bears her husband's children according to schedule.

Consequences of this hypothetical situation are difficult to predict. Given the move toward more sexual permissiveness, the whole idea of infidelity may change, so that infidelity comes to mean only that a child is conceived by someone other than the spouse, or only applies when both spouses are together between trips. On the other hand, the reluctance of husbands to leave in such a flexible situation may encourage the development of communes within the space community, where continued surveillance of the wife assures her faithfulness.

Still another solution may be sending married couples on long range space expeditions. In this case both spouses would have to be space technologists, since there will be no room for "free loaders." The implications here for the mate selection process are great. Of what good is a woman's culinary art with no kitchen, her taste in fashion when confined to a space suit, her scintillating personality if she is no good at astrophysics or celestial mechanics?

We might find trial periods developing to discover whether two people can stand each other confined to a room without windows and without doors for days on end. Imagine the consequences of a couple deciding they can no longer live together the fifth year out on a ten year trip!

The technological problems of handling childbirth and child care aboard a spaceship would probably be too immense to allow reproduction during the expedition. But now we have both husband and wife removed during their prime reproduction period. They either must desire to remain childless or utilize the sperm and egg banks, with the fertilized egg implanted in a substitute mother or artificial womb. In this way, their babies could be born as they would have them and be waiting for them on their return. This, of course, would require the maintenance of children's houses by the Space Agency.

Perhaps, considering these difficulties, one of the requirements for participation in space exploration will be commitment to the single life, until age makes him (or her) earthbound. This would definitely introduce a selective factor into the recruitment of personnel.

Colonization. When we look even farther into the future to the day when colonization may be possible (perhaps mining colonies on the moon, first) the imagination is stretched all the more. The relationship between the technological structure and family structure becomes even more apparent. What kind of family conditions can develop will of necessity be contingent upon the kind of controlled environment the technology can provide. It seems almost certain, however, that present husband–wife roles will be greatly altered, as everyone is expected to contribute to the colonizing enterprise. This may bring us full circle back to the close-knit, tribal kind of community living, where the sense of family extends to the whole colony, and the nuclear family is de-emphasized. Controlled by a completely technological perspective, however, the way is opened for the development of a "Brave New World" (Huxley, 1932). Instead of sending family units, a group of well-trained technologists supplied with sperm and egg banks and artificial wombs may be sent to develop their own population according to specifications. Prevailing values here on earth will be the deciding factor in the direction we go—not just the development of the technology.

THE PRINCIPLE OF VALUE RELEVANCE

The future promises both hope and despair, depending upon the value system of the individual. The family is not completely at the mercy of the other institutions in the society; it also influences the direction those institutions will develop. It influences, however, not through organized action but through the expression of its values in everyday interaction, through decisions its members make as they interact in other systems, and through transmittal of these values to the children. When there is severe conflict between the values held and transmitted by individual families, the influence of the family institution is reduced. As the strength of values instilled in children is weakened the influence of the family on society is weakened. But as individual families come closer together on the values they express and transmit, and as the strength of values transmitted grows stronger, the influence of the family institution increases.

Whether one would like to see the family influence weakened or strengthened depends upon his evaluation of the values he sees as being transmitted by it. Obviously there is no single set of values transmitted by *the* family today. They vary according to the past traditions and the interrelations of the individual family with the other social systems.

Whatever the outcome, the direction the family takes will be inextricably tied to the direction the total society takes. The complex interaction between the economic, educational, religious, and political systems shapes the environment within which families may either flourish, stagnate, or perish. On the other hand, millions of individuals living in and shaped by family groups express their values in what they contribute to, how they use, and what they demand of the economic, educational, religious, and political systems. Barring the interference of wars or economic disaster, the content and strength of the value systems being put into children in our families today will to a large extent determine the future of both the family and society tomorrow.

SUMMARY

Changes occurring in the family over time can be related to changes occurring in other social activities and institutions—the economic, the educational, the religious, and the political. It has been pointed out that the family is both a conservative and an adaptive institution—making adjustments to the pressures coming from changes in the other systems and preserving past forms through the socialization process.

The relative strengths of the conservative and adaptive functions are related to the direction and rapidity with which change occurs. There have been four major revolutions taking place in our society which have had a tremendous impact on our whole way of life, including family life. These are: the technological revolution, the population revolution, the democratic revolution, and the secular revolution.

Using these past trends and their effects on the family, many sociologists have attempted to predict the future of the family. Predictions concerning the future are always hazardous since it is impossible to anticipate all the changes which will occur in a society or their consequences. It is not surprising, then, that the predictions do not always agree. Factors seen to contribute to the increased stability of the family include: (1) decline of teen-age marriages; (2) decrease in age difference between spouses which, combined with increased medical knowledge, should reduce the incidence of widowhood; and (3) increased level of living.

Factors seen to contribute to family instability are: (1) lessened external control because of heightened mobility and shifting friendship groups; (2) heightened external pulls because of needs to achieve and increased interaction between the sexes both at work and in voluntary associational membership; and (3) the conflict between economic and humanistic values. Hobart sees the value conflict being resolved by the ascendancy of humanistic values which will open the way for the development of marriages which stress the importance of people over things.

Edwards, however, anticipates that the conflict will not be resolved since the valuing of economic rewards will result in more and more people expecting rewards for everything they do. Since being able to extract rewards is related to low commitment to a relationship, he sees a decline in the marriage rate, with those who do marry doing so more on rational considerations than on impulse or habit. Both perspectives, however, include the anticipation of much more flexible and variable family structures in the future. Whether this will result in more freedom in satisfying personal needs or increased value conflict and instability, or both, remains to be seen.

Another of the important current developments which should have an enormous impact on the future of the family is the advance in biological knowledge, especially as this affects reproduction and control over characteristics of the unborn child. Since reproduction is central to the organization of the family, whatever affects this will in turn affect the family.

Looking far into the future, the consequences of the Space Age can only be imagined. The technological advances necessary to develop space exploration and colonization will provide the pressure and possibility for many variations of our present family form.

Whatever the outcome, the direction the family takes will be bound up with the direction the total society takes. The future of the family will reflect the adaptations of millions of individuals to the pressures and opportunities offered by changes in the complex web of societal institutions. These adaptations, however, will be greatly influenced by the content and strength of the value systems instilled by today's families in their children.

QUESTIONS AND PROJECTS

1. Describe the major societal trends affecting the family given in this chapter. Would you include any other trends among these? Explain.

2. Discuss the conflict between family values and economic values. If you agree these values are actually contradictory, toward which direction do you think this conflict will be resolved? Explain.

3. How do you think the increased "external pulls" will affect family sta-

bility? Will they affect marital satisfaction? Are there any conflicts between the effects? Explain.

4. If marriages and families do develop more variability in form in the future, what will be the impact on socialization for marriage? On mate selection?

5. What is your opinion of the statement that the family is no longer adapted to modern society? What changes would you suggest? Why?

6. Consider the most recent biological advances and suggest changes in marriage and the family which might flow from them. Which of these changes do you think are most likely to occur? Why?

7. What impact do you think the "space age" will have on family life? Consider both those involved in space projects and those not involved. Give reasons for your answers.

8. Let your imagination run wild and construct an "ideal" family form. What kind of society would be necessary to support it? What would be its major advantages over the present form? Its greatest difficulties? Do you think we are moving closer to or farther away from your hypothetical construct?

Appendix:

Family Changes Reflected in Statistical Trends

The broad changes in family structure were discussed in Chapter 2. If these generalizations are correct, they should be substantiated by statistical trends. The trends discussed here are not exhaustive, nor are the items mutually exclusive, but together they describe the directions in which the American family is moving.

MORE AND EARLIER MARRIAGES

Almost two-thirds of all Americans fourteen years of age and over are married, and the great majority of these are living with their spouse (see Figure A–1). One-fourth are single, nearly one-twelfth are widowed, and only slightly more than one-thirty-fifth are divorced. In terms of absolute numbers, the 1969 Census figures show 88,880,000 persons married and living with spouse; 1,814,000 married but separated due to working conditions, military service, and the like; 2,695,000 married but separated because of marital discord; 4,076,000 divorced; 11,741,000 widowed; and 35,415,000 single.

The numbers just given are for persons fourteen years of age and over. If higher ages were used as breaking points, the figures would be different. For example, for persons aged twenty and over only 14,652,000, or 12.0 per cent, were single; and for persons aged thirty and over only 6,244,000, or 6.6 per cent, were single in 1969.

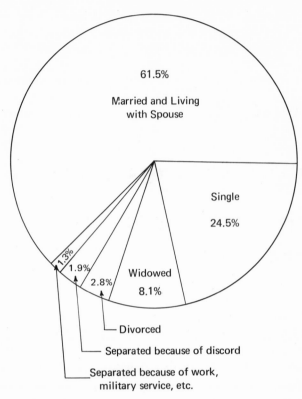

Fig. A–1. Marital composition of the population for persons fourteen years and over, including members of armed forces who were living off post or with their families on post. (Computed from Bureau of the Census, March, 1970, p. 11.)

Of special interest are the percentages in Table A–1, showing time trends in marital composition. It will be observed that for more than half a century, from 1890 to 1955, the single portion of the population had been declining, and the married, widowed, and divorced portions had been expanding. In the period from 1955 to 1969, however, there appears to have been a reversal. This is probably due to the tremendous increase in the 14 to 17 age-groups during these years. Since only about .5 per cent of the males and 2.7 per cent of the females aged 14 to 17 are married, it serves to raise the single category when all persons fourteen and over are used as the base. We get a clearer picture if we select the age group between 30 and 54. This grouping, in 1890 as well as now, includes the majority of those who will *ever* marry, and by excluding the large percentage of widows above age 54 we have a better comparison of

Table A–1

Marital Status in the United States
(Percentage Distribution by Sex and Year)*

Sex and Year	Single	Married	Widowed	Divorced
MALE				
1969	27.4	67.0	3.3	2.3
1965	26.6	67.9	3.3	2.2
1960	25.3	69.5	3.4	2.1
1955	24.1	69.9	4.2	1.8
1950	26.2	68.2	4.0	1.6
1940	34.8	59.7	4.2	1.2
1890	43.6	52.1	3.8	0.2
FEMALE				
1969	21.8	62.3	12.5	3.3
1965	20.7	63.9	12.5	2.9
1960	19.0	66.0	12.1	2.9
1955	18.2	66.9	12.6	2.3
1950	19.6	66.1	12.1	2.2
1940	27.6	59.5	11.3	1.6
1890	34.1	54.8	10.6	0.4

* Percentages are based on the population aged fourteen and over.

SOURCE: Bureau of the Census, 1960, Vol. 1, "Characteristics of the Population," Part I, U. S. Summary, pp. 436–38; "Marital Status and Family Status: March, 1965"; *Current Population Reports,* Series P–20, No. 144 (November 10, 1965), p. 10; and *Current Population Reports,* Series P–20, No. 198 (March 25, 1970), p. 4.

families during the period when children are likely to be present in the household (Table A–2).

Looking at this group (which represents the period of childrearing) the per cent married has increased and the per cent single and widowed has declined for both males and females. These percentages represent those in the particular status at the time the census was taken. Although over the entire period there is a slight decrease in proportion of families broken by widowhood and divorce combined, this does not mean that those now married have not experienced divorce or widowhood. Fourteen per cent of both males and females ever married in 1965 had been married more than once.

Contrary to popular opinion, people are marrying younger today than in earlier generations (see Figure A–2). Average age at first marriage declined for more than fifty years for both sexes. The lowering of the median age at marriage for the male has been greater than for the female, however. During the last decade, the decline has not continued and even shows a slight upward trend. Age difference between the spouses has also decreased. There was, on the average, a four year differential in

Table A–2

Marital Status in the United States of Persons
Between the Ages of 30 and 54
(Percentage Distribution by Sex and Year)

Sex and Year	Single	Married	Widowed	Divorced
MALE				
1969	8.2	87.6	0.9	3.3
1965	8.7	87.6	0.8	2.9
1960	8.6	87.7	1.0	2.7
1950	10.1	85.9	1.5	2.6
1940	14.5	81.3	2.3	1.8
1930	14.9	80.3	3.1	1.5
1920	16.7	78.6	3.6	0.9
1910	17.3	77.9	3.8	0.7
1900	17.7	77.5	4.2	0.5
1890	16.6	79.2	3.7	0.3
FEMALE				
1969	5.2	85.5	4.6	4.7
1965	5.3	86.1	4.5	4.2
1960	6.7	84.8	4.7	3.8
1950	8.4	82.4	5.8	3.4
1940	10.8	79.1	7.6	2.5
1930	10.5	79.5	8.2	1.8
1920	11.7	78.3	8.9	1.1
1910	11.8	78.2	9.1	0.9
1900	11.6	77.4	10.2	0.7
1890	10.4	78.3	10.6	0.5

SOURCE: Computed from Bureau of the Census, 1960, Vol. 1, "Characteristics of the Population," Part I, U. S. Summary, pp. 436–38. 1965 and 1969 data added.

1890, which decreased to approximately two and one-half years in 1965 and 1969.

There is some indication that the female's median age at marriage may continue to increase for the next several years, with perhaps an additional increase in percentage of single women. This may result from what is called the "marriage squeeze" resulting from the maturing of the "baby boom" children of the late 1940's and early 1950's. Because women typically marry at earlier ages than men, there is an increase of the number of marriageable females somewhat earlier than the increase in the number of marriageable males. For example, in 1969 there were 9.1 million females in the age group 15–19. They should be looking for husbands roughly in the 20–24 age group, since comparatively few males marry before age 20 and at these ages they marry females, on the average, from 2 to 4 years younger. There were, however, only 7.6 million males in this age group.

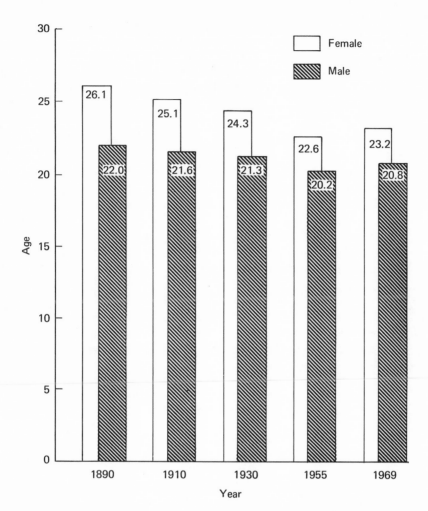

Fig. A–2. Median age at marriage. (Bureau of the Census, March, 1970, p. 2.)

The excess women will either have to wait for males in their own age group to reach marriageable age, thereby decreasing the age difference between spouses and raising the median age of first marriage for females, or remain unmarried. If the males continue to marry women several years younger than themselves, then we could expect an increase in the number of single women. An excess of about a million females over males in the next older age group continues down to age 10-14 for the females when there are 10 million girls aged 10–14 and 9.2 million males aged 15-19 (Bureau of the Census, September, 1970, p. 10).

NUCLEAR FAMILIES MORE PREVALENT

About 99 per cent of married couples living together live in their own households—and these are likely to include children. Of all the 70.6 million children under 18 in 1969, 84.8 per cent of them were living with two parents. At the same time that there has been an increase in the primary family units, there has been a steady rise in the number of persons living alone or sharing living quarters with non-related persons. In 1969 this number was about 11.4 million persons fourteen years old and older. In close to two-thirds of these households the head was 55 years old or over. The number has doubled since 1950 (Bureau of the Census, March, 1970, p. 15). This rapid increase reflects the increasing proportion of older persons in the population as well as the increasing tendency of older persons to maintain their own home rather than live with relatives. During the same period there has been a steady decline in the number of unrelated individuals living in households as lodgers, or resident employees, and in the number of family units living in the households of either relatives or non-relatives. These trends seem to give a clear indication of the rise of the nuclear family unit, composed almost exclusively of husband, wife, and single children under 18. This does not necessarily mean that both husband and wife are the biological parents of the children living with them, however.

GREATER DISRUPTION

Marriage and divorce rates, illustrated in Figure A–3, tend to fluctuate together. They both took a dip during the depression years in the early thirties; they both reached an all-time peak in 1946, following World War II; and they both declined somewhat since that time until 1969.

Another way of presenting the picture is in terms of marriage–divorce ratios. At the beginning of the present century there averaged only about one divorce for every twelve marriages. By 1930 the ratio had become one to six. More recently it has been approaching one to four. Now over one-half of a million divorces occur every year in the United States.[1] However, this overrepresents the proportion of the married population which experiences divorce. Some of these are repeated divorces, describing the marriage pattern prevalent among a few who marry–divorce–remarry–divorce–remarry and so on. This has been spoken of by some as

---

[1] In 1967 divorces for the first time exceeded one-half million (534,000). In 1969, the preliminary estimate was 660,000. Marriages also increased from 1,913,000 to a preliminary estimate of 2,146,000 (Bureau of the Census, 1970, p. 60).

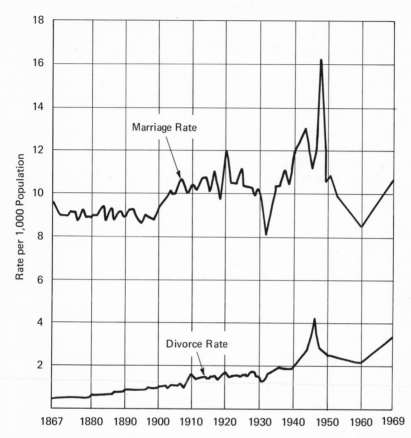

Fig. A–3. Estimated marriage and divorce rates for the United States, 1867–1969. (Department of Health, Education, and Welfare, Public Health Service, *Vital Statistics of the United States,* "Marriages," vol. 3, section 1, p. 7; "Divorces," vol. 3, section 3, p. 5. Data for 1960 and 1969 from Bureau of the Census, September, 1970, p. 60.)

sequential polygamy—never more than one mate at a time, but a succession of mates over time.

There is a tendency for those remarried to be overrepresented in the divorce statistics. About one-third in 1958 and about 25 per cent in 1965 of all divorcing persons had been involved in a previous marriage. Although there appears to have been a slight decline in the tendency for those remarried to divorce, the percentage of persons entering a second or third marriage is remaining constant. In 1958, about 20.5 per cent of both brides and grooms were remarrying. This had risen only to about

21.8 in 1965 (Department of Health, Education, and Welfare, October, 1969, p. 38).

Divorces tend to be prevalent in certain segments of the population. They are higher among non-whites, women under 20, and men under 25. Among the states supplying statistics on age at divorce, a divorce rate of 8.8 per 1,000 married men and 8.7 per 1,000 married women was registered as compared with 24.5 for married men under age 25 and 27.7 for married women under age 25.

Marriages seem somewhat more stable if we look from the other direction. In 1960, three-fourths of the males ever married were still living with their first wife. Two-thirds of the ever-married females were still living with their first husband. The lower proportion for females is due mainly to the larger proportion of women who were widowed—about 16 per cent of the ever-married women and only 3 per cent of the ever-married men were widowed. The difference between marital stability in white and non-white groups is shown by the difference in percentage of women ever-married at ages 45 to 49 still living with their first husband. This percentage was 48 per cent for non-whites and 73 per cent for whites.

Although the divorce rate appeared to have leveled off at about 2.2 per 1,000 population during the 1950's, it has taken another rise in the 1960's. Even when the rate was stable the numbers representing disrupted families continued to climb. The pool of divorced persons aged 14 and older in 1969 totaled approximately 4 million, about a million and a half more than in 1950. Those married but separated due to marital discord totaled another 2.7 million. We can say, roughly, that since these figures include both males and females, we have 3.4 million *families* disrupted by marital discord. Add to this another 1.8 million persons who are married but separated due to military service, employment, hospitalization, and other reasons, and the 11.7 million widowed persons. This gives roughly 16 or 17 million *families* disrupted by marital discord, death, or the absence of one of the spouses for other reasons (Bureau of the Census, March 27, 1970, p. 11).

As far as the stability of the family is concerned, we are more concerned with those which contain minor children. Not all the divorces involved children, although the ratio of children to total divorces has been steadily increasing from .85 in 1953 to 1.18 in 1960 to 1.32 in 1965 (Department of Health, Education, and Welfare, 1969, p. 13). Over 600,000 children were involved in divorces in 1965 alone. It is estimated that in 1969, 84.8 per cent of the children under 18 were living with both mother and father. But the 12.1 per cent with one parent missing accounts for approximately 8.2 million children under eighteen. Another 1.2 million live with neither parent, in foster homes, in institutions, with relatives, and so forth. Although the percentage in broken homes is small, the numbers continue to grow as our population becomes larger and larger (Bureau of the Census, 1970, p. 21).

SMALLER FAMILIES

On the average families have been growing smaller. In census usage, a family consists of two or more persons living together who are related by marriage, blood, or adoption. Classified in this way, average family size decreased from 5.7 in 1790 to 4.7 in 1900 to 3.7 in 1965 to 3.62 in 1970 (1970 data from Bureau of the Census, *Current Population Reports*, July, 1970, p. 13). However, the difference in number of children per family is more readily seen by comparing the number of children ever-born to women 45–49 years old. By this time the childbearing period is over and we can view their childbearing history.

From Table A–3, we see that the per cent of childless couples increased considerably until the 1950's and then began to decline. If we look only at those between the ages of 30–34 in 1960, it is apparent that, although their fertile period was not yet over, they had reduced the per cent child-less to about the same percentage as for 1910. By 1969, only 8 per cent of this younger group were still childless—lower than the 1910 percentage (Bureau of the Census, September, 1970, p. 51). The 30–34 age group had already surpassed the completed families in all the previous years in percentages of two, three, and four child families. They were drastically underrepresented in the very large families, however. In 1910, about 29 per cent of the ever-married women had produced seven or more children. Only 5.3 per cent of the 45–49 group had produced this many in 1960, and only 3.3 per cent of those aged 30–34. It is of interest to note that almost half the ever-married women had produced over 5 children by the end of their fertile period in 1910, while only about one-eighth had done so in 1960. Women today, however, are more likely to rear the children they bear to maturity. The infant mortality rate dropped from 98.2 per thousand live births in 1915 to 23.4 in 1966.

BIRTH RATE DOWN, NUMBERS UP

The crude birth rate (number of births per 1,000 population) declined steadily from 37.0 per thousand population in 1875 to 17.9 in 1940. During the 1940's and early 1950's, a rising birth rate reflected the end of World War II. The rate declined some in the later 1950's, and has declined rapidly in the first five years of the 1960's. But the *number* of babies born has increased. Between 1960 and 1965 the birth rate fell

Table A–3

Per Cent Distribution of Ever-Married Women Aged 45–49 by Number of Children Ever Born and Year

Children Ever Born	Age 30–34 1960	Age 45–49			
		1960	1950	1940	1910
No children	10.4	18.1	20.4	16.7	9.5
1 child	14.7	19.4	19.8	16.2	10.3
2 children	27.4	24.7	21.7	19.1	12.1
3 children	22.5	15.8	13.8	14.7	11.3
4 children	12.7	8.9	8.7	10.3	10.7
5–6 children	9.2	7.8	8.4	12.2	17.3
7–9 children			5.0	7.7	17.6
10 or more children	3.3	5.3	2.2	3.1	11.2

SOURCE: Donald J. Bogue, *Population of the United States* (New York: Free Press of Glencoe, 1959), p. 289. 1960 data added.

from 23.7 per thousand to 19.4 while the population grew by 14.1 million. This reflects a change in the structure of the population stemming from the "baby boom" of the late 40's and 50's.

A comparison of 1932 with 1965 emphasizes the effects of the number and structure of the population on the birth rate. The birth rate was about the same for both years but 1932 registered 2.4 million births, while the comparable number in 1965 was 3.8 million. This results from the percentages of women of childbearing age (15–44) in the population and their fertility rate. In 1932, they comprised 23 per cent of the population and had a fertility rate (number of live births per 1,000 women of childbearing age) of 81.7. In 1965, they comprised 20 per cent of the population with a fertility rate of 96.8. The number of women in the prime reproductive period (ages 20–29) has changed little since the mid-1930's. There were 11.1 million of them in 1935 and 11.0 million in 1960. But as the "boom" babies reach maturity, the numbers increase rapidly. In 1970, they totaled 15.5 million. By 1980, they will total 20 million. If they elect to continue the childbearing pattern of age group 30–34, shown in Table A–3, the population will increase extremely rapidly. The very recent decrease in *numbers* of births after 1965 appears related to the decrease in women in the prime reproductive period as a result of the lowered birth rate in the early 1940's. This condition is not expected to continue unless age at marriage and delayed childbearing increase.

There is some indication that the recent trend of more children per family as indicated by the 30–34-year-old cohort will not continue, however. According to the number of children expected, in 1955, the youngest wives (18–24) expected the largest families—an average of 3.2 children. In 1960, the youngest wives (18–24) expected the smallest families (3.0). It would be extremely hazardous to predict the future trends of childbearing, however, since the *ideal* family remains the same, with the most popular number being four children. In 1941 the most popular number was two, and in 1945, three (Population Reference Bureau, 1966). We have not seen what the effect of recent movements to hold family size to two children will be.

Looking back over the past century, the statistics reflect a decrease in the reproduction function of the family. But the population trends indicate a strength in *responsible* reproduction, in that the number of children produced per family has adjusted to the declining mortality rate, keeping the population growth within social and economic limits so that the level of living has not decreased. The adjustment of family size to mortality rates and longer life expectancies has contributed significantly to the orderly development of the economic system. The August, 1966, *Population Bulletin* presents a graphic illustration of what would have happened had the fertility pattern present a century or two ago continued. The reproduction history of an old order Amish couple, where the traditional fertility pattern still continues, illustrates the possible consequences of unchecked family size.

When he died on the eve of his 95 birthday, Miller had 410 living descendants and their number was being increased by about one a week. The Millers were married in 1888, a year when about 535,000 marriages were consummated in the United States. Had each of these couples and their descendants followed the fertility pattern of the Miller clan, the offspring of this one year's marriage cohort would have amounted to about 219 million living descendants in 1960. Had the Amish pattern been copied by all American families in the 12 years remaining until 1900, the population of the United States today would be much larger than that of China.

This footnote to demographic history illustrates how the critical interplay between births and deaths affects the social, economic, and political fate of nations. Obviously to have 'out chinaed' China would not have been in the National interest. It has been clear for some years that the 1960's will be a decade of demographic decision, for this nation, for the world, in setting the pattern of future population growth (Population Reference Bureau, 1966).

The future trend in birth rate and family size will be the result of millions of individual decisions. But those decisions will be influenced by a number of factors—peace, war, prosperity, and depression at the national level; the individual couple's contact with religion, education, and the economic system. These will influence the number of children they desire, as well as their willingness and ability to keep the number they have in conformity to the number they desire.

Bibliography

ALBRECHT, RUTH, "Relationships of Older Parents with Their Children," *Marriage and Family Living*, 16 (February, 1954a), pp. 32–35.
——, "The Parental Responsibilities of Grandparents," *Marriage and Family Living*, 16 (August, 1954b), pp. 201–4.
BARNETT, LARRY D., "Research on International and Interracial Marriages," reprinted in J. Ross Eshleman (ed.), *Perspectives in Marriage and the Family* (Boston: Allyn and Bacon, Inc., 1969).
BATES, ALAN, "Parental Roles in Courtship," *Social Forces*, 20 (May, 1942), pp. 483–86.
BEHRMAN, SAMUEL J., and JOHN R. G. GOSLING, *Fundamentals of Gynecology*, 2nd ed. (New York: Oxford University Press, 1966).
BELL, ROBERT R., and JACK V. BUERKLE, "Mother and Daughter Attitudes Toward Premarital Sexual Behavior," *Marriage and Family Living*, 23 (November, 1961), pp. 340–42.
——, and JAY B. CHASKES, "Premarital Sexual Experience Among Coeds, 1958 and 1968," *Journal of Marriage and the Family*, 32 (February, 1970), pp. 81–84.
BERARDO, FELIX M., "Widowhood Status in the United States: Perspective on a Neglected Aspect of the Family Life Cycle," *The Family Coordinator*, 17 (July, 1968), pp. 191–203.
BERNARD, JESSIE, *Remarriage: A Study of Marriage* (New York: The Dryden Press, 1956).
——, "The Adjustment of Marriage Mates," in Harold T. Christensen (ed.), *Handbook of Marriage and the Family* (Chicago: Rand McNally & Co., 1964), pp. 675–740.
——, "Note on Educational Homogamy in Negro–White and White–Negro Marriages, 1960," *Journal of Marriage and the Family*, 28 (August, 1966a), pp. 274–76.
——, "Marital Stability and Patterns of Status Variables," *Journal of Marriage and the Family*, 28 (November, 1966b), pp. 421–39.
BIEGEL., H., "Romantic Love," *American Sociological Review*, 16 (June, 1951), pp. 326–34.
BILLINGSLEY, ANDREW W., *Black Families in White America* (Englewood Cliffs, N. J.: Prentice-Hall, Inc., 1969).
BIRDWHISTLE, MIRIAM, "Adolescents and the Pill Culture," *The Family Coordinator*, 17 (January, 1968), pp. 27–32.
BLOOD, JR., ROBERT O., *Marriage*, 2nd ed. (New York: The Free Press of Glencoe, Inc., 1969).
——, and DONALD M. WOLFE, *Husbands and Wives: The Dynamics of Married Living* (New York: The Free Press of Glencoe, Inc., 1960).
BOGUE, DONALD J., *Population of the United States* (New York: The Free Press of Glencoe, Inc., 1959).
BOLTON, CHARLES D., "Mate Selection as the Development of a Relationship," *Marriage and Family Living*, 23 (August, 1961), pp. 234–40.
BOSSARD, JAMES H. S., and WINOGENE SANGER, "The Large Family System—A Research Report," *American Sociological Review*, 17 (February, 1952), pp. 3–9.

BOWMAN, HENRY A., *Marriage for Moderns,* 3rd ed. (New York: McGraw-Hill Book Co., Inc., 1954).

BRECHER, RUTH, and EDWARD BRECHER (eds.), *An Analysis of Human Sexual Response* (New York: New American Library, Signet Books, 1966).

BRODERICK, CARLFRED B., and JESSIE BERNARD (eds.), *The Individual, Sex, and Society* (Baltimore: The Johns Hopkins Press, 1969).

BRODERICK, CARLFRED B., and STANLEY E. FOWLER, "New Patterns of Relationships Between the Sexes Among Preadolescents," *Marriage and Family Living,* 23 (February, 1961), pp. 27–30.

BRONFENBRENNER, URIE, "The Split Level American Family," reprinted in J. Ross Eshleman (ed.), *Perspectives in Marriage and the Family* (Boston: Allyn and Bacon, Inc., 1969), pp. 521–35.

BROWN, DANIEL B., "Female Orgasm and Sexual Inadequacy," in Ruth and Edward Brecher (eds.), *An Analysis of Human Sexual Response* (New York: New American Library, Signet Books, 1966).

BURCHINAL, LEE G., "The Premarital Dyad and Love Involvement," in H. T. Christensen (ed.), *Handbook of Marriage and the Family* (Chicago: Rand McNally & Co., 1964), pp. 623–74.

————, and LOREN E. CHANCELLOR, "Proportions of Catholics, Urbanism and Mixed Catholic Marriage Rates Among Iowa Counties," *Social Problems,* No. 4 (1962), pp. 359–65.

————, "Survival Rates Among Religiously Homogamous and Interreligious Marriages," *Social Forces,* 41 (May, 1963), pp. 353–62.

BUREAU OF THE CENSUS, "Characteristics of the Population," 1960, Part 1, U. S. Summary.

————, "Marital Status and Family Status, March, 1965," *Current Population Reports,* Series P-20, No. 144 (November, 1965).

————, "Household and Family Characteristics, March, 1965," *Population Characteristics,* Series P-20, No. 153 (August, 1966).

————, "Marital Status and Family Status," *Current Population Reports,* Series P-20, No. 198 (March, 1970).

————, *The Statistical Abstract of the United States,* 1970.

BURGESS, ERNEST W., and LEONARD S. COTTRELL, *Predicting Success or Failure in Marriage* (Englewood Cliffs, N. J.: Prentice-Hall, Inc., 1939).

BURGESS, ERNEST W., and PAUL WALLIN, *Engagement and Marriage* (Philadelphia: J. B. Lippincott Co., 1953).

CAMERON, WILLIAM J., and WILLIAM F. KENKEL, "High School Dating: A Study in Variation," *Marriage and Family Living,* 22 (February, 1960), pp. 74–76.

CAMPBELL, ARTHUR A., "Population Dynamics and Family Planning," *Journal of Marriage and the Family,* 30 (May, 1968), pp. 202–6.

CAPLOW, THEODORE, *Two Against One—Coalitions in Triads* (Englewood Cliffs, N. J.: Prentice-Hall, Inc., 1968).

CARPENTER, GEORGE R., "Cross-Cultural Values as a Factor in Premarital Intimacy," unpublished Ph.D. dissertation, Purdue University, 1960.

CARTER, HUGH, PAUL C. GLICK, and SARAH LEWIT, "Some Demographic Characteristics of Recently Married Persons: Comparisons of Registration Data and Sample Survey Data," *American Sociological Review,* 20 (April, 1955), pp. 165–72.

CATTON, JR., W. R., and R. J. SMIRCICH, "A Comparison of Mathematical Models for the Effect of Residential Propinquity on Mate Selection," *American Sociological Review,* 29 (August, 1964), pp. 522–29.

CAVAN, RUTH SCHONLE, "Family Tensions Between the Old and the Middle-Aged," *Marriage and Family Living,* 18 (November, 1956), pp. 323–27.

CHENG, C. K., and DOUGLAS S. YAMAMURA, "Interracial Marriage and Divorce in Hawaii," *Social Forces,* 36 (October, 1957), pp. 77–84.

CHILMAN, CATHERINE S., "Child-Rearing and Family Relationship Patterns of the Very Poor," in Marvin B. Sussman (ed.), *Sourcebook in Marriage and the Family,* 3rd ed. (Boston: Houghton Mifflin Co., 1968a), pp. 201–10.

———, "Fertility and Poverty in the United States: Some Implications for Family-Planning Programs, Evaluation and Research," *Journal of Marriage and the Family*, 30 (May, 1968), pp. 207–27.

CHRISTENSEN, HAROLD T. "Dating Behavior as Evaluated by High-School Students," *American Journal of Sociology*, 57 (May, 1952), pp. 580–86.

———, "Rural–Urban Differences in the Spacing of the First Birth from Marriage: A Repeat Study," *Rural Sociology*, 18 (March, 1953a), p. 60.

———, "Studies in Child Spacing: I—Premarital Pregnancy as Measured by the Spacing of the First Birth from Marriage," *American Sociological Review*, 18 (February, 1953b), pp. 53–59.

———, "Pregnant Brides—Record Linkage Studies," in Evelyn M. Duvall and Sylvanus M. Duvall (eds.), *Sex Ways—in Fact and Faith* (New York: Association Press, 1961), pp. 129–39, Chapter 8.

———, "The Intrusion of Values," in Harold T. Christensen (ed.), *Handbook of Marriage and the Family* (Chicago: Rand McNally & Co., 1964), pp. 969–1006.

———, "Children in the Family: Relationship of Number and Spacing to Marital Success," *Journal of Marriage and the Family*, 30 (May, 1968), pp. 283–89.

———, "The Changing American Family," unpublished, 1970.

———, and KENNETH E. BARBER, "Interfaith Versus Intrafaith Marriage in Indiana," *Journal of Marriage and the Family*, 29 (August, 1967), pp. 461–69.

CHRISTENSEN, HAROLD T., and OLIVE P. BOWDEN, "Studies in Child Spacing: II—The Time-Interval Between Marriage of Parents and Birth of Their First Child, Tippecanoe County, Ind.," *Social Forces*, 31 (May, 1953), pp. 346–51.

CHRISTENSEN, HAROLD T., and GEORGE R. CARPENTER, "Value-Behavior Discrepancies Regarding Premarital Coitus in Three Western Cultures," *American Sociological Review*, 27 (February, 1962), pp. 66–74.

CHRISTENSEN, HAROLD T., and CHRISTINA F. GREGG, "Changing Sex Norms in America and Scandinavia," *Journal of Marriage and the Family*, 32 (November, 1970), pp. 616–27.

CHRISTENSEN, HAROLD T., and HANNA H. MEISSNER, "Studies in Child Spacing: III—Premarital Pregnancy as a Factor in Divorce," *American Sociological Review*, 18 (December, 1953), pp. 641–44.

CHRISTENSEN, HAROLD T., and ROBERT E. PHILBRICK, "Family Size as a Factor in the Marital Adjustments of College Couples," *American Sociological Review*, 17 (June, 1952), pp. 306–12.

CHRISTENSEN, HAROLD T., and BETTE B. RUBINSTEIN, "Premarital Pregnancy and Divorce: A Follow-up Study by the Interview Method," *Marriage and Family Living*, 18 (May, 1956), pp. 114–23.

CLAUSEN, JOHN A., "Perspectives on Childhood Socialization," in John A. Clausen (ed.), *Socialization and Society* (Boston: Little, Brown, and Co., 1968), pp. 139–41.

COOMBS, ROBERT H., "Value Consensus and Partner Satisfaction Among Dating Couples," *Journal of Marriage and the Family*, 28 (May, 1966), pp. 166–73.

———, and WILLIAM F. KENKEL, "Sex Differences in Dating Aspirations and Satisfaction with Computer Arranged Partners," *Journal of Marriage and the Family*, 28 (February, 1966), pp. 62–66.

CRIST, JOHN R., "High School Dating as a Behavior System," *Marriage and Family Living*, 15 (February, 1953), pp. 23–28.

CUBER, JOHN F., and PEGGY HARROFF, *The Significant Americans: A Study of Sexual Behavior Among the Affluent* (New York: Meredith Press, 1965).

DAGER, EDWARD Z., "Socialization and Personality Development in the Child," in Harold T. Christensen (ed.), *Handbook of Marriage and the Family* (Chicago: Rand McNally & Co., 1964), pp. 740–81.

DAVIS, KATHERINE B., *Factors in the Sex Life of Twenty-Two Hundred Women* (New York: Harper and Row, 1929).

DEPARTMENT OF HEALTH, EDUCATION AND WELFARE, PUBLIC HEALTH SERVICE, "Divorces," *Vital Statistics of the United States*, Vol. III, 1960, Section 3.

DEPARTMENT OF HEALTH, EDUCATION AND WELFARE, PUBLIC HEALTH SERVICE, "Marriages," *Vital Statistics of the United States,* Vol. III, 1960, Section 1.

————, *Divorce Statistics Analysis, United States, 1964 and 1965,* Series 21, No. 17 (October, 1969).

DEUTSCHER, IRWIN, "The Quality of Postparental Life: Definitions of the Situation," *Journal of Marriage and the Family,* 26 (February, 1964), pp. 52–59.

DEVEREAUX, EDWARD C., URIE BRONFENBRENNER, and ROBERT R. RODGERS, "Childrearing in England and the United States; a Cross National Comparison," *Journal of Marriage and the Family,* 31 (May, 1969), pp. 257–70.

DINITZ, SIMON, FRANKLIN BANKS, and BENJAMIN PASAMANICK, "Mate Selection and Social Class: Changes During the Last Quarter Century," *Marriage and Family Living,* 22 (November, 1960), pp. 348–51.

DOUVAN, ELIZABETH, "Employment and the Adolescent," in F. Ivan Nye and Lois Hoffman, *The Employed Mother in America* (Chicago: Rand McNally & Co., 1963), pp. 142–64.

DUVALL, EVELYN M., *In-Laws: Pro and Con* (New York: Association Press, 1954).

DYER, EVERETT D., "Parenthood as Crisis: A Restudy," *Marriage and Family Living,* 25 (May, 1963), pp. 196–201.

DYER, WILLIAM G., "Analyzing Marital Adjustment Using Role Theory," *Marriage and Family Living,* 24 (November, 1962), pp. 371–75.

————, "Family Reactions to the Father's Job," in Arthur B. Shostak and William Gomberg (eds.), *Blue-Collar World* (Englewood Cliffs, N. J.: Prentice-Hall, Inc., 1964), pp. 86–91.

EDWARDS, HARRY, "Black Muslim and Negro Christian Family Relationships," *Journal of Marriage and the Family,* 30 (November, 1968), pp. 604–11.

EDWARDS, JOHN N., "The Future of the Family Revisited," *Journal of Marriage and the Family,* 29 (August, 1967), pp. 505–11.

———— (ed.), *The Family and Change* (New York: Alfred A. Knopf, Inc., 1969).

EHRLICH, PAUL R. *The Population Bomb* (New York: Ballantine Books, Inc., 1968).

EHRMANN, WINSTON, *Premarital Dating Behavior* (New York: Holt, Rinehart & Winston, Inc., 1959).

————, "Marital and Nonmarital Sexual Behavior," in Harold T. Christensen (ed.), *Handbook of Marriage and the Family* (Chicago: Rand McNally & Co., 1964), pp. 585–622.

ELLIS, JULIE, *Revolt of the Second Sex* (New York: Lancer Books, 1970).

EMERSON, RICHARD M., "Power-Dependence Relations," *American Sociological Review,* 27 (February, 1962), pp. 31–40.

EMMERICH, WALTER, "Young Children's Discrimination of Parent and Child Roles," *Child Development,* 30 (1959), pp. 403–19.

ERIKSON, ERIK H., *For Every Child a Healthy Personality: A Digest of the Fact Finding Report* (Washington, D.C.: Midcentury White House Conference on Children and Youth, 1950).

————, "Growth and Crises of the Healthy Personality," in Clyde Kluckhohn and Henry A. Murray (eds.) with the collaboration of David M. Schneider, *Personality in Nature, Society, and Culture,* 2nd ed. (New York: Alfred A. Knopf, Inc., 1964), pp. 185–226.

FELDMAN, HAROLD, "Development of the Husband–Wife Relationship: A Research Report," Cornell University, Mimeograph, no date. Cited on p. 530 in Gerald R. Leslie, *The Family in Social Context* (New York: Oxford University Press, 1967).

FOLSOM, JOSEPH K., *The Family and Democratic Society* (New York: John Wiley and Sons, 1943).

FOOTE, NELSON N., "Matching of Husbands and Wives in Phases of Development," in Marvin B. Sussman (ed.), *Sourcebook of Marriage and the Family,* 2nd ed. (Boston: Houghton Mifflin Co., 1963), pp. 13–21.

FRANKLIN, R. D., and H. H. REMMERS, "Youth's Attitudes Toward Courtship and Marriage," Poll No. 62 of *The Purdue Opinion Panel,* Purdue University (April, 1961).

FREEDMAN, RONALD, PASKAL K. WHELPTON, and ARTHUR A. CAMPBELL, *Family Planning, Sterility, and Population Growth* (New York: McGraw-Hill Book Co., 1959).

GEBHARD, PAUL H., WARDELL B. POMEROY, CLYDE E. MARTIN, and CORNELIA V. CHRISTENSON, *Pregnancy, Birth, and Abortion* (New York: Harper & Row, 1950).

GERTH, HANS, and C. WRIGHT MILLS, *Character and Social Structure* (New York: Harcourt Brace Jovanovich, Inc., 1953), Chapter 5.

GIANOPULOS, ARTIE, and HOWARD E. MITCHELL, "Marital Disagreement in Working Wife Marriages as a Function of Husband's Attitude Toward Wife's Employment," *Marriage and Family Living*, 19 (November, 1957), pp. 373–78.

GLASSER, PAUL H., and LOIS N. GLASSER, "Role Reversal and Conflict Between Aged Parents and Their Children," *Marriage and Family Living*, 24 (February, 1962), pp. 46–51.

GLICK, PAUL C., "The Family Cycle," *American Sociological Review*, 12 (April, 1947), pp. 164–69.

———, "The Life Cycle of the Family," *Marriage and Family Living*, 17 (February, 1955), pp. 3–9.

———, *American Families* (New York: John Wiley & Sons, Inc., 1957).

———, "Marriage, Socio-economic Status and Health," in Egon Szabady (ed.), *World Views of Population Problems* (Budapest: Hungarian Academy of Sciences, 1968), pp. 127–37.

GOLDBERG, PHILIP, "Are Women Prejudiced Against Women?" *Trans-action*, 6 (April, 1968).

GOLLIN, GILLIAN LINDT, "Family Surrogates in Colonial America: The Moravian Experiment," *Journal of Marriage and the Family*, 31 (November, 1969), pp. 650–58.

GOODE, WILLIAM J., *After Divorce* (New York: The Free Press of Glencoe, Inc., 1956).

———, "The Sociology of the Family—Horizons in Family Theory," in Robert K. Merton, Leonard Bloom, and Leonard S. Cottrell, Jr. (eds.), *Sociology Today* (New York: Basic Books, Inc., 1959), pp. 178–96.

———, *The Family* (Englewood Cliffs, N. J.: Prentice-Hall, Inc., 1965).

———, "Family Disorganization," in Robert K. Merton and Robert A. Nisbet (eds.), *Contemporary Social Problems*, 2nd ed. (New York: Harcourt Brace Jovanovich, Inc., 1966), pp. 479–552.

GOODMAN, MARVIN, "Expressed Self-Acceptance and Interspousal Needs: A Basis for Mate Selection," *Journal of Counseling Psychology*, 11, No. 2 (Summer, 1964), pp. 129–35.

GORDON, ALBERT I., *Intermarriage—Interfaith, Interracial, Interethnic* (Boston: Beacon Press, 1966).

GORER, GEOFFREY, *The American People, A Study in National Character* (New York: W. W. Norton & Co., 1948).

GREEN, MORRIS, and PATRICIA BEALL, "Paternal Deprivation: A Disturbance in Fathering," *Pediatrics*, 30 (July, 1962), pp. 91–99.

GROVES, ERNEST R., and WILLIAM F. OGBURN, *American Marriage and Family Relationships* (New York: Henry Holt & Company, 1928).

GUYON, RENÈ, "Chastity and Virginity: The Case Against," in Albert Ellis and Albert Abarband (eds.), *The Encyclopedia of Sexual Behavior* (New York: Hawthorn Books, Inc., 1961), pp. 253–57.

HALLENBECK, PHYLLIS N., "An Analysis of Power Dynamics in Marriage," *Journal of Marriage and the Family*, 28 (May, 1966), pp. 200–3.

HALLOWELL, POPE, "Negro–White Differences in Decisions Regarding Illegitimate Children," *Journal of Marriage and the Family*, 31 (November, 1969), pp. 756–64.

HAMILTON, GILBERT V., *A Research in Marriage* (New York: Albert and Charles Boni, Inc., 1929).

HANDEL, GERALD (ed.), *The Psychosocial Interior of the Family* (Chicago: Aldine Publishing Co., 1967), pp. 332–469.

———, and LEE RAINWATER, "Persistence and Change in Working-Class Life Style,"

528 BIBLIOGRAPHY

in Arthur B. Shostak and William Gomberg (eds.), *Blue-Collar World* (Englewood Cliffs, N. J.: Prentice-Hall, Inc., 1964), pp. 36–41.

HARPER, ROBERT A., "Communication Problems in Marriage and Marriage Counseling," *Marriage and Family Living*, 20 (May, 1958), pp. 107–12.

HARRIS, DANIEL, "Age and Occupational Factors in the Residential Propinquity of Marriage Partners," *Journal of Social Psychology*, 6 (May, 1935), pp. 131–50.

HARTLEY, RUTH E., "Sex Role Pressures and the Socialization of the Male Child," *Psychological Reports*, 5 (1959), pp. 457–68.

————, "Some Implications of Current Changes in Sex Role Patterns," in Marvin B. Sussman (ed.), *Sourcebook in Marriage and the Family*, rev. ed. (Boston: Houghton Mifflin Co., 1963), pp. 133–38.

HASTINGS, DONALD W., "Can Specific Training Procedures Overcome Sexual Inadequacy?," in Ruth and Edward Brecher (eds.), *An Analysis of Human Sexual Response* (New York: Signet Books, 1966), pp. 223–26.

HAWKINS, JAMES L., and KATHRYN P. JOHNSEN, "Perception of Behavioral Conformity, Imputation of Consensus, and Marital Satisfaction," *Journal of Marriage and the Family*, 31 (August, 1969), pp. 507–11.

HEER, DAVID M., "Negro–White Marriage in the United States," *Journal of Marriage and the Family*, 28 (August, 1966), pp. 262–73.

HEISS, JEROLD S., "Premarital Characteristics of the Religiously Intermarried, An Urban Area," *American Sociological Review*, 25 (February, 1960a), pp. 47–55.

————, "Variations in Courtship Progress Among High School Students," *Marriage and Family Living*, 22 (May, 1960b), pp. 165–70.

————, "Degree of Intimacy and Male–Female Interaction," *Sociometry*, 25 (June, 1962), pp. 197–208.

HENRY, JULES, *Culture Against Man* (New York: Random House, 1963).

HERMAN, R. D., "The Going Steady Complex: A Reexamination," *Marriage and Family Living*, 17 (February, 1955), pp. 36–40.

HERMANN, ROBERT O., "Families in Bankruptcy—A Survey of Recent Studies," *Journal of Marriage and the Family*, 28 (August, 1966), pp. 324–30.

HILL, REUBEN, "Campus Norms in Mate Selection," *Journal of Home Economics*, 37 (November, 1945), pp. 368–73.

————, "Decision Making and the Family Life Cycle," in Ethel Shanas and Gordon F. Streib, *Social Structure and the Family: Generational Relations* (Englewoods Cliffs, N. J.: Prentice-Hall, Inc., 1965).

HOBART, CHARLES W., "Disillusionment in Marriage and Romanticism," *Marriage and Family Living*, 20 (May, 1958), pp. 156–62.

————, "Commitment, Value Conflict and the Future of the American Family," *Marriage and Family Living*, 25 (November, 1963), pp. 405–12.

HOBBS, DANIEL F., JR., "Parenthood as Crisis: A Third Study," *Journal of Marriage and the Family*, 27 (August, 1965), pp. 367–72.

HOFFMAN, LOIS W., "Effects of Maternal Employment on the Child," *Child Development*, 32 (1961), pp. 187–97.

————, "Effects Upon Children: Summary and Discussion," in F. Ivan Nye and Lois Hoffman, *The Employed Mother in America* (Chicago: Rand McNally & Co., 1963), pp. 190–212.

————, and MARTIN L. HOFFMAN, *Review of Child Development Research*, Vol. 1 (New York: Russell Sage Foundation, 1966).

HORNER, MATINA S., "Woman's Will to Fail," *Psychology Today*, 62 (November, 1969), pp. 36–38.

HUDSON, JOHN W., and LAURA F. HENZE, "Campus Values in Mate Selection: A Replication," *Journal of Marriage and the Family*, 31 (November, 1969), pp. 772–75.

HURVITZ, NATHAN, "Marital Strain in the Blue-Collar Family," in Arthur B. Shostak and William Gomberg (eds.), *Blue-Collar World* (Englewood Cliffs, N. J.: Prentice-Hall, Inc., 1964), pp. 92–109.

HUXLEY, ALDOUS, *Brave New World* (New York, Harper & Row, 1932).

JACOBSOHN, PETER, and ADAM P. MATHENY, JR., "Mate Selection in Open Marriage Systems," *International Journal of Comparative Sociology,* 3 (September, 1962), pp. 98–123.

JOHANNIS, THEODORE B., JR., "The Marital Adjustment of a Sample of Married College Students," *Family Life Coordinator,* 4 (June, 1956), pp. 29–32.

JOHNSEN, KATHRYN P., *An Analysis of Factors Contributing to Within-Class Differences in Maternal Role Change Over Two Generations,* unpublished Ph.D. thesis, Purdue University, 1966.

———, "Self-Concept Validation as the Focus of Marriage Counseling," *Family Life Coordinator,* 17 (July, 1968), pp. 174–80.

———, "A Progress Report on a Study of the Factors Associated With the Male's Tendency To Negatively Stereotype the Female," *Sociological Focus,* 3 (Spring, 1969), pp. 21–35.

JOHNSON, VIRGINIA E., and WILLIAM H. MASTERS, "Intravaginal Contraceptive Study: Phase 1. Anatomy," *Western Journal of Surgery, Obstetrics, and Gynecology* (1962), pp. 202–7.

JORDAN, JOAN, "Comment: Working Women and the Equal Rights Amendment," *Trans-action,* 8 (November–December, 1970), pp. 16–22.

Journal of Marriage and the Family, 29 (February, 1967), entire issue.

KAATS, GILBERT R., and KEITH E. DAVIS, "The Dynamics of Sexual Behavior of College Students," *Journal of Marriage and the Family,* 32 (August, 1970), pp. 390–99.

KAHL, JOSEPH A., *The American Class Structure* (New York: Holt, Rinehart & Winston, Inc., 1957).

KANIN, EUGENE J., KAREN R. DAVIDSON, and SONIA R. SCHECK, "A Research Note on Male–Female Differentials in the Experience of Heterosexual Love," *The Journal of Sex Research,* 6 (February, 1970), pp. 64–72.

KANIN, EUGENE J., and DAVID H. HOWARD, "Post-marital Consequences of Premarital Sex Adjustments," *American Sociological Review,* 23 (October, 1958), pp. 556–62.

KEPHART, WILLIAM M., "Some Variables in Cases of Reported Sexual Maladjustment," *Marriage and Family Living,* 26 (August, 1954a), pp. 241–43.

———, "The Duration of Marriage," *American Sociological Review,* 19 (June, 1954b), pp. 287–95.

———, "Legal and Procedural Aspects of Marriage and Divorce," in Harold T. Christensen (ed.), *Handbook of Marriage and the Family* (Chicago: Rand McNally & Co., 1964), pp. 944–68.

———, and ROLF B. STROHM, "The Stability of Gretna Green Marriages," *Sociology and Social Research,* 36 (May–June, 1952), pp. 291–96.

KERCKHOFF, ALAN C., "Notes and Comments on the Meaning of Residential Propinquity as a Factor in Mate Selection," *Social Forces,* 34 (March, 1956), pp. 207–13.

———, and KEITH E. DAVIS, "Value Consensus and Need Complementarity in Mate Selection," *American Sociological Review,* 27 (June, 1962), pp. 295–303.

KINSEY, ALFRED C., WARDELL B. POMEROY, CLYDE MARTIN, and PAUL GEBHARD, *Sexual Behavior in the Human Male* (Philadelphia: W. B. Saunders Co., 1948).

———, *Sexual Behavior in the Human Female* (Philadelphia: W. B. Saunders Co., 1953).

———, "Premarital Coitus: Some Arguments and Attitudes," original text from pp. 307–10 and 314–21 in Kinsey, *et al.* (1953), reprinted under this title in Edwin M. Schur (ed.), *The Family and the Sexual Revolution* (Bloomington: Indiana University Press, 1964), pp. 19–29.

KIRKENDALL, LESTER A., "Sex Education of Adolescents; An Exchange," *Marriage and Family Living,* 22 (November, 1960), pp. 317–22.

———, *Premarital Intercourse and Interpersonal Relationships* (New York: Julian Press, Inc., 1961).

KIRKPATRICK, CLIFFORD, *The Family as Process and Institution,* rev. ed. (New York: The Ronald Press Co., 1963).

———, and EUGENE J. KANIN, "Male Sex Aggression on a University Campus," *American Sociological Review,* 23 (February, 1952), pp. 52–58.

KLEMER, RICHARD H., "Factors of Personality and Experience Which Differentiate Single from Married Persons," *Marriage and Family Living,* 26 (February, 1954), pp. 41–44.

KNUDSEN, DEAN D., "The Declining Status of Women: Popular Myths and the Failure of Functionalist Thought," *Social Forces,* 48 (December, 1969), pp. 183–93.

KOHN, MELVIN L., "Social Class and Parental Values," *American Journal of Sociology,* 64 (January, 1959), pp. 337–52.

————, "Social Class and Parent–Child Relationships: An Interpretation," *American Journal of Sociology,* 68 (March, 1963), pp. 471–80.

————, "Social Class, Occupation and Parental Values," *American Sociological Review,* 31 (August, 1966), pp. 466–79.

KOMAROVSKY, MIRRA, *Blue-Collar Marriage* (New York: Random House, Inc., 1964).

LAIRD, R. D., H. PHILLIPSON, and A. R. LEE, *Interpersonal Perception* (New York: Springer Publishing Co., Inc., 1966), Chapter 1.

LANDIS, JUDSON T., "On the Campus," *Survey Midmonthly,* 84 (January, 1948), pp. 17–19.

————, "The Trauma of Children When Parents Divorce," *Marriage and Family Living,* 22 (February, 1960), pp. 7–13.

————, and MARY G. LANDIS, *Building A Successful Marriage,* 4th ed. (Englewood Cliffs, N. J.: Prentice-Hall, Inc., 1963).

LANDIS, JUDSON T., and THOMAS and SHIRLEY POFFENBERGER, "The Effects of First Pregnancy upon the Sexual Adjustment of 212 Couples," *American Sociological Review,* 15 (December, 1950), pp. 766–72.

LANG, R. O., *The Rating of Happiness in Marriage,* M.A. Thesis, University of Chicago, Chicago, 1932.

LANSING, JOHN B., and JAMES M. MORGAN, "Consumer Finances over the Life Cycle," in Lincoln H. Clark (ed.), *Consumer Behavior* (New York: New York University Press, 1955), Vol. II, pp. 36–51.

LARSSON, CLOYTE M., *Marriage Across the Color Line* (Boston: Houghton Mifflin Co., 1965).

LeMASTERS, ERSAL E., "Parenthood as Crisis," *Marriage and Family Living,* 29 (November, 1957), pp. 352–55.

LESLIE, GERALD R., *The Family in Social Context* (New York: Oxford University Press, 1967).

————, HAROLD T. CHRISTENSEN, and GLENN L. PEARMAN, "Studies in Child Spacing: IV. The Time-Interval Separating All Children in Completed Families of Purdue University Graduates," *Social Forces,* 34 (October, 1955), pp. 77–82.

LEVINGER, GEORGE, "Marital Cohesiveness and Dissolution: An Integrative Review," *Journal of Marriage and the Family,* 27 (February, 1965), pp. 19–28.

————, "Sources of Marital Dissatisfaction Among Applicants for Divorce," *American Journal of Orthopsychiatry,* 1966, pp. 803–7; also reproduced in Jeffrey K. Hadden and Marie L. Borgatta (eds.), *Marriage and the Family: A Comprehensive Reader* (Itasca, Ill.: F. E. Peacock Publishers, Inc., 1969), pp. 517–21.

Life's Science Editor, "Challenge to the Miracle of Life," *Life,* 66, No. 23 (June 13, 1969), pp. 39–50; adapted from Albert Rosenfeld, *The Second Genesis; The Coming Control of Life* (Englewood Cliffs, N. J.: Prentice-Hall, Inc., 1969).

LIND, ANDREW W., "Interracial Marriage as Affecting Divorce in Hawaii," *Sociology and Social Research,* 49 (October, 1964), pp. 17–26.

LINDESMITH, ALFRED R., and ANSELM L. STRAUSS, *Social Psychology,* rev. ed. (New York: Holt, Rinehart & Winston, Inc., 1956), Chapter 4, pp. 105–34; Chapter 18, pp. 512–32.

LOCKE, HARVEY J., *Predicting Adjustment in Marriage* (New York: Holt, Rinehart & Winston, Inc., 1951).

LOWRIE, SAMUEL H., "Early and Late Dating: Some Conditions Associated with Them," *Marriage and Family Living,* 23 (August, 1961), pp. 284–91.

LUCKEY, ELEANOR B., "Marital Satisfaction and Congruent Self-Spouse Concepts," *Social Forces,* 39 (December, 1960), pp. 153–57.

LYNN, DAVID B., "A Note on Sex Differences in the Development of Masculine and Feminine Identification," *Psychological Review*, 66 (March, 1959), pp. 126–35.

———, "Sex Differences in Identification Development," *Sociometry*, 24 (December, 1961), pp. 372–81.

———, "Divergent Feedback and Sex Role Identification in Boys and Men," *Merrill Palmer Quarterly*, 10 (January, 1964), pp. 17–24.

———, and W. L. SAWYER, "The Effects of Father–Son Absence on Norwegian Boys and Girls," *Journal of Abnormal and Social Psychology*, 59 (September, 1959), pp. 258–62.

MACCOBY, ELEANOR E., "Women's Intellect," in Seymour M. Farber and R. H. L. Wilson (eds.), *The Potential of Woman* (New York: McGraw-Hill Book Co., Inc., 1963), pp. 24–39.

MACE, DAVID R., "Chastity and Virginity; The Case For," in Albert Ellis and Albert Abarband (eds.), *The Encyclopedia of Sexual Behavior*, Vol. 1 (New York: Hawthorn Books, Inc., 1961), pp. 247–52.

McGINNIS, ROBERT, "Campus Values in Mate Selection: A Repeat Study," *Social Forces*, 36 (May, 1958), pp. 368–73.

McKEE, JOHN P., and ALEX C. SHERIFFS, "Men and Women's Beliefs, Ideals and Self Concepts," in Jerome M. Seidman (ed.), *The Adolescent*, rev. ed. (New York: Holt, Rinehart & Winston, Inc., 1960).

MARTINSON, FLOYD M., "Ego Deficiency as a Factor in Marriage," *American Sociological Review*, 20 (April, 1955), pp. 161–64.

MARVIN, D. M., "Occupational Propinquity as a Factor in Marriage Selection," *American Statistical Association*, 16 (September, 1918), pp. 131–50.

MASTERS, WILLIAM H., and VIRGINIA E. JOHNSON, "Counseling with Sexually Incompatible Marriage Partners," in Ruth and Edward Brecher (eds.), *An Analysis of Human Sexual Response* (New York: Signet Books, 1966a), pp. 210–13.

———, *Human Sexual Response* (Boston: Little, Brown, and Co., 1966b).

———, *Human Sexual Inadequacy* (Boston: Little, Brown, and Co., 1970).

MATTHEWS, VINCENT D., and CLEMENT S. MIHANOVICH. "New Orientations on Marital Adjustment," *Marriage and Family Living*, 25 (August, 1963), pp. 300–4.

MAYER, JOHN E., *Jewish–Gentile Courtship: An Exploratory Study of a Social Process* (New York: The Free Press of Glencoe, Inc., 1961).

MEAD, MARGARET, "Marriage in Two Steps," *Redbook Magazine* (July, 1966), pp. 48–49, 84–85.

METROPOLITAN LIFE INSURANCE COMPANY, "How Often Do Multiple Births Occur?," *Statistical Bulletin* (April, 1954).

———, *Statistical Bulletin* (August, 1967).

———, *Statistical Bulletin* (June, 1968).

———, *Statistical Bulletin* (September, 1969).

MILLER, DANIEL R., and GUY E. SWANSON, *The Changing American Parent* (New York: John Wiley and Sons, Inc., 1959).

MILLER, S. M., "The American Lower Classes: A Typological Approach," in Arthur B. Shostak and William Gomberg (eds.), *Blue-Collar World* (Englewood Cliffs, N. J.: Prentice-Hall, Inc., 1964a), pp. 9–23.

MILLER, S. M., and FRANK RIESSMANN, "The Working Class Subculture: A New View," in Arthur B. Shostak and William Gomberg (eds.), *Blue-Collar World* (Englewood Cliffs, N. J.: Prentice-Hall, Inc., 1964b), pp. 24–35.

MILLER, WALTER B., "Lower Class Culture as a Generating Milieu of Gang Delinquency," *Journal of Social Issues*, 14, No. 3 (1958), pp. 5–19.

———, "Implications of Urban Lower-Class Culture for Social Work," *Social Service Review*, 33 (September, 1959), pp. 219–36.

MOORE, BARRINGTON, "Thoughts on the Future of the Family," in John N. Edwards, (ed.), *The Family and Change* (New York: Alfred A. Knopf, Inc., 1969), pp. 455–67.

MOORE, BERNICE MILBURN, and WAYNE H. HOLTZMAN, *Tomorrow's Parents* (Austin, Texas: University of Texas Press, 1965).

MORGAN, EDMUND S., "Puritan Love and Marriage," in William J. Goode (ed.), *Readings on the Family and Society* (Englewood Cliffs, N. J.: Prentice-Hall, Inc., 1964), pp. 132–35.

MORGAN, ROBIN (ed.), *Sisterhood Is Powerful* (New York: Random House, Inc., Vintage Books, 1970), pp. 512–14.

MURSTEIN, BERNARD I., "Empirical Tests of Role, Complementary Needs and Homogamy Theories of Marital Choice," *Journal of Marriage and the Family*, 29 (November, 1967a), pp. 689–96.

———, "The Relationship of Marital Choice and Courtship Progress," *Journal of Marriage and the Family*, 29 (August, 1967b), pp. 447–51.

———, "Stimulus–Value–Role: A Theory of Marital Choice," *Journal of Marriage and the Family*, 32 (August, 1970), pp. 465–81.

MUSSEN, PAUL, and LUTHER DISTLER, "Masculinity, Identification, and Father–Son Relationships," in Jerold Heiss (ed.), *Family Roles and Interaction: An Anthology* (Chicago: Rand McNally & Co., 1968), pp. 358–73.

NAVRAN, LESLIE, "Communication and Adjustment in Marriage," *Family Process*, 6 (September, 1967), pp. 173–84.

NEUBECK, GERHARD, and VERA M. SCHLETZER, "A Study of Extramarital Relationships," *Marriage and Family Living*, 24 (August, 1962), pp. 279–81.

NEUGARTEN, BERNICE L., and KAROL K. WEINSTEIN, "The Changing American Grandparent," *Journal of Marriage and the Family*, 26 (May, 1964), pp. 199–204.

NIMKOFF, MEYER F., "Biological Discoveries and the Future of the Family: A Reappraisal," *Social Forces*, 41 (December, 1962), pp. 121–27.

NYE, F. IVAN, "Adolescent–Parent Adjustment: Age, Sex, Sibling Number, Broken Homes, and Employed Mothers as Variables, *Marriage and Family Living*, 14 (November, 1952), pp. 327–32.

———, "Child Adjustment in Broken and in Unhappy Unbroken Homes," *Marriage and Family Living*, 19 (November, 1957), pp. 356–61.

———, "Marital Interaction," in F. Ivan Nye and Lois W. Hoffman (eds.), *The Employed Mother in America* (Chicago: Rand McNally & Co., 1963a), pp. 278–80.

———, "The Adjustment of Adolescent Children," in F. Ivan Nye and Lois Hoffman (eds.), *The Employed Mother in America* (Chicago: Rand McNally & Co., 1963b), pp. 133–41.

ORDEN, SUSAN R., and NORMAN M. BRADBURN, "Working Wives and Marriage Happiness," *American Journal of Sociology*, 74 (January, 1969), pp. 392–407.

ORT, ROBERT S., "A Study of Role Conflicts as Related to Happiness in Marriage," *Journal of Abnormal and Social Psychology*, 45 (1950), pp. 691–99.

OSMUNDSON, JOHN A., in the *New York Times* (November 7, 1965).

PARKE, JR., ROBERT, and PAUL C. GLICK, "Prospective Changes in Marriage and the Family," *Journal of Marriage and the Family*, 29 (May, 1967), pp. 249–56.

PARSONS, TALCOTT, "Certain Primary Sources and Patterns of Aggression in the Social Structure of the Western World," in *Essays in Sociological Theory*, rev. ed. (New York: The Free Press of Glencoe, Inc., 1954), pp. 298–322.

PETERSON, EVAN T., "The Impact of Maternal Employment on the Mother–Daughter Relationship," *Marriage and Family Living*, 23 (November, 1961), pp. 355–61.

PHILLIPS, BERNARD S., "A Role Theory Approach to Adjustment in Old Age," *American Sociological Review*, 22 (April, 1957), pp. 212–17.

PILPEL, HARRIET F., and THEODORA SAVIN, *Your Marriage and the Law* (New York: Holt, Rinehart & Winston, Inc., 1952).

PINEO, PETER C., "Disenchantment in the Later Years of Marriage," *Marriage and Family Living*, 23 (February, 1961), pp. 3–11.

PLATERIS, ALEXANDER A., *Divorce Statistics Analysis* (*United States, 1963*), Vital and Health Statistics, Series 21, No. 13 (Washington, D. C.: GPO: U. S. Department of Health, Education, and Welfare, October, 1967), pp. 1–40; also reprinted in Jeffrey K. Hadden and Marie L. Borgatta (eds.), *Marriage and the Family: A*

Comprehensive Reader (Itasca, Ill.: F. E. Peacock Publishers, Inc., 1969), pp. 506–17.

POFFENBERGER, SHIRLEY, THOMAS POFFENBERGER, and JUDSON T. LANDIS, "Intent Toward Conception and the Pregnancy Experience," *American Sociological Review,* 17 (October, 1952), pp. 616–20.

POFFENBERGER, THOMAS, "Individual Choice in Adolescent Premarital Sex Behavior," *Marriage and Family Living,* 22 (November, 1960), pp. 324–30.

———, "Going Steady in High School," in Ruth S. Cavan, (ed.), *Marriage and the Family in the Modern World: A Book of Readings* (New York: Thomas Y. Crowell and Co., 1965), pp. 112–24.

POPENOE, PAUL, and R. H. JOHNSON, *Applied Eugenics,* rev. ed. (New York: The MacMillan Co., 1953).

POPPY, JOHN, "It's OK to Cry in the Office,"*Look* (July, 1968), pp. 64–76.

POPULATION REFERENCE BUREAU, "Marriage and the American Woman," *Population Profile* (June 3, 1963).

———, "Boom Babies Come of Age: The American Family at the Crossroads," in *Population Bulletin,* No. 3 (August, 1966).

PRICE, DOROTHY Z., "A Technique for Analyzing the Economic Value System," *Journal of Marriage and the Family,* 30 (August, 1968), pp. 467–72.

RABKIN, RICHARD, "Uncoordinated Communication between Marriage Partners," *Family Process,* 6 (March, 1967), pp. 10–15.

RAINWATER, LEE, *And the Poor Get Children* (Chicago: Quadrangle Books, 1960).

———, "Crucible of Identity: The Negro Lower Class Family," in Gerald Handel (ed.), *The Psychosocial Interior of the Family* (Chicago: Aldine Publishing Co., 1967, pp. 362–400. Also in *Daedalus* (Winter, 1966), pp. 172–216.

———, *Family Design: Marital Sexuality, Family Size, and Contraception* (Chicago: Aldine Publishing Co., 1965).

RAINWATER, LEE, and GERALD HANDEL, "Changing Family Roles in the Working Class," in Arthur B. Shostak and William Gomberg (eds.), *Blue-Collar World* (Englewood Cliffs, N. J.: Prentice-Hall, Inc., 1964), pp. 70–74.

RAINWATER, LEE, R. P. COLEMAN, and GERALD HANDEL, *The Workingman's Wife— Her Personality, World and Life Style* (New York: Oceana Publications, Inc., 1959).

RAINWATER, LEE, and WILLIAM L. YANCY, *The Moynihan Report and the Politics of Controversy* (Cambridge: The M.I.T. Press, 1967).

RAPOPORT, RHONA, and ROBERT N. RAPOPORT, "New Light on the Honeymoon," *Human Relations,* 17, No. 1 (1964), pp. 33–56.

———, "Work and Family in Contemporary Society," *American Sociological Review,* 30 (June, 1965), pp. 381–94.

READ, GRANTLEY DICK, *Childbirth Without Fear* (New York: Harper and Row, 1944).

REISS, IRA L., "Toward a Sociology of the Heterosexual Love Relationship," *Marriage and Family Living,* 22 (May, 1960), pp. 139–45.

———, "The Universality of the Family: A Conceptual Analysis," *Journal of Marriage and the Family,* 27 (November, 1965), pp. 443–53.

———, *The Social Context of Sexual Permissiveness* (New York: Holt, Rinehart & Winston, Inc., 1967).

RODKIN, I. D., "Sexual Characteristics of a Cervical Cancer Population," *American Journal of Public Health,* 57 (May, 1967), pp. 815–29.

RODMAN, HYMAN, "Middle-Class Misconceptions About Lower-Class Families," in Arthur B. Shostak and William Gomberg (eds.), *Blue-Collar World* (Englewood Cliffs, N. J.: Prentice-Hall, Inc., 1964), pp. 59–69.

ROGERS, EVERETT M., and A. EUGENE HAVENS, "Prestige Rating and Mate Selection on a College Campus," *Marriage and Family Living,* 22 (February, 1960), pp. 55–59.

ROLLINS, BOYD C., and HAROLD FELDMAN, "Marital Satisfaction over the Life Cycle," *Journal of Marriage and the Family,* 32 (February, 1970), pp. 20–28.

RORVIK, DAVID M., and LANDRUM B. SHETTLES, M.D., "You Can Choose Your Baby's

Sex," *Look* (April 21, 1970), pp. 88–98. Excerpted from *Your Baby's Sex: Now You Can Choose* (Dodd, Mead & Co., Inc., 1970).

ROSE, ARNOLD M., "Factors Associated with the Life Sastisfactions of Middle-Class, Middle-Aged Persons," *Marriage and Family Living*, 17 (February, 1955), pp. 15–19.

ROSENBERG, MORRIS, "The Broken Family and the Adolescent Self-Image," in Morris Rosenberg, *Society and the Adolescent Self-Image*, (Princeton, N. J.: Princeton University Press, 1965), pp. 85–106, Chapter 5.

ROSENGREEN, WILLIAM R., "Social Sources of Pregnancy as Illness or Normality," *Social Forces*, 39 (March, 1961), pp. 260–67.

ROSSI, ALICE S., "Status of Women in Graduate Departments of Sociology, 1968–1969," *The American Sociologist*, 5 (February, 1970), pp. 1–12.

ROTH, JULIUS, and ROBERT F. PECK, "Social Class and Social Mobility Factors Related to Marital Adjustment," *American Sociological Review*, 16 (August, 1951), pp. 478–87.

RUBIN, ISADORE, "Transition in Sex Values—Implication for the Education of Adolescents," *Journal of Marriage and the Family*, 27 (May, 1965), pp. 185–89.

———, "Sex After Forty—and After Seventy," in Ruth and Edward Brecher (eds.), *Analysis of Human Sexual Response* (New York: Signet Books, 1966), pp. 251–66.

RUDY, ARTHUR J., "Sex-Role Perception in Early Adolescence," *Adolescence*, 3 (Winter, 1968/69), pp. 453–70.

RYDER, NORMAN B., and CHARLES F. WESTOFF, "Use of Oral Contraception in the United States, 1965," *Science* (September 9, 1966), pp. 1199–1205.

SCANZONI, JOHN, "Family Organization and the Probability of Disorganization," *Journal of Marriage and the Family*, 28 (November, 1966), pp. 407–11.

———, "A Social System Analysis of Dissolved and Existing Marriages," *Journal of Marriage and the Family*, 30 (August, 1968), pp. 452–61.

SCHECK, SONIA, "An Investigation of the Heterosexual Affectional Response," unpublished Master's Thesis, Purdue University, August, 1967.

SCHLEIN, JOHN M., "Mother-in-Law: A Problem in Kinship Terminology," *ETC*, 19 (July, 1962), pp. 161–71.

SCHOFIELD, MICHAEL, *The Sexual Behavior of Young People* (London: Longmans, Green, 1965).

SCHORR, ALVIN L., "Family Policy in the U.S.," *UNESCO International Social Science Journal*, 14, No. 3 (1962), pp. 452–68.

SCOTT, JOHN F., "The American College Sorority: Its Role in Class and Ethnic Endogamy," *American Sociological Review*, 30 (August, 1965), pp. 514–27.

SEARS, ROBERT R., ELEANOR E. MACCOBY, and HARRY LEVIN, *Patterns of Childrearing* (New York: Harper and Row, 1957).

SEELEY, JOHN R., R. ALEXANDER SIM, and ELIZABETH W. LOOSLEY, *Crestwood Heights* (New York: John Wiley and Sons, Inc., Science Edition, 1963).

SEWELL, WILLIAM H., "Infant Training and the Personality of the Child," *American Journal of Sociology*, 58 (September, 1952), pp. 150–59.

SHOPE, DAVID F., and CARLFRED B. BRODERICK, "Level of Sexual Experience and Predicted Adjustment in Marriage," *Journal of Marriage and the Family*, 29 (August, 1967), pp. 424–27.

SIEGEL, ALBERTA E., LOIS M. STOLZ, ETHEL A. HITCHCOCK, and JEAN ADAMSON, "Dependence and Independence in Children," in F. Ivan Nye and Lois Hoffman, *The Employed Mother in America* (Chicago: Rand McNally and Co., 1963), pp. 67–81.

SKIPPER, JAMES K. JR., and GILBERT NASS, "Dating Behavior, a Framework for Analysis and Illustration," *Journal of Marriage and the Family*, 28 (1966), pp. 412–20.

SLATER, PHILIP, "Social Limitations on Libidinal Withdrawal," *American Journal of Sociology*, 67 (November, 1961), pp. 296–311.

SMITH, S., "Age and Sex Differences in Children's Opinions Concerning Sex Differences," *Journal of Genetic Psychology*, 54 (January, 1939), pp. 17–25.

STANNARD, UNA, "Adam's Rib, or the Woman Within," *Trans-action*, 8 (November–December, 1970), pp. 28–35.

STENDLER, CELIA B., "Sixty Years of Child Training Practices," *Journal of Pediatrics*, 36 (January, 1950), pp. 122–34.

STEWART, GEORGE, *Storm* (New York: Random House, Inc., 1941).

STRAUSS, ANSELM, "The Ideal and the Chosen Mate," *American Journal of Sociology*, 52 (November, 1946), pp. 204–8.

———, "Personality Needs and Marital Choice," *Social Forces*, 24 (March, 1947), pp. 332–35.

———, "Strain and Harmony in American–Japanese war Bride Marriages," *Marriage and Family Living*, 16 (May, 1954), pp. 99–106.

STREIB, GORDON F., "Family Patterns in Retirement," *Journal of Social Issues*, 14 No. 2 (1958), pp. 46–60.

———, "Intergenerational Relations: Perspectives of the Two Generations on the Older Parent," *Journal of Marriage and the Family*, 27 (November, 1965), pp. 469–76.

STUCKERT, ROBERT P., "Role Perception and Marital Saitsfaction—A Configurational Approach," *Marriage and Family Living*, 25 (November, 1963), pp. 415–19.

SUELZLE, MARIJEAN, "Women in Labor," *Trans-action*, 8 (November–December, 1970), pp. 50–59.

SULLIVAN, HARRY STACK, H. PERRY and M. GAMEL (eds.), *The Impersonal Theory of Psychiatry* (New York: W. W. Norton, 1953).

SUSSMAN, MARVIN B., "Activity Patterns of Post Parental Couples and Their Relationship to Family Continuity," *Marriage and Family Living*, 17 (November, 1955), pp. 338–41.

———, "The Isolated Nuclear Family: Fact or Fiction," in Robert F. Winch, Robert McGinnis, and Herbert Barringer (eds.), *Selected Studies in Marriage and the Family* (New York: Holt, Rinehart and Winston, Inc., 1962), pp. 49–57.

———, Family Continuity: *A Study of Factors Which Affect Relationships Between Families at Generational Levels*, Ph.D. Dissertation, Yale University, 1951.

SWITZER, ALAN L., *Some Factors Related to In-Law Difficulty and Conflict*, unpublished M.S. thesis, Purdue University, 1966.

TERMAN, LEWIS M., *Psychological Factors in Marital Happiness* (New York: McGraw-Hill Book Co., Inc., 1938).

THOMLINSON, RALPH, *Population Dynamics: Causes and Consequences of World Demographic Change* (New York: Random House, Inc., 1965).

TIBBITTS, CLARK, *The Older Person in the Family: Challenges and Conflicts* (Iowa City, Iowa: The Institute of Gerontology, 1965).

TILLER, P. O., "Father-Absence and Personality Development of Children in Sailor Families: A Preliminary Research Report," in N. Anderson (ed.), *Studies of the Family*, Vol. 2 (Gottingen: Vandenhoeck and Ruprecht, 1957), pp. 115–33.

———, "The Changing Roles of Men and Women," in Edmund Dahlstrom (ed.), (London: Gerald Duckworth & Co., Ltd., 1967).

Time, "Man into Superman" (April 19, 1971), pp. 33–52.

Trans-action, Special combined issue, 8 (November–December, 1970).

TROST, JAN, "Some Data on Mate Selection: Homogamy and Perceived Homogamy," *Journal of Marriage and the Family*, 29 (November, 1967), pp. 739–55.

TUCKMAN, JACOB, and IRVING LORGE, "Old People's Appraisal of Adjustment Over the Life Span," *Journal of Personality*, 22 (March, 1954), pp. 417–22.

UDRY, J. RICHARD, "The Influence of Ideal Mate Images on Mate Selection," *Journal of Marriage and the Family*, 27 (November, 1965), pp. 477–82.

———, *The Social Context of Marriage* (Philadelphia: J. B. Lippincott Co., 1966).

VAN DEN HAAG, ERNEST, "Love or Marriage," *Harper's Magazine*, 224 (May, 1962), pp. 43–47.

VERNON, GLENN M., and JACK A. BROADWAY, "Attitudes toward Artificial Insemination and Some Variables Associated Therewith," *Marriage and Family Living*, 21 (February, 1959), pp. 43–47.

VINCENT, CLARK E., "Social and Interpersonal Sources of Symptomatic Frigidity," *Marriage and Family Living*, 18 (November, 1956), pp. 355–60.

——, *Unmarried Mothers* (New York: Free Press of Glencoe, Inc., 1961).

——, "Familia Spongia: The Adaptive Function," *Journal of Marriage and the Family*, 28 (February, 1966a), pp. 29–36.

——, "Teen-age Unwed Mothers in American Society," *The Journal of Social Issues*, 22 (April, 1966b), pp. 22–33.

VON HENTIG, HANS, "The Sociological Function of the Grandmother," *Social Forces*, 24 (May, 1946), pp. 389–92.

WALLER, WILLARD, *The Old Love and the New* (New York: Liveright Publishing Corp., 1930).

——, "The Rating and Dating Complex," *American Sociological Review*, 2 (October, 1937), pp. 729–34.

——, *The Family—A Dynamic Interpretation* (New York: Dryden Press, 1938).

——, and REUBEN HILL, *The Family: A Dynamic Interpretation*, rev. ed. (New York: The Dryden Press, Inc., 1951).

WALLIN, PAUL, "Sex Differences in Attitudes to In-Laws: A Test of a Theory," *American Journal of Sociology*, 59 (March, 1954), pp. 466–69.

——, "Religiosity, Sexual Gratification, and Marital Satisfaction," *American Sociological Review*, 22 (June, 1957), pp. 300–5.

——, and ALEXANDER L. CLARK, "Religiosity, Sexual Gratification, and Marital Satisfaction in the Middle Years of Marriage," *Social Forces*, 42 (March, 1964), pp. 303–9.

WEST, JAMES, *Plainsville, U.S.A.* (New York: Columbia University Press, 1945).

WESTOFF, CHARLES, ROBERT POTTER, PHILLIP SAGI, and ELLIOT MISHLER, *Family Growth in Metropolitan America* (Princeton, N. J.: Princeton University Press, 1961).

WHELPTON, PASKAL K., ARTHUR A. CAMPBELL, and JOHN E. PATTERSON, *Fertility and Family Planning in the United States* (Princeton, N. J.: Princeton University Press, 1966).

WILENSKY, HAROLD L., "Work, Careers, and Social Integration," *International Social Science Journal*, 12 (Fall, 1960), pp. 543–60.

WILLIAMS, M. J., "Personal and Family Problems of High School Youth and Their Bearing upon Family Education Needs," *Social Forces*, 27 (March, 1949), pp. 779–85.

WINCH, ROBERT F., "The Theory of Complementary Needs in Mate Selection: Final Results on the Test of the General Hypotheses," *American Sociological Review*, 20 (October, 1955), pp. 552–55.

——, *Identification and its Familial Determinants* (Indianapolis, Ind.: Bobbs-Merrill, 1962).

——, *The Modern Family* (New York: Holt, Rinehart & Winston, Inc., 1963).

WINSTON, SANFORD, "Birth Control and Sex-Ratio at Birth," *American Journal of Sociology*, 38 (September, 1932), pp. 225–31.

WOLFENSTEIN, MARTHA, "The Emergence of Fun Morality," *The Journal of Social Issues*, No. 4 (1951), pp. 15–25.

WORTHY, M., A. L. GARY, and G. M. KAHN, "Self-disclosure as an Exchange Process," *Journal of Personality and Social Psychology*, 13 (September, 1969), pp. 59–63.

ZIMMERMAN, CARLE C., and LUCIUS F. CERVANTES, *Successful American Families* (New York: Pageant, 1960).

Name Index

Albrecht, Ruth, 453, 458

Banks, Franklin, 216
Barber, Kenneth E., 205, 254, 377
Barnett, Larry D., 382
Bates, Alan, 212
Beall, Patricia, 437
Behrman, Samuel J., 396, 403
Bell, Robert R., 174, 192
Berardo, Felix M., 469–70
Bernard, Jessie, 63–64, 215–16, 468
Biegel, H., 33–34
Billingsley, Andrew W., 64
Blood, Jr., Robert O., 51, 57, 62–63, 279–80, 288–89, 294, 300–1, 306, 310–11, 340, 342, 345–46, 362, 364–65, 374, 377, 380, 391, 450
Bogue, Donald J., 520
Bolton, Charles D., 230
Bossard, James H. S., 424
Bowman, Henry A., 130
Bradburn, Norman M., 343
Brecher, Edward, 324, 412–14
Brecher, Ruth, 324, 412–14
Broadway, Jack A., 403
Broderick, Carlfred B., 153, 250
Bronfenbrenner, Urie, 438, 440–41, 444
Buerkle, Jack V., 192
Burchinal, Lee G., 172, 376, 378–79
Burgess, Ernest W., 242–43, 247–48, 331–32, 390

Cameron, William J., 152
Campbell, Arthur A., 391, 396
Caplow, Theodore, 424
Carpenter, George R., 186, 188, 190, 192
Carter, Hugh, 485
Cavan, Ruth Schonle, 453
Cervantes, Lucius F., 380
Chancellor, Loren E., 376, 378–79
Chaskes, Jay B., 174
Cheng, C. K., 383
Chilman, Catherine S., 339, 396–97

Christensen, Harold T., 71, 141, 157, 163, 186, 188–90, 192, 201, 205–6, 254, 377, 389, 391, 494
Clark, Alexander L., 320
Clausen, John A., 425
Coombs, Robert H., 220–21
Cottrell, Jr., Leonard S., 390
Crist, John R., 157
Cuber, John F., 83–85, 88, 488, 501

Dager, Edward Z., 123, 428–29
Davis, Katherine B., 248
Davis, Keith E., 188, 217, 248
Deutscher, Irwin, 450–51
Dinitz, Simon, 216
Distler, Luther, 437
Douvan, Elizabeth, 440
Duvall, Evelyn M., 357, 359, 362
Dyer, Everett D., 422
Dyer, William G., 270

Edwards, Harry, 65
Edwards, John N., 499–502
Ehrlich, Paul R., 390
Ehrmann, Winston, 33, 152, 165, 194–95
Ellis, Julie, 136–37
Emmerich, Walter, 123
Erikson, Erik H., 96, 430, 433, 436

Feldman, Harold, 295–96, 298, 311, 422, 451–52
Folsom, Joseph K., 303, 475
Fowler, Stanley E., 153
Franklin, R. D., 163
Freedman, Ronald, 389, 401–2

Gebhard, Paul H., 202, 204
Gerth, Hans, 110
Gianopulos, Artie, 342
Glasser, Lois N., 458
Glasser, Paul H., 458
Glick, Paul C., 448, 474, 484–85, 497
Goldberg, Philip, 126

Goode, William J., 234, 464–66, 473, 483–84
Goodman, Marvin, 222
Gordon, Albert I., 380
Gorer, Geoffrey, 152, 165
Gosling, John R. G., 396, 403
Green, Morris, 437
Gregg, Christina F., 188, 190
Groves, Ernest R., 214
Guyon, Renè, 248

Hamilton, Gilbert V., 248
Handel, Gerald, 48, 51–52, 305
Harris, Daniel, 213
Harroff, Peggy, 83–85, 88, 488, 501
Hartley, Ruth E., 124, 143, 440
Hastings, Donald W., 326
Havens, A. Eugene, 217
Hawkins, James L., 299
Heer, David M., 215, 382
Heiss, Jerold S., 173, 376
Henry, Jules, 170
Henze, Laura F., 163
Herman, R. D., 173
Hermann, Robert O., 352
Hill, Reuben, 108, 163, 450, 457
Hobart, Charles W., 268, 498–500
Hobbs, Daniel F., Jr., 422
Hoffman, Lois W., 115, 439–40
Hoffman, Martin L., 115
Holtzman, Wayne H., 12
Horner, Matina S., 128–29
Howard, David H., 191, 249
Hudson, John W., 163
Hurvitz, Nathan, 75–76
Huxley, Aldous, 506

Johannis, Theodore B., Jr., 268
Johnsen, Kathryn P., 126, 299, 427
Johnson, R. H., 252
Johnson, Virginia E., 319, 321–24, 326–27, 330, 395, 413

Kaats, Gilbert R., 188
Kahl, Joseph A., 54, 58–60
Kanin, Eugene J., 191, 198, 249
Kenkel, William F., 152, 221
Kephart, William M., 254, 269, 333, 466, 468
Kerckhoff, Alan C., 217
Kinsey, Alfred C., 183–86, 192, 194, 197, 202, 204, 207, 247–50, 321, 333–35
Kirkendall, Lester A., 165, 201, 248–50
Kirkpatrick, Clifford, 29, 31–32, 198, 272, 423
Klemer, Richard H., 474
Knudsen, Dean D., 142–43

Kohn, Melvin L., 109, 427
Komarovsky, Mirra, 48–53, 55, 75, 79, 293, 374

Laird, R. D., 106
Landis, Judson T., 268, 412, 472
Lang, R. O., 390
Lansing, John B., 341
Larsson, Cloyte M., 382
Lee, A. R., 106
LeMasters, Ersal E., 422–23
Leslie, Gerald R., 227, 303, 305, 321, 360
Levinger, George, 462–63, 467
Lewit, Sarah, 485
Lind, Andrew W., 383
Locke, Harvey J., 248
Loosley, Elizabeth W., 59
Lowrie, Samuel H., 173
Luckey, Eleanor B., 299
Lynn, David B., 124–26, 437

Maccoby, Eleanor E., 128
Mace, David R., 248
McGinnis, Robert, 163
McKee, John P., 122
Martinson, Floyd M., 474
Marvin, D. M., 213
Masters, William H., 319, 321–24, 326–27, 330, 395, 413
Matthews, Vincent D., 288–89
Mayer, John E., 380
Mead, Margaret, 502
Mihanovich, Clement S., 288–89
Miller, Daniel R., 426
Miller, S. M., 49
Miller, Walter B., 437–38
Mills, C. Wright, 110
Mitchell, Howard E., 342
Moore, Barrington, 502
Moore, Bernice Milburn, 12
Morgan, Edmund S., 37
Morgan, James M., 341
Morgan, Robin, 136
Murstein, Bernard I., 218, 228–29
Mussen, Paul, 437

Navran, Leslie, 297
Neubeck, Gerhard, 335
Neugarten, Bernice L., 453–55
Nye, F. Ivan, 342, 440, 470–71

Ogburn, William F., 214
Orden, Susan R., 343
Ort, Robert S., 299
Osmundson, John A., 215

Parke, Jr., Robert, 497

Parsons, Talcott, 123
Pasamanick, Benjamin, 216
Patterson, John E., 440
Peck, Robert F., 373
Peterson, Evan T., 440
Philbrick, Robert E., 391
Phillips, Bernard S., 457
Phillipson, H., 106
Pineo, Peter C., 51, 450
Plateris, Alexander A., 468
Poffenberger, Shirley, 412
Poffenberger, Thomas, 165, 248, 412
Popenoe, Paul, 252
Poppy, John, 235
Price, Dorothy Z., 350

Rabkin, Richard, 290
Rainwater, Lee, 48, 51–52, 56–58, 62,
    86–87, 307–10, 318–20, 339, 391,
    397–401
Rapoport, Rhona, 76, 262–63
Rapoport, Robert N., 76, 262–63
Read, Grantley Dick, 411
Reiss, Ira L., 182–83, 189–94, 196–98,
    227–29, 230, 244
Remmers, H. H., 163
Riessmann, Frank, 49
Rodkin, I. D., 200
Rogers, Everett M., 217
Rollins, Boyd C., 295–96, 298, 311, 451–
    52
Rorvik, David M., 406–7
Rose, Arnold M., 449
Rosenberg, Morris, 471–72
Rosengreen, William R., 412
Rossi, Alice S., 132
Roth, Julius, 373
Rubin, Isadore, 207, 324–26
Rudy, Arthur J., 126
Ryder, Norman B., 126

Sanger, Winogene, 424
Sawyer, W. L., 437
Scanzoni, John, 341–42, 344, 346
Scheck, Sonia R., 191
Schlein, John M., 357
Schletzer, Vera M., 335
Schofield, Michael, 165
Schorr, Alvin L., 12
Sears, Robert R., 426
Seeley, John R., 42, 59–61
Sewell, William H., 424
Sheriffs, Alex C., 122

Shettles, Landrum B., 406–7
Shope, David F., 250
Siegel, Alberta E., 440
Sim, R. Alexander, 59
Smith, S., 126
Stendler, Celia B., 426
Strauss, Anselm L., 213, 383
Streib, Gordon F., 458
Strohm, Rolf B., 254
Stuckert, Robert P., 299
Suelzle, Marijean, 143
Sullivan, Harry Stack, 180
Sussman, Marvin B., 362, 449
Swanson, Guy E., 426
Switzer, Alan L., 360–62

Terman, Lewis M., 184, 248
Thomlinson, Ralph, 495
Tibbitts, Clark, 457, 459
Tiller, P. O., 437–38
Trost, Jan, 218

Udry, J. Richard, 142, 151, 153, 165,
    213, 240, 374, 403

van den Haag, Ernest, 34
Vernon, Glenn M., 403
Vincent, Clark E., 4, 28, 202–4, 318, 323
Von Hentig, Hans, 453

Waller, Willard, 108, 152, 165, 227,
    481–84
Wallin, Paul, 242–43, 247–49, 320, 331–
    32, 360
Weinstein, Karol K., 453–55
West, James, 152
Westoff, Charles F., 396
Whelpton, Paskal K., 389
Wilensky, Harold L., 58
Williams, M. J., 157
Winch, Robert F., 219–20, 437
Winston, Sanford, 392
Wolfe, Donald M., 51, 57, 62–63, 279–
    80, 288–89, 294, 300–1, 306, 310–11,
    340, 342, 345–46, 365, 374, 391,
    450
Wolfenstein, Martha, 426
Worthy, M., 228–29

Yancy, William L., 339
Yamamura, Douglas S., 383

Zimmerman, Carle C., 380

Subject Index

Abortion, 32, 201–2, 393
Adolescence, 101–2, 125–27, 151, 432–35
Adoption, 404–5
Aging, and in-law relationships, 366; see also Middle years; Old age
Anger, 111–15
Annulment, 253; see also Divorce
Anxiety, 97–103, 113–14, 121, 124–27
Arranged marriage, 33, 211–12
Artificial insemination, 403
Authority structure
    differentiated from power structure, 268–69
    and marital roles, 273–78, 344
    relation to family functions, 24
    student attitudes toward, 138, 140–42
Autosexuality, 178, 179, 334

Bachelor; see Permanently unmarried
Bereavement, 481–82
Birth, 405–14; see also Pregnancy
    determining date of, 410–11
    labor, 411
    process of, 405–11
Birth control, 394–405; see also Contraception; Family planning
Birth rates, 42
    downward trend, 519–21
Black subculture; see Negro family culture

Childrearing; see Children; Parenthood
Children; see also Adoption; Artificial insemination; Family planning; Parenthood
    boys preferred, 392
    developmental stages, 430, 436
    discipline of, 39–40, 115
    effect on
        of broken homes, 470–73
        of father absence, 437–38
        of mother employment, 438–41
        of parents, 428–29

number of, 423–24
reaching adulthood, 436
rearing of, 426–28
spacing of, 421, 424
Civil Rights Act of 1964, 135–36
College marriages, 475
Common-law marriage, 62, 251, 253
Communication, 286–301; see also Marriage; Sex in marriage; Value conflict
    defined, 106–7
    in in-law relationships, 362–63
    in love development, 230–31
    in marital sex, 320, 328–29, 331
    in marriage, 50–51, 103, 286–301
    problems in, 290–95
    relation to habits, 109–12, 118–19
    relation to marital happiness, 295–99
Conception, 393–94
Conflict; see also Marriage
    areas of, 306–10
    covert, 305–6
    overt, 303–5
    resolution of, 310–13
Contraception, 200–1, 395–401; see also Birth control; Family planning
    effect of spouses' attitudes, 400–1
    effectiveness of, 396–401
    methods of, 395–96
    and religion, 397–400
    and social class, 397–400
Counseling, 468–69
Courtship, 153; see also Dating; Mate selection
Crisis; see also Family; Social change
    family affected by, 41–42
    parenthood as, 421–25

Dating, 149–76; see also Engagement; Going steady; Love; Mate selection; Premarital sex
    changes in, 150–53
    conduct during, 163–68
    cross-sex criticisms in, 154–60

Dating (*Continued*)
 defined, 149–50, 165–68
 effects on sex behavior, 193–96
 power-dependence relationship in, 168–72
 preferences in date selection, 160–63
Death, 458–59, 469–70; *see also* Widowhood
Democratic revolution, 495–96
Desertion, 62–64, 465–66, 467
Discipline; *see* Children
Divergent feedback, 124
Division of labor; *see* Sex roles
Divorce, 33, 35, 466–69; *see also* Annulment; Desertion; Marital disruption; Separation
 actual reasons for, 467–68
 adjustment problems, 482–84, 488
 avoidance of, 468–69
 grounds for, 466–67
 and interfaith marriage, 378–80
 and interracial marriage, 382–83
 rates, 42, 516–19
 relation to premarital pregnancy, 205–6
 and social class, 47, 63–65, 467
Double standard; *see* Sex

Economic factors in marriage; *see* Family; Institutions; Marriage; Money and marriage
Educational factors in marriage; *see* Family; Institutions; Marriage
Elopement, 240, 254
Engagement, 238–57
 adjustments during, 240–43
 broken, 238, 243–44
 commitments preliminary to, 238–39
 function of the public announcement, 238–39
 and marital success, 239–40
 sexual behavior during, 244–50
Environmental crisis, 390, 521; *see also* Population revolution
Environmental influences; *see* Social context
Equal Rights Amendment, 135
Expectations; *see* Role expectations
Exploitation; *see* Power-dependency relationship, in dating; Principle of least interest
Extended family, 20–23, 40, 46–47, 234; *see also* Family
Extra-marital sex; *see* Infidelity

Family; *see also* Future of the family; Institutions; Marriage; Social class; Values

adaptive quality of, 28–29
 affected by social trends, 494–97
 authority structure in, 24
 biological needs of, 23–24
 conservative nature of, 28–29
 crises and the, 41–42
 defined, 20
 diversity in, 20
 in early America, 34–37, 150
 influences on
  economic, 10, 48–49, 54–55, 58–59, 63–65, 73–82
  educational, 11–12, 58–59, 63–65, 73–82
  political, 12
  religious, 10–11
 emotional maintenance by, 27
 functions of, 21–30, 37–42
 patriarchal pattern, 31–32, 37, 46–47
 social control by, 27–28
 trends in, 30–42, 511–21
 types of, 20–23
Family change, 20–44; *see also* Family; Future of the family; Social change
Family courts, 468–69
Family culture, 12–13, 94–95, 110–11
Family life cycle, 446
 in-law adjustments during, 365–66
 marital conflict during, 306–7
 marital satisfaction during, 295–97, 449–52
 role changes in, 279–82
Family life education, functional approach, 3, 8; *see also* Sex education
Family planning, 393–405; *see also* Contraception
Family size, 389–93, 519–21; *see also* Birth rates; Children; Contraception; Family planning
 changing norms, 389–93
 downward trend, 519–20
 and marital adjustment, 390–93, 423–25
Family stability, 82, 462–65, 516–19; *see also* Marital disruption; Value conflict
 racial differences in, 63–64
Fantasies, 266–67
Feminist movement, 151
Femininity, 121–46; *see also* Sex roles
Frigidity, 197, 321, 327–29, 332–34
Future of the family, 235, 493–509
 anticipated structural changes, 498–502
 demographic projections, 497–98, 521
 influence of the space age, 504–6
 question of being outmoded, 502
 proposed "marriage in two stages," 502

prospects through the biological revolution, 503–4

Genetics; *see* Heredity
Going steady, 165–68, 172–74; *see also* Dating; Engagement
Grandparenthood, 451–55; *see also* Middle years; Old age; Postparenthood
contrasting styles, 454–55

Habits, 106–20, 271; *see also* Interaction; Sex roles
defined, 108–9
development of, 111–17
systems of, 108–17, 121
Heredity, 92, 405–9; *see also* Twinning
genetic principles, 405–6
Rh factor, 408–9
sex determination, 406–8
Heterosexuality, 178–79, 180–81
Homosexuality, 178, 180
Honeymoon, 249, 261–63
Husband–wife roles, 261–85; *see also* Conflict; Marriage; Sex roles
changes over the family cycle, 279–82
cultural definitions of, 272–78
differences in expectation, 265–70
in early marriage, 264–72, 279
and effective family planning, 400–1
levels of expectation, 270–72
problems in segregated relationships, 307–10, 320
and social class, 49–50, 55–57, 59–61
types of, 273–78

Ideal-mate image, 212
Identification, 123–27; *see also* Role models; Sex roles
Identity; *see* Self-concept
Illegitimacy, 42, 62, 202–4
Impotence, 197, 325–26, 332–34
Individual; *see* Personality
Infanticide, 393
Infidelity, 334–35
In-law relationships, 70, 356–69
changes over the life cycle, 365–66
a feminine problem, 357–61
problem of communication, 362–63
problem of feeling included, 363–64
role readjustments in, 356–61
time allocations in, 364–65
value conflict in, 361–65
Institutions; *see also* Family; Marriage
definition of, 10
family dependency on, 37–38, 42
universality of, 20–21

Interaction; *see also* Family; Marriage
family, 421–89
habits of, 14, 106–20, 149
marital, 261–417
premarital, 149–257
Interclass marriage, 216–17, 373–75, 383–84
Interfaith marriage, 216–17, 375–81, 383–84
Intergenerational continuity, 265–66; *see also* Socialization
Intergenerational interaction, 457–59; *see also* Adolescence; Parenthood
Interracial marriage, 215, 381–84

Judeo-Christian tradition, 31–33, 34

Kinship groupings, 21–22, 46–47

Labor; *see* Birth
Legal requirements; *see* Divorce; Marriage
Leisure time activities, 51
Level of living defined, 339
Life styles; *see* Family; Marriage; Sex
Love, 223–36; *see also* Dating; Mate selection
ambivalence in, 233
developmental processes, 227–34
as distinguished from friendship, 230–31
elements and types, 225–27
external influences on, 231–32
fallacies concerning, 224–25
importance to nuclear family, 234–35
meaning of, 223–27
recognition and measurement, 233–34
romantic emphasis, 33–34, 224–25
wheel theory of, 227–32, 421

Male-female comparisons; *see* Infidelity; Marital Sex; Premarital sex; Sex; Sex Roles
Male preference; *see* Children; Sex roles
Marital composition and trends in, 511–21
Marital disruption, 253, 462–70; *see also* Death; Desertion; Divorce; Separation
effects on children, 470–73
increasing rates of, 516–19
lack of internal and external supports, 462–65
Marital happiness, as related to communication, 288–90; 295–301; *see also* Communication; Marriage

Marriage; *see also* Family; Husband–wife roles; Sexual adjustments; Social class
communication problems in, 290–301
conflict in, 70, 73–85, 301–10
conflict resolution in, 310–13
criteria for success in, 3–8
defined, 20
definition of success, 7
disillusionment in, 268
factors in adjustment, 50–51, 86
influence of mobility on, 103
interaction in, 14–15
legal aspects of, 6, 250–53
pattern variations, 82–85
power structure in, 268–69, 273–78, 311–13, 345–48, 365
problems in, 86–87
rates, 42, 214, 511–13, 517
reality factors in, 286–87
satisfaction in, 53
trends in age at marriage, 513–15
trends in per cent married, 511–14
Marriage analysis, 8–19
Marriage education; *see* Family life education
Masculinity, 121–46; *see also* Sex roles
Masturbation; *see* Autosexuality
Mate selection, 37, 211–37; *see also* Arranged marriage
complementary needs theory, 219–22
endogamy in, 214–17
homogamy in, 218
legal restrictions, 212
parental influence over, 212–13
personality matching in, 117–19, 222–23
place of dating in, 149–50
propinquity in, 213–14
reciprocity in, 219
value consensus in, 220–22
Mating gradient, 217, 475
Menopause, 451
Middle years, 446–61; *see also* Aging; Family life cycle; Postparenthood
"empty nest" stage, 448
marital adjustment in, 448–51
Mixed marriages, 370–88; *see also* Interclass marriage; Interfaith marriage; Interracial marriage; Mate selection
achieving pair identity in, 385–86
cultural gap handicap, 371–72
non-normative combinations, 384–86
selectivity advantage, 372
social pressures against, 370–71
Mobility and the family
geographic, 51–52, 58

social, 102–3
Money and marriage, 338–55
bankruptcy, 352
changes during the life cycle, 340
changing norms and values, 348–52
decision making power, 345–47
effect of poverty, 339–40
problems with, and social class, 307–10
source of income, 341–44
systems for handling money, 347
working wife, 342–44
Morals; *see* Sex; Values
Multiple conceptions; *see* Twinning

National Organization of Women (NOW), 135
Natural childbirth; *see* Birth
Negro family culture, 61–65, 215–16
contraception, 397–400
family disruption, 63–64, 518
marital problems, 307–9
marriage with Caucasians, 381–83
premarital sex, 192, 202–4
Norms, 6–13, 30–31, 68–69
Nuclear family, 20–23, 40–41; *see also* Family
importance of love in, 234–35
prevalence of, 516

Old age, 446–61; *see also* Aging; Family life cycle; Middle years; Postparenthood
the aging process, 455–57
disadvantages in a youth-oriented culture, 456
lack of meaningful roles, 459
Oriental-Caucasian marriages, 383–84

Parent–child relationships; *see* Parenthood
Parenthood; *see also* Children
changing norms concerning, 426–27
crisis of, 421–25
goals of, 425–28
initial adjustments, 280, 422–23
intergenerational conflicts, 434–35
the launching stage, 447–48
shifting family coalitions, 423–25
Parent–youth conflict; *see* Adolescence; Parenthood
Permanently unmarried, 35, 474–79
adjustment problems, 477–79, 488
Permissiveness in training, 428–29; *see also* Children; Parenthood
Personality, 91–146; *see also* Children; Parenthood; Self-concept; Self-system

defined, 13
parental effects on, 428–29
as a variable in family success, 13–14
Petting; see Dating; Premarital sex
Political factors; see Family; Institutions; Marriage
Population revolution, 494–95; see also Birth rates; Environmental crisis; Family planning
Pornography, 185
Postparenthood, 446–61; see also Family life cycle; Middle years; Old age; Parenthood
Power-dependency relationship, in dating, 168–72; see also Marriage
Pregnancy, 409–14; see also Birth
coitus during, 412–14
determination of, 409–10
fetal development during, 410–11
husband–wife adjustments to, 412–14
Premarital pregnancy, 174, 200–6, 377
Premarital sex, 40, 174, 177–210; see also Sex
aggressiveness in, 198
attitudes, 182–83
behavior, 183–96
cancer associated with, 200
classification of standards, 182
consequences of, 196–206, 247–50
control over, 198
decisions regarding, 169–72
during engagement, 244–50
male–female comparisons, 185–86, 190, 244–47
petting, 196–98
religious effect on, 190–92
trends in, 184
Principle of least interest, 168, 314
Principle of value relevance, 15–18, 70–71, 85–87, 117–19, 143–44, 174–75, 206–9, 235–36, 250, 254–55, 282–84, 313–14, 329–30, 335, 353, 367–68, 386–87, 414–15, 441–42, 459–60, 486–87, 506–7; see also Values; Value-behavior discrepancy
Prostitution, 179, 199

Rating and dating complex, 165
Record linkage, 205
Religious factors; see Contraception; Family; Institutions; Marriage; Premarital sex; Sex in marriage; Wedding
Remarriage, 33, 36, 484–86, 517–18
effect on children, 372–73
probability of success, 485–86
Reproduction, as a family function, 21–23

Retirement, 451; see also Family life cycle
Role conflict, 277–78, 280–82; see also Value conflict
Role expectations, 265–72, 280–82
Role models, 116–17, 123–27
Role taking, 106–8
Roles; see Husband–wife roles; Sex roles

Secular revolution, 496–97
Self-concept, 7, 13, 78–80, 91–108, 121, 149, 433
background influences, 92–95
changes in, 100–3
development of, 95–100
effects of dating on, 170–72
effects of marriage on, 269–70, 288–90
Self-system, 97–100; see also Self-concept
Separation, 465–66, 518; see also Desertion; Divorce; Marital disruption
Sequential polygamy, 516
Sex; see also Premarital pregnancy; Premarital sex; Sex in marriage; Sexual adjustment
aversion toward, 32
double versus single standard, 40, 181, 187–89, 194–95, 244–46
freedom in, 40, 184
life cycle patterns, 184–85
during pregnancy, 412–14
standards, 181–83
types of behavior, 178–79
Sex education, 199, 207–9; see also Family life education
Sex in marriage, 317–37; see also Sex; Sexual adjustment
adjustments, 331–34
attitudinal difficulties, 329–30
disturbances, 325–31
effects on
of aging, 324–25
of education, 319
of religion, 320
of role type, 320
interrelated with other areas, 332–34
male–female differences, 320–21, 323–24
physiological aspects, 321–25
relationship difficulties, 330–31
the response cycle, 322–23
social context of, 317–21
Sex ratio, 406–8
effect on marriage rate, 214
Sex roles; see also Habits; Husband–wife roles; Personality; Sex ratio
argument for differentiated equality, 133

Sex roles (*Continued*)
　changing patterns in, 133–43
　conflict over, 141–42
　division of labor in, 23, 122–23, 138–42
　female negatively stereotyped, 130–32
　learning of, 117, 121–27
　male–female differences, 127–33
　persistent inequality, 142–43
　position of women, 32, 36, 38–39, 129–43
　preference for male children, 392
Sexual aberrations, 180, 185
Sexual adjustment, 52–53, 57–58, 262–63
Sexual development, 179–81
Shotgun wedding; *see* Wedding
Social change, 4–6, 30–42, 494–97
Social class, 45–67, 73–85; *see also* Interclass marriage; Mixed marriages; Status
　and childrearing, 427
　and contraception, 397–400
　and extra-marital sex, 334
　and marital problems, 86–87, 307–10
　and marital sex, 318–19
　middle-class family, 53–61, 80–82
　upper class family, 46–47
　working class family, 47–53, 73–80
Social context, 3–88
　effects on habit formation, 109–11
　elements in, 9–13, 93–95
　of marital sex, 317–21
Socialization; *see also* Self-concept
　effect of father's work upon, 109–10
　as a family function, 26–28
　for sex roles, 122–27
　and social class, 46, 55
Spinster; *see* Permanently unmarried
Standard of living defined, 339
Status; *see also* Social class
　change in, 102–3
　positional placement by family, 24–26
Sterility, 401–2; *see also* Adoption; Artificial insemination

Technological revolution, 494
Trends; *see* Family; Future of the family; Social change
Twinning, 408

Value conflict, 17–18, 68–88, 207, 246–47, 269–70, 338–39, 361–65, 493–94, 496
　resolution of, 82–85, 241–43
　types of, 68–73
Value consensus
　importance in mate selection, 220–22
　movement toward in engagement, 241–42
Value-behavior discrepancy, 186–90, 206, 247–50, 342–44, 352, 391, 392–93
Values, 9–10, 68–88; *see also* Norms; Principle of value relevance; Value conflict
　changes in, 31–42, 348–51
　differing meanings of money, 349–52
　effects on sexual behavior, 186–96
　neutrality concerning, 18
　and social class, 49, 55, 59, 76
　transmittal of, 29–30, 193
Venereal disease, 199–200, 252

Wedding
　age falsification at, 205
　civil versus religious, 254
　forced by a pregnancy, 204–6
　types of, 253–54
Widowhood, 36, 469–70
　adjustment problems, 477, 479–82, 488
Women, position of; *see* Sex roles
Women's Liberation Movement, 136–37; *see also* Sex roles
Working wife–mother, 71–73, 139–40, 342–44, 438–41; *see also* Children; Money and marriage; Sex roles

Youth; *see* Adolescence
Youthful marriage, 205, 376–77